THE
DARK
AND
TANGLED
PATH:

RACE
IN
AMERICA

THE
DARK
AND
TANGLED
PATH:
RACE
IN
AMERICA

DAVID D. ANDERSON

ROBERT L. WRIGHT

Department of American
Thought and Language
Michigan State University

HOUGHTON
MIFFLIN
COMPANY

BOSTON
New York
Atlanta

Geneva, Illinois
Dallas
Palo Alto

Printed in the U.S.A.

Library of Congress Catalog Card Number: 76–121711

ISBN: 0–395–04108–2

ACKNOWLEDGMENTS

Acknowledgment is gratefully made to the following authors and publishers:

C. LAWSON CROWE, *Rights and Differences: Some Notes for Liberals.* Copyright 1964 Christian Century Foundation. Reprinted by permission from the November 4, 1964 issue of *The Christian Century.*

ROGER DANIELS, from *The Politics of Prejudice.* Reprinted by permission of The Regents of the University of California.

ANTHONY DOWNS, *Alternative Futures for the American Ghetto.* Reprinted by permission from *Daedalus,* Journal of the American Academy of Arts & Sciences, Boston, Massachusetts, Volume 97, Number 4.

NATHAN HARE, *Brainwashing of Black Men's Minds. Liberator,* vol. 6, no. 9 (September 1966). Copyright © 1966 by *Liberator* magazine. Reprinted by permission.

DANIEL HENNINGER and NANCY ESPOSITO, *Regimented Non-Education: Indian Schools.* Reprinted by permission of *The New Republic,* © 1969, Harrison-Blaine of New Jersey, Inc.

LANGSTON HUGHES, *Big Round World.* Reprinted by permission of Harold Ober Associates Incorporated. Copyright © 1953, 1954, 1955, 1956, 1957 by Langston Hughes.

MARTIN LUTHER KING, JR., *A Testament of Hope.* Reprinted by permission of Joan Daves. Copyright © 1968 by the Estate of Martin Luther King, Jr.

JAMES M. LACY, *Folklore of the South and Racial Discrimination.* Reprinted by permission of the Texas Folklore Society from *A Good Tale and a Bonnie Tune,* Publication of the Texas Folklore Society, XXXII (1964).

C. ERIC LINCOLN, from *The Black Muslims in America.* Reprinted by permission of the Beacon Press, copyright © 1961 by C. Eric Lincoln.

NEWSWEEK, *"My Kountry"—Klonsel's Kreed.* Reprinted from the May 17, 1965 issue of *Newsweek.* Copyright Newsweek Inc., May, 1965.

EARL RAAB, from *The Black Revolution and the Jewish Question.* Reprinted from *Commentary,* by permission; Copyright © 1969 by the American Jewish Committee.

BAYARD RUSTIN, *The Failure of Black Separatism.* Copyright © 1969, by Harper's Magazine, Inc. Reprinted from the January, 1970 issue of Harper's Magazine by permission of the author.

W. D. SNODGRASS, *Powwow.* From *After Experience* by W. D. Snodgrass. Copyright © 1963 by W. D. Snodgrass. Originally appeared in *The New Yorker* and reprinted by permission of Harper & Row, Publishers.

KENNETH M. STAMPP ET AL, *The Negro in American History Textbooks.* From *The Negro History Bulletin,* October, 1968. Reprinted with the permission of The Association for the Study of Negro Life and History. Copyright © by ASNLH.

TIME, *The Angry American Indian.* Reprinted by permission from *Time,* the Weekly Newsmagazine; Copyright Time Inc., 1970.

MELVIN M. TUMIN, from *Race and Intelligence.* Reprinted with permission from the Anti-Defamation League of B'nai B'rith.

MARK TWAIN, *Niagara.* From *Sketches New and Old* (Harper & Row).

MARK TWAIN, from *Roughing It* (Harper & Row).

ERNEST VAN DEN HAAG, from *Intelligence or Prejudice?* Reprinted in part from the December 1, 1964 issue of *National Review* with the permission of the author.

ROBERT PENN WARREN, *The Briar Patch* from *I'll Take My Stand* by Twelve Southerners. Copyright, 1930 by Harper & Brothers; renewed 1958 by Donald Davidson. Reprinted by permission of the publisher.

MIN YEE, *Chinatown in Crisis.* Reprinted from the February 23, 1970 issue of *Newsweek.* Copyright Newsweek Inc., February, 1970.

All art by Bob Owens.

CONTENTS

3. THE TWENTIETH CENTURY: THE SEARCH FOR RESOLUTION / 273

BLACK CRISIS

SEEDS FOR THE FUTURE

INTRODUCTION

The reality and the importance of race, racial attitudes, and racism in the history of the United States need neither definition nor emphasis in this introduction; the scope and significance of both have shadowed America from its inception to the present, leading it to violence on many occasions. This volume is an attempt to collect and present the documents, selected from more than three hundred years of American history, that illuminate that shadow cast by race in America as it has made its continuing presence felt.

The documents included in this collection are concerned with race as it has been commonly thought of in America, that is, as a matter of skin pigmentation. The focus of the documents is confined to those groups generally called Mongolian or yellow, American Indian or red, and Negroid or black. Race in this context is not a matter of language or culture; it is determined by color, and the history of race in America is the history of these groups in relation to the powerful Caucasians or whites who very quickly became and remain the majority.

The Caucasian or white race, although not native to this continent, began almost immediately, through numbers, aggressiveness, philosophy, and technology, to dominate it. Today, for example, white Americans make up nearly nine-tenths of the population in the United States and almost completely dominate the material, cultural, and technological aspects of American society. With roughly the same conditions prevailing for three hundred years, it is not surprising that the documentary record reveals the white man's assessments of the other races more often than the reverse, and minority assessments are primarily those of treatment by the dominant whites.

Such assessments invariably include misconceptions, rationalizations, sentimentalism, faulty interpretations, *non-sequiturs*, stereotyped ideas, self interest, and sheer lack of information, often in attempts at honest, objective appraisal. Although the reactions of Cotton Mather to the American Indians are not surprising, dominated as they are by the tenets of Calvinism, nevertheless a moment of shock is inevitable when it becomes apparent that even Jefferson, possessed of the most transcendent mind of his time and place, could not escape the widely-held opinion that blacks were by nature intellectually inferior to whites.

Any attempt to classify presents problems, and the attempt to deal with race systematically is particularly hazardous. The editors of this book are not concerned primarily with those physiological features—head size and shape, for example—normally considered in racial classification. Neither do they share the confidence with which many Americans assign their fellows to racial groups through combinations of factors involving appearance, speech patterns, legalisms (in X state, how many drops of Y blood must a person have to be legally a member of that race?), and folklore. Clearly, however, skin color is the most widespread popular criterion for racial classification in America, as the documents reveal, and it provides the most enduring basis for the awareness of "difference" upon which attitudes toward race, often "scientific" as well as popular, are based.

What matters most in the collection of historical documents concerned with race is that many persons react to racial "differences" whether such differences are definable or not or whether they in fact exist. The differences that can be demonstrated are almost invariably related to color, and the bulk of the documents included in this collection reveal the nature and significance of those reactions while demonstrating the continuous presence of the awareness of racial differences in American life and development.

In limiting the scope of the book to clearly distinguishable racial minorities, the editors have excluded such ethnic minority groups as Jews (except in their relation to Negroes), Puerto Ricans, Eskimos, and Spanish-Americans, although these segments of our population have had to face many of the same problems. Attention will be given, nevertheless, to certain issues not directly related to racial considerations, but demonstrably growing out of them. For example, despite abortive attempts to establish Indian slavery in America, slavery on this continent has historically been that of blacks. (Curiously, the word *slave* owes its existence to the enslavement of one white group by another.) Insistence on inherent inferiorities of black people may have served to rationalize the institution of slavery. In time, such attempts at justification become premises—quite mysterious to observers who do not comprehend the original motivations.

Principles for selection of documents entailed, first of all, a search for materials concerned with distinct features of race as seen against the American setting. Consequently, at times the selected documents may seem offensive, absurd or overstated, but the task of editors is not to make history or to rewrite it, but to report it; and these documents, the raw material of history, indicate not what is or should be; they make graphically clear what men have believed in the course of the evolution of human ideas.

Dozens of new books attempt to give long overdue and justified credit to various racial groups, to blacks in particular. Much of the material in this collection provides insight into the influences which delayed that credit, and it shows the gradual evolution of ideas that makes that credit possible now. Thought patterns that involve racial prejudice and ego involvement change slowly, as American Indians and blacks are well aware. This book documents what was, it portrays change, and it presents what has come to be.

No attempt has been made to pre-determine the general tone of the selections by limiting them to sources or journals classified as "liberal" or "conservative," "professional" or "popular." Included in the documents are factual accounts, essays, biographies, and other non-fictional, sometimes sub-literary forms. In addition, fiction and poetry are also included because the editors believe that literary materials can often express reality more vigorously and effectively than other documents. The literary materials are drawn not only from *belles lettres* but also from popular songs and ballads, and even from jingles, including those that illustrate, sometimes with wry humor, an ultimate equality that transcends difference:

> White gal rides in the Pullman car,
> Yellow gal she try to do the same,
> Black gal rides in the Jim Crow car,
> But she gets there just the same.

Finally, there can be no valid reason for choosing only authors who represent a single common point of view or who straddle issues and matters of race. Attitudes represented by Elijah Mohammed are neither more nor less revealing and hence valid for purposes of examination and illustration than those of the Ku Klux Klan, and the editors believe that the range of attitudes is both wide and comprehensive. At the same time the arbitrary limits of length and taste have forced the exclusion of much relevant material.

Problems of selection have been intensified by other, more substantive problems that have bemused and often puzzled us as editors, forcing us to consider origins and relationships as well as specific attitudes and statements. The role of language in prejudice and in indoctrination of attitudes is one such problem only cursorily explored and which demands treatment beyond the scope of this book. The problem has become obvious: to what degree have the attitudes of white Americans toward black Americans been shaped by color prejudice inherent in the English language?

A definitive answer must await the expert testimony of linguists, anthropologists, and sociologists of the future, but it is impossible to ignore the fact that darkness and blackness carry certain consistent linguistic connotations. Consider, for example, the following common phrases: in the dark, the darkness of despair, dark deeds, the Dark Ages, black sheep, the Black Death, the Black Plague, Black Monday, black-hearted, a black mood, blackmail, blackball, black magic, black mark, and countless other similar expressions.

To be sure, some of these terms express other than figurative meanings, but neither their number nor their frequency can be ignored or dismissed. The Black Knight of the past was seen immediately to be sinister, and the symbolism of the black hat or the white hat is obvious to today's television viewer, a continuation of an old allegory become cliché. White lies are still differentiated from the evil nature of their black equivalents. And today the S.D.S. banner of anarchy is black rather than the red of traditional revolt.

It is wise not to belabor English alone as the culprit in establishing negative attitudes toward things black, however. The connection between the darkness of night, sin, and death, and the lightness of their counterparts goes back to antiquity and beyond. However, it is interesting and speculatively intriguing to note that blackness and death are not interrelated in all non-Western societies.

Nevertheless, persons of all cultures associate that which is good with the familiar and with themselves, just as they associate the bad with whatever seems most dissimilar or strange. In consequence, it is clear that the English and other Northern Europeans, encountering their first black man, ascribed to him, in obvious linguistic allegory, the physical appearance of evil. At the same time, purity and innocence were pictured as white; Snow White became an altogether suitable name for a folk heroine, and William Blake feared no misunderstanding when he wrote:

> And I am black, but O! My soul is white;
> White as angel is the English child . . .

As obvious as the importance of dark and black as allegorical expressions in English is the fact that red and yellow as words and as allegory are far less significant and less consistent. Red is as likely to be compared to a rose as to blood (although both similes are representational), while "in the red" and "seeing red" are literal. Yellow as the symbol of cowardice seems to have as little relationship to human beings as the white feather. Although it is true that ghosts are usually represented as white and the peculiar and awesome ambiguity of Moby Dick is well known, the connotation of white is highly positive in America as in Europe, while red and yellow are generally inconsistent, and black is distinctly negative.

As provocative as the language and color connotations are the stereotyped views of members of racial groups, particularly when mutually contradictory or exclusive. Often several views appear in the same document, each obviously subscribed to by substantial groups of Americans. Thus, although blacks were considered incapable of abstract learning by most whites in the nineteenth century, the law in many southern states forbade teaching them to read and write. Blacks were considered lazy, but to "work like a nigger" connoted back-breaking toil. Slave revolts were widely feared by whites, resulting in much oppressive legislation, yet blacks were invariably shown on the minstrel stage, in popular literature, and in the film classic *Birth of a Nation* as good-natured, light-hearted, happy, and loyal.

Indians, however, although victimized by similar stereotypes, were rarely interpreted in such mutually contradictory terms in the same document or by the same observer. Instead, the Indian was seen either as the Noble Savage of romanticism, brave, virtuous, clean, and intuitively wise in his closeness to Nature, or as the treacherous animal, indolent, dirty, cruel, and good only when dead. Occasionally it was acknowledged that Indians were members of various tribes and that some differences might be perceived in the behavior of Zunis when contrasted with Sioux. This type of tribal or regional identification, although permitted Indians, was denied to Negro slaves, in part to reduce the possibility of uprisings and to prevent "savage" cultural continuity.

Orientals have also been victimized and depersonalized by often contradictory stereotypes. Every American schoolboy knows that Orientals have incredible dietary habits, and they are inscrutable, industrious, willing to work for low wages (akin to stupidity in the American lexicon of stereotypes), and dangerous competition for American workmen. White Americans know that Chinese and Japanese are not the same but are not clear about the differences, a confusion that is compounded by shifting national alliances that characterize Chinese as "good" and Japanese as "bad" and then reverse the two. Further confusion comes from Hollywood, which is itself uncertain about the differences and with blithe practicality uses Chinese to play Japanese and vice versa, compounding confusion further by casting various Orientals as Koreans, Vietnamese, Filipinos, and whatever else is demanded by the contingencies of casting. But then, Americans have never been precise about national identifications; typical of American uncertainty is the Swede of Stephen Crane's "The Blue Hotel," referred to by a cowboy as "some kind of Dutchman."

The Pavlovian reactions of many white Americans to persons of other races might strike one as intriguingly peculiar and archaic, were they not part of the cultural continuation that has produced the bitter fruit of the present. Extract black people from their own complex cultural milieu; transport them against their will to an unfamiliar continent and culture; deny their language, heritage, and identity; and exploit them to subsidize an archaic agricultural system, rationalizing such actions as justified by the propagation of Christianity among them. Create myths (of extraordinary sexual proficiency, for example) which lead to complex love-hate relationships. After the abolition of slavery, a movement not without its sentimental aspects, proceed as if slavery had been the best possible preparation for citizenship. Finally, after generations of promises ignored or incompletely kept, react with self-flagellating guilt to that historical relationship.

Such a sequence of events, admittedly oversimplified in its outline form, is nevertheless the foundation of relations between black and white Americans today. Such a foundation is more conducive to continued misunderstanding and apprehension than to acceptance, and it increases the difficulty of acknowledging members of either race as individual human beings rather than collectively defining them by the pigmentation that has provided easy identification in past centuries. Science and social science are moving toward definitive answers to the complexities of race, but the transmutation of those answers to popularly-accepted fact has yet to happen.

The problem of the relationship between red man and white is at once more complex and brutally simpler than that between black and white. Originally the victim of theological speculation on whether or not he had a soul, the future of the Indian was resolved quickly and pragmatically—he was considered as a sub-human species. As a species he stood, figuratively as well as literally, in the path of progress; consequently, as Thomas Hart Benton, Andrew Jackson, and others made clear, the Indian could only be banished to reservations or eliminated. Manifest Destiny had room only for the white vision, and the remaining Indians began their inexorable movement toward the tar paper shacks of the peculiar rural ghettoes they have received in exchange for a continent.

Although a "Chinaman's chance" is no chance at all, the position of the yellow man is the aspect of racial relations that comes closest to a happy ending in the present (although the presence on campuses of so-called Third World Groups denies it). Feared, taunted, bullied, excluded from citizenship, relegated to menial positions, many banished by government action to concentration camps at the start of World War II (an experience unique in modern American history), the yellow man has persisted in his quiet attempts to rise and prosper, and in many respects he has done so. A larger proportion of Orientals than of any other racial minority has found America to be the "land of opportunity" of American folklore.

Skeptical, disillusioned, frustrated members of racial minorities continue to battle the unique handicaps posed by the peculiar history of racial attitudes in this country. Perhaps this battle may ultimately be resolved in their rejection of the Horatio Alger myth of middle-class American material success and the creation of new myths peculiarly and satisfyingly their own.

Yet at the same time, the past has shown a change in attitudes, evolutionary rather than revolutionary, and a search for a common identity. The dark and tangled path depicted by the following documents may lead in either direction. Perhaps a better understanding of the past can help ensure a path to the future that is straight and bright.

East Lansing, Michigan   *David D. Anderson*
                                            Robert L. Wright

1

THE
COLONIAL
PERIOD
TO
1800:
BEGINNINGS

SHORTLY AFTER THE beginning of permanent settlement in North America, the three major racial groups that still occupy that continent found themselves facing a confrontation that was to determine the nature of their relationship for the next hundred years. As pre-Columbian America became post-Columbian and a century of discovery and exploration followed, the pattern of relations between the aboriginal inhabitants and the European explorers, whether French, Spanish, English or Dutch, was virtually identical. That is, the American Indians were objects of curiosity, subjects for trade and barter, potential sources of cheap labor, colonial subjects, and ultimately annoyances or barriers to settlement and progress, fit only for extermination. In addition they quickly became the subject of theological speculation and subsequent conversion or condemnation, depending on whether or not it was concluded that they were human and had souls.

By the time of the first permanent English settlements in North America, those that were later to provide the foundations for the United States, the nature of the relationship was established. William Bradford describes a reasonably good relationship between the Indians and the Pilgrims in his *History of Plimouth Plantation;* but this was not to continue, despite the fact that the story of Squanto and Massasoit has taken on epic proportions in the folklore of American history. Rather, in New England, particularly among the Puritans of Massachusetts Bay who quickly absorbed the smaller Plymouth band in the 1830's, as well as in Virginia a generation before, the Indians seemed eminently suited to solve what was one of the demanding problems faced by the colonists: the need for cheap, docile labor.

The exploitation of man by his fellow man through servile labor, whether voluntary or not, was an unquestioned fact of economic and social life in seventeenth century Europe, and virtually none of the colonists saw any need for questioning or challenging the idea in America. The idea of master and servant was a natural one, and to the colonial Englishman, whether Anglican or Puritan, it was scripturally sanctioned, as was the similar but permanent relationship between master and slave. Thus, as the need for labor appeared, attempts to provide it were natural and immediate. There were few distinctions between limited servitude, usually of voluntary indentured European servants, pledged to serve for a definite period of years in exchange for passage to the New World, and involuntary indefinite servitude, which was to evolve into chattel slavery. One major difference did appear, however: those subjected to involuntary, indefinite servitude were non-European.

5

The first attempts at involuntary servitude in the English colonies, as in the Spanish and to a lesser extent the French, were directed at the Indians. With clear Biblical evidence demonstrating to the Puritan mind that the Indians were savage subjects of the devil whose energies must be redirected toward the service of God, His people, and His Commonwealth Upon Earth, Indians conquered or captured as a result of the hostility described by John Winthrop and Cotton Mather, were reverently, even religiously forced into slavery. The same attempts, with perhaps less theological sanction and more denial of the equality of man, became commonplace in Jamestown to the south.

But it quickly became evident in both colonies that the Indians, by temperament and by a peculiar susceptibility to disease, were not a suitable solution to the demand for labor, and the labor supply provided by the indenture system was insufficient. An apparently more satisfying solution became evident in the colonies soon after the first Negro slaves were sold on the docks of Jamestown in 1619. This was the beginning of the system that was to subjugate and degrade vast numbers of a people, brutalize and degrade vast numbers of another, divide and nearly destroy a great nation, and provide the foundation for another succeeding system of prejudice and segregation that was to continue to degrade, to brutalize, and to threaten the existence of that nation.

But in the seventeenth century, the system of involuntary indefinite servitude quickly evolved into chattel slavery with much economic, social, and theological support and virtually no opposition. The Indians were subjected to almost constant pressure from a growing English settlement, and a state of war between the English and the Indians eventually resulted, partially due to a growing alliance between the Indians and the French, traditional enemies of the English. It appeared, therefore, that the demands for labor, particularly by the thriving agricultural enterprises of the middle and southern colonies, could best be met by the importation of Negroes.

Such importation was to reduce human beings to a commodity and become a profitable leg of the triangular trade route that developed between the North American colonies, the West Indies, and the West Coast of Africa. The exchange of molasses, rum and Negroes laid the foundation of much New England prosperity and many individual New England fortunes.

Nevertheless, by 1700 a measure of public opinion in New England began to voice opposition to slavery. In that year Samuel Sewall published *The Selling of Joseph,* an eloquent condemnation of the legal recognition of property rights to human beings. But he was answered by his contemporaries, most notably by John Saffin, who cited numerous Biblical passages and incidents to establish the divine approval of the peculiar institution. In this emphasis Saffin not only pleased many of his Puritan contemporaries, who were not to follow Sewall's lead for more than half a century, but he also provided the basis for Biblical arguments for the approval of slavery. Saffin's arguments were to contribute to disunion in the Protestant churches a century later and to provide much of the rationale for slavery until the outbreak of the Civil War.

During the eighteenth century, chattel slavery established itself firmly in South Carolina and the new colony of Georgia. It was less firmly entrenched elsewhere in the colonies, but it became at the same time an institution restricted to blacks, many of them the victims of tribal wars and greedy local rulers on the West Coast of Africa. During that century what opposition to the perniciousness of the institution existed in the British North American colonies was led by Quakers, whose recognition of Godhood in themselves and all men made the evil of slavery evident.

Among the Quakers who opposed the institution were Ralph Sandiford, Benjamin Say, John Woolman, and Anthony Benezet. Sandiford's *Brief Exposition of the Times,* published by Benjamin Franklin in 1729, condemned slavery as an abomination, a view apparently subscribed to by Franklin at that comparatively early date. Say's *All Slave Keepers that Keep the Innocent in Bondage, Apostates . . . ,* also printed by Franklin, in 1737, was even more outspoken in condemning both the institution and those who refused to see its true nature. Woolman's *Journal,* published in 1774, and his *Some Considerations on the Keeping of Negroes* (1754) are eloquent humanitarian documents, and the latter pleads for the innocent victims of the dehumanizing institution.

By 1776, at the instigation of Benezet, the author of a number of antislavery tracts, the Society of Friends as a whole condemned slavery. Benjamin Rush, Benjamin Franklin and other followers of the Enlightenment responded with a rational condemnation of the institution. In 1776, in the first draft of the Declaration of Independence, Thomas Jefferson attempted to make this theological and philosophical opposition to slavery part of the public policy of the new Country. But political necessity, resulting in the first of almost a century of compromises, forced Jefferson to consent to delete that clause from the final draft of that statement of the American ideal. Its removal, however, did not detract from the eloquence with which Jefferson defined the nature and equality of man.

Quakers and members of the Enlightenment alike based their arguments against slavery on the principle that Negroes are human beings and, as such, are entitled to control their own destiny insofar as God, either the intensely personal God of the Quakers or the aloof, rational God of Deists, permits man to direct the course of his life. To the Quakers slavery denied the Godhood in man as it brutalized and degraded slave and slaveholder alike; to the rationalists such an institution denied both the intrinsic equality of all men and the natural rights of the slaves, and it was consequently irrational. To both groups, slavery was an offense against the very nature of man, a denial of man's humanity, and a mockery of the image of God found in man.

Both groups found fertile ground for the seeds of their opposition; in 1780 Pennsylvania, largely under the influence of the Quakers, passed a law providing for gradual, orderly emancipation in that state, and Southern rationalists, particularly in Virginia, sought the same effect. Arthur Lee condemned slavery as depraving for both slave and master as early as 1764, and Jefferson sought unsuccessfully to direct the Virginia delegates to the Continental Congress to pursue an anti-slavery clause course, but, like his abortive effort to include his anti-slavery clause in the Declaration of Independence, it was unsuccessful.

During the Revolution Negroes served in the Continental Army and militia under some circumstances, and they were forbidden to do so under others; and, although Negro blood was among the first shed by British arms, the Revolution was ineffectual in advancing the cause of human freedom for all men. At the conclusion of the war, the slave's position rapidly became solidified in custom as well as law in the new country. Anti-slavery sentiment, led by Jefferson, sought unsuccessfully in 1785 to exclude slaves from the territories after 1800, but two years later the Northwest Ordinance, which provided for the government of the territory north and west of the Ohio River, successfully excluded the institution of slavery—but not individual slaves—from that vast area.

The Constitution of the United States, the document designed to bring an orderly, harmonious government to the new country by emu-lating the rationality and balance of the universe, as the political phi-losophers of the Enlightenment insisted government must, is, on the issue of race, or, more properly, slavery, a study in ambiguity. Con-structed to be a practical political document that would apply rational theory to practical reality, provide checks and balances that would prevent tyranny, and insure liberty to all Americans, the Constitution did none of those things for the slave. In spite of active anti-slavery sentiment widespread in the colonies, particularly in the northern and middle colonies, and in spite of the proclamations concerning the na-ture and the rights of man subscribed to by the members of the Enlight-enment and proclaimed by the Declaration of Independence, the Con-stitution met the issue of that anachronistic institution, a mockery of the Declaration of Independence and the faith of the Enlightenment, by evasion.

As in the debate over adoption of the Declaration by the Continental Congress, the members of the Constitutional Convention compromised with the pro-slavery states of the Deep South. Curiously, the words slaves and slavery do not appear in the Constitution in the three clauses in which the role of slavery in the new nation was defined. This omission, capable of interpretation in a number of ways and ultimately responsible for the constitutional crisis of the 1850's and for the secession of the South, is actually a reflection of the majority view of the members of the Convention: that slavery, an institution rejected by the science and philosophy of the age as irrational and proven uneconomical in most states, would disappear quickly in the new nation. To hasten its end, the Constitution provided for an end, in 1808, to the further importation of slaves. With its demise assured, there seemed to be no urgent need to risk the hard-won harmony of the Convention by standing on an issue that might destroy it or to mar the new document by the inclusion of words that reflected the harsh, irrational and inhuman reality of the moment.

Consequently, hindsight makes clear the fact that the Constitution, in its euphemisms "other persons" and "persons held to service," statements of condition based not on race or color but upon legal fact at the moment, provided for the continuation of the institution until it became so firmly established that its eradication could come only through force. In their conscious attempt to make the document other than a racist document, the framers of the Constitution planted the seeds that were to bear the poisonous national fruit that would threaten the national existence for two centuries.

Just as Negro rights were denied by omission in the document, so were those of the indigenous Indians. In this case, too, it seems evident that the failure of the framers of the Constitution to define the nature of the relationship between the new country and this sizable group of original inhabitants left to chance and to pragmatic and often inhuman solutions problems that should have been anticipated and solved. But even in the Bill of Rights, the ten amendments appended at the insistence of Jeffersonian liberals, there is no recognition of the reality of racial relations at the time.

This is not to imply that the Constitution is a "racist" document, nor does it suggest that its framers were bigots or hypocrites; indeed, the preponderance of evidence points to the contrary. But it does make clear the fact that both document and framers, in spite of their determination to build well and to emulate the order of the Universe, fell short in a crucial aspect of a government proclaimed to be devoted to the protection of the natural rights of man.

However, as the eighteenth century closed under the administrations of George Washington and John Adams there was no suggestion of what was to come. During those twelve years the country sought, largely through crisis, to transmute the words of the Constitution into workable political fact. In those crucial years the foundations of competing political philosophies were laid, and major political threats to the rights of man were written into law. At the close of the decade the alien and sedition laws were part of America's evolving legal structure, and the idealistic pronouncements of the Declaration of Independence were far from the American reality. But in the election of 1800, the revolution of 1800 that reversed the course of the previous twelve years, the path that the country was to take, the devious, gradual, often almost impossible path toward the remote goal of human freedom, was marked out.

The reality for the white man, and certainly for the common man, was grim enough at the end of the eighteenth century. For the black man, however, there was not even the glimpse of hope provided by Thomas Jefferson; the reality was that described by Gustavus Vassa. But at the same time, almost unnoticed in proportion to the magnitude of the reality of oppression, there was the quiet lyric beauty of Phillis Wheatley's poems, sure evidence that the lot of the black man was not permanent nor his fate hopeless.

FIRST
ENCOUNTERS

From
HISTORY OF PLIMOUTH PLANTATION (1606-1646)
WILLIAM BRADFORD

William Bradford (1590–1657) was governor of Plymouth Colony for most of his life; he maintained friendly relationships with the Indians, provided capable leadership in developing the colony, and exhibited a measure of tolerance greater than that of his Puritan contemporaries. His History of Plimouth Plantation, *first published completely in 1856, is the best single source of Pilgrim attitudes and incidents.*

All this while the Indians came skulking about them, and would sometimes show them selves aloofe of, but when any approached near them, they would rune away. And once they stoale away their tools wher they had been at worke, and were gone to diner. But about the 16. of March certaine Indian came bouldly amongst them, and spoke to them in broken English, which they could well understand, but marvelled at it. At length they understood by discourse with him, that he was not of these parts, but belonged to the eastrene parts, wher some English-ships came to fhish, with whom he was acquainted, and could name sundrie of them by their names, amongst whom he had gott his language. He became proftable to them in aquainting them with many things concerning the state of the cuntry in the east-parts wher he lived, which was afterwards profitable unto them; as also of the people hear, of their names, number, and strength; of their situation and distance from this place, and who was cheefe amongst them. His name was Samaset; he tould them also of another Indian whos name was Squanto, a native of this place, who had been in England and could speake better English then him selfe. Being, after some time of entertainmente and gifts, dismist, a while after he came againe, and 5. more with him, and they brought againe all the tooles that were stolen away before, and made way for the coming of their great Sachem, called Massasoyt; who, about 4. or 5. days after, came with the cheefe of his freinds and other attendance, with the aforesaid Squanto. With whom, after frendly entertainment, and some gifts given him, they made a peace with him (which hath now continued this 24. years) in these terms.

1. That neither he nor any of his, should injurie or doe hurte to any of their peopl.

2. That if any of his did any hurte to any of theirs, he should send the offender, that they might punish him.

3. That if any thing were taken away from any of theirs, he should cause it to be restored; and they should doe the like to his.

4. If any did unjustly warr against him, they would aide him; if any did warr against them, he should aide them.

5. He should send to his neighbours confederats, to certifie them of this, that they might not wrong them, but might be likewise comprised in the conditions of peace.

6. That when ther men came to them, they should leave their bows and arrows behind them.

After these things he returned to his place caled Sowams, some 40. mile from this place, but Squanto continued with them, and was their interpreter, and was a spetiall instrument sent of God for their good beyond their expectation. He directed them how to set their corne, wher to take fish, and to procure other comodities, and was also their pilott to bring them to unknowne places for their profitt, and never left them till he dyed. He was a native of this place, and scarce any left alive besids him selfe. He was caried away with diverce others by one Hunt, a m^r of a ship, who thought to sell them for slaves in Spaine; but he got away for England, and was entertained by a marchante in London, and imployed to New-foundland and other parts, and lastly brought hither into these parts by one Mr. Dermer, a gentle-man imployed by Sr. Ferdinando Gorges and others, for discovery, and other designes in these parts. Of whom I shall say some thing, because it is mentioned in a booke set forth An^o: 1622. by the Presidente and Counsell for New-England, that he made the peace betweene the salvages of these parts and the English; of which this plantation, as it is intimated, had the benefite. But what a peace it was, may apeare by what befell him and his men.

This Mr. Dermer was hear the same year that these people came, as apears by a relation written by him, and given me by a freind, bearing date June 30. An^o: 1620. And they came in Novemb^r: following, so ther was but 4. months differance. In which relation to his honored freind, he hath these passages of this very place.

I will first begine (saith he) with that place from whence Squanto, or Tisquantem, was taken away; which in Cap: Smiths mape is called Plimoth: and I would that Plimoth had the like comodities. I would that the first plantation might hear be seated, if ther come to the number of 50. persons, or upward. Otherwise at Charlton, because ther the savages are lese to be feared. The Pocanawkits, which live to the west of Plimoth, bear an inveterate malice to the English, and are of more strength then all the savags from thence to Penobscote. Their desire of revenge was occasioned by an English man, who having many of them on bord, made a great slaughter with their murderers and smale shot, when as (they say) they offered no injurie on their parts. Whether they were English or no, it may by douted; yet they beleeve they were, for the Frenche have so possest them; for which cause Squanto cannot deney but they would have kiled me when I was at Namasket, had he not entreated hard for me. The soyle of the borders of this great bay, may be compared to most of the plantations which I have seene in Virginia. The land is of diverce sorts; for Patuxite is a hardy but strong soyle, Nawset and Saughtughtett are for the most part a blakish and deep mould, much like that wher groweth the best Tobacco in Virginia. In the botume of that great bay is store of Codd and basse, or mulett, etc.

But above all he comends Pacanawkite for the richest soyle, and much open ground fitt for English graine, etc.

Massachussets is about 9. leagues from Plimoth, and situate in the mids betweene both, is full of ilands and peninsules very fertill for the most parte.

With sundrie shuch relations which I forbear to transcribe, being now better knowne then they were to him.

He was taken prisoner by the Indeans at Manamoiak (a place not farr from hence, now well knowne). He gave them what they demanded for his liberty, but when they had gott what they desired, they kept him still and indevored to kill his men; but he was freed by seasing on some of them, and kept them bound till they gave him a cannows load of corne. Of which, see Purch: lib. 9. fol. 1778. But this was An°: 1619.

After the writing of the former relation he came to the Ile of Capawack (which lyes south of this place in the way to Virginia), and the foresaid Squanto with him, wher he going a shore amongst the Indans to trad, as he used to doe, was betrayed and assaulted by them, and all his men slaine, but one that kept the boat; but him selfe gott abord very sore wounded, and they had cut of his head upon the cudy of his boat, had not the man reskued him with a sword. And so they got away, and made shift to gett into Virginia, wher he dyed; whether of his wounds or the diseases of the cuntrie, or both togeather, is uncertaine. By all which it may appeare how farr these people were from peace, and with what danger this plantation was begune, save as the powerfull hand of the Lord did protect them. These thing[s] were partly the reason why they kept aloofe and were so long before they came to the English. An other reason (as after them selvs made known) was how aboute 3. years before, a French-ship was cast away at Cap-Codd, but the men gott ashore, and saved their lives, and much of their victails, and other goods; but after the Indeans heard of it, they geathered togeather from these parts, and never left watching and dogging them till they got advantage, and kild them all but 3. or 4. which they kept, and sent from one Sachem to another, to make sporte with, and used them worse then slaves; (of which the foresaid Mr. Dermer redeemed 2. of them;) and they conceived this ship was now come to revenge it.

Also, (as after was made knowne,) before they came to the English to make freindship, they gott all the Powachs of the cuntrie, for 3. days togeather, in a horid and divellish maner to curse and execrate them with their cunjurations, which asembly and service they held in a darke and dismale swampe.

But to returne. The spring now approaching, it pleased God the mortalitie begane to cease amongst them, and the sick and lame recovered apace, which put as it were new life into them; though they had borne their sadd affliction with much patience and contentednes, as I thinke any people could doe. But it was the Lord which upheld them, and had beforehand prepared them; many having long borne the yoake, yea from their youth. Many other smaler maters I omite, sundrie of them having been allready published in a Jurnall made by one of the company; and some other passages of jurneys and relations allredy published, to which I referr those that are willing to know them more perticulerly. And being now come to the 25. of March I shall begine the year 1621.

ANNO. 1621.

They now begane to dispatch the ship away which brought them over, which lay tille aboute this time, or the begining of Aprill. The reason on their parts why she stayed so long, was the necessitie and danger that lay upon them, for it was well towards the ende of Desember before she could land any thing hear, or they able to receive any thing ashore. Afterwards, the 14. of Jan: the house which they had made for a generall randevoze by casulty fell afire, and some were faine to retire abord for shilter. Then the sicknes begane to fall sore amongst them, and the weather so bad as they could not make much sooner any dispatch. Againe, the Govr and cheefe of them, seeing so many dye, and fall downe sick dayly, thought it no wisdom to send away the ship, their condition considered, and the danger they stood in from the Indeans, till they could procure some shelter; and therfore thought it better to draw some more charge upon them selves and freinds, then hazard all. The m^r and sea-men likewise, though before they hasted the passengers a shore to be goone, now many of their men being dead, and of the ablest of them, (as is before noted,) and of the rest many lay sick and weake, the m^r durst not put to sea, till he saw his men begine to recover, and the hart of winter over.

Afterwards they (as many as were able) began to plant ther corne, in which servise Squanto stood them in great stead, showing them both the maner how to set it, and after how to dress and tend it. Also he tould them excepte they gott fish and set with it (in these old grounds) it would come to nothing, and he showed them that in the midle of

Aprill they should have store enough come up the brooke, by which they begane to build, and taught them how to take it, and wher to get other provissions necessary for them; all which they found true by triall and experience. Some English seed they sew, as wheat and pease, but it came not to good, eather by the badnes of the seed, or latenes of the season, or both, or some other defecte.

In this month of Aprill whilst they were bussie about their seed, their Govr (Mr. John Carver) came out of the feild very sick, it being a hott day; he complained greatly of his head, and lay downe, and within a few howers his sences failed, so as he never spake more till he dyed, which was within a few days after. Whoss death was much lamented, and caused great heavines amongst them, as ther was cause. He was buried in the best maner they could, with some vollies of shott by all that bore armes; and his wife, being a weak woman, dyed within 5. or 6. weeks after him.

Shortly after William Bradford was chosen Gove^r in his stead, and being not yet recoverd of his ilnes, in which he had been near the point of death, Isaak Allerton was chosen to be an Asistante unto him, who, by renewed election every year, continued sundry years togeather, which I hear note once for all.

May 12. was the first mariage in this place, which, according to the laudable custome of the Low-Cuntries, in which they had lived, was thought most requisite to be performed by the magistrate, as being a civill thing, upon which many questions aboute inheritances doe depende, with other things most proper to their cognizans, and most consonante to the scripturs, Ruth 4. and no wher found in the gospell to be layed on the ministers as a part of their office. "This decree or law about mariage was published by the Stats of the Low-Cuntries An°: 1590. That those of any religion, after lawfull and open publication, coming before the magistrats, in the Town or Stat-house, were to be orderly (by them) maried one to another." Petets Hist. fol: 1029. And this practiss hath continued amongst, not only them, but hath been followed by all the famous churches of Christ in these parts to this time, —An°: 1646.

Haveing in some sorte ordered their bussines at home, it was thought meete to send some abroad to see their new freind Massasoyet, and to bestow upon him some gratuitie to bind him the faster unto them; as also that hearby they might veiw the countrie, and see in what maner he lived, what strength he had aboute him, and how the ways were to his place, if at any time they should have occasion. So the 2. of July they sente Mr. Edward Winslow and Mr. Hopkins, with the foresaid Squanto for ther guid, who gave him a suite of cloaths, and a horsemans coate, with some other small things, which were kindly accepted; but they found but short commons, and came both weary and hungrie home. For the Indeans used then to have nothing so much corne as they have since the English have stored them with their hows, and seene their industrie in breaking up new grounds therwith. They found his place to be 40. miles from hence, the soyle good, and the people not many, being dead and abundantly wasted in the late great mortalitie which fell in all these parts aboute three years before the coming of the English, wherein thousands of them dyed, they not being able to burie one another; ther sculs and bones were found in many places lying still above ground, where their houses and dwellings had been; a very sad spectackle to behould. But they brought word that the Narighansets lived but on the other side of that great bay, and were a strong people, and many in number, living compacte togeather, and had not been at all touched with this wasting plague.

Aboute the later end of this month, one John Billington lost him selfe in the woods, and wandered up and downe some 5. days, living on beries and what he could find. At length he light on an Indean plantation, 20. mils south of this place, called Manamet, they conveid him furder of, to Nawsett, among those peopl that had before set upon the English when they were costing, whilest the ship lay at the Cape, as is before noted. But the Gove^r caused him to be enquired for among the Indeans, and at length Massassoyt sent word wher he was, and the Gove^r sent a shalop for him, and had him delivered. Those people also came and made their peace; and they gave full satisfaction to those whose corne they had found taken when they were at Cap-Codd.

Thus ther peace and acquaintance was pretty well establisht with the natives aboute them; and ther was an other Indean called Hobamack come to live amongst them, a proper lustie man, and a man of accounte for his vallour and parts amongst the Indeans, and continued very faithfull and constant to the English till he dyed. He and Squanto being gone upon bussines amonge the Indeans, at their returne (whether it was out of envie to them or malice to the English) ther was a Sachem called Corbitant, alyed to Massassoyte, but never any good freind to the English to this day, mett with them at an Indean towne caled Namassakett 14. miles to the west of this place, and begane to quarell with them, and offered to stabe Hobamack; but being a lusty man, he cleared him selfe of him, and came running away all sweating and tould the Govr what had befalne him, and he feared they had killed Squanto, for they threatened them both, and for no other cause but because they were freinds to the English, and servisable unto them. Upon this the Gove^r taking counsell, it was conceivd not fitt to be borne; for if they should suffer their freinds and messengers thus to be wronged, they should have none would cleave unto them, or give them any inteligence, or doe them serviss afterwards; but nexte they would fall upon them selves. Whereupon it was resolved to send the Captaine and 14. men well armed, and to goe and fall upon them in the night; and if they found that Squanto was kild, to cut of Corbitants head, but not to hurt any but those that had a hand in it. Hobamack was asked if he would goe and be their guid, and bring them ther before day. He said he would, and bring them to the house wher the man lay, and show them which was he. So they set forth the 14. of August, and beset the house round; the Captin giving charg to let none pass out, entred the house to search for him. But he was goone away that day, so they mist him; but understood that Squanto was alive, and that he had only threatened to kill him, and made an offer to stabe him but did not. So they withheld and did no more hurte, and the people came trembling, and brought them the best provissions they had, after they were aquainted by Hobamack what was only intended. Ther was 3. sore wounded which broak out of the house, and asaid to pass through the garde. These they brought home with them, and they had their wounds drest and cured, and sente home. After this they had many gratulations from diverce sachims, and much firmer peace; yea, those of the Iles of Capawack sent to make frendship; and this Corbitant him selfe used the mediation of Massassoyte to make his peace, but was shie to come neare them a longe while after.

After this, the 18. of Sepemb^r: they sente out ther shalop to the Massachusets, with 10. men, and Squanto for their guid and interpreter, to discover and veiw that bay, and trade with the natives; the which they performed, and found kind entertainement. The people were much affraid of the Tarentins, a people to the eastward which used to come in harvest time and take away their corne, and many times kill their persons. They returned in saftie, and brought home a good quanty of beaver, and made reporte of the place, wishing they had been ther seated; (but it seems the Lord, who assignes to all men the bounds of their habitations, had apoynted it for an other use). And thus they found the Lord to be with them in all their ways, and to blesse their outgoings and incommings, for which let his holy name have the praise for ever, to all posteritie.

They begane now to gather in the small harvest they had, and to fitte up their houses and dwellings against winter, being all well recovered in health and strenght, and had all things in good plenty; for as some were thus imployed in affairs abroad, others were excersisted in fishing, aboute codd, and bass, and other fish, of which they tooke good store, of which every family had their portion. All the sommer ther was no wante. And now begane to come in store of foule, as winter aproached, of which this place did abound when they came first (but afterward decreased by degrees). And besids water foule, ther was great store of wild Turkies, of which they tooke many, besids venison, etc. Besids they had aboute a peck a meale a weeke to a person, or now since harvest, Indean corne to that proportion. Which made many afterwards write so largly of their plenty hear to their freinds in England, which were not fained, but true reports.

In Novemb^r, about that time twelfe month that them selves came, ther came in a small ship to them unexpected or loked for, in which came Mr. Cushman (so much spoken of before) and with him 35. persons to remaine and live in the plantation; which did not a litle rejoyce them. And they when they came a shore and found all well, and saw plenty of vitails in every house, were no less glade. For most of them were lusty yonge men, and many of them wild enough, who litle considered whither or aboute what they wente, till they came into the harbore at Cap-Codd, and ther saw nothing but a naked and barren place. They then begane to thinke what should become of them, if the people here were dead or cut of by the Indeans. They begane to consulte (upon some speeches that some of the sea-men had cast out) to take the sayls from the yeard least the ship should gett away and leave them ther. But the m^r hereing of it, gave them good words, and tould them if any thing but well should have befallne the people hear, he hoped he had vitails enough to cary them to Virginia, and whilst he had a bitt they should have their parte; which gave them good satisfaction. So they were all landed; but ther was not so much as bisket-cake or any other victialls for them, neither had they any bed-ing, but some sory things they had in their cabins, nor pot, nor pan, to drese any meate in; nor overmany cloaths, for many of them had brusht away their coats and cloaks at Plimoth as they came. But ther was sent over some burching-lane suits in the ship, out of which they were supplied. The plantation was glad of this addition of strenght, but could have wished that many of them had been of beter condition, and all of them beter furnished with provissions; but that could not now be helpte.

In this ship Mr. Weston sent a large leter to Mr. Carver, the late Gove^r, now deseased, full of complaints and expostulations aboute former passagess at Hampton; and the keeping the shipe so long in the country, and returning her without lading, etc., which for brevitie I omite. The rest is as followeth:

PART OF MR. WESTONS LETTER.

I durst never aquainte the adventurers with the alteration of the condi-tions first agreed on betweene us, which I have since been very glad of, for I am well assured had they knowne as much as I doe, they would not have adventured a halfe-peny of what was necesary for this ship. That you sent no lading in the ship is wonderfull, and worthily distasted. I know you^r weaknes was the cause of it, and I beleeve more weaknes of judgmente, then weaknes of hands. A quarter of the time you spente in discoursing, arguing, and consulting, would have done much more; but that is past, etc. If you mean, bona fide, to performe the conditions agreed upon, doe us the favore to coppy them out faire, and subscribe them with the principall of your names. And likwise give us accounte as perticulerly as you can how our moneys were laid out. And then I shall be able to give them some satisfaction, whom I am now forsed with good words to shift of. And consider that the life of the bussines depends on the lading of this ship, which, if you doe to any good purpose, that I may be freed from the great sums I have disbursed for the former, and must doe for the later, *I promise you I will never quit the bussines, though all the other adventurers should.*

We have procured you a Charter, the best we could, which is beter then your former, and with less limitation. For any thing that is els worth writting, Mr. Cushman can informe you. I pray write instantly for Mr. Robinson to come to you. And so praying God to blesse you with all graces nessessary both for this life and that to come, I rest

Your very loving frend,
THO. WESTON.

London, July 6. 1621.

This ship (caled the *Fortune*) was speedily dispatcht away, being laden with good clapbord as full as she could stowe, and 2. hoggsheads of beaver and otter skins, which they gott with a few trifling comodities brought with them at first, being altogeather unprovided for trade; neither was ther any amongst them that ever saw a beaver skin till they came hear, and were informed by Squanto. The fraight was estimated to be worth near 500*li*. Mr. Cushman returned backe also with this ship, for so Mr. Weston and the rest had apoynted him, for their better information. And he doubted not, nor them selves neither, but they should have a speedy supply; considering allso how by Mr. Cushmans perswation, and letters received from Leyden, wherin they willed them so to doe, they yeel[d]ed to the afforesaid conditions, and subscribed them with their hands. But it proved other wise, for Mr. Weston, who had made that large promise in his leter, (as is before noted,) that if all the rest should fall of, yet he would never quit the bussines, but stick to them, if they yeelded to the conditions, and sente some lading in the ship; and of this Mr. Cushman was confident, and confirmed the same from his mouth, and serious protestations to him selfe before he came. But all proved but wind, for he was the first and only man that forsooke them, and that before he so much as heard of the returne of this ship, or knew what was done; (so vaine is the confidence in man.) But of this more in its place.

A leter in answer to his write to Mr. Carver, was sente to him from the Govr, of which so much as is pertenente to the thing in hand I shall hear inserte.

Sr: Your large letter writen to Mr. Carver, and dated the 6. of July, 1621, I have received the 10. of Novembr, wherein (after the apologie made for your selfe) you lay many heavie imputations upon him and us all. Touching him, he is departed this life, and now is at rest in the Lord from all those troubls and incoumbrances with which we are yet to strive. He needs not my appologie; for his care and pains was so great for the commone good, both ours and yours, as that therwith (it is thought) he oppressed him selfe and shortened his days; of whose loss we cannot sufficiently complaine. At great charges in this adventure, I confess you have beene, and many losses may sustaine; but the loss of his and many other honest and industrious mens lives, cannot be vallewed at any prise. Of the one, ther may be hope of recovery, but the other no recompence can make good. But I will not insiste in generalls, but come more perticulerly to the things them selves. You greatly blame us for keping the ship so long in the countrie, and then to send her away emptie. She lay 5. weks at Cap-Codd, whilst with many a weary step (after a long journey) and the indurance of many a hard brunte, we sought out in the foule winter a place of habitation. Then we went in so tedious a time to make provission to sheelter us and our goods, aboute which labour, many of our armes and leggs can tell us to this day we were not necligent. But it pleased God to vissite us then, with death dayly, and with so generall a disease, that the living were scarce able to burie the dead; and the well not in any measure sufficiente to tend the sick. And now to be so greatly blamed, for not fraighting the ship, doth indeed goe near us, and much discourage us. But you say you know we will pretend weaknes; and doe you think we had not cause? Yes, you tell us you beleeve it, but it was more weaknes of judgmente, then of hands. Our weaknes herin is great we confess, therfore we will bear this check patiently amongst the rest, till God send us wiser men. But they which tould you we spent so much time in discoursing and consulting, etc., their harts can tell their toungs, they lye. They cared not, so they might salve their owne sores, how they wounded others. Indeed, it is our callamitie that we are (beyound expectation) yoked with some ill conditioned people, who will never doe good, but corrupte and abuse others, etc.

The rest of the letter declared how they had subscribed those conditions according to his desire, and sente him the former accounts very perticulerly; also how the ship was laden, and in what condition their affairs stood; that the coming of these people would bring famine upon them unavoydably, if they had not supply in time (as Mr. Cushman could more fully informe him and the rest of the adventurers). Also that seeing he was now satisfied in all his demands, that offences would be forgoten, and he remember his promise, etc.

After the departure of this ship, (which stayed not above 14. days,) the Gove^r and his assistante haveing disposed these late commers into severall families, as they best could, tooke an exacte accounte of all their provissions in store, and proportioned the same to the number of persons, and found that it would not hould out above 6. months at halfe alowance, and hardly that. And they could not well give less this winter time till fish came in againe. So they were presently put to half alowance, one as well as an other, which begane to be hard, but they bore it patiently under hope of supply.

Soone after this ships departure, the great people of the Narigansets, in a braving maner, sente a messenger unto them with a bundl of arrows tyed aboute with a great sneak-skine; which their interpretours tould them was a threatening and a chaleng. Upon which the Govr, with the advice of others sente them a round answere, that if they had rather have warre then peace, they might begine when they would; they had done them no wrong, neither did they fear them, or should they find them unprovided. And by another messenger sente the sneake-skine back with bulits in it; but they would not receive it, but sent it back againe. But these things I doe but mention, because they are more at large allready put forth in printe, by Mr. Winslow, at the requeste of some freinds. And it is like the reason was their owne ambition, who, (since the death of so many of the Indeans,) thought to dominire and lord it over the rest, and conceived the English would be a barr in their way, and saw that Massasoyt took sheilter allready under their wings.

But this made them the more carefully to looke to them selves, so as they agreed to inclose their dwellings with a good strong pale, and make flankers in convenient places, with gates to shute, which were every night locked, and a watch kept and when neede required ther was also warding in the day time. And the company was by the Captaine and the Govr advise, devided into 4. squadrons, and every one had ther quarter apoynted them, unto which they were to repaire upon any suddane alarme. And if ther should be any crie of fire, a company were appointed for a gard, with muskets, whilst others quenchet the same, to prevent Indean treachery. This was accomplished very cherfully, and the towne impayled round by the begining of March, in which evry family had a prety garden plote secured. And herewith I shall end this year. Only I shall remember one passage more, rather of mirth then of waight. One the day called Chrismasday, the Govr caled them out to worke, (as was used,) but the most of this new-company excused them selves and said it wente against their consciences to work on that day. So the Govr tould them that if they made it mater of conscience, he would spare them till they were better informed. So he led-away the rest and left them; but when they came home at noone from their worke, he found them in the streete at play, openly; some pitching the barr and some at stoole-ball, and shuch like sports. So he went to them, and tooke away their implements, and tould them that was against his conscience, that they should play and others worke. If they made the keeping of it mater of devotion, let them kepe their houses, but ther should be no gameing or reveling in the streets. Since which time nothing hath been atempted that way, at least openly.

ANNO. 1622.

At the spring of the year they had apointed the Massachusets to come againe and trade with them, and begane now to prepare for that vioag about the later end of March. But upon some rumors heard, Hobamak, their Indean, tould them upon some jealocies he had, he feared they were joyned with the Narighansets and might betray them if they were not carefull. He intimated also some jealocie of Squanto, by what he gathered from some private whisperings betweene him and other Indeans. But they resolved to proseede, and sente out their shalop with 10. of their cheefe men aboute the begining of Aprill, and both Squanto and Hobamake with them, in regarde of the jelocie betweene them. But they had not bene gone longe, but an Indean belonging to Squantos family came runing in seeming great fear, and tould them that many of the Narihgansets, with Corbytant, and he thought also Massasoyte, were coming against them; and he gott away to tell them, not without danger. And being examined by the Govr, he made as if they were at hand, and would still be looking back, as if they were at his heels. At which the Govr caused them to take armes and stand on their garde, and supposing the boat to be still within hearing (by reason it was calme) caused a warning peece or 2. to be shote of, the which they heard and came in. But no Indeans apeared; watch was kepte all night, but nothing was seene. Hobamak was confidente for Massasoyt, and thought all was false; yet the Govr caused him to send his wife privatly, to see what she could observe (pretening other occasions), but ther was nothing found, but all was quiet. After this they proseeded on their vioge to the Massachusets, and had good trade, and returned in saftie, blessed be God.

But by the former passages, and other things of like nature, they begane to see that Squanto sought his owne ends, and plaid his owne game, by putting the Indeans in fear, and drawing gifts from them to enrich him selfe; making them beleeve he could stur up warr against whom he would, and make peece for whom he would. Yea, he made them beleeve they kept the plague buried in the ground, and could send it amongs whom they would, which did much terrifie the Indeans, and made them depend more on him, and seeke more to him then to Massasoyte, which proucured him envie, and had like to have cost him his life. For after the discovery of his practises, Massasoyt sought it both privatly and openly; which caused him to stick close to the English, and never durst goe from them till he dyed. They also made good use of the emulation that grue betweene Hobamack and him, which made them cary more squarely. And the Govr seemed to countenance the one, and the Captaine the other, by which they had better intelligence, and made them both more diligente.

JOHN WINTHROP

John Winthrop (1588–1649), Puritan and governor of the Massachu-setts Bay Colony, was largely responsible for developing and directing the theocratic government of the colony. He rejected democracy and toleration, and regarded Indians as evil. His journal, first published in its entirety in 1853, is a major source for colonial material, and The Life and Letters of John Winthrop *is a valuable supplement.*

JOHN WINTHROP TO WILLIAM BRADFORD
From *Life and Letters of John Winthrop (1630-1649)*

"WORTHY SIR,—I received your loving letter, and am much provoked to express my affections towards you, but straightness of time forbids me, for my desire is to acquaint you with the Lord's great mercy to-wards us, in our prevailing against his & our enemies, that you may rejoice & praise his name with us. About fourscore of our men, having coasted along towards the Dutch Plantation, sometimes by water but most by land, met here & there with some Pequots, whom they slew or took prisoners. Two Sachems they took & beheaded; & not hearing of Sassacus, the chief Sachem, they gave a prisoner his life to go & find him out: He went & brought them word where he was, but Sassacus suspecting him to be a spy, after he was gone, fled away with some twenty more to the Mohawks, so our men missed of him; yet dividing themselves & ranging up & down as the providence of God guided them, for the Indians were all gone, save three or four, & they knew not whither to find them, or else would not, upon the thirteenth of this month, they lighted upon a great company, viz. eighty strong men, & two hundred women & children, in a small Indian town, fast by a hideous swamp, which they all slipped into, before our men could get to them.

"Our Captains were not then come together; but there was Mr. Lud-low & Captain Mason, with some ten of their men, Captain Patrick, with some twenty or more of his, who, shooting at the Indians, Captain Trask, with fifty more, came soon in at the noise. Then they gave order to surround the swamp, it being about a mile round; but Lieutenant Davenport, & some twelve more, not hearing that command, fell into the swamp amongst the Indians. The swamp was so thick with shrubs, & boggy withal, that some stuck fast, & received many shot.

"Lieutenant Davenport was dangerously wounded about his arm hole, & another shot in the head, so as fainting, they were in great dan-ger to have been taken by the Indians; but Sergeant Riggs and Sergeant Jeffery, & two or three more, rescued them, & slew divers of the Indians with their swords. After they were drawn out, the Indians desired parley, & were offered by Thomas Stanton, our interpreter, that if they would come out & yield themselves, they should have their lives that had not their hand in the English blood. Whereupon the Sachem of the place came forth, & an old man or two, & their wives & children, & so they spake two hours, till it was night. Then Thomas Stanton was sent to them again, to call them forth, but they said they would sell their lives there; & so shot at him so thick, as, if he had not been presently relieved & rescued, on his crying out, they would have slain him.

"Then our men cut off a place of swamp with their swords, & cooped up the Indians into a narrow compass, so as they could easier kill them through the thickets. So they continued all the night, standing about twelve foot one from another, & the Indians coming up close to our men, shot their arrows so thick, as they pierced their hat brims, & their sleeves & stockings, & other parts of their clothes; yet so miraculously did the Lord preserve them, as not one of them was wounded, save those there who rashly went into the swamp as aforesaid. When it was near day it grew very dark, so as those of them that were left, dropped away, though they stood but twelve or fourteen foot asunder, & were presently discovered, & some killed in the pursuit. In the searching of the swamp the next morning, they found nine slain, & some they pulled up, whom the Indians had buried in the mire; so as they do think that of all their company not twenty did escape, for they afterwards found some who died in the fight, of their wounds received. The prisoners were divided, some to those of the river, & the rest to us of these parts. We send the male children to Bermuda[1] by Mr. William Pierce, & the women & maid children are disposed about in the towns. There have been slain & taken in all, about seven hundred, the rest are dispersed, & the Indians, in all quarters, so terrified, as all their friends are afraid to receive them. Two of the Sachems of Long Island came to Mr. Stoughton, & tendered themselves to be under our protection; & two of the Neponset Sachems have been with me to seek our friendship. Among the prisoners we have the wife & children of Mononotto, a woman of very modest countenance & behaviour. It was by her mediation, that two English maids were spared from death, & were kindly used by her. One of her first requests was, that the English would not abuse her body, & that her children might not be taken from her. Those which were wounded we fetched soon off, by John Gallop, who came with his boat in a happy hour, to bring them victuals, & to carry their wounded men to the barque, where our chief surgeon was, with Mr. Wilson, being about eight leagues off. Our people are all in health, the Lord be praised. And although they had marched in their arms all the day, & had been in fight all the night, yet they professed they found themselves so, as they would willingly have gone to such another business. The Captains report we have slain thirteen Sachems, but Sasacus

& Mononotto are still living. This is the substance of what I have received, though I am forced to omit many considerable circumstances. So being in much straightness of time, the ships being to depart within this four days, & in them Lord Lee & Mr. Vane; I here break off, & with hearty salutations, &c. I rest

"Your assured friend,

"JOHN WINTHROP.

"JULY 28, 1637"

From
LAST WILL AND TESTAMENT

"I give to my son Adam my island called the Governour's Garden, to have to him and his heirs forever; not doubting but he will be dutiful and loving to his mother, and kind to his brethren in letting them partake in such fruits as grow there. I give him also my Indians there and my boat and such household as is there.

DIARY ENTRY, 1646

"Mention was made before of some beginning to instruct the Indians, etc. Mr. John Eliot, teacher of the church of Roxbury, found such encouragement, as he took great pains to get their language, and in a few months could speak of the things of God to their understanding; and God prospered his endeavors, so as he kept a constant lecture to them in two places, one week at the wigwam of one Wabon, a *new* sachem near Watertown mill, and the other the next week in the wigwam of Cutshamekin near Dorchester mill. And for the furtherance of the work of God, divers of the English resorted to his lecture, and the governour and other of the magistrates and elders sometimes; and the Indians began to repair thither from other parts. His manner of proceeding was thus; he would persuade one of the other elders or some magistrate to begin the exercise with prayer in English; then he took a text, and read it first in the Indian language, and after in English; then he preached to them in Indian about an hour; (but first I should have spoke of the catechising their children, who were soon brought to answer him some short questions, whereupon he gave each of them an apple or a cake) then he demanded of some of the chiefs, if they understood him; if they answered, yea, then he asked of them if they had any questions to propound. And they had usually two or three or more questions, which he did resolve. At one time (when the governour was there and about two hundred people, Indian and English, in one wigwam of Cutshamekin's) an old man asked him, if God would receive such an old man as he was; to whom he answered by opening the parable of the workmen that were hired into the vineyard; and when he had opened it, he asked the old man, if he did believe it, who answered he did, and was ready to *weep*. A second question was, what was the reason, that when all Englishmen did know God, yet some of them were poor. His answer was, 1. that God knows it is better for his children to be good than to be rich; he knows withal, that if some of them had riches, they would abuse them, and wax proud and wanton, etc., therefore he gives them no more riches than may be needful for them, that they may be kept from pride, etc., to depend upon him, 2. he would hereby have men know, that he hath better blessings to bestow upon good men than riches, etc., and that their best portion is in heaven, etc. A third question was, if a man had two wives, (which was ordinary with them,) seeing he must put away one, which he should put away. To this it was answered, that by the law of God the first is the true wife, and the other is no wife; but if such a case fell out, they should then repair to the magistrates, and they would direct them what to do, for it might be, that the first wife might be an adulteress, etc., and then she was to be put away. When all their questions were resolved, he concluded with prayer in the Indian language.

"The Indians were usually very attentive, and kept their children so quiet as caused no disturbance. Some of them began to be seriously affected, and to understand the things of God, and they were generally ready to reform whatsoever they were told to be against the word of God, as their sorcery, (which they call powwowing,) their whoredoms, etc., idleness, etc. The Indians grew very inquisitive after knowledge both in things divine and also human, so as one of them, meeting with an honest plain Englishman, would needs know of him, what were the first beginnings (which we call principles) of a commonwealth. The Englishman, being far short in the knowledge of such matters, yet ashamed that an Indian should find an Englishman ignorant of any thing, bethought himself what answer to give him, at last resolved upon this, viz. that the first principle of a commonwealth was salt, for (saith he) by means of salt we can keep our flesh and fish, to have it ready when we need it, whereas you lose much for want of it, and are sometimes ready to starve. A second principle is iron, for thereby we fell trees, build houses, till our land, etc. A third is, ships, by which we carry forth such commodities as we have to spare, and fetch in such as we need, as cloth, wine, etc. Alas! (saith the Indian) then I fear, we shall never be a commonwealth, for we can neither make salt, nor iron, nor ships."

From
NARRATIVES OF THE INDIAN WARS (1669)
COTTON MATHER

Cotton Mather (1663–1728), Puritan clergyman and theologian, was a powerful voice and force in the theocracy. A firm believer in witchcraft and the omnipresence of the devil, he was convinced that opposition to Puritan programs and policies, particularly by the Indians as well as other non-believers, was action contrary to God's will.

INTRODUCTION.

Twenty Three Years have Rolled away since the Nations of Indians within the Confines of New England, generally began a fierce War upon the English Inhabitants of that Country. The Flame of War then Raged thro' a great part of the Country, whereby many whole Towns were Laid in Ashes, and many Lives were Sacrificed. But in little more than one years Time, the United Colonies of Plymouth, Massachusetts, and Connecticut, with their United Endeavours, bravely Conquered the Salvages. The Evident Hand of Heaven appearing on the Side of a people whose Hope and Help was alone in the Almighty Lord of Hosts, Extinguished whole Nations of the Salvages at such a rate, that there can hardly any of them now be found under any Distinction upon the face of the Earth. Onely the Fate of our Northern and Eastern Regions in that War was very different from that of the rest. The Desolations of the War had overwhelmed all the Settlements to the North-East of Wells. And when the Time arrived, that all hands were weary of the War, a sort of a Peace was patched up, which Left a Body of Indians, not only with Horrible Murders Unrevenged, but also in the possession of no little part of the Countrey, with circumstances which the English might think not very Honourable. Upon this Peace the English returned unto their Plantations; their Number increased; they Stock'd their Farms, and Sow'd their Fields; they found the Air as Healthful, as the Earth was Fruitful; their Lumber and their Fishery became a considerable Merchandize; continual Accessions were made unto them, until Ten or a Dozen Towns in the Province of Main, and the County of Cornwall, were suddenly Started up into something of Observation.

But in the Year 1688, the Indians which dwelt after the Indian manner among them, Commenced another War upon these Plantations which hath broke them up, and strangely held us in play for Ten Years together. In these Ten Years there hath been a variety of Remarkable Occurrences; and because I have supposed that a Relation of those Occurrences may be Acceptable and Profitable to some of my Country men, I shall now with all Faithfulness Endeavour it. With all Faithfulness, I say; because tho' there should happen any Circumstantial Mistake in our Story, (for 'tis a rare thing for any Two men concern'd in the same Action, to give the Story of it without some Circumstantial Difference) yet even this also I shall be willing to Retract and Correct, if there be found any just occasion: But for any one Material Error in the whole Composure, I challenge the most Sagacious Malice upon Earth to detect it, while matters are yet so fresh as to allow the Detection of it. I disdain to make the Apology once made by the Roman Historian, *Nemo Historicus non aliquid mentitus, et habiturus sum mendaciorum Comites, quos Historiœ et eloquentiœ miramur Authores.* No, I will write with an Irreproachable and Incontestable Veracity; and I will write not one Thing but what I am furnished with so good Authority for, that any Reasonable man, who will please to Examine it, shall say, I do well to insert it as I do: And I will hope that my reader hath not been Studying of Godefridus de Valle's book, *De arte nihil Credendi;* About The Art of Believing Nothing. Wherefore having at the very Beginning thus given such a Knock upon thy Head, O Malice, that thou canst never with Reason Hiss at our History, we will proceed unto the several Articles of it.

Article I.

The Occasion and Beginning of the War.

If Diodorus Siculus had never given it as a great Rule of History, *Historiœ primum Studium, primariaq' consideratioesse videtur, insoliti gravisq' Casus principio causas investigare,* Yet my Reader would have expected that I should Begin the History of our War, with an History of the Occurrences and Occasions which did Begin the War. Now, Reader, I am at the very first fallen upon a Difficult Point; and I am in danger of pulling a War upon my self, by Endeavouring of thy Satisfaction. In Truth, I had rather be called a Coward, than undertake my self to Determine the Truth in this matter; but having Armed my self with some good Authority for it, I will Transcribe Two or Three Reports of the matter, now in my Hands, and Leave it unto thy own Determination.

One Account I have now lying by me, Written by a Gentleman of Dover, in these Terms.

The Eastern Indians, and especially those of Saco and Ammonoscoggin pretend many Reasons for the late Quarrel against the English, which began this long and bloody War.

1. Because the English refused to pay that yearly Tribute of Corn, agreed upon in the Articles of Peace formerly concluded with them by the English Commissioners.

2. Because they were Invaded in their Fishery, at Saco River, by certain Gentlemen, who stop'd the Fish from coming up the River with their Nets and Sains. This they were greatly Affronted at, saying, They thought (though the English had got away their Lands as they had, yet) the Fishery of the Rivers had been a priviledge Reserved Entire unto themselves.

3. Because they were Abused by the English, in Suffering, if not Turning, their Cattel over to a certain Island to destroy their Corn.

4. But the Fourth and Main provocation was, The Granting or Pattenting of their Lands to some English; at which they were greatly Enraged, threatning the Surveyor to knock him on the Head if he came to lay out any Lands there.

5. To these may be added the Common Abuses in Trading, *viz.* Drunkeness, Cheating, etc. which such as Trade much with them are seldom Innocent of.

Doubtless these Indian Allegations may be answered with many English Vindications. But I shall at present Intermeddle no further than to offer another Account, which also I have in my Hands, written by a Gentleman of Casco. It runs in such terms as these.

Many were the Outrages and Insultings of the Indians upon the English, while Sir E. A. was Governour. At North-Yarmouth, and other places at the Eastward, the Indians killed sundry Cattel, came into Houses, and threatned to knock the people on the Head; and at several Times gave out Reports that they would make a War upon the English, and that they were animated to do so by the French. The Indians, behaving themselves so insultingly, gave just occasion of great suspicion. In order for the finding out the Truth, and to Endeavour the preventing of a War, Capt. Blackman, Justice of Peace, with some of the Neighbourhood of Saco River, Seized several Indians that had been bloody murderous Rogues in the first Indian War, being the chief Ring-Leaders, and most capable to do mischief. The said Capt. Blackman Seized to the Number of between Sixteen and Twenty, in order for their Examination, and to bring the rest to a Treaty. The said Blackman soon sent the said Indians with a Good Guard to Falmouth in Casco-bay, there to be Secured, until orders could come from Boston concerning them. And in the mean Time the said Indians were well provided with Provisions and Suitable Necessaries. The rest of the Indians Robb'd the English, and took some English Prisoners: Whereupon Post was sent to Boston. Sir Edmond Andross being at New-York, the Gentlemen of Boston sent to Falmouth some Souldiers for the Defence of the Country, and also the Worshipful Mr. Stoughton, with others, to Treat with the Indians in order for the Setting of a Peace, and getting in of our English Captives. As soon as the said Gentlemen arrived to the East-ward, they sent away one of the Indian Prisoners to the rest of the Indians, to Summon them to bring in the English they had taken; Also that their Sachims should come in to treat with the English, in order that a Just Satisfaction should be made on both sides. The Gentlemen waited the Return of the Indian Messenger; and when he Returned he brought Answer, That they would meet our English at a place called Macquoit, and there they would bring in the English Captives, and Treat with the English. And although the place appointed by the Indians for the Meeting was some Leagues distant from Falmouth, yet our English Gentlemen did condescend to it, in hope of getting in our Captives, and putting a stop to further Trouble. They Dispatch'd away to the place, and carried the Indian Prisoners with them, and staid at the place appointed, expecting the coming of the Indians that had promised a Meeting. But they, like false perfidious Rogues, did not appear. Without doubt they had been counselled what to do by the French and their Abettors, as the Indians did declare afterwards; and that they were near the place, and saw our English that were to Treat with them, but would not shew themselves; but did Endeavour to take an Opportunity to Destroy our English that were to Treat [with] them. Such was their Treachery! Our Gentlemen staid days to wait their coming; but seeing they did not appear at the place appointed, they Returned to Falmouth, and brought the Indian Prisoners, expecting that the other Indians would have sent down some Reason why they did not appear at the place appointed, and to make some excuse for themselves. But instead of any compliance, they fell upon North Yarmouth, and there kill'd several of our English. Whereupon the Eastern parts were ordered to get into Garrisons, and to be upon their Guard until further Orders from Sir Edmond Andros; and that the Indian Prisoners should be sent to Boston, which was done with great care, and not one of them hurt; and care taken daily for provision. But Sir E. A. Returning from New-York, set them all at Liberty; not so much as taking care to Redeem those of our English for them, that were in their hands. I had kept one at Falmouth a Prisoner, to be a Guide into the Woods for our English, to find out the Haunts of our Heathen Enemies. But Sir E. A. sent an Express to me, that upon my utmost peril I should set the said Indian at Liberty, and take care that all the Arms that were taken from him, and all the rest of those Capt. Blackman had seized, should be delivered up to them, without any Orders to Receive the like of ours from them.

It will be readily Acknowledged, that here was enough done to render the Indians Inexcusable for not coming in upon the Proclamation, which Sir Edmond Andros, then Governour of New-England, immediately Emitted thereupon, requiring them to Surrender the Murderers now among them. A Spaniard, that was a Souldier, would say, That if we have a good Cause, the smell of Gunpowder in the Field is as sweet as the Incense at the Altar. Let the Reader judge after these things, what scent there was in the Gunpowder spent for Nine or Ten years together in our War with the Indian Salvages.

Now that while we are upon this Head, we may at once dispatch it; I will unto these two Accounts add certain passages of one more, which was published in September, 1689.

Such were the Obscure Measures taken at that Time of Day, that the Rise of this War hath been as dark as that of the River Nilus; only the Generality of Thinking People through the Country can Remember When and Where every one did foretel A War. If any Wild English (for there are such as well as of another nation) did then Begin to Provoke and Affront the Indians, yet those Indians had a fairer way to come by Right than that of Bloodshed, nothing worthy of, or calling for, any Such Revenge was done unto them. The most Injured of them all, (if there were any Such) were afterwards dismissed by the English with Favours, that were then Admirable even to Our selves; and These too, instead of Surrendring the Persons, did increase the Numbers of the Murderers. But upon the Revolution of the Government (April, 1689.) the State of the War became wholly New: and we are more arrived unto Righteousness as the Light, and Justice as the Noon day. A great Sachem of the East we then immediately Applied our selves unto, and with no small Expences to our selves, we Engaged Him to Employ his Interest for a Good Understanding between us, and the party of Indians then in Hostility against us. This was the Likely, the Only way of coming at those Wandring Salvages: But That very Sachem now treacherously of an Embassador became a Traitor, and annexed himself with his People to the Heard of our Enemies, which have since been Ravaging, Pillaging and Murdering, at a rate which we ought to count Intolerable. The Penacook Indians, of whom we were Jealous, we likewise Treated with; and while we were by our Kindnesses and Courtesies Endeavouring to render them utterly Inexcusable, if ever they sought our Harm; Even They, did Those also by some Evil Instigation, (the Devils, no doubt!) quickly Surprize a Plantation where they had been Civilly treated a Day or Two before, and Commit at once more Plunder and Murder than can be heard with patience.

Reader, Having so placed these Three Accounts as to defend my Teeth, I think I may safely proceed with our Story. But because Tacitus teaches us to distinguish between the meer Occasions and the real Causes of a War, it may be some will go a little Higher up in their Enquiries: They will Enquire whether no body seized a parcel of Wines that were Landed at a French Plantation to the East ward? Whether an Order were not obtained from the King of England, at the Instance of the French Embassador, to Restore these Wines? Whether upon the Vexation of this Order, we none of us ran a New Line for the Bounds of the Province? Whether we did not contrive our New Line so as to take in the Country of Monsieur St. Casteen? Whether Monsieur St. Casteen, flying from our Encroachments, we did not seize upon his Arms and Goods, and bring them away to Pemmaquid? And Who were the We which did these things? And whether the Indians, who were Extremely under the Influence of St. Casteen, that had Married a Sagamore's Daughter among them, did not from this very Moment begin to be obstreperous? And whether all the Sober English in the

Country did not from this very Moment foretel a War? But for any Answer to all these Enquiries I will be my self a Tacitus.

ARTICLE II.

The first Acts of Hostility between the Indians and the English.

When one Capt. Sargeant had Seized some of the principal Indians about Saco by order of Justice Blackman, presently the Indians fell to Seizing as many of the English, as they could catch. Capt. Rowden, with many more, in one place, and Capt. Gendal, with sundry more, in another place, particularly fell into the Hands of these desperate Man-catchers. Rowden, with many of his Folks, never got out of their Cruel Hands; but Gendal, with his, got a Release, one can scarce too, How, upon the Return of those which had been detain'd in Boston. Hitherto there was no Spilling of Blood! But some Time in September following, this Capt. Gendal went up, with Soldiers and others, to a place above Casco, called North Yarmouth, having Orders to build Stockados on both sides the River, for Defence of the place, in case of any Sudden Invasion. While they were at work, an English Captive came to 'em with Information, that Seventy or Eighty of the Enemy were just coming upon 'em; and he advised 'em, To yield quietly, that they might Save their Lives. The Soldiers that went thither from the Southward being terrifyed at this Report, Ran with an Hasty Terror to get over the River; but with more Hast than good speed; for they ran directly into the Hands of the Indians. The Indians dragging along these their Prisoners with 'em, came up towards the Casconians; who, having but a very Little Time to Consult, yet in this Time Resolved; First, That they would not be Siezed by the Salvages: Next, That they would free their Friends out of the Hands of the Salvages, if it were possible; Thirdly, That if it were possible they would use all other Force upon the Salvages, without coming to down right Fight. Accordingly They laid hold on their Neighbours, whom the Salvages had Siezed, and this with so much Dexterity that they cleared them all, Except one or Two; whereof the whole Number was about a Dozen. But in the Scuffle one Sturdy and Surly Indian held his prey so fast, that one Benedict Pucifer gave the Mastiff a Blow with the Edge of his Broad Ax upon the Shoulder, upon which they fell to't with a Vengeance, and Fired their Guns on both sides, till some on both sides were Slain. These were, as one may call them, the Scower-pit of a long War to follow. At last, the English Victoriously chased away the Salvages, and Returned safely unto the other side of the River. And Thus was the Vein of New-England first opened, that afterwards Bled for Ten years together!

The Skirmish being over, Captain Gendal in the Evening passed over the River in a Canoo, with none but a Servant; but Landing where the Enemy lay hid in the Bushes, they were both Slain immediately. And the same Evening, one Ryal, with another man, fell unawares into the Hands of the Enemy; Ryal was afterwards Ransomed by Monsieur St. Casteen, but the other man, was barbarously Butchered. Soon after this, the Enemy went Eastward unto a place call'd Merry-Meeting, (from the Concourse of divers Rivers there) where several English had a Sad-Meeting with them; for they were killed several of them even in Cold Blood, after the Indians had Seized upon their Houses and their Persons. And about this Time, the Town call'd Sheepscote was entered by these Rapacious Wolves, who burnt all the Houses of the Town, save Two or Three. The People saved themselves by getting into the Fort, all but one Man, who going out of the Fort, for to Treat with 'em, was Treacherously Assassinated. Thus the place, which was counted, The Garden of the East, was infested by Serpents; and a Sword Expell'd the poor Inhabitants. Little more Spoil was done by the Salvages before Winter, Except only, that a place called Kennebunk, near Winter-harbour, they cut off Two Families, to wit, Barrows, and Bussies; but Winter coming on, the Serpents retired into their Holes. When Summer comes, Reader, look for Tornadoes enough to overset a greater Vessel, than little New-England.

ARTICLE III.

The First Expedition of the English against the Indians.

When the Keeper of the Wild Beasts, at Florence, has entertain'd the Spectators with their Encounters on the Stage, he has this Device to make 'em Retire into the several Dens of their Seraglio. He has a fearful Machin of Wood, made like a Great Green Dragon, which a man within it rouls upon Wheels, and holding out a Couple of Lighted Torches at the Eyes of it, frights the fiercest Beast of them all into the Cell that belongs unto him. Sir Edmond Andros, the Governour of New-England, that he might Express his Resolutions, to force the Wild Beasts of the East into order, in the Winter now coming on, turned upon them as Effectual a Machin as the Green Dragon of Florence; that is to say, An Army of near a Thousand men. With this Army he marched himself in Person into the Caucasæan Regions, where he built a Fort at Pemmaquid, and another Fort at Pechypscot Falls, besides the Fort at Sheepscote. He, and his Army underwent no little Hardship, thus in the Depth of Winter to Expose themselves unto the Circumstances of a Campaign, in all the Bleak Winds and Thick Snows of that

Northern Country. But it was Hop'd That Good Forts being thus Garrison'd with Stout Hearts in several Convenient places, the Indians might be kept from their usual Retreats, both for Planting and for Fishing, and lye open also to perpetual Incursions from the English, in the fittest seasons thereof: and it was Thought by the most sensible, this method would in a little while compel the Enemy to Submit unto any Terms: albeit others considering the Vast Woods of the Wilderness, and the French on the back of these Woods, fancied that this was but a project to Hedge in the Cuckow. However, partly the Army, and partly the Winter, frighted the salvages into their Inaccessible Dens: and yet not one of the Indians was killed; but Sickness and Service kill'd it may be more of our English, than there were Indians then in Hostility against them. The News of matters approaching towards a Revolution in England, caused the Governor to Return unto Boston in the Spring, and upon his Return, there fell out several odd Events, with Rumours, whereof I have now nothing to say, but, that I love my eyes too well, to mention them. Some of the Soldiers took Advantage from the Absence of the Governor to desert their Stations in the Army; and tho' this Action was by Good men generally condemned, as an Evil Action, yet their Friends began to gather together here and there in Little Bodies to protect them from the Governor, concerning whom, abundance of odd Stories then buzz'd about the Country, made 'em to imagine, that he had carried 'em out only to Sacrifice 'em. Some of the principal Gentlemen in Boston, consulting what was to be done, in this Extraordinary Juncture, They Agreed, that altho' New-England had as much to Justifie a Revolution as old, yet they would, if it were possible, extinguish all Essays in the people, towards an Insurrection; in daily hopes of Orders from England for our Safety: but that if the Country people, by any unrestrainable Violences pushed the business on so far, as to make a Revolution unavoidable, Then to prevent the Shedding of Blood by an ungoverned Mobile, some of the Gentlemen present, should appear at the Head of it, with a Declaration accordingly prepared. He that Reads the Narrative of Grievances under the Male Administrations of the Government then Tyrannizing, Written and Signed by the Chief Gentlemen of the Governour's Council, will not wonder at it, that a Revolution was now rendered indeed unavoidable. It was a Government whereof New Randolph, a Bird of their own Feather, confess'd as we find in one of his published Letters, That they were as Arbitrary as the Great Turk. And for such a Government a better Similitude cannot perhaps be thought on than that of Mons. Souligne; 'Tis like the Condition of persons possessed with Evil Spirits, which will go an Hundred Leagues in less time than others can Ten; but at the Journeys End find themselves to be so Bruised that they never can Recover it. The Revolution (and ye

Tories, a Just one) was accordingly Made on the Eighteenth of April, which their Majesties, then happily Seated on the British Throne, kindly Accepted and Approved. The Governor and Magistrates of the Massachusets-Colony, which were in power Three years and Half before, (a period often observed!) did some Time after this Resume their places, and apply themselves to such Acts of Government, as Emergencies made necessary for them, Fortified with a Letter from the King to Authorize and Empower them in their Administrations. Thus they waited for further Directions from the Authority of England, and such a Settlement as would most Conduce (which were the words of the King's Letter, bearing Date Aug. 12, 1689.) to the Security and Satisfaction of the Subjects in that Colony.

HUMANISTIC
AND
SCIENTIFIC
CONCERNS

From
THE SELLING OF JOSEPH (1700)
SAMUEL SEWALL

A political leader in Massachusetts for most of his life, Samuel Sewall (1652–1730), was a political and economic conservative. Nevertheless, his determination to see that the Indians were shown just treatment and his eloquent The Selling of Joseph *reflect a deep and liberal humanitarianism rare in New England at the time.*

"Forasmuch as Liberty *is in real value next unto* Life: *None ought to part with it themselves, or deprive others of it, but upon most mature Consideration.*

"The Numerousness of Slaves at this day in the Province, and the Uneasiness of them under their Slavery, hath put many upon thinking whether the Foundation of it be firmly and well laid; so as to sustain the Vast Weight that is built upon it. It is most certain that all Men, as they are the Sons of *Adam,* are Co-heirs; and have equal Right unto Liberty, and all other outward Comforts of Life. *GOD hath given the Earth* (with all its Commodities) *unto the Sons of* Adam, *Psal.* 115. 16. *And hath made of One Blood, all Nations of Men, for to dwell on all the face of the Earth, and hath determined the Times before appointed, and the bounds of their habitation: That they should seek the Lord. Forasmuch then as we are the Offspring of GOD &c. Act* 17. 26, 27, 29. Now although the Title given by the last *ADAM,* doth infinitely better Mens Estates, respecting GOD and themselves; and grants them a most beneficial and inviolable Lease under the Broad Seal of Heaven, who were before only Tenants at Will: Yet through the Indulgence of GOD to our First Parents after the Fall, the outward Estate of all and every of their Children, remains the same, as to one another. So that Originally, and Naturally, there is no such thing as Slavery. *Joseph* was rightfully no more a Slave to his Brethren, than they were to him: and they had no more Authority to *Sell* him, than they had to *Slay* him. And if *they* had nothing to do to Sell him; the Ishmaelites bargaining with them, and paying down Twenty pieces of Silver, could not make a Title. Neither could *Potiphar* have any better interest in him than the *Ishmaelites* had. *Gen.* 37. 20, 27, 28. For he that shall in this case plead *Alteration of Property,* seems to have forfeited a great part of his own claim to Humanity. There is no proportion between Twenty Pieces of Silver, and LIBERTY. The Commodity itself is the Claimer. If *Arabian* Gold be imported in any quantities, most are afraid to meddle with it, though they might have it at easy rates; lest if it should have been wrongfully taken from the Owners, it should kindle a fire to the Consumption of their whole Estate. 'Tis pity there should be more Caution used in buying a Horse, or a little lifeless dust; than there is in purchasing Men and Women: Whenas they are the Offspring of GOD, and their Liberty is,

" '. . . *Auro pretiosior Omni.*'

"And seeing GOD hath said, *He that Stealeth a Man and Selleth him, or if he be found in his hand, he shall surely be put to Death.* *Exod.* 21. 16. This Law being of Everlasting Equity, wherein Man Stealing is ranked amongst the most atrocious of Capital Crimes: What louder Cry can there be made of that Celebrated Warning,

" *'Caveat Emptor!'*

"And all things considered, it would conduce more to the Welfare of the Province, to have White Servants for a Term of Years, than to have Slaves for Life. Few can endure to hear of a Negro's being made free; and indeed they can seldom use their freedom well; yet their continual aspiring after their forbidden Liberty, renders them Unwilling Servants. And there is such a disparity in their Conditions, Colour & Hair, that they can never embody with us, and grow up into orderly Families, to the Peopling of the Land: but still remain in our Body Politick as a kind of extravasat Blood. As many Negro men as there are among us, so many empty places there are in our Train Bands, and the places taken up of Men that might make Husbands for our Daughters. And the Sons and Daughters of *New England* would become more like *Jacob,* and *Rachel,* if this Slavery were thrust quite out of doors. Moreover it is too well known what Temptations Masters are under, to connive at the Fornication of their Slaves; lest they should be obliged to find them Wives, or pay their Fines. It seems to be practically pleaded that they might be Lawless; 'tis thought much of, that the Law should have Satisfaction for their Thefts, and other Immoralities; by which means, *Holiness to the Lord,* is more rarely engraven upon this sort of Servitude. It is likewise most lamentable to think, how in taking Negros out of *Africa,* and Selling of them here, That which GOD has joyned together men do boldly rend asunder; Men from their Country, Husbands from their Wives, Parents from their Children. How horrible is the Uncleanness, Mortality, if not Murder, that the Ships are guilty of that bring great Crouds of these miserable Men, and Women. Methinks, when we are bemoaning the barbarous Usage of our Friends and Kinsfolk in *Africa:* it might not be unseasonable to enquire whether we are not culpable in forcing the Africans to become Slaves amongst our selves. And it may be a question whether all the Benefit received by *Negro* Slaves, will balance the Accompt of Cash laid out upon them; and for the Redemption of our own enslaved Friends out of *Africa.* Besides all the Persons and Estates that have perished there.

"Obj. 1. *These Blackamores are of the Posterity* of Cham, *and therefore are under the Curse of Slavery.* Gen. 9. 25, 26, 27.

"*Answ.* Of all Offices, one would not begg this; *viz.* Uncall'd for, to be an Executioner of the Vindictive Wrath of God; the extent and duration of which is to us uncertain. If this ever was a Commission; How do we know but that it is long since out of Date? Many have found it to their Cost, that a Prophetical Denunciation of Judgment against a Person or People, would not warrant them to inflict that evil. If it would, *Hazael* might justify himself in all he did against his Master, and the *Israelites,* from 2 *Kings* 8. 10, 12.

"But it is possible that by cursory reading, this Text may have been mistaken. For *Canaan* is the Person Cursed three times over, without the mentioning of *Cham.* Good Expositors suppose the Curse entail'd on him, and that this Prophesie was accomplished in the Extirpation of the *Canaanites,* and in the Servitude of the *Gibeonites. Vide Pareum.* Whereas the Blackmores are not descended of *Canaan,* but of *Cush.* Psal. 68. 31. *Princes shall come out of Egypt* [Misraim], *Ethiopia* [Cush] *shall soon stretch out her hands unto God.* Under which Names, all *Africa* may be comprehended; and their Promised Conversion ought to be prayed for. Jer. 13. 23. *Can the Ethiopian change his skin?* This shows that Black Men are the Posterity of *Cush:* Who time out of mind have been distinguished by their Colour. And for want of the true, Ovid assigns a fabulous cause of it.

" '*Sanguine tum credunt in corpora summa vocato Æthiopum populus nigrum traxisse colorem.*'

Metamorph. lib. 2.

"Obj. 2. *The Nigers are brought out of a Pagan Country, into places where the Gospel is Preached.*

"*Answ.* Evil must not be done, that good may come of it. The extraordinary and comprehensive Benefit accruing to the Church of God, and to *Joseph* personally, did not rectify his brethrens Sale of him.

"Obj. 3. *The* Africans *have Wars one with another: Our Ships bring lawful Captives taken in those Wars.*

"*Answ.* For ought is known, their Wars are much such as were between *Jacob's* Sons and their Brother *Joseph.* If they be between Town and Town; Provincial, or National: Every War is upon one side Unjust. An Unlawful War can't make lawful Captives. And by Receiving, we are in danger to promote, and partake in their Barbarous Cruelties. I am sure, if some Gentlemen should go down to the Brewsters to take the Air, and Fish: and a stronger party from *Hull* should Surprise them, and Sell them for Slaves to a Ship outward bound: they would think themselves unjustly dealt with; both by Sellers and Buyers. And yet 'tis to be feared, we have no other kind of Title to our *Nigers.*

Therefore all things whatsoever ye would that men should do to you, do ye even so to them: for this is the Law and the Prophets. Matt. 7. 12.

"Obj. 4. Abraham *had servants bought with his Money, and born in his House.*

"*Answ.* Until the Circumstances of *Abraham's* purchase be recorded, no Argument can be drawn from it. In the mean time, Charity obliges us to conclude, that He knew it was lawful and good.

"It is Observable that the *Israelites* were strictly forbidden the buying or selling one another for Slaves. *Levit.* 25. 39. 46. *Jer.* 34 8. . . . 22. And *GOD* gaged His Blessing in lieu of any loss they might conceipt they suffered thereby. *Deut.* 15. 18. And since the partition Wall is broken down, inordinate Self love should likewise be demolished. GOD expects that Christians should be of a more Ingenuous and benign frame of spirit. Christians should carry it to all the World, as the Israelites were to carry it one towards another. And for men obstinately to persist in holding their Neighbours and Brethren under the Rigor of perpetual Bondage, seems to be no proper way of gaining Assurance that God has given them Spiritual Freedom. Our Blessed Saviour has altered the Measures of the ancient Love-Song, and set it to a most Excellent New Tune, which all ought to be ambitious of Learning. *Matt.* 5. 43, 44, *John* 13. 34. These Ethiopians, as black as they are; seeing they are the Sons and Daughters of the First *Adam,* the Brethren and Sisters of the Last ADAM, and the Offspring of GOD; They ought to be treated with a Respect agreeable.

From
CONCERNING THE SAVAGES OF NORTH AMERICA (1784)
BENJAMIN FRANKLIN

Benjamin Franklin (1706–1790), statesman, scientist, writer, philosopher and Revolutionary leader, epitomized the American success story as he rose to power and wealth, and as a son of the Enlightenment he avidly pursued and freely disseminated knowledge. Consequently, he was one of the first to regard the Indian society as a unique culture and to attempt scientific description of its habits. Deeply humanitarian, he opposed slavery and the persecution of the Indians.

Savages we call them, because their manners differ from ours, which we think the perfection of civility; they think the same of theirs.

Perhaps, if we could examine the manners of different nations with impartiality, we should find no people so rude as to be without rules of politeness; nor any so polite as not to have some remains of rudeness.

The Indian men, when young, are hunters and warriors; when old, counsellors, for all their government is by counsel of the sages; there is no force, there are no prisons, no officers to compel obedience or inflict punishment. Hence they generally study oratory, the best speaker having the most influence. The Indian women till the ground, dress the food, nurse and bring up the children, and preserve and hand down to posterity the memory of public transactions. These employments of men and women are accounted natural and honorable. Having few artificial wants, they have abundance of leisure for improvement by conversation. Our laborious manner of life, compared with theirs, they esteem slavish and base; and the learning, on which we value ourselves, they regard as frivolous and useless. An instance of this occurred at the treaty of Lancaster, in Pennsylvania, *anno* 1744, between the government of Virginia and the Six Nations. After the principal business was settled, the commissioners from Virginia acquainted the Indians by a speech that there was at Williamsburg a college, with a fund for educating Indian youth; and that, if the Six Nations would send down half a dozen of their young lads to that college, the government would take care that they should be well provided for, and instructed in all the learning of the white people. It is one of the Indian rules of politeness not to answer a public proposition the same day that it is made; they think it would be treating it as a light matter, and that they show it respect by taking time to consider it, as of a matter important. They therefore deferred their answer till the day following; when their speaker began, by expressing their deep sense of the kindness of the Virginia government, in making them that offer; "for we know," says he, "that you highly esteem the kind of learning taught in those colleges, and that the maintenance of our young men, while with you, would be very expensive to you. We are convinced, therefore, that you mean to do us good by your proposal, and we thank you heartily. But you, who are wise, must know that different nations have different conceptions of things; and you will therefore not take it amiss, if our ideas of this kind of education happen not to be the same with yours. We have had some experience of it; several of our young people were formerly brought up at the colleges of the northern provinces; they were instructed in all your sciences; but when they came back to us they were bad runners, ignorant of every means of living in the woods, unable to bear cold or hunger, knew neither how to build a cabin, take a deer, nor kill an enemy, spoke our language imperfectly, were therefore neither fit for hunters, warriors, nor counsellors; they were totally good for nothing. We are however not the less obliged by your kind offer, though we decline accepting it; and, to show our grateful sense of it, if the gentlemen of Virginia will send us a dozen of their sons, we will take great care of their education, instruct them in all we know, and make *men* of them."

Having frequent occasions to hold public councils, they have acquired great order and decency in conducting them. The old men sit in the foremost ranks, the warriors in the next, and the women and children in the hindmost. The business of the women is to take exact notice of what passes, imprint it in their memories (for they have no writing), and communicate it to their children. They are the records of the council, and they preserve the tradition of the stipulations in treaties a hundred years back; which, when we compare with our writings, we always find exact. He that would speak, rises. The rest observe a profound silence. When he has finished and sits down, they leave him five or six minutes to recollect that, if he has omitted any thing he intended to say, or has any thing to add, he may rise again and deliver it. To interrupt another, even in common conversation, is reckoned highly indecent. How different this is from the conduct of a polite British House of Commons, where scarce a day passes without some confusion, that makes the Speaker hoarse in calling *to order;* and how different from the mode of conversation in many polite companies in Europe, where, if you do not deliver your sentence with great rapidity, you are cut off in the middle of it by the impatient loquacity of those you converse with, and never suffered to finish it!

The politeness of these savages in conversation is indeed carried to excess, since it does not permit them to contradict or deny the truth of what is asserted in their presence. By this means they indeed avoid disputes; but then it becomes difficult to know their minds, or what impression you made upon them. The missionaries who have attempted to convert them to Christianity, all complain of this as one of the great difficulties of their mission. The Indians hear with patience the truths of the Gospel explained to them, and give their usual tokens of assent and approbation; you would think they were convinced. No such matter. It is mere civility.

A Swedish minister, having assembled the chiefs of the Susquehanna Indians, made a sermon to them, acquainting them with the principal historical facts on which our religion is founded; such as the fall of our first parents by eating an apple, the coming of Christ to repair the mischief, his miracles and sufferings, etc. When he had finished, an Indian orator stood up to thank him. "What you have told us," says he, "is all very good. It is indeed bad to eat apples. It is better to make them all into cider. We are much obliged by your kindness in coming so far, to tell us those things which you have heard from your mothers. In return, I will tell you some of those we have heard from ours: In the beginning, our fathers had only the flesh of animals to subsist on; and if their hunting was unsuccessful, they were starving. Two of our young hunters, having killed a deer, made a fire in the woods to broil some parts of it. When they were about to satisfy their hunger, they beheld a beautiful young woman descend from the clouds, and seat herself on that hill which you see yonder among the Blue Mountains. They said to each other, it is a spirit that perhaps has smelt our broiling venison and wishes to eat of it; let us offer some to her. They presented her with the tongue; she was pleased with the taste of it, and said: 'Your kindness shall be rewarded; come to this place after thirteen moons, and you shall find something that will be of great benefit in nourishing you and your children to the latest generations.' They did so, and, to their surprise, found plants they had never seen before; but which, from that ancient time, have been constantly cultivated among us, to our great advantage. Where her right hand had touched the ground, they found maize; where her left hand had touched it, they found kidney-beans; and where her backside had sat on it, they found tobacco." The good missionary, disgusted with this idle tale, said: "What I delivered to you were sacred truths; but what you tell me is mere fable, fiction, and falsehood." The Indian, offended, replied: "My brother, it seems your friends have not done you justice in your education; they have not well instructed you in the rules of common civility. You saw that we, who understand and practise those rules, believed all your stories; why do you refuse to believe ours?"

When any of them come into our towns, our people are apt to crowd round them, gaze upon them, and incommode them, where they desire to be private; this they esteem great rudeness, and the effect of want of instruction in the rules of civility and good manners. "We have," say they, "as much curiosity as you, and when you come into our towns, we wish for opportunities of looking at you; but for this purpose we hide ourselves behind bushes, where you are to pass, and never intrude ourselves into your company."

Their manner of entering one another's village has likewise its rules. It is reckoned uncivil in travelling strangers to enter a village abruptly, without giving notice of their approach. Therefore, as soon as they arrive within hearing, they stop and halloo, remaining there till invited to enter. Two old men usually come out to them, and lead them in. There is in every village a vacant dwelling, called *the strangers' house*. Here they are placed, while the old men go round from hut to hut, acquainting the inhabitants that strangers are arrived who are probably hungry and weary; and every one sends them what he can spare of victuals, and skins to repose on. When the strangers are refreshed, pipes and tobacco are brought, and then, but not before, conversation begins, with inquiries who they are, whither bound, what news, etc.; and it usually ends with offers of service, if the strangers have occasion for guides, or any necessaries for continuing their journey; and nothing is exacted for the entertainment.

The same hospitality, esteemed among them as a principal virtue, is practised by private persons; of which Conrad Weiser, our interpreter, gave me the following instance. He had been naturalized among the Six Nations, and spoke well the Mohock language. In going through the Indian country, to carry a message from our governor to the council at Onondaga, he called at the habitation of Canassetego, an old acquaintance, who embraced him, spread furs for him to sit on, and placed before him some boiled beans and venison, and mixed some rum and water for his drink. When he was well refreshed, and had lit his pipe, Canassetego began to converse with him; asked how he had fared the many years since they had seen each other, whence he then came, what occasioned the journey, etc. Conrad answered all his questions; and when the discourse began to flag, the Indian, to continue it, said: "Conrad, you have lived long among the white people, and know something of their customs; I have been sometimes at Albany, and have observed that once in seven days they shut up their shops and assemble all in the great house; tell me what it is for. What do they do there?" "They meet there," says Conrad, "to hear and learn *good things.*" "I do not doubt," says the Indian, "that they tell you so; they have told me the same; but I doubt the truth of what they say, and I will tell you my reasons. I went lately to Albany to sell my skins and buy blankets, knives, powder, rum, etc. You know I used generally to deal with Hans Hanson; but I was a little inclined this time to try some other merchants. However, I called first upon Hans, and asked what he would give for beaver. He said he could not give any more than four shillings a pound; 'but,' says he, 'I cannot talk on business now; this is the day when we meet together to learn *good things*, and I am going to meeting.' So I thought to myself: 'Since I cannot do any business to-day, I may as well go to the meeting too,' and I went with him. There stood up a man in black, and began to talk to the people very angrily. I did not understand what he said; but, perceiving that he looked much at me and at Hanson, I imagined he was angry at seeing me there; so I went out, sat down near the house, struck fire, and lit my pipe, waiting till the meeting should break up. I thought, too, that the man had mentioned something of beaver, and I suspected it might be the subject of their meeting. So when they came out I accosted my merchant. 'Well, Hans,' says I, 'I hope you have agreed to give more than four shillings a pound.' 'No,' says he, 'I cannot give so much; I cannot give more than three shillings and sixpence.' I then spoke to several other dealers, but they all sung the same song,—three and sixpence—three and sixpence. This made it clear to me that my suspicion was right; and that whatever they pretended of meeting to learn *good things*, the real purpose was to consult how to cheat Indians in the price of beaver. Consider but a little, Conrad, and you must be of my opinion. If they met so often to learn *good things*, they would certainly have learned some before this time. But they are still ignorant. You know our practice. If a white man, in travelling through our country, encounters one of our cabins, we all treat him as I treat you; we dry him if he is wet, we warm him if he is cold, we give him meat and drink that he may allay his thirst and hunger, and spread soft furs for him to rest and sleep on; we demand nothing in return.[1] But if I go into a white man's house at Albany, and ask for victuals and drink, they say, 'Where is your money?' and if I have none, they say, 'Get out, you Indian dog!' You see they have not yet learned those little *good things*, that we need no meetings to be instructed in, because our mothers taught them to us when we were children; and therefore it is impossible their meetings should be, as they say, for any such purpose, or have any such effect; they are only to contrive *the cheating of Indians in the price of beaver.*"

[1] It is remarkable that in all ages and countries hospitality has been allowed as the virtue of those whom the civilized were pleased to call barbarians.

The Greeks celebrated the Scythians for it. The Saracens possessed it eminently, and it is to this day the reigning virtue of the wandering Arabs.

St. Paul, too, in the relation of his voyage and shipwreck on the Island of Melita, says: *The barbarous people showed us no little kindness; for they kindled a fire and received every one because of the present rain and because of the cold.*— Acts, ch. xxviii.   F.

From *Letters* (*1791-1815*)
THOMAS JEFFERSON

Thomas Jefferson (1743–1826), was statesman, scientist, farmer, Revolutionary leader, author of the Declaration of Independence and third President of the United States. Politically and philosophically liberal, he opposed slavery and supported education and advancement for Negroes. His Notes on the State of Virginia (*1785*) *is an attempt to describe that state (including its western areas now detached) and its Indian inhabitants in a scientific, objective manner.*

TO CONDORCET

August 30, 1791   *Philadelphia*

Dear Sir, I am to acknowledge the receipt of your favor on the subject of the element of measure adopted by France. Candor obliges me to confess that it is not what I would have approved. It is liable to the inexactitude of mensuration as to that part of the quadrant of the earth which is to be measured, that is to say as to one tenth of the quadrant, and as to the remaining nine tenths they are to be calculated on conjectural data, presuming the figure of the earth which has not yet been proved. It is liable too to the objection that no nation but your own can come at it; because yours is the only nation within which a meridian can be found of such extent crossing the 45th degree and terminating at both ends in a level. We may certainly say then that this measure is uncatholic, and I would rather have seen you depart from Catholicism in your religion than in your philosophy.

I am happy to be able to inform you that we have now in the United States a Negro, the son of a black man born in Africa, and of a black woman born in the United States, who is a very respectable mathematician.[1] I procured him to be employed under one of our chief directors in laying out the new federal city on the Potomac, and in the intervals of his leisure, while on that work, he made an almanac for the next year, which he sent me in his own handwriting,† and which I enclose to you. I have seen very elegant solutions of geometrical problems by him.[2] Add to this that he is a very worthy and respectable member of society. He is a free man. I shall be delighted to see these instances of moral eminence so multiplied as to prove that the want of talents observed in them is merely the effect of their degraded condition, and not proceeding from any difference in the structure of the parts on which intellect depends.

I am looking ardently to the completion of the glorious work in

[1] The reference is to Benjamin Banneker—sometimes spelled Bannaker—(1731–1806), a self-educated Negro freeman, who became a mathematician and astronomer and assisted his patron and neighbor, Major Andrew Ellicott, in the surveying of the District of Columbia. See Saul K. Padover, "Benjamin Banneker: Unschooled Wizard," in *New Republic,* February 2, 1948.

[2] Upon receipt of Banneker's *Almanac and Ephemeris,* Secretary of State Jefferson, on August 30, 1791, replied:

"Sir, I thank you sincerely for your letter of the 19th instant and for the Almanac it contained. Nobody wishes more than I do to see such proofs as you exhibit, that nature has given to our black brethren, talents equal to those of the other-colors of men, and that the appearance of a want of them is owing merely to the degraded condition of their existence, both in Africa and America. I can add with truth, that nobody wishes more ardently to see a good system commenced for raising the condition of both their body and mind to what it ought to be, as fast as the imbecility of their present existence, and other circumstances which cannot be neglected, will admit. I have taken the liberty of sending your Almanac to Monsieur de Condorcet, Secretary of the Academy of Sciences at Paris . . . , because I considered it as a document to which your whole color had a right for their justification against the doubts which have been entertained of them. I am with great esteem, Sir, Your most obedient humble servant." This letter was written on the same day as the one above to Condorcet.

which your country is engaged [the French Revolution]. I view the general condition of Europe as hanging on the success or failure of France. Having set such an example of philosophical arrangement within, I hope it will be extended without your limits also, to your dependents and to your friends in every part of the earth.

TO HENRI GRÉGOIRE

February 25, 1809   *Washington*

Sir, I have received the favor of your letter of August 17th, and with it the volume you were so kind as to send me on the "Literature of Negroes." Be assured that no person living wishes more sincerely than I do, to see a complete refutation of the doubts I have myself entertained and expressed on the grade of understanding allotted to them by nature, and to find that in this respect they are on a par with ourselves. My doubts were the result of personal observation on the limited sphere of my own State, where the opportunities for the development of their genius were not favorable, and those of exercising it still less so. I expressed them therefore with great hesitation; but whatever be their degree of talent, it is no measure of their rights.[1] Because Sir Isaac Newton was superior to others in understanding, he was not therefore lord of the person or property of others. On this subject they are gaining daily in the opinions of nations, and hopeful advances are making towards their reestablishment on an equal footing with the other colors of the human family. I pray you, therefore, to accept my thanks for the many instances you have enabled me to observe of respectable intelligence in that race of men, which cannot fail to have effect in hastening the day of their relief.

[1] Yet years later Jefferson expressed doubts about Banneker's skill and abilities. In a letter to Joel Barlow, written on October 8, 1809, and discussing Bishop Grégoire's friendly book on Negroes, Jefferson wrote:

"His [Grégoire's] credulity has made him gather up every story he could find of men of color . . . , however slight the mention, or light the authority on which they are quoted. The whole do not amount, in point of evidence, to what we know ourselves of Banneker. We know he had spherical trigonometry enough to make almanacs, but not without the suspicion of aid from Ellicott, who was his neighbor and friend, and never missed an opportunity of puffing him. I have a long letter from Banneker, which shows him to have had a mind of very common stature indeed."

TO FRANCIS C. GRAY

March 4, 1815   *Monticello*

You asked me in conversation, what constituted a mulatto by our law? And I believe I told you four crossings with the whites. I looked afterwards into our law, and found it to be in these words: "Every person, other than a Negro, of whose grandfathers or grandmothers anyone shall have been a Negro, shall be deemed a mulatto, and so every such person who shall have one-fourth part or more of Negro blood, shall in like manner be deemed a mulatto;" L. Virgà 1792, December 17: the case put in the first member of this paragraph of the law is *exempli gratiâ*. The latter contains the true canon, which is that one-fourth of Negro blood, mixed with any portion of white, constitutes the mulatto. As the issue has one-half of the blood of each parent, and the blood of each of these may be made up of a variety of fractional mixtures, the estimate of their compound in some cases may be intricate, it becomes a mathematical problem of the same class with those on the mixtures of different liquors or different metals; as in these, therefore, the algebraical notation is the most convenient and intelligible. Let us express the pure blood of the white in the capital letters of the printed alphabet, the pure blood of the Negro in the small letters of the printed alphabet, and any given mixture of either, by way of abridgment in MS. letters.

Let the first crossing be of *a*, pure Negro, with A, pure white. The unit of blood of the issue being composed of the half of that of each parent, will be $\frac{a}{2} + \frac{A}{2}$. Call it, for abbreviation, *h* (half blood).

Let the second crossing be of *h* and B, the blood of the issue will be $\frac{h}{2} + \frac{B}{2}$, or substituting for $\frac{h}{2}$ its equivalent, it will be $\frac{a}{4} + \frac{A}{4} + \frac{B}{2}$ call it *q* (quarteroon) being ¼ Negro blood.

Let the third crossing be of *q* and C, their offspring will be $\frac{q}{2} + \frac{C}{2} = \frac{a}{8} + \frac{A}{8} + \frac{B}{4} + \frac{C}{2}$, call this *e* (eighth), who having less than ¼ of *a*, or of pure Negro blood, to wit ⅛ only, is no longer a mulatto, so that a third cross clears the blood.

From these elements let us examine their compounds. For example, let *h* and *q* cohabit, their issue will be $\frac{h}{2} + \frac{q}{2} = \frac{a}{4} + \frac{A}{4} + \frac{a}{8} + \frac{A}{8} + \frac{B}{4} = \frac{^3a}{8} + \frac{^3A}{8} + \frac{B}{4}$ wherein we find ⅜ of *a*, or Negro blood.

Let h and e cohabit, their issue will be $\dfrac{h}{2} + \dfrac{e}{2} = \dfrac{a}{4} + \dfrac{A}{4} + \dfrac{a}{16} + \dfrac{A}{16} +$ $\dfrac{B}{8} + \dfrac{c}{4} = \dfrac{^5a}{16} + \dfrac{^5A}{16} + \dfrac{B}{8} + \dfrac{c}{4}$, wherein $\frac{5}{16}\,a$ makes still a mulatto.

Let q and e cohabit, the half of the blood of each will be $\dfrac{q}{2} + \dfrac{e}{2} =$ $\dfrac{a}{8} + \dfrac{A}{8} + \dfrac{B}{4} + \dfrac{a}{16} + \dfrac{A}{16} + \dfrac{B}{8} + \dfrac{C}{4} = \dfrac{^3a}{16} + \dfrac{^3A}{16} + \dfrac{^3B}{8} + \dfrac{C}{4}$, wherein $\frac{3}{16}$ of a is no longer a mulatto, and thus may every compound be noted and summed, the sum of the fractions composing the blood of the issue being always equal to unit. It is understood in natural history that a fourth cross of one race of animals with another gives an issue equivalent for all sensible purposes to the original blood. Thus a Merino ram being crossed, first with a country ewe, second with his daughter, third with his granddaughter, and fourth with the great-granddaughter, the last issue is deemed pure Merino, having in fact but $\frac{1}{16}$ of the country blood. Our canon considers two crosses with the pure white, and a third with any degree of mixture, however small, as clearing the issue of the Negro blood. But observe, that this does not re-establish freedom, which depends on the condition of the mother, the principle of the civil law, *partus sequitur ventrem*, being adopted here. But if e emancipated, he becomes a free *white* man, and a citizen of the United States to all intents and purposes. So much for this trifle by way of correction.

PRODUCTIONS MINERAL, VEGETABLE AND ANIMAL
From *Notes on the State of Virginia* (1785)

Hitherto I have considered this hypothesis as applied to brute animals only, and not in its extension to the man of America, whether aboriginal or transplanted. It is the opinion of Mons. de Buffon that the former furnishes no exception to it: "Although the savage of the new world is about the same height as man in our world, this does not suffice for him to constitute an exception to the general fact that all living nature has become smaller on that continent. The savage is feeble, and has small organs of generation; he has neither hair nor beard, and no ardor whatever for his female; although swifter than the European because he is better accustomed to running, he is, on the other hand, less strong in body; he is also less sensitive, and yet more timid and cowardly; he has no vivacity, no activity of mind; the activity of his body is less an exercise, a voluntary motion, than a necessary action caused by want; relieve him of hunger and thirst, and you deprive him of the active principle of all his movements; he will rest stupidly upon his legs or lying down entire days. There is no need for seeking further the cause of the isolated mode of life of these savages and their repugnance for society: the most precious spark of the fire of nature has been refused to them; they lack ardor for their females, and consequently have no love for their fellow men: not knowing this strongest and most tender of all affections, their other feelings are also cold and languid; they love their parents and children but little; the most intimate of all ties, the family connection, binds them therefore but loosely together; between family and family there is no tie at all; hence they have no communion, no commonwealth, no state of society. Physical love constitutes their only morality; their heart is icy, their society cold, and their rule harsh. They look upon their wives only as servants for all work, or as beasts of burden, which they load without consideration with the burden of their hunting, and which they compel without mercy, without gratitude, to perform tasks which are often beyond their strength. They have only few children, and they take little care of them. Everywhere the original defect appears: they are indifferent because they have little sexual capacity, and this indifference to the other sex is the fundamental defect which weakens their nature, prevents its development, and—destroying the very germs of life—uproots society at the same time. Man is here no exception to the general rule. Nature, by refusing him the power of love, has treated him worse and lowered him deeper than any animal." An afflicting picture indeed, which, for the honor of human nature, I am glad to believe has no original. Of the Indian of South America I know nothing; for I would not honor with the appelation of knowledge, what I derive from the fables published of them. These I believe to be just as true as the fables of Æsop. This belief is founded on what I have seen of man, white, red, and black, and what has been written of him by authors, enlightened themselves, and writing amidst an enlightened people. The Indian of North America being more within our reach, I can speak of him somewhat from my own knowledge, but more from the information of others better acquainted with him, and on whose truth and judgment I can rely. From these sources I am able to say, in contradiction to this representation, that he is neither more defective in ardor, nor more impotent with his female, than the white reduced to the same diet and exercise: that he is brave, when an enterprize depends on bravery; education with him making the point of honor consist in the destruction of an enemy by stratagem, and in the preservation of his own person free from injury; or perhaps this is nature; while it is education which teaches us to honor force more than finesse; that he will defend himself against an host of enemies, always chusing to be killed, rather than to surrender, though it be to the whites, who he knows will treat him well: that in other situations also he meets death with more deliberation, and endures tortures with a firmness unknown almost to religious enthusiasm with us: that he is affectionate to his children, careful of them, and indulgent in the extreme: that his affections comprehend his other connections, weakening, as with us, from circle to circle, as they recede from the center: that his friendships are strong and faithful to the uttermost extremity: that his sensibility is keen, even the warriors weeping most bitterly on the loss of their children, though in general they endeavour to appear superior to human events: that his vivacity and activity of mind is equal to ours in the same situation; hence his eagerness for hunting, and for games of chance. The women are submitted to unjust drudgery. This I believe is the case with every barbarous people. With such, force is law. The stronger sex therefore imposes on the weaker. It is civilization alone which replaces women in the enjoyment of their natural equality. That first teaches us to subdue the selfish passions, and to respect those rights in others which we value in ourselves. Were we in equal barbarism, our females would be equal drudges. The man with them is less strong than with us, but their woman stronger than ours; and both for the same obvious reason; because our man and their woman is habituated to labour, and formed by it. With both races the sex which is indulged with ease is least athletic. An Indian man is small in the hand and wrist for the same reason for which a sailor is large and strong in the arms and shoulders, and a porter in the legs and thighs.—They raise fewer children than we do. The causes of this are to be found, not in a difference of nature, but of circumstance. The women very frequently attending the men in their parties of war and of hunting, child-bearing becomes extremely inconvenient to them. It is said, therefore, that they have learnt the practice of procuring abortion by the use of some vegetable; and that it even extends to prevent conception for a considerable time after. During these parties they are exposed to numerous hazards, to excessive exertions, to the greatest extremities of hunger. Even at their homes the nation depends for food, through a certain part of every year, on the gleanings of the forest: that is, they experience a famine once in every year. With all animals, if the female be badly fed, or not fed at all, her young perish: and if both male and female be reduced to like want, generation becomes less active, less productive. To the obstacles then of want and hazard, which nature has opposed to the multiplication of wild animals, for the purpose of restraining their numbers within certain bounds, those of labour and of voluntary abortion are added with the Indian. No wonder then if they multiply less than we do. Where food is regularly supplied, a single farm will shew more of cattle, than a whole country of forests can of buffaloes. The same Indian women, when married to white traders, who feed them and their children plentifully and regularly, who exempt them from excessive drudgery, who keep them stationary and unexposed to accident, produce and raise as many children as the white women. Instances are known, under these circumstances, of their rearing a dozen children. An inhuman practice once prevailed in this country of making slaves of the Indians. (This practice commenced with the Spaniards with the first discovery of America). It is a fact well known with us, that the Indian women so enslaved produced and raised as numerous families as either the whites or blacks, among whom they lived.—It has been said, that Indians have less hair than the whites, except on the head. But this is a fact of which fair proof can scarcely be had. With them it is disgraceful to be hairy on the body. They say it likens them to hogs. They therefore pluck the hair as fast as it appears. But the traders who marry their women, and prevail on them to discontinue this practice, say, that nature is the same with them as with the whites. Nor, if the fact be true, is the consequence necessary which has been drawn from it. Negroes have notoriously less hair than the whites; yet they are more ardent. But if cold and moisture be the agents of nature for diminishing the races of animals, how comes she all at once to suspend their operation as to the physical man of the new world, whom the Count acknowledges to be "about the same size as the man of our hemisphere," and to let loose their influence on his moral faculties? How has this "combination of the elements and other physical causes, so contrary to the enlargement of animal nature in this new world, these obstacles to the developement and formation of great germs," been arrested and suspended, so as to permit the human body to acquire its just dimensions, and by what inconceivable process has their action been directed on his mind alone? To judge of the truth of this, to form a just estimate of their genius and mental powers, more facts are wanting, and great allowance to be made for those circumstances of their situation which call for a display of particular talents only. This done, we shall probably find that they are formed in mind as well as in body, on the same module with the "Homo sapiens Europæus." The principles of their society forbidding all compulsion, they are to be led to duty and to enterprize by personal influence and persuasion. Hence eloquence in council, bravery and address in war, become the foundations of all consequence with them. To these acquirements all their faculties are directed. Of their bravery and address in war we have multiplied proofs, because we have been the subjects on which they were exercised. Of their eminence in oratory we have fewer examples, because it is displayed chiefly in their own councils. Some, however, we have of very superior lustre. I may challenge the whole orations of Demosthenes and Cicero, and of any more eminent orator, if Europe has furnished more eminent, to produce a single passage, superior to the speech of Logan, a Mingo chief, to Lord Dunmore, when governor of this state. And, as a testimony of their talents in this line, I beg leave to introduce it, first stating the incidents necessary for understanding it. In the spring of the year 1774, a robbery was committed by some Indians on certain land-adventurers on the river

Ohio. The whites in that quarter, according to their custom, undertook to punish this outrage in a summary way. Captain Michael Cresap, and a certain Daniel Great-house, leading on these parties, surprized, at different times, travelling and hunting parties of the Indians, having their women and children with them, and murdered many. Among these were unfortunately the family of Logan, a chief celebrated in peace and war, and long distinguished as the friend of the whites. This unworthy return provoked his vengeance. He accordingly signalized himself in the war which ensued. In the autumn of the same year a decisive battle was fought at the mouth of the Great Kanhaway, between the collected forces of the Shawanese, Mingoes, and Delawares, and a detachment of the Virginia militia. The Indians were defeated, and sued for peace. Logan however disdained to be seen among the suppliants. But, lest the sincerity of a treaty should be distrusted, from which so distinguished a chief absented himself, he sent by a messenger the following speech to be delivered to Lord Dunmore.

"I appeal to any white man to say, if ever he entered Logan's cabin hungry, and he gave him not meat; if ever he came cold and naked, and he clothed him not. During the course of the last long and bloody war, Logan remained idle in his cabin, an advocate for peace. Such was my love for the whites, that my countrymen pointed as they passed, and said, 'Logan is the friend of white men.' I had even thought to have lived with you, but for the injuries of one man. Col. Cresap, the last spring, in cold blood, and unprovoked, murdered all the relations of Logan, not sparing even my women and children. There runs not a drop of my blood in the veins of any living creature. This called on me for revenge. I have sought it: I have killed many: I have fully glutted my vengeance. For my country, I rejoice at the beams of peace. But do not harbour a thought that mine is the joy of fear. Logan never felt fear. He will not turn on his heel to save his life. Who is there to mourn for Logan?—Not one."

Before we condemn the Indians of this continent as wanting genius, we must consider that letters have not yet been introduced among them. Were we to compare them in their present state with the Europeans North of the Alps, when the Roman arms and arts first crossed those mountains, the comparison would be unequal, because, at that time, those parts of Europe were swarming with numbers; because numbers produce emulation, and multiply the chances of improvement, and one improvement begets another. Yet I may safely ask, How many good poets, how many able mathematicians, how many great inventors in arts or sciences, had Europe North of the Alps then produced? And it was sixteen centuries after this before a Newton could be formed. I do not mean to deny, that there are varieties in the race of man, distinguished by their powers both of body and mind. I believe there are, as I see to be the case in the races of other animals. I only mean to suggest a doubt, whether the bulk and faculties of animals depend on the side of the Atlantic on which their food happens to grow, or which furnishes the elements of which they are compounded? Whether nature has enlisted herself as a Cis or Trans-Atlantic partisan? I am induced to suspect, there has been more eloquence than sound reasoning displayed in support of this theory; that it is one of those cases where the judgment has been seduced by a glowing pen: and whilst I render every tribute of honor and esteem to the celebrated Zoologist, who has added, and is still adding, so many precious things to the treasures of science, I must doubt whether in this instance he has not cherished error also, by lending her for a moment his vivid imagination and bewitching language.

So far the Count de Buffon has carried this new theory of the tendency of nature to belittle her productions on this side of the Atlantic. Its application to the race of whites, transplanted from Europe, remained for the Abbé Raynal. "One must be astonished (he says) that America has not yet produced one good poet, one able mathematician, one man of genius in a single art or a single science." "America has not yet produced one good poet." When we shall have existed as a people as long as the Greeks did before they produced a Homer, the Romans a Virgil, the French a Racine and Voltaire, the English a Shakespeare and Milton, should this reproach be still true, we will enquire from what unfriendly causes it has proceeded, that the other countries of Europe and quarters of the earth shall not have inscribed any name in the roll of poets. But neither has America produced "one able mathematician, one man of genius in a single art or a single science." In war we have produced a Washington, whose memory will be adored while liberty shall have votaries, whose name will triumph over time, and will in future ages assume its just station among the most celebrated worthies of the world, when that wretched philosophy shall be forgotten which would have arranged him among the degeneracies of nature. In physics we have produced a Franklin, than whom no one of the present age has made more important discoveries, nor has enriched philosophy with more, or more ingenious solutions of the phænomena of nature. We have supposed Mr. Rittenhouse second to no astronomer living: that in genius he must be the first, because he is self-taught. As an artist he has exhibited as great a proof of mechanical genius as the world has ever produced. He has not indeed made a world; but he has by imitation approached nearer its Maker than any man who has lived from the creation to this day. As in philosophy and war, so in government, in oratory, in painting, in the plastic art, we might shew that America, though but a child of yesterday, has already given hopeful proofs of genius, as well of the nobler kinds, which arouse the best feelings of man, which call him into action, which substantiate his freedom, and conduct him to happiness, as of the subordinate, which serve to amuse him only. We therefore suppose, that this reproach is as un-just as it is unkind; and that, of the geniuses which adorn the present age, America contributes its full share. For comparing it with those countries, where genius is most cultivated, where are the most excel-lent models for art, and scaffoldings for the attainment of science, as France and England for instance, we calculate thus. The United States contain three millions of inhabitants; France twenty millions; and the British islands ten. We produce a Washington, a Franklin, a Ritten-house. France then should have half a dozen in each of these lines, and Great-Britain half that number, equally eminent. It may be true, that France has: we are but just becoming acquainted with her, and our acquaintance so far gives us high ideas of the genius of her in-habitants. It would be injuring too many of them to name particularly a Voltaire, a Buffon, the constellation of Encyclopedists, the Abbé Ray-nal himself, &c. &c. We therefore have reason to believe she can pro-duce her full quota of genius. The present war having so long cut off all communication with Great-Britain, we are not able to make a fair estimate of the state of science in that country. The spirit in which she wages war is the only sample before our eyes, and that does not seem the legitimate offspring either of science or of civilization. The sun of her glory is fast descending to the horizon. Her philosophy has crossed the Channel, her freedom the Atlantic, and herself seems passing to that awful dissolution, whose issue is not given human foresight to scan.

REFLECTIONS ON NEGRO SLAVERY

From *Letters from an American Farmer* (*1782*)
HECTOR ST. JOHN DE CREVECOEUR

Hector St. John de Crevecoeur (1735–1813), an American farmer, ex-perimenter and social observer, traveled widely and described and in-terpreted his observations in his Letters from an American Farmer. *A liberal humanitarian, his opposition to slavery became evident in his letters.*

While all is joy, festivity, and happiness in Charles-Town, would you imagine that scenes of misery overspread in the country? Their ears by habit are become deaf, their hearts are hardened; they neither see, hear, nor feel for the woes of their poor slaves, from whose painful labours all their wealth proceeds. Here the horrors of slavery, the hard-ship of incessant toils, are unseen; and no one thinks with compassion of those showers of sweat and of tears which from the bodies of Africans, daily drop, and moisten the ground they till. The cracks of the whip urging these miserable beings to excessive labour, are far too distant from the gay Capital to be heard. The chosen race eat, drink, and live happy, while the unfortunate one grubs up the ground, raises indigo, or husks the rice; exposed to a sun full as scorching as their native one; without the support of good food, without the cordials of any chearing liquor. This great contrast has often afforded me subjects of the most afflicting meditation. On the one side, behold a people enjoying all that life affords most bewitching and pleasurable, without labour, without fatigue, hardly subjected to the trouble of wishing. With gold, dug from Peruvian mountains, they order vessels to the coasts of Guinea; by virtue of that gold, wars, murders, and devastations are committed in some harmless, peaceable African neighbourhood, where dwelt innocent people, who even knew not but that all men were black. The daughter torn from her weeping mother, the child from the wretched parents, the wife from the loving husband; whole families swept away and brought through storms and tempests to this rich metropolis! There, arranged like horses at a fair, they are branded like cattle, and then driven to toil, to starve, and to languish for a few years on the different plantations of these citizens. And for whom must they work? For persons they know not, and who have no other power over them than that of violence; no other right than what this accursed metal has given them! Strange order of things! Oh, Nature, where art thou?—Are not these blacks thy children as well as we? On the other side, nothing is to be seen but the most diffusive misery and wretchedness, unrelieved even in thought or wish! Day after day they drudge on without any prospect of ever reaping for themselves; they are obliged to devote their lives, their limbs, their will, and every vital exertion to swell the wealth of masters; who look not upon them with half the kindness and affection with which they consider their dogs and horses. Kindness and affection are not the portion of those who till the earth, who carry the burdens, who convert the logs into useful boards. This reward, simple and natural as one would conceive it, would border on humanity; and planters must have none of it!

If negroes are permitted to become fathers, this fatal indulgence only tends to increase their misery: the poor companions of their scanty pleasures are likewise the companions of their labours; and when at some critical seasons they could wish to see them relieved, with tears in their eyes they behold them perhaps doubly oppressed, obliged to bear the burden of nature—a fatal present—as well as that of unabated tasks. How many have I seen cursing the irresistible propensity, and regretting, that by having tasted of those harmless joys, they had become the authors of double misery to their wives. Like their masters, they are not permitted to partake of those ineffable sensations with which nature inspires the hearts of fathers and mothers; they must repel them all, and become callous and passive. This unnatural state often occasions the most acute, the most pungent of their afflictions; they have no time, like us, tenderly to rear their helpless offspring, to nurse them on their knees, to enjoy the delight of being parents. Their paternal fondness is embittered by considering, that if their children live, they must live to be slaves like themselves; no time is allowed them to exercise their pious office, the mothers must fasten them on their backs, and, with this double load, follow their husbands in the fields, where they too often hear no other sound than that of the voice or whip of the task-master, and the cries of their infants, broiling in the sun. These unfortunate creatures cry and weep like their parents, without a possibility of relief; the very instinct of the brute, so laudable, so irresistible, runs counter here to their master's interest; and to that god, all the laws of nature must give way. Thus planters get rich; so raw, so unexperienced am I in this mode of life, that were I to be possessed of a plantation, and my slaves treated as in general they are here, never could I rest in peace; my sleep would be perpetually disturbed by a retrospect of the frauds committed in Africa, in order to entrap them; frauds surpassing in enormity every thing which a common mind can possibly conceive. I should be thinking of the barbarous treatment they meet with on ship-board; of their anguish, of the despair necessarily inspired by their situation, when torn from their friends and relations; when delivered into the hands of a people differently coloured, whom they cannot understand; carried in a strange machine over an ever agitated element, which they had never seen before; and finally delivered over to the severities of the whippers, and the excessive labours of the field. Can it be possible that the force of custom should ever make me deaf to all these reflections, and as insensible to the injustice of that trade, and to their miseries, as the rich inhabitants of this town seem to be? What then is man; this being who boasts so much of the excellence and dignity of his nature, among that variety of unscrutable mysteries, of unsolvable problems, with which he is surrounded? The reason why man has been thus created, is not the least astonishing! It is said, I know that they are much happier here than in the West-Indies; because land being cheaper upon this continent than in those islands, the fields allowed them to raise their subsistence from, are in general more extensive. The only possible chance of any alleviation depends on the humour of the planters, who, bred in the midst of slaves, learn from the example of their parents to despise them; and seldom conceive either from religion or philosophy, any ideas that tend to make their fate less calamitous; except some strong native tenderness of heart, some rays of philanthropy, overcome the obduracy contracted by habit.

I have not resided here long enough to become insensible of pain for the objects which I every day behold. In the choice of my friends and acquaintance, I always endeavour to find out those whose dispositions are somewhat congenial with my own. We have slaves likewise in our northern provinces; I hope the time draws near when they will be all emancipated: but how different their lot, how different their situation, in every possible respect! They enjoy as much liberty as their masters, they are as well clad, and as well fed; in health and sickness they are tenderly taken care of; they live under the same roof, and are, truly speaking, a part of our families. Many of them are taught to read and write, and are well instructed in the principles of religion; they are the companions of our labours, and treated as such; they enjoy many perquisites, many established holidays, and are not obliged to work more than white people. They marry where inclination leads them; visit their wives every week; are as decently clad as the common people; they are indulged in educating, cherishing, and chastising their children, who are taught subordination to them as to their lawful parents: in short, they participate in many of the benefits of our society, without being obliged to bear any of its burthens. They are fat, healthy, and hearty, and far from repining at their fate; they think themselves happier than many of the lower class whites: they share with their masters the wheat and meat provision they help to raise; many of those whom the good Quakers have emancipated, have received that great benefit with tears of regret, and have never quitted, though free, their former masters and benefactors.

But is it really true, as I have heard it asserted here, that those blacks are incapable of feeling the spurs of emulation, and the chearful sound of encouragement? By no means; there are a thousand proofs existing of their gratitude and fidelity: those hearts in which such noble dispositions can grow, are then like ours, they are susceptible of every generous sentiment, of every useful motive of action; they are capable of receiving lights, of imbibing ideas that would greatly alleviate the weight of their miseries. But what methods have in general been made use of to obtain so desirable an end? None; the day in which they arrive and are sold, is the first of their labours; labours, which from that hour admit of no respite; for though indulged by law with relaxation on Sundays, they are obliged to employ that time which is intended for rest, to till their little plantations. What can be expected from wretches in such circumstances? Forced from their native country, cruelly treated when on board, and not less so on the plantations to which they are driven; is there any thing in this treatment but what must kindle all the passions, sow the seeds of inveterate resentment, and nourish a wish of perpetual revenge? They are left to the irresistible effects of those strong and natural propensities; the blows they receive are they conducive to extinguish them, or to win their affections? They are neither soothed by the hopes that their slavery will ever terminate but with their lives; or yet encouraged by the goodness of their food, or the mildness of their treatment. The very hopes held out to mankind by religion, that consolatory system, so useful to the miserable, are never presented to them; neither moral nor physical means are made use of to soften their chains; they are left in their original and untutored state; that very state where in the natural propensities of revenge and warm passions, are so soon kindled. Cheered by no one single motive that can impel the will, or excite their efforts; nothing but terrors and punishments are presented to them; death is denounced if they run away; horrid delaceration if they speak with their native freedom; perpetually awed by the terrible cracks of whips, or by the fear of capital punishments, while even those punishments often fail of their purpose.

THE
AFRICAN
BECOMES
AMERICAN

PHILLIS WHEATLEY

*Phillis Wheatley (1753–1784), an American Negro poet, was brought
from Africa in 1761 and sold to a Boston merchant, John Wheatley, who
educated her. Her verse, typical of neoclassic verse of the eighteenth
century, has been published in several editions. The following selections are from* Poems *(1802).*

TO THE RIGHT HONORABLE WILLIAM, EARL OF DARTMOUTH, HIS MAJESTY'S PRINCIPAL SECRETARY OF STATE FOR NORTH-AMERICA, &C. (1772)

Hail, happy day, when, smiling like the morn,
Fair *Freedom* rose *New-England* to adorn:
The northern clime beneath her genial ray,
Dartmouth, congratulates thy blissful sway:
Elate with hope her race no longer mourns,
Each soul expands, each grateful bosom burns,
While in thine hand with pleasure we behold
The silken reins, and *Freedom's* charms unfold.
Long lost to realms beneath the northern skies
She shines supreme, while hated *faction* dies:
Soon as appear'd the *Goddess* long desir'd,
Sick at the view, she lanquish'd and expir'd;
Thus from the splendors of the morning light
The owl in sadness seeks the caves of night.

No more, *America,* in mournful strain
Of wrongs, and grievance unredress'd complain,
No longer shalt thou dread the iron chain,
Which wanton *Tyranny* with lawless hand
Had made, and with it meant t' enslave the land.

Should you, my lord, while you peruse my song,
Wonder from whence my love of *Freedom* sprung,
Whence flow these wishes for the common good,
By feeling hearts alone best understood,
I, young in life, by seeming cruel fate
Was snatch'd from *Afric's* fancy'd happy seat:
What pangs excruciating must molest,
What sorrows labour in my parent's breast?

Steel'd was that soul and by no misery mov'd
That from a father seiz'd his babe belov'd:
Such, such my case. And can I then but pray
Others may never feel tyrannic sway?

For favours past, great Sir, our thanks are due,
And thee we ask thy favours to renew,
Since in thy pow'r, as in thy will before,
To sooth the griefs, which thou did'st once deplore.
May heav'nly grace the sacred sanction give
To all thy works, and thou for ever live
Not only on the wings of fleeting *Fame,*
Though praise immortal crowns the patriot's name,
But to conduct heav'ns refulgent fane,
May fiery coursers sweep th' ethereal plain,
And bear thee upwards to that blest abode,
Where, like the prophet, thou shalt find thy God.

ON BEING BROUGHT FROM AFRICA TO AMERICA

'Twas mercy brought me from my *Pagan* land,
Taught my benighted soul to understand
That there's a God, that there's a *Saviour* too;
Once I redemption neither sought nor knew.
Some view our sable race with scornful eye,
"Their color is a diabolic die."
Remember, *Christians, Negroes,* black as *Cain,*
May be refined, and join th' angelic train.

KIDNAPPING AND ENSLAVEMENT

From *The Interesting Narrative* (*1789*)

GUSTAVUS VASSA

Gustavus Vassa (1745–1801?), an American Negro slave born in West Africa and brought to America at eleven, was educated by his owner, a British naval officer, and later by a Philadelphia merchant who helped him purchase his freedom. Later he settled in England and became active in anti-slavery work. His Interesting Narrative *was extremely popular, appearing in eight editions in five years.*

I hope the reader will not think I have trespassed on his patience in introducing myself to him, with some account of the manners and customs of my country. They had been implanted in me with great care, and made an impression on my mind which time could not erase, and which all the adversity and variety of fortune I have since experienced served only to rivet and record; for, whether the love of one's country be real or imaginary, or a lesson of reason, or an instinct of nature, I still look back with pleasure on the first scenes of my life, though that pleasure has been for the most part mingled with sorrow.

I have already acquainted the reader with the time and place of my birth. My father, besides many slaves, had a numerous family, of which seven lived to grow up, including myself and a sister, who was the only daughter. As I was the youngest of the sons, I became, of course, the greatest favorite with my mother, and was always with her; and she used to take particular pains to form my mind. I was trained up from my earliest years in the arts of agriculture and war: my daily exercise was shooting and throwing javelins; and my mother adorned me with emblems, after the manner of our greatest warriors. In this way I grew up till I was turned the age of eleven, when an end was put to my happiness in the following manner:—Generally, when the grown people in the neighborhood were gone far in the fields to labour, the children assembled together in some of the neighbors' premises to play; and commonly some of us used to get up a tree to look out for any assailant or kidnapper that might come upon us; for they sometimes took those opportunities of our parents' absence, to attack and carry off as many as they could seize. One day, as I was watching at the top of a tree in our yard, I saw one of those people come into the yard of our next neighbor but one, to kidnap, there being many stout young people in it. Immediately, on this, I gave the alarm of the rogue, and he was surrounded by the stoutest of them, who entangled him with cords, so that he could not escape till some of the grown people came and secured him. But alas! ere long, it was my fate to be thus attacked, and to be carried off, when none of our grown people were nigh. One day, when all our people were gone out to their works as usual, and only I and my dear sister were left to mind the house, two men and a woman got over our walls, and in a moment seized us both; and without giving us time to cry out, or make resistance, they stopped our mouths and ran off with us into the nearest wood. Here they tied our hands, and continued to carry us as far as they could, till night came on, when we reached a small house, where the robbers halted for refreshment, and spent the night. We were then unbound, but were unable to take any food; and being quite overpowered by fatigue and grief, our only relief was some sleep, which allayed our misfortune for a short time. The next morning we left the house, and continued traveling all the day. For a long time we had kept the woods, but at last we came into a road which I believed I knew. I now had some hopes of being delivered; for we had advanced but a little way when I discovered some people at a distance, on which I began to cry out for their assistance; but my cries had no other effect than to make them tie me faster and stop my mouth, and then they put me into a large sack. They also stopped my sister's mouth and tied her hands; and in this manner we proceeded till we were out of the sight of these people.—When we went to rest the following night they offered us some victuals, but we refused them; and the only comfort we had was in being in one another's arms all that night, and bathing each other with our tears. But alas! we were soon deprived of even the small comfort of weeping together. The next day proved a day of greater sorrow than I had yet experienced; for my sister and I were then separated, while we lay clasped in each other's arms: it was in vain that we besought them not to part us; she was torn from me, and immediately carried away, while I was left in a state of distraction not to be described. I cried and grieved continually; and for several days did not eat any thing but what they forced into my mouth. At length, after many days traveling, during which I had often changed masters, I got into the hands of a chieftain, in a very pleasant country. This man had two wives and some children, and they all used me extremely well, and did all they could to comfort me; particularly the first wife, who was something like my mother. Although I was a great many days journey from my father's house, yet these people spoke exactly the same language with us. This first master of mine, as I may call him, was a smith, and my principal employment was working his bellows, which was the same kind as I had seen in my vicinity. They were in some respects not unlike the stoves here in gentlemen's kitchens; and were covered over with leather; and in the middle of that leather a stick was fixed, and a person stood up, and worked it, in the same manner as is done to pump water out of a cask with a hand pump. I believe it was gold he worked, for it was of a lovely bright yellow colour, and was worn by the women on their wrists and ancles. I was there I suppose about a month, and they at last used to trust me some little distance from the house. This liberty I used in embracing every opportunity to inquire the way to my own home: and I also sometimes, for the same purpose, went with the maidens, in the cool of the evenings, to bring pitchers of water from the springs for the use of the house. I had also remarked where the sun rose in the morning, and set in the evening, as I had travelled along; and I had observed that my father's house was towards the rising of the sun. I therefore determined to seize the first opportunity of making my escape, and to shape my course for that quarter; for I was quite oppressed and weighed down by grief after my mother and friends; and my love of liberty, ever great, was strengthened by the mortifying circumstance of not daring to eat with the free-born children, although I was mostly their companion.—While I was projecting my escape one day, an unlucky event happened, which quite disconcerted my plan, and put an end to my hopes. I used to be sometimes employed in assisting an elderly woman slave to cook and take care of the poultry; and one morning while I was feeding some chickens, I happened to toss a small pebble at one of them, which hit it on the middle, and directly killed it. The old slave, having soon after missed the chicken, inquired after it; and on my relating the accident, (for I told her the truth, because my mother would never suffer me to tell a lie), she flew into a violent passion, threatened that I should suffer for it; and, my master being out, she immediately went and told her mistress what I had done. This alarmed me very much, and I expected an instant flogging, which to me was uncommonly dreadful; for I had seldom been beaten at home. I therefore resolved to fly; and accordingly I ran into a thicket that was hard by, and hid myself in the bushes. Soon afterwards my mistress and the slave returned, and, not seeing me, they searched all the house, but not finding me, and I not making answer when they called to me, they thought I had run away, and the whole neighborhood was raised in the pursuit of me. In that part of the country (as well as ours) the houses and villages were skirted with woods or shrubberies, and the bushes were so thick, that a man could readily conceal himself in them, so as to elude the strictest search. The neighbors continued the whole day looking for me, and several times many of them came within a few yards of the place where I lay hid. I expected every moment, when I heard a rustling among the trees, to be found out, and punished by my master; but they never discovered me, though they were often so near that I even heard their conjectures as they were looking about for me; and I now learned from them that any attempt to return home would be hopeless. Most of them supposed I had fled towards home; but the distance was so great, and the way so intricate, that they thought I could never reach it, and that I should be lost in the woods. When I heard this I was seized with a violent panic, and abandoned myself to despair. Night too began to approach, and aggravated all my fears. I had before entertained hopes of getting home, and had determined when it should be dark to make the attempt; but I was now convinced that it was fruitless, and began to consider that, if possibly I could escape all other animals, I could not those of the human kind; and that, not knowing the way, I must perish in the woods.—Thus was I like the hunted deer:

> —"Ev'ry leaf, and ev'ry whisp'ring breath
> "Convey'd a foe, and ev'ry foe a death."

I heard frequent rustlings among the leaves; and being pretty sure they were snakes, I expected every instant to be stung by them.—This increased my anguish; and the horror of my situation became now quite insupportable. I at length quitted the thicket, very faint and hungry, for I had not eaten or drank anything all the day, and crept to my master's kitchen, from whence I set out at first, and which was an open shed, and laid myself down in the ashes with an anxious wish for death to relieve me from all my pains. I was scarcely awake in the morning, when the old woman slave, who was the first up, came to light the fire, and saw me in the fireplace. She was very much surprised to see me, and could scarcely believe her own eyes. She now promised to intercede for me, and went for her master, who soon after came, and having lightly reprimanded me, ordered me to be taken care of, and not ill treated.

Soon after this my master's only daughter and child by his first wife sickened and died, which affected him so much that for some time he was almost frantic, and really would have killed himself, had he not been watched and prevented. However, in a small time afterwards he recovered and I was again sold. I was now carried to the left of the sun's rising, through many dreary wastes and dismal woods, amidst the hideous roaring of wild beasts.—The people I was sold to used to carry me very often, when I was tired, either on their shoulders or on their backs. I saw many convenient well-built sheds along the road, at proper distances, to accommodate the merchants and travellers, who lay in those buildings along with their wives, who often accompany them; and they always go well armed.

From the time I left my own nation I always found somebody that understood me till I came to the sea coast. The languages of different nations did not totally differ, nor were they so copious as those of the Europeans, particularly the English. They were therefore easily learned; and while I was journeying thus through Africa, I acquired two or three different tongues. In this manner I had been travelling for a considerable time, when one evening to my great surprise, whom should I see brought to the house where I was but my dear sister? As soon as she saw me she gave a loud shriek, and ran into my arms. I was quite overpowered: neither of us could speak, but, for a considerable time, clung to each other in mutual embraces, unable to do anything but weep. Our meeting affected all who saw us; and indeed I must acknowledge, in honour of those sable destroyers of human rights, that I never met with any ill treatment, or saw any offered to their slaves, except tying them, when necessary to keep them from running away. When these people knew we were brother and sister, they indulged us to be together; and the man, to whom I supposed we belonged, lay with us, he in the middle, while she and I held one another by the hands across his breast all night; and thus for awhile we forgot our misfortunes in the joy of being together; but even this small comfort was soon to have an end; for scarcely had the fatal morning appeared, when she was again torn from me for ever! I was now more miserable, if possible, than before. The small relief which her presence gave me from pain was gone, and the wretchedness of my situation was redoubled by my anxiety after her fate, and my apprehensions lest her sufferings should be greater than mine, when I could not be with her to alleviate them. Yes, thou dear partner of my childish sports! thou sharer of my joys and sorrows! happy should I have ever esteemed myself to encounter every misery for you, and to procure your freedom by the sacrifice of my own! Though you were early forced from my arms, your image has been always rivetted in my heart, from which neither *time nor fortune* have been able to remove it: so that, while the thoughts of your suffering have dampened my prosperity, they have mingled with adversity and increased its bitterness.—To that Heaven which protects the weak from the strong, I commit the care of your innocence and virtues, if they have not already received their full reward, and if your youth and delicacy have not long since fallen victims to the violence of the African trader, the pestilential stench of a Guinea ship, the seasoning in the European colonies, or the lash and lust of a brutal and unrelenting overseer.

I did not long remain after my sister. I was again sold, and carried through a number of places, till after travelling a considerable time, I came to a town called Tinmah, in the most beautiful country I had yet seen in Africa. It was extremely rich, and there were many rivulets which flowed through it, and supplied a large pond in the centre of the town, where the people washed. Here I first saw and tasted cocoa nuts, which I thought superior to any nuts I had ever tasted before; and the trees which were loaded were also interspersed among the houses, which had commodious shades adjoining, and were in the same manner as ours, the insides being neatly plastered and whitewashed. Here I also saw and tasted for the first time, sugar cane. Their money consisted of little white shells, the size of the finger nail. I was sold here for one hundred and seventy-two of them, by a merchant who lived and brought me there. I had been about two or three days at his house, when a wealthy widow, a neighbor of his, came there one evening, and brought with her an only son, a young gentleman about my own age and size. Here they saw me; and having taken a fancy to me, I was bought of the merchant, and went home with them. Her house and premises were situated close to one of those rivulets I have mentioned, and were the finest I ever saw in Africa: they were very extensive, and she had a number of slaves to attend her. The next day I was washed and perfumed, and when meal time came, I was led into the presence of my mistress, and ate and drank before her with her son. This filled me with astonishment; and I could scarce help expressing my surprise that the young gentleman should suffer me, who was bound, to eat with him who was free; and not only so, but that he would not at any time either eat or drink till I had taken first, because I was the eldest, which was agreeable to our custom. Indeed, everything here, and all their treatment of me, made me forget that I was a slave. The language of these people resembled ours so nearly, that we understood each other perfectly. They had also the same customs as we. There were likewise slaves daily to attend us, while my young master and I, with other boys, sported with our darts and bows and arrows, as I had been used to do at home. In this resemblance to my former happy state, I passed about two months; and I now began to think I was to be adopted into the family, and was beginning to be reconciled to my situation, and to forget by degrees my misfortunes, when all at once the delusion vanished; for, without the least previous knowledge, one morning early, while my dear master and companion was still asleep, I was awakened out of my reverie to fresh sorrow, and hurried away even amongst the uncircumcised.

Thus at the very moment I dreamed of the greatest happiness, I found myself most miserable; and it seemed as if fortune wished to give me this taste of joy only to render the reverse more poignant.— The change I now experienced, was as painful as it was sudden and unexpected. It was a change indeed, from a state of bliss to a scene which is inexpressible by me, as it discovered to me an element I had never before beheld, and till then had no idea of, and wherein such instances of hardship and cruelty occurred, as I can never reflect on but with horror.

All the nations and people I had hitherto passed through, resembled our own in their manners, customs and language; but I came at length to a country, the inhabitants of which differed from us in all those particulars. I was very much struck with this difference, especially when I came among a people who did not circumcise, and ate without washing their hands. They cooked also in iron pots, and had European cutlasses and cross bows, which were unknown to us, and fought with their fists among themselves. Their women were not so modest as ours, for they ate and drank, and slept with their men. But, above all, I was amazed to see no sacrifices or offerings among them. In some of these places the people ornamented themselves with scars, and likewise filed their teeth very sharp. They wanted sometimes to ornament me in the same manner, but I would not suffer them; hoping that I might some time be among a people who did not thus disfigure themselves, as I thought they did. At last I came to the banks of a large river which was covered with canoes, in which the people appeared to live with their household utensils, and provisions of all kinds. I was beyond measure astonished at this, as I had never before seen any water larger than a pond or a rivulet: and my surprise was mingled with no small fear when I was put into one of these canoes, and we began to paddle and move along the river. We continued going on thus till night, when we came to land, and made fires on the banks, each family by them-selves; some dragged their canoes on shore, others stayed and cooked in theirs, and laid in them all night. Those on the land had mats, of which they made tents, some in the shape of little houses; in these we slept; and after the morning meal, we embarked again and proceeded as before. I was often very much astonished to see some of the women, as well as the men, jump into the water, dive to the bottom, come up again, and swim about.—Thus I continued to travel, sometimes by land, sometimes by water, through different countries and various na-tions, till, at the end of six or seven months after I had been kidnapped, I arrived at the sea coast. It would be tedious and uninteresting to re-late all the incidents which befell me during this journey, and which I have not yet forgotten; of the various hands I passed through, and the manners and customs of all the different people among whom I lived. I shall therefore only observe, that in all the places where I was, the soil was exceedingly rich; the pumpkins, eadas, plaintains, yams, etc., were in great abundance, and of incredible size. There were also vast quantities of different gums, though not used for any purpose, and every where a great deal of tobacco. The cotton even grew quite wild, and there was plenty of red-wood. I saw no mechanics whatever in all the way, except such as I have mentioned. The chief employment in all these countries was agriculture, and both the males and females, as with us, were brought up to it, and trained in the arts of war.

The first object which saluted my eyes when I arrived on the coast, was the sea, and a slave ship, which was then riding at anchor, and waiting for its cargo. These filled me with astonishment, which was soon converted into terror, when I was carried on board. I was imme-diately handled, and tossed up to see if I were sound, by some of the crew; and I was now persuaded that I had gotten into a world of bad spirits, and that they were going to kill me. Their complexions, too, differing so much from ours, their long hair, and the language they spoke, (which was very different from any I had ever heard) united to confirm me in this belief. Indeed, such were the horrors of my views and fears at the moment, that, if ten thousand worlds had been my own, I would have freely parted with them all to have exchanged my condition with that of the meanest slave in my own country. When I looked round the ship too, and saw a large furnace of copper boiling, and a multitude of black people of every description chained together, every one of their countenances expressing dejection and sorrow, I no longer doubted of my fate; and quite overpowered with horror and anguish, I fell motionless on the deck and fainted. When I recovered a little, I found some black people about me, who I believed were some of those who had brought me on board, and had been receiving their pay; they talked to me in order to cheer me, but all in vain. I asked them if we were not to be eaten by those white men with horrible looks, red faces and long hair. They told me I was not: and one of the crew brought me a small portion of spirituous liquor in a wine glass, but, being afraid of him, I would not take it out of his hand. One of the blacks, therefore, took it from him and gave it to me, and I took a little down my palate, which, instead of reviving me, as they thought it would, threw me into the greatest consternation at the strange feeling it produced, having never tasted any such liquor before. Soon after this, the blacks who brought me on board went off, and left me abandoned to despair.

I now saw myself deprived of all chance of returning to my native country, or even the least glimpse of hope of gaining the shore, which I now considered as friendly; and I even wished for my former slavery in preference to my present situation, which was filled with horrors of every kind, still heightened by my ignorance of what I was to undergo. I was not long suffered to indulge my grief; I was soon put down under the decks, and there I received such a salutation in my nostrils as I had never experienced in my life: so that, with the loathsomeness of the stench and crying together, I became so sick and low that I was not able to eat, nor had I the least desire to taste any thing. I now wished for the last friend, death, to relieve me; but soon, to my grief, two of the white men offered me eatables; and, on my refusing to eat, one of them held me fast by the hands, and laid me across, I think the windlass, and tied my feet, while the other flogged me severely. I had never experienced any thing of this kind before, and although not being used to the water, I naturally feared that element the first time I saw it, yet, nevertheless, could I have got over the nettings, I would have jumped over the side, but I could not; and besides, the crew used to watch us very closely who were not chained down to the decks, lest we should leap into the water; and I have seen some of these poor African prisoners most severely cut, for attempting to do so, and hourly whipped for not eating. This indeed was often the case with myself. In a little time after, amongst the poor chained men, I found some of my own nation, which in a small degree gave ease to my mind. I inquired of these what was to be done with us? They gave me to understand, we were to be carried to these white people's country to work for them. I then was a little revived, and thought, if it were no worse than working, my situation was not so desperate; but still I feared I should be put to death, the white people looked and acted, as I thought, in so savage a manner; for I had never seen among any people such instances of brutal cruelty; and this not only shown towards us blacks, but also to some of the whites themselves. One white man in particular I saw, when we were permitted to be on deck, flogged so unmercifully with a large rope near the foremast, that he died in consequence of it; and they tossed him over the side as they would have done a brute. This made me fear these people the more; and I expected nothing less than to be treated in the same manner. I could not help expressing my fears and apprehensions to some of my countrymen; I asked them if these people had no country, but lived in this hollow place? (the ship) they told me they did not, but came from a distant one. 'Then," said I, "how comes it in all our country we never heard of them?" They told me because they lived so very far off. I then asked where were their women? had they any like themselves? I was told they had. "And why," said I, "do we not see them?" They answered, because they were left behind. I asked how the vessel could go? they told me they could not tell; but that there was cloth put upon the masts by the help of the ropes I saw, and then the vessel went on; and the white men had some spell or magic they put in the water when they liked in order to stop the vessel. I was exceedingly amazed at this account, and really thought they were spirits. I therefore wished much to be from amongst them, for I expected they would sacrifice me; but my wishes were vain, for we were so quartered that it was impossible for any of us to make our escape.

While we stayed on the coast I was mostly on deck; and one day, to my great astonishment, I saw one of these vessels coming in with the sails up. As soon as the whites saw it, they gave a great shout, at which we were amazed; and the more so, as the vessel appeared larger by approaching nearer. At last, she came to an anchor in my sight, and when the anchor was let go, I and my countrymen who saw it, were lost in astonishment to observe the vessel stop—and were now convinced it was done by magic. Soon after this the other ship got her boats out, and they came on board of us, and the people of both ships seemed very glad to see each other.—Several of the strangers also shook hands with us black people, and made motions with their hands, signifying, I suppose, we were to go to their country, but we did not understand them.

At last, when the ship we were in, had got in all her cargo, they made ready with many fearful noises, and we were all put under deck, so that we could not see how they managed the vessel. But this disappointment was the least of my sorrow. The stench of the hold while we were on the coast was so intolerably loathsome, that it was dangerous to remain there for any time, and some of us had been permitted to stay on the deck for the fresh air; but now that the whole ship's cargo were confined together, it became absolutely pestilential. The closeness of the place, and the heat of the climate, added to the number in the ship, which was so crowded that each had scarcely room to turn himself, almost suffocated us. This produced copious perspirations, so that the air soon became unfit for respiration, from a variety of loathsome smells, and brought on a sickness among the slaves, of which many died—thus falling victims to the improvident avarice, as I may call it, of their purchasers. This wretched situation was again aggravated by the falling of the chains, now become insupportable; and the filth of the necessary tubs, into which the children often fell, and were almost suffocated. The shrieks of the women, and the groans of the dying, rendered the whole a scene of horror almost inconceivable. Happily perhaps, for myself, I was soon reduced so low here that it was thought necessary to keep me almost always on deck; and from my extreme youth I was not put in fetters. In this situation I expected every hour to share the fate of my companions, some of whom were almost daily brought upon the deck at the point of death, which I began to hope would soon put an end to my miseries. Often did I think many of the inhabitants of the deep much more happy than myself. I envied them the freedom they enjoyed, and as often wished I could change my condition for theirs. Every circumstance I met with, served only to render my state more painful, and heightened my apprehensions, and my opinion of the cruelty of the whites.

One day they had taken a number of fishes; and when they had killed and satisfied themselves with as many as they thought fit, to our astonishment, who were on deck, rather than give any of them to us to eat, as we expected, they tossed the remaining fish into the sea again, although we begged and prayed for some as well as we could, but in vain; and some of my countrymen, being pressed by hunger, took an opportunity, when they thought no one saw them, of trying to get a little privately; but they were discovered, and the attempt procured them some very severe floggings. One day, when we had a smooth sea and moderate wind, two of my wearied countrymen who were chained together, (I was near them at the time,) preferring death to such a life of misery, somehow made through the nettings and jumped into the sea: immediately, another quite dejected fellow, who, on account of his illness, was suffered to be out of irons, also followed their example; and I believe many more would very soon have done the same, if they had not been prevented by the ship's crew, who were instantly alarmed. Those of us that were the most active, were in a moment put down under the deck, and there was such a noise and confusion amongst the people of the ship as I never heard before, to stop her and get the boat out to go after the slaves. However, two of the wretched were drowned, but they got the other, and afterwards flogged him unmercifully, for thus attempting to prefer death to slavery. In this manner we continued to undergo more hardships than I can now relate, hardships which are inseparable from this accursed trade. Many a time we were near suffocation from the want of fresh air, which we were often without for whole days together. This and the stench of the necessary tubs, carried off many.

During our passage, I first saw flying fishes, which surprised me very much; they used frequently to fly across the ship, and many of them fell on the deck. I also now first saw the use of the quadrant; I had often with astonishment seen the mariners make observations with it, and I could not think what it meant. They at last took notice of my surprise; and one of them, willing to increase it, as well as to gratify my curiosity, made me one day look through it. The clouds appeared to me to be land, which disappeared as they passed along. This heightened my wonder; and I was now more persuaded than ever, that I was in another world, and that every thing about me was magic. At last, we came in sight of the island of Barbadoes, at which the whites on board gave a great shout, and made many signs of joy to us. We did not know what to think of this; but as the vessel drew nearer, we plainly saw the harbor, and other ships of different kinds and sizes, and we soon anchored amongst them, off Bridgetown. Many merchants and planters now came on board, though it was in the evening. They put us in separate parcels, and examined us attentively. They also made us jump, and pointed to the land, signifying we were to go there. We thought by this, we should be eaten by these ugly men, as they appeared to us; and, when soon after we were all put down under the deck again, there was much dread and trembling among us, and nothing but bitter cries to be heard all the night from these apprehensions, insomuch that at last the white people got some old slaves from the land to pacify us. They told us we were not to be eaten, but to work, and were soon to go on land, where we should see many of our country people. This report eased us much. And sure enough, soon after we were landed, there came to us Africans of all languages.

We were conducted immediately to the merchant's yard, where we were all pent up together, like so many sheep in a fold, without regard to sex or age. As every object was new to me, everything I saw filled me with surpise. What struck me first, was that the houses were built with bricks and stories, and in every other respect different from those I had seen in Africa; but I was still more astonished on seeing people on horseback. I did not know what this could mean; and, indeed, I thought these people were full of nothing but magical arts. While I was in this astonishment, one of my fellow-prisoners spoke to a country-man of his, about the horses, who said they were the same kind they had in their country. I understood them, though they were from a distant part of Africa; and I thought it odd I had not seen any horses there; but afterwards, when I came to converse with different Africans, I found they had many horses amongst them, and much larger than those I then saw.

We were not many days in the merchant's custody, before we were sold after their usual manner, which is this:—On a signal given, (as the beat of a drum,) the buyers rush at once into the yard where the slaves are confined, and make choice of that parcel they like best. The noise and clamor with which this is attended, and the eagerness visible in the countenance of the buyers, serve not a little to increase the apprehension of terrified Africans, who may well be supposed to consider them as the ministers of that destruction to which they think themselves devoted. In this manner, without scruple, are relations and friends separated, most of them never to see each other again. I remember in the vessel in which I was brought over, in the men's apartment, there were several brothers, who, in hte sale, were sold in different lots; and it was very moving on this occasion, to see and hear their cries at parting. O, ye nominal Christians; might not an African ask you—Learned you this from your God, who says unto you, Do unto all men as you would men should do unto you? Is it not enough that we are torn from our country and friends, to toil for your luxury and lust of gain? Must every tender feeling be likewise sacrificed to your avarice? Are the dearest friends and relations, now rendered more dear by their separation from their kindred, still to be parted from each other, and thus prevented from cheering the gloom of slavery, with the small comfort of being together, and mingling their sufferings and sorrows? Why are parents to lose their children, brothers their sisters, or husbands their wives? Surely, this is a new refinement in cruelty, which, while it has no advantage to atone for it, thus aggravates distress, and adds fresh horrors even to the wretchedness of slavery.

2

THE NINETEENTH CENTURY: ATTEMPTS AT DEFINITION

As THE NINETEENTH century opened, the United States was an obscure nation precariously perched on the eastern seacoast of North America, uncertain of its identity, its destiny, or its relationship in fact to the lofty ideals stated by Thomas Jefferson in the Declaration of Independence that marked its founding a quarter century before. When the century closed, the United States was a major industrial nation spanning the North American continent, and it had expanded its sphere of influence and domination to include the eastern coast of Asia and the Western Hemisphere. During that century the United States had forged a national identity out of its unique frontier experience and Civil War; it had become convinced that its destiny was to provide moral and political guidance to the world; and it had moved, however ineptly, toward making those eighteenth century ideals the American reality in the nineteenth. But a wide gulf remained between them.

The central problems faced by the new country in 1800 were the attempt to determine the identity of "the people," and the attempt to determine the place of the individual in society. The two major factions that had begun alignment in the constitutional debates—the conservative Adams-Hamilton faction that sought to limit the role of the individual, and the liberal Jefferson faction that sought to increase it— emerged as the nucleus of the two party system that has become enshrined in the American political system. Each faction asserted that it had found its rationale and principles in the political philosophy of the Enlightenment, and each sought to define the nature of the nation's ruling group according to its interpretation of that philosophy. Although each said that "the people" should rule, and although both factions interpreted that group more broadly than had their English forebears, they disagreed over the means of determining the membership of that group. Jefferson's criteria were broader than those of Adams, but neither man was willing to include everybody.

Significantly, in these debates over the identity of "the people" and the role of the individual, race as a criterion for exclusion or inclusion was not a matter for contention, although it was to become increasingly important in the later years of the nineteenth century and throughout the twentieth. The nation had no Indian policy, and westward migration had not yet become great enough to demand one, but that migration was beginning. In 1800 only five percent of the American population lived beyond the mountains; by 1828, however, the numbers would increase to one-third of the population.

The other major racial group, the Negro, was still almost entirely in chains, a factor disturbing to the leaders of both major political factions, each of whom found slavery, in John Quincy Adams's words, "morally and politically vicious, inconsistent with the principles upon which the Revolution was justified." Yet the implications of the influence of technological change upon Southern agriculture, particularly the invention of the cotton gin by Eli Whitney in 1792, did not affect the thinking of either Adams or Jefferson. To each, it was axiomatic that natural political progress, supported by the Constitution, insured the demise of the institution. The Northwest Ordinance of 1787 had made the area north and west of the Ohio River forever free, thus preventing the expansion of the institution, and the non-importation clause of the Constitution, to take effect in 1808, was to cut off its sources of supply. If morality demanded that the institution die, they were convinced that reason had insured, through law, that it would die without turmoil.

Yet the Constitution was a compromise. It did permit the continued existence of the institution through compromise, as did the Declaration of Independence, from which Jefferson's anti-slavery clause was deleted in deference to South Carolina and Georgia. As a result, legality and technology began their long conflict with reason and morality, with the manhood of the slave as the stake, long before Adams and Jefferson died on the fiftieth anniversary of the acceptance of the first illogical and ultimately fatal compromise of July 4, 1776.

By 1800 the Indians were not yet an obstacle of expansion and progress, the Negro was apparently provided for by the Constitution (he was acknowledged as 3/5 of a person for purposes of representation and taxation), and the occasional oriental was only a curiosity. The new nation was therefore ready, under the guidance of a minority of its residents—white adult male property owners—to embark on the progress the Enlightenment had foreseen for it.

The previous twelve years, under the Washington and Adams administrations, had been marked by conservative legislative and judicial branches of the federal government and increasing popular unrest. The excesses of the French Revolution abroad and such domestic disturbances as the Whiskey Rebellion in Pennsylvania in 1794 led to such repressive, limiting acts of legislation as the Naturalization Act, the Alien Act, the Alien Enemies Act, and the Sedition Act, all under the Adams administration. There was real fear that the nation was on the verge of a social revolution like that which had afflicted France.

The revolution came, but it was not that anticipated by Adams. Instead it was the revolution sought by Jefferson; and his election in 1800, called with some justification the revolution of 1800, marked its beginning. It was to alter the course of American history, and it was to

affect and in turn be affected by every aspect of a society characterized from its onset by change. Ultimately and inevitably it was to influence and be influenced by the fact that America was to be not a
simple monocultural society but that it was to be increasingly complex.
Important in this complexity was to be the racial nature of the country,
as men became increasingly aware that there was not a single race, but
three, and ultimately four, in conflict.

With the election of Jefferson, progress began to accelerate in several
dimensions. Economic expansion began in the East with the beginnings
of the industrial revolution; geographic expansion saw rapid movement
across the mountains, into the Northwest, the Ohio country that was
forever free, and into the rich valleys of the trans-mountain South. In
1803, the illegal, unconstitutional, but inevitable Louisiana Purchase
marked the beginning of a century of territorial expansion.

As Jeffersonian democracy, the product of the stable, orderly East,
faded into the dynamic Jacksonian democracy of the frontier, progress
in the franchise and in increasing popular domination of the forces of
the country was matched by an increasingly romantic view of the
world. The two combined with the optimism of the age of Jackson to
produce an age of reform unmatched in human history. Between 1830
and the outbreak of the Civil War the tremendous moral energy of reform activity, together with the dominant romantic philosophy of the
age, began to examine the nature of American society and see it for the
first time as it was, a society of several races struggling for existence
or dominance, rather than of a single ruling race.

After the War of 1812 closed, with its confirmation of American independence, western expansion increased rapidly; Louisiana, Indiana,
Mississippi, Illinois, and Alabama were admitted to the Union in rapid
succession, and once more American concern with the aboriginal population, those who now stood in the path of progress, began to intensify.
Two major points of view concerning the Indians emerged; these views
continued through the last Indian war in 1890 and the closing of the
frontier, when the Indians experienced the ultimate humiliation of becoming wards of the government on inhospitable reservations. The Indian's image became a stereotype of the western pulp magazines, wild
west shows, and eventually movies and television.

The major policy toward the Indians was one that publicly proclaimed respect for Indian rights, particularly those of property, and
privately denied them. The result was a long series of treaties, each one
of which resulted in further loss of land, and more tribes being displaced to the West, while the private attitude insisted that the Indian
was a savage, subhuman beast, and that consequently the only good
Indian was a dead one.

John Wilbarger and John Hall reflected this policy in their writings.
At the same time that they denied the humanity of the Indian, they

pointed the way for the development of governmental Indian policy under Jackson, which included the forced westward migration of the civilized Cherokee and Creek tribes from the rich cotton land of Georgia, Alabama, and Mississippi. Elias Boudinot's eloquent plea for justice went unheeded.

They denied, too, often with a great deal of bitterness, the view of the Indian presented by romantic writers of the East and of Europe. This was the concept, stemming from Rousseau, that the Indian was a noble savage, a child of nature unspoiled by the corruption of civilized society and possessed of a virtue and beauty unsurpassed in human history. In practice, in spite of the sympathetic good intentions of writers like Washington Irving and James Fenimore Cooper and artists like Frederick Remington, this romantic view of the Indian denied his humanity as effectively as did the harsher view.

It remained for certain dedicated writers of fiction particularly Owen Wister and Joaquin Miller, to define the Indian as their insights saw him to be—not in the sense of savage, noble or otherwise, nor as the children seen by government, even by Abraham Lincoln, but as human beings. Not since the pleas of Elias Boudinot had such a definition been made, and as the century closed it went unheard in the plethora of pulp magazines and wild west shows, just as in Boudinot's day it was drowned in the cries of Indian haters and apologists alike. But at the time, with the Indians safely on the reservations, their numbers decimated and their spirits battered, it appeared that the problem presented to the European settlers by the Indians had at last been solved. Reform activity, which had ignored the Indians in the 19th Century, was to continue to do so until well into the twentieth. And ghettoized reservations remained.

Another minority group—Orientals—were concentrated on the West Coast after 1850. Primarily Chinese, this group was a remnant of the Gold Rush. For the majority of Americans, Orientals were of less concern than the Indians. This was in spite of recurrent curiosity that sometimes took the form of vicious humor and of a slowly emerging fear that resulted in limiting immigration and contributing to the growth of Chinatowns filled with exotic folklore.

Conversely, however, the existence of slavery, the peculiar institution that denied the humanity of almost all black men in America, was to become the major focal point of American attention in the century. Although slavery was widespread in the rich black belt of the South, contributing to the expulsion of the Creeks and Cherokees, who themselves owned slaves, that expansion of the institution did not cause concern. But by 1820, it was obvious that not only was slavery not dying out, but that it was embarked on its period of most rapid expansion. At the same time the peculiar combination of romantic insight into the nature of man, reform energy dedicated to his redemption, and the righteous indignation that was one of the few remnants of American puritanism slowly began to emerge. In 1816 the American Colonizing Society was founded, largely by Southerners. By 1820, confrontation and ultimate conflict between expanding slavery and militant opposition, each supported by a social, economic, and political structure growing constantly more complex, was inevitable. But moderates sought to prevent it.

The first attempt was a continuation of the efforts at compromise that had marked the Continental Congress and the Constitutional Convention. That compromise, the Missouri Compromise of 1820, was the first of those that sought to denationalize the institution. For all time, according to its provisions, political balance would be insured between slave and free states. But "for all time" was destined to mean less than thirty years. Nevertheless, the decade of the 1820's was quiet.

But by 1831 anti-slavery forces had begun to make their voices heard as the abolition movement began to take its place alongside the temperance movement, peace societies, women's rights societies, and those devoted to social reform. William Lloyd Garrison established *The Liberator* in 1831, marking the beginning of serious propaganda efforts ranging from the memoirs of Austin Steward and Frederick Douglass to the vivid harshness of *Uncle Tom's Cabin*. The stereotyped "darkie" of popular ballads and folklore slowly began to give way to the image of the enslaved man. The New England Anti-Slavery Society was founded in 1832 and the American Anti-Slavery Society in 1833. Although reformers of various emphases generally supported one another, ironically the American Anti-Slavery Society split over the role of women within it.

By 1850, however, Texas and Mexico's northern province had been annexed, and slavery threatened to expand westward. A few years later there appeared the pro-slavery propaganda of George Fitzhugh, Chancellor Harper and others. The decade from 1850 to 1860 marked the inexorable march to war as another compromise failed. By 1858, although Abraham Lincoln and Stephen Douglas debated the issue, each attempting to define the nature and role of the black man in the process, war was inevitable. In 1859 John Brown raided Harpers Ferry, and in the fall and winter of 1860–61, with the election of Lincoln, a member of a regional political party of declared hostility to slavery, the secession of the South, war and the destruction of slavery were inevitable.

In five years the Emancipation Proclamation, the defeat of the South, and Constitutional amendment had freed the slave and made him a citizen, but his social, economic, and political role had not yet been defined. The America that emerged from the war, suddenly an industrial power dedicated to another kind of expansion than that which marked the first half of the nineteenth century, gave cursory support to the cause of dignity for the freeman. David Ross Locke and others examined the problem seriously or satirically. But the Gilded Age, the age of the bloody shirt, and the conflicts between agrarianism and industrialism, between the new exploiters and the newly exploited, began to dominate the American consciousness. The black man, ghettoized in the rural South, was subject to a new kind of domination, beginning with the fear of *The Klansman* and ending in Jim Crow, the result of custom and legal sanction and disenfranchisement. By the end of the century, although Negro troopers of the 10th United States Cavalry had stormed San Juan Hill alongside Theodore Roosevelt's Rough Riders, those troopers were invisible. The Negro problem, like the Indian problem, was apparently solved. But social pressures were already forming to resurrect it. The century that had begun with a social revolution and had been convulsed by a major war in the cause of human freedom concluded by denying the need for continuing those movements.

GENERAL
STATEMENTS

A MIGHTY QUESTION (1809)

From *History of New York*

WASHINGTON IRVING

---

*Washington Irving (1783–1859), was America's first major literary fig-
ure. Essayist, satirist, historical and romantic traveler, he was one of the
first to establish the romantic view of the Indian as a noble savage and
to oppose popular policies toward him.*

(*A Mighty Question*) **in which the author puts a mighty question to
the rout by the assistance of the man in the moon—which not only
delivers thousands of people from great embarrassment, but likewise
concludes this introductory book.**

The writer of a history may, in some respects, be likened unto an adventurous knight, who, having undertaken a perilous enterprise, by
way of establishing his fame, feels bound in honor and chivalry to turn
back for no difficulty nor hardship, and never to shrink or quail, whatever enemy he may encounter. Under this impression, I resolutely draw
my pen, and fall to, with might and main, at those doughty questions
and subtle paradoxes, which, like fiery dragons and bloody giants, beset
the entrance to my history, and would fain repulse me from the very
threshold. And at this moment a gigantic question has started up,
which I must needs take by the beard and utterly subdue, before I can
advance another step in my historic undertaking; but I trust this will
be the last adversary I shall have to contend with, and that in the next
book I shall be enabled to conduct my readers in triumph into the body
of my work.

The question which has thus suddenly arisen is, what right had the
first discoverers of America to land and take possession of a country,
without first gaining the consent of its inhabitants, or yielding them an
adequate compensation for their territory?—a question which has with-
stood many fierce assaults, and has given much distress of mind to multitudes of kind-hearted folk. And, indeed, until it be totally vanquished,
and put to rest, the worthy people of America can by no means enjoy
the soil they inhabit with clear right and title, and quiet, unsullied consciences.

The first source of right, by which property is acquired in a country,
is DISCOVERY. For as all mankind have an equal right to anything which
has never before been appropriated, so any nation that discovers an
uninhabited country, and takes possession thereof, is considered as
enjoying full property, and absolute, unquestionable empire therein.

86

This proposition being admitted, it follows clearly that the Europeans who first visited America were the real discoverers of the same; nothing being necessary to the establishment of this fact but simply to prove that it was totally uninhabited by man. This would, at first, appear to be a point of some difficulty, for it is well known that this quarter of the world abounded with certain animals that walked erect on two feet, had something of the human countenance, uttered certain unintelligible sounds very much like language; in short, had a marvelous resemblance to human beings. But the zealous and enlightened fathers, who accompanied the discoverers, for the purpose of promoting the kingdom of heaven by establishing fat monasteries and bishoprics on earth, soon cleared up this point, greatly to the satisfaction of his holiness the Pope and of all Christian voyagers and discoverers.

They plainly proved, and as there were no Indian writers arose on the other side the fact was considered as fully admitted and established, that the two-legged race of animals before mentioned were mere cannibals, detestable monsters, and many of them giants—which last description of vagrants have, since the time of Gog, Magog, and Goliath, been considered as outlaws, and have received no quarter in either history, chivalry, or song. Indeed, even the philosophic Bacon declared the Americans to be people proscribed by the laws of nature, inasmuch as they had a barbarous custom of sacrificing men and feeding upon man's flesh.

Nor are these all the proofs of their utter barbarism: among many other writers of discernment, Ulloa tells us, "their imbecility is so visible that one can hardly form an idea of them different from what one has of the brutes. Nothing disturbs the tranquillity of their souls, equally insensible to disasters and to prosperity. Though half naked, they are as contented as a monarch in his most splendid array. Fear makes no impression on them, and respect as little." All this is furthermore supported by the authority of M. Bouguer: "It is not easy," says he "to describe the degree of their indifference for wealth and all its advantages. One does not well know what motives to propose to them, when one would persuade them to any service. It is vain to offer them money; they answer that they are not hungry." And Vanegas confirms the whole, assuring us that "ambition they have none, and are more desirous of being thought strong than valiant. The objects of ambition with us—honor, fame, reputation, riches, posts and distinctions—are unknown among them. So that this powerful spring of action, the cause of so much *seeming* good and *real* evil in the world, has no power over them. In a word, these unhappy mortals may be compared to children, in whom the development of reason is not completed."

Now all these peculiarities, although in the unenlightened states of Greece they would have entitled their possessors to immortal honor, as having reduced to practice those rigid and abstemious maxims, the mere talking about which acquired certain old Greeks the reputation of sages and philosophers;—yet, were they clearly proved in the present instance to betoken a most abject and brutified nature, totally beneath the human character. But the benevolent fathers, who had undertaken to turn these unhappy savages into dumb beasts by dint of argument, advanced still stronger proofs; for as certain divines of the sixteenth century, and among the rest, Lullus, affirm—the Americans go naked and have no beards!—"They have nothing," says Lullus, "of the reasonable animal, except the mask."—And even that mask was allowed to avail them but little, for it was soon found that they were of a hideous copper complexion—and being of a copper complexion, it was all the same as if they were negroes—and negroes are black, "and black," said the pious fathers, devoutly crossing themselves, "is the color of the Devil!" Therefore, so far from being able to own property, they had no right even to personal freedom—for liberty is too radiant a deity to inhabit such gloomy temples. All which circumstances plainly convinced the righteous followers of Cortes and Pizarro that these miscreants had no title to the soil that they infested—that they were a perverse, illiterate, dumb, beardless, black-seed—mere wild beasts of the forests, and, like them, should either be subdued or exterminated.

From the foregoing arguments, therefore, and a variety of others equally conclusive, which I forbear to enumerate, it is clearly evident that this fair quarter of the globe, when first visited by Europeans, was a howling wilderness, inhabited by nothing but wild beasts; and that the transatlantic visitors acquired an incontrovertible property therein, by the *right of discovery*.

This right being fully established, we now come to the next, which is the right acquired by *cultivation*. "The cultivation of the soil," we are told, "is an obligation imposed by nature on mankind. The whole world is appointed for the nourishment of its inhabitants: but it would be incapable of doing it, was it uncultivated. Every nation is then obliged by the law of nature to cultivate the ground that has fallen to its share. Those people, like the ancient Germans and modern Tartars, who, having fertile countries, disdain to cultivate the earth and choose to live by rapine, are wanting to themselves, and *deserve to be exterminated as savage and pernicious beasts.*"

Now it is notorious that the savages knew nothing of agriculture, when first discovered by the Europeans, but lived a most vagabond, disorderly, unrighteous life—rambling from place to place, and prodigally rioting upon the spontaneous luxuries of nature, without tasking her generosity to yield them anything more; whereas it has been most unquestionably shown that Heaven intended the earth should be plowed and sown, and manured, and laid out into cities, and towns, and farms, and country-seats, and pleasure grounds, and public gardens, all which the Indians knew nothing about—therefore, they did not improve the talents Providence had bestowed on them—therefore, they were careless stewards—therefore, they had no right to the soil—therefore, they deserved to be exterminated.

It is true the savages might plead that they drew all the benefits from the land which their simple wants required—they found plenty of game to hunt, which, together with the roots and uncultivated fruits of the earth, furnished a sufficient variety for their frugal repasts;—and that as Heaven merely designed the earth to form the abode and satisfy the wants of man, so long as those purposes were answered the Will of Heaven was accomplished.—But this only proves how undeserving they were of the blessings around them—they were so much the more savages for not having more wants; for knowledge is in some degree an increase of desires, and it is this superiority, both in the number and magnitude of his desires, that distinguishes the man from the beast. Therefore, the Indians in not having more wants, were very unreasonable animals; and it was but just that they should make way for the Europeans, who had a thousand wants to their one, and, therefore, would turn the earth to more account, and, by cultivating it, more truly fulfill the will of Heaven. Besides—Grotius and Lauterbach, and Puffendorf, and Titus, and many wise men besides, who have considered the matter properly, have determined that the property of a country cannot be acquired by hunting, cutting wood, or drawing water in it—nothing but precise demarcation of limits and the intention of cultivation can establish the possession. Now, as the savages (probably from never having read the authors above quoted) had never complied with any of these necessary forms, it plainly followed that they had no right to the soil, but that it was completely at the disposal of the first comers, who had more knowledge, more wants, and more elegant, that is to say artificial, desires than themselves.

In entering upon a newly-discovered, uncultivated country, therefore, the newcomers were but taking possession of what, according to the aforesaid doctrine, was their own property—therefore, in opposing them, the savages were invading their just rights, infringing the immutable laws of Nature, and counteracting the will of Heaven—therefore, they were guilty of impiety, burglary, and trespass on the case—therefore, they were hardened offenders against God and man—therefore, they ought to be exterminated.

But a more irresistible right than either that I have mentioned, and one which will be the most readily admitted by my reader, provided he be blessed with bowels of charity and philanthropy, is the right acquired by civilization. All the world knows the lamentable state in which these poor savages were found—not only deficient in the comforts of life, but, what is still worse, most piteously and unfortunately blind to the miseries of their situation. But no sooner did the benevolent inhabitants of Europe behold their sad condition than they immediately went to work to meliorate and improve it. They introduced among them rum, gin, brandy, and the other comforts of life—and it is astonishing to read how soon the poor savages learned to estimate these blessings—they likewise made known to them a thousand remedies, by which the most inveterate diseases are alleviated and healed; and that they might comprehend the benefits and enjoy the comforts of these medicines, they previously introduced among them the diseases which they were calculated to cure. By these and a variety of other methods was the condition of these poor savages wonderfully improved; they acquired a thousand wants of which they had before been ignorant; and as he has most sources of happiness who has most wants to be gratified, they were doubtlessly rendered a much happier race of beings.

But the most important branch of civilization, and which has most strenuously been extolled by the zealous and pious father of the Romish Church, is the introduction of the Christian faith. It was truly a sight that might well inspire horror, to behold these savages stumbling among the dark mountains of paganism, and guilty of the most horrible ignorance of religion. It is true they neither stole nor defrauded; they were sober, frugal, continent, and faithful to their word; but though they acted right habitually, it was all in vain, unless they acted so from precept. The newcomers, therefore, used every method to induce them to embrace and practice the true religion—except indeed that of setting them the example.

But notwithstanding all these complicated labors for their good, such was the unparalleled obstinacy of these stubborn wretches, that they ungratefully refused to acknowledge the strangers as their benefactors, and persisted in disbelieving the doctrines they endeavored to inculcate; most insolently alleging that from their conduct the advocates of Christianity did not seem to believe in it themselves. Was not this too much for human patience?—would not one suppose that the benign visitants from Europe, provoked at their incredulity, and discouraged by their stiff-necked obstinacy, would forever have abandoned their shores and consigned them to their original ignorance and misery?—But no— so zealous were they to effect the temporal comfort and eternal salvation of these pagan infidels, that they even proceeded from the milder means of persuasion to the more painful and troublesome one of persecution, let loose among them whole troops of fiery monks and furious bloodhounds—purified them by fire and sword, by stake and fagot; in consequence of which indefatigable measures the cause of Christian love and charity was so rapidly advanced that in a very few years not one-fifth of the number of unbelievers existed in South America that were found there at the time of its discovery.

What stronger right need the European settlers advance to the country than this? Have not whole nations of uninformed savages been made acquainted with a thousand imperious wants and indispensable comforts, of which they were before wholly ignorant?—Have they not been literally hunted and smoked out of the dens and lurking-places of ignorance and infidelity, and absolutely scourged into the right path? —Have not the temporal things, the vain baubles and filthy lucre of this world, which were too apt to engage their worldly and selfish thoughts, been benevolently taken from them? and have they not, instead thereof been taught to set their affections on things above?—And finally, to use the words of a reverend Spanish father, in a letter to his superior in Spain—"Can any one have the presumption to say that these savage pagans have yielded anything more than an inconsiderable recompense to their benefactors, in surrendering to them a little pitiful tract of this dirty sublunary planet, in exchange for a glorious inheritance in the kingdom of heaven!"

Here, then, are three complete and undeniable sources of right established, any one of which was more than ample to establish a property in the newly-discovered regions of America. Now, so it has happened in certain parts of this delightful quarter of the globe, that the right of discovery has been so strenuously asserted—the influence of cultivation so industriously extended, and the progress of salvation and civilization so zealously prosecuted that, what with their attendant wars, persecutions, oppressions, diseases and other partial evils that often hang on the skirts of great benefits—the savage aborigines have, somehow or another, been utterly annihilated—and this all at once brings me to a fourth right, which is worth all the others put together.—For the original claimants to the soil being all dead and buried, and no one remaining to inherit or dispute the soil, the Spaniards, as the next immediate occupants, entered upon the possession as clearly as the hangman succeeds to the clothes of the malefactor—and as they have Blackstone, and all the learned expounders of the law on their side, they may set all actions of ejectment at defiance—and this last right may be entitled the RIGHT BY EXTERMINATION, or, in other words, the RIGHT BY GUNPOWDER.

But lest any scruples of conscience should remain on this head, and to settle the question of right forever, his holiness Pope Alexander VI. issued a bull, by which he generously granted the newly-discovered quarter of the globe to the Spaniards and Portuguese; who, thus having law and gospel on their side, and being inflamed with great spiritual zeal, showed the pagan savages neither favor nor affection, but prosecuted the work of discovery, colonization, civilization and extermination, with ten times more fury than ever.

Thus were the European worthies who first discovered America clearly entitled to the soil; and not only entitled to the soil, but likewise to the eternal thanks of these infidel savages, for having come so far, endured so many perils by sea and land, and taken such unwearied pains, for no other purpose but to improve their forlorn, uncivilized, and heathenish condition—for having made them acquainted with the comforts of life; for having introduced among them the light of religion; and, finally, for having hurried them out of the world, to enjoy its reward!

But as argument is never so well understood by us selfish mortals as when it comes home to ourselves, and as I am particularly anxious that this question should be put to rest forever, I will suppose a parallel case, by way of arousing the candid attention of my readers.

Let us suppose, then, that the inhabitants of the moon, by astonishing advancement in science, and by profound insight into that lunar philosophy, the mere flickerings of which have of late years dazzled the feeble optics and addled the shallow brains of the good people of our globe—let us suppose, I say, that the inhabitants of the moon, by these means, had arrived at such a command of their *energies*, such an enviable state of *perfectibility,* as to control the elements and navigate the boundless regions of space. Let us suppose a roving crew of these soaring philosophers, in the course of an aerial voyage of discovery among the stars, should chance to alight upon this outlandish planet.

And here I beg my readers will not have the uncharitableness to smile, as is too frequently the fault of volatile readers, when perusing the grave speculations of philosophers. I am far from indulging in any sportive vein at present; nor is the supposition I have been making so wild as many may deem it. It has long been a very serious and anxious question with me, and many a time and oft, in the course of my overwhelming cares and contrivances for the welfare and protection of this my native planet, have I lain awake whole nights debating in my mind whether it were most probable we should first discover and civilize the moon or the moon discover and civilize our globe. Neither would the prodigy of sailing in the air and cruising among the stars be a whit more astonishing and incomprehensible to us, than was the European mystery of navigating floating castles through the world of waters to the simple savages. We have already discovered the art of coasting along the aerial shores of our planet, by means of balloons, as the savages had of venturing along their seacoasts in canoes; and the disparity between the former, and the aerial vehicles of the philosophers from the moon, might not be greater than that between the bark canoes of the savages and the mighty ships of their discoverers. I might here pursue an endless chain of similar speculations; but as they would be unimportant to my subject, I abandon them to my reader, particularly if he be a philosopher, as matters well worthy of his attentive consideration.

To return then to my supposition—let us suppose that the aerial visitants I have mentioned, possessed of vastly superior knowledge to ourselves; that is to say, possessed of superior knowledge in the art of extermination—riding on hippogriffs—defended with impenetrable armor—armed with concentrated sunbeams, and provided with vast engines, to hurl enormous moonstones: in short, let us suppose them, if our vanity will permit the supposition, as superior to us in knowledge, and consequently in power, as the Europeans were to the Indians, when they first discovered them. All this is very possible; it is only our self-sufficiency that makes us think otherwise; and I warrant the poor savages, before they had any knowledge of the white men, armed in all the terrors of glittering steel and tremendous gunpowder, were as perfectly convinced that they themselves were the wisest, the most virtuous, powerful, and perfect of created beings, as are at this present moment the lordly inhabitants of Old England, the volatile populace of France, or even the self-satisfied citizens of this most enlightened republic.

Let us suppose, moreover, that the aerial voyagers, finding this planet to be nothing but a howling wilderness, inhabited by us, poor savages and wild beasts, shall take formal possession of it in the name of his most gracious and philosophic excellency, the man in the moon. Finding, however, that their numbers are incompetent to hold it in complete subjection, on account of the ferocious barbarity of its inhabitants, they shall take our worthy President, the King of England, the Emperor of Hayti, the mighty Bonaparte, and the great King of Bantam, and returning to their native planet, shall carry them to court, as were the Indian chiefs led about as spectacles in the courts of Europe.

Then making such obeisance as the etiquette of the court requires, they shall address the puissant man in the moon, in, as near as I can conjecture, the following terms:

"Most serene and mighty Potentate, whose dominions extend as far as eye can reach, who rideth on the Great Bear, useth the sun as a looking-glass, and maintaineth unrivaled control over tides, madmen and sea-crabs: We, thy liege subjects, have just returned from a voyage of discovery, in the course of which we have landed and taken possession of that obscure little dirty planet which thou beholdest rolling at a distance. The five uncouth monsters which we have brought into this august presence were once very important chiefs among their fellow-savages, who are a race of beings totally destitute of the common attributes of humanity; and differing in everything from the inhabitants of the moon, inasmuch as they carry their heads upon their shoulders, instead of under their arms—have two eyes instead of one—are utterly destitute of tails, and a variety of unseemly complexions, particularly of a horrible whiteness—instead of pea-green.

"We have, moreover, found these miserable savages sunk into a state of the utmost ignorance and depravity, every man shamelessly living with his own wife, and rearing his own children, instead of indulging in that community of wives enjoined by the law of nature, as expounded by the philosophers of the moon. In a word, they have scarcely a gleam of true philosophy among them, but are, in fact, utter heretics, ignoramuses, and barbarians. Taking compassion, therefore, on the sad condition of these sublunary wretches, we have endeavored, while we remained on their planet, to introduce among them the light of reason—and the comforts of the moon. We have treated them to mouthfuls of moonshine, and draughts of nitrous oxide, which they swallowed with incredible voracity, particularly the females; and we have likewise endeavored to instil into them the precepts of lunar philosophy. We have insisted upon their renouncing the contemptible shackles of religion and common sense, and adoring the profound, omnipotent, and all-perfect energy, and the ecstatic, immutable, immovable perfection. But such was the unparalleled obstinacy of these wretched savages that they persisted in cleaving to their wives, and adhering to their religion, and absolutely set at naught the sublime doctrines of the moon—nay, among other abominable heresies, they even went so far as blasphemously to declare that this ineffable planet was made of nothing more nor less than green cheese!"

At these words, the great man in the moon (being a very profound philosopher) shall fall into a terrible passion, and possessing equal authority over things that do not belong to him, as did whilom his holiness the Pope, shall forthwith issue a formidable bull, specifying "That, whereas a certain crew of Lunatics have lately discovered, and taken possession of, a newly discovered planet called *the earth*—and that whereas it is inhabited by none but a race of two-legged animals, that carry their heads on their shoulders instead of under their arms; cannot talk the lunatic language; have two eyes instead of one; are destitute of tails, and of a horrible whiteness, instead of pea-green—therefore, and for a variety of other excellent reasons, they are considered incapable of possessing any property in the planet they infest, and the right and title to it are confirmed to its original discoverers.—And furthermore, the colonists who are now about to depart to the aforesaid planet are authorized and commanded to use every means to convert these infidel savages from the darkness of Christianity, and make them thorough and absolute Lunatics."

In consequence of this benevolent bull, our philosophic benefactors go to work with hearty zeal. They seize upon our fertile territories, scourge us from our rightful possessions, relieve us from our wives, and when we are unreasonable enough to complain, they will turn upon us and say: Miserable barbarians! ungrateful wretches! have we not come thousands of miles to improve your worthless planet? have we not fed you with moonshine? have we not intoxicated you with nitrous oxide? does not our moon give you light every night, and have you the baseness to murmur when we claim a pitiful return for all these benefits? But finding that we not only persist in absolute contempt of their reasoning and disbelief in their philosophy, but even go so far as daringly to defend our property, their patience shall be exhausted, and they shall resort to their superior powers of argument; hunt us with hippogriffs, transfix us with concentrated sunbeams, demolish our cities with moonstones; until having, by main force, converted us to the true faith, they shall graciously permit us to exist in the torrid deserts of Arabia, or the frozen regions of Lapland, there to enjoy the blessings of civilization and the charms of lunar philosophy, in much the same manner as the reformed and enlightened savages of this country are kindly suffered to inhabit the inhospitable forests of the north, or the impenetrable wilderness of South America.

Thus, I hope, I have clearly proved, and strikingly illustrated, the right of the early colonists to the possession of this country; and thus is this gigantic question completely vanquished. So, having manfully surmounted all obstacles, and subdued all opposition, what remains but that I should forthwith conduct my readers into the city which we have been so long in a manner besieging? But hold—before I proceed another step, I must pause to take breath, and recover from the excessive fatigue I have undergone, in preparing to begin this most accurate of histories. And in this I do but imitate the example of a renowned Dutch tumbler of antiquity, who took a start of three miles for the purpose of jumping over a hill, but having run himself quietly down for a few moments to blow, and then walked over it at his leisure.

THE SUPERIORITY OF THE WHITE RACE (1846)
From *Speech in the Senate*
THOMAS HART BENTON

Thomas Hart Benton (1782–1858), American statesman, followed the frontier west to Tennessee and Missouri, from whence he was elected to the United States Senate. An expansionist, he supported American "manifest destiny" and believed firmly in the superiority of the Anglo-Saxons.

The effect of the arrival of the Caucasian, or White race, on the western coast of America, opposite the eastern coast of Asia, remains to be mentioned among the benefits which the settlement of the Columbia will produce; and that a benefit, not local to us, but general and universal to the human race. Since the dispersion of man upon earth, I know of no human event, past or present, which promises a greater, and more beneficent change upon earth than the arrival of the van of the Caucasian race (the Celtic-Anglo-Saxon division) upon the border of the sea which washes the shore of the eastern Asia. The Mongolian, or Yellow race, is there, four hundred millions in number, spreading almost to Europe; a race once the foremost of the human family in the arts of civilization, but torpid and stationary for thousands of years. It is a race far above the Ethiopian, or Black—above the Malay, or Brown, (if we must admit five races)—and above the American Indian, or Red: it is a race far above all these, but still, far below the White; and, like all the rest, must receive an impression from the superior race whenever they come in contact. It would seem that the White race alone received the divine command, to subdue and replenish the earth; for it is the only race that has obeyed it—the only one that hunts out new and distant lands, and even a New World, to subdue and replenish. Starting from western Asia, taking Europe for their field, and the Sun for their guide, and leaving the Mongolians behind, they arrived, after many ages, on the shores of the Atlantic, which they lit up with the lights of science and religion, and adorned with the useful and the elegant arts. Three and a half centuries ago, this race, in obedience to the great command, arrived in the New World, and found new lands to subdue and replenish. For a long time, it was confined to the border of the new field, (I now mean the Celtic-Anglo-Saxon division;) and even fourscore years ago the philosophic Burke was considered a rash man because he said the English colonists would top the Alleghanies, and descend into the valley of the Mississippi, and occupy without parchment if the Crown refused to make grants of land. What was considered a rash declaration eighty years ago, is old history, in our young country, at this day. Thirty years ago I said the same thing of the Rocky Mountains and the Columbia: it was ridiculed then: it is becoming history to-day. The venerable Mr. Macon has often told me that he remembered a line low down in North Carolina, fixed by a royal governor as a boundary between the whites and the Indians: where is that boundary now? The van of the Caucasian race now top the Rocky Mountains, and spread down to the shores of the Pacific. In a few years a great population will grow up there, luminous with the accumulated lights of European and American civilization. Their presence in such a position cannot be without its influence upon eastern Asia. The sun of civilization must shine across the sea: socially and commercially, the van of the Caucasians, and the rear of the Mongolians, must intermix. They must talk together, and trade together, and marry together. Commerce is a great civilizer—social intercourse as great—and marriage greater. The White and Yellow races can marry together, as well as eat and trade together. Moral and intellectual superiority will do the rest: the White race will take the ascendant, elevating what is susceptible of improvement—wearing out what is not. The Red race has disappeared from the Atlantic coast: the tribes that resisted civilization, met extinction. This is a cause of lamentation with many. For my part, I cannot murmur at what seems to be the effect of divine law. I cannot repine that this Capitol has replaced the wigwam—this Christian people, replaced the savages—white matrons, the red squaws—and that such men as Washington, Franklin, and Jefferson, have taken the place of Powhattan, Opechonecanough, and other red men, howsoever respectable they may have been as savages. Civilization, or extinction, has been the fate of all people who have found themselves in the track of the advancing Whites, and civilization, always the preference of the Whites, has been pressed as an object, while extinction has followed as a consequence of its resistance. The Black and the Red races have often felt their ameliorating influence. The Yellow race, next to themselves in the scale of mental and moral excellence, and in the beauty of form, once their superiors in the useful and elegant arts, and in learning, and still respectable though stationary; this race cannot fail to receive a new impulse from the approach of the Whites, improved so much since so many ages ago they left the western borders of Asia. The apparition of the van of the Caucasian race, rising upon them in the east after having left them on the west, and after having completed the circumnavigation of the globe, must wake up and reanimate the torpid body of old Asia. Our position and policy will commend us to their hospitable reception: political considerations will aid the action of social and commercial influences. Pressed upon by the great Powers of Europe—the same that press upon us—they must in our appoach see the advent of friends, not of foes—of benefactors, not of invaders. The moral and intellectual superiority of the White race will do the rest: and thus, the youngest people, and the newest land, will become the reviver and the regenerator of the oldest.

It is in this point of view, and as acting upon the social, political, and religious condition of Asia, and giving a new point of departure to her ancient civilization, that I look upon the settlement of the Columbia river by the van of the Caucasian race as the most momentous human event in the history of man since his dispersion over the face of the earth. . . .

From
ASIA AND AFRICA IN AMERICA (1912)
HUBERT HOWE BANCROFT

Hubert Howe Bancroft (1832–1918), American historian, publisher, and archivist, reflects much of the popular social and scientific thought of the nineteenth century in his works. As coordinator of a massive survey of America written by twelve others, he did little actual writing but he collected vast amounts of information and made it accessible.

Of the several dark-skinned races that met western civilization in America the Japanese though latest to arrive were quickest to respond to its influence; the African was the slowest; while the Chinaman, the most advanced of the three, and as an economic asset the best for low-grade labor in the world, was so sterilized by ages of inaction as to be impervious to the modifying influences of progress.

In 1848 there were but three Chinese in California; 700 came in 1849, 3000 in 1850, about the same number in 1851, and 10,000 in 1852. Then a sharp decline, the tide setting in the other way, and that without expulsion laws. More came later, and again the tide turned; whence it appears that California is not altogether and forever a paradise for the celestial.

Nippon did not even awake at the call of gold, nor yet until Commodore Perry knocked so loudly at her portal, threatening if not opened to break it down.

A true story of the Asiatics in America illustrates not only the elasticity of our old puritan principles, and certain glaring defects in our republican systems, but it brings home to us as well the amazing gullibility of the American people. "A century of dishonor" Helen Hunt calls our treatment of the Indians; she might add another century and include the Chinese.

The first reception of these ancients of the Asiatics by the best men of San Francisco,—or should I say by the white devils of this weird environment as best befitting the thoughts of the visitors,—may be better described in the words of an eye-witness than in a report at second hand.

Albert Williams, the founder of the First Presbyterian church in San Francisco, 1849, a good man of sound mind and practical ability, minister of Christ, friend of the sick and suffering, friend of the stranger, working for no earthly reward, working with other good men in this sometime hellhole of gold and gambling, working with Frederick Billings, with Governor Mason, with George W. P. Bissel and others of that stamp, thus writes:—

"Very naturally the trade of California with the opposite shore of the Pacific originated. Soon as the news of the discovery of gold reached its ports, ships lying in them were loaded and dispatched to the California market. Arriving at a time when goods of all kinds almost were in demand, cargoes were readily disposed of, and the vessels returned for second loadings. Here was demand, there was supply. An active though limited trade with China engaged leading mercantile houses in San Francisco. Finley Johnson & Co., Osborn and Brannan, G. B. Post & Co. and others embarked in the trade. Articles of American and European growth and manufacture in the Chinese market found their opportunity to meet the new demand, products of China, tea, sugar, rice, and fruits were sent in quantities. This course of trade became settled, the importance of the business was felt and commented upon. At length communication with China by steamship was mooted. J. H. Osborn of San Francisco was foremost in urging upon the United States government the establishment of a mail steamship line between San Francisco and Hong-Kong. The end was accomplished.

"Looking back to its commencement, it is seen that in the track of the newly opened trade the Chinese themselves came to our shores. At first the number was few, so few as hardly to attract attention. Like other immigrants they came as adventurers, they were importers and jobbers. Very few were in other employments. Nearly all were merchants. They were intelligent, and by their orderly demeanor they commended themselves to the public confidence and respect, their number steadily though slowly increased. In the summer of 1850 there were about one hundred Chinese in San Francisco. The first public recognition of their presence in our city was made an occasion of general interest. Consignments of the Chinese books and tracts, secular and religious, having been sent to us, it was suggested by their consular agent, Frederick A. Woodworth, that a public distribution should be made of the publications among the resident Chinese. Arrangements were accordingly made by a committee consisting of Mr. Woodworth, Mayor Geary, and Mr. Williams. In the afternoon of the 28th of August, 1850, their entire number assembled and were conducted in procession, two by two, to a large platform on Portsmouth square. In their rich national costume, not omitting the costly fan to shelter them from the sun, they were objects of marked observation. In turn they were addressed, through Ah Sing, the interpreter, by Mr. Woodworth, Mayor Geary, Mr. Hunt, and Mr. Williams, the several speakers united in expressing the pleasure shared in common by the citizens of San Francisco in their presence, the encouraging omen of opening friendly intercourse with their country, the hope that more of their people would follow their example in crossing the ocean to our shore, and finally charging them with a message to their friends in China that in coming to this country they would find welcome and protection. The dignified manners and general attractive bearing of the China boys, as Mr. Woodworth familiarly styled them,—others said they bore the appearance of mandarins,—called forth universal commendation. The *California Courier* making note concerning them expressed the general sentiment. 'We have never seen a finer-looking body of men collected together in San Francisco,' it said; 'in fact, this portion of our population is a pattern for sobriety, order, and obedience to laws, not only to other foreign residents but to Americans themselves.'"

Such was the estimate of the situation placed by these representatives of the American people then in San Francisco, a newly opened port of the advanced civilization, and nearest the celestial regions of the cultured heathen who now for the first time timidly approached our shores in response to pledges of good faith and courtesy.

It was the voice not of aliens or demagogues but of true men not yet demoralized by prosperity, of true Americans, sons of those who had come for conscience sake, and had called from the wilds to all the world, "Come over to us and be free!"

It was the voice of humanity, of fraternity, calling to the victims of the old world despotisms and superstitions. More to the point, perhaps, in the minds of these utilitarian occupants of the San Francisco dunes, it was the voice of good business. Here for the first time in history met upon the most friendly and favorable terms the latest civilization of the West and the remotest civilization of the East.

It was an opportunity such as could come but once to any people, an opportunity such as the powers of Europe would have fought for if fighting could accomplish the purpose; an opportunity for the statesman, the merchant, the manufacturer, the philanthropist, the proselytist, an opportunity for us to make the whole of China our sphere of influence, and give us the beneficent guardianship of half a continent older than England and richer than India.

And we threw the chance away. The insensate folly of it! Congress was occupied with that dismal curse of Africa, the enslaved black man and his master, and had no time to talk of continents; besides, the celestial empire was far away. The politician was thinking of place, the journalist of patronage, and the agitator of his dinner; these, the masters of the situation, united their strength for pelf. What cared they for principalities and powers, for the glory of Yankeedom, for the prosperity of the United States, or even for remote advantages to themselves!

The friendly emissaries from far Cathay returned home and reported. They told their people, the mild-eyed dwellers upon the streams of paradise, and the sterner inhabitants of the celestial hills, that the foreign devils lately arrived upon the opposite shores though white and bearded were not evil-minded beings, but good devils, friendly and kind, ready to share with them their gold and give them their clothes to wash, their ditches to dig, and lordly aliens to wait upon. So with the rest of the world came the Chinese to California, specially invited thither, though spurned and scourged on their arrival, and for fifty years thereafter.

The Japanese, their emergence from exclusiveness at the call of Commodore Perry, their marvelous development, their deeds at arms and their coming hither in unwelcomed numbers are incidents known to all, but the story of the Chinese in America has never been fully or fairly told. It is a tale not particularly pleasing, not specially creditable to a people professing broad benevolence, love of equity, and filled with a desire to benefit the world, to enlighten and civilize and Christianize every nation of whatsoever color or creed.

It is a tale of patient endurance on the part of a people not altogether lovely, and by no means altogether vile; a people whose nation, buried under the accumulations of its own numbers, is still dreaming life away in its old half-civilization, and yet with vitality enough, with temerity hitherto unknown among its members, for some to pledge dearly loved wife and children for passage to the wilderness across the fearful waters, where they might gather a little gold with which to return and make them all happy forever after.

The rude encounter they were called upon to undergo at the outset with a dominant race, which too often delights in its rudeness, was small as compared with their relentless persecution by demagogues and politicians high and low, by a servile press and a thoughtless people, all under protection of a great and good government that delights in dealing out fair justice to the white man and to the black man, but which balks when up against the yellow man. Color-blind, or color-wise, or color-crazed, which? The anarchistic Italian, called white; the cannibalistic African, known to be black, fine material for American citizenship even though fresh from his native jungle and of the proper shade, but pale yellow is an off color in federal dispensations. So decreed the sapient law-makers at Washington, incited thereunto by alien agitators and a prostituted press.

In the face of these influences what could they do, the merchant, the farmer, the manufacturer, the professor, the preacher. A true expression of opinion would bring upon them unpopularity and loss of patronage; it were easier to float with the tide. So the iniquity must be continued, not for ourselves or for the good of the country, but to please the fancy and gratify the passions of low-grade Europeans who had no more right to dictate terms than had those they would drive away.

It was in the placer mines of California, in the early gold-gathering days, that Chinese working-men first made their appearance in any considerable numbers in America. To the somewhat unlearned and in-experienced mid-continent Americans who came hither from the op-posite direction upon the same errand, they were a queer humanity. Eyes aslant and long tail of braided hair; half-shaved scalp with black stubs standing in the scraped yellow skin; fuzzy face with flat nose and wide-extended mouth; raiment brilliant and baggy; shuffling gait and clattering feet, high squeaking voice,—this for first glance and the out-side; later, after many deep soundings for fresh iniquities to be used in their undoing, they were found to be mild and unoffending; self-centred and retiring, yet, when cornered ready to fight with reckless indifference to danger; hard workers, economical and thrifty,—or as others would say low-wage grinders, parsimonious and niggardly.

Temperate, preferring a little of the divine drug to great measures of brain-burning drink; never seen staggering on the street, or joining in noisy riot, or begging for bed-money, or lying dead drunk with up-turned bloated face in the gutter as their vilifiers are sometimes found; pagan in mind and morals and yet more Christian than many Chris-tians;—or if one chooses, opium-smoking, devil-worshiping heathen, —yet void of small revenges, void of the many outrages that the white and black indulge in; declining to intermeddle in politics; declining citizenship, assimilation, or amalgamation; declining any new religion yet never attempting to enforce their own; declining boycotts, strikes, and dynamiting; declining theft of franchise, looting, and the usual official vileness; asking but little in the way of free education, free pris-ons, hospitals, or asylums.

From an industrial point of view they are the best class for certain work that comes to this country, and if our morals and Americanism cannot survive their indifference, we had better reconstruct ourselves. Indeed that they do not desire close relationship, but are satisfied to do our drudgery, disturbing nothing, stealing nothing, and then retire, is one of the best features of the case.

When the American miners saw these strange beings from the an-cient east pecking at the placers, they cried "Scat!" as to ground-squir-rels in a field of grain. For was not this their country, for which some-body sometime had bled and died; was not this the land looted from Mexico by Polk's politicians, and was not the gold thereof their very own? True, there were present other foreigners, who were likewise in-terlopers, Mexicans, Kanakas, and tropical islanders, English, French, and Germans.

The Europeans, however, did not fly away so readily at the shouting of "Scat!' but seemed able to take care of themselves; so the patriotism of the Americans might all be saved to discharge at those of dusky skin.

While the yield was plentiful and the gold-picking easy it seemed scarcely worth while to quarrel over the relative rights of American citizens and foreigners. A little way back in the Sierra there were probably many mother lodes, mountains of metal, perhaps, from which pieces and particles had been brought down to the foot-hills by the water and the ice, places where mule trains might be loaded with gold and ships bear away cargoes of it. But the gold mountains could not be found, and the weary prospectors came back from their wanderings, and the miners returned to their old claims, driving out those who had taken possession during their absence.

Other rumors of other great gold deposits were heard, and away rush the mercurial miners only again to return, which they must do or starve. At first a claim that did not pay an ounce a day to the man was not worth having, but when forced to it they were content with eight dollars, and then with four dollars a day, below which returns white men would not work, though the Chinamen held on, scratching around abandoned claims and working over several times the old tailings, content to secure even a dollar a day. So the Chinese remained at their gold-gleanings long after the white men had given them up, and still the press and politicians baited them.

Meanwhile among the miners whenever sport was afoot there were plenty of participants. And what could be better fun for a band of patriots in defense of their new gold-giving country, on a warm Sunday afternoon, filled with Sunday whiskey, than a raid on a Chinese camp to see the celestials fly? Mounted on mustangs with pistols popping, away they go, into the valley of death, the brave fellows; when shall their glory fade? "What in hell are these heathen doing here any way, carrying off our gold, and leaving only a hole in the ground!"

But when it came to knife practice pure and simple, if peradventure some unlucky wight got his queue cut off too near the shoulders, the raiders were always ready to apologize for the mistake like gentlemen.

No one dare frown and say "infamous" on their return, and get a pistol-ball in his hat for his pains. The rumseller would not say so, nor the store-keeper who sold them goods, nor the hotel man, nor the humble ones who found profit in minding their own business.

The aspirant to legislative honors laughed loudly over these brave exploits, promising laws that should fix the foreigners, and so reaping a harvest of votes.

After all it was only a freak of the miners which started it, and which led to such unhappy results both in the United States and in the British colonies, for had no steps been taken in the one case they would not have been taken in the other. The migratory gold-diggers really cared nothing for the little that could be gathered from their leavings; the farmers always wanted Chinese help, particularly in their households, and few factories could long continue without them. The press and politicians found profit and patronage in keeping up the agitation; nothing was to be gained by taking up the other side; there were few to speak a good word for the Chinamen; so that it was thought that more were against them than was really the case.

In the city streets likewise, Johns and demijons appeared as funny fellows as they with their almond-eyes and pigtails, their wooden shoes and shiny dress, a candle-snuffer on the head and a balancing-pole with baskets over the shoulder. It made them laugh and play, the nice little boys on their way home from Sunday-school, who would throw stones at them and pull their pigtails, while the big boys to show their bravery would give them a kick or throw dirt in their eyes, the tormented strangers making no resistance.

Then up sprang Dennis Kearney, out of the bogs came he, and his one cry from first to last was, "The Chinese must go!"

Why must the Chinese go, Mr. Kearney; and by what authority do you come hither all the way from Kilkenny to order any one out of America?

"Bedad they take the work from our wives, and the bread from our childer, and lave us no cesspools to clane, and we wouldn't clane 'em if they did."

And if they do thus and so have they not as much right here as you? Is it the mission of the American people to find work for the Irish? Are we commissioned by the Almighty to provide for the European and drive out the Asiatic?

Suppose you talk less, Mr. Kearney, and go to work. Regard the Chinese with an unprejudiced eye; there is much you may learn from them to your advantage if you will profit by their example. There is room here for both of you if you will step back a little way and not place yourself quite so much in evidence.

Yet ever and forever, on this Market street sand-lot in San Francisco at the triangular Yerba Buena cemetery, in front of where the city hall was later placed, mounted on a drygoods box the cry goes forth from this blatant Irishman, "The Chinese must go!"

Standing by listening to the chaste eloquence of Dennis, and meditating thereon were the impecunious politician, the demagogue, and the embryo walking delegate, for here sprang up in a night these several champions of labor, each to depend forever after on the labor of others for his food and clothes.

Then the white working-man, who had votes and spent money, fancying himself ill-used as he was constantly kept informed, took up the cry, and soon there was not a newspaper or politician in the country that dared speak a favorable word for the Chinese.

It was the irony of impudence the appearance upon the sand-lots of the city hall of the scum of Europe crying out orders to the American people, and stranger still that the American people should hear and obey.

The charges formulated against the Chinese were false in every particular, or if true were not serious. Far worse might be said of their accusers. All were predicated upon the hypothesis that Europe and Africa have rights in the United States which Asia has not, and that it is our duty as between the Irish and the Chinese to consider the welfare of the former alone. The same line of argument, if arguments such assertions can be called, was followed by all, sand-lotter, demagogues, statesmen, and editors; yet the only true reason why the presence of the Asiatic among us was undesirable was because he did not vote, although none of them took the trouble so to state it.

If all these fatuous charges failed to convince, the demagogues would sometimes fall back upon the truth, and give the real reasons why they opposed the coming of the Asiatics, which were solely individual and selfish—it would not pay them to do otherwise.

Even the white working-man did not care how many of these little yellow things came to America, well knowing they were no match for him, until he was persuaded by his masters, the politicians and labor leaders, that some sort of wrong was being perpetrated against him. Then on the sand-lots, the intelligence thence radiating throughout the state, throughout the world, the Chinese were everything that was wicked and undesirable, while their virtues were turned into grossest vice. "The Chinese must go!" cried Dennis, demagogues repeating, "The Chinese must go!" a subservient press echoing "must go" and from distant Washington the wail of elusive votes "must go!"

Ah, men of sense, is this your boasted republicanism, a government by the people for the people? Rather a government by wild Irishmen, for wild Irishmen and self-serving labor leaders!

Wherefore it appears that some of us do not want the Asiatic in America. We will take his tea, his silks, and his works of art but we do not want him. The nations of Christendom are willing to exploit his country and parcel out his lands among them, retaining the inhabitants to work them, though they abhor slavery, unless it be such slavery as India enjoys.

Should admittance to the celestial lands on these or other satisfactory terms be denied them, they could batter down the doors with their guns as did England when out with a chip on her shoulder peddling her India opium, or as gallant Commodore Perry threatened to do if the little apes delayed him too long while standing on their holy dignity. True, we deny them admittance to our shores; but that is different.

What is the matter with the Chinese working-man? Is he lazy and ultra-amorous like the negro, anarchistic dirty and revengeful like the Italian, thieving and vermiparous like the Slav, or impudent and intermeddling like the Celt and Teuton?

Are not their merchants as honorable as our high-crime bankers and corporate capitalists, and are their dens of vice more repulsive than our Barbary coast and classic Tenderloin? Is it because they are not quarrelsome, do not indulge in street brawls, or stagger about drunk in public places, or fill our hospitals and penitentiaries that we so dislike them?

The Chinese will not amalgamate we are told. They care nothing for our doctrine of race suicide; they will not make love to our matrons nor marry our maids, nor breed a few millions of yellow piccaninnies for American citizenship.

They will not assimilate politically; they do not care to become voters, play policeman, or lean upon a shovel-handle over public works at three dollars a day. They do not care to control whiskey-shops, guard gambling dens, or protect restaurant palaces of ill-fame; they do not care to steal a franchise, or loot the public treasury, or buy a seat in the United States senate. They do not care for our cathedrals, but prefer their Josh house with its thirty thousand devils. They love their own country better than ours; being outsiders and un-American, they only wish to return to their own country at the proper time, failing in which their bones must be made into a fragrant little package and sent there.

Lacking these accomplishments, lacking the essentials of American citizenship, the lords high demagogue of the nation adopt the proper means to efface them, and with their effacement to efface the most promising industries of western America, delaying economic development for half a century if not for all time.

The truth is that for common labor, factory work, and fruit farming, industries necessary to our civilization but which cannot pay a high wage and live, and which first-class American artisans and mechanics will not touch at any price, the Chinaman has no equal. He is faithful, efficient, and honest; he is cleanly, thrifty, and decent.

His alleged faults are among his most valued qualities. The fact that he does more work for less pay, that he saves his earnings and in sickness becomes a charge to no one, and that he has no desire to mix in society or intermeddle in politics are all points in his favor. For surely we should be satisfied with the dregs of humanity we have already absorbed into our body politic without desiring more. We want the Asiatic for our low-grade work, and when it is finished we want him to go home and stay there until we want him again.

This is exactly what the Chinaman himself wishes; the Japanese, on the contrary, has more subtle pretensions. He is captious, clamorous of his rights, and would like to become the equal or superior of the white race. He anticipates war, and is prying into hidden things and on the alert to learn. He is more frivolous and unreliable than the Chinese, and is not so good as a working-man, but to the half-stranded farmer or manufacturer he is better than none.

The white race proposes to control the earth. When that time comes the working-man of to-day will want men to work for him; will he employ all white labor or use the Asiatics for some things? And will his children work or remain idle? He will control the tropics but he cannot work there. Neither will the African work tropical lands unless driven to it. If the white man would possess the tropics he must employ Asiatic labor.

We want some men in the United States for work alone. We do not need them all for governing or for breeding purposes, least of all low grade foreigners, Asiatic or European. We want some who are not for ornament, and whose aspirations are to do something for their employer, and not to overturn or supersede him.

The Chinese are the best material obtainable for domestic service. They are the solution of the domestic problem. The daughters of working-men prefer factory or other work at a less wage but with more leisure and independence, while the present class of immigrants are not good for much at anything. More than 100,000 Chinese are needed throughout the United States for household service alone, to say nothing of such occupations as hop-picking, fruit-gathering and scores of menial and mechanical industries in town and country essential to the comfort and prosperity of the people, and without the slightest injury, but rather a benefit to the American working-man.

And to this labor the farmer, the householder, the manufacturer have a right, as much right as has the southern cotton planter to employ the African, without whom, or his equivalent, which it would be difficult to find for that place, his plantation would be valueless and the nation be deprived of one of its great industries.

The American and European are best for high grade work; the Chinaman is best for low grade labor. In agriculture and horticulture the lines are distinctly drawn; the Asiatic is good for fruit-growing but is worth nothing in grain-growing or stockraising.

The value of an alien element to a new country depends upon its adaptability to unite with the best and not with the worst classes in the community. The low European gravitates toward the lowest; the Asiatic does not; he does not gravitate at all, but remains here as at home, stationary. There are two kinds of assimilation, assimilation upward and assimilation downward. The Asiatic will not assimilate downward.

If the interests of the nation are considered, if the rights of the farmer and manufacturer as opposed to the hollow and frenzied demonstrations of press and politicians are considered, and especially if the economic development of the Pacific is worthy of attention, then steps should be taken for the protection of industries vital to the progress of this section of the commonwealth. A system of passports, or other device, might easily be arranged so that the needed Asiatic laborers could be admitted as required, and sent away when no longer needed.

The origin of the infamy, as we have seen, was in the overweening conceit of unfledged Americans turned loose in the California mines, and in the aggressive unrest of the Irish transplantation.

Passing the question of the tacit consent of the United States to the unassessed presence of foreigners working in the mines the American miner chose to feel aggrieved, or to make a pretense of suffering at the presence of interlopers, especially of timid and unoffending strangers.

In the cities the crusader was continued with greater virulence and with more disastrous effect.

Impecunious politicians standing by and hearing Dennis talk saw the opportunity for gathering for themselves a little cheap fame. They could extol the Irish and denounce the Chinese as well as any one. Some of them could even shout louder than Dennis. It was but the bray of asses, yet men listened to the bray, shutting their ears to the words of wisdom and their hearts to every generous impulse.

During inflammatory times it is easier to incite a riot than to institute a reform. Both may be at times important agencies and Kearney adopted both. Was it a stroke of genius or simply Irish blundering that with the principle laid down of "America for Americans"—an Irishism truly—the cry was raised "The Chinese must go."

So it was not in the mines but in legislative circles on the sand-lots before the city hall and in the sanctum of editors that the real baiting of the Chinese in American was carried on.

It was in the towns and cities of the United States that the idea originated of a crusade upon a people whose barriers of exclusiveness were but a short time before broken down by Christian cannon mainly at the moment for the enforced introduction of Christian opium.

. . .

Turning to the African in our midst we find conditions never elsewhere existing in the history of humanity.

The Anglo-African presents a pathetic picture, a picture more touching than that of Russian Jew or Armenian Christian. However white within he must forever appear in black without. However learned he may become, however lofty his ideals or high his aspirations he must wear the badge of ignorance and servitude, he and his children forever. God hath made him so; man has re-stamped him; time brings no relief. It was a cruel kindness to enslave him; it was cruelty pure and simple to enfranchise him.

Sentimentalists say that our forefathers did the African a wrong when they enslaved him, and that we owe him reparation. It does not so appear to me. Slaves were obtained from different tribes constantly at war with each other, as Mandinga, Congo, Senegal, and Nard, each speaking a language which the other did not understand.

The slaver found the object of his pursuit, as a rule, an enslaved cannibal in the hands of cannibals, to be sold or else to be killed and eaten. On the horrible slave-ships his condition was but little improved. It was from such atrocities as these that the southern planter rescued him, gave him work and made him happy. True, he did not buy him from benevolence but for profit. It was not the purpose of the slave-trade, the most infamous of human deeds since the coming of Christ, to make the negro happy. Further, only a few thousand were rescued from cannibalism, whereas millions became slaves.

It is right and proper that we should do what we can for the amelioration of the condition of that unfortunate people, but not on the ground of the cruelties or injustice practised by others.

For if ever we owed the negro aught we paid the debt many times in the war which though not for him was because of him.

When all is said, the fact remains that had the early slave-traders read and followed the American declaration of human rights, so emphasized by human wrongs, the progenitors of our Africans would have been killed and eaten, and these United States thereby have been saved much trouble, past and future. But fate willed it otherwise, and the end is not yet.

Race friction will increase; there is nothing to soothe but everything to aggravate. And so race troubles will continue to grow with the growth of antagonistic populations; serious uprisings will come and continue until either the black or the white will have to efface himself.

Between the poor white trash of the south and the idle rich of the north there are certain analogies as well as comparisons to be drawn. The one has passed the other is passing. Or shall we say that the entire south at present is poor white trash, that is if work or doing something useful makes them so. Privilege to-day is ruining the north as slavery ruined the south. The idle rich are the poor white trash and slaves combined, though they do not know it. From the poor white trash have emanated able and useful men; I know of none who have come from the idle rich.

It was right for us to set the negro free. It was our necessity, not his. We have passed the period when we can hold our fellow-man in slavery and live. But we bungled more in liberating than in enslaving him. Brazil had only to declare that henceforth all children born of slave parents were born free, the parents still remaining slaves, and the thing was done.

The tragedy of enfranchisement stares the republican party in the face like the ghost of Hamlet's father.

Were it not better frankly to admit that the freed African in America is a failure, and that when made free he should have been sent away?

He is a failure here, for effective work is not to be obtained from him except under compulsion. As an American citizen he is a monstrosity.

If we could utilize our African citizens in factories and on farms it would be an advantage to all concerned, but the negro is good for nothing as a working-man, or for anything else, except on the southern plantations, and he is not all that he might be there.

The African is lazy and licentious. It is not altogether the fault of the white man that he is so, nor yet altogether his own fault. It is kismet. The animal in him over-balances the mental. He will work only as necessity requires. At least three millions out of the ever-increasing ten millions encamped upon us live without work. The black man is trifling; he lacks application: he has neither continuous purpose nor continuous effort; he is satisfied simply to live and enjoy. And why not? Wall street might profit by his philosophy.

We are told by good people of the sentimental school, as before remarked, that we have wronged the African, that notwithstanding the clothes and colored schools we have given him, the lessons in grace and refinement, and the several other gifts of the intellectual life, to say nothing of the bestowal of equal rights and American citizenship, that we are still in his debt.

This is discouraging.

To our fair land of America he was brought a captive—a happy captive one would think—and in a genial clime was given work, not too severe, as the change from meat diet to corn must be considered, and though for wholesome discipline cut with the whip a little sometimes when he moved too slowly.

And on his part, did he pine away and grow pale under his inhuman wrongs? Ah, no! He laughed and grew fat, threw care to the winds, and slept undisturbed by thoughts of having to go into the boiling pot for somebody's breakfast in the morning. Thus on these southern plantations for a century or more he was made the happiest of mortals, as indeed from first to last he was the most fortunate. His troubles came with emancipation; more came with enfranchisement; but he had to be emancipated; it was necessity; civilization must be allowed to move on unobstructed.

We did more than that. We gave him religion, which he took to greedily. We gave him his freedom, but he did not know what to do with it, and he gained from it no new happiness. We gave him American citizenship, the cheapest thing we had—what was left over after supplying the Europeans, and which the Chinese would not take. And with the franchise in his pocket, price of votes from fifty cents to two dollars, he was left to propagate piccaninnies and idle life away in peace and happiness.

However horrid the crime of human slavery, however repulsive in all its forms and unprofitable in its operations, the fact remains that the negro was never so well off, so happy and contented as when he was the chattel of the chivalrous south. It was as if God's curse of Canaan was but a covert benediction, for until he found the blessings of bondage in North America his lot was truly a piteous one, a savage, and the master or the slave of savages.

A million of the finest young men the sun ever shone upon, slaughtered because of these Africans, and some billions of money and property sacrificed—all together more than the whole continent of Africa and all its people are worth. I should call the debt paid, if indeed it ever existed.

We are a queer lot, we Yankees, in common with the rest of the world; even the best of us, the Boston sort, are sometimes a little queer, as when we mob William Lloyd Garrison and Wendell Phillips for speaking abolitionism that hurts our trade in the south, whilom taking the black man in our arms when that helps trade in the north or soothes our conscience in the sanctuary.

In all this I mean no unkindness to the negro, and offer no excuse for his enslavement. I have never forgotten his wrongs as they were told to me at my mother's knee. I have never wavered in my loyalty to him since as a small boy I used to drive wagon loads of him on his way to freedom hidden under the straw, but I cannot change from hot to cold and back again so often or so quickly as some of my super-sensitive friends.

The boy, becoming man, though always anti-slavery, was never so rabid an abolitionist as were his parents and others of his native town. He could no more join the mob in pelting anti-slavery speakers with stones or rotten eggs than he could later, dissolved in a spasm of repentant sentimentalism, clasp to his bosom the bad-smelling black man, or set him up as a ruler over his former masters.

One of the most intricate problems of population before the American people, and one likely to be with us, is that of the African. The subject varies with the varying mood of the American mind, sentimentalism having entered into it largely of late. Every one knows that as an economic asset the freed slave diminished in value, while in the end the employer gained, as free labor is cheaper than slave labor.

The relative influence for good or evil of the African, the Asiatic, and the European in our midst lies chiefly in the difference between adoption and absorption. If we could disabuse our minds of the sentiment that it is necessary forever to debase American blood and institutions by the infusion of low alien elements, whether in colors black, white, or yellow, receive and hold foreigners as foreigners for whatsoever they prove themselves to be worth, not necessarily to be admitted into our political household as members with all rights and privileges; assigning them their proper place, treating them fairly, without being forced to divide and re-divide with them our patrimony, we might better be able to preserve our own integrity while giving higher service to them.

The great mistake has been in religiously or sentimentally regarding this Republic, its lands and institutions, as the world's common property. So long as the land was limitless, and better inhabited than lying waste, and our liberal principles and free institutions preserved in their integrity by the inherent force that originated them, the constant dilution has been endurable. But it cannot always last. How fast and how far in one brief century have we drifted from the plans and purposes of the founders of this Republic! We have made ten millions of negroes, of a servile race and antecedents, whose fathers were slaves and themselves in intellect, in natural proclivities, not too far removed from the jungles of Africa, our equals, politically and some would have it so socially were it possible—a blot upon our name and nation, and now we know not what to do with them. We cannot kill them, or lose them, and they will not be driven by any force at our present command to herd themselves on some distant island or continent.

Further, we do not need the negro for any purpose, and never shall. We did not need the Indian and so eliminated him. We cannot so dispose of the negro. He is too incompetent and unreliable for any use; as a citizen of the commonwealth he is an unmitigated nuisance, and judging from the past he will so remain. The ultra susceptible, who alternately scourge and weep will say otherwise, but the facts stand plainly out that he who runs may read if he chooses. Neither do we need any more of the scum of Europe. But we do need the Asiatic, not for his society or citizenship, not to marry our daughters or manage our government, but for work, work which our citizens, whether African or Anglo-Saxon, will not do. Agriculture and manufactures both languish for lack of laborers, and illogical as it may be and strangely absurd, the government selects its foreign population not by merit or capability, but by color; the white and black may come but not the yellow. The only class the labor leaders fear, because of its competency, because they think it is the only labor that can compete with or break up their labor monopoly. Docile statesmen, demagogues, and unprincipled agitators acquiesce and aid for patronage or some other selfish motives. Meanwhile the whole country, laborers and high livers alike, cries out against the high prices of food. Labor, ever insistent in its demands for more, is cutting its own throat by killing the industries by which it lives, and sending up prices of commodities upon which depend the welfare of wives and children as well as of the workmen themselves.

African economics are regulated by geographic influence. Slavery never could have flourished in the northern states, even if the people had been in favor of it. Neither is the free negro of much use anywhere except on the plantations of the south.

As a laborer, bond or free, the negro is of economic value only in certain localities and under certain conditions. The labor must be agricultural and upon a large scale, so that he can be worked in gangs under the eye of an overseer. Then he needs to live in a warm climate. The cotton and tobacco fields of the south alone meet his requirements. In plantation life alone he finds happiness. To live together under compulsion on some allotted territory would not suit the Americanized negro. He depends upon the white man to do his mental work, his thinking and managing for him, preferring himself only to serve. He is by nature and habit a servant, not alone because of his long period of enslavement, but because of his mental inferiority.

There are those who claim for the African race an intellectual equality with Europeans, but they make out a poor case of it. Even to Asiatics the Africans are inferior in every respect, else why when every opportunity and encouragement was given them did they remain stationary, when Japan surged forward to the front the moment her reluctant doors were forced open by western civilization?

Finally, as a last word to the fathers of our future, if you wish to keep your Republic sweet and clean you will not be forever emptying into it the cesspools of Europe, forbidding even celestials to come in and scrub.

THE
RED
MAN

AN ADDRESS TO THE WHITES (1826)

ELIAS BOUDINOT

Elias Boudinot (1803?–1839), a full-blooded Cherokee Indian born as Galagina in Georgia, studied at the Mission School, Cornwall, Connecticut, and Andover Theological Seminary. He established a bilingual English-Cherokee newspaper and became an educational leader of his people. When the Cherokees were forced out of Georgia, he protested eloquently. In the West he was murdered by a group of angry young Indians because of his white ways and education.

To those who are unacquainted with the manners, habits and improvements of the Aborigines of this country, the term *Indian* is pregnant with ideas the most repelling and degrading. But such impressions, originating as they frequently do, from infant prejudices although they hold too true when applied to some, do great injustice to many of this race of beings.

Some there are, perhaps even in this enlightened assembly, who at the bare sight of an Indian, or at the mention of the name, would throw back their imaginations to ancient times, to the savages of savage warfare, to the yells pronounced over the mangled bodies of women and children, thus creating an opinion, inapplicable and highly injurious to those for whose temporal interest and eternal welfare, I come to plead.

What is an Indian? Is he not formed of the same materials with yourself? For "Of one blood God created all the nations that dwell on the face of the earth." Though it be true that he is ignorant, that he is a heathen, that he is a savage; yet he is no more than all others have been under similar circumstances. Eighteen centuries ago what were the inhabitants of Great Britain?

You here behold an *Indian,* my kindred are *Indians,* and my fathers sleeping in the wilderness grave—they too were Indians. But I am not as my fathers were—broader means and nobler influences have fallen upon me. Yet I was not born as thousands are, in a stately dome and amid the congratulations of the great, for on a little hill, in a lonely cabin, overspread by the forest oak I first drew my breath; and in a language unknown to learned and polished nations, I learnt to lisp my fond mother's name. In after days, I have had greater advantages than most of my race; and I now stand before you delegated by my native country to seek her interest, to labour for her respectability, and by my public efforts to assist in raising her to an equal standing with other nations of the earth.

The time has arrived when speculations and conjectures as to the practicability of civilizing the Indians must forever cease. A period is

116

fast approaching when the stale remark—"Do what you will, an Indian will still be an Indian," must be placed no more in speech. With whatever plausibility this popular objection may have heretofore been made, every candid mind must now be sensible that it can no longer be uttered, except by those who are uninformed with respect to us, who are strongly prejudiced against us, or who are filled with vindictive feelings towards us; for the present history of the Indians, particularly of that nation to which I belong, most incontrovertibly establishes the fallacy of this remark. I am aware of the difficulties which have ever existed to Indian civilization, I do not deny the almost insurmountable obstacles which we ourselves have thrown in the way of this improvement, nor do I say that difficulties no longer remain; but facts will permit me to declare that there are none which may not easily be overcome, by strong and continued exertions. It needs not abstract reasoning to prove this position. It needs not the display of language to prove to the minds of good men, that Indians are susceptible of attainments necessary to the formation of polished society. It needs not the power of argument on the nature of man, to silence forever the remark that "It is the purpose of the Almighty that the Indians should be exterminated." It needs only that the world should know what we have done in the few last years, to foresee what yet we may do with the assistance of our white brethren, and that of the common Parent of us all.

It is not necessary to present to you a detailed account of the various aboriginal tribes, who have been known to you only on the pages of history, and there but obscurely known. They have gone; and to revert back to their days, would be only to disturb their oblivious sleep; to darken these walls with deeds at which humanity must shudder; to place before your eyes the scenes of Muskingum Sahta-goo and the plains of Mexico, to call up the crimes of the bloody Cortes and his infernal host; and to describe the animosity and vengeance which have overthrown, and hurried into the shades of death those numerous tribes. But here let me say, that however guilty these unhappy nations may have been, yet many and unreasonable were the wrongs they suffered, many the hardships they endured, and many their wanderings through the trackless wilderness. Yes "Notwithstanding the obloquy with which the early historians of the colonies have overshadowed the character of the ignorant and unfortunate natives, some bright gleams will occasionally break through, that throw a melancholy lustre on their memories. Facts are occasionally to be met with in their rude annals, which though recorded with all the colouring of prejudice and bigotry, yet speak for themselves, and will be dwelt upon with applause and sympathy when prejudice shall have passed away."

Nor is it my purpose to enter largely into the consideration of the remnants, of those who have fled with time and are no more. They stand as monuments of the Indian's fate. And should they ever become extinct, they must move off the earth, as did their fathers. My design is to offer a few disconnected facts relative to the present improved state, and to the ultimate prospects of that particular tribe called Cherokees to which I belong.

The Cherokee nation lies within the charted limits of the states of Georgia, Tennessee, and Alabama. Its extent as defined by treaties is about 200 miles in length from East to West, and about 120 in breadth. This country which is supposed to contain about 10,000,000 of acres exhibits great varieties of surface, the most part being hilly and mountainous, affording soil of no value. The valleys however, are well watered and afford excellent land, in many parts particularly on the large streams, that of the first quality. The climate is temperate and healthy, indeed I would not be guilty of exaggeration were I to say that the advantages which this country possesses to render it salubrious, are many and superior. Those lofty and barren mountains, defying the labour and ingenuity of man, and supposed by some as placed there only to exhibit omnipotence, contribute to the healthiness and beauty of the surrounding plains, and give us that free air and pure water which distinguish our country. These advantages, calculated to make the inhabitants healthy, vigorous, and intelligent, cannot fail to cause this country to become interesting. And there can be no doubt that the Cherokee Nation, however obscure and trifling it may now appear, will finally become, if not under its present occupants, one of the Garden spots of America. And here, let me be indulged in the fond wish, that she may thus become under those who now possess her; and ever be fostered, regulated and protected by the generous government of the United States.

The population of the Cherokee Nation increased for the year 1810 to that of 1824, 2,000 exclusive of those who emigrated in 1818 and '19 to the west of the Mississippi—of those who reside on the Arkansas the number is supposed to be about 5,000.

The rise of these people in their movement toward civilization, may be traced as far back as the relinquishment of their towns; when game became incompetent to their support, by reason of the surrounding white population. They then betook themselves to the woods and commenced the opening of small clearings, and the raising of stock; still however following the chase. Game has since become so scarce that little dependence for subsistence can be placed upon it. They have gradually and I could almost say universally forsaken their ancient employment. In fact, there is not a single family in the nation, that can be said to subsist on the slender support which the wilderness would afford. The love and the practice of hunting are not now carried to a higher degree, than among all frontier people whether white or red. It cannot be doubted, however, that there are many who have commenced a life of agricultural labour from mere necessity, and if they could, would gladly resume their former course of living. But these are individual failings and ought to be passed over.

On the other hand it cannot be doubted that the nation is improving, rapidly improving in all those particulars which must finally constitute the inhabitants an industrious and intelligent people.

It is a matter of surprise to me, and must be to all those who are properly acquainted with the condition of the Aborigines of this country, that the Cherokees have advanced so far and so rapidly in civilization. But there are yet powerful obstacles, both within and without, to be surmounted in the march of improvement. The prejudices in regard to them in the general community are strong and lasting. The evil effects of their intercourse with their immediate white neighbours, who differ from them chiefly in name, are easily to be seen, and it is evident that from this intercourse proceed those demoralizing practices which in order to surmount, peculiar and unremitting efforts are necessary. In defiance, however, of these obstacles the Cherokees have improved and are still rapidly improving. To give you a further view of their condition, I will here repeat some of the articles of the two statistical tables taken at different periods.

In 1810 there were 19,500 cattle; 6,100 horses; 19,600 swine; 1,037 sheep; 467 looms; 1,600 spinning wheels; 30 wagons; 500 ploughs; 3 saw-mills; 13 grist-mills, etc. At this time there are 22,000 cattle; 7,600 horses; 46,000 swine; 2,500 sheep; 762 looms; 2,488 spinning wheels; 172 wagons; 2,943 ploughs; 10 saw-mills; 31 grist-mills; 62 blacksmith-shops; 8 cotton machines; 18 schools; 18 ferries; and a number of public roads. In one district there were, last winter, upwards of 1,000 volumes of good books; and 11 different periodical papers both religious and political, which were taken and read. On the public roads there are many decent inns, and few houses for convenience, etc., would disgrace any country. Most of the schools are under the care and tuition of Christian missionaries, of different denominations, who have been of great service to the nation, by inculcating moral and religious principles into the minds of the rising generation. In many places the word of God is regularly preached and explained, both by missionaries and natives; and there are numbers who have publicly professed their belief in the merits of the great Savior of the world. It is worthy of remark, that in no ignorant country have the missionaries undergone less trouble and difficulty, in spreading a knowledge of the Bible than in this. Here, they have been welcomed and encouraged by the proper authorities of the nation, their persons have been protected, and in very few instances have some individual vagabonds threatened violence to them. Indeed it may be said with truth, that among no heathen people has the faithful minister of God experienced greater success, greater reward for his labour, than in this. He is surrounded by attentive hearers, the words which flow from his lips are not spent in vain. The Cherokees have had no established religion of their own, and perhaps to this circumstance we may attribute, in part, the facilities with which missionaries have pursued their ends. They cannot be called idolators; for they never worshipped Images. They believed in a Supreme Being, the Creator of all, the God of the white, the red, and the black man. They also believed in the existence of an evil spirit who resided, as they thought, in the setting sun, the future place of all who in their life time had done iniquitously. Their prayers were addressed alone to the Supreme Being, and which if written would fill a large volume, and display much sincerity, beauty, and sublimity. When the ancient customs of the Cherokees were in their full force, no warrior thought himself secure, unless he had addressed his guardian angel; no hunter could hope for success, unless before the rising sun he had asked the assistance of his God, and on his return at eve he had offered his sacrifice to him.

There are three things of late occurrence, which must certainly place the Cherokee Nation in a fair light, and act as powerful argument in favor of Indian improvement.

First. The invention of letters.

Second. The translation of the New Testament into Cherokee.

Third. The organization of a Government.

The Cherokee mode of writing lately invented by George Guess, who could not read any language nor speak any other than his own, consists of eighty-six characters, principally syllabic, the combinations of which form all the words of the language. Their terms may be greatly simplified, yet they answer all the purposes of writing, and already many natives use them.

The translation of the New Testament, together with Guess's mode of writing, has swept away that barrier which has long existed, and opened a spacious channel for the instruction of adult Cherokees. Persons of all ages and classes may now read the precepts of the Almighty in their own language. Before it is long, there will scarcely be an individual in the nation who can say, "I know not God neither understand I what thou sayest," for all shall know him from the greatest to the least. The aged warrior over whom has rolled three score and ten years of savage life, will grace the temple of God with his hoary head; and the little child yet on the breast of its pious mother shall learn to lisp its Maker's name.

The shrill sound of the Savage yell shall die away as the roaring of far distant thunder; and Heaven-wrought music will gladden the affrighted wilderness. "The solitary place will be glad for them, and the desert shall rejoice and blossom as a rose." Already do we see the morning star, forerunner of approaching dawn, rising over the tops of deep forests in which for ages have echoed the warrior's whoop. But has not God said it, and will he not do it? The Almighty decrees his purposes, and man cannot with all his ingenuity and device countervail them. They are more fixed in their course than the rolling sun—more durable than the everlasting mountains.

The Government, though defective in many respects, is well suited to the condition of the inhabitants. As they rise in information and refinement, changes in it must follow, until they arrive at that state of advancement, when I trust they will be admitted into all the privileges of the American family.

The Cherokee Nation is divided into eight districts, in each of which are established courts of justice, where all disputed cases are decided by a jury, under the direction of a circuit Judge, who has jurisdiction over two districts. Sheriffs and other public officers are appointed to execute the decisions of the courts, collect debts, and arrest thieves and other criminals. Appeals may be taken to the Superior Court, held annually at the seat of Government. The Legislative authority is vested in General Court, which consists of the National Committee and Council. The National Committee consists of thirteen members who are generally men of sound sense and fine talents. The National Council consists of thirty-two members, besides the speaker, who act as the representatives of the people. Every bill passing these two bodies, becomes the law of the land. Clerks are appointed to do the writings, and record the proceedings of the Council. The executive power is vested in two principal chiefs, who hold their office during good behaviour, and sanction all the decisions of the legislative council. Many of the laws display some degree of civilization, and establish the respectability of the nation.

Polygamy is abolished. Female chastity and honor are protected by law. The Sabbath is respected by the Council during session. Mechanics are encouraged by law. The practice of putting aged persons to death for witchcraft is abolished and murder has now become a governmental crime.

From what I have said, you will form but a faint opinion of the true state and prospects of the Cherokees. You will, however, be convinced of three important truths.

First, that the means which have been employed for the christianization and civilization of this tribe, have been greatly blessed. Second, that the increase of these means will meet with final success. Third, that it has now become necessary, that efficient and more than ordinary means should be employed.

Sensible of this last point, and wishing to do something for themselves, the Cherokees have thought it advisable that there should be established, a Printing Press and a Seminary of respectable character;

and for these purposes your aid and patronage are now solicited. They wish the types, as expressed in their resolution, to be composed of English letters and Cherokee characters. Those characters have now become extensively used in the nation; their religious songs are written in them; there is an astonishing eagerness in people of all classes and ages to acquire a knowledge of them; and the New Testament has been translated into their language. All this impresses on them the immediate necessity of procuring types. The most informed and judicious of our nation, believe that such a press would go further to remove ignorance, and her offspring superstitution and prejudice, than all other means. The adult part of the nation will probably grovel on in ignorance and die in ignorance, without any fair trial upon them, unless the proposed means are carried into effect. The simplicity of this method of writing, and the eagerness to obtain a knowledge of it, are evinced by the astonishing rapidity with which it is acquired, and by the numbers who do so. It is about two years since its introduction, and already there are a great many who can read it. In the neighbourhood in which I live, I do not recollect a male Cherokee, between the ages of fifteen and twenty-five, who is ignorant of this mode of writing. But in connexion with type for Cherokee characters, it is necessary to have type for English letters. There are many who already speak and read the English language, and can appreciate the advantages which would result from the publication of their laws and transactions in a well conducted newspaper. Such a paper, comprising a summary of religious and political events, etc. on the one hand; and on the other, exhibiting the feelings, disposition, improvements, and prospects of the Indians; their traditions, their true character, as it once was and as it now is; the ways and means most likely to throw the mantle of civilization over all tribes; and such other matter as will tend to diffuse proper and correct impressions in regard to their condition—such a paper could not fail to create much interest in the American community, favourable to the aborigines, and to have a powerful influence, on the advancement of the Indians themselves. How can the patriot or the philanthropist devise efficient means, without full and correct information as to the subjects of their labour. And I am inclined to think, after all that has been said of the aborigines, after all that has been written in narratives, professedly to elucidate the leading traits of their character, that the public knows little of that character. To obtain a correct and complete knowledge of these people, there must exist a vehicle of Indian intelligence, altogether different from those which have heretofore been employed. Will not a paper published in an Indian country, under proper and judicious regulations, have the desired effect? I do not say that Indians will produce learned and elaborate dissertations in explanation and vindication of their own character; but they may exhibit specimens of their intellectual efforts, of their eloquence, of their moral, civil, and physical advancement, which will do quite as much to remove prejudice and to give profitable information.

The Cherokees wish to establish their Seminary, upon a footing which will insure to it all the advantages, that belong to such institutions in the state. Need I spend one moment in arguments, in favor of such an institution; need I speak one word of the utility, of the necessity, of an institution of learning; need I do more than simply to ask the patronage of benevolent hearts, to obtain that patronage.

When before did a nation of Indians step forward and ask for the means of civilization? The Cherokee authorities have adopted the measures already stated, with a sincere desire to make their nation an intelligent and a virtuous people, and with a full hope that those who have already pointed out to them the road of happiness, will now assist them to pursue it. With that assistance, what are the prospects of the Cherokees? Are they not indeed glorious, compared to that deep darkness in which the nobler qualities of their souls have slept? Yes, methinks I can view my native country, rising from the ashes of her degradation, wearing her purified and beautiful garments, and taking her seat with the nations of the earth. I can behold her sons bursting the fetters of ignorance and unshackling her from the voice of heathenism. She is at this instant, risen like the first morning sun, which grows brighter and brighter, until it reaches its fullness of glory.

She will become not a great, but a faithful ally of the United States. In time of peace she will plead the common liberties of America. In time of war her intrepid sons will sacrifice their lives in your defense. And because she will be useful to you in coming time, she asks you to assist her in her present struggles. She asks not for greatness; she seeks not wealth; she pleads only for assistance to become respectable as a nation, to enlighten and ennoble his sons, and to ornament her daughters with modesty and virtue. She pleads for this assistance, too, because on her destiny hangs that of many nations. If she completes her civilization—then may we hope that all our nations will—then, indeed, may true patriots be encouraged in their efforts to make this world of the West, one continuous abode of enlightened, free, and happy people.

There are, with regard to the Cherokees and other tribes, two alternatives; they must either become civilized and happy, or sharing the fate of many kindred nations, become extinct. If the General Government continues its protection, and the American people assist them in their humble efforts, they will, they must rise. Yes, under such protection, and with such assistance, the Indian must rise like the Phoenix, after having wallowed for ages in ignorant barbarity. But should this Government withdraw its care, and the American people their aid, then, to use the words of a writer, "They will go the way that so many tribes have gone before them; for the hordes that still linger about the shores of Huron, and the tributary streams of the Mississippi will share the fate of those tribes that once lorded it along the proud banks of the Hudson; of that gigantic race that is said to have existed on the borders of the Susquehanna; of those various nations that flourished about the Potomac and the Rhappahannoc, and that peopled the forests of the vast valley of Shenandoah. They will vanish like a vapour from the face of the earth, their very history will be lost in forgetfulness, and the places that now know them will know them no more."

There is, in Indian history, something very melancholy, and which seems to establish a mournful precedent for the future events of the few sons of the forest, now scattered over this vast continent. We have seen every where the poor aborigines melt away before the white population. I merely speak of the fact, without at all referring to the cause. We have seen, I say, one family after another, one tribe after another, nation after nation pass away; until only a few solitary creatures are left to tell the sad story of extinction.

Shall this precedent be followed? I ask you, shall red men live, or shall they be swept from the earth? With you and this public at large, the decision chiefly rests. Must they perish? Must they all, like the unfortunate Creeks (victims of the unchristian policy of certain persons), go down in sorrow to their graves?

They hang upon your mercy as to a garment. Will you push them from you, or will you save them? Let humanity answer.

AN INDIAN PLEA FOR CHRISTIAN KNOWLEDGE (1833)

WILLIAM WALKER

G. P. DISOWAY

William Walker and G. P. Disoway, supporters of Christianizing the Indians, were the cause of much spiritual agitation among churches back in the East. This letter by Disoway, including Walker's letter in it, was first published in The Christian Advocate and Zion's Herald *on March 1, 1833. It was responsible for the movement of missionaries, including Daniel Lee, Marcus Whitman, and Father DeSmet, into the Oregon country.*

THE FLATHEAD INDIANS

[*To The Christian Advocate*]

New York, February 18, 1833.

The plans to civilize the savage tribes of our country are among the most remarkable signs of the times. To meliorate the condition of the Indians and to preserve them from gradual decline and extinction, the government of the United States have proposed and already commenced removing them to the region westward of the Mississippi. Here it is intended to establish them in a permanent residence. Some powerful nations of these aborigines, having accepted the proposal, have already emigrated to their new lands, and others are now preparing to follow them. Among those who still remain are the Wyandots, a tribe long distinguished as standing at the head of the great Indian family. . . .

The wonderful effects of the Gospel among the Wyandots are well known. Providence has blessed in a most remarkable manner the labors of our missionaries for their conversion. Knowledge, civilization, and social comforts have followed the introduction of Christianity into their regions. To all of the Indians residing within the jurisdiction of the states or territories, the United States propose to purchase their present possessions and improvements, and in return to pay them acre for acre with lands west of the Mississippi River. Among the inducements to make the exchange are the following: perpetuity in their new abodes, as the faith of the government is pledged never to sanction another removal; the organization of a territorial government for their use like those in Florida, Arkansas, and Michigan, and the privilege to send delegates to Congress, as is now enjoyed by the other territories. Could the remaining tribes of the original possessors of this country place implicit reliance upon these assurances and prospects, this scheme to meliorate their condition, and to bring them within the pale of civilized life, might safely be pronounced great, humane, and rational.

The Wyandots, after urgent and often repeated solicitations of the government for their removal, wisely resolved to send agents to explore the region offered them in exchange, before they made any decision upon the proposal. In November last the party started on the exploring expedition, and visited their proposed residence. This was a tract of country containing about 200,000 acres, and situated between the western part of Missouri and the Missouri River. The location was found to be one altogether unsuitable to the views, the necessities, and the support of the nation. They consequently declined the exchange.

Since their return, one of the exploring party, Mr. William Walker, an interpreter and himself a member of the [Wyandot] nation, has sent me a communication. As it contains some valuable facts of a region from which we seldom hear, the letter is now offered for publication:

[*To G. P. Disoway*]

Upper Sandusky, January 19th, 1833.

. . . The country we explored is truly a land of savages. It is wild and romantic; it is a champaign, but beautifully undulated country. You can travel in some parts for whole days and not find timber enough to afford a riding switch, especially after you get off the Missouri and her principal tributary streams. The soil is generally a dark loam, but not of a durable kind for agriculture. As a country for agricultural pursuits, it is far inferior to what it has been represented to be. It is deplorably defective in timber. There are millions of acres on which you cannot procure timber enough to make a chicken coop. Those parts that are timbered are on some of the principal streams emptying into the great Missouri, and are very broken, rough, and cut up with deep ravines; and the timber, what there is of it, is of an inferior quality, generally a small growth of white, black, and bur oaks; hickory, ash, buckeye, mulberry, linwood, coffee bean, a low scrubby kind of birch, red and slippy elm, and a few scattering walnut trees. It is remarkable, in all our travels west of the Mississippi river, we never found even one solitary poplar, beech, pine, or sassafras tree, though we were informed that higher up the Missouri river, above Council Bluffs, pine trees abound to a great extent, especially the nearer you approach the Rocky mountains. The immense country embraced between the western line of the State of Missouri, and the Territory of Arkansas, and the eastern base of the Rocky mountains on the west, and Texas and Santa Fe on the south, is inhabited by the Osage, Sioux (pronounced Sooz), Pawnees, Comanches, Panchas, Arrapohoes, Assinaboins, Riccarees, Yanktons, Omahaws, Blackfeet, Ottoes, Crow Indians, Sacs, Foxes, and

Iowas: all a wild, fierce, and war-like people. West of the mountains reside the Flatheads, and many other tribes, whose names I do not now recollect.

I will here relate an anecdote, if I may so call it. Immediately after we landed in St. Louis, on our way to the West, I proceeded to Gen. Clark's, superintendent of Indian affairs, to present our letters of introduction from the Secretary of War, and to receive the same from him to the different Indian agents in the upper country. While in his office and transacting business with him, he informed me that three chiefs from the Flathead nation were in his house, and were quite sick, and the one (the fourth) had died a few days ago. They were from the west of the Rocky mountains. Curiosity prompted me to step into the adjoining room to see them, having never seen any, but often heard of them. I was struck with their appearance. They differ in appearance from any tribe of Indians I have ever seen: small in size, delicately formed, small limbs, and the most exact symmetry throughout, except the head. I had always supposed from their being called "Flatheads," that the head was actually flat on top; but this is not the case. The head is flattened thus:

From the point of the nose to the apex of the head, there is a perfect straight line, the protuberance of the forehead is flattened or leveled. . . . This is produced by a pressure upon the cranium while in infancy. The distance they had traveled on foot was nearly three thousand miles to see General Clark, their great father, as they called him, he being the first American officer they ever became acquainted with, and having much confidence in him, they had come to consult him as they said, upon very important matters. Gen. Clark related to me the object of their mission, and, my dear friend, it is impossible for me to describe to you my feelings while listening to his narrative. I will here relate it as briefly as I well can. It appeared that some white man had penetrated into their country, and happened to be a spectator at one of their religious ceremonies, which they scrupulously perform at stated periods. He informed them that their mode of worshipping the Supreme Being was radically wrong, and instead of being acceptable and pleasing, it was displeasing to him; he also informed them that the white people away toward the rising of the sun had been put in possession of the true mode of worshipping the Great Spirit. They had a book containing directions how to conduct themselves in order to enjoy his favor and hold converse with him; and with this guide, no one need go astray; but every one that would follow the directions laid down there could enjoy, in this, his favor, and after death would be received into the country where the Great Spirit resides, and live for ever with him.

Upon receiving this information, they called a national council to take this subject into consideration. Some said, if this be true, it is certainly high time we were put in possession of this mode, and if our mode of worshipping be wrong and displeasing to the Great Spirit, it is time we had laid it aside. We must know something about this; it is a matter that cannot be put off; the sooner we know it the better. They accordingly deputed four of the chiefs to proceed to St. Louis to see their great father, General Clark, to inquire of him, having no doubt but he would tell them the whole truth about it.

They arrived at St. Louis, and presented themselves to Gen. Clark. The latter was somewhat puzzled, being sensible of the responsibility that rested on him; he, however, proceeded by informing them that what they had been told by the white man in their own country was true. Then he went into a succinct history of man, from his creation down to the advent of the Savious; explained to them all the moral precepts contained in the Bible, expounded to them the decalogue; informed them of the advent of the Saviour, his life, precepts, his death, resurrection, ascension, and the relation he now stands to man as a mediator—that he will judge the world, etc.

Poor fellows, they were not all permitted to return home to their people with the intelligence. Two died in St. Louis, and the remaining two, though somewhat indisposed, set out for their native land. Whether they reached home or not is not known. The change of climate and diet operated very severely upon their health. Their diet when at home is chiefly vegetables and fish.

If they died on their way home, peace be to their manes! They died inquirers after the truth. . . .

Yours in haste,
WM. WALKER.

. . . How deeply touching is the circumstance of the four natives traveling on feet 3,000 miles through thick forests and extensive prairies, sincere searchers after truth! The story has scarcely a parallel in history. What a touching theme does it form for the imagination and pen! . . . With what intense concern will men of God, whose souls are fired with holy zeal for the salvation of their fellow beings, read their history! There are immense plains, mountains, and forests in regions whence they came, the abodes of numerous savage tribes. But no apostle of Christ has yet had the courage to penetrate into their moral darkness. Adventurous and daring fur traders only have visited these regions, unknown to the rest of the world, except from their own accounts of them. If the Father of spirits, as revealed by Jesus Christ, is not known in these interior wilds of America, they nevertheless often resound the praises of the unknown, invisible Great Spirit, as he is denominated by the savages. They are not ignorant of the immortality of their souls, and speak of some future delicious island or country where departed spirits rest. May we not indulge the hope that the day is not far distant when the missionaries will penetrate into these wilds where the Sabbath bell has never yet tolled since the world began!

WHAT THE INDIAN MEANS TO AMERICA (ca. 1877)

CHIEF STANDING BEAR

Chief Standing Bear (1829–1908), chief of the Oglala Sioux, protested the forced movement of his people, the Lakotas, from Nebraska to Indian Territory in Kansas in 1877. He gained much popular support, and his pleas were incorporated in Land of the Spotted Eagle *(Boston, 1933) by his son, Luther Standing Bear (1863–1939).*

The feathered and blanketed figure of the American Indian has come to symbolize the American continent. He is the man who through centuries has been moulded and sculped by the same hand that shaped its mountains, forests, and plains, and marked the course of its rivers.

The American Indian is of the soil, whether it be the region of forests, plains, pueblos, or mesas. He fits into the landscape, for the hand that fashioned the continent also fashioned the man for his surroundings. He once grew as naturally as the wild sunflowers; he belongs just as the buffalo belonged.

With a physique that fitted, the man developed fitting skills—crafts which today are called American. And the body had a soul, also formed and moulded by the same master hand of harmony. Out of the Indian approach to existence there came a great freedom—an intense and absorbing love for nature; a respect for life; enriching faith in a Supreme Power; and principles of truth, honesty, generosity, equity, and brotherhood as a guide to mundane relations.

Becoming possessed of a fitting philosophy and art, it was by them that native man perpetuated his identity; stamped it into the history and soul of this country—made land and man one.

By living—struggling, losing, meditating, imbibing, aspiring, achieving—he wrote himself into inerasable evidence—an evidence that can be and often has been ignored, but never totally destroyed. Living— and all the intangible forces that constitute that phenomenon—are brought into being by Spirit, that which no man can alter. Only the hand of the Supreme Power can transform man; only Wakan Tanka can transform the Indian. But of such deep and infinite graces finite man has little comprehension. He has, therefore, no weapons with which to slay the unassailable. He can only foolishly trample.

The white man does not understand the Indian for the reason that he does not understand America. He is too far removed from its formative processes. The roots of the tree of his life have not yet grasped the rock and soil. The white man is still troubled with primitive fears; he still has in his consciousness the perils of this frontier continent, some of its fastnesses not yet having yielded to his questing footsteps and inquiring eyes. He shudders still with the memory of the loss of his forefathers upon its scorching deserts and forbidding mountain-tops. The man from Europe is still a foreigner and an alien. And he still hates the man who questioned his path across the continent.

But in the Indian the spirit of the land is still vested; it will be until other men are able to divine and meet its rhythm. Men must be born and reborn to belong. Their bodies must be formed of the dust of their forefathers' bones.

The attempted transformation of the Indian by the white man and the chaos that has resulted are but the fruits of the white man's disobedience of a fundamental and spiritual law. The pressure that has been brought to bear upon the native people, since the cessation of armed conflict, in the attempt to force conformity of custom and habit has caused a reaction more destructive than war, and the injury has not only affected the Indian, but has extended to the white population as well. Tyranny, stupidity, and lack of vision have brought about the situation now alluded to as the 'Indian Problem.'

There is, I insist, no Indian problem as created by the Indian himself. Every problem that exists today in regard to the native population is due to the white man's cast of mind, which is unable, at least reluctant, to seek understanding and achieve adjustment in a new and a significant environment into which it has so recently come.

The white man excused his presence here by saying that he had been guided by the will of his God; and in so saying absolved himself of all responsibility for his appearance in a land occupied by other men.

Then, too his law was a written law; his divine decalogue reposed in a book. And what better proof that his advent into this country and his subsequent acts were the result of divine will! He brought the Word! There ensued a blind worship of written history, of books, of the written word, that has denuded the spoken word of its power and sacredness. The written word became established as a criterion of the superior man—a symbol of emotional fineness. The man who could write his name on a piece of paper, whether or not he possessed the spiritual fineness to honor those words in speech, was by some miraculous formula a more highly developed and sensitized person than the one who had never had a pen in hand, but whose spoken word was inviolable and whose sense of honor and truth was paramount. With false reasoning was the quality of human character measured by man's ability to make with an implement a mark upon paper. But granting this mode of reasoning be correct and just, then where are to be placed the thousands of illiterate whites who are unable to read and write? Are they, too, 'savages'? Is not humanness a matter of heart and mind, and is it not evident in the form of relationship with men? Is not kindness more powerful than arrogance; and truth more powerful than the sword?

True, the white man brought great change. But the varied fruits of his civilization, though highly colored and inviting, are sickening and deadening. And if it be the part of civilization to maim, rob, and thwart, then what is progress?

I am going to venture that the man who sat on the ground in his tipi meditating on life and its meaning, accepting the kinship of all creatures, and acknowledging unity with the universe of things was infusing into his being the true essence of civilization. And when native man left off this form of development, his humanization was retarded in growth.

Another most powerful agent that gave native man promise of developing into a true human was the responsibility accepted by parenthood. Mating among Lakotas was motivated, of course, by the same laws of attraction that motivate all beings; however, considerable thought was given by parents of both boy and girl to the choosing of mates. And a still greater advantage accrued to the race by the law of self-mastery which the young couple voluntarily placed upon themselves as soon as they discovered they were to become parents. Immediately, and for some time after, the sole thought of the parents was in preparing the child for life. And true civilization lies in the dominance of self and not in the dominance of other men.

How far this idea would have gone in carrying my people upward and toward a better plane of existence, or how much of an influence it was in the development of their spiritual being, it is not possible to say. But it had its promises. And it cannot be gainsaid that the man who is rising to a higher estate is the man who is putting into his being the essence of humanism. It is self-effort that develops, and by this token the greatest factor today in dehumanizing races is the manner in which the machine is used—the product of one man's brain doing the work for another. The hand is the tool that has built man's mind; it, too, can refine it.

THE SAVAGE

After subjugation, after dispossession, there was cast the last abuse upon the people who so entirely resented their wrongs and punishments, and that was the stamping and the labeling of them as savages.

To make this label stick has been the task of the white race and the greatest salve that it has been able to apply to its sore and troubled conscience now hardened through the habitual practice of injustice.

But all the years of calling the Indian a savage has never made him one; all the denial of his virtues has never taken them from him; and the very resistance he has made to save the things inalienably his has been his saving strength—that which will stand him in need when justice does make its belated appearance and he undertakes rehabilitation.

All sorts of feeble excuses are heard for the continued subjection of the Indian. One of the most common is that he is not yet ready to accept the society of the white man—that he is not yet ready to mingle as a social entity.

This, I maintain, is beside the question. The matter is not one of making-over the external Indian into the likeness of the white race— a process detrimental to both races. Who can say that the white man's way is better for the Indian? Where resides the human judgment with the competence to weigh and value Indian ideals and spiritual concepts; or substitute for them other values?

Then, has the white man's social order been so harmonious and ideal as to merit the respect of the Indian, and for that matter the thinking class of the white race? Is it wise to urge upon the Indian a foreign social form? Let none but the Indian answer!

Rather, let the white brother face about and cast his mental eye upon a new angle of vision. Let him look upon the Indian world as a human world; then let him see to it that human rights be accorded to the Indians. And this for the purpose of retaining for his own order of society a measure of humanity. . . .

THE LIVING SPIRIT OF THE INDIAN—HIS ART

The spiritual health and existence of the Indian was maintained by song, magic, ritual, dance, symbolism, oratory (or council), design, handicraft, and folk-story.

Manifestly, to check or thwart this expression is to bring about spiritual decline. And it is in this condition of decline that the Indian people are today. There is but a feeble effort among the Sioux to keep alive their traditional songs and dances, while among other tribes there is but a half-hearted attempt to offset the influence of the Government school and at the same time recover from the crushing and stifling régime of the Indian Bureau.

One has but to speak of Indian verse to receive uncomprehending and unbelieving glances. Yet the Indian loved verse and into this mode of expression went his deepest feelings. Only a few ardent and advanced students seem interested; nevertheless, they have given in book form enough Indian translations to set forth the character and quality of Indian verse.

Oratory receives a little better understanding on the part of the white public, owing to the fact that oratorical compilations include those of Indian orators.

Hard as it seemingly is for the white man's ear to sense the differences, Indian songs are as varied as the many emotions which inspire them, for no two of them are alike. For instance, the Song of Victory is spirited and the notes high and remindful of an unrestrained hunter or warrior riding exultantly over the prairies. On the other hand, the song of the Cano *unye* is solemn and full of urge, for it is meant to inspire the young men to deeds of valor. Then there are the songs of death and the spiritual songs which are connected with the ceremony of initiation. These are full of the spirit of praise and worship, and so strong are some of these invocations that the very air seems as if surcharged with the presence of the Big Holy.

The Indian loved to worship. From birth to death he revered his surroundings. He considered himself born in the luxurious lap of Mother Earth and no place was to him humble. There was nothing between him and the Big Holy. The contact was immediate and personal, and the blessings of Wakan Tanka flowed over the Indian like rain showered from the sky. Wakan Tanka was not aloof, apart, and ever seeking to quell evil forces. He did not punish the animals and the birds, and likewise He did not punish man. He was not a punishing God. For there was never a question as to the supremacy of an evil power over and above the power of Good. There was but one ruling power, and that was *Good.*

Of course, none but an adoring one could dance for days with his face to the sacred sun, and that time is all but done. We cannot have back the days of the buffalo and beaver; we cannot win back our clean blood-stream and superb health, and we can never again expect that beautiful *rapport* we once had with Nature. The springs and lakes have dried and the mountains are bare of forests. The plow has changed the face of the world. Wi-wila is dead! No more may we heal our sick and comfort our dying with a strength founded on faith, for even the animals now fear us, and fear supplants faith.

And the Indian wants to dance! It is his way of expressing devotion, of communing with unseen power, and in keeping his tribal identity. When the Lakota heart was filled with high emotion, he danced. When he felt the benediction of the warming rays of the sun, he danced. When his blood ran hot with success of the hunt or chase, he danced. When his heart was filled with pity for the orphan, the lonely father, or bereaved mother, he danced. All the joys and exaltations of life, all his gratefulness and thankfulness, all his acknowledgments of the mysterious power that guided life, and all his aspirations for a better life, culminated in one great dance—the Sun Dance.

Today we see our young people dancing together the silly jazz—dances that add nothing to the beauty and fineness of our lives and certainly nothing to our history, while the dances that record the life annals of a people die. It is the American Indian who contributes to this country its true folk-dancing, growing, as we did, out of the soil. The dance is far older than his legends, songs, or philosophy.

Did dancing mean much to the white people they would better understand ours. Yet at the same time there is no attraction that brings people from such distances as a certain tribal dance, for the reason that the white mind senses its mystery, for even the white man's inmost feelings are unconsciously stirred by the beat of the tomtom. They are heart-beats, and once all men danced to its rhythm.

When the Indian has forgotten the music of his forefathers, when the sound of the tomtom is no more, when noisy jazz has drowned the melody of the flute, he will be a dead Indian. When the memory of his heroes are no longer told in story, and he forsakes the beautiful white buckskin for factory shoddy, he will be dead. When from him has been taken all that is, all that he has visioned in nature, all that has come to him from infinite sources, he then, truly, will be a dead Indian. His spirit will be gone, and though he walk crowded streets, he will, in truth, be—*dead!*

But all this must not perish; it must live, to the end that America shall be educated no longer to regard native production of whatever tribe—folk-story, basketry, pottery, dance, song, poetry—as curios, and native artists as curiosities. For who but the man indigenous to the soil could produce its song, story, and folk-tale; who but the man who loved the dust beneath his feet could shape it and put it into undying, ceramic form; who but he who loved the reeds that grew beside still waters, and the damp roots of shrub and tree, could save it from seasonal death, and with almost superhuman patience weave it into enduring objects of beauty—into timeless art!

Regarding the 'civilization' that has been thrust upon me since the days of reservation, it has not added one whit to my sense of justice; to my reverence for the rights of life; to my love for truth, honesty, and generosity; nor to my faith in Wakan Tanka—God of the Lakotas. For after all the great religions have been preached and expounded, or have been revealed by brilliant scholars, or have been written in books and embellished in fine language with finer covers, man—all man—is still confronted with the Great Mystery.

So if today I had a young mind to direct, to start on the journey of life, and I was faced with the duty of choosing between the natural way of civilization, I would, for its welfare, unhesitatingly set that child's feet in the path of my forefathers. I would raise him to be an Indian!

From
GREYSLAER, A ROMANCE OF THE MOHAWK (1849)
CHARLES F. HOFFMAN

Charles F. Hoffman (1806–1884) founded and edited The Knicker-bocker *(1833) and the* American Monthly Magazine *(1835–1837). His travel book* A Winter in the West *(1835) and his novel* Greyslaer: A Romance of the Mohawk *were popular works presenting the romantic view of the Indian and the frontier.*

"Your tribesmen, noble Mohawk, if indeed you be an Indian," answered Greyslaer, touched by the proud yet feeling tone with which the last words were uttered, "your red brethren had indeed better keep aloof from us, alike in war or in peace, for they seem to acquire only the worst attributes of civilized life by attempting to mingle with us as one people; and their share in this struggle must——"

"Ay, you speak well, young man," interrupted the Indian, now wholly thrown off his dignified reserve of manner by what appeared to be a theme of great excitement with him; "if your vaunted civilization be not all a fraud, your perverted learning but a shallow substitute for the wisdom of the heart, your so-called social virtues but a loose covering for guile, like the frail thatch of leaves that hides the traps of an Indian hunter; if your religion be not a bitter satire upon the lives of all of ye; if, in a word, all your conflicting teachings and practices be indeed reconcilable to *Truth* and pleasing to THE SPIRIT, then hath he created Truth of as many colors as he hath man; and his red children should still rest content with the simple system which alone their hearts are fitted to understand."

Greyslaer was precisely at that age when most men of an imaginative cast of mind mistake musing for philosophizing, sentiment for religion; and with that ready confidence in the result of one's own reflections and mental experience which is the darling prerogative of youth and immaturity of thought, he did not hesitate to assume the attitude of a teacher in reply to the last remark of the Indian. "Truth, noble Mohawk, hath ever been, will ever be the same. But the truths of the other world, as well as of this, are often wrapped in mystery. God has, in two dispensations of light from above, revealed to mortals so much of his holy truth as the human mind was fitted to receive.

"The first revelation was like a dawn in the forest, where the young day shoots its horizontal rays beneath the dusky canopy of tree-tops, and, glancing between the columned trunks, streams upon the path of the benighted wanderer of the wilderness. That matin-light—those holy rays of the virgin morn of true religion—I am willing to believe, illumined the lake-girdled mountains of the Iroquois hunter as well as the cedar-crowned hills of the Hebrew shepherd. It shone alike, perhaps, upon the pathway of either, if indeed they were not one and the same people. But the realm of glory to which that pathway led; the snares that beset it; the solace and refreshment that lay within reach of the traveller, alternating his perils, these it required a second revelation to bring to light: when the sun of righteousness, fairly uprisen, should throw the blaze of noontide into that forest, revealing now, in stern reality, its yawning caverns, its precipices and pitfalls; now touching with mellow beauty its mossy resting-places, or sparkling with cheerful radiance upon its refreshing wayside waters; and now bathing with glorious effulgence the region beyond the wilderness, where lay the final rest and reward of the wanderer. The good men of my race, therefore, preach not a new Truth to the Indian! they seek out to share with him that broader light which has been vouchsafed to us regarding the same one Eternal Truth."

The Mohawk listened with an air of deep respect to the earnest language of the youth, but his own feelings and prejudices were too deeply excited to permit the discussion long to preserve the abstract character which Greyslaer attempted to give it.

"I spoke not against the truths of Christianity," said he; "for they may have their sanctuary as well in the desert and the forest as in the city; I spoke not, I say, of the pure light of Christianity, which your mobbled faith no more resembles than do the stained and distorted rays that struggle through a dungeon's window resemble the beams of the noontide sun. The holy teachings of your Master come to us like those unwholesome airs which, travelling out pure and invigorating from the skies, are polluted and made pestiferous by traversing some noxious march before they reach the unfortunate mortal who is doomed to breathe them. It is your vaunted social system from which I recoil with loathing. Your so-called civilization is, in its very essence, a tyrant and enthraller of the soul; it merges the individual in the mass, and moulds him to the purposes, not of God, but of a community of men. It follows the guidance of true religion so far only as that ministers to its own ends, and then it turns and fashions anew its belief from time to time, to suit the 'improved' mechanism of its artificial system. In crowded Europe the evil is irremediable; for man the machine occupies less room than man the herdsman or hunter; but your mode of existence is not less a curse to ye—the white man's curse, which he would fain share with his red brother! But have I not seen how it works among you? Have I not been to your palaces and your churches, and seen there a deformed piece of earth assume airs that become none but the great Spirit above? Have I not been to your prisons, and seen the wretched debtor peering through the bars? You call the Indian nations cruel! Yet liberty to a rational creature as much exceeds property in value as does the light of the sun that of the smallest twinkling star! But you put them on a level, to the everlasting disgrace of human nature. I have seen the white captive writhing at the Indian stake, and rending the air with shrieks of agony;—strange that the unhappy man did not endeavor, by his fortitude, to atone in some degree for the crimes committed during the life thus justly shortened;—I have witnessed all the hideous torments you ascribe to such a death, and yet I had rather die by the most severe tortures ever inflicted by the Indian than languish in one of your prisons a single year! Great Spirit of the Universe! and do you call yourselves Christians? Does the religion of him whom you call your Saviour inspire this spirit and lead to these practices?"

Greyslaer, who listened with curious attention to this strange harangue, as coming from the lips of an Indian, was completely bewildered by the fluency and energy with which the magician delivered his tirade, and he scrutinized his features and complexion, as if expecting to discover the lineaments of some disguised renegado white, who, with talents fitted for a better sphere, had, induced by caprice or compelled by crime, banished himself from society, and assumed the character of one of the aborigines. But the natural and easy manner in which the object of his suspicions turned the next moment and addressed the Indian woman in her own language, not less than the veneration with which the squaw received his behests, dispelled the idea, while little opportunity was given him for making a more minute examination. The Medicine-man, smiling blandly, as if he read what was passing in the mind of his patient, approached to his side, and telling him that he was now about to consign him to the care of others, asked Greyslaer, as the only return expected for any service he might have rendered him, to curb his tongue hereafter in speaking of Joseph Brant!

Before the patriot officer could reply, the magician had turned upon his heel and gained the door; but, as if struck with an after-thought, he instantly returned, and ere Greyslaer was aware of his intention, he had bared his arm to the shoulder, produced a stained flint from his pouch, and branded an uncouth device, that made the skin smart with pain as the blood oozed through.

"He who loves the Red-man may die by rifle or tomahawk, but he will never be disgraced by the scalping-knife or tortured at the stake if he shows this mark to the followers of Thayendanagea!"

And, before Greyslaer could find language to express his astonishment, either at the act or the words which accompanied it, he was alone with the old woman, who busied herself in reverentially picking up and putting away the mumming tools of his profession which the pseudo magician had flung upon the ground as he disappeared through the door.

From
NOTIONS OF THE AMERICANS (1828)
JAMES FENIMORE COOPER

Novelist James Fenimore Cooper (1789–1851) first became known for his sea and Revolutionary tales and later for his still popular romantic Leatherstocking Tales *of the frontier and the Indians (1823–1841).* Notions of the Americans *(1828) is a spirited defense of his countrymen engendered by his stay in France as American consul, but in later works, most notably* The American Democrat *(1838), he was quite critical of America.*

As a rule, the red man disappears before the superior moral and physical influence of the white, just as I believe the black man will eventually do the same thing, unless he shall seek shelter in some other region. In nine cases in ten, the tribes have gradually removed west; and there is now a confused assemblage of nations and languages collected on the immense hunting grounds of the Prairies. . . .

The ordinary manner of the disappearance of the Indian, is by a removal deeper into the forest. Still, many linger near the graves of their fathers, to which their superstitions, no less than a fine natural feeling, lend a deeper interest. The fate of the latter is inevitable; they become victims to the abuses of civilization, without ever attaining to any of its moral elevation.

As might be supposed, numberless divisions of these people, when the country was discovered, were found in possession of districts along the coast, and deriving a principal means of support from the ocean. They were fishermen rather than hunters, though the savage state ordinarily infers a resort to both pursuits. Most of these people, too, retired reluctantly from a view of "the great salt lake," but some were environed by the whites before they were properly aware of the blighting influence of the communion; and, getting gradually accustomed to their presence, they preferred remaining near the places where they had first drawn breath. Trifling districts of territory have been, in every instance in which they were sufficiently numerous to make such a provision desirable, secured to them, and on these little tracts of land many of them still remain. I have visited one or two of their establishments.

In point of civilization, comforts, and character, the Indians, who remain near the coasts, are about on a level with the lowest classes of European peasantry. Perhaps they are somewhat below the English, but I think not below the Irish peasants. They are much below the condition of the mass of the slaves. It is but another proof of the wayward vanity of man, that the latter always hold the Indians in contempt, though it is some proof that they feel their own condition to be physically better: morally, in one sense, it certainly is not.

Many of these Atlantic Indians go to sea. They are quite often found in the whalers, and, in some instances, in the vessels of war. An officer in the navy has told me that he once knew a Montauk Indian who was a captain of the main-top in a sloop of war; and in another instance, a flag officer had his gig manned by Indians. They make active and very obedient seamen, but are never remarkable for strength. The whole number of them who now go to sea, does not, however, probably exceed a hundred or two.[1]

I accompanied Cadwallader on a visit to a connexion, who lives within forty miles of New-York, on the adjacent island of Nassau (Long Island). The uncle of my friend was a man of extensive hereditary estate, on which there might have been a reservation of a few thousand acres of woods. While shooting over this forest, one day, the proprietor asked me if I felt any desire to see an Indian king. Surprised at such a question, in such a place, an explanation was requested. He told me that an Indian, who claimed to be a descendant of the ancient Sachems, then held his court in his woods, and that a walk of fifteen minutes would bring us into the presence of King Peter. We went.

I found this Indian, dwelling with his family, in a wigwam of a most primitive construction. It was in the form of a bee-hive, or rather of a very high dome. The covering was made of a long, tough grass, that grows near the sea, and the texture was fine and even beautiful. A post in the centre supported the fabric, which was shaped by delicate curving poles. A hole in the top admitted the light, and allowed the smoke to pass out; and the fire was near enough to the upright post to permit a kettle to be suspended from one of its knots (or cut branches) near enough to feel the influence of the heat. The door was a covering of mats, and the furniture consisted of a few rude chairs, baskets, and a bed, that was neither savage, nor yet such as marks the civilized man.

---

[1] The writer, while in America, heard an anecdote which may give some idea of the notions of retributive justice which linger so long in the philosophy of an Indian, and which is, probably, the basis of his desire for revenge, since he is well known to be as eminently grateful as he is vindictive. The whalers always take their reward in a portion of the profits of the voyage. An Indian made several voyages in succession, in the same ship; he found, at his return, that bad luck, advances, and the supplies of an extravagant family at home, left him always in debt. "What shall I do?" was the question put to his owner, as each unfortunate balance was exhibited. "You must go to sea." To sea he went, and, as stated, for four or five years, always with the same result. At length, good fortune, with a proper amount of preventive castigation on his improvident wife, before he sailed, brought the balance on his side. The money was of course tendered; but for a long time he refused to receive it, insisting that justice required that his owners should now go to sea, where it would seem he had not enjoyed himself quite as much as he believed the other party to the contract had done on shore.

The attire of the family was partly that of the one condition, and partly that of the other. The man himself was a full-blooded Indian, but his manner had that species of sullen deportment that betrays the disposition without the boldness of the savage. He complained that "basket stuff" was getting scarce, and spoke of an intention of removing his wigwam shortly to some other estate.

The manufacture of baskets and brooms is a common employment of all the Indians who reside near the settlements. They feed on game, and, sometimes, like the gypsies, they make free with poultry, though in common they are rigidly honest; nearly always so, unless corrupted by much intercourse with the whites. With the proceeds of their labour they purchase blankets, powder, and such other indulgences as exceed their art to manufacture. King Peter, I was told, claimed a right, in virtue of his royal descent, to cut saplings to supply his materials, on any estate in the island. He was permitted to enjoy this species of feudal privilege in quiet, it being well understood that he was not to exceed a certain discretion in its exercise.

In the more interior parts of the country, I frequently met families of the Indians, either travelling, or proceeding to some village, with their wares. They were all alike, a stunted, dirty, and degraded race. Sometimes they encamped in the forests, lighted their fires, and remained for weeks in a place; and at others, they kept roaming daily, until the time arrived when they should return to their reservations.

The reservations in the old States, and with tribes that cannot aspire to the dignity of nations, are managed on a sufficiently humane principle. The laws of the State, or of the United States, have jurisdiction there, in all matters between white men, or between a white man and an Indian; but the Indians themselves are commonly permitted to control the whole of their own internal policy. Bargains, exceeding certain amounts, are not valid between them and the whites, who cannot, for instance, purchase their lands. Schools are usually provided, in the more important tribes, by the general government, and in the less, by charity. Religious instruction is also furnished by the latter means.

I saw reservations in which no mean advances had been made in civilization. Farms were imperfectly tilled, and cattle were seen grazing in the fields. Still, civilization, advances slowly among a people who consider labour a degradation, in addition to the bodily dislike that all men have to its occupations.

There are many of these tribes, however, who fill a far more important, and altogether a remarkable position. There is certainly no portion of country within the admitted boundaries of the United States, in which their laws are not paramount, if they choose to exert them. Still, savage communities do exist within these limits, with whom they make treaties, against whom they wage open war, and with whom they make solemn peace. As a treaty is, by the constitution, the paramount law of the land, the several States are obliged to respect their legal provisions.

That neither the United States, nor any individual State, has ever taken possession of any land that, by usage or construction, might be decreed the property of the Indians, without a treaty and a purchase, is, I believe, certain. How far an equivalent is given, is another question: though I fancy that these bargains are quite as just as any that are ever driven between the weak and the strong, the intelligent and the ignorant. It is not pretended that the value of the territory gained is paid for; but the purchase is rather a deference to general principles of justice and humanity, than a concession to a right in the Indians, which itself might admit of a thousand legal quibbles. The treaties are sufficiently humane, and, although certain borderers, who possess the power of the white man with the disposition of the savage, do sometimes violate their conditions, there is no just reason to distrust the intentions or the conduct of the government. . . .

There is a bureau of the war department that is called the "office of the Indian affairs." A humane and discreet individual is at its head, and a good deal is endeavoured to be done in mitigating the sufferings and in meliorating the condition of the Indians, though, owing to the peculiar habits and opinions of these people, but little, I fear, is effected. I see by the report of the current year, (1827) that, in nine months, requisitions towards the support of the objects of this bureau, were made to the amount of 759, 116 dollars, or at the rate of a little more than a million of dollars a year. This, you will remember, is one-tenth of the current expenditure of the whole government, and nearly as much as is paid for the support of the whole civil list, strictly speaking. . . .

The government, it would appear by the reports, puts the utmost latitude on the construction of their constitutional powers, by even paying money for the support of missionaries among the Indians. I believe, however, that the alleged and legal object of this charge, is for general instruction, though in point of fact, the teachers are missionaries. They are of all sects, Protestant and Catholic, the question of creed being never discussed at all. I see by the reports, that (in 1827) there were 1291 scholars in the different schools that come under the superintendence of the government. It is not probable that all the Indians belonging to the tribes that receive this instruction much exceed, if indeed they reach, the total number of 30,000. I think it is therefore apparent, that quite as good provision for elementary instruction is made in behalf of the Indians, as is commonly made for the people of any country, except those of the United States themselves. There is no reason to suppose that all the children who present themselves, are not taught; and there is much reason for believing that efforts are constantly making to induce all to come. The number of teachers is 293, which is quite enough to instruct ten times the number. You are not to suppose, however, that all these teachers are men hired expressly for that purpose. They are the missionaries, their wives and families, and some of them are for the purpose of instructing in the arts of life, as well as in reading and writing. Much of the expense is defrayed by charitable associations. The sum actually paid by the government for the express object of instruction, is 7,150 dollars, or enough to maintain rather more than forty teachers of stipends of 150 dollars each. It is probable that some receive more, and some less. It is said that the schools are generally in a flourishing condition.

Where there is much intercourse between the very strong and very weak, there is always a tendency in the human mind to suspect abuses of power. I shall not descend into the secret impulses that give rise to these suspicions; but in this stage of the world, there is no necessity for suspecting a nation like this of any unprovoked wrongs against a people like the savages. The inroad of the whites of the United States has never been marked by the gross injustice and brutality that have distinguished similar inroads elsewhere. The Indians have never been slain except in battle, unless by lawless individuals; never hunted by blood-hounds, or in any manner aggrieved, except in the general, and, perhaps, in some degree, justifiable invasion of a territory that they did not want, nor could not use. If the government of the United States was poor and necessitous, one might suspect it of an unjust propensity; but not only the facts, but the premises, would teach us to believe the reverse.

A great, humane, and, I think, rational project, is now in operation to bring the Indians within the pale of civilization. I shall furnish you with its outline as it is detailed in a recent report of the head of the Indian office.

Most, if not all of the Indians who reside east of the Mississippi, live within the jurisdiction of some State or of some territory. In most cases they are left to the quiet enjoyment of the scanty rights which they retain, but the people of their vicinity commonly wish to get rid of neighbours that retard civilization, and who are so often troublesome. The policy of States is sometimes adverse to their continuance. Though there is no power, except that of the United States, which can effect their removal without their own consent, the State authorities can greatly embarrass the control of the general government. A question of policy, and, perhaps, of jurisdiction, lately arose on this subject between Georgia and the general government. In the course of its disposal, the United States, in order to secure the rights of the Indians more effectually, and to prevent any future question of this sort, appear to have hit on the following plan.

West of the Mississippi they still hold large regions that belong to no State or territory. They propose to several tribes (Choctaws, Chickasaws, Cherokees, &c.) to sell their present possessions, improvements, houses, fences, stock, &c., and to receive, in return, acre for acre, with the same amount of stock, fences, and every other auxiliary of civilization they now possess. The inducements to make this exchange are as follows:—Perpetuity to their establishments, since a pledge is given that no title shall ever be granted that may raise a pretext for another removal; an organization of a republican, or, as it is termed, a territorial government for them, such as now exist in Florida, Arkansas, and Michigan; protection, by the presence of troops; and a right to send delegates to Congress, similar to that now enjoyed by the other territories.

If the plan can be effected, there is reason to think that the constant diminution in the numbers of the Indians will be checked, and that a race, about whom there is so much that is poetic and fine in recollection, will be preserved. Indeed, some of the southern tribes have already endured the collision with the white man, and are still slowly on the increase. As one of these tribes, at least, (the Chickasaws,) is included in this plan, there is just ground to hope that the dangerous point of communication has been passed, and that they may continue to advance in civilization to maturity. The chief of the bureau on Indian affairs gives it as his opinion that they (the Chickasaws) have increased about ten per cent within six years. Their whole number is computed at four thousand souls.

Should such a territory be formed, a nucleus will be created, around which all the savages of the west, who have any yearnings for a more meliorated state of existence, can rally. As there is little reluctance to mingle the white and red blood, (for the physical difference is far less than in the case of the blacks, and the Indians have never been menial slaves,) I think an amalgamation of the two races would in time occur. Those families of America who are thought to have any of the Indian blood, are rather proud of their descent, and it is a matter of boast among many of the most considerable persons of Virginia, that they are descended from the renowned Pocahontas.

The character of the American Indian has been too often faithfully described to need any repetition here. The majority of them, in or near the settlements, are an humbled and much degraded race. As you recede from the Mississippi, the finer traits of savage life become visible; and, although most of the natives of the Prairies, even there, are far from being the interesting and romantic heroes that poets love to paint, there are specimens of loftiness of spirit, of bearing, and of savage heroism, to be found among the chiefs, that might embarrass the fertility of the richest invention to equal. I met one of those heroes of the desert, and a finer physical and moral man, allowing for peculiarity of condition, it has rarely been my good fortune to encounter.

From
INDIAN DEPREDATIONS IN TEXAS (1889)
JOHN WESLEY WILBARGER

John Wesley Wilbarger, together with his two brothers, one of whom was scalped by the Indians just east of what is now Austin, Texas, was an early Texas pioneer. His Indian Depredations in Texas, *written when he was an old man, is typical of the frontiersman's view of the Indians, and it is a remarkable example of the literature produced by the frontier.*

There is a certain class of maudlin, sentimental writers who are forever bewailing the rapid disappearance of the Indian tribes from the American continent. We must confess we don't fraternize with our brother scribblers on this point. They have evidently taken their ideas of the Indian character from Cooper's novels and similar productions, which give about as correct delineation of it as are the grotesque figures a school boy draws on his slate of the animals or objects he intends to represent. There may have been, and no doubt there have been, some individuals among the Indians like those described by Cooper, *et id omne genus,* but they have been like angels' visits, few and far between. His general character may be summarily stated in Byron's words, when speaking of his hero, the Corsair: "He had one virtue linked to a thousand crimes." This solitary virtue may have been physical courage, hospitality or something else, but among his unquestionable vices may be reckoned cruelty, treachery, vindictiveness, brutality, indolence (except when spurred to action by his thirst for rapine and blood) and his utter inability to advance beyond the condition in which nature had originally placed him. There is, however, one notable exception to this general rule, which is most singular and difficult to account for. We mean the Pueblo Indians of New Mexico, who physically are similar to all the other North American tribes, but differ from them as widely in all other respects as any of the Caucasian races.

It is true there are a few remnants of tribes, as the Cherokees and Choctaws in the Indian Territory, who have made some advances towards civilization, but this is largely, if not wholly, owing to the fact that their blood has been mingled to a great extent with that of the whites. In our opinion, the aborigines of the American continent, pure and simple, were all naturally incapable of progress, and that their existence was only intended to be a temporary one, and that it should cease as soon as their places could be filled by a progressive people, such as the Anglo-Saxon race. The very fact of their rapid disappearance, that they are fast fading away under the action of that inexorable law, the "survival of the fittest," is the best proof of this.

144

A COMANCHE PRINCESS

In the spring of 1843, the Republic of Texas, Sam Houston being president, dispatched Colonel J. C. Eldridge, Commissioner of Indian Affairs, and Mr. Tom Torrey, Indian Agent, to visit the several wild tribes on the frontier of Texas, and induce them to make peace and conclude treaties with the Republic. General H. P. Bee accompanied the expedition, but in no official capacity. A recent conversation with him disclosed to us the following touching scene as one of many incidents of that perilous and adventurous trip: At the house of a frontier settler, near where the town of Marlin stands, the commissioners received two Comanche children who had been captured by Colonel Moore, a famous and valiant soldier of the old Republic, in one of his forays on the upper waters of the Colorado in 1840. These children had been ordered to be returned to their people. One of them, a boy fourteen years old, named Bill Hockley, in honor of the veteran Colonel Hockley, then high in command of the army of the Republic, who had adopted the boy and taken care of him; the other was a girl eleven years old, named Maria. The parting of the little girl from the good people who had evidently been kind to her, was very affecting; she cried bitterly and begged that she would not be carried away. She had forgotten her native tongue, spoke only our language, and had the same dread of an Indian that any of the white children had. Her little nature had been cultivated by the hand of civilization until it drooped at the thought of the rough Indian life, as a delicately nurtured flower will droop in the strong winds of the prairies. There being no excuse, however, for retaining her among the white people, a pretty, gentle Indian pony, with a little side saddle, was procured for her, and she was taken from her friends. On arriving at a camp in Tanaconi, above where the town of Waco is now located, the party met the first Indians, a mixture of Delawares, Wacos, etc. The appearance of the little girl on horseback created great amusement among the Indians. She was so shy and timid, and the very manner in which she was seated on the side saddle was different from that of the brown skinned woman of her race. The next morning after the arrival at the camp, Bill Hockley came out in full Indian costume, having exchanged his citizen clothes for buckskin jacket, pants, etc. He at once resumed his Indian habits, and from that day during the long trip of months, Bill was noticed as the keenest eye of the party. He could tell an object at a greater distance, a horse from a buffalo, a horse without a rider, etc., quicker than an Indian in camp.

The journey proceeded with its varied scenes of excitement, danger and interest for four months, and the barometer of the party was the little Comanche princess. The object of the expedition was to see the head chief of the Comanches, and of course, as the search was to be made in the boundless prairies, it was no easy or certain task; yet they could tell the distance from or proximity to the Comanches by the conduct of the little girl. When news would come that the Indians were near, the childish voice would not be heard in its joyous freshness, caroling around the fire; but when news arrived that they could not be found, her spirits would revive, and her joy would show itself in gambols as merry as those of the innocent fawn that sports around its mother on the green bosom of the prairie.

At last the goal was reached, and the party was in the Comanche camp, the village of Pay-ha-hu-co, the head chief of all the Comanches. Maria's time had come, but the little girl tried to avoid notice, and kept as close as possible. Her appearance, however, was the cause of great sensation, and a few days fixed the fact that she was the daughter of the former head chief of the nation, who died on the forks of the Brazos from wounds received at the battle of Plum creek, in 1840. Thus, unknown to her or themselves, they had been associating with a royal princess, No-sa-co-oi-ash, the long lost and beloved child of the nation. This extraordinary good luck for the little girl brought no assuagement to her grief. Her joy was gone. She spoke not a word of Comanche, and could not reciprocate the warm greetings she received. On arriving at the village, Bill Hockley determined he would not talk Comanche, although he spoke it perfectly well, not having, like little Maria, forgotten his native language. During the week they remained in the village, Bill, contrary to his usual custom, kept close to the party, and did not speak a word to those around him; nor could he be induced to do so.

On one occasion a woman brought a roasting ear, which was of great value in her eyes, as it had come probably one hundred and fifty miles, and presented it to Bill, who sat in one of the tents. The boy gave not the slightest attention to the woman or her gift, but kept his eyes fixed on the ground. Finally, she put the roasting ear under his eyes, so that, as he looked down, he must see it. Then, talking all the time, she walked off and watched him. But Bill, from under his eyes, noted her movements, and not until she was out of sight did he get up and say: "That ugly old woman is not Mammie, but I will eat her roasting ear."

When the chief came home (he was absent for several days after the party arrived) he asked to see the children, and when they were presented he spoke to Bill in a very peremptory tone of voice, and Bill at once answered, being the first word of Comanche he had spoken since his arrival. This broke the ice, and the boy went among his people, not returning to his white friends until he was wanted to take part in the ceremony of being finally delivered over to his tribe, and afterward never going to tell them good bye. So there and then Bill Hockley passed from the scene. The day before the grand council with the Comanches the skill and ingenuity of the party of three white men were taxed to its fullest extent to make a suitable dress for the Comanche Princess, whose clothes, it may be supposed, had become old and shabby. Their lady friends would have been vastly amused at their efforts. There was no "pull-back," to be sure. Whether the body was too short we are unable to say, but it was one or the other. The skirt was a success, but the sleeves would not work, so they cut them off at the elbow. The next morning they dressed the little princess in a flaming red calico dress, put strings of brass beads on her neck, brass rings on her arms, a wreath of prairie flowers on her head, tied a red ribbon around her smooth, nicely plaited hair, and painted her face with vermilion, until she looked like the real princess that she was. All this, however, was no pleasure to poor Maria. She was like a lamb dressed in flowers for the sacrifice.

Finally, the time came when in the full council, Colonel Eldridge stood holding the hands of the two children, in front of the chief, and said to him that as an evidence of the desire of the Great White Father (Houston) to make peace, and be friendly with the great Comanche nation, he had sent them two children, captives in war, back to their people. After these words he attempted to place the hands of both in the extended hand of the chief, but at that moment the most distressing screams burst from Maria. She ran behind Colonel Eldridge and begged him for God's sake not to give her to those people—to have mercy, and not to leave her. Then the poor child fell on her knees and shrieked, and clung to him with all the madness of despair. A death-like silence prevailed in the council. The Indians stood by in stern stoicism, the voices of the white men were silent with emotion, and nothing but the cries of the poor lamb of sacrific pierced the distance of the bloom scented prairies. Her white friends, as soon as possible, attemped to quiet the child. Of course the comforting words were spoken in their own language, but they were evidently understood by all, for theirs was the language of nature. Finding their efforts useless, the chief said:

"This is the child of our long-mourned chief; she is of our blood; her aged grandmother stands ready to receive her, but she has forgotten her people. She does not want to come to us, and if the Great White Chief only sent her for us to see that she is fat and well taken care of, tell him I thank him, and she can go back."

This was an opportunity, and General Bee suggested to Colonel Eldridge to save the child; but although the latter's heart was bursting with grief and sympathy, his sense of duty told him his work was unfinished, and he replied to the chief: "I have been ordered to give you this child. I have done so, and my duty is fulfilled. But you see she is no longer a Comanche. Child in years when she was taken from you by the stern hand of war, she had learned the language of another people, and I implore you to give her to me, and let me take her to my home and care for her all the days of my life." "No," said the chief, "if she is my child I will keep her"; he swung her roughly behind him into the arms of the old grandmother, who bore her, screaming, from the council tent. And thus the princess was delivered to her people; but the last sound the party heard on leaving that Comanche camp was the wail of the poor, desolate child.

Years after, General Bee received a message from Maria, and sent her a few presents by way of remembrance. She had become the main interpreter of her nation, and often met our people in council. So it ended well at last. She became an instrument of good, and fulfilled her destiny on the stage of action for which she was born.

MASSACRE OF THE KEENON AND PASCHAL FAMILIES

The story of this sad tragedy is given as related by A. J. Sowell, author of "Texas Rangers." Mr. Sowell, who was in the ranging service at the time, arrived at the scene of the bloody tragedy soon after it occurred, and ought to be prepared to give a true version of all the particulars.

"While in camp on Big Sandy, news was brought to us of a fearful massacre of women and children on a small creek about thirty miles north of our camp, near the line of Montague and Wise counties. We lost no time in getting off, with eighteen men, well mounted and armed, to the scene of the slaughter, and by rapid riding arrived at the place before night, which was at Keenon's ranch but we soon discovered that it would be impossible for us to follow the trail, as it had been snowing since the Indians were there. As we rode up we saw seven new made graves on the north side of the cabin, under some trees. The settlers from down the country had buried the dead. There were only two ranches west of there—Colonel Bean's and O. T. Brown's. Bean was absent at the time. His ranch was about two miles from Keenon's. The Keenon house consisted of only one room, about twelve by fourteen feet, made out of logs. There was a small field south of the cabin, at the foot of the hill near the creek. On the northwest side, about two hundred yards from the house, was a small lake of water, at the foot of some hills; on the east was a crib of corn. Keenon himself was not at home when the Indians made the attack on his ranch and massacred the helpless inmates.

"We dismounted, entered the yard, walked to the door and looked in. It was a horrible sight. The door was torn from its hinges, and lay in the yard covered with blood. Blood on the door steps, blood everywhere, met our sight. The inside of the cabin was like a butcher pen. Quilts and pillows were scattered about over the floor, stiff with clotted blood. The dress which Mrs. Keenon wore was hanging across the girder which extended from one wall to the other. It had been hung there by some party who buried the victims. The dead were as follows: Mrs. Keenon and two of her children; the widow Paschal, who was living with the Keenon family, and her three children.

"We obtained the particulars of the attack from one of the Keenon children, a boy about eight years old, who made his escape on that fearful night. He said it was about ten o'clock at night; the ground was covered with snow, and it was very cold. The inmates had all gone to bed except Mrs. Keenon, who was sitting by the fire smoking. On the north side of the cabin was a small window with a shutter which fastened on the inside with a wooden pin entering a hole in one of the logs. The door was in the south side. Everything was still and quiet on that cold winter night. The children were all asleep, probably dreaming sweet dreams, which seldom visit the couch except of innocent childhood; when suddenly crash came the end of a rail through the frail shutter, bursting it wide open, and the hideous painted face of an Indian looked in and began to crawl through into the cabin. One brave man or resolute woman, armed with an ax or hatchet, could have held them at bay; but poor Mrs. Keenon was timid, and instantly sank on her knees and began to pray and beg for her life. As fast as one Indian got through another followed, until nine hideous wretches stood inside. By this time the balance of the inmates were aroused. The children began screaming and the work of death commenced.

"Pen can not describe the scene. The cold and lonely night, far out in the western wilds; the painted faces of the Indians lit up by the wood fire; the frantic and heart-rending cries of the women and children; the sickening blows of the tomahawks, etc., make one shudder to think of it. Who can blame a Texas ranger for placing his six shooter to the head of a wounded savage and pulling the trigger, as they often do in battle when they are victors.

"It was during the confusion that the little boy made his escape through the window by which the Indians had entered. He received a severe cut in the hip with a knife as he went through, but succeeded in getting clear of the house, and was able to run off and hide himself until the Indians left. Crouched in some bushes near the corn crib, and bleeding profusely, he waited and listened until all was still. The work was done; the fiends had reveled in blood.

"This boy displayed a presence of mind that was truly astonishing for one of his tender years before he made his escape from the house. He noticed the number of Indians that entered, and when they came out to take their departure, counted them to see if they were all leaving. The Indians had left their horses at the lake and came to the house on foot, and as the ground was covered with snow he could plainly see each form standing out in bold relief against the white back ground. He left his place of concealment and watched them until they mounted their horses and disappeared over the snow clad hills towards the west, and being satisfied that they would not return came back to the house and entered.

"What a sight for a boy of his age to behold. His mother lay near the hearth with three arrows in her breast, tomahawked and scalped. Some of the children were killed in bed, others lay on the floor in pools of blood; one of his sisters was crouched in a corner with her throat cut. There was at least a quart of blood in that corner when we were there. The widow Paschal was lying on the door shutter in the yard. She had three broken arrows in her breast. She had broken them off in attempting to pull them out; she was also scalped. The youngest child, about eighteen months old, was taken by the legs and its head dashed against the wall of the house and then thrown out through the window on the frozen ground. But the boy brought his little sister back in the house and laid her down before the fire and she recovered. While in the house attending to his sister he heard a noise in the yard, and on going to the door saw Mrs. Paschal sitting upon the door shutter, upon which she had been lying. She looked horrible, covered with blood and scalp taken off. But the brave boy went to her and she asked him for a drink of water, and there being none at the house he took a gourd and went to the lake and brought the water. Mrs. Paschal drank the water and immediately expired. On looking around in the house while we were there I saw the old lady's pipe lying on the hearth, about half smoked out, where she had dropped it on that fatal night. We also saw a bent arrow spike in one of the logs, just above the bed. It had been shot at some of the children on the bed and missed. The shaft had been removed. The next evening after the massacre a settler passed the house and was hailed by the boy, who soon told his tale of woe.

"The man took a hasty view of the victims and then galloped off to give the alarm. The next day the dead were buried and the news carried to the ranger camp, and when we arrived the ranch was deserted, the children having been taken away and cared for until their father arrived, who was off somewhere with a wagon and had one of his children with him, which circumstance saved its life, no doubt. As we could accomplish nothing, the trail being covered with a fresh fall of snow, after about an hour's stay we mounted and set out for camp, vowing vengeance if we should ever meet the red man face to face. Some time after our first visit to the Keenon place a small party of us returned after a load of corn. Keenon had returned and was preparing to move away from the frontier. Our Captain hearing of it had purchased his corn crop, which amounted to about three hundred bushels. I was detailed on this trip as one of the guards and saw the little girl who was thrown out of the window and so nearly killed by the Indians. She was very lively and when we asked her where the Indians hit her she would tuck down her head so we could see the back of it, which still looked discolored and bruised. The boy looked pale and thin; his wound was not yet healed."

THE NOBLE RED MAN
From *Western Wilds* (*1877*)

J. H. BEADLE

John Hanson Beadle, traveler and author of several of the many travel books about Western America that poured from the presses in the second half of the nineteenth century, attempts an objective view of Indians, frontiersmen, and Mormons, the three groups of people whom Easterners were eager to read about. In Western Wilds *he combines history, geography, anthropology, and current biases to produce a work more stimulating than most of its type.*

A glance at the map of Aboriginal America will show that very few of the Indian nations have retained their original locations; but it must not be judged therefrom that numerous tribes have become extinct. The Indian population of this country at the landing of Columbus has been greatly exaggerated. It is demonstrable that all that part of the United States east of the Mississippi never contained half a million Indians; some authorities say a quarter of a million. It is apparent at a glance that a country like Ohio will sustain four hundred times as many people in the civilized as in the savage state. When men live upon game and the spontaneous products of the earth, it must be a fertile land indeed which will sustain an average of one person to the square mile. When we pass to the Indian of the plains the original population was sparser still. But there we find some of the races on the soil where first discovered. The Sioux have steadily contracted their eastern border, while maintaining their western border intact. But if, leaving history we take tradition, we find that the Indian tribes have been engaged for centuries in a series of migrations, the northern ones as a rule slowly pushing southward. As all our mountain chains run north and south, it follows that the people of this country can not grow into distinct races as in Europe, where different climates and soils are partitioned off by natural barriers. Hence the Indian, from Manitoba to the Gulf of Mexico is *one;* hence, too, half a million men of the West rose in arms to prevent the mouth of the Mississippi being "held by an alien government." Of the Indian migrations, the best authenticated are those of the Shoshonees and Sioux, which are referred to in the following legend, as related to the interpreter by Susuceicha, a Sioux chief:

"Ages past the Lacotas (or Dakotas, *i. e.*, Sioux) lived in a land far above the sun of winter.

"Here then the Shoshonee had all, but these basins were yet full of water, and the buffalo ranged even to the Salt Land (Utah).

151

"Ages passed. The Shoshonees gave place to the Scarred Arms (Cheyennes). The Lacotas came toward the sun and fought long with the Scarred Arms. A great party came far into the inner plain (Laramie) and fell into a snare; all were killed by the Scarred Arms but six; these hid in a hole in the mountain.

"They built a fire and dressed their wounds; they hoped to stay many days till the Scarred Arms left the plain. But a form rose from the dark corner of the cave; it was a woman—old as the red mountain that was scarred by Waukan. Her hair was like wool; she was feeble and wrinkled. She spoke:

" 'Children, you have been against the Scarred Arms. You alone live. I know it all. But your fire has waked me, and the full time of my dream has come. Listen:

" 'Long ago the Shoshonees visited the Lacotas; the prairie took in the blood of many Lacota braves, and I was made captive. The Shoshonees brought me here, but I was not happy. I fled. I was weak. I took refuge in this cave.

" 'But look! Where are the Shoshonees? The Lacotas will soon know them, and bring from their lodges many scalps and medicine dogs. They have fled before the Scarred Arms. One-half crossed the snow hills toward sunset; the other went toward the sun, and now hunt the buffalo east of the Ispanola's earth lodges. But my eyes were sealed for ages till my people should come. The Scarred Arms have long thought this land their own, but it is not. Waukantunga gives it to the Lacotas; they shall possess the land of their daughter's captivity. But why wait ye? Go gather your warriors and attack the Scarred Arms. Fear not, their scalps are yours.'

"The warriors did return. They found the Scarred Arms at the foot of the mountain, and drove them to the South. Our grateful braves then sought the mountain to reverence the medicine woman, who told them so many good things. But woman and cave were gone. There was only a cleft in the mountain side from which came a cold stream of water. Then the Lacotas made peace with the Scarred Arms. Each year our warriors visit the Shoshonees for scalps and medicine dogs, and each of our braves, as he passes the old woman's spring, stops to quench his thirst and yield a tribute of veneration."

The Shoshonees not only have a legend answering to this, but name the various times when the Comanches, Arapahoes, and Apaches seceded from the main body. Thus this great colony of the Athabascan race, slowly moving southward, has sent off branches right and left, from the Saskatchewan to the Rio Grande and Gulf of California.

It would surprise some people who have been indignant over the death of Custer and his companions to learn how small, comparatively, is the number of hostile Indians. A strip of 500 miles wide, from the Missouri to the Pacific, is rarely visited by hostiles; and at no time for the past ten years have more than one-fifth of the race been in arms or even threatening. All the border States except Texas are free from hostiles. Of the nine Territories only three have been seriously troubled since 1867, and the three Pacific States have had even a longer exemption. Within that time Indian hostilities have been confined to three districts. First, and greatest, is that strip of mountain, forest, and desert including all Northern Wyoming, South-eastern and Eastern Montana, and a small portion of Western Dakota. Next are the highlands of Western Texas, raided by the Comanches and their allies; and lastly that part of New Mexico and Arizona dominated by the Apaches. To judge how contemptible a performance an Indian war is, how small the glory in proportion to the aggravation, be it noted that the whole Apache race numbers less than 8,000, and can not possibly mount 2,000 warriors.

If it be decided that the 300,000 Indians in the United States (or rather the 200,000 wild ones) are to "die off," then by all means let a "feeding policy" be pursued; it is so much cheaper to kill them by kindness than by war. Since 1860 the average cost of killing Indians has been about $500,000 each. One-tenth that amount would stuff one to death. If, I say, the theory of final extermination be adopted, the most Christian and, by all odds, the cheapest plan would be this: Let central depots be established along the Pacific Railway and at other accessible points, and give general notice that every Indian who will come there and live shall have all the bread, meat, coffee, sugar, whisky and tobacco he can consume. The last man of them would be dead in ten years, and at a cost not exceeding twenty per cent. of the killing price. Since the Mormons began the feeding policy with their nearest Indian neighbors the latter have died off much faster than when at war. They can't stand petting any more than a rabbit.

From
THE CONFIDENCE MAN (1857)
HERMAN MELVILLE

Herman Melville (1819–1891), one of America's greatest novelists, best known for Moby-Dick *(1851) and other novels based on his experiences at sea, has been the subject of intensive scholarly examination in recent years. In* The Confidence Man, *as in his other works, he wrestles with the question of the nature of good and evil in the universe.*

Chapter 26 Containing *The Metaphysics of Indian Hating,* According to the Views of One Evidently Not So Prepossessed as Rousseau in Favor of Savages.

"The judge always began in these words: "The backwoodsman's hatred of the Indian has been a topic for some remark. In the earlier times of the frontier the passion was thought to be readily accounted for. But Indian rapine having mostly ceased through regions where it once prevailed, the philanthropist is surprised that Indian-hating has not in like degree ceased with it. He wonders why the backwoodsman still regards the red man in much the same spirit that a jury does a murderer, or a trapper a wild cat—a creature, in whose behalf mercy were not wisdom; truce is vain; he must be executed.

" 'A curious point,' the judge would continue, 'which perhaps not everybody, even upon explanation, may fully understand; while, in order for any one to approach to an understanding, it is necessary for him to learn, or if he already know, to bear in mind, what manner of man the backwoodsman is; as for what manner of man the Indian is, many know, either from history or experience.

" 'The backwoodsman is a lonely man. He is a thoughtful man. He is a man strong and unsophisticated. Impulsive, he is what some might call unprincipled. At any rate, he is self-willed; being one who less hearkens to what others may say about things, than looks for himself, to see what are things themselves. If in straits, there are few to help; he must depend upon himself; he must continually look to himself. Hence self-reliance, to the degree of standing by his own judgment, though it stand alone. Not that he deems himself infallible; too many mistakes in following trails prove the contrary; but he thinks that nature destines such sagacity as she has given him, as she destines it to the 'possum. To these fellow-beings of the wilds their untutored sagacity is their best dependence. If with either it prove faulty, if the 'possum's betray it to the trap, or the backwoodsman's mislead him into ambuscade, there are consequences to be undergone, but no self-blame. As with the 'possum, instincts prevail with the backwoodsman over

154

precepts. Like the 'possum, the backwoodsman presents the spectacle of a creature dwelling exclusively among the works of God, yet these, truth must confess, breed little in him of a godly mind. Small bowing and scraping is his, further than when with bent knee he points his rifle, or picks its flint. With few companions, solitude by necessity his lengthened lot, he stands the trial—no slight one, since, next to dying, solitude, rightly borne, is perhaps of fortitude the most rigorous test. But not merely is the backwoodsman content to be alone, but in no few cases is anxious to be so. The sight of smoke ten miles off is provocation to one more remove from man, one step deeper into nature. Is it that he feels that whatever man may be, man is not the universe? that glory, beauty, kindness, are not all engrossed by him? that as the presence of man frights birds away, so, many bird-like thoughts? Be that how it will, the backwoodsman is not without some fineness to his nature. Hairy Orson as he looks, it may be with him as with the Shetland seal—beneath the bristles lurks the fur.

" 'Though held in a sort a barbarian, the backwoodsman would seem to America what Alexander was to Asia—captain in the vanguard of conquering civilization. Whatever the nation's growing opulence or power, does it not lackey his heels? Pathfinder, provider of security to those who come after him, for himself he asks nothing but hardship. Worthy to be compared with Moses in the Exodus, or the Emperor Julian in Gaul, who on foot, and barebrowed, at the head of covered or mounted legions, marched so through the elements, day after day. The tide of emigration, let it roll as it will, never overwhelms the backwoodsman into itself; he rides upon advance, as the Polynesian upon the comb of the surf.

" 'Thus, though he keeps moving on through life, he maintains with respect to nature much the same unaltered relation throughout; with her creatures, too, including panthers and Indians. Hence, it is not unlikely that, accurate as the theory of the Peace Congress may be with respect to those two varieties of beings, among others, yet the backwoodsman might be qualified to throw out some practical suggestions.

" 'As the child born to a backwoodsman must in turn lead his father's life—a life which, as related to humanity, is related mainly to Indians—it is thought best not to mince matters, out of delicacy; but to tell the boy pretty plainly what an Indian is, and what he must expect from him. For however charitable it may be to view Indians as members of the Society of Friends, yet to affirm them such to one ignorant of Indians, whose lonely path lies a long way through their lands, this, in the event, might prove not only injudicious but cruel. At least something of this kind would seem the maxim upon which backswoods' education is based. Accordingly, if in youth the backwoodsman incline to knowledge, as is generally the case, he hears little from his schoolmasters, the old chroniclers of the forest, but histories of Indian lying,

Indian theft, Indian double-dealing, Indian fraud and perfidy, Indian want of conscience, Indian blood-thirstiness, Indian diabolism—histories which, though of wild woods, are almost as full of things unangelic as the Newgate Calendar or the Annals of Europe. In these Indian narratives and traditions the lad is thoroughly grounded. "As the twig is bent the tree's inclined." The instinct of antipathy against an Indian grows in the backwoodsman with the sense of good and bad, right and wrong. In one breath he learns that a brother is to be loved, and an Indian to be hated.

" 'Such are the facts,' the judge would say, 'upon which, if one seek to moralize, he must do so with an eye to them. It is terrible that one creature should so regard another, should make it conscience to abhor an entire race. It is terrible; but is it surprising? Surprising, that one should hate a race which he believes to be red from a cause akin to that which makes some tribes of garden insects green? A race whose name is upon the frontier a *memento mori;* painted to him in every evil light; now a horse-thief like those in Moyamensing; now an assassin like a New York rowdy; now a treaty-breaker like an Austrian; now a Palmer with poisoned arrows; now a judicial murderer and Jeffries, after a fierce farce of trial condemning his victim to bloody death; or a Jew with hospitable speeches cozening some fainting stranger into ambuscade, there to burke him, and account it a deed grateful to Manitou, his god.

" 'Still, all this is less advanced as truths of the Indians than as examples of the backwoodsman's impression of them—in which the charitable may think he does them some injustice. Certain it is, the Indians themselves think so; quite unanimously, too. The Indians, indeed, protest against the backwoodsman's view of them; and some think that one cause of their returning his antipathy so sincerely as they do, is their moral indignation at being so libeled by him, as they really believe and say. But whether, on this or any point, the Indians should be permitted to testify for themselves, to the exclusion of other testimony, is a question that may be left to the Supreme Court. At any rate, it has been observed that when an Indian becomes a genuine proselyte to Christianity (such cases, however, not being very many; though, indeed, entire tribes are sometimes nominally brought to the true light), he will not in that case conceal his enlightened conviction, that his race's portion by nature is total depravity; and, in that way, as much as admits that the backwoodsman's worst idea of it is not very far from true; while, on the other hand, those red men who are the greatest sticklers for the theory of Indian virtue, and Indian loving-kindness, are sometimes the arrantest horse-thieves and tomahawkers among them. So, at least, avers the backwoodsman. And though, knowing the Indian nature, as he thinks he does, he fancies he is not ignorant that an Indian may in some points deceive himself almost as effectually as in bush-tactics he can another, yet his theory and his practice as above

contrasted seem to involve an inconsistency so extreme, that the backwoodsman only accounts for it on the supposition that when a toma-
hawking red man advances the notion of the benignity of the red race,
it is but part and parcel with that subtle strategy which he finds so
useful in war, in hunting, and the general conduct of life.'

"In further explanation of that deep abhorrence with which the backwoodsman regards the savage, the judge used to think it might perhaps
a little help, to consider what kind of stimulus to it is furnished in those
forest histories and traditions before spoken of. In which behalf, he
would tell the story of the little colony of Wrights and Weavers, originally seven cousins from Virginia, who, after successive removals with
their families, at last established themselves near the southern frontier
of the Bloody Ground, Kentucky: 'They were strong, brave men; but,
unlike many of the pioneers in those days, theirs was no love of conflict for conflict's sake. Step by step they had been lured to their lonely
resting-place by the ever-beckoning seductions of a fertile and virgin
land, with a singular exemption, during the march, from Indian moles-
tation. But clearings made and houses built, the bright shield was soon
to turn its other side. After repeated persecutions and eventual hostilities, forced on them by a dwindled tribe in their neighborhood—persecutions resulting in loss of crops and cattle; hostilities in which they
lost two of their number, illy to be spared, besides others getting painful wounds—the five remaining cousins made, with some serious concessions, a kind of treaty with Mocmohoc, the chief—being to this induced by the harryings of the enemy, leaving them no peace. But they
were further prompted, indeed, first incited, by the suddenly changed
ways of Mocmohoc, who, though hitherto deemed a savage almost perfidious as Caesar Borgia, yet now put on a seeming the reverse of this,
engaging to bury the hatchet, smoke the pipe, and be friends forever;
not friends in the mere sense of renouncing enmity; but in the sense of
kindliness, active and familiar.

" 'But what the chief now seemed, did not wholly blind them to what
the chief had been; so that, though in no small degree influenced by
his change of bearing, they still distrusted him enough to covenant with
him, among other articles on their side, that though friendly visits
should be exchanged between the wigwams and the cabins, yet the five
cousins should never, on any account, be expected to enter the chief's
lodge together. The intention was, though they reserved it, that if ever,
under the guise of amity, the chief should mean them mischief, and
effect it, it should be but partially; so that some of the five might survive, not only for their families' sake, but also for retribution's. Nevertheless, Mocmohoc did, upon a time, with such fine art and pleasing
carriage win their confidence, that he brought them all together to a
feast of bear's meat, and there, by stratagem, ended them. Years after,
over their calcined bones and those of all their families, the chief, re-
proached for his treachery by a proud hunter whom he had made cap-

tive, jeered out, "Treachery? pale face! 'Twas they who broke their covenant first, in coming all together; they that broke it first, in trusting Mocmohoc.' "

"At this point the judge would pause, and lifting his hand, and rolling his eyes, exclaim in a solemn enough voice, 'Circling wiles and bloody lusts. The acuteness and genius of the chief but make him the more atrocious.'

"After another pause, he would begin an imaginary kind of dialogue between a backwoodsman and a questioner:

" 'But are all Indians like Mocmohoc?—Not all have proved such; but in the least harmful may lie his germ. There is an Indian nature. "Indian blood is in me," is the half-breed's threat.—But are not some Indians kind?—Yes, but kind Indians are mostly lazy, and reputed simple—at all events, are seldom chiefs; chiefs among the red men being taken from the active, and those accounted wise. Hence, with small promotion, kind Indians have but proportionate influence. And kind Indians may be forced to do unkind biddings. So "beware the Indian, kind or unkind," said Daniel Boone, who lost his sons by them.—But, have all you backwoodsmen been some way victimized by Indians?— No.—Well, and in certain cases may not at least some few of you be favored by them?—Yes, but scarce one among us so self-important, or so selfish-minded, as to hold his personal exemption from Indian outrage such a set-off against the contrary experience of so many others, as that he must needs, in a general way, think well of Indians; or, if he do, an arrow in his flank might suggest a pertinent doubt.

" 'In short,' according to the judge, 'if we at all credit the backwoodsman, his feeling against Indians, to be taken aright, must be considered as being not so much on his own account as on others', or jointly on both accounts. True it is, scarce a family he knows but some member of it, or connection, has been by Indians maimed or scalped. What avails, then, that some one Indian, or some two or three, treat a backwoodsman friendly-like? He fears me, he thinks. Take my rifle from me, give him motive, and what will come? Or if not so, how know I what involuntary preparations may be going on in him for things as unbeknown in present time to him as me—a sort of chemical preparation in the soul for malice, as chemical preparation in the body for malady.'

"Not that the backwoodsman ever used those words, you see, but the judge found him expression for his meaning. And this point he would conclude with saying, that, 'what is called a "friendly Indian" is a very rare sort of creature; and well it was so, for no ruthlessness exceeds that of a "friendly Indian" turned enemy. A coward friend, he makes a valiant foe.

" 'But, thus far the passion in question has been viewed in a general way as that of a community. When to his due share of this the backwoodsman adds his private passion, we have then the stock out of which is formed, if formed at all, the Indian-hater *par excellence*.'

"The Indian-hater *par excellence* the judge defined to be one 'who, having with his mother's milk drank in small love for red men, in youth or early manhood, ere the sensibilities become osseous, receives at their hand some signal outrage, or, which in effect is much the same, some of his kin have, or some friend. Now, nature all around him by her solitudes wooing or bidding him muse upon this matter, he accordingly does so, till the thought develops such attraction, that much as straggling vapors troop from all sides to a storm-cloud, so straggling thoughts of other outrages troop to the nucleus thought, assimilate with it, and swell it. At last, taking counsel with the elements, he comes to his resolution. An intenser Hannibal, he makes a vow, the hate of which is a vortex from whose suction scarce the remotest chip of the guilty race may reasonably feel secure. Next, he declares himself and settles his temporal affairs. With the solemnity of a Spaniard turned monk, he takes leave of his kin; or rather, these leave-takings have something of the still more impressive finality of death-bed adieus. Last, he commits himself to the forest primeval; there, so long as life shall be his, to act upon a calm, cloistered scheme of strategical, implacable, and lonesome vengeance. Ever on the noiseless trail; cool, collected, patient; less seen than felt; snuffing, smelling—a Leatherstocking Nemesis. In the settlements he will not be seen again; in eyes of old companions tears may start at some chance thing that speaks of him; but they never look for him, nor call; they know he will not come. Suns and seasons fleet; the tiger-lily blows and falls; babes are born and leap in their mothers' arms; but, the Indian-hater is good as gone to his long home, and "Terror" is his epitaph.'

"Here the judge, not unaffected, would pause again, but presently resume: 'How evident that in strict speech there can be no biography of an Indian-hater *par excellence*, any more than one of a sword-fish, or other deep-sea denizen; or, which is still less imaginable, one of a dead man. The career of the Indian-hater *par excellence* has the impenetrability of the fate of a lost steamer. Doubtless, events, terrible ones, have happened, must have happened; but the powers that be in nature have taken order that they shall never become news.

" 'But, luckily for the curious, there is a species of diluted Indian-hater, one whose heart proves not so steely as his brain. Soft enticements of domestic life too often draw him from the ascetic trail; a monk who apostatizes to the world at times. Like a mariner, too, though much abroad, he may have a wife and family in some green harbor which he does not forget. It is with him as with the Papist converts in Senegal; fasting and mortification prove hard to bear.'

"The judge, with his usual judgment, always thought that the intense solitude to which the Indian-hater consigns himself, has, by its overawing influence, no little to do with relaxing his vow. He would relate instances where, after some months' lonely scoutings, the Indian-hater is suddenly seized with a sort of calenture; hurries openly towards the first smoke, though he knows it is an Indian's, announces himself as a lost hunter, gives the savage his rifle, throws himself upon his charity, embraces him with much affection, imploring the privilege of living a while in his sweet companionship. What is too often the sequel of so distempered a procedure may be best known by those who best know the Indian. Upon the whole, the judge, by two and thirty good and sufficient reasons, would maintain that there was no known vocation whose consistent following calls for such self-containings as that of the Indian-hater *par excellence*. In the highest view, he considered such a soul one peeping out but once an age.

"For the diluted Indian-hater, although the vacations he permits himself impair the keeping of the character, yet, it should not be overlooked that this is the man who, by his very infirmity, enables us to form surmises, however inadequate, of what Indian-hating in its perfection is."

"One moment," gently interrupted the cosmopolitan here, "and let me refill my calumet."

Which being done, the other proceeded:—

SPEECH TO INDIANS (1863)

ABRAHAM LINCOLN

Abraham Lincoln (1809–1865) devoted most of his attention during his presidency to slavery, secession and war. But he accepted, virtually without question, the paternal relationship between the government and the Indians, tempering law with mercy after the abortive revolt of the Minnesota Indians.

March 27, 1863

"You have all spoken of the strange sights you see here, among your pale-faced brethren; the very great number of people that you see; the big wigwams; the difference between our people and your own.

Washington *Daily Morning Chronicle,* March 28, 1863. The *Chronicle* account of the ceremonies which preceded Lincoln's speech reads in part:

"The Executive Mansion was yesterday morning the scene of a very interesting ceremony. The Indian chiefs now in the city met the President of the United States and had a formal interview with him. The meeting took place in the East room. Quite a number of persons were present, among whom we noticed Secretaries Seward, Chase, and Welles. Daniel S. Dickinson, of New York, Professor Henry, and other celebrated personages. The Indians were all seated on the floor in a line, and around them the spectators formed a ring which, notwithstanding the assiduous yet polite efforts of Mr. Nicolay, was still too contracted to permit all to see the principal actors. The silence, which would seem to be the part of common propriety on such an occasion, was by no means observed by the restless and eager crowd of visitors. Everybody seemed to find some one's bonnet or shoulder in the way, and to think himself or herself entitled to the best and most conspicuous place. The ladies, too, could not refrain from audible comments on the speeches.

"Still everything went off very well. These Indians are fine-looking men. They have all the hard and cruel lines in their faces which we might expect in savages; but they are evidently men of intelligence and force of character. They were both dignified and cordial in their manner, and listened to everything with great interest. At half-past eleven the President entered the circle, and each one of the chiefs came forward and shook him by the hand, some of them adding a sort of salaam or salutation by spreading out the hands, and some contenting themselves with a simple shake of the hand and the inevitable "how" of the Indians of the Plains. The following is a list of the chiefs:

"*Cheyennes.*—Lean Bear, War Bonnet, and Standing Water.

"*Kiowais.*—Yellow Buffalo, Lone Wolf, Yellow Wolf, White Bull, and Little Heart.

"*Arapahoes.*—Spotted Wolf and Nevah.

"*Comanches.*—Pricked Forehead and Ten Bears.

"*Apache.*—Poor Bear.

"*Caddo.*—Jacob

"Mr. Commissioner Dole introduced them. . . .

"The President said: 'Say to them I am very glad to see them, and if they have anything to say, it will afford me great pleasure to hear them.'"

Speeches were made by Lean Bear and Spotted Wolf, through an interpreter, and by Lincoln as reported above.

161

But you have seen but a very small part of the pale-faced people. You may wonder when I tell you that there are people here in this wigwam, now looking at you, who have come from other countries a great deal farther off than you have come.

"We pale-faced people think that this world is a great, round ball, and we have people here of the pale-faced family who have come almost from the other side of it to represent their nations here and conduct their friendly intercourse with us, as you now come from your part of the round ball."

Here a globe was introduced, and the President, laying his hand upon it, said:

"One of our learned men will now explain to you our notions about this great ball, and show you where you live."

Professor Henry then gave the delegation a detailed and interesting explanation of the formation of the earth, showing how much of it was water and how much was land; and pointing out the countries with which we had intercourse. He also showed them the position of Washington and that of their own country, from which they had come.

The President then said:

"We have people now present from all parts of the globe—here, and here, and here. There is a great difference between this pale-faced people and their red brethren, both as to numbers and the way in which they live. We know not whether your own situation is best for your race, but this is what has made the difference in our way of living.

"The pale-faced people are numerous and prosperous because they cultivate the earth, produce bread, and depend upon the products of the earth rather than wild game for a subsistence.

"This is the chief reason of the difference; but there is another. Although we are now engaged in a great war between one another, we are not, as a race, so much disposed to fight and kill one another as our red brethren.

"You have asked for my advice. I really am not capable of advising you whether, in the providence of the Great Spirit, who is the great Father of us all, it is best for you to maintain the habits and customs of your race, or adopt a new mode of life.

"I can only say that I can see no way in which your race is to become as numerous and prosperous as the white race except by living as they do, by the cultivation of the earth.

"It is the object of this Government to be on terms of peace with you, and with all our red brethren. We constantly endeavor to be so. We make treaties with you, and will try to observe them; and if our children should sometimes behave badly, and violate these treaties, it is against our wish.

"You know it is not always possible for any father to have his children do precisely as he wishes them to do.

"In regard to being sent back to your own country, we have an officer, the Commissioner of Indian Affairs, who will take charge of that matter, and make the necessary arrangements."

The President's remarks were received with frequent marks of applause and approbation. "Ugh," "Aha" sounded along the line as the interpreter proceeded, and their countenances gave evident tokens of satisfaction.

NIAGARA (1871)

MARK TWAIN

Mark Twain (1835–1910), American humorist and satirist, probed the ironies of American life with a fond humor in his early writing, as characterized by "Niagara." His last works What is Man *(1906) and* The Mysterious Stranger *(1916) reflect the bitter condemnation and despair that later permeated his writing.*

Niagara Falls is a most enjoyable place of resort. The hotels are excellent, and the prices not at all exorbitant. The opportunities for fishing are not surpassed in the country; in fact, they are not even equaled elsewhere. Because, in other localities, certain places in the streams are much better than others; but at Niagara one place is just as good as another, for the reason that the fish do not bite anywhere, and so there is no use in your walking five miles to fish, when you can depend on being just as unsuccessful nearer home. The advantages of this state of things have never heretofore been properly placed before the public.

The weather is cool in summer, and the walks and drives are all pleasant and none of them fatiguing. When you start out to "do" the Falls you first drive down about a mile, and pay a small sum for the privilege of looking down from a precipice into the narrowest part of the Niagara River. A railway "cut" through a hill would be as comely if it had the angry river tumbling and foaming through its bottom. You can descend a staircase here a hundred and fifty feet down, and stand at the edge of the water. After you have done it, you will wonder why you did it; but you will then be too late.

The guide will explain to you, in his blood-curdling way, how he saw the little steamer, *Maid of the Mist*, descend the fearful rapids— how first one paddle-box was out of sight behind the raging billows and then the other, and at what point it was that her smokestack toppled overboard, and where her planking began to break and part asunder—and how she did finally live through the trip, after accomplishing the incredible feat of traveling seventeen miles in six minutes, or six miles in seventeen minutes, I have really forgotten which. But it was very extraordinary, anyhow. It is worth the price of admission to hear the guide tell the story nine times in succession to different parties, and never miss a word or alter a sentence or a gesture.

Then you drive over to Suspension Bridge, and divide your misery between the chances of smashing down two hundred feet into the river below, and the chances of having the railway-train overhead smashing down onto you. Either possibility is discomforting taken by itself, but, mixed together, they amount in the aggregate to positive unhappiness.

On the Canada side you drive along the chasm between long ranks of photographers standing guard behind their cameras, ready to make an ostentatious frontispiece of you and your decaying ambulance, and your solemn crate with a hide on it, which you are expected to regard in the light of a horse, and a diminished and unimportant background of sublime Niagara; and a great many people *have* the incredible effrontery or the native depravity to aid and abet this sort of crime.

Any day, in the hands of these photographers, you may see stately pictures of papa and mamma, Johnny and Bub and Sis, or a couple of country cousins, all smiling vacantly, and all disposed in studied and uncomfortable attitudes in their carriage, and all looming up in their awe-inspiring imbecility before the snubbed and diminished presentment of that majestic presence whose ministering spirits are the rainbows, whose voice is the thunder, whose awful front is veiled in clouds, who was monarch here dead and forgotten ages before this hackful of small reptiles was deemed temporarily necessary to fill a crack in the world's unnoted myriads, and will still be monarch here ages and decades of ages after they shall have gathered themselves to their blood-relations, the other worms, and been mingled with the unremembering dust.

There is no actual harm in making Niagara a background whereon to display one's marvelous insignificance in a good strong light, but it requires a sort of superhuman self-complacency to enable one to do it.

When you have examined the stupendous Horseshoe Fall till you are satisfied you cannot improve on it, you return to America by the new Suspension Bridge, and follow up the bank to where they exhibit the Cave of the Winds.

Here I followed instructions, and divested myself of all my clothing, and put on a waterproof jacket and overalls. This costume is picturesque, but not beautiful. A guide, similarly dressed, led the way down a flight of winding stairs, which wound and wound, and still kept on winding long after the thing ceased to be a novelty, and then terminated long before it had begun to be a pleasure. We were then well down under the precipice, but still considerably above the level of the river.

We now began to creep along flimsy bridges of a single plank, our persons shielded from destruction by a crazy wooden railing, to which I clung with both hands—not because I was afraid, but because I wanted to. Presently the descent became steeper, and the bridge flimsier, and sprays from the American Fall began to rain down on us in fast increasing sheets that soon became blinding, and after that our progress was mostly in the nature of groping. Now a furious wind began to rush out from behind the waterfall, which seemed determined to sweep us from the bridge, and scatter us on the rocks and among the torrents below. I remarked that I wanted to go home; but it was too late. We were almost under the monstrous wall of water thundering down from above, and speech was in vain in the midst of such a pitiless crash of sound.

In another moment the guide disappeared behind the deluge, and, bewildered by the thunder, driven helplessly by the wind, and smitten by the arrowy tempest of rain, I followed. All was darkness. Such a mad storming, roaring, and bellowing of warring wind and water never crazed my ears before. I bent my head, and seemed to receive the Atlantic on my back. The world seemed going to destruction. I could not see anything, the flood poured down so savagely. I raised my head, with open mouth, and the most of the American cataract went down my throat. If I had sprung a leak now I had been lost. And at this moment I discovered that the bridge had ceased, and we must trust for a foothold to the slippery and precipitous rocks. I never was so scared before and survived it. But we got through at last, and emerged into the open day, where we could stand in front of the laced and frothy and seething world of descending water, and look at it. When I saw how much of it there was, and how fearfully in earnest it was, I was sorry I had gone behind it.

The noble Red Man has always been a friend and darling of mine. I love to read about him in tales and legends and romances. I love to read of his inspired sagacity, and his love of the wild free life of mountain and forest, and his general nobility of character, and his stately metaphorical manner of speech, and his chivalrous love for the dusky maiden, and the picturesque pomp of his dress and accoutrements. Especially the picturesque pomp of his dress and accoutrements. When I found the shops at Niagara Falls full of dainty Indian beadwork, and stunning moccasins, and equally stunning toy figures representing human beings who carried their weapons in holes bored through their arms and bodies, and had feet shaped like a pie, I was filled with emotion. I knew that now, at last, I was going to come face to face with the noble Red Man.

A lady clerk in a shop told me, indeed, that all her grand array of curiosities were made by the Indians, and that they were plenty about the Falls, and that they were friendly, and it would not be dangerous to speak to them. And sure enough, as I approached the bridge leading over to Luna Island, I came upon a noble Son of the Forest sitting under a tree, diligently at work on a bead reticule. He wore a slouch hat and brogans, and had a short black pipe in his mouth. Thus does the baneful contact with our effeminate civilization dilute the picturesque pomp which is so natural to the Indian when far removed from us in his native haunts. I addressed the relic as follows:

"Is the Wawhoo-Wang-Wang of the Whack-a-Whack happy? Does the great Speckled Thunder sigh for the war-path, or is his heart contented with dreaming of the dusky maiden, the Pride of the Forest? Does the mighty Sachem yearn to drink the blood of his enemies, or is he satisfied to make bead reticules for the pappooses of the paleface? Speak, sublime relic of bygone grandeur—venerable ruin, speak!"

The relic said:

"An' is it mesilf, Dennis Hooligan, that ye'd be takin' for a dirty Injin, ye drawlin', lantern-jawed, spider-legged divil! By the piper that played before Moses, I'll ate ye!"

I went away from there.

By and by, in the neighborhood of the Terrapin Tower, I came upon a gentle daughter of the aborigines in fringed and beaded buckskin moccasins and leggins, seated on a bench with her pretty wares about her. She had just carved out a wooden chief that had a strong family resemblance to a clothespin, and was now boring a hole through his abdomen to put his bow through. I hesitated a moment, and then addressed her:

"Is the heart of the forest maiden heavy? Is the Laughing Tadpole lonely? Does she mourn over the extinguished council-fires of her race, and the vanished glory of her ancestors? Or does her sad spirit wander afar toward the hunting-grounds whither her brave Gobbler-of-the-Lightnings is gone? Why is my daughter silent? Has she aught against the paleface stranger?"

The maiden said:

"Faix, an' is Biddy Malone ye dare to be callin' names? Lave this, or I'll shy your lean carcass over the cataract, ye sniveling blaggard!"

I adjourned from there also.

"Confound these Indians!" I said. "They told me they were tame; but, if appearances go for anything, I should say they were all on the warpath."

I made one more attempt to fraternize with them, and only one. I came upon a camp of them gathered in the shade of a great tree, making wampum and moccasins, and addressed them in the language of friendship:

"Noble Red Men, Braves, Grand Sachems, War Chiefs, Squaws, and High Muck-a-Mucks, the paleface from the land of the setting sun greets you! You, Beneficent Polecat—you, Devourer of Mountains— you, Roaring Thundergust—you, Bully Boy with a Glass eye—the pale- face from beyond the great waters greets you all! War and pestilence have thinned your ranks and destroyed your once proud nation. Poker and seven-up, and a vain modern expense for soap, unknown to your glorious ancestors, have depleted your purses. Appropriating, in your simplicity, the property of others has gotten you into trouble. Misrepre- senting facts, in your simple innocence, has damaged your reputation with the soulless usurper. Trading for forty-rod whisky, to enable you to get drunk and happy and tomahawk your families, has played the everlasting mischief with the picturesque pomp of your dress, and here you are, in the broad light of the nineteenth century, gotten up like the ragtag and bobtail of the purlieus of New York. For shame! Re- member your ancestors! Recall their mighty deeds! Remember Uncas! —and Red Jacket!—and Hole in the Day!—and Whoopdedoodledo! Emulate their achievements! Unfurl yourselves under my banner, noble savages, illustrious guttersnipes—"

"Down wid him!" "Scoop the blaggard!" "Burn him!" Hang him!" "Dhround him!"

It was the quickest operation that ever was. I simply saw a sudden flash in the air of clubs, brickbats, fists, bead-baskets, and moccasins— a single flash, and they all appeared to hit me at once, and no two of them in the same place. In the next instant the entire tribe was upon me. They tore half the clothes off me; they broke my arms and legs; they gave me a thump that dented the top of my head till it would hold coffee like a saucer; and, to crown their disgraceful proceedings and add insult to injury, they threw me over the Niagara Falls, and I got wet.

About ninety or a hundred feet from the top, the remains of my vest caught on a projecting rock, and I was almost drowned before I could get loose. I finally fell, and brought up in a world of white foam at the foot of the Fall, whose celled and bubbly masses towered up several inches above my head. Of course I got into the eddy. I sailed round and round in it forty-four times—chasing a chip and gaining on it—each round trip a half-mile—reaching for the same bush on the bank forty- four times, and just exactly missing it by a hair's-breadth every time.

At last a man walked down and sat down close to that bush, and put a pipe in his mouth, and lit a match, and followed me with one eye and kept the other on the match, while he sheltered it in his hands from the wind. Presently a puff of wind blew it out.. The next time I swept around he said:

"Got a match?"

"Yes; in my other vest. Help me out, please."

"Not for Joe."

When I came round again, I said:

"Excuse the seemingly impertinent curiosity of a drowning man, but will you explain this singular conduct of yours?"

"With pleasure. I am the coroner. Don't hurry on my account. I can wait for you. But I wish I had a match."

I said: "Take my place, and I'll go and get you one."

He declined. This lack of confidence on his part created a coldness between us, and from that time forward I avoided him. It was my idea, in case anything happened to me, to so time the occurrence as to throw my custom into the hands of the opposition coroner on the American side.

At last a policeman came along, and arrested me for disturbing the peace by yelling at people on shore for help. The judge fined me, but I had the advantage of him. My money was with my pantaloons, and my pantaloons were with the Indians.

Thus I escaped. I am now lying in a very critical condition. At least I am lying anyway—critical or not critical. I am hurt all over, but I cannot tell the full extent yet, because the doctor is not done taking inventory. He will make out my manifest this evening. However, thus far he thinks only sixteen of my wounds are fatal. I don't mind the others.

Upon regaining my right mind, I said:

"It is an awful savage tribe of Indians that do the beadwork and moccasins for Niagara Falls, doctor. Where are they from?"

"Limerick, my son."

BLOOD ON THE SNOW
From *My Own Story* (*1890*)
JOAQUIN MILLER

Joaquin Miller (1839–1913) became famous for his graphic treatment of Western subject matter and themes. A local colorist, as well as poet, short story writer and playwright, he contributed to the rise of realistic treatment of such themes. "Blood on the Snow" is typical of his attempt to recreate with a strong atmosphere of verisimilitude.

There was a tribe of Indians camped down on the rapid, rocky Klamat River—a sullen, ugly set were they, too: at least so said The Forks. Never social, hardly seeming to notice the whites, who were now thick about them, below them, above them, on the river all around them.

Sometimes we would meet one on the narrow trail; he would gather his skins about him, hide his bow and arrows under their folds, and, without seeming to see any one, would move past us still as a shadow. I do not remember that I ever saw one of these Indians laugh, not even to smile. A hard-featured, half-starved set of savages, of whom the wise men of the camp prophesied no good.

The snow, unusually deep this winter, had driven them all down from the mountains, and they were compelled to camp on the river.

The game, too, had been driven down along with the Indians, but it was of but little use to them. Their bows and arrows did poor competition with the rifles of the whites in the killing of the game. The whites had fairly filled the cabins with deer and elk in their season, got the lion's share, and left the Indians almost destitute.

Another thing that made it rather more hard on the Indians than anything else, was the utter failure of the annual run of salmon the summer before, on account of the muddy water. The Klamat, which had poured from the mountain lakes to the sea as clear as glass, was now made muddy and turbid from the miners washing for gold on its banks and tributaries. The trout turned on their sides and died; the salmon from the sea came in but rarely on account of this; and what few did come were pretty safe from the spears of the Indians, because of the colored water; so that the supply, which was more than all others their bread and their meat, was entirely cut off. . . .

What made matters worse, there was a set of men, low men, of the lowest type, who would hang around those lodges at night, give the Indians whisky of the vilest sort, debauch their women, and cheat the men out of their skins and bows and arrows.

Perhaps there was a grim sort of philosophy in the red man so disposing of his bows and arrows now that the game was gone and they were of no further use. Sold them for bread for his starving babes, maybe. How many tragedies are hidden here? How many tales of devotion, self-denial, and sacrifice, as true as the white man ever lived, as pure, and brave, and beautiful as ever gave tongue to eloquence or pen to song, sleep here with the dust of these sad and silent people on the bank of the stormy river!

In this condition of things, about mid-winter, when the snow was deep and crusted stiff, and all nature seemed dead and buried in a ruffled shroud, there was a murder. The Indians had broken out! The prophesied massacre had begun!

Killed by the Indians! It swept like a telegram through the camp. Confused and incoherent, it is true, but it gathered force and form as the tale flew on from tongue to tongue, until it assumed a frightful shape.

A man had been killed by the Indians down at the rancheria. Not much of a man, it is true.

Killed, too, down in the Indian camp when he should have been in bed, or at home, or at least in company with his kind.

All this made the miners hesitate a bit as they hurriedly gathered in at The Forks, with their long Kentucky rifles, their pistols capped and primed, and bowie-knives in their belts.

But as the gathering storm that was to sweep the Indians from the earth took shape and form, these honest men stood out in little knots, leaning on their rifles in the streets, and gravely questioned whether, all things considered, the death of the "Chicken," for that was the dead man's name, was sufficient cause for interference.

To their eternal credit these men mainly decided that it was not, and two by two they turned away, went back to their cabins, hung their rifles up on the rack, and turned their thoughts to their own affairs.

But the hangers-on about the town were terribly enraged. "A man has been killed!" they proclaimed aloud. "A man has been murdered by the savages!! We shall all be massacred! butchered! burnt!!"

In one of the saloons where men were wont to meet at night, have stag-dances, and drink lightening, a short, important man, with the print of a glass-tumbler cut above his eye, arose and made a speech.

"Fellow-miners [he had never touched a pick in his life], I am ready to die for me country! [He was an Irishman sent out to Sydney at the Crown's expense.] What have I to live for? [Nothing whatever, as far as any one could tell.] Fellow-miners, a man has been kilt by the treacherous savages—kilt in cold blood! Fellow-miners, let us advance upon the inemy. Let us—let us—fellow-miners, let us take a drink and advance upon the inemy."

"Range around me. Rally to the bar and take a drink, every man of you, at me own ixpense."

The barkeeper, who was also proprietor of the place, a man not much above the type of the speaker, ventured a mild remonstrance at this wholesale generosity; but the pistol, flourished in a very suggestive way, settled the matter, and, with something of a groan, he set his decanters to the crowd, and became a bankrupt.

This was the beginning; they passed from saloon to saloon, or, rather, from door to door; the short, stout Irishman making speeches, and the mob gathering force and arms as it went, and then, wild with drink and excitement, moved down upon the Indians, some miles away on the bank of the river.

"Come," said the Prince to me, as they passed out of town, "let us see this through. Here will be blood. We will see from the hill overlooking the camp. I hope the Indians are armed—hope to God they are 'heeled,' and that they will receive the wretches warmly as they deserve."

Maybe his own wretchedness had something to do with his wrath; but I think not. I should rather say that, had he been in strength and spirits, and had his pistols, which had long since been disposed of for bread, he had met this mob face to face, and sent it back to town.

We followed not far behind the crowd of fifty or sixty men armed with pistols, rifles, knives, and hatchets.

The trail led to a little point overlooking the bar on which the Indian huts were huddled.

The river made a bend about there. It ground and boiled in a crescent blocked with running ice and snow. The Indians were out in the extreme curve of a horse-shoe made by the river, and we advanced from without. They were in a net. They had only a choice of deaths; death by drowning, or death at the hands of their hereditary foe.

It was nearly night; cold and sharp the wind blew up the river, and the snow flew around like feathers. Not an Indian to be seen. The thin, blue smoke came slowly up, as if afraid to leave the wigwams, and the traditional, everwatchful and wakeful Indian dog was not to be seen or heard. The men hurried down upon the camp, spreading out upon the horse-shoe as they advanced in a run.

"Stop here," said the Prince; and we stood from the wind behind a boulder that stood, tall as a cabin, upon the bar. The crowd advanced to within half a pistol shot, and gave a shout as they drew and leveled their arms. Old squaws came out—bang! bang! bang! shot after shot, and they were pierced and fell, or turned to run.

The whites, yelling, howling, screaming, were now among the lodges, shooting down at arm's length man, woman, or child. Some attempted the river, I should say, for I afterward saw streams of blood upon the ice, but not one escaped; nor was a hand raised in defense. It was all done in a little time. Instantly, as the shots and shouts began, we two advanced, we rushed into the camp, and when we reached the spot, only now and then a shot was heard within a lodge, dispatching a wounded man or woman.

The few surviving children—for nearly all had been starved to death —had taken refuge under skins and under lodges overthrown, hidden away as little kittens will hide just old enough to spit and hiss, and hide when they first see the face of man. These were now dragged forth and shot. Not all these men who made this mob, bad as they were, did this—only a few; but enough to leave, as far as they could, no living thing.

The babies did not scream. Not a wail, not a sound. The murdered men and women, in the few minutes that the breath took leave, did not even groan.

As we came up a man named "Shon"—at least, that was all the name I knew for him—held up a baby by the leg, a naked, bony little thing, which he had dragged from under a lodge—held it up with one hand, and with the other blew its head to pieces with his pistol.

I must stop here to say that this man Shon soon left camp, and was afterward hung by the Vigilance Committee near Lewiston, Idaho Territory; that he whined for his life like a puppy, and he died like a coward he was. I chronicle this fact with a feeling of delight. . . .

This man threw down the body of the child among the dead, and rushed across to where a pair of ruffians had dragged up another, a little girl, naked, bony, thin as a shadow, starved into a ghost. He caught her by the hair with a howl of delight, placed the pistol to her head, and turned around to point the muzzle out of range of his companions who stood around on the other side.

The child did not cry—she did not even flinch. Perhaps she did not know what it meant; but I should rather believe she had seen so much of death there, so much misery, the steady, silent work of the monster famine through the village day after day that she did not care. I saw her face; it did not even wince. Her lips were thin and fixed, and firm as iron.

The villain, having turned her around, now lifted his arm, cocked the pistol, and—

"Stop that! Stop that, or die! You damned assassin, let go that child, or I will pitch you neck and crop into the Klamat."

The Prince had him by the throat with one hand, and with the other he wrested the pistol from his grasp and threw it into the river. The Prince had not even so much as a knife. The man did not know this, nor did the Prince care, or he had not thrown away the weapon he wrung from his hand. The Prince pushed the child behind him, and advanced toward the short, fat Sydney convict, who had turned, pistol in hand, in his direction.

"Keep your distance, or I will send you to hell across lots in a second."

The man turned away cowed and baffled. He had looked in the Prince's face, and seen his master.

As for myself, I was not only helpless, but, as was always the case on similar occasions, stupid, awkward, speechless. I went up to the little girl, however, got a robe out of one of the lodges—for they had not yet set fire to the village—and put it around her naked little body. After that, as I moved about among the dead, or stepped aside to the river to see the streams of blood on the snow and ice, she followed close as a shadow behind me, but said nothing.

Suddenly there was a sharp yell, a volley of oaths, exclamations, a scuffle, and blows.

"Scalp him! Scalp him! the little savage! Scalp him and throw him in the river!"

From out of the piles of dead somewhere, no one could tell exactly where or when, an apparition had sprung up—a naked little Indian boy, that might have been all the way from twelve to twenty, armed with a knotted war-club, and had fallen upon his foes like a fury.

The poor little hero, starved into a shadow, stood little show there, though he had been a very Hercules in courage. He was felled almost instantly by kicks and blows; and the very number of his enemies saved his life, for they could neither shoot nor stab him with safety, as they crowded and crushed around him.

How or why he was finally spared, was always a marvel. Quite likely the example of the Prince had moved some of the men to more humanity.

When the crowd that had formed a knot about him had broken up, and I first got sight of him, he was sitting on a stone with his hands between his naked legs, and blood dripping from his long hair, which fell down in strings over his forehead. He had been stunned by a grazing shot, no doubt, and had fallen among the first. He came up to his work, though, like a man, when his senses returned, and, without counting the chances, lifted his two hands to do with all his might the thing he had been taught.

Valor, such valor as that, is not a cheap or common thing. It is rare enough to be respected even by the worst of men. It is only the coward who affects to despise such courage.

The boy sat there on the stone as the village burned, the smoke from burning skins, the wild-rye straw, willow-baskets and Indian robes, ascended, and a smell of burning bodies went up to the Indians' God and the God of us all, and no one said nay, and no one approached him; the men looked at him from under their slouched hats as they moved around, but said nothing.

I pitied him. God knows I pitied him. I was a boy myself, alone, helpless, in an army of strong and unsympathetic men. I would have gone up and put my arms about the wild and splendid little savage, bloody and desperate as he was, so lonely now, so intimate with death, so pitiful! if I had dared, dared the reproach of men-brutes.

There was a sort of nobility about him; his recklessness, his desire to die, lifting his little arms against an army of strong and reckless men, his proud and defiant courage, that made me feel at once that he was above me, stronger, somehow better, than I. Still, he was a boy, and I was a boy—the only boys in the camp, and my heart went out, strong and true, toward him.

The work of destruction was now too complete. There was not found another living thing—nothing but two or three Indians that had been shot and shot, and yet seemed determined never to die, that lay in the bloody snow down toward the rim of the river.

Naked nearly, they were, and only skeletons, with the longest and blackest hair tangled and tossed, and blown in strips and strings, or in clouds out on the white and the blood-red snow, or down their tawny backs, or over their bony breasts, about their dusky forms, fierce and unconquered, with the bloodless lips set close, and blue, and cold, and firm, like steel.

The dead lay around us, piled up in places, limbs twisted with limbs in the wrestle with death; a mother embracing her boy here; an arm thrown around a neck there; as if these wild people could love as well as die.

In the village, some of the white men claimed to have found something that had been stolen. I have no idea there is any truth in it. I wish there was; then there might be some shadow of excuse for all the murders that made up this cruel tragedy, all of which is, I believe, literally true; truer than nine-tenths of the history and official reports written, wherein these people are mentioned; and I stand ready to give names, dates, and detail to all whom it may concern.

Let me not here be misunderstood. An Indian is no better than a white man. If he sins let him suffer. But I do protest against this custom of making up a case—this custom of deciding the case against him in favor of the white man, forever, on the evidence of the white man only; even though that custom be, in the language of the law, so old "that the memory of man runneth not to the contrary."

The white man and red man are much alike, with one great difference, which you must and will set down to the advantage of the latter.

The Indian has no desire for fortune; he has no wish in his wild state to accumulate wealth; and it is in his wild state that he must be judged, for it is in this condition that he is said to sin. If "money is the root of all evil," as Solomon hath it, then the Indian has not that evil, or that root of evil, or any desire for it.

It is the white man's monopoly. If an Indian love you, trusts you, or believes in you at all, he will serve you, guide you through the country, follow you to battle, fight for you, he and all his sons and kindred, and never think of the pay or profit. He would despise it if offered, beyond some presents, some tokens of remembrance, decorations, or simplest articles of use.

Again, I do vehemently protest against taking the testimony of border Indians or any Indians with whom the white man comes in constant contact, and to whom he has taught the use of money and the art of lying.

And most particularly I do protest against taking these Indians— renegades—who affiliate, mix and strike hands with the whites, as representative Indians. Better take our own "camp followers" as respectable and representative soldiers.

When you reflect that for centuries the Indians in almost every lodge on the continent, at almost every council, have talked of the whites and their aggressions, and of these things chiefly, and always with that bitterness which characterizes people who look at and see only one side of the case, then you may come to understand, a little, their eternal hatred of their hereditary enemy—how deeply seated this is, how it has become a part of their nature, and, above all, how low, fallen, and how unlike a true Indian one must be who leaves his retreating tribe and lingers in a drunken and debauched fellowship with the whites, losing all his virtues, and taking on all the vices of his enemy.

The true Indian retires before the white man's face to the forest and to the mountain tops. It is very true he leaves a surf, a sort of kelp and driftwood, and trash, the scum, the idlers, and the cowards and prostitutes of his tribe, as the sea leaves weeds and drift and kelp. But the true Indian is to be found only in his fastnesses or on the heights, gun in hand.

THE
BLACK
MAN

From
TWENTY-TWO YEARS A SLAVE (1857)
AUSTIN STEWARD

Negro anti-slavery leader Austin Steward (1794–1860) escaped from slavery into Canada and became president of Wilberforce Colony, a colony of ex-slaves and sympathizers. His autobiography was typical of the anti-slavery memoirs of ex-slaves in its emphasis upon the dehumanizing effects of the institution.

I was born in Prince William County, Virginia. At seven years of age, I found myself a slave on the plantation of Capt. William Helm. Our family consisted of my father and mother—whose names were Robert and Susan Steward—a sister, Mary, and myself. As was the usual custom, we lived in a small cabin, built of rough boards, with a floor of earth, and small openings in the sides of the cabin were substituted for windows. The chimney was built of sticks and mud; the door, of rough boards; and the whole was put together in the rudest possible manner. As to the furniture of this rude dwelling, it was procured by the slaves themselves, who were occasionally permitted to earn a little money after their day's toil was done. I never knew Capt. H. to furnish his slaves with household utensils of any description.

The amount of provision given out in the plantation per week, was invariably one peck of corn or meal for each slave. This allowance was given in meal when it could be obtained; when it could not, they received corn, which they pounded in mortars after they returned from their labor in the field. The slaves on our plantation were provided with very little meat. In addition to the peck of corn or meal, they were allowed a little salt and a few herrings. If they wished for more, they were obliged to earn it by over-work. They were permitted to cultivate small gardens, and were thereby enabled to provide themselves with many trifling conveniences. But these gardens were only allowed to some of the more industrious. Capt. Helm allowed his slaves a small quantity of meat during harvest time, but when the harvest was over they were obliged to fall back on the old allowance.

It was usual for men and women to work side by side on our plantation; and in many kinds of work, the women were compelled to do as much as the men. Capt. H. employed an overseer, whose business it was to look after each slave in the field, and see that he performed his task. The overseer always went around with a whip, about nine feet long, made of the toughest kind of cowhide, the but-end of which was loaded with lead, and was about four or five inches in circumference, running to a point at the opposite extremity. This made a dreadful instrument of torture, and, when in the hands of a cruel overseer, it was truly fearful. With it, the skin of an ox or a horse could be cut through. Hence, it was no uncommon thing to see the poor slaves with their backs mangled in a most horrible manner. Our overseer, thus armed with his cowhide, and with a large bull-dog behind him, followed the slaves all day; and, if one of them fell in the rear from any cause, this cruel weapon was plied with terrible force. He would strike the dog one blow and the slave another, in order to keep the former from tearing the delinquent slave in pieces,—such was the ferocity of his canine attendant.

It was the rule for the slaves to rise and be ready for their task by sun-rise, on the blowing of a horn or conch-shell; and woe be to the unfortunate, who was not in the field at the time appointed, which was in thirty minutes from the first sounding of the horn. I have heard the poor creatures beg for their lives, of the inhuman overseer, to desist from his cruel punishment. Hence, they were usually found in the field "betimes in the morning," (to use an old Virginia phrase), where they worked until nine o'clock. They were then allowed thirty minutes to eat their morning meal, which consisted of a little bread. At a given signal, all hands were compelled to return to their work. They toiled until noon, when they were permitted to take their breakfast, which corresponds to our dinner.

On our plantation, it was the usual practice to have one of the old slaves set apart to do the cooking. All the field hands were required to give into the hands of the cook a certain portion of their weekly allowance, either in dough or meal, which was prepared in the following manner. The cook made a hot fire and rolled up each person's portion in some cabbage leaves, when they could be obtained, and placed it in a hole in the ashes, carefully covered with the same, where it remained until done. Bread baked in this way is very sweet and good. But cabbage leaves could not always be obtained. When this was the case, the bread was little better than a mixture of dough and ashes, which was not very palatable. The time allowed for breakfast, was one hour. At the signal, all hands were obliged to resume their toil. The overseer was always on hand to attend to all delinquents, who never failed to feel the blows of his heavy whip.

The usual mode of punishing the poor slaves was, to make them take off their clothes to the bare back, and then tie their hands before them with a rope, pass the end of the rope over a beam, and draw them up till they stood on the tips of their toes. Sometimes they tied their legs together and placed a rail between. Thus prepared, the overseer proceeded to punish the poor, helpless victim. Thirty-nine was the number of lashes ordinarily inflicted for the most trifling offence.

Who can imagine a position more painful? Oh, who, with feelings of common humanity, could look quietly on such torture? Who could remain unmoved, to see a fellow-creature thus tied, unable to move or to raise a hand in his own defence; scourged on his bare back, with a cowhide, until the blood flows in streams from his quivering flesh? And for what? Often for the most trifling fault; and, as sometimes occurs, because a mere whim or caprice of his brutal overseer demands it. Pale with passion, his eyes flashing and his stalwart frame trembling with rage, like some volcano, just ready to belch forth its fiery contents, and, in all its might and fury, spread death and destruction all around, he continues to wield the bloody lash on the broken flesh of the poor, pleading slave, until his arm grows weary, or he sinks down, utterly exhausted, on the very spot where already stand the pools of blood which his cruelty has drawn from the mangled body of his helpless victim, and within the hearing of those agonized groans and feeble cries of "Oh do, Massa! Oh do, Massa! Do, Lord, have mercy! Oh, Lord, have mercy!" &c.

Nor is this cruel punishment inflicted on the bare backs of the male portion of slaves only. Oh no! The slave husband must submit without a murmur, to see the form of his cherished, but wretched wife, not only exposed to the rude gaze of a beastly tyrant, but he must unresistingly see the heavy cowhide descend upon her shrinking flesh, and her man- acled limbs writhe in inexpressible torture, while her piteous cries for help ring through his ears unanswered. The wild throbbing of his heart must be suppressed, and his righteous indignation find no voice, in the presence of the human monster who holds dominion over him.

After the infuriated and heartless overseer had satiated his thirst for vengeance, on the disobedient or delinquent slave, he was untied, and left to crawl away as best he could; sometimes on his hands and knees, to his lonely and dilapidated cabin, where, stretched upon the cold earth, he lay weak and bleeding and often faint from the loss of blood, without a friend who dare administer to his necessities, and groaning in the agony of his crushed spirit. In his cabin, which was not as good as many of our stables at the North, he might lie for weeks before re- covering sufficient strength to resume the labor imposed upon him, and all this time without a bed or bed clothing, or any of the necessaries considered so essential to the sick.

Perhaps some of his fellow-slaves might come and bathe his wounds in warm water, to prevent his clothing from tearing open his flesh anew, and thus make the second suffering well nigh equal to the first; or they might from their scanty store bring him such food as they could spare, to keep him from suffering hunger, and offer their sym- pathy, and then drag their own weary bodies to their place of rest, after their daily task was finished.

Oh, you who have hearts to feel; you who have kind friends around you, in sickness and in sorrow, think of the sufferings of the helpless, destitute, and down-trodden slave. Has sickness laid its withering hand upon you, or disappointment blasted your fairest earthly prospects, still, the outgushings of an affectionate heart are not denied you, and you may look forward with hope to a bright future. Such a hope seldom animates the heart of the poor slave. He toils on, in his unrequited labor, looking only to the grave to find a quiet resting place, where he will be free from the oppressor.

From
NARRATIVE OF THE LIFE OF FREDERICK DOUGLASS (1845)
FREDERICK DOUGLASS

Negro abolitionist Frederick Douglass (1817–1895) was born a slave and escaped to New England in 1838. In 1841 he became an agent of the Massachusetts Anti-Slavery Society, and four years later he published his narrative, a powerful anti-slavery document. During and after the Civil War, he was a civil rights leader and Republican office holder.

If at any one time of my life more than another, I was made to drink the bitterest dregs of slavery, that time was during the first six months of my stay with Mr. Covey. We were worked in all weathers. It was never too hot or too cold; it could never rain, blow, hail, or snow, too hard for us to work in the field. Work, work, work, was scarcely more the order of the day than of the night. The longest days were too short for him, and the shortest nights too long for him. I was somewhat un-manageable when I first went there, but a few months of this discipline tamed me. Mr. Covey succeeded in breaking me. I was broken in body, soul, and spirit. My natural elasticity was crushed, my intellect lan-guished, the disposition to read departed, the cheerful spark that lin-gered about my eye died; the dark night of slavery closed in upon me; and behold a man transformed into a brute!

Sunday was my only leisure time. I spent this in a sort of beast-like stupor, between sleep and wake, under some large tree. At times I would rise up, a flash of energetic freedom would dart through my soul, accompanied with a faint beam of hope, that flickered for a mo-ment, and then vanished. I sank down again, mourning over my wretched condition. I was sometimes prompted to take my life, and that of Covey, but was prevented by a combination of hope and fear. My sufferings on this plantation seem now like a dream rather than a stern reality.

Our house stood within a few rods of the Chesapeake Bay, whose broad bosom was ever white with sails from every quarter of the habitable globe. Those beautiful vessels, robed in purest white, so delightful to the eye of freemen, were to me so many shrouded ghosts, to terrify and torment me with thoughts of my wretched condition. I have often, in the deep stillness of a summer's Sabbath, stood all alone upon the lofty banks of that noble bay, and traced, with saddened heart and tearful eye, the countless number of sails moving off to the mighty ocean. The sight of these always affected me powerfully. My thoughts would compel utterance; and there, with no audience but the Almighty, I would pour out my soul's complaint, in my rude way, with an apostrophe to the moving multitude of ships:—

"You are loosed from your moorings, and are free; I am fast in my chains, and am a slave! You move merrily before the gentle gale, and I sadly before the bloody whip! You are freedom's swift-winged angels. that fly round the world; I am confined in bands of iron! O that I were free! O, that I were on one of your gallant decks, and under your protecting wing! Alas! betwixt me and you, the turbid waters roll. Go on, go on. O that I could also go! Could I but swim! If I could fly! O, why was I born a man, of whom to make a brute! The glad ship is gone; she hides in the dim distance. I am left in the hottest hell of unending slavery. O God, save me! God, deliver me! Let me be free! Is there any God? Why am I a slave? I will run away. I will not stand it. Get caught, or get clear, I'll try it. I had as well die with ague as the fever. I have only one life to lose. I had as well be killed running as die standing. Only think of it; one hundred miles straight north, and I am free! Try it? Yes! God helping me, I will. It cannot be that I shall live and die a slave. I will take to the water. This very bay shall yet bear me into freedom. The steamboats steered in a north-east course from North Point. I will do the same; and when I get to the head of the bay, I will turn my canoe adrift, and walk straight through Delaware into Pennsylvania. When I get there, I shall not be required to have a pass; I can travel without being disturbed. Let but the first opportunity offer, and, come what will, I am off. Meanwhile, I will try to bear up under the yoke. I am not the only slave in the world. Why should I fret? I can bear as much as any of them. Besides, I am but a boy, and all boys are bound to some one. It may be that my misery in slavery will only increase my happiness when I get free. There is a better day coming."

Thus I used to think, and thus I used to speak to myself; goaded almost to madness at one moment, and at the next reconciling myself to my wretched lot.

I have already intimated that my condition was much worse, during the first six months of my stay at Mr. Covey's, than in the last six. The circumstances leading to the change in Mr. Covey's course toward me form an epoch in my humble history. You have seen how a man was made a slave; you shall see how a slave was made a man. On one of the hottest days of the month of August, 1833, Bill Smith, William Hughes, a slave named Eli, and myself, were engaged in fanning wheat. Hughes was clearing the fanned wheat from before the fan. Eli was turning, Smith was feeding, and I was carrying wheat to the fan. The work was simple, requiring strength rather than intellect; yet, to one entirely unused to such work, it came very hard. About three o'clock of that day, I broke down; my strength failed me; I was seized with a violent aching of the head, attended with extreme dizziness; I trembled in every limb. Finding what was coming, I nerved myself up, feeling it would never do to stop work. I stood as long as I could stagger to the hopper with grain. When I could stand no longer, I fell, and felt as if held down by an immense weight. The fan of course stopped; every one had his own work to do; and no one could do the work of the other, and have his own go on at the same time.

Mr. Covey was at the house, about one hundred yards from the treading-yard where we were fanning. On hearing the fan stop, he left immediately, and came to the spot where we were. He hastily inquired what the matter was. Bill answered that I was sick, and there was no one to bring wheat to the fan. I had by this time crawled away under the side of the post and rail-fence by which the yard was enclosed, hoping to find relief by getting out of the sun. He then asked where I was. He was told by one of the hands. He came to the spot, and, after looking at me awhile, asked me what was the matter. I told him as well as I could, for I scarce had strength to speak. He then gave me a savage kick in the side, and told me to get up. I tried to do so, but fell back in the attempt. He gave me another kick, and again told me to rise. I again tried, and succeeded in gaining my feet; but, stooping to get the tub with which I was feeding the fan, I again staggered and fell. While down in this situation, Mr. Covey took up the hickory slat with which Hughes had been striking off the half-bushel measure, and with it gave me a heavy blow upon the head, making a large wound, and the blood ran freely; and with this again told me to get up. I made no effort to comply, having now made up my mind to let him do his worst. In a short time after receiving this blow, my head grew better. Mr. Covey had now left me to my fate. At this moment I resolved, for the first time, to go to my master, enter a complaint, and ask his protection. In order to do this, I must that afternoon walk seven miles; and this, under the circumstances, was truly a severe undertaking. I was exceedingly feeble; made so as much by the kicks and blows which I received, as by the severe fit of sickness to which I had been subjected. I, however, watched my chance, while Covey was looking in an opposite direction, and started for St. Michael's. I succeeded in getting a considerable distance on my way to the woods, when Covey discovered me, and called after me to come back, threatening what he would do if I did not come. I disregarded both his calls and his threats, and made my way to the woods as fast as my feeble state would allow; and thinking I might be overhauled by him if I kept the road, I walked through the woods, keeping far enough from the road to avoid detection, and near enough to prevent losing my way. I had not gone far before my little strength again failed me. I could go no farther. I fell down, and lay for a considerable time. The blood was yet oozing from the wound on my head. For a time I thought I should bleed to death; and think now that I should have done so, but that the blood so matted my hair as to stop the wound. After lying there about three quarters of an hour, I nerved myself up again, and started on my way, through bogs and briers, barefooted and bareheaded, tearing my feet sometimes at nearly every step; and after a journey of about seven miles, occupying some five hours to perform it, I arrived at master's store. I then presented an appearance enough to affect any but a heart of iron. From the crown of my head to my feet, I was covered with blood. My hair was all clotted with dust and blood; my shirt was stiff with blood. My legs and feet were torn in sundry places with briers and thorns, and were also covered with blood. I suppose I looked like a man who had escaped a den of wild beasts, and barely escaped them. In this state I appeared before my master, humbly entreating him to interpose his authority for my protection. I told him all the circumstances as well as I could, and it seemed, as I spoke, at times to affect him. He would then walk the floor, and seek to justify Covey by saying he expected I deserved it. He asked me what I wanted. I told him, to let me get a new home; that as sure as I lived with Mr. Covey again, I should live with but to die with him; that Covey would surely kill me; he was in a fair way for it. Master Thomas ridiculed the idea that there was any danger of Mr. Covey's killing me, and said that he knew Mr. Covey; that he was a good man, and that he could not think of taking me from him; that, should he do so, he would lose the whole year's wages; that I belonged to Mr. Covey for one year, and that I must go back to him, come what might; and that I must not trouble him with any more stories, or that he would himself *get hold of me.* After threatening me thus, he gave me a very large dose of salts, telling me that I might remain in St. Michael's that night, (it being quite late,) but that I must be off back to Mr. Covey's early in the morning; and that if I did not, he would *get hold of me,* which meant that he would whip me. I remained all night, and, according to his orders, I started off to Covey's in the morning, (Saturday morning,) wearied in body and broken in spirit. I got no supper that night, or breakfast that morning. I reached

Covey's about nine o'clock; and just as I was getting over the fence that divided Mrs. Kemp's fields from ours, out ran Covey with his cowskin, to give me another whipping. Before he could reach me, I succeeded in getting to the cornfield; and as the corn was very high, it afforded me the means of hiding. He seemed very angry, and searched for me a long time. My behavior was altogether unaccountable. He finally gave up the chase, thinking, I suppose, that I must come home for something to eat; he would give himself no futher trouble in looking for me. I spent that day mostly in the woods, having the alternative before me,—to go home and be whipped to death, or stay in the woods and be starved to death. That night, I fell in with Sandy Jenkins, a slave with whom I was somewhat acquainted. Sandy had a free wife who lived about four miles from Mr. Covey's; and it being Saturday, he was on his way to see her. I told him my circumstances, and he very kindly invited me to go home with him. I went home with him, and talked this whole matter over, and got his advice as to what course it was best for me to pursue. I found Sandy an old adviser. He told me, with great solemnity, I must go back to Covey; but that before I went, I must go with him into another part of the woods, where there was a certain *root*, which, if I would take some of it with me, carrying it *always on my right side*, would render it impossible for Mr. Covey, or any other white man, to whip me. He said he had carried it for years; and since he had done so, he had never received a blow, and never expected to while he carried it. I at first rejected the idea, that the simple carrying of a root in my pocket would have any such effect as he had said, and was not disposed to take it; but Sandy impressed the necessity with much earnestness, telling me it could do no harm, if it did no good. To please him, I at length took the root, and, according to his direction, carried it upon my right side. This was Sunday morning. I immediately started for home; and upon entering the yard gate, out came Mr. Covey on his way to meeting. He spoke to me very kindly, bade me drive the pigs from a lot near by, and passed on towards the church. Now, this singular conduct of Mr. Covey really made me begin to think that there was something in the *root* which Sandy had given me; and had it been on any other day than Sunday, I could have attributed the conduct to no other cause than the influence of that root; and as it was, I was half inclined to think the *root* to be something more than I at first had taken it to be. All went well till Monday morning. On this morning, the virtue of the *root* was fully tested. Long before daylight, I was called to go and rub, curry, and feed, the horses. I obeyed, and was glad to obey. But whilst thus engaged, whilst in the act of throwing down some blades from the loft, Mr. Covey entered the stable with a long rope; and just as I was half out of the loft, he caught hold of my legs, and was about tying me. As soon as I found what he was up to, I gave a sudden spring, and as I did so, he holding to my legs, I was brought sprawling on the stable floor. Mr. Covey seemed now to think he had me, and could do what he pleased; but at this moment—from whence came the spirit I don't know—I resolved to fight; and, suiting my action to the resolution, I seized Covey hard by the throat; and as I did so, I rose. He held on to me, and I to him. My resistance was so entirely unexpected, that Covey seemed taken all aback. He trembled like a leaf. This gave me assurance, and I held him uneasy, causing the blood to run where I touched him with the ends of my fingers. Mr. Covey soon called out to Hughes for help. Hughes came, and, while Covey held me, attempted to tie my right hand. While he was in the act of doing so, I watched my chance, and gave him a heavy kick close under the ribs. This kick fairly sickened Hughes, so that he left me in the hands of Mr. Covey. This kick had the effect of not only weakening Hughes, but Covey also. When he saw Hughes bending over with pain, his courage quailed. He asked me if I meant to persist in my resistance. I told him I did, come what might; that he had used me like a brute for six months, and that I was determined to be used so no longer. With that, he strove to drag me to a stick that was lying just out of the stable door. He meant to knock me down. But just as he was leaning over to get the stick, I seized him with both hands by his collar, and brought him by a sudden snatch to the ground. By this time, Bill came. Covey called upon him for assistance. Bill wanted to know what he could do. Covey said, "Take hold of him, take hold of him!" Bill said his master hired him out to work, and not to help to whip me; so he left Covey and myself to fight our own battle out. We were at it for nearly two hours. Covey at length let me go, puffing and blowing at a great rate, saying that if I had not resisted, he would not have whipped me half so much. The truth was, that he had not whipped me at all. I considered him as getting entirely the worst end of the bargain; for he had drawn no blood from me, but I had from him. The whole six months afterwards, that I spent with Mr. Covey, he never laid the weight of his finger upon me in anger. He would occasionally say, he didn't want to get hold of me again. "No," thought I, "you need not; for you will come off worse than you did before."

This battle with Mr. Covey was the turning-point in my career as a slave. It rekindled the few expiring embers of freedom, and revived within me a sense of my own manhood. It recalled the departed self-confidence, and inspired me again with a determination to be free. The gratification afforded by the triumph was a full compensation for whatever else might follow, even death itself. He only can understand the deep satisfaction which I experienced, who has himself repelled by force the bloody arm of slavery. I felt as I never felt before. It was a glorious resurrection, from the tomb of slavery, to the heaven of freedom. My long-crushed spirit rose, cowardice departed, bold defiance took its place; and I now resolved that, however long I might remain a slave in form, the day had passed forever when I could be a slave in fact. I did not hesitate to let it be known of me, that the white man who expected to succeed in whipping, must also succeed in killing me.

From this time I was never again what might be called fairly whipped, though I remained a slave four years afterwards. I had several fights, but was never whipped.

It was for a long time a matter of surprise to me why Mr. Covey did not immediately have me taken by the constable to the whipping-post, and there regularly whipped for the crime of raising my hand against a white man in defence of myself. And the only explanation I can now think of does not entirely satisfy me; but such as it is, I will give it. Mr. Covey enjoyed the most unbounded reputation for being a first-rate overseer and negro-breaker. It was of considerable importance to him. That reputation was at stake; and had he sent me—a boy about sixteen years old—to the public whipping-post, his reputation would have been lost; so, to save his reputation, he suffered me to go unpunished.

My term of actual service to Mr. Edward Covey ended on Christmas day, 1833. The days between Christmas and New Year's day are allowed as holidays; and, accordingly, we were not required to perform any labor, more than to feed and take care of the stock. This time we regarded as our own, by the grace of our masters; and we therefore used or abused it nearly as we pleased. Those of us who had families at a distance, were generally allowed to spend the whole six days in their society. This time, however, was spent in various ways. The staid, sober, thinking and industrious ones of our number would employ themselves in making corn-brooms, mats, horse-collars, and baskets; and another class of us would spend the time in hunting opossums, hares, and coons. But by far the larger part engaged in such sports and merriments as playing ball, wrestling, running foot-races, fiddling, dancing, and drinking whisky.

NEGRO SLAVERY
From *Sociology for the South* (*1854*)
GEORGE FITZHUGH

George Fitzhugh (1806–1881) was a Southern social theorist and sup-
porter of socialist experimentation. Maintaining that laissez faire *capi-*
talism was a failure and that Southern chattel slavery provided an ideal
social and economic structure in which all labor and produce are shared
according to needs, he introduced the "politive good" interpretation of
the slave system. Sociology for the South *provided major support for*
the Southern defense of slavery.

We have already stated that we should not attempt to introduce any
new theories of government and of society, but merely try to justify old
ones, so far as we could deduce such theories from ancient and almost
universal practices. Now it has been the practice in all countries and in
all ages, in some degree, to accommodate the amount and character of
government control to the wants, intelligence, and moral capacities of
the nations or individuals to be governed. A highly moral and intellectual people, like the free citizens of ancient Athens, are best governed
by a democracy. For a less moral and intellectual one, a limited and
constitutional monarchy will answer. For a people either very ignorant
or very wicked, nothing short of military despotism will suffice. So
among individuals, the most moral and well-informed members of
society require no other government than law. They are capable of
reading and understanding the law, and have sufficient self-control and
virtuous disposition to obey it. Children cannot be governed by mere
law; first, because they do not understand it, and secondly, because
they are so much under the influence of impulse, passion and appetite,
that they want sufficient self-control to be deterred or governed by the
distant and doubtful penalties of the law. They must be constantly
controlled by parents or guardians, whose will and orders shall stand
in the place of law for them. Very wicked men must be put into penitentiaries; lunatics into asylums, and the most wild of them into strait-
jackets, just as the most wicked of the sane are manacled with irons;
and idiots must have committees to govern and take care of them. Now,
it is clear the Athenian democracy would not suit a negro nation, nor
will the government of mere law suffice for the individual negro. He is
but a grown up child, and must be governed as a child, not as a lunatic
or criminal. The master occupies towards him the place of parent or
guardian. We shall not dwell on this view, for no one will differ with us
who thinks as we do of the negro's capacity, and we might argue till
dooms-day, in vain, with those who have a high opinion of the negro's
moral and intellectual capacity.

Secondly. The negro is improvident; will not lay up in summer for the wants of winter; will not accumulate in youth for the exigencies of age. He would become an insufferable burden to society. Society has the right to prevent this, and can only do so by subjecting him to domestic slavery. In the last place, the negro race is inferior to the white race, and living in their midst, they would be far outstripped or outwitted in the chase of free competition. Gradual but certain extermination would be their fate. We presume the maddest abolitionist does not think the negro's providence of habits and money-making capacity at all to compare to those of the whites. This defect of character would alone justify enslaving him, if he is to remain here. In Africa or the West Indies, he would become idolatrous, savage and cannibal, or be devoured by savages and cannibals. At the North he would freeze or starve.

We would remind those who deprecate and sympathize with negro slavery, that his slavery here relieves him from a far more cruel slavery in Africa, or from idolatry and cannibalism, and every brutal vice and crime that can disgrace humanity; and that it christianizes, protects, supports and civilizes him; that it governs him far better than free laborers at the North are governed. There, wife-murder has become a mere holiday pastime; and where so many wives are murdered, almost all must be brutally treated. Nay, more: men who kill their wives or treat them brutally, must be ready for all kinds of crime, and the calendar of crime at the North proves the inference to be correct. Negroes never kill their wives. If it be objected that legally they have no wives, then we reply, that in an experience of more than forty years, we never yet heard of a negro man killing a negro woman. Our negroes are not only better off as to physical comfort than free laborers, but their moral condition is better.

But abolish negro slavery, and how much of slavery still remains. Soldiers and sailors in Europe enlist for life; here, for five years. Are they not slaves who have not only sold their liberties, but their lives also? And they are worse treated than domestic slaves. No domestic affection and self-interest extend their ægis over them. No kind mistress, like a guardian angel, provides for them in health, tends them in sickness, and soothes their dying pillow. Wellington at Waterloo was a slave. He was bound to obey, or would, like admiral Byng, have been shot for gross misconduct, and might not, like a common laborer, quit his work at any moment. He had sold his liberty, and might not resign without the consent of his master, the king. The common laborer may quit his work at any moment, whatever his contract; declare that liberty is an alienable right, and leave his employer to redress by a useless suit for damages. The highest and most honorable position on earth was that of the slave Wellington; the lowest, that of the free man who cleaned his boots and fed his hounds. The African cannibal, caught, christianized and enslaved, is as much elevated by slavery as was Wellington. The kind of slavery is adapted to the men enslaved. Wives and apprentices are slaves; not in theory only, but often in fact. Children are slaves to their parents, guardians and teachers. Imprisoned culprits are slaves. Lunatics and idiots are slaves also. Three-fourths of free society are slaves, no better treated, when their wants and capacities are estimated, than negro slaves. The masters in free society, or slave society, if they perform properly their duties, have more cares and less liberty than the slaves themselves. "In the sweat of thy face shalt thou earn thy bread!" made all men slaves, and such all *good men* continue to be.

Negro slavery would be changed immediately to some form of peonage, serfdom or villienage, if the negroes were sufficiently intelligent and provident to manage a farm. No one would have the labor and trouble of management, if his negroes would pay in hires and rents one-half what free tenants pay in rent in Europe. Every negro in the South would be soon liberated, if he would take liberty on the terms that white tenants hold it. The fact that he cannot enjoy liberty on such terms, seems conclusive that he is only fit to be a slave.

But for the assaults of the abolitionists, much would have been done ere this to regulate and improve Southern slavery. Our negro mechanics do not work so hard, have many more privileges and holidays, and are better fed and clothed than field hands, and are yet more valuable to their masters. The slaves of the South are cheated of their rights by the purchase of Northern manufacturers which they could produce. Besides, if we would employ our slaves in the coarser processes of the mechanic arts and manufacturers, such as brick making, getting and hewing timber for ships and houses, iron mining and smelting, coal mining, grading railroads and plank roads, in the manufacture of cotton, tobacco, &c., we would find a vent in new employments for their increase, more humane and more profitable than the vent afforded by new states and territories. The nice and finishing processes of manufactures and mechanics should be reserved for the whites, who only are fitted for them, and thus, by diversifying pursuits and cutting off dependence on the North, we might benefit and advance the interests of our whole population. Exclusive agriculture has depressed and impoverished the South. We will not here dilate on this topic, because we intend to make it the subject of a separate essay. Free trade doctrines, not slavery, have made the South agricultural and dependent, given her a sparse and ignorant population, ruined her cities, and expelled her people.

Would the abolitionists approve of a system of society that set white children free, and remitted them at the age of fourteen, males and females, to all the rights, both as to person and property, which belong to adults? Would it be criminal or praiseworthy to do so? Criminal, of course, Now, are the average of negroes equal in formation, in native intelligence, in prudence or providence, to well-informed white children of fourteen? We who have lived with them for forty years, think not. The competition of the world would be too much for the children. They would be cheated out of their property and debased in their morals. Yet they would meet every where with sympathizing friends of their own color, ready to aid, advise and assist them. The negro would be exposed to the same competition and greater temptations, with no greater ability to contend with them, with these additional difficulties. He would be welcome nowhere; meet with thousands of enemies and no friends. If he went North, the white laborers would kick and cuff him, and drive him out of employment. If he went to Africa, the savages would cook him and eat him. If he went to the West Indies, they would not let him in, or if they did, they would soon make of him a savage and idolater.

We have a further question to ask. If it be right and incumbent to subject children to the authority of parents and guardians, and idiots and lunatics to committees, would it not be equally right and incumbent to give the free negroes masters, until at least they arrive at years of discretion, which very few ever did or will attain? What is the difference between the authority of a parent and of a master? Neither pay wages, and each is entitled to the services of those subject to him. The father may not sell his child forever, but may hire him out till he is twenty-one. The free negro's master may also be restrained from selling. Let him stand *in loco parentis*, and call him papa instead of master. Look closely into slavery, and you will see nothing so hideous in it; or if you do, you will find plenty of it at home in its most hideous form.

The earliest civilization of which history gives account is that of Egypt. The negro was always in contact with that civilization. For four thousand years he has had opportunities of becoming civilized. Like the wild horse, he must be caught, tamed and domesticated. When his subjugation ceases he again runs wild, like the cattle on the Pampas of the South, or the horses on the prairies of the West. His condition in the West Indies proves this.

It is a common remark, that the grand and lasting architectural structures of antiquity were the results of slavery. The mighty and continued association of labor requisite to their construction, when mechanic art was so little advanced, and labor-saving processes unknown, could only have been brought about by a despotic authority, like that of the master over his slaves. It is, however, very remarkable, that whilst in taste and artistic skill the world seems to have been retrograding ever since the decay and abolition of feudalism, in mechanical invention and in great utilitarian operations requiring the wielding of immense capital and much labor, its progress has been unexampled. Is it because capital is more despotic in its authority over free laborers than Roman masters and feudal lords were over their slaves and vassals?

Free society has continued long enough to justify the attempt to generalize its phenomena, and calculate its moral and intellectual influences. It is obvious that, in whatever is purely utilitarian and material, it incites invention and stimulates industry. Benjamin Franklin, as a man and a philosopher, is the best exponent of the working of the system. His sentiments and his philosophy are low, selfish, atheistic and material. They tend directly to make man a mere "featherless biped," well-fed, well-clothed and comfortable, but regardless of his soul as "the beasts that perish."

Since the Reformation the world has as regularly been retrograding in whatever belongs to the departments of genius, taste and art, as it has been progressing in physical science and its application to mechanical construction. Mediæval Italy rivalled if it did not surpass ancient Rome, in poetry, in sculpture, in painting, and many of the fine arts. Gothic architecture reared its monuments of skill and genius throughout Europe, till the 15th century; but Gothic architecture died with the Reformation. The age of Elizabeth was the Augustan age of England. The men who lived then acquired their sentiments in a world not yet deadened and vulgarized by puritanical cant and levelling demagoguism. Since then men have arisen who have been the fashion and the go for a season, but none have appeared whose names will descend to posterity. Liberty and equality made slower advances in France. The age of Louis XIV. was the culminating point of French genius and art. It then shed but a flickering and lurid light. Frenchmen are servile copyists of Roman art, and Rome has no art of her own. She borrowed from Greece; distorted and deteriorated what she borrowed; and France imitates and falls below Roman distortions. The genius of Spain disappeared with Cervantes; and now the world seems to regard nothing as desirable except what will make money and what costs money. There is not a poet, an orator, a sculptor, or painter in the world. The tedious elaboration necessary to all the productions of high art would be ridiculed in this money-making, utilitarian, charlatan age. Nothing now but what is gaudy and costly excites admiration. The public taste is debased.

But fare the worst feature of modern civilization, which is the civilization of free society, remains to be exposed. Whilst labor-saving processes have probably lessened by one half, in the last century, the amount of work needed for comfortable support, the free laborer is compelled by capital and competition to work more than he ever did before, and is less comfortable. The organization of society cheats him of his earnings, and those earnings go to swell the vulgar pomp and pageantry of the ignorant millionaires, who are the only great of the present day. These reflections might seem, at first view, to have little connexion with negro slavery; but it is well for us of the South not to be deceived by the tinsel glare and glitter of free society, and to employ ourselves in doing our duty at home, and studying the past, rather than in insidious rivalry of the expensive pleasures and pursuits of men whose sentiments and whose aims are low, sensual and grovelling.

Human progress consisting in moral and intellectual improvement, and there being no agreed and conventional standard weights or measures of moral and intellectual qualities and quantities, the question of progress can never be accurately decided. We maintain that man has not improved, because in all save the mechanic arts he reverts to the distant past for models to imitate, and he never imitates what he can excel.

We need never have white slaves in the South, because we have black ones. Our citizens, like those of Rome and Athens, are a privileged class. We should train and educate them to deserve the privileges and to perform the duties which society confers on them. Instead of, by a low demagoguism, depressing their self-respect by discourses on the equality of man, we had better excite their pride by reminding them that they do not fulfil the menial offices which white men do in other countries. Society does not feel the burden of providing for the few helpless paupers in the South. And we should recollect that here we have but half the people to educate, for half are negroes; whilst at the North they profess to educate all. It is in our power to spike this last gun of the abolitionists. We should educate all the poor. The abolitionists say that it is one of the necessary consequences of slavery that the poor are neglected. It was not so in Athens, and in Rome, and should not be so in the South. If we had less trade with and less dependence on the North, all our poor might be profitably and honorably employed in trades, professions and manufactures. Then we should have a rich and denser population. Yet we but marshal her in the way that she was going. The South is already aware of the necessity of a new policy, and has begun to act on it. Every day more and more is done for education, the mechanic arts, manufactures and internal improvements. We will soon be independent of the North.

We deem this peculiar question of negro slavery of very little importance. The issue is made throughout the world on the general subject of slavery in the abstract. The argument has commenced. One set of ideas will govern and control after awhile the civilized world. Slavery will every where be abolished, or every where be re-instituted. We think the opponents of practical, existing slavery, are stopped by their own admission; nay, that unconsciously, as socialists, they are the defenders and propagandists of slavery, and have furnished the only sound arguments on which its defence and justification can be rested. We have introduced the subject of negro slavery to afford us a better opportunity to disclaim the purpose of reducing the white man any where to the condition of negro slaves here. It would be very unwise and unscientific to govern white men as you would negroes. Every shade and variety of slavery has existed in the world. In some cases there has been much of legal regulation, much restraint of the master's authority; in others, none at all. The character of slavery necessary to protect the whites in Europe should be much milder than negro slavery, for slavery is only needed to protect the white man, whilst it is more necessary for the government of the negro even than for his protection. But even negro slavery should not be outlawed. We might and should have laws in Virginia, as in Louisiana, to make the master subject to presentment by the grand jury and to punishment, for any inhuman or improper treatment or neglect of his slave.

We abhor the doctrine of the "Types of Mankind;" first, because it is at war with scripture, which teaches us that the whole human race is descended from a common parentage; and, secondly, because it encourages and incites brutal masters to treat negroes, not as weak, ignorant and dependent brethren, but as wicked beasts, without the pale of humanity. This Southerner is the negro's friend, his only friend. Let no intermeddling abolitionist, no refined philosophy, dissolve this friendship.

ABRAHAM LINCOLN

Neither an abolitionist nor a revolutionist, Abraham Lincoln based his opposition to slavery on personal humanitarian grounds and insisted that the path to freedom lay through legislation and Constitutional interpretation.

LINCOLN AT CHICAGO, JULY 10, 1858
From *Lincoln-Douglas Debates*

. . . These 4th of July gatherings I suppose have their uses. If you will indulge me, I will state what I suppose to be some of them.

We are now a mighty nation, we are thirty—or about thirty millions of people, and we own and inhabit about one-fifteenth part of the dry land of the whole earth. We run our memory back over the pages of history for about eighty-two years and we discover that we were then a very small people in point of numbers, vastly inferior to what we are now, with a vastly less extent of country,—with vastly less of everything we deem desirable among men,—we look upon the change as exceedingly advantageous to us and to our posterity, and we fix upon something that happened away back, as in some way or other being connected with this rise of prosperity. We find a race of men living in that day whom we claim as our fathers and grandfathers; they were iron men, they fought for the principle that they were contending for; and we understood that by what they then did it has followed that the degree of prosperity that we now enjoy has come to us. We hold this annual celebration to remind ourselves of all the good done in this process of time, of how it was done and who did it, and how we are historically connected with it; and we go from these meetings in better humor with ourselves—we feel more attached the one to the other, and more firmly bound to the country we inhabit. In every way we are better men in the age, and race, and country in which we live for these celebrations. But after we have done all this we have not yet reached the whole. There is something else connected with it. We have besides these men—descended by blood from our ancestors—among us perhaps half our people who are not descendants at all of these men, they are men who have come from Europe—German, Irish, French and Scandinavian—men that have come from Europe themselves, or whose ancestors have come hither and settled here, finding themselves our equals in all things. If they look back through this history to trace their connections with those days by blood, they find they have none, they cannot carry themselves back into that glorious epoch and make themselves feel that they are part of us, but when they look through that old Declaration of Independence they find that those old men say that "We hold these truths to be self-evident, that all men are created equal," and then they feel that that moral sentiment taught in that day evidences their relation to those men, that it is the father of all moral principle in them, and that they have a right to claim it as though they were blood of the blood, and flesh of the flesh of the men who wrote that Declaration, (loud and long continued applause) and so they are. This is the electric cord in that Declaration that links the hearts of patriotic and liberty-loving men together, that will link those patriotic hearts as long as the love of freedom exists in the minds of men throughout the world. [Applause.]

Now, sirs, for the purpose of squaring things with this idea of "don't care if slavery is voted up or voted down," for sustaining the Dred Scott decision [A voice—"Hit him again"], for holding that the Declaration of Independence did not mean anything at all, we have Judge Douglas giving his exposition of what the Declaration of Independence means, and we have him saying that the people of America are equal to the people of England. According to his construction, you Germans are not connected with it. Now I ask you in all soberness, if all these things, if indulged in, if ratified, if confirmed and endorsed, if taught to our children, and repeated to them, do not tend to rub out the sentiment of liberty in the country, and to transform this government into a government of some other form. Those arguments that are made, that the inferior race are to be treated with as much allowance as they are capable of enjoying; that as much is to be done for them as their condition will allow. What are these arguments? They are the arguments that kings have made for enslaving the people in all ages of the world. You will find that all the arguments in favor of king-craft were of this class; they always bestrode the necks of the people, not that they wanted to do it, but because the people were better off for being ridden. That is their argument, and this argument of the Judge is the same old serpent that says you work and I eat, you toil and I will enjoy the fruits of it. Turn it whatever way you will—whether it come from the mouth of a king, an excuse for enslaving the people of his country, or from the mouth of men of one race as a reason for enslaving the men of another race, it is all the same old serpent, and I hold if that course of argumentation that is made for the purpose of convincing the public mind that we should not care about this, should be granted, it does not stop with the negro. I should like to know if taking this old Declaration of Independence, which declares that all men are equal upon principle and making exceptions to it where will it stop. If one man says it does not mean a negro, why not another say it does not mean some other man? If that Declaration is not the truth, let us get the statute book, in which we find it and tear it out! Who is so bold as to do it! [Voices— "me," "no one," &c.] If it is not true let us tear it out! [cries of "no, no,"] let us stick to it then, [cheers] let us stand firmly by it then. [Applause.]

It may be argued that there are certain conditions that make necessities and impose them upon us, and to the extent that a necessity is imposed upon a man he must submit to it. I think that was the condition in which we found ourselves when we established this government. We had slavery among us, we could not get our constitution unless we permitted them to remain in slavery, we could not secure the good we did secure if we grasped for more, and having by necessity submitted to that much, it does not destroy the principle that is the charter of our liberties. Let that charter stand as our standard.

My friend has said to me that I am a poor hand to quote Scripture. I will try it again, however. It is said in one of the admonitions of the Lord, 'As your Father in Heaven is perfect, be ye also perfect." The Savior, I suppose, did not expect that any human creature could be perfect as the Father in Heaven; but He said, "As your Father in Heaven is perfect, be ye also perfect." He set that up as a standard, and he who did most towards reaching that standard, attained the highest degree of moral perfection. So I say in relation to the principle that all men are created equal, let it be as nearly reached as we can. If we cannot give freedom to every creature, let us do nothing that will impose slavery upon any other creature. [Applause.] Let us turn this government back into the channel in which the framers of the Constitution originally placed it. Let us stand firmly by each other. If we do not do so we are turning in the contrary direction, that our friend Judge Douglas proposes—not intentionally—as working in the traces tend to make this one universal slave nation. [A voice—"that is so."] He is one that runs in that direction, and as such I resist him.

My friends, I have detained you about as long as I desired to do, and I have only to say, let us discard all this quibbling about this man and the other man—this race and that race and the other race being inferior, and therefore they must be placed in an inferior position—discarding our standard that we have left us. Let us discard all these things, and unite as one people throughout this land, until we shall once more stand up declaring that all men are created equal.

My friends, I could not, without launching off upon some new topic, which would detain you too long, continue to-night. [Cries of "go on."] I thank you for this most extensive audience that you have furnished me to-night. I leave you, hoping that the lamp of liberty will burn in your bosoms until there shall no longer be a doubt that all men are created free and equal.

FRAGMENT ON PRO-SLAVERY THEOLOGY (1858)

October 1, 1858

Suppose it is true, that the negro is inferior to the white, in the gifts of nature; is it not the exact reverse justice that the white should, for that reason, take from the negro, any part of the little which has been given him? "*Give* to him that is needy" is the christian rule of charity; but "Take from him that is needy" is the rule of slavery.

PRO-SLAVERY THEOLOGY

The sum of pro-slavery theology seems to be this: "Slavery is not universally *right*, nor yet universally *wrong*; it is better for *some* people to be slaves; and, in such cases, it is the Will of God that they be such."

Certainly there is no contending against the Will of God; but still there is some difficulty in ascertaining, and applying it, to particular cases. For instance we will suppose the Rev. Dr. Ross has a slave named Sambo, and the question is "Is it the Will of God that Sambo shall remain a slave, or be set free?" The Almighty gives no audible answer to the question, and his revelation—the Bible—gives none—or, at most, none but such as admits of a squabble, as to it's meaning. No one thinks of asking Sambo's opinion on it. So, at last, it comes to this, that *Dr. Ross* is to decide the question. And while he consider[s] it, he sits in the shade, with gloves on his hands, and subsists on the bread that Sambo is earning in the burning sun. If he decides that God Wills Sambo to continue a slave, he thereby retains his own comfortable position; but if he decides that God will's Sambo to be free, he thereby has to walk out of the shade, throw off his gloves, and delve for his own bread. Will Dr. Ross be actuated by that perfect impartiality, which has ever been considered most favorable to correct decisions?

But, slavery is good for the people!!! As a *good* thing, slavery is strikingly perculiar, in this, that it is the only good thing which no man ever seeks the good of, *for himself.*

Nonsense! Wolves devouring lambs, not because it is good for their own greedy maws, but because it [is] good for the lambs!!!

STEPHEN A. DOUGLAS

Stephen A. Douglas (1813–1861), statesman and Democratic leader, sought, in spite of personal dislike of the institution of slavery, to eliminate it as a national problem by determining that state and local governmental units should accept or reject it. But the intensity of emotions and the terminology of the Declaration of Independence and the Bill of Rights made it a problem that demanded national solution.

OTTAWA: DOUGLAS' OPENING SPEECH (AUGUST 21, 1858)
From *Lincoln-Douglas Debates*

. . . Washington, Jefferson, Franklin, Madison, Hamilton, Jay, and the great men of that day, made this government divided into free states and slave states, and left each state perfectly free to do as it pleased on the subject of slavery. ("Right, right.") Why can it not exist on the same principles on which our fathers made it? ("It can.") They knew when they framed the Constitution that in a country as wide and broad as this, with such a variety of climate, production and interest, the people necessarily required different laws and institutions in different localities. They knew that the laws and regulations which would suit the granite hills of New Hampshire would be unsuited to the rice plantations of South Carolina, ("right, right,") and they, therefore, provided that each state should retain its own legislature, and its own sovereignty with the full and complete power to do as it pleased within its own limits, in all that was local and not national. (Applause.)

One of the reserved rights of the states, was the right to regulate the relations between master and servant, on the slavery question. At the time the Constitution was formed, there were thirteen states in the Union, twelve of which were slaveholding states and one a free state. Suppose this doctrine of uniformity preached by Mr. Lincoln, that the states should all be free or all be slave had prevailed and what would have been the result? Of course, the twelve slaveholding states would have overruled the one free state, and slavery would have been fastened by a constitutional provision on every inch of the American Republic, instead of being left as our fathers wisely left it, to each state to decide for itself. ("Good, good," and three cheers for Douglas.) Here I assert that uniformity in the local laws and institutions of the different states is neither possible or desirable. If uniformity had been adopted when the government was established, it must inevitably have been the uniformity of slavery everywhere, or else the uniformity of negro citizenship and negro equality everywhere.

We are told by Lincoln that he is utterly opposed to the Dred Scott decision, and will not submit to it, for the reason that he says it deprives the negro of the rights and privileges of citizenship. (Laughter and applause.) That is the first and main reason which he assigns for his warfare on the Supreme Court of the United States and its decision. I ask you, are you in favor of conferring upon the negro the rights and privileges of citizenship? ("No, no.") Do you desire to strike out of our state constitution that clause which keeps slaves and free negroes out of the state, and allow the free negroes to flow in, ("never,") and cover your prairies with black settlements? Do you desire to turn this beautiful state into a free negro colony, ("no, no,") in order that when Missouri abolishes slavery she can send one hundred thousand emancipated slaves into Illinois, to become citizens and voters, on an equality with yourselves? ("Never," "no.") If you desire negro citizenship, if you desire to allow them to come into the state and settle with the white man, if you desire them to vote on an equality with yourselves, and to make them eligible to office, to serve on juries, and to adjudge your rights, then support Mr. Lincoln and the Black Republican party, who are in favor of the citizenship of the negro. ("Never, never.") For one, I am opposed to negro citizenship in any and every form. (Cheers.) I believe this government was made on the white basis. ("Good.") I believe it was made by white men, for the benefit of white men and their posterity for ever, and I am in favor of confining citizenship to white men, men of European birth and descent, instead of conferring it upon negroes, Indians and other inferior races. ("Good for you." "Douglas forever.")

Mr. Lincoln, following the example and lead of all the little Abolition orators, who go around and lecture in the basements of schools and churches, reads from the Declaration of Independence, that all men were created equal, and then asks how can you deprive a negro of that equality which God and the Declaration of Independence awards to him. He and they maintain that negro equality is guaranteed by the laws of God, and that it is asserted in the Declaration of Independence. If they think so, of course they have a right to say so, and so vote. I do not question Mr. Lincoln's conscientious belief that the negro was made his equal, and hence is his brother, (laughter,) but for my own part, I do not regard the negro as my equal, and positively deny that he is my brother or any kin to me whatever. ("Never." "Hit him again," and cheers.) Lincoln has evidently learned by heart Parson Lovejoy's catechism. (Laughter and applause.) He can repeat it as well as Farnsworth,[1] and he is worthy of a medal from father Giddings and Fred Douglass for his abolitionism. (Laughter.) He holds that the negro was born his equal and yours, and that he was endowed with equality by the Almighty, and that no human law can deprive him of these rights which were guaranteed to him by the Supreme Ruler of the universe. Now, I do not believe that the Almighty ever intended the negro to be the equal of the white man. ("Never, never.") If he did, he has been a long time demonstrating the fact. (Cheers.) For thousands of years the negro has been a race upon the earth, and during all that time, in all latitudes and climates, wherever he has wandered or been taken, he has been inferior to the race which he has there met. He belongs to an inferior race, and must always occupy an inferior position. ("Good," "that's so," &c.) I do not hold that because the negro is our inferior that therefore he ought to be a slave. By no means can such a conclusion be drawn from what I have said. On the contrary, I hold that humanity and Christianity both require that the negro shall have and enjoy every right, every privilege, and every immunity consistent with the safety of the society in which he lives. ("That's so.") On that point, I presume, there can be no diversity of opinion. You and I are bound to extend to our inferior and dependent being every right, every privilege, every facility and immunity consistent with the public good. The question then arises what rights and privileges are consistent with the public good. This is a question which each state and each territory must decide for itself—Illinois has decided it for herself. We have provided that the negro shall not be a slave, and we have also provided that he shall not be a citizen, but protect him in his civil rights, in his life, his person and his property, only depriving him of all political rights whatsoever, and refusing to put him on an equality with the white man. ("Good.") That policy of Illinois is satisfactory to the Democratic party and to me, and if it were to the Republicans, there would then be no question upon the subject; but the Republicans say that he ought to be made a citizen, and when he becomes a citizen he

[1] John F. Farnsworth of Chicago, Congressman from Illinois.

becomes your equal, with all your rights and privileges. ("He never shall.") They assert the Dred Scott decision to be monstrous because it denies that the negro is or can be a citizen under the Constitution. Now, I hold that Illinois had a right to abolish and prohibit slavery as she did, and I hold that Kentucky has the same right to continue and protect slavery that Illinois had to abolish it. I hold that New York had as much right to abolish slavery as Virginia has to continue it, and that each and every state of this Union is a sovereign power, with the right to do as it pleases upon this question of slavery, and upon all its domestic institutions. Slavery is not the only question which comes up in this controversy. There is a far more important one to you, and that is, what shall be done with the free negro? We have settled the slavery question as far as we are concerned; we have prohibited it in Illinois forever, and in doing so, I think we have done wisely, and there is no man in the state who would be more strenuous in his opposition to the introduction of slavery than I would; (cheers) but when we settled it for ourselves, we exhausted all our power over that subject. We have done our whole duty, and can do no more. We must leave each and every other state to decide for itself the same question. In relation to the policy to be pursued towards the free negroes, we have said that they shall not vote; whilst Maine, on the other hand, has said that they shall vote. Maine is a sovereign state, and has the power to regulate the qualifications of voters within her limits. I would never consent to confer the right of voting and of citizenship upon a negro, but still I am not going to quarrel with Maine for differing from me in opinion. Let Maine take care of her own negroes and fix the qualifications of her own voters to suit herself, without interfering with Illinois, and Illinois will not interfere with Maine. So with the state of New York. She allows the negro to vote provided he owns two hundred and fifty dollars worth of property, but not otherwise. While I would not make any distinction whatever between a negro who held property and one who did not; yet if the sovereign state of New York chooses to make that distinction it is her business and not mine, and I will not quarrel with her for it. She can do as she pleases on this question if she minds her own business, and we will do the same thing. Now, my friends, if we will only act conscientiously and rigidly upon this great principle of popular sovereignty which guarantees to each state and territory the right to do as it pleases on all things local and domestic instead of Congress interfering, we will continue at peace one with another. Why should Illinois be at war with Missouri, or Kentucky with Ohio, or Virginia with New York, merely because their institutions differ? Our fathers intended that our institutions should differ. They knew that the North and the South having different climates, productions and interests, required different institutions. This doctrine of Mr. Lincoln's of uniformity among the institutions of the different states is a new doctrine, never dreamed of by Washington, Madison, or the framers of this government. Mr. Lincoln and the Republican party set themselves up as wiser than these men who made this government, which has flourished for seventy years under the principle of popular sovereignty, recognizing the right of each state to do as it pleased. Under that principle, we have grown from a nation of three or four millions to a nation of about thirty millions of people; we have crossed the Allegheny mountains and filled up the whole North West, turning the prairie into a garden, and building up churches and schools, thus spreading civilization and Christianity where before there was nothing but savage-barbarism. Under that principle we have become from a feeble nation, the most powerful on the face of the earth, and if we only adhere to that principle, we can go forward increasing in territory, in power, in strength and in glory until the Republic of America shall be the North Star that shall guide the friends of freedom throughout the civilized world. ("Long may you live," and great applause.) And why can we not adhere to the great principle of self-government, upon which our institutions were originally based. ("We can.") I believe that this new doctrine preached by Mr. Lincoln and his party will dissolve the Union if it succeeds. They are trying to array all the Northern states in one body against the South, to excite a sectional war between the free states and the slave states, in order that the one or the other may be driven to the wall.

I am told that my time is out. Mr. Lincoln will now address you for an hour and a half, and I will then occupy a half hour in replying to him. (Three times three cheers were here given for Douglas.)

OTTAWA: LINCOLN'S REPLY (AUGUST 21, 1858)

My Fellow Citizens:
When a man hears himself somewhat misrepresented, it provokes him —at least, I find it so with myself; but when the misrepresentation becomes very gross and palpable, it is more apt to amuse him. [Laughter.] The first thing I see fit to notice, is the fact that Judge Douglas alleges, after running through the history of the old Democratic and the old Whig parties, that Judge Trumbull and myself made an arrangement in 1854, by which I was to have the place of Gen. Shields in the United States Senate, and Judge Trumbull was to have the place of Judge Douglas. Now all I have to say upon that subject is, that I think no man—not even Judge Douglas—can prove it, *because it is not true.* [Cheers.] I have no doubt he is "*conscientious*" in saying it. [Laughter.] As to those resolutions that he took such a length of time to read, as being the platform of the Republican party in 1854, I say I

never had anything to do with them, and I think Trumbull never had. [Renewed laughter.] Judge Douglas cannot show that either one of us ever did have any thing to do with them. I believe *this* is true about those resolutions: There was a call for a convention to form a Republican party at Springfield, and I think that my friend Mr. Lovejoy, who is here upon this stand, had a hand in it. I think this is true, and I think if he will remember accurately, he will be able to recollect that he tried to get me into it, and I would not go in. [Cheers and laughter.] I believe it is also true, that I went away from Springfield when the convention was in session, to attend court in Tazewell County. It is true they did place my name, though without authority, upon the committee, and afterwards wrote me to attend the meeting of the committee, but I refused to do so, and I never had anything to do with that organization. This is the plain truth about all that matter of the resolutions.

Now, about this story that Judge Douglas tells of Trumbull bargaining to sell out the old Democratic party, and Lincoln agreeing to sell out the old Whig party, I have the means of *knowing* about that; [laughter] Judge Douglas cannot have; and I know there is no substance to it whatever. [Applause.] Yet I have no doubt he is "*conscientious*" about it. [Laughter.] I know that after Mr. Lovejoy got into the legislature that winter, he complained of me that I had told all the old Whigs in his district that the old Whig party was good enough for them, and some of them voted against him because I told them so. Now I have no means of totally disproving such charges as this which the Judge makes. A man cannot prove a negative, but he has a right to claim that when a man makes an affirmative charge, he must offer some proof to show the truth of what he says. I certainly cannot introduce testimony to show the negative about things, but I have a right to claim that if a man says he *knows* a thing, then he must show *how* he knows it. I always have a right to claim this, and it is not satisfactory to me that he may be "conscientious" on the subject. [Cheers and Laughter.]

Now gentlemen, I hate to waste my time on such things, but in regard to that general abolition tilt that Judge Douglas makes, when he says that I was engaged at that time in selling out and abolitionizing the old Whig party—I hope you will permit me to read a part of a printed speech that I made then at Peoria, which will show altogether a different view of the position I took in that contest of 1854.

Voice—Put on your specs.

Mr. Lincoln—Yes, sir, I am obliged to do so. I am no longer a young man. [Laughter.]

This is the *repeal* of the Missouri Compromise. The foregoing history may not be precisely accurate in every particular; but I am sure it is sufficiently so, for all the uses I shall attempt to make of it, and in it, we have before us, the chief materials enabling us to correctly judge whether the repeal of the Missouri Compromise is right or wrong.

I think, and shall try to show, that it is wrong; wrong in its direct effect, letting slavery into Kansas and Nebraska—and wrong in its prospective principle, allowing it to spread to every other part of the wide world, where men can be found inclined to take it.

This *declared* indifference, but as I must think, covert *real* zeal for the spread of slavery, I can not but hate. I hate it because of the monstrous injustice of slavery itself. I hate it because it deprives our republican example of its just influence in the world—enables the enemies of free institutions, with plausibility, to taunt us as hypocrites—causes the real friends of freedom to doubt our sincerity, and especially because it forces so many really good men amongst ourselves into an open war with the very fundamental principles of civil liberty—criticising the Declaration of Independence, and insisting that there is no right principle of action but *self-interest*.

Before proceeding, let me say I think I have no prejudice against the Southern people. They are just what we would be in their situation. If slavery did not now exist amongst them, they would not introduce it. If it did now exist amongst us, we should not instantly give it up. This I believe of the masses North and South. Doubtless there are individuals, on both sides, who would not hold slaves under any circumstances; and others who would gladly introduce slavery anew, if it were out of existence. We know that some Southern men do free their slaves, go north, and become tip-top Abolitionists; while some Northern ones go south, and become most cruel slave-masters.

When Southern people tell us they are no more responsible for the origin of slavery, than we; I acknowledge the fact. When it is said that the institution exists, and that it is very difficult to get rid of it, in any satisfactory way, I can understand and appreciate the saying. I surely will not blame them for not doing what I should not know how to do myself. If all earthly power were given me, I should not know what to do, as to the existing institution. My first impulse would be to free all the slaves, and send them to Liberia,—to their own native land. But a moment's reflection would convince me, that whatever of high hope, (as I think there is) there may be in this, in the long run, its sudden execution is impossible. If they were all landed there in a day, they would all perish in the next ten days; and there are not surplus shipping and surplus money enough in the world to carry them there in many times ten days. What then? Free them all, and keep them among us as underlings? Is it quite certain that this betters their condition? I think I would not hold one in slavery, at any rate; yet the point is not clear enough to me to denounce people upon. What next? Free them, and make them politically and socially, our equals? My own feelings will not admit of this; and if mine would, we well know that those of the great mass of white people will not. Whether this feeling accords with justice and sound judgment, is not the sole issue, if indeed, it is any part of it. A universal feeling, whether well or ill-founded, can not be safely disregarded. We can not, then, make them equals. It does seem to me that systems of gradual emancipation might be adopted; but for their tardiness in this, I will not undertake to judge our brethren of the South.

When they remind us of their constitutional rights, I acknowledge them, not grudgingly, but fully, and fairly; and I would give them any legislation for the reclaiming of their fugitives, which should not, in its stringency, be more likely to carry a free man into slavery, than our ordinary criminal laws are to hang an innocent one.

But all this, to my judgment, furnishes no more excuse for permitting slavery to go into our own free territory, than it would for reviving the African slave trade by law. The law which forbids the bringing of slaves *from* Africa; and that which has so long forbid the taking them *to* Nebraska, can hardly be distinguished on any moral principle; and the repeal of the former could find quite as plausible excuses as that of the latter.

I have reason to know that Judge Douglas *knows* that I said this. I think he has the answer here to one of the questions he put to me. I do not mean to allow him to catechise me unless he pays back for it in kind. I will not answer questions one after another unless he reciprocates, but as he made this inquiry and I have answered it before, he has got it without my getting anything in return. He has got my answer on the fugitive slave law.

Now gentlemen, I don't want to read at any greater length, but this is the true complexion of all I have ever said in regard to the institution of slavery and the black race. This is the whole of it, and anything that argues me into his idea of perfect social and political equality with the negro, is but a specious and fantastic arrangement of words, by which a man can prove a horse chestnut to be a chestnut horse. [Laughter.] I will say here, while upon this subject, that I have no purpose directly or indirectly to interfere with the institution of slavery in the states where it exists. I believe I have no lawful right to do so, and I have no inclination to do so. I have no purpose to introduce political and social equality between the white and the black races. There is a physical difference between the two, which in my judgment will probably forever forbid their living together upon the footing of perfect equality, and inasmuch as it becomes a necessity that there must be a difference, I, as well as Judge Douglas, am in favor of the race to which I belong, having the superior position. I have never said anything to the contrary, but I hold that notwithstanding all this, there is no reason in the world why the negro is not entitled to all the natural rights enumerated in the Declaration of Independence, the right to life, liberty and the pursuit of happiness. [Loud cheers.] I hold that he is as much entitled to these as the white man. I agree with Judge Douglas he is not my equal in many respects—certainly not in color, perhaps not in moral or intellectual endowment. But in the right to eat the bread, without leave of anybody else, which his own hand earns, *he is my equal and the equal of Judge Douglas, and the equal of every living man.* [Great applause.] . . .

GALESBURG: DOUGLAS' OPENING SPEECH (OCTOBER 7, 1858)

From *Lincoln-Douglas Debates*

. . . I tell you that this Chicago doctrine of Lincoln's—declaring that the negro and the white man are made equal by the Declaration of Independence and by Divine Providence—is a monstrous heresy. ("That's so," and terrific applause.) The signers of the Declaration of Independence never dreamed of the negro when they were writing that document. They referred to white men, to men of European birth and European descent, when they declared the equality of all men. I see a gentleman there in the crowd shaking his head. Let me remind him that when Thomas Jefferson wrote that document he was the owner, and so continued until his death, of a large number of slaves. Did he intend to say in that Declaration that his negro slaves, which he held and treated as property, were created his equals by Divine law, and that he was violating the law of God every day of his life by holding them as slaves? ("No, no.") It must be borne in mind that when that Declaration was put forth every one of the thirteen colonies were slaveholding colonies, and every man who signed that instrument represented a slaveholding constituency. Recollect, also, that no one of them emancipated his slaves, much less put them on an equality with himself, after he signed the Declaration. On the contrary, they all continued to hold their negroes as slaves during the Revolutionary war. Now, do you believe—are you willing to have it said—that every man who signed the Declaration of Independence declared the negro his equal, and then was hypocrite enough to continue to hold him as a slave, in violation of what he believed to be the divine law? ("No, no,") And yet when you say that the Declaration of Independence includes the negro, you charge the signers of it with hypocrisy.

I say to you, frankly, that in my opinion this government was made by our fathers on the white basis. It was made by white men for the benefit of white men and their posterity forever, and was intended to be administered by white men in all time to come. ("That's so," and cheers.) But while I hold that under our constitution and political system the negro is not a citizen, cannot be a citizen, and ought not to be a citizen, it does not follow by any means that he should be a slave. On the contrary it does follow that the negro, as an inferior race, ought to possess every right, every privilege, every immunity which he can safely exercise consistent with the safety of the society in which he lives. ("That's so," and cheers.) Humanity requires, and Christianity commands that you shall extend to every inferior being, and every dependent being, all the privileges, immunities and advantages which can be granted to them consistent with the safety of society. If you ask me the nature and extent of these privileges, I answer that it is a question which the people of each state must decide for themselves. ("That's it.") Illinois has decided that question for herself. We have said that in this state the negro shall not be a slave, nor shall he be a citizen. Kentucky holds a different doctrine. New York holds one different from either, and Maine one different from all. Virginia, in her policy on this question, differs in many respects from the others, and so on, until there is hardly two states whose policy is exactly alike in regard to the relation of the white man and the negro. Nor can you reconcile them and make them alike. Each state must do as it pleases. Illinois had as much right to adopt the policy which we have on that subject as Kentucky had to adopt a different policy. The great principle of this government is that each state has the right to do as it pleases on all these questions, and no other state, or power on earth has the right to interfere with us, or complain of us merely because our system differs from theirs. In the compromise measures of 1850, Mr. Clay declared that this great principle ought to exist in the territories as well as in the states, and I reasserted his doctrine in the Kansas and Nebraska Bill in 1854.

But Mr. Lincoln cannot be made to understand, and those who are determined to vote for him, no matter whether he is a pro-slavery man in the south and a negro equality advocate in the north, cannot be made to understand how it is that in a territory the people can do as they please on the slavery question under the Dred Scott decision. Let us see whether I cannot explain it to the satisfaction of all impartial men. Chief Justice Taney has said in his opinion in the Dred Scott case, that a negro slave being property, stands on an equal footing with other property, and that the owner may carry them into United States territory the same as he does other property. . . .

BALLADS (ca. 1860)

The Negro in America and the institution of slavery were responsible for an outpouring of songs, popular, secular and religious, that were disseminated by popular broadsides, by entertainers and by word of mouth. Typical ballads are those dealing with Negro stereotypes in the pre-war years and with the theme of freedom as the war neared its close.

THE DARKEY'S SERENADE

> Oh! come, my lovely Dinah
>   Come, hasten, love, to me:
> The moon shines bright and beautiful
>   Across the rippling sea.

I love you as the stars of night,
  That shine in heaven above.
Then come away with me this night,
  My best, my only love.
Chorus: Then come away, my Dinah dear,
      Oh! come away with me:
    For, all the world is fast asleep,
      And the moon shines o'er the sea.

Oh! Dinah dear, you know for years
  I loved you long and well—
And now I've come, this very night,
  My love to you to tell—
And if you do not say, this night,
  You love this darkey swain,
I'll throw myself into the sea,
  And I'll ne'er come back again!
    Then come away, my Dinah dear, &c.

HAPPY LITTLE DARKEYS

Happy little nigs are we,
Just as gay as gay can be;
Always laughing, never sigh,
Twist our heel and wink our eye.
    Chorus.
    Dat's my notion,
    Whatch dis motion:
Happy little darkeys, and I want you all to know,
With de scientific movement of de heel and toe.

When, at night, our day's work's done,
Dat's de time we have our fun;
Den we are merry, light and free,
Sorrow never comes to we.
      Dat's my notion, &c.

All de world's de same to we,
Joy in every ting we see:
Snow or cloudy, wet or dry,
Always laughing, never sigh.
      Dat's my notion, &c.

HAPPY NIGGER JOE

P. H. MOWREY

Song and Dance

Oh! I've jist come out to dance a while
And sing a little song;
So, give me your attention,
And I won't detain you long.
Oh! de gals are all in lub wid me:
Ax dem, dey'll tell you so;
For, a red-hot hunkey-dora nig
Is Happy Nigger Joe!
    Chorus: For, when I sing, (Symphony)
                Dis foot I sling: (do.   )
           For, when I sing, dis foot I sling:
           It pleases all, you know;
           For, a red-hot hunkey-dora nig
           Is Happy Nigger Joe!

I'm in lub wid a pretty yellar gal
I met de oder day,
While gazing on de fashions,
A-walking down Broadway.
De last time dat I saw her,
She said she lubbed me so,
Dat soon she would be married to
Happy Nigger Joe.   Chorus.

Now, white folks, I think I'd better stop:
Too much at once won't do;
So, I hope dat I have pleased
And not offended you.
And if ever around dis way you drop,
Stop in, as a-past you go:
And listen to the song and dance
Of Happy Nigger Joe.   Chorus.

DAY OF JUBILEE

A. G. DUNCAN

Roll on, thou joyful day,
When tyranny's proud sway,
Stern as the grave,
Shall to the ground be hurled,
And Freedom's flag unfurled
Shall wave throughout the world,
O'er every slave!

Trump of glad jubilee,
Echo o'er land and sea,
Freedom for all!
Let the glad tidings fly,
And every tribe reply,
Glory to God on high,
At Slavery's fall!

VIRGINIA

From *A Journey in the Slave States* (*1856*)

FREDERICK LAW OLMSTED

*Frederick Law Olmsted (1822–1903) was a landscape architect, writer
and social critic. His journeys through the South immediately preceding the Civil War resulted in several volumes of observations that are
among the most objective and realistic of the period. He attempted to
bring rationality to bear on the slavery controversy, but it had gone
beyond the possibility of rational appraisal.*

SLAVE LABOR

The labor of this farm was entirely performed by slaves. I did not
inquire their number, but I judged there were from twenty to forty.
Their "quarters" lined the approach-road to the mansion, and were
well-made and comfortable log cabins, about thirty feet long by twenty
wide, and eight feet tall, with a high loft and shingle roof. Each, divided in the middle, and having a brick chimney outside the wall at
each end, was intended to be occupied by two families. There were

square windows closed by wooden ports, having a single pane of glass in the center. The house-servants were neatly dressed, but the field-hands wore very coarse and ragged garments.

During three hours or more in which I was in company with the proprietor, I do not think there were ten consecutive minutes uninterrupted by some of the slaves requiring his personal direction or assistance. He was even obliged three times to leave the dinner-table.

"You see," said he, smiling, as he came in the last time, "a farmer's life, in this country, is no sinecure." This turning the conversation to Slavery, he observed, in answer to a remark of mine, "I only wish your philanthropists would contrive some satisfactory plan to relieve us of it; the trouble and the responsibility of properly taking care of our negroes, you may judge, from what you see yourself here, is anything but enviable. But what can we do that is better? Our free negroes—and, I believe it is the same at the North as it is here—are a miserable set of vagabonds, drunken, vicious, worse off, it is my honest opinion, than those who are retained in slavery. I am satisfied, too, that our slaves are better off as they are, than the majority of your free laboring classes at the North."

I expressed my doubts.

"Well, they certainly are better off than the English agricultural laborers or, I believe, those of any other Christian country. Free labor might be more profitable to us: I am inclined to think it would be. The slaves are excessively careless and wasteful, and, in various ways—which, without you lived among them, you could hardly be made to understand—subject us to very annoying losses.

"To make anything by farming here, a man has got to live a hard life. You see how constantly I am called upon—and often it is as bad at night as by day. Last night I did not sleep a wink till near morning; I am quite worn out with it, and my wife's health is failing. But I cannot rid myself of it."

OVERSEERS

I asked why he did not employ an overseer.

"Because I do not think it right to trust to such men as we have to use, if we use any, for overseers."

"Is the general character of overseers bad?"

"They are the curse of this country, sir; the worst men in the community. * * * * But lately, I had another sort of fellow offer—a fellow like a dancing-master, with kid gloves, and wrist-bands turned up over his coat-sleeves, and all so nice that I was almost ashamed to talk to him in my old coat and slouched hat. Half a bushel of recommendations he had with him, too. Well, he was not the man for me—not half the gentleman, with all his airs, that Ned here is"—(a black servant, who was bursting with suppressed laughter, behind his chair).

"Oh, they are interesting creatures, sir," he continued, "and, with all their faults, have many beautiful traits. I can't help being attached to them, and I am sure they love us." In his own case, at least, I did not doubt it; his manner towards them was paternal—familiar and kind; and they came to him like children who have been given some task and constantly are wanting to be encouraged and guided, simply and confidently. At dinner, he frequently addressed the servant familiarly and drew him into our conversation as if he were a family friend, better informed, on some local and domestic points, than himself.

He informed me that able-bodied field-hands were hired out, in this vicinity, at the rate of one hundred dollars a year and their board and clothing. Four able-bodied men that I have employed the last year on my farm in New York, I pay, on an average, one hundred and five dollars each, and board them; they clothe themselves at an expense, I think, of twenty dollars a year;—probably slaves' clothing costs twice that. They constitute all the force of my farm, hired by the year (except a boy, who goes to school in Winter), and, in my absence, have no overseer except one of themselves, whom I appoint. I pay the fair wages of the market, more than any of my neighbors, I believe, and these are no lower than the average of what I have paid for the last five years. It is difficult to measure the labor performed in a day by one with that of the other, on account of undefined differences in the soil and in the bulk and weight of articles operated upon. But, here, I am shown tools that no man in his senses, with us, would allow a laborer, to whom he was paying wages, to be encumbered with, and the excessive weight and clumsiness of which, I would judge, would make work at least ten per cent greater than those ordinarily used with us. And I am assured that, in the careless and clumsy way they must be used by the slaves, anything lighter or less rude could not be furnished them with good economy, and that such tools as we constantly give our laborers, and find our profit in giving them, would not last out a day in a Virginia corn-field—much lighter and more free from stones though it be than ours.

So, too, when I ask why mules are so universally substituted for horses on the farm, the first reason given, and confessedly the most conclusive one, is that horses cannot bear the treatment they always *must* get from negroes; horses are always soon foundered or crippled by them, while mules will bear cudgeling and lose a meal now and then and not be materially injured, and they do not take cold or get sick if neglected or overworked. But I do not need to go further than to the window of the room in which I am writing to see, at almost any time, treatment of cattle that would insure the immediate discharge of the driver by almost any farmer owning them at the North.

A Coal Mine—Negro and English Miners

Yesterday I visited a coal-pit: the majority of the mining laborers are slaves, and uncommonly athletic and fine-looking negroes, but a considerable number of white hands are also employed, and they occupy all the responsible posts. The slaves are, some of them, owned by the Mining Company; but the most are hired of their owners at from $120 to $200 a year, the company boarding and clothing them. (I have the impression that I heard it was customary to give them a certain allowance of money and let them find their own board).

The white hands are mostly English or Welchmen. One of them with whom I conversed told me that he had been here several years; he had previously lived some years at the North. He got better wages here than he had earned at the North, but he was not contented, and did not intend to remain. On pressing him for the reason of his discontent, he said, after some hesitation, that he had rather live where he could be more free; a man had to be too *"discreet"* here: if one happened to say anything that gave offense, they thought no more of drawing a pistol or a knife upon him, than they would of kicking a dog that was in their way. Not long since, a young English fellow came to the pit, and was put to work along with a gang of negroes. One morning, about a week afterwards, twenty or thirty men called on him and told him that they would allow him fifteen minutes to get out of sight, and if they ever saw him in those parts again they would "give him hell." They were all armed, and there was nothing for the young fellow to do but to move "right off."

"What reason did they give him for it?"

"They did not give him any reason."

"But what had he done?"

"Why I believe they thought he had been too free with the niggers; he wasn't used to them, you see, sir, and he talked to 'em free like, and they thought he'd make 'em think too much of themselves."

He said the slaves were very well fed, and well treated—not worked over hard. They were employed night and day, in relays.

The coal from these beds is of special value for gas manufacture and is shipped for that purpose to all the large towns on the Atlantic seaboard, even to beyond Boston. It is delivered to shipping at Richmond at fifteen cents a bushel: about thirty bushels go to a ton.

Valuable Servants

The hotel at which I am staying, "the American," Milberger Smith from New York, proprietor, is a very capital one. I have never, this side the Atlantic, had my comforts provided for better, in my private room, with so little annoyance from the servants. The chamber-servants are negroes, and are accomplished in their business; (the dining-room servants are Irish). A man and a woman attend together upon a few assigned rooms in the hall adjoining which they are constantly in waiting; your bell is answered immediately, your orders are quickly and quietly followed, and your particular personal wants anticipated as much as possible and provided for, as well as the usual offices performed, when you are out. The man becomes your servant while you are in your room; he asks, at night, when he comes to request your boots, at what time he shall come in the morning, and then, without being very exactly punctual, he comes quietly in, makes your fire, set the boots before it, brushes and arranges your clothes, lays out your linen, arranges your washing and dressing gear, asks if you want anything else of him before breakfast, opens the shutters and goes off to the next room. I took occasion to speak well of him to my neighbor one day, that I might judge whether I was particularly favored.

"Oh yes," he said. "Henry was a very good boy, very—valuable servant—quite so—would be worth two thousand dollars if he was a little younger—easy."

At dinner, a respectable-looking, gray-headed man asked another:

"Niggers are going high now, aint they?"

"Yes, sir."

"What would you consider a fair price for a woman thirty years old, with a young-one two years old?"

"Depends altogether on her physical condition, you know.—Has she any other children?"

"*Yes; four.*"

"——Well—I reckon about seven to eight hundred."

"I bought one yesterday—gave six hundred and fifty."

"Well, sir, if she's tolerable likely, you did well."

DRESS AND STYLE OF PEOPLE

What is most remarkable in the appearance of the people of the better class, is their invariably *high-dressed* condition; look down the opposite side of the table, even at breakfast, and you will probably see thirty men drinking coffee, all in full funeral dress, not an easy coat amongst them. It is the same in the street, and the same with ladies as with gentlemen; silk and satin, under umbrellas, rustle along the sidewalk, or skip across it between carriages and the shops, as if they were going to a dinner-party, at eleven o'clock in the morning. The last is only New York repeated, to be sure, but the gentlemen carry it further than in New York, and seem never to indulge in undress.

I have rarely seen a finer assemblage of people than filled the theatre one night, at the benefit of the Bateman children, who are especial favorites of the public here. As the Legislature is in session, I presume there was a fair representation of the Virginians of all parts of the State. A remarkable proportion of the men were very tall and of animated expression—and of the women, fair, refined and serene. The men, however, were very deficient in robustness, and the women, though graceful and attractive, had none of that dignity and stateliness for which the dames of Virginia were formerly much distinguished.

In *manners*, I notice that between man and man more ceremony and form is sustained in familiar conversation than well-bred people commonly use at the North.

Among the people you see in the streets, full half, I should think, are more or less of negro blood, and a very decent, civil people these seem, in general, to be; more so than the laboring class of whites, among which there are many very ruffianly looking fellows. There is a considerable population of foreign origin, generally of the least valuable class; very dirty German Jews, especially, abound, and their characteristic shops (with their characteristic smells, quite as bad as in Cologne), are thickly set in the narrowest and meanest streets, which seem to be otherwise inhabited mainly by negroes. . . .

The Great Southern Route and Its Fast Train

The train was advertised to leave at 3.30 P.M. At that hour the cars were crowded with passengers, and the engineer, punctually at the minute, gave notice that he was at his post, by a long, loud whistle of the locomotive. Five minutes afterwards he gave us an impatient jerk; ten minutes afterwards we advanced three rods; twelve minutes afterwards, returned to first position: continued "backing and filling" upon the bridge over the rapids of the James river for half an hour. At precisely four o'clock, crossed the bridge and fairly started for Petersburg.

Ran twenty miles in exactly an hour and thirty minutes, (thirteen miles an hour; mail train, especially recommended by advertisement as "fast"). Brakes on, three times, for cattle on the track; twenty minutes spent at way-stations. Flat rail. Locomotive built at Philadelphia. I am informed that most of those used on the road—perhaps all those of the *slow* trains—are made at Petersburg.

At one of the stoppages, smoke was to be seen issuing from the truck of a car. The conductor, on having his attention called to it, nodded his head sagely, took a morsel of tobacco, put his hands in his pocket, looked at the truck as if he would mesmerize it, spat upon it, and then stept upon the platform and shouted "All right! Go ahead!" At the next stoppage, the smoking was furious; conductor bent himself over it with

an evidently strong exercise of his will, but not succeeding to tran-
quilize the subject at all, he suddenly relinquished the attempt, and,
deserting Mesmer for Preisnitz, shouted, "Ho! boy! bring me some
water here." A negro soon brought a quart of water in a tin vessel.

"Hain't got no oil, Columbus?"

"No, sir."

"Hum—go ask Mr. Smith for some: this yer's a screaking so, I durst-
n't go on. You Scott! get some salt. And look here, some of you boys,
get me some more water. D'ye hear?"

Salt, oil and water, were crowded into the box, and, after five minutes longer delay, we went on, the truck still smoking, and the water
and oil boiling in the box, until we reached Petersburg. The heat was
the result, I suppose, of a neglect of sufficient or timely oiling. While
waiting, in a carriage, for the driver to get my baggage, I saw a negro
oiling all the trucks of the train; as he proceeded from one to the
other, he did not give himself the trouble to elevate the outlet of his
oiler, so that a stream of oil costing probably a dollar and a half a gal-
lon was poured out upon the ground the whole length of the train.

One of the Law-Givers.

While on the bridge at Richmond, the car in which I was seated was
over-full—several persons standing; among them one considerably "excited" who informed the company that he was a Member of the House
of Delegates, and that he would take advantage of this opportune collection of the people to expose an atrocious attempt on the part of the
minority to jump a Bill through the Legislature which was not in accordance with true Democratic principles. He continued for some time to
address them in most violent, absurd, profane and meaningless language; the main point of his oration being to demand the popular gratitude for himself for having had the sagacity and courage to prevent the
accomplishment of the nefarious design. He afterwards attempted to
pass into the ladies' car, but was dissuaded from doing so by the conductor who prevailed on a young man to give him his seat. Having
taken it, he immediately lifted his feet upon the back of the seat before
him, resting them upon the shoulders of its occupant. This gentleman
turning his head, he begged his pardon; but, hoping it would not occasion him inconvenience, he said he would prefer to keep them there,
and did so; soon afterwards falling asleep.

Freight Taken—The Slave Trade.

There were in the train two first-class passenger cars and two freight
cars. The latter were occupied by about forty negroes, most of them be-

longing to traders, who were sending them to the cotton States to be sold. Such kind of evidence of activity in the slave trade of Virginia is to be seen every day; but particulars and statistics of it are not to be obtained by a stranger here. Most gentlemen of character seem to have a special disinclination to converse on the subject; and it is denied, with feeling, that slaves are often reared, as is supposed by the Abolitionists, with the intention of selling them to the traders. It appears to me evident, however, from the manner in which I hear the traffic spoken of incidentally, that the cash value of a slave for sale, above the cost of raising it from infancy to the age at which it commands the highest price, is generally considered among the surest elements of a planter's wealth. Such a nigger is worth such a price, and such another is too old to learn to pick cotton, and such another will bring so much, when it has grown a little more. I have frequently heard people say, in the street, or the public-houses. That a slave woman is commonly esteemed least for her laboring qualities, most for those qualities which give value to a brood-mare is also constantly made apparent.[1]

By comparing the average decennial ratio of slave increase in all the States with the difference in the number of the actual slave-population of the slave-breeding States, as ascertained by the census, it is apparent that the number of slaves exported to the cotton States is considerably more than twenty thousand a year.

While calling on a gentleman occupying an honorable official position at Richmond, I noticed upon his table a copy of Professor Johnson's Agricultural Tour in the United States. Referring to a paragraph in it, where some statistics of the value of the slaves raised and annually exported from Virginia were given. I asked if he knew how these had been obtained, and whether they were reliable. "No," he replied; "I don't know anything about it; but if they are anything unfavorable to the institution of slavery, you may be sure they are false." This is but an illustration, in extreme, of the manner in which I find a desire to obtain more correct but *definite* information on the subject of slavery is usually met, by gentlemen otherwise of enlarged mind and generous qualities.

A gentleman who was a member of the "Union Safety Committee" of New York during the excitement which attended the discussion of the Fugitive Slave Act of 1850, told me that, as he was passing through Virginia this winter, a man entered the car in which he was seated,

[1] A slaveholder writing to me with regard to my cautious statements on this subject, made in the *Daily Times,* says:—"In the States of Maryland, Virginia, North Carolina, Kentucky, Tennessee and Missouri, as much attention is paid to the breeding and growth of negroes as to that of horses and mules. Further south, we raise them both for use and for market. Planters command their girls and women (married or unmarried) to have children; and I have known a great many negro girls to be sold off, because they did not have children. A breeding women is worth from one-sixth to one-fourth more than one who does not breed."

leading in a negro girl, whose manner and expression of face indicated
dread and grief. Thinking she was a criminal, he asked the man what
she had done:

"Done? Nothing."

"What are you going to do with her?"

"I'm taking her down to Richmond, to be sold."

"Does she belong to you?"

"No; she belongs to————; he raised her."

"Why does he sell her—has she done anything wrong?"

"Done anything? No: she's no fault, I reckon."

"Then, what does he want to sell for?"

"Sell her for! Why shouldn't he sell her? He sells one or two every
year; wants the money for 'em, I reckon."

The irritated tone and severe stare with which this was said, my
friend took as a caution not to pursue his investigation.

A gentleman with whom I was conversing on the subject of the cost
of slave labor in answer to an inquiry—what proportion of all the stock
of slaves of an old plantation might be reckoned upon to do full work?
—answered that he owned ninety-six negroes; of these, only thirty-five
were field-hands, the rest being either too young or too old for hard
work. He reckoned his whole force as only equal to twenty-one strong
men, or *"prime* field-hands." But this proportion was somewhat smaller
than usual, he added, "because his women were uncommonly good
breeders; he did not suppose there was a lot of women anywhere that
bred faster than his; he never heard of babies coming so fast as they
did on his plantation; it was perfectly surprising; and every one of
them, in his estimation, was worth two hundred dollars, as negroes
were selling now, the moment it drew breath."

I asked what he thought might be the usual proportion of workers to
slaves supported on plantations throughout the South. On the large
cotton and sugar plantations of the more Southern States, it was very
high, he replied; because their hands were nearly all bought and
picked for work; he supposed, on those, it would be about one-half;
but on any old plantation, where the stock of slaves had been an inheritance, and none had been bought or sold, he thought the working force
would rarely be more than one-third, at most, of the whole number.

This gentleman was out of health, and told me, with frankness, that
such was the trouble and annoyance his negroes occasioned him—although he had an overseer—and so wearisome did he find the lonely
life he led on his plantation, that he could not remain upon it; and, as
he knew everything would go to the dogs if he did not, he was seriously
contemplating to sell out, retaining only his foster-mother and a body-
servant. He thought of taking them to Louisiana and Texas, for sale;
but, if he should learn that there was much probability that Lower
California would be made a slave State, he supposed it would pay him
to wait, as probably, if that should occur, he could take them there and

sell them for twice as much as they would now bring in New Orleans. He knew very well, he said, that, as they were, raising corn and to-bacco, they were paying nothing at all like a fair interest on their value.[2]

Some of his best hands he now rented out to work in a furnace, and for the best of these he had been offered, for next year, two hundred dollars. He did not know whether he ought to let them go, though. They were worked hard, and had too much liberty, and were acquiring bad habits. They earned money by overwork, and spent it for whisky, and got a habit of roaming about and *taking care of themselves;* because, when they were not at work in the furnace, nobody looked out for them.

I begin to suspect that the great trouble and anxiety of Southern gentlemen is:—How, without quite destroying the capabilities of the negro for any work at all, to prevent him from learning to take care of himself.

From
THE CLANSMAN (1905)
THOMAS DIXON

Baptist clergyman and writer Thomas Dixon (1864–1946) is best known for The Clansman, *a sentimental novel of Reconstruction as the white South saw it. Later made into the classic motion picture* The Birth of a Nation *(1915), directed by D. W. Griffith, the novel was influential in affecting the popular view of the Reconstruction period and the original Ku Klux Klan.*

The Hunt for the Animal

Aunt Cindy came at seven o'clock to get breakfast, and finding the house closed and no one at home, supposed Mrs. Lenoir and Marion had remained at the Cameron House for the night. She sat down on the steps, waited grumblingly an hour, and then hurried to the hotel to scold her former mistress for keeping her out so long.

Accustomed to enter familiarly, she thrust her head into the dining-room, where the family were at breakfast with a solitary guest, muttering the speech she had been rehearsing on the way:

[2] Mr. Wise is reported to have stated in his electioneering tour when candidate for Governor in 1855, that if slavery were permitted, negroes would sell for $5,000 apiece.

"I lak ter know what sort er way dis—whar's Miss Jeannie?"

Ben leaped to his feet.

"Isn't she at home?"

"Been waitin' dar two hours."

"Great God!" he groaned, springing through the door and rushing to saddle the mare. As he left he called to his father: "Let no one know till I return."

At the house he could find no trace of the crime he had suspected. Every room was in perfect order. He searched the yard carefully and under the cedar by the window he saw the barefoot tracks of a negro. The white man was never born who could make that track. The enormous heel projected backward, and in the hollow of the instep where the dirt would scarcely be touched by an Aryan was the deep wide mark of the African's flat foot. He carefully measured it, brought from an out-house a box, and fastened it over the spot.

It might have been an ordinary chicken thief, of course. He could not tell, but it was a fact of big import. A sudden hope flashed through his mind that they might have risen with the sun and strolled to their favorite haunt at Lover's Leap.

In two minutes he was there, gazing with hard-set eyes at Marion's hat and handkerchief lying on the shelving rock.

The mare bent her glistening neck, touched the hat with her nose, lifted her head, dilated her delicate nostrils, looked out over the cliff with her great soft half-human eyes and whinnied gently.

Ben leaped to the ground, picked up the handkerchief, and looked at the initials, "M. L.," worked in the corner. He knew what lay on the river's brink below as well as if he stood over the dead bodies. He kissed the letters of her name, crushed the handkerchief in his locked hands, and cried:

"Now, Lord God, give me strength for the service of my people!"

He hurriedly examined the ground, amazed to find no trace of a struggle or crime. Could it be possible they had ventured too near the brink and fallen over?

He hurried to report to his father his discoveries, instructed his mother and Margaret to keep the servants quiet until the truth was known, and the two men returned along the river's brink to the foot of the cliff.

They found the bodies close to the water's edge. Marion had been killed instantly. Her fair blonde head lay in a crimson circle sharply defined in the white sand. But the mother was still warm with life. She had scarcely ceased to breathe. In one last desperate throb of love the trembling soul had dragged the dying body to the girl's side, and she had died with her head resting on the fair round neck as though she had kissed her and fallen asleep.

Father and son clasped hands and stood for a moment with uncovered heads. The doctor said at length:

"Go to the coroner at once and see that he summons the jury *you* select and hand to him. Bring them immediately. I will examine the bodies before they arrive."

Ben took the negro coroner into his office alone, turned the key, told him of the discovery, and handed him the list of the jury.

"I'll hatter see Mr. Lynch fust, sah," he answered.

Ben placed his hand on his hip pocket and said coldly:

"Put your cross-mark on those forms I've made out there for you, go with me immediately, and summon these men. If you dare put a negro on this jury, or open your mouth as to what has occurred in this room, I'll kill you."

The negro tremblingly did as he was commanded.

The coroner's jury reported that the mother and daughter had been killed by accidentally falling over the cliff.

In all the throng of grief-stricken friends who came to the little cottage that day, but two men knew the hell-lit secret beneath the tragedy.

When the bodies reached the home, Doctor Cameron placed Mrs. Cameron and Margaret outside to receive visitors and prevent any one from disturbing him. He took Ben into the room and locked the doors.

"My boy, I wish you to witness an experiment."

He drew from its case a powerful microscope of French make.

"What on earth are you going to do, sir?"

The doctor's brilliant eyes flashed with a mystic light as he replied:

"Find the fiend who did this crime—and then we will hang him on a gallows so high that all men from the rivers to ends of the earth shall see and feel and know the might of an unconquerable race of men."

"But there's no trace of him here."

"We shall see," said the doctor, adjusting his instrument.

"I believe that a microscope of sufficient power will reveal on the retina of these dead eyes the image of this devil as if etched there by fire. The experiment has been made successfully in France. No word or deed of man is lost. A German scholar has a memory so wonderful he can repeat whole volumes of Latin, German, and French without an error. A Russian officer has been known to repeat the roll-call of any regiment by reading it twice. Psychologists hold that nothing is lost from the memory of man. Impressions remain in the brain like words written on paper in invisible ink. So I believe of images in the eye if we can trace them early enough. If no impression were made subsequently on the mother's eye by the light of day, I believe the fire-etched record of this crime can yet be traced."

Ben watched him with breathless interest.

He first examined Marion's eyes. But in the cold azure blue of their pure depths he could find nothing.

"It's as I feared with the child," he said. "I can see nothing. It is on the mother I rely. In the splendour of life, at thirty-seven she was the full-blown perfection of womanhood, with every vital force at its highest tension————"

He looked long and patiently into the dead mother's eye, rose and wiped the perspiration from his face.

"What is it, sir?" asked Ben.

Without reply, as if in a trance, he returned to the microscope and again rose with the little, quick, nervous cough he gave only in the greatest excitement, and whispered:

"Look now and tell me what you see."

Ben looked and said:

"I can see nothing."

"Your powers of vision are not trained as mine," replied the doctor, resuming his place at the instrument.

"What do you see?" asked the younger man, bending nervously.

"The bestial figure of a negro—his huge black hand plainly defined—the upper part of the face is dim, as if obscured by a gray mist of dawn—but the massive jaws and lips are clear—merciful God—yes—it's Gus!"

The doctor leaped to his feet livid with excitement.

Ben bent again, looked long and eagerly, but could see nothing.

"I'm afraid the image is in your eye, sir, not the mother's," said Ben sadly.

"That's possible, of course," said the doctor, "yet I don't believe it."

"I've thought of the same scoundrel and tried blood hounds on that track, but for some reason they couldn't follow it. I suspected him from the first, especially since learning that he left for Columbia on the early morning train on pretended official business."

"Then I'm not mistaken," insisted the doctor, trembling with excitement. "Now do as I tell you. Find when he returns. Capture him, bind, gag, and carry him to your meeting-place under the cliff, and let me know."

On the afternoon of the funeral, two days later, Ben received a cypher telegram from the conductor on the train telling him that Gus was on the evening mail due at Piedmont at nine o'clock.

The papers had been filled with accounts of the accident, and an enormous crowd from the county and many admirers of the fiery lyrics of the poet father had come from distant parts to honour his name. All business was suspended, and the entire white population of the village followed the bodies to their last resting place.

As the crowds returned to their homes, no notice was taken of a dozen men on horseback who rode out of town by different ways about dusk. At eight o'clock they met in the woods near the first little flag-station located on McAllister's farm four miles from Piedmont, where a buggy awaited them. Two men of powerful build, who were strangers in the county, alighted from the buggy and walked along the track to board the train at the station three miles beyond and confer with the conductor.

The men, who gathered in the woods, dismounted, removed their saddles, and from the folds of the blankets took a white disguise for horse and man. In a moment it was fitted on each horse, with buckles at the throat, breast, and tail, and the saddles replaced. The white robe for the man was made in the form of an ulster overcoat with cape, the skirt extending to the top of the shoes. From the red belt at the waist were swung two revolvers which had been concealed in their pockets. On each man's breast was a scarlet circle within which shone a white cross. The same scarlet circle and cross appeared on the horse's breast, while on his flanks flamed the three red mystic letters, K. K. K. Each man wore a white cap, from the edges of which fell a piece of cloth extending to the shoulders. Beneath the visor was an opening for the eyes and lower down one for the mouth. On the front of the caps of two of the men appeared the red wings of a hawk as the ensign of rank. From the top of each cap rose eighteen inches high a single spike held erect by a twisted wire. The disguises for man and horse were made of clean unbleached domestic and weighed less than three pounds. They were easily folded within a blanket and kept under the saddle in a crowd without discovery. It required less than two minutes to remove the saddles, place the disguises, and remount.

At the signal of a whistle, the men and horses arrayed in white and scarlet swung into double-file cavalry formation and stood awaiting orders. The moon was now shining brightly, and its light shimmering on the silent horses and men with their tall spiked caps made a picture such as the world had not seen since the Knights of the Middle Ages rode on their Holy Crusades.

As the train neared the flag-station, which was dark and unattended, the conductor approached Gus, leaned over, and said: "I've just gotten a message from the sheriff telling me to warn you to get off at this station and slip into town. There's a crowd at the depot there waiting for you and they mean trouble."

Gus trembled and whispered:

"Den fur Gawd's sake lemme off here."

The two men who got on at the station below stepped out before the negro, and as he alighted from the car, seized, tripped, and threw him to the ground. The engineer blew a sharp signal, and the train pulled on.

In a minute Gus was bound and gagged.

One of the men drew a whistle and blew twice. A single tremulous call like the cry of an owl answered. The swift beat of horses' feet followed, and four white-and-scarlet clansmen swept in a circle around the group.

One of the strangers turned to the horseman with red-winged ensign on his cap, saluted, and said:

"Here's your man, Night Hawk."

"Thanks, gentlemen," was the answer. "Let us know when we can be of service to your county."

The strangers sprang into their buggy and disappeared toward the North Carolina line.

The clansmen blindfolded the negro, placed him on a horse, tied his legs securely, and his arms behind him to the ring of the saddle.

The Night Hawk blew his whistle four sharp blasts, and his pickets galloped from their positions and joined him.

Again the signal rang, and his men wheeled with the precision of trained cavalrymen into column formation three abreast, and rode toward Piedmont, the single black figure tied and gagged in the centre of the white-and-scarlet squadron.

From
PETROLEUM VESUVIUS NASBY (1866)
DAVID ROSS LOCKE

David Ross Locke, (1833–1888), humorist and political satirist, was creator of Petroleum Vesuvius Nasby, the most popular humorous character of the Civil War period. An ardent Republican and abolitionist, Locke was merciless in his denunciation of slavery, secession, and Southern sympathies. He remained active in civil rights movements after the war.

SAINT'S REST, (wich is in the Stait uv Noo Gersey,)
September the 24th, 1865.

Whenever yoo ask the people to adopt any given line uv ackshen, yoo hev got to give em a tolable good reason therefor. Troo, this never hez bin so nessary in the Dimekratik party, whose members hev alluz follered their leeders, without askin the why or wherefore, with a fidelity beautiful to behold. But people, ginrally, are inquisitive, and wun reason why we hev never succeeded with the slavery question, is becoz we never hev yet given a good reason why the nigger shood be held in slavery.

Wunst it wuz sought to be defended on the ground that the nigger wuz inferior to the white man, but it woodent do. Why? Becoz the full-blown Dimekrat thot to hisself to wunst, "Ef the stronger shel own the weaker—ef the intellectooally sooperior shel hold in slavery the intellectooally inferior, LORD HELP ME! Why, I might ez well go into a Ablishn township and select my master to wunst."

The same argument won't do ez to nigger equality. Why shood we say that the nigger shan't vote, on the skore uv his not bein fitted by eddicashen or intelligence, when the fust and cheefest qualificashen uv a strate Dimekrat is his not knowin how to read? Why, to-day, in my county, ef a Dimekrat kin rite his name without runnin his tongue out, we alluz refooze to elect him a delegate in the county convenshun. It exposes him to the suspishun uv knowin too much.

I hev quit all these shaller dodges, long ago. We must hev the nigger, for jest at this time there ain't no uther cappitle for us to run on; but he must be put on maintainable ground. I put my foot on him, on the ground uv the DIVERSITY UV THE RACES! He is not wun uv us. He is not a descendant uv Adam. Goddlemity probably made him, ez he did the ox, and the ass, and the dorg, and the babboon, but not at the same time, nor for the same purposes. He is not, in enny sence uv the word, a MAN! His kulor is different, the size uv his head is diffrent, his foot is longer, and his hand is bigger. He wuz created a beast, and the fiat uv the Almity give us dominion over him, the same ez over other beasts.

Does the theologian say that this doctrine undermines the Christian religion? I to wunst reply, that that don't matter to us. Dimokrasy and religion shook hands and bid each other a affekshunate farewell, years ago. Uv what comparison is religion to a Dimekratik triumph?

Doth the ethnologist say that the diffrence atween the Caucassian and Afrikin is no greater than atween the Caucassian and Mongolian? I anser to wunst that he is rite—that the Mongolian is likewise a beest; becoz, don't yoo see there ain't no Mongolians in this seckshun uv country to disprove it.

Doth the Ablishnist pint to a nigger who kin read and rite, and figure through to division, and in sich other partickelers show hisself sooperior to the majority uv Dimekrats? I alluz draw myself up to my full hite, assoom a virchusly indignant look, and exclaim, "He's nuthin but a d—d nigger, anyhow!" which is the only effective argument we hev hed for ten years.

Doth the besotted nigger-lover pint to the mulatter, and say, "What will yoo do with him, who is half beest and half man, who hez half a sole that is to be saved—for one-half uv whom Christ died?" I anser at wunst, that I don't deal in abstrackshuns, and git out ez soon ez possible, for there is a weak pint there, that I hevent ez yit bin able to git over.

This wun weak pint is no argument agin my theory, for happy is the Dimekrat who kin propound a theory that hezent a skore, instid uv wun, weak places in it.

This doctrine kivers the whole ground. Ef the nigger is a beest, Dimekrats hev a good excuse for not givin to mishnary sosieties, for uv what use is it to undertake to Christianize beests, who hev no soles to save and no interest in the blood uv Christ? It gives us a perfek rite to re-establish slavery, for doth not Blackstun, who wuz supposed to know ez much law ez a Noo Gersey justis uv the peece, say that we hev a rite to ketch and tame the wild beest, and bend him to our uses?

Also, he can't vote; for wood the lowest white man consent to vote alongside uv a beest, even ef he did walk on 2 legs? Not enny.

Let this doctrine be vigerusly preechd, and I hev no doubt suthin will result from it.

Petroleum V. Nasby,
Lait Paster uv the Church uv the Noo Dispensashun.

THE TRAINING OF THE NEGRO (1906)
ROBERT BENNETT BEAN

Anthropologist Robert Bennett Bean (1874–1944), particularly concerned with anatomical differences between races, was author of The Races of Man *(1935),* The Racial Anatomy of the Philippine Islands *(1910), and other studies having in common the conviction that understanding such differences in character and ability is the first step toward improving race relations.*

The negro in America may be classified in four racial groups: the true negro, of which there are several types (Guinea coast, Hottentot, Bushman), constitutes the majority in the South; the Hamitic negro (Bantu, Zulu, Kafir), is found in small numbers throughout the whole country, particularly in Virginia and the Carolinas; the Semitic negro (Sudanese, Dahomian), is also found in small numbers scattered over wide areas in the United States; the Caucasian negroes (sambo, mulatto, octoroon, etc.) are found in large and constantly increasing numbers both North and South, but predominate specially in the North.

In any training of the negro, cognizance should be taken of these elements in the colored people, as well as of the natural endowments and qualifications of the race. In order to obtain a just estimate of the different factors, it may be well to trace the origins of the peoples that make up the present negro population of America.

Mankind may be grouped primarily into two classes, the black and the white. The yellow, the red, and the brown races are secondary classes. There are several distinct types of the black race: the Australian, the African, etc., only one of which, the African, concerns us. There are three types of the white race: Hamitic, Semitic, and Caucasian. The Caucasian is the white race of Europe and America, although this has become mixed with the prehistoric Hamitic of Europe. The Semitic comprises the Jews, Arabs, and Gipsies. The Hamitic stock in prehistoric times peopled the region of the Sahara and the great lakes of Africa. This was then a habitable area, with an altitude of several thousand feet, three great rivers, a salubrious climate, and probably abundant vegetation. From this primitive home the stock spread in all directions. To the east, the fair-skinned Libyans settled on the upper Nile and assisted in founding one of the most flourishing civilizations of antiquity. The most recent exhumations in Egypt point to this fact. To the west, prehistoric men were Hamitic, being represented to-day by the Berbers of northern Africa, as well as by the fair-haired, blue-eyed, white-skinned inhabitants of the Atlas Mountains. To the north, they crossed the land bridges of the Mediterranean, which existed at Gibraltar, Italy, and Crete; and as the late prehistoric man of Europe they settled in the south, west, and north, as well as in the British Isles, and assisted in founding Grecian, Roman, Carthaginian, European, English, and American civilizations, through combinations with other peoples. To the south, the Hamitic race peopled the land of Sheba and of King Solomon's mines, as well as Madagascar, where Mongolian, negro, and Semitic elements, have been added, and are represented in the Madagascar negro of America.

In the course of many centuries,—many thousands of years, perhaps, —there has been an interminable intermingling of the Hamitic and negro stocks in Africa, while at present the pure negro is found only in isolated places along the west coast and in the jungles. This is indicated by the color map of Africa. Elsewhere the Hamitic negro prevails, and many of the relics of a previous civilization may be determined in the existing institutions, arts, and industries of the natives. Starting along the eastern coast, this element has fought its way to the southern extremities of the continent, then up the western coast to the region of the Congo, virtually exterminating the Bushmen and the Hottentots. The Dutch, German, and English are continually harassed by this warlike people, who are just at present engaged in a general uprising throughout South Africa.

More recently, in the last fifteen hundred years, the Semitic element has pervaded the north and west of Africa, conquering and proselyting, subduing and mingling with, the natives. The Semitic negro is more inclined to domesticity, and many states south of the Sudan are found where culture abounds, trades flourish, and laws are made and obeyed.

Before the negroes reached America, then, we see that two divisions of the white race had mixed with them for centuries. Since their arrival, the third has become more intimately incorporated with them, until now it is fair to say that perhaps two thirds or three fourths of the negroes in America have white blood in varying proportions.

Thus are evolved the four classes of negroes previously mentioned. The members of these four classes are so diverse in their characteristics and capabilities that it would be unfair and unjust to demand the same treatment, training, and education for each class; and in the processes of development and evolution, through natural selection, economic selection, and competition, the different classes are shifting to various levels, according to their capabilities and limitations. "The Hamitic negro has been warlike and dominant in Africa, and he is warlike and dominant in his own race in America. The Semitic negro is inclined to peace and domesticity wherever he is found. Because of faulty perspective, the Caucasian negro is of too recent origin to be judged fairly; but many noted men of this class indicate great possibilities, although their longevity is questionable and their stability doubtful. The characteristics of the true negro have been briefly outlined in a previous consideration of the negro brain, fundamental racial differences having been shown, with their consequent characteristics. These may be elaborated, in order to understand better the negro character.

The anterior association center, which was found smaller in the negro brain than in the Caucasian, is designated by Flechsig, the great German anatomist, as the seat of apperception, the ego, the personality, self-control, reason, and ethical and esthetic judgment. Wundt, the German psychologist, considers this center to be the seat of apperception. Professor Pillsbury of Ann Arbor declares that attention disappears or is affected when the frontal lobes are diseased. Dr. Allen Starr denotes the result of lesions of this center as follows: loss of interest in environment, loss of memory, of reason, and of spontaneity of action. Goltz, Hitzig, and Fritsch demonstrated virtually the same facts in monkeys. Cunningham, the foremost English anatomist, indicates the size of the frontal lobes to be the great and distinguishing difference between man and the lower animals. Broca, the eminent French anthropologist, considers skull formation to be due to brain development in a general way, stating that when a lobe of the brain increases in size, it tends to dilate the whole skull, but the dilation produced is at its maximum where the lobe is found. The frontal region of the negro skull has been repeatedly shown to be much smaller than the Caucasian.

Considering these facts, the conclusion is reached that the negro has a smaller proportion of the faculties pertaining to the frontal lobe than the Caucasian. The negro, then, lacks reason, judgment, apperception, attention, self-control, will power, orientation, ethical and esthetic attributes, and the relations of the ego (of personality, of self) to environment.

On the other hand, the posterior association center and the adjacent areas are slightly larger in the negro brain than in the Caucasian.

This center is concerned in the rudimentary connections of the parts of consciousness, in the coordination of the sense centers (sight, hearing, touch, taste, and smell), in the complex reflexes, and in the coordination of the perceptions of language (seeing, hearing, or, as in the blind, feeling the words). The posterior association center coordinates the perceptions of the senses, but without relating them to the personality, which is affected by the anterior association center, where they are allied with all previous experiences of the individual, and made effective in the processes of reasoning. The rudimentary connections of the parts of consciousness establish complex reflexes by uniting two or more widely separated areas of the brain, enabling a person to react to stimuli. Thus one dodges a ball or catches it when it is seen coming, because the seat of sight in the brain is coordinated with the seat for controlling the muscles, probably through the medium of the posterior association center. Each one of the senses reacts similarly. On hearing a sudden noise, one starts and listens with attention; on smelling a bad odor, one holds the breath and draws away. On the prick of a pin, one jumps aside.

Destruction of the posterior part of the brain results in a loss of the senses, a loss of the perception of language, in a confusion in the relations of time and space, in a lack of recognition of objects or persons, and general trouble in the complex reflexes and in the connections of ordinary association. Concrete perception is impossible. The objective conditions of consciousness are affected, but subjective control remains normal as long as the frontal lobes are normal. There is no confusion of the individuality in relation to environment; there is no loss of power of spoken or written language. Reason, will, judgment, apperception, attention, and the ethical and esthetic faculties are normal.

The indications are, then, that the negro is equal to the white in the development of the special senses (sight, hearing, touch, taste, smell, pain, heat, cold, muscle and tendon sense, thirst, hunger, and the sense of equilibrium of the body); in the perception of concrete objects, facts, ideas, and a good memory for them; in a ready response to stimuli (simple and complex reflexes), resulting in good automatic power; and in love for music and appreciation of art.

His vocabulary is generally limited to concrete terms, more or less, and is mainly monosyllabic, as witness the description of the game of "prisoners' base" by a colored boy sixteen years of age. "The way you play is to have equal numbers on each side of the street, and one has to show a lead; if he get caught, he has to hol' out his hands; and if he falls, he will say 'broken bones.'"

Individual observations have determined that certain concrete terms have the following associated ideas in the mind of the negro, the latter being readily obtained on mentioning the former, as: pole, north; boots, black; pencil, lead; paper, reading; fire, place; hat, white; horse, brown;

and bear, grizzly. Abstract terms are largely lacking, although the simple ones may be understood. After repeated trials, the following may be obtained: strength, man's; time, piece; courage, dogs; dear, not; love, he.

Abstract terms and difficult words are either not known or seldom used, or misapplied when used. The negro readily grasps single ideas, retains one idea to the exclusion of others, or else fails to correlate the various ideas when more than one is grasped. The negro is a good laborer under compulsion, or a good soldier with white officers, where his one idea is to work and obey.

In automatic power and in reflex response to stimuli, the negro exceeds the white, especially in youth, as every one will admit, this having been repeatedly demonstrated even in the laboratory. The negro also had a good memory for concrete facts, learning readily by repetition. The sense of color, of form, of rhythm, of melody, and of tactile impressions is acute, as is the sense of taste and of smell. Their aptitude for rhythm and melody appears in their remarkable dancing and singing, and in their playing of certain kinds of musical instruments. Their acuteness of taste and smell and of tactile impressions is shown in their relish of savory viands and in their sensitiveness to heat, cold, and pain.

Experiments have shown that the negro surpasses the white in the detection of shades of color, as in rearranging color cards that had been examined for half a minute, and then shuffled, the test being to replace them in their original positions.

Their rough carvings and drawings show no mean artistic skill, and their ability in the trades adds strength to this assertion. Should all these natural aptitudes be properly controlled and directed, much value might be made of them as assets in the struggle for existence. As they now exist, many of them are only phantom wiles that lure the child of color to a visionary and fleeting satisfaction of sensory impulses in unrestraint.

Moreover, the negro is lacking in apperception, faulty in reasoning, and deficient in judgment. A negro youth nearly twenty years of age called the Malay race the "malaria race," and could not be made to realize his error. This was told to a white girl of about ten years, who immediately exclaimed, with evident amusement, "Oh, he mistook a disease for a people." This example illustrates well the concrete perception of the negro as contrasted with the abstract reasoning of the white, and shows the lack of apperception in the one and the ready application of apperception by the other.

The negro has not become adapted to his new position or conditions. Lack of the proper appreciation of environment, or failure to become *en rapport* with surroundings, is continually evident in a particularly characteristic peculiarity of the negro which has been termed "bumptiousness." For instance, one evening coming home late on the trolley, four Germans were singing such songs as "Tannenbaum," "Die Lorelei," etc., in German, when a negro student entered the car. Presently the negro (a mulatto) blurted out a very indecent and inelegant expression of opprobrium relating to cowherds and aimed at the Germans. They immediately stopped singing, and one by one they cautioned the youth that sometimes one said too much. Needless to say the negro remained quiet after that, and the Germans resumed their singing, to the delight of the other occupants of the car. Bumptiousness continually embroils the negroes with one another and with the lower classes of whites, and embitters all sects and sections wherever there is contact between the races.

As the brain is divided into two parts, anterior and posterior, so the mind may be divided into two faculties, subjective and objective, active and passive, intellectual and sensory, voluntary and involuntary, or, better still, that which depends upon external forces and that which depends upon the mental attitude or interest. The negro has a well developed posterior brain, and good objective faculties, which are passive, sensory, involuntary, and depend upon external forces; and he has less of the frontal brain and subjective faculties, which are active, intellectual, voluntary, and depend upon the mental attitude.

A mind well organized, as in the Caucasian, is a mind in which the lines of demarcation of the experience are nearly effaced, and in which each bit of knowledge is founded on a unity equally effective at any moment to control the course of the mental life. When the parts of the mind are limited and rigidly distinct, as is apparent in the negro, a great part of the knowledge of the person is almost without value, and necessarily this person takes a narrowed and partial attitude toward all questions.

These generalizations all relate to the true negro, and not to the Hamitic, Semitic, or Caucasian negro. The object to be attained in training the true negro is to cultivate his natural endowments and to fit him for positions that he can fill. The training should be in manual labor of various kinds, useful in the industrial development of the South, and in intellectual pursuits for the production of men of affairs among their own people. But the true negro is capable of learning in only one way—objectively, by concrete perception, by repetition, and by memory of individual facts. He should be taught practical subjects in a practical way. His sensibilities may be controlled and guided, and his musical and artistic tastes may be directed into channels of usefulness to himself and pleasure to others. Hampton and Tuskegee are the schools in the South that teach the true negroes in the proper way and fit them for such occupations as they are properly qualified to conduct. Many Hamitic, Semitic, and Caucasian negroes, however, have good minds, and naturally become the leaders of their race. These men are trained in scores of colleges North and South, and are rapidly becoming an important factor in the negro problem. They control the religious and secular press of the race; they are rapidly acquiring the balance of financial power among their people; and they practise medicine, teach, and preach among those of their color. Many of their efforts do harm. It is expedient that this class be properly trained in order that they may exert a right influence over their fellows. Neither the rudiments of education nor the classics can alter the negro's brain, change his mental capacity, create a reform, or cure his diseases.

But one thing of signal service may be done. Since ignorance, immorality, and disease are the besetting evils of the negro, it behooves us to improve his mental, moral, and physical condition. This may be done by three groups of properly qualified men—teachers, preachers, and doctors. That these men may reach the home-life of the people and exert the greatest influence, it is necessary that they be negroes who have a consecrated zeal to devote their lives to the service of their fellows for the elevation of their race.

In order that such men may be impressed with the condition of their own people and their needs, they should study the problem in some large city like Baltimore, Washington, or New Orleans, where the negro is at home in large numbers. They should study disease at first hand among their own people. They should learn the social evils of their race. They should be brought face to face with the mockery of religion practised in many of their churches—a mere emotionalism. In order to avoid gross evil, they should know the practices of their own clergy. They should learn to teach practical subjects in a practical way. It would be well if a university for the higher education of the negro could be established in Baltimore or Washington, with the three departments of pedagogy, theology, and medicine. The requirements for entrance should be, first, maturity, morality, and mentality; second, determined purpose and consecration to the uplifting of the race from their threefold plague of ignorance, immorality, and disease; and, third, the possession of a degree equivalent to that of A.B. at the recognized American colleges. The chairs of the departments should be filled by white male teachers of the highest moral caliber, most earnest zeal, and greatest mental ability obtainable. The courses given should be mainly objective, so that the students may learn well the lessons of practical experience by concrete perception in the use of eyes, ears, and fingers. Life, and not books, should be read. Facts, as well as ideals, should be learned. Morality, and not emotionalism, should be encouraged.

A strong body of negro men so trained and at work leavening the race would do much good. This should be done not only for the good of the negro, but as a matter of self-protection. The negro is being educated by the thousand to-day, and it would be better to direct that education in the proper way rather than to allow it to breed mischief, as it has done in the past.

Out of the hundreds of negroes who are being graduated each year, there are surely some who would do well thus to consecrate their lives. The negroes in the South prepare our food, and in this way tuberculosis, or worse contagious diseases, may be transmitted. They tend our children, and not only convey the great white plague, but, worse still, by intimate contact they affect the morals of the young. As washerwomen, they contaminate our clothes. They are foci of infection in any community. For our own preservation and purity, then, we should foster such education as tends to the cleansing of the nation. It would be easier to change the ignorance, immorality, and diseased condition of the negro than to alter his brain or mental capacity, remove his past, eradicate race prejudice, change the attitude of the races, eliminate the mulatto element, perfect the habits of the negro, or provide the administration of justice to all alike. In alleviating the three great evils of the race, we ameliorate the other evils.

Taking a dip into the future, one sees the gradual forcing of the true negro, by competition, into the most degraded and least remunerative occupations. The large cities, with their inevitable blight of squalor and disease, will destroy great multitudes. Pitiless competition, merciless corporations, disease, and other afflictions will cause a constantly decreasing negro population. Continual youthful aberrations and intermarriage will keep the ranks of the mulattoes recruited until they form a very considerable proportion of the colored people. The cross-breed negro will probably find a place in the economy of commercial life in the future. An ever increasing proportion of them are learning agriculture and the trades. A great many are becoming doctors, lawyers, and teachers among their own people. The negro business man is yearly increasing in numbers. Natural traders, they take to business like a horse to grass. The number of negro landowners is rapidly increasing.

Here, then, is opportunity for stability, something to build on, and hope for the future. Much depends on the guiding hand and the brain behind it. Mr. Alfred H. Stone has demonstrated on his plantation in Mississippi that negro labor can be made as efficient as white labor in the cotton-fields, although other Southern planters have offered proofs to the contrary. Many prefer negro labor to white in large undertakings, because the negro is more effective than the white under compulsion.

An intelligent physician, on being called to a patient, will do three things: make a diagnosis (if possible), locate the primary cause of the trouble, and prescribe a remedy. In the case of the negro, the diagnosis is the three-fold evil in the race—ignorance, immorality, and disease. Among the most evident causes are the past history of the race, present racial antipathy, resulting in the dominant attitude of the Caucasian and the servile condition of the negro throughout the world; a difference in the brain and mental capacity of the two races; a difference in the administration of justice to the two; the habits of the negro (laziness, licentiousness, and unrestraint); the mulatto element; and lack of proper education. The remedy is legitimate restraint; an attitude of sympathy and altruistic guidance on the part of the white; a responsive effort to improve on the part of the negro; and proper education for him. The white man occupies the relation of physician toward this patient. Faith in the physician is a prime requisite for a cure. The attitude of the negro toward the white is all-important.

The differences of the brain and mental traits as fundamental conditions may be the primary cause of everything relating to the race question, other causes being secondary or merely symptoms resulting from this elemental condition. If this be true, the remedy should be applied to the brain and mind of the negro. But is the condition hereditary and fixed, or is it due to environment and alterable? Is it capable of change or is it stable? Is the negro capable of mental development in the same way as is the Caucasian? Time alone can answer these questions. History, investigations, experiments, and existing conditions indicate that the traits are hereditary and stable, and that the negro is not capable of mental development in the same way that the Caucasian is. The remedy should be to develop the negro along the lines of natural inclination and fitness, which lines must be established scientifically, not sentimentally.

Happily, whatever may be the final outcome, our duty lies in the present. Facing actual facts, seeing conditions as they are, we should endeavor to improve these conditions for the sake of our ideals, for the sake of humanity, for the sake of the negro, and for our own sakes. Our efforts must be directed in a different way from that heretofore pursued. We have viewed the race question in America as extremists: the North has been idealistic, the South realistic. The North has consistently claimed for the negro all the so-called inalienable rights of man, while the South has as persistently denied them. It is high time to unite on a common middle ground.

The negro needs restraint, moral and physical. As a child, he must learn to crawl before he can walk. Moral restraint may be made serviceable by a body of earnest and honest negroes, trained to a realization of the evils of the race and the means of eradicating them, and working from within toward an uplift. Physical restraint may be made effective by a body of rural police, such as the mounted police of Northwest Canada, keeping order in sparsely settled districts, or where the negro is preponderant. The police may be whites, but there can be no objection to negroes, allowing them jurisdiction over their own race. Such a thoroughly organized body would be a safeguard to rural communities and a conservator of peace, as well as a great relief to anxious absentees from home.

Local conditions are such that the attitude of the two races cannot be the same in all parts of the country. There are four or five States and many counties in the South where it is a matter of self-preservation, and not of ideals, in dealing with the negro. Suppose there were 5,000,000 negroes in Boston: would the attitude of the white inhabitants be the same there, I wonder? Or if New York City had 30,000,000 negroes, would there be no difference? And suppose that instead of the refined and intelligent negro, many of whom at present live in these cities, the millions were common laborers, with uncouth habits and uncultivated ways would that make any difference? Even then the conditions would not reach the extremes encountered in some of the counties of the South. However, even with such extremes, justice, tempered with mercy and administered with a kind heart and a firm hand, may do good.

Two things are essential to a peaceful solution of existing difficulties. The attitude of the white man toward the negro must be one of restraint and control, combined with humane interest, sympathetic and altruistic guidance, and a good example, while the negro must work out his own salvation with fear and trembling; for he is at the bar of public opinion, and, if tried and found wanting, is in imminent danger of losing all.

THE
YELLOW
MAN

From
ACROSS THE CONTINENT (1866)
SAMUEL BOWLES

---

*Samuel Bowles (1826–1878) was one of a distinguished family of jour-
nalists who edited the* Springfield Republican *for three generations.
Strongly opposed to slavery, he repudiated his Whig Party and denounced the Know Nothings, becoming a firm Republican. His first
western trip led to publication of* Across the Continent, *a collection of
sharp, objective observations, including one of the earliest fair ap-
praisals of the new Chinese culture in San Francisco.*

San Francisco, August 18.
I have been waiting before writing of the Chinese in these Pacific
States, till my experience of them had culminated in the long-promised
grand dinner with their leaders and aristocrats. This came last night,
and while I am full of the subject,—shark's fins and resurrected fungus
digest slowly,—let me write of this unique and important element in
the population and civilization of this region. There are no fewer than
sixty to eighty thousand Chinamen here. They are scattered all over
the States and Territories of the Coast, and number from one-eighth
to one-sixth of the entire population. We began to see them at Austin,
in Nevada, and have found them everywhere since, in country and city,
in the woods, among the mines, north in the British dominions, on the
Coast, in the mountains,—everywhere that work is to be done, and
money gained by patient, plodding industry. They have been coming
over from home since 1852, when was the largest emigration, (twenty
thousand.) A hundred thousand in all have come, but thirty thousand
to forty thousand have gone back. None come really to stay; they do
not identify themselves with the country; but to get work, to make
money, and go back. They never, or very rarely, bring their wives. The
Chinese woman here are prostitutes, imported as such by those who
make a business of satisfying the lust of men. Nor are their customers
altogether Chinese; base white men patronize their wares as well. Some
of these women are taken as "secondary" wives by the Chinese residents, and a sort of family life established; but, as a general rule, there
are no families among them, and few children.

The occupations of these people are various. There is hardly anything that they cannot turn their hands to,—the work of women as well
as men. They do the washing and ironing for the whole population;
and sprinkle the clothes as they iron them, by squirting water over
them in a fine spray from their mouths. Everywhere, in village and
town, you see rude signs, informing you that See Hop or Ah Thing or

Sam Sing or Wee Lung or Cum Sing wash and iron. How Tie is a doctor, and Hop Chang and Chi Lung keep stores. They are good house servants; cooks, table-waiters, and nurses; better, on the whole, than Irish girls, and as cheap,—fifteen to twenty-five dollars a month and board. One element of their usefulness as cooks is their genius for imitation; show them once how to do a thing, and their education is perfected; no repetition of the lesson is needed. But they seem to be more in use as house servants in the country than the city; they do not share the passion of the Irish girls for herding together, and appear to be content to be alone in a house, in a neighborhood, or a town.

Many are vegetable gardeners, too. In this even climate and with this productive soil, their painstaking culture, much hoeing and constant watering, makes little ground very fruitful, and they gather in three, four and five crops a year. Their garden patches, in the neighborhood of cities and villages, are always distinguishable from the rougher and more carelessly cultured grounds of their Saxon rivals. The Pacific Railroad is being built by Chinese labor; several thousand Chinamen are now rapidly grading the track through the rocks and sands of the Sierra Nevadas,—without them, indeed, this great work would have to wait for years, or move on with slow, hesitating steps. They can, by their steady industry, do nearly as much in a day, even in this rough labor, as the average of white men, and they cost only about half as much, say thirty dollars a month against fifty dollars. Besides, white labor is not to be had in the quantities necessary for such a great job as this. Good farm hands are the Chinese, also; and in the simpler and routine mechanic arts they have proven adepts;— there is hardly any branch of labor in which, under proper tuition, they do not or cannot succeed most admirably. The great success of the woolen manufacture here is due to the admirable adaptation and comparative cheapness of Chinese labor for the details. They are quick to learn, quiet, cleanly and faithful, and have no "off days," no sprees to get over. As factory operatives they receive twenty and twenty-five dollars a month, and board themselves, though quarters are provided for them on the mill grounds. Fish, vegetables, rice and pork are the main food, which is prepared and eaten with such economy that they live for about one-third what Yankee laborers can.

Thousands of the Chinese are gleaners in the gold fields. They follow in crowds after the white miners, working and washing over their deserted or neglected sands, and thriving on results that their predecessors would despise. A Chinese gold washer is content with one to two dollars a day; while the white man starves or moves on disgusted with twice that. A very considerable portion of the present gold production of California must now be the work of Chinese painstaking and moderate ambition. The traveler meets these Chinese miners everywhere on his road through the State; at work in the deserted ditches, or moving from one to another, on foot with their packs, or often in the stage, sharing the seats and paying the price of their aristocratic Saxon rivals.

Labor, cheap labor, being the one great palpable need of the Pacific States,—far more indeed than capital the want and necessity of their prosperity,— we should all say that these Chinese would be welcomed on every hand, their emigration encouraged, and themselves protected by law. Instead of which, we see them the victims of all sorts of prejudice and injustice. Ever since they began to come here, even now, it is a disputed question with the public, whether they should not be forbidden our shores. They do not ask or wish for citizenship; they have no ambition to become voters; but they are even denied protection in persons and property by the law. Their testimony is inadmissible against the white man; and, as miners, they are subject to a tax of four dollars a month, or nearly fifty dollars a year, each, for the benefit of the County and State treasuries. Thus ostracized and burdened by the State, they, of course, have been the victims of much meanness and cruelty from individuals. To abuse and cheat a Chinaman; to rob him; to kick and cuff him; even to kill him, have been things not only done with impunity by mean and wicked men, but even with vain glory. Terrible are some of the cases of robbery and wanton maiming and murder reported from the mining districts. Had "John,"—here and in China alike the English and Americans nickname every Chinaman "John,"—a good claim, original or improved, he was ordered to "move on,"—it belonged to somebody else. Had he hoarded a pile, he was ordered to disgorge; and, if he resisted, he was killed. Worse crimes even are known against them; they have been wantonly assaulted and shot down or stabbed by bad men, as sportsmen would surprise and shoot their game in the woods. There was no risk in such barbarity; if "John" survived to tell the tale, the law would not hear him or believe him. Nobody was so low, so miserable, that he did not despise the Chinaman, and could not outrage him. Ross Browne has an illustration of the status of poor "John," that is quite to the point. A vagabond Indian comes upon a solitary Chinaman, working over the sands of a deserted gulch for gold. "Dish is my land,"—says he,—"you pay me fifty dollar." The poor celestial turns, deprecatingly, saying: "Melican man (American) been here, and took all,—no bit left." Indian, irate and fierce,— "D—— Melican man,—you pay me fifty dollar, or I killee you."

Through a growing elevation of public opinion, and a reactionary experience towards depression, that calls for study of the future, the Californians are beginning to have a better appreciation of their Chinese immigrants. The demand for them is increasing. The new State, to be built upon manufactures and agriculture, is seen to need their cheap and reliable labor; and more pains will be taken to attract them to the country. But even now, a man who aspires to be a political leader, till lately a possible United States Senator, and the most widely circulated daily paper of this city, pronounce against the Chinese, and would drive them home. Their opposition is based upon the prejudices and jealousy of ignorant white laborers,—the Irish particularly,—who regard the Chinese as rivals in their field, and clothes itself in that cheap talk, so common among the bogus democracy of the East, about this being a "white man's country," and no place for Africans or Asiatics. But our national democratic principle, of welcoming hither the people of every country and clime, aside, the white man needs the negro and the Chinaman more than they him; the pocket appeal will override the prejudices of his soul,—and we shall do a sort of rough justice to both classes, because it will pay. The political questions involved in the negro's presence, and pressing so earnestly for solution, do not yet arise with regard to the Chinese,—perhaps will never be presented. As I have said, the Chinese are ambitious of no political rights, no citizenship,—it is only as our merchants go to China that they come here. Their great care, indeed, is to be buried at home; they stipulate with anxiety for that; and the great bulk of all who die on these shores are carried back for final interment.

There is no ready assimilation of the Chinese with our habits and modes of thought and action. Their simple, narrow though not dull minds have run too long in the old grooves to be easily turned off. They look down even with contempt upon our newer and rougher civilization, regarding us barbaric in fact, and calling us in their hearts, if not in speech, "the foreign devils." And our conduct towards them has inevitably intensified these feelings,—it has driven them back upon their naturally self-contained natures and habits. So they bring here and retain all their home ways of living and dressing, their old associations and religion. Their streets and quarters in town and city are China reproduced, unalleviated. Christian missionaries make small inroads among them. There is an intelligent and faithful one here (Rev. Mr. Loomis,) who has an attractive chapel and school, but his followers are few, and not rapidly increasing. But he and his predecessors and assistants have been and are doing a good work in teaching the two diverse races to better understand each other and in showing them how they can be of value to one another. They have been the constant and urgent advocates of the personal rights of the Chinese.

The religion of these people is a cheap, showy idolatry, with apparently nothing like fanaticism in it, and not a very deep hold in itself on their natures. "Josh" is their god or idol, and the "Josh" houses are small affairs, fitted up with images and altars a good deal after the style of cheap Catholic churches in Europe. Their whole civilization impresses me as a low, disciplined, perfected, sensuous sensualism. Everything in their life and their habits seems cut and dried like their food. There is no sign of that abandonment to an emotion, to a passion, good or bad, that marks the western races. Their great vice is gambling; that is going on constantly in their houses and shops; and commerical women and barbaric music minister to its indulgence. Cheap lotteries are a common form of this passion. Opium-smoking ranks next; and this is believed to be indulged in more extensively among them here than at home, since there is less restraint from relatives and authorities, and the means of procuring the article are greater. The wildly brilliant eye, the thin, haggard face, and the broken nervous system betray the victim to opium-smoking; and all tense, all excited, staring in eye and expression, he was almost a frightful object, as we peered in through the smoke of his half-lighted little room, and saw him lying on his mat in the midst of his fatal enjoyment.

But as laborers in our manufactories and as servants in our houses, beside their constant contact with our life and industry otherwise, these emigrants from the East cannot fail to get enlargement of ideas, freedom and novelty of action, and familiarity with and then preference for our higher civilization. Slowly and hardly but still surely this work must go on; and their constant going back and forth between here and China must also transplant new elements of thought and action into the home circles. Thus it is that we may hope and expect to reach this great people with the influences of our better and higher life. It is through modification and revolution in materialities, in manner of living, in manner of doing, that we shall pave the way for our thought and our religion. Our missionaries to the Five Points have learned to attack first with soap and water and clean clothes. The Chinese that come here are unconsciously beseiged at first with better food and more of it than they have at home. The bath-house and the restaurant are the avant couriers of the Christian civilization.

The Chinese that come to these States are among the best of the peasantry from the country about Canton and Hong Kong. None of them are the miserable coolies that have been imported by the English to their Indian colonies as farm laborers. They associate themselves here into companies, based upon the village or neighborhood from which they come at home. These companies have headquarters in San Francisco; their presidents are men of high intelligence and character; and their office is to afford a temporary refuge for all who belong to their bodies, to assist them to work, to protect them against wrong, and send the dead back to their kindred at home. Beside these organizations, there are guilds or trade associations among the Chinese engaged in different occupations. Thus the laundry-men and the cigar-makers have organizations, with heavy fees from the members, power over the common interests of the business, and an occasional festivity.

The impressions these people make upon the American mind, after close observation of their habits, are very mixed and contradictory. They unite to many of the attainments and knowledge of the highest civilization, in some of which they are models for ourselves, many of the incidents and most of the ignorance of a simple barbarism. It may yet prove that we have as much to learn from them as they from us. Certainly here in this great field, this western half of our continental Nation, their diversified labor is a blessing and a necessity. It is all, perhaps more even, than the Irish and the Africans have been and are to our eastern wealth and progress. At the first, at least, they have greater adaptability and perfection than either of these classes of laborers, to whom we are so intimately and sometimes painfully accustomed.

There are quite a number of heavy mercantile houses here in the hands of the Chinese. The managers are intelligent, superior men. Their business is in supplies for their countrymen and in teas and silks and curiosities for the Americans. They import by the hundreds of thousands, even millions, yearly; and their reputation for fair and honest dealing is above that of the American merchants generally. These are the men, with the presidents of the six companies, into which the whole Chinese population is organized, as I have described, with whom Mr. Colfax and his friends dined last night. There were formalities and negotiations enough in the preliminary arrangements of the entertainment to have sufficed for a pacification of Kentucky politics, or the making of a new map of Europe; but when these were finally adjusted, questions of precedence among the Chinese settled, and a proper choice made among the many Americans who were eager to be bidden to the feast, all went as smooth as a town school examination that the teacher has been drilling for a month previous.

The party numbered from fifty to sixty, half Chinese, half white folks. The dinner was given in the second story of a Chinese restaurant, in a leading street of the city. Our hosts were fine-looking men, with impressive manners. While their race generally seems not more than two-thirds the size of our American men, these were nearly if not quite as tall and stout as their guests. Their eyes and their faces beamed with intelligence, and they were quick to perceive everything, and alert and *au fait* in all courtesies and politeness. An interpreter was present for the heavy talking; but most of our Chinese entertainers spoke a little English, and we got on well enough so far as that was concerned; though handshaking and bowing and scraping and a general flexibility of countenance, bodies and limbs had a very large share of the conversation to perform. Neither here nor in China is it common for the English and Americans to learn the Chinese language. The Chinese can and do more readily acquire ours, sufficiently at least for all business intercourse. Their broken or "pigeon" English, as it is called, is often very grotesque, and always very simple. Here is a specimen—a "pigeon-English" rendering of "My name is Norval," etc.:—

My namee being Norval topside that Glampian Hillee,
My father you sabee my father, makee pay chow-chow he sheep,
He smallo heartee man, too muchee take care that dolla, gallo?

So fashion he wantchee keep my, counta one piece chilo stop he own side
My no wantchee long that largee mandoli, go knockee alla man;
Littee turn Jose pay my what thing my father no like pay
That mourn last nightee get up loune, alla same my hat,
No go full up, no got square; that plenty piece
That lobbie man, too muchee qui-si, alla same that tiger
Chop-chop come down that hillee, catchie that sheep long that cow,
That man, custom take care, too muchie quick lun away
My one piecie owne spee eye, look see that landlone man what side he walkee
Hi-yah! No good chancie, findie he, lun catchie my flew:
Too piecie loon choon lun catchie that lobbie man! he
No can walkee welly quick, he pocket too much full up.
So fashion knockee he largee.
  He head man no got shuttee far
My knockie he head, Hi-yah! my No. 1 strong man,
Catchie he jacket, long he toousa, galo! You likee look see?
My no likee takee care that sheep, so fashion my hear you got fightee this
      side.
My takee one servant, come your country, come helpie you,
He heart all same cow, too muchie fear lun away.
Masquie, Joss take care pay my come you house.

We were seated for the dinner around little round tables, six to nine at the table, and hosts and guests evenly mixed. There was a profusion of elegant China dishes on each table; each guest had two or three plates and saucers, all delicate and small. Choice sauces, pickles, sweetmeats and nuts were plentifully scattered about. Each guest had a saucer of flowers, a China spoon or bowl with a handle, and a pair of chop-sticks, little round and smooth ivory sticks about six inches long. Chi Sing-Tong, President of the San Yup Company, presided at Mr. Colfax's table.

Now the meal began. It consisted of three different courses, or dinners rather, between which was a recess of half an hour, when we retired to an anteroom, smoked and talked, and listened to the simple, rough, barbaric music from coarse guitar, viol drum, and violin, and meanwhile the tables were reset and new food provided.

Each course or dinner comprised a dozen to twenty different dishes, served generally one at a time, though sometimes two were brought on at once. There were no joints, nothing to be carved. Every article of food was brought on in quart bowls, in a sort of hash form. We dove into it with our chop-sticks, which, well handled, took up about a mouthful, and, transferring this to our plates, worked the chop-sticks again to get it or parts of it to our mouths. No one seemed to take more than a single taste or mouthful of each dish; so that, even if one relished the food, it would need something like a hundred different dishes to satisfy an ordinary appetite. Some of us took very readily to the chopsticks; others did not,—perhaps were glad they could not; and for these a Yankee fork was provided, and our Chinese neighbors at the table were also prompt to offer their own chop-sticks to place a bit of each dish upon our plates. But as these same chop-sticks were also used to convey food into the mouths of the Chinese, the service did not always add to the relish of the food.

These were the principal dishes served for the first course, and in the order named: Fried shark's fins and grated ham, stewed pigeon with bamboo soup, fish sinews with ham, stewed chicken with water-cress, sea-weed, stewed ducks and bamboo soup, sponge cake, omelet cake, flower cake and banana fritters, bird-nest soup, tea. The meats seemed all alike; they had been dried or preserved in some way; were cut up into mouthfuls, and depended for all savoriness upon their accompaniments. The sea-weed, shark's fins and the like had a glutinous sort of taste; not repulsive, nor very seductive. The sweets were very delicate, but like everything else had a very artificial flavor; every article, indeed, seemed to have had its original and real taste and strength dried or cooked out of it, and a common Chinese flavor put into it. The bird-nest soup looked and tasted somewhat as a very delicate vermicelli soup does. The tea was delicious,—it was served without milk or sugar, did not need any such amelioration, and was very refreshing. Evidently it was made from the most delicate leaves or flowers of the tea plant, and had escaped all vulgar steeping or boiling.

During the first recess, the presidents of the companies,—the chief entertainers,—took their leave, and the merchants assumed the post of leading hosts; such being the fashion of the people. The second dinner opened with cold tea, and a white rose-scented liquor, very strong, and served in tiny cups, and went on with lichens and a fungus-like moss, more shark's fins, stewed chestnuts and chickens, Chinese oysters, yellow and resurrected from the dried stage, more fungus stewed, a stew of flour and white nuts, stewed mutton, roast ducks, rice soup, rice and ducks' eggs and pickled cucumbers, ham and chicken soup. Between the second and third parts, there was an exchange of complimentary speeches by the head Chinaman and Mr. Colfax, at which the interpreter had to officiate. The third and last course consisted of a great variety of fresh fruits; and the unique entertainment ended about eleven o'clock, after a sitting of full five hours. The American resident guests furnished champagne and claret, and our Chinese hosts, invariably at the entrance and departure of each dish, invited us, with a gracious bow, to a sip thereof, in the which they all faithfully joined themselves.

The dinner was unquestionably a most magnificent one after the Chinese standard; the dishes were many of them rare and expensive; and everything was served in elegance and taste. It was a curious and interesting experience, and one of the rarest of the many courtesies extended to Mr. Colfax on this coast. But as to any real gastronomic satisfaction to be derived from it, I certainly "did not see it." Governor Bross's fidelity to the great principle of "when you are among the Romans to do as the Romans do," led him to take the meal seriatim, and eat of everything; but my own personal experience is perhaps the best commentary to be made upon the meal, as a meal. I went to the table weak and hungry; but I found the one universal odor and flavor soon destroyed all appetite; and I fell back resignedly on a constitutional incapacity to use the chop-sticks, and was sitting with a grim politeness through dinner number two, when there came an angel in disguise to my relief. The urbane chief of police of the city appeared and touched my shoulder: "There is a gentleman at the door who wishes to see you, and would have you bring your hat and coat." There were visions of violated city ordinances and "assisting" at the police court next morning. I thought, too, what a polite way this man has of arresting a stranger to the city. But, bowing my excuses to my pig-tail neighbor, I went joyfully to the unknown tribunal. A friend, a leading banker, who had sat opposite to me during the evening, and had been called out a few moments before, welcomed me at the street door with: "B——, I knew you were suffering, and were hungry—let us go and get something to eat—a good square meal!" So we crossed to an American restaurant; the lost appetite came back; and mutton chops, squabs, fried potatoes and a bottle of champagne soon restored me. My friend insisted that the second course of the Chinese dinner was only the first warmed over, and that that was the object of the recess. However that might be,—this is how I went to the grand Chinese dinner, and went out, when it was two-thirds over, and "got something to eat."

From
ROUGHING IT (1872)
MARK TWAIN

Mark Twain (1835–1910) was noted for his sympathetic defense of the Chinese on the West Coast when such defenses were unpopular. Roughing It *is particularly pointed in its denunciation of those who persecuted and exploited the Chinese.*

CHINESE IN VIRGINIA CITY—WASHING BILLS—HABIT OF IMITATION—
CHINESE IMMIGRATION—A VISIT TO CHINATOWN—MESSRS. AH SING,
HONG WO, SEE YUP, &c.

Of course there was a large Chinese population in Virginia—it is the case with every town and city on the Pacific coast. They are a harmless race when white men either let them alone or treat them no worse than dogs; in fact they are almost entirely harmless anyhow, for they seldom think of resenting the vilest insults or the cruelist injuries. They are quiet, peaceable, tractable, free from drunkenness, and they are as industrious as the day is long. A disorderly Chinaman is rare, and a lazy one does not exist. So long as a Chinaman has strength to use his hands he needs no support from anybody; white men often complain of want of work, but a Chinaman offers no such complaint; he always manages to find something to do. He is a great convenience to everybody—even to the worst class of white men, for he bears the most of their sins, suffering fines for their petty thefts, imprisonment for their robberies, and death for their murders. Any white man can swear a Chinaman's life away in the courts, but no Chinaman can testify against a white man. Ours is the "land of the free"—nobody denies that—nobody challenges it. [Maybe it is because we won't let other people testify.] As I write, news comes that in broad daylight in San Francisco, some boys have stoned an inoffensive Chinaman to death, and that although a large crowd witnessed the shameful deed, no one interfered.

There are seventy thousand (and possibly one hundred thousand) Chinamen on the Pacific coast. There were about a thousand in Virginia. They were penned into a "Chinese quarter"—a thing which they do not particularly object to, as they are fond of herding together. Their buildings were of wood; usually only one story high, and set thickly together along streets scarcely wide enough for a wagon to pass through. Their quarter was a little removed from the rest of the town. The chief employment of Chinamen in towns is to wash clothing. They always send a bill pinned to the clothes. It is mere ceremony, for it does not enlighten the customer much. Their price for washing was $2.50 per dozen—rather cheaper than white people could afford to wash for at that time. A very common sign on the Chinese houses was: "See Yup, Washer and Ironer"; "Hong Wo, Washer"; "Sam Sing & Ah Hop, Washing." The house servants, cooks, etc., in California and Nevada, were chiefly Chinamen. There were few white servants and no Chinawomen so employed. Chinamen make good house servants, being quick, obedient, patient, quick to learn and tirelessly industrious. They do not need to be taught a thing twice, as a general thing. They are imitative. If a Chinaman were to see his master break up a centre table, in a passion, and kindle a fire with it, that Chinaman would be likely to resort to the furniture for fuel forever afterward.

All Chinamen can read, write and cipher with easy facility—pity but all our petted *voters* could. In California they rent little patches of ground and do a deal of gardening. They will raise surprising crops of vegetables on a sand pile. They waste nothing. What is rubbish to a Christian, a Chinaman carefully preserves and makes useful in one way or another. He gathers up all the old oyster and sardine cans that white people throw away, and procures marketable tin and solder from them by melting. He gathers up old bones and turns them into manure. In

California he gets a living out of old mining claims that white men have abandoned as exhausted and worthless—and then the officers come down on him once a month with an exorbitant swindle to which the legislature has given the broad, general name of "foreign" mining tax, but it is usually inflicted on no foreigners but Chinamen. This swindle has in some cases been repeated once or twice on the same victim in the course of the same month—but the public treasury was not additionally enriched by it, probably.

Chinamen hold their dead in great reverence—they worship their departed ancestors, in fact. Hence, in China, a man's front yard, back yard, or any other part of his premises, is made his family burying ground, in order that he may visit the graves at any and all times. Therefore that huge empire is one mighty cemetery; it is ridged and wringled from its centre to its circumference with graves—and inasmuch as every foot of ground must be made to do its utmost, in China, lest the swarming population suffer for food, the very graves are cultivated and yield a harvest, custom holding this to be no dishonor to the dead. Since the departed are held in such worshipful reverence, a Chinaman cannot bear that any indignity be offered the places where they sleep. Mr. Burlingame said that herein lay China's bitter opposition to railroads; a road could not be built anywhere in the empire without disturbing the graves of their ancestors or friends.

A Chinaman hardly believes he could enjoy the hereafter except his body lay in his beloved China; also, he desires to receive, himself, after death, that worship with which he has honored his dead that preceded him. Therefore, if he visits a foreign country, he makes arrangements to have his bones returned to China in case he dies; if he hires to go to a foreign country on a labor contract, there is always a stipulation that his body shall be taken back to China if he dies: if the government sells a gang of Coolies to a foreigner for the usual five-year term, it is specified in the contract that their bodies shall be restored to China in case of death. On the Pacific coast the Chinamen all belong to one or another of several great companies or organizations, and these companies keep track of their members, register their names, and ship their bodies home when they die. The See Yup Company is held to be the largest of these. The Ning Yeong Company is next, and numbers eighteen thousand members on the coast. Its headquarters are at San Francisco, where it has a costly temple, several great officers (one of whom keeps regal state in seclusion and cannot be approached by common humanity), and a numerous priesthood. In it I was shown a register of its members, with the dead and the date of their shipment to China duly marked. Every ship that sails from San Francisco carries away a heavy freight of Chinese corpses—or did, at least, until the legislature, with an ingenious refinement of Christian cruelty, forbade the shipments, as a neat underhanded way of deterring Chinese immigration. The bill was offered, whether it passed or not. It is my impression that it passed. There was another bill—it became a law—compelling every incoming Chinaman to be vaccinated on the wharf and pay a duly appointed quack (no decent doctor would defile himself with such legalized robbery) ten dollars for it. As few importers of Chinese would want to go to an expense like that, the lawmakers thought this would be another heavy blow to Chinese immigration.

What the Chinese quarter of Virginia was like—or, indeed, what the Chinese quarter of any Pacific coast town was and is like—may be gathered from this item which I printed in the *Enterprise* while reporting for that paper:

CHINATOWN.—Accompanied by a fellow reporter, we made a trip through our Chinese quarter the other night. The Chinese have built their portion of the city to suit themselves; and as they keep neither carriages nor wagons, their streets are not wide enough, as a general thing, to admit of the passage of vehicles. At ten o'clock at night the Chinaman may be seen in all his glory. In every little cooped-up, dingy cavern of a hut, faint with the odor of burning Josh-lights and with nothing to see the gloom by save the sickly, guttering tallow candle, were two or three yellow, long-tailed vagabonds, coiled up on a sort of short truckle-bed, smoking opium, motionless and with their lustreless eyes turned inward from excess of satisfaction—or rather the recent smoker looks thus, immediately after having passed the pipe to his neighbor—for opium-smoking is a comfortless operation, and requires constant attention. A lamp sits on the bed, the length of the long pipestem from the smoker's mouth; he puts a pellet of opium on the end of a wire, sets it on fire, and plasters it into the pipe much as a Christian would fill a hole with putty; then he applies the bowl to the lamp and proceeds to smoke—and the stewing and frying of the drug and the gurgling of the juices in the stem would wellnigh turn the stomach of a statue. John likes it, though; it soothes him, he takes about two dozen whiffs, and then rolls over to dream, Heaven only knows what, for we could not imagine by looking at the soggy creature. Possibly in his visions he travels far way from the gross world and his regular washing, and feasts on succulent rats and birds'-nests in Paradise.

Mr. Ah Sing keeps a general grocery and provision store at No. 13 Wang street. He lavished his hospitality upon our party in the friendliest way. He had various kinds of colored and colorless wines and brandies, with unpronounceable names, imported from China in little crockery jugs, and which he offered to us in dainty little miniature wash-basins of porcelain. He offered us a mess of birds'-nests; also, small, neat sausages, of which we could have swallowed several yards if we had chosen to try, but we suspected that each link contained the corpse of a mouse, and therefore refrained. Mr. Sing had in his store a thousand articles of merchandise, curious to behold, impossible to imagine the use of, and beyond our ability to describe.

His ducks, however, and his eggs, we could understand; the former were split open and flattened out like codfish, and came from China in that shape, and the latter were plastered over with some kind of paste which kept them fresh and palatable through the long voyage.

We found Mr. Hong Wo, No. 37 Chow-chow street, making up a lottery scheme—in fact we found a dozen others occupied in the same way in various parts of the quarter, for about every third Chinaman runs a lottery, and the balance of the tribe "buck" at it. "Tom," who speaks faultless English, and used to be chief and only cook to the *Territorial Enterprise,* when the establishment kept bachelor's hall two years ago, said that "Sometime Chinaman buy ticket one dollar hap, ketch um two tree hundred, sometime no ketch um anyting; lottery like one man fight um seventy—may-be he whip, may-be he get whip heself, welly good." However, the percentage being sixty-nine against him, the chances are, as a general thing, that "he get whip heself." We could not see that these lotteries differed in any respect from our own, save that the figures being Chinese, no ignorant white man might ever hope to succeed in telling "t'other from which;" the manner of drawing is similar to ours.

Mr. See Yup keeps a fancy store on Live Fox street. He sold us fans of white feathers, gorgeously ornamented; perfumery that smelled like Limburger cheese, Chinese pens, and watch-charms made of a stone unscratchable with steel instruments, yet polished and tinted like the inner coat of a sea-shell.[1] As tokens of his esteem, See Yup presented the party with gaudy plumes made of gold tinsel and trimmed with peacocks' feathers.

We ate chow-chow with chop-sticks in the celestial restaurants; our comrade chided the moon-eyed damsels in front of the houses for their want of feminine reserve; we received protecting Josh-lights from our hosts and "dickered" for a pagan God or two. Finally, we were impressed with the genius of a Chinese book-keeper; he figured up his accounts on a machine like a gridiron with buttons strung on its bars; the different rows represented units, tens, hundreds and thousands. He fingered them with incredible rapidity—in fact, he pushed them from place to place as fast as a musical professor's fingers travel over the keys of a piano.

They are a kindly disposed, well-meaning race, and are respected and well treated by the upper classes, all over the Pacific coast. No Californian *gentleman or lady* ever abuses or oppresses a Chinaman, under any circumstances, an explanation that seems to be much needed in the East. Only the scum of the population do it—they and their children; they, and, naturally and consistently, the policemen and politicians, likewise, for these are the dust-licking pimps and slaves of the scum, there as well as elsewhere in America.

[1] A peculiar species of the "jade-stone"—to a Chinaman peculiarly precious.

BRET HARTE

Bret Harte (1836–1902), American humorist and Western local color writer, explored the Western phenomena, largely unknown in the East, of mining camps, gamblers, and Chinese miners. An extremely popular writer, his attempts to be objective in his portrayals are limited by sentimentality rather than sympathy.

THE LATEST CHINESE OUTRAGE (1875)

It was noon by the sun; we had finished our game,
And was passin' remarks goin' back to our claim;
Jones was countin' his chips, Smith relievin' his mind
Of ideas that a "straight" should beat "three of a kind,"
When Johnson of Elko came gallopin' down,
With a look on his face 'twixt a grin and a frown,
And he calls, "Drop your shovels and face right about,
For them Chinees from Murphy's are cleanin' us out—
      With their ching-a-ring-chow
      And their chic-colorow
      They're bent upon making
      No slouch of a row."

Then Jones—my own pardner—looks up with a sigh;
"It's your wash-bill," sez he, and I answers, "You lie!"
But afore he could draw or the others could arm,
Up tumbles the Bates boys, who heard the alarm.
And a yell from the hill-top and roar of a gong,
Mixed up with remarks like "Hi! yi! Chang-a-wong,"
And bombs, shells, and crackers, that crashed through the trees,
Revealed in their war-togs four hundred Chinees!
      Four hundred Chinee;
      We are eight, don't ye see!
      That made a square fifty
      To just one o' we.

They were dressed in their best, but I grieve that that same
Was largely made up of our own, to their shame;
And my pardner's best shirt and his trousers were hung
On a spear, and above him were tauntingly swung;
While that beggar, Chey Lee, like a conjurer sat
Pullin' out eggs and chickens from Johnson's best hat;
And Bates's game rooster was part of their "loot,"
And all of Smith's pigs were skyugled to boot;

251

But the climax was reached and I like to have died
When my demijohn, empty, came down the hillside,—
    Down the hillside—
    What once held the pride
    Of Robertson County
    Pitched down the hillside!

Then we axed for a parley. When out of the din
To the front comes a-rockin' that heathen, Ah Sin!
"You owe flowty dollee—me washee you camp,
You catchee my washee—me catchee no stamp;
One dollar hap dozen, me no catchee yet,
Now that flowty dolee—no hab?—how can get?
Me catchee you pigee—me sellee for cash,
It catchee me licee—you catchee no 'hash;'
Me belly good Sheliff—me lebbee when can,
Me allee same halp pin as Melican man!
    But Melican man
    He washee him pan
    On *bottom* side hillee
    And catchee—how can?"

"Are we men?" says Joe Johnson, "and list to this jaw,
Without process of warrant or color of law?
Are we men or—a-chew!"—here he gasped in his speech,
For a stink-pot had fallen just out of his reach.
"Shall we stand here as idle, and let Asia pour
Her barbaric hordes on this civilized shore?
Has the White Man no country? Are we left in the lurch?
And likewise what's gone of the Established Church?
One man to four hundred is great odds, I own,
But this 'yer's a White Man—I plays it alone!
And he sprang up the hillside—to stop him none dare—
Till a yell from the top told a "White Man was there!"
    A White Man was there!
    We prayed he might spare
    Those misguided heathens
    The few clothes they wear.

They fled, and he followed, but no matter where;
They fled to escape him,—the "White Man was there,"—
Till we missed first his voice on the pine-wooded slope,
And we knew for the heathen henceforth was no hope;
And the yells they grew fainter, when Petersen said,
"It simply was human to bury his dead."

And then, with slow tread,
We crept up, in dread,
But found nary mortal there,
Living or dead.

But there was his trail, and the way that they came,
And yonder, no doubt, he was bagging his game.
When Jones drops his pickaxe, and Thompson says "Shoo!"
And both of 'em points to a cage of bamboo
Hanging down from a tree, with a label that swung
Conspicuous, with letters in some foreign tongue,
Which, when freely translated, the same did appear
Was the Chinese for saying, "A White Man is here!"
    And as we drew near,
    In anger and fear,
    Bound hand and foot, Johnson
    Looked down with a leer!

In his mouth was an opium pipe—which was why
He leered at us so with a drunken-like eye!
They had shaved off his eyebrows, and tacked on a cue,
They had painted his face of a coppery hue,
And rigged him all up in a heathenish suit,
And softly departed, each man with his "loot."
    Yes, every galoot,
    And Ah Sin, to boot,
    Had left him hanging
    Like ripening fruit.

At a mass meeting held up at Murphy's next day
There were seventeen speakers and each had his say;
There were twelve resolutions that instantly passed,
And each resolution was worse than the last;
There were fourteen petitions, which, granting the same,
Will determine what Governor Murphy's shall name;
And the man from our district that goes up next year
Goes up on one issue—that's patent and clear:
    "Can the work of a mean,
    Degraded, unclean
    Believer in Buddah
    Be held as a lien?"

WAN LEE, THE PAGAN (1875)

As I opened Hop Sing's letter there fluttered to the ground a square strip of yellow paper covered with hieroglyphics, which at first glance I innocently took to be the label from a pack of Chinese fire-crackers. But the same envelope also contained a smaller strip of rice paper, with two Chinese characters traced in India ink, that I at once knew to be Hop Sing's visiting card. The whole, as afterwards literally translated, ran as follows:

To the stranger the gates of my house are not closed; the rice-jar is on the
  left, and the sweetmeats on the right, as you enter.
Two sayings of the Master:
  Hospitality is the virtue of the son and the wisdom of the ancestor.
  The superior man is light-hearted after the crop-gathering; he makes a
  festival.
When the stranger is in your melon patch observe him not too closely; in-
  attention is often the highest form of civility.
    Happiness, Peace, and Prosperity.   HOP SING.

Admirable, certainly, as was this morality and proverbial wisdom, and although this last axiom was very characteristic of my friend Hop Sing, who was that most sombre of all humorists, a Chinese philosopher, I must confess that, even after a very free translation, I was at a loss to make any immediate application of the message. Luckily I discovered a third inclosure in the shape of a little note in English and Hop Sing's own commercial hand. It ran thus:—

The pleasure of your company is requested at No. —. Sacramento Street, on
Friday evening at eight o'clock. A cup of tea at nine—sharp.   HOP SING.

This explained all. It meant a visit to Hop Sing's warehouse, the opening and exhibition of some rare Chinese novelties and curios, a chat in the back office, a cup of tea of a perfection unknown beyond these sacred precincts, cigars, and a visit to the Chinese Theater or Temple. This was in fact the favorite programme of Hop Sing when he exercised his functions of hospitality as the chief factor or superintendent of the Ning Foo Company.

At eight o'clock on Friday evening I entered the warehouse of Hop Sing. here was that deliciously commingled mysterious foreign odor that I had so often noticed; there was the old array of uncouth-looking objects, the long procession of jars and crockery, the same singular blending of the grotesque and the mathematically neat and exact, the same endless suggestions of frivolity and fragility, the same want of harmony in colors that were each, in themselves, beautiful and rare. Kites in the shape of enormous dragons and gigantic butterflies; kites so ingeniously arranged as to utter at intervals, when facing the wind, the cry of a hawk; kites so large as to be beyond any boy's power of restraint—so large that you understood why kite-flying in China was an amusement for adults; gods of china and bronze so gratuitously ugly as to be beyond any human interest or sympathy from their very impossibility; jars of sweetmeats covered all over with moral sentiments from Confucious; hats that looked like baskets, and baskets that looked like hats; silk so light that I hesitate to record the incredible number of square yards that you might pass through the ring on your little finger—these and a great many other indescribable objects were all familiar to me. I pushed my way through the dimly lighted warehouse until I reached the back office or parlor, where I found Hop Sing waiting to receive me.

Before I describe him I want the average reader to discharge from his mind any idea of a Chinaman that he may have gathered from the pantomine. He did not wear beautifully scalloped drawers fringed with little bells—I never met a Chinaman who did; he did not habitually carry his forefinger extended before him at right angles with his body, nor did I ever hear him utter the mysterious sentence, "Ching a ring a ring chaw," nor dance under any provocation. He was, on the whole, a rather grave, decorous, handsome gentleman. His complexion, which extended all over his head except where his long pig-tail grew, was like a very nice piece of glazed brown paper-muslin. His eyes were black and bright, and his eyelids set at an angle of 15°; his nose straight and delicately formed, his mouth small, and his teeth white and clean. He wore a dark blue silk blouse, and in the streets on cold days a short jacket of Astrakhan fur. He wore also a pair of drawers of blue brocade gathered tightly over his calves and ankles, offering a general sort of suggestion that he had forgotten his trousers that morning, but that, so gentlemanly were his manners, his friends had forborne to mention the fact to him. His manner was urbane, although quite serious. He spoke French and English fluently. In brief, I doubt if you could have found the equal of this Pagan shopkeeper among the Christian traders of San Francisco.

There were a few others present: a Judge of the Federal Court, an editor, a high government official, and a prominent merchant. After we had drunk our tea, and tasted a few sweetmeats from a mysterious jar, that looked as if it might contain a preserved mouse among its other nondescript treasures, Hop Sing arose, and gravely beckoning us to follow him, began to descend to the basement. When we got there, we were amazed at finding it brilliantly lighted, and that a number of chairs were arranged in a half-circle on the asphalt pavement. When he had courteously seated us, he said,—

"I have invited you to witness a performance which I can at least promise you no other foreigners but yourselves have ever seen. Wang, the court juggler, arrived here yesterday morning. He has never given a performance outside of the palace before. I have asked him to entertain my friends this evening. He requires no theatre, stage, accessories, or any confederate—nothing more than you see here. Will you be pleased to examine the ground yourselves, gentlemen."

Of course we examined the premises. It was the ordinary basement or cellar of the San Francisco storehouse, cemented to keep out the damp. We poked our sticks into the pavement and rapped on the walls to satisfy our polite host, but for no other purpose. We were quite content to be the victims of any clever deception. For myself, I knew I was ready to be deluded to any extent, and if I had been offered an explanation of what followed, I should have probably declined it.

Although I am satisfied that Wang's general performance was the first of that kind ever given on American soil, it has probably since become so familiar to many of my readers that I shall not bore them with it here. He began by setting to flight, with the aid of his fan, the usual number of butterflies made before our eyes of little bits of tissue-paper, and kept them in the air during the remainder of the performance. I have a vivid recollection of the judge trying to catch one that had lit on his knee, and of its evading him with the pertinacity of a living insect. And even at this time Wang, still plying his fan, was taking chickens out of hats, making oranges disappear, pulling endless yards of silk from his sleeve, apparently filling the whole area of the basement with goods that appeared mysteriously from the ground, from his own sleeves, from nowhere! He swallowed knives to the ruin of his digestion for years to come; he dislocated every limb of his body; he reclined in the air, apparently upon nothing. But his crowning performance, which I have never yet seen repeated, was the most weird, mysterious, and astounding. It is my apology for this long introduction, my sole excuse for writing this article, the genesis of this veracious history.

He cleared the ground of its encumbering articles for a space of about fifteen feet square, and then invited us all to walk forward and again examine it. We did so gravely; there was nothing but the cemented pavement below to be seen or felt. He then asked for the loan of a handkerchief, and, as I chanced to be nearest him, I offered mine. He took it and spread it open upon the floor. Over this he spread a large square of silk, and over this again a large shawl covering the space he had cleared. He then took a position at one of the points of this rectangle, and began a monotonous chant, rocking his body to and fro in time with the somewhat lugubrious air.

We sat still and waited. Above the chant we could hear the striking of the city clocks, and the occasional rattle of a cart in the street overhead. The absolute watchfulness and expectation, the dim, mysterious half-light of the cellar, falling in a gruesome way upon the

misshapen bulk of a Chinese diety in the background, a faint smell
of opium smoke mingling with spice, and the dreadful uncertainty
of what we were really waiting for, sent an uncomfortable thrill down
our backs, and made us look at each other with a forced and unnatural
smile. This feeling was heightened when Hop Sing slowly rose, and,
without a word, pointed with his finger to the centre of the shawl.

There was something beneath the shawl! Surely—and something
that was not there before. At first a mere suggestion in relief, a faint
outline, but growing more and more distinct and visible every
moment. The chant still continued, the perspiration began to roll
from the singer's face, gradually the hidden object took upon itself
a shape and bulk that raised the shawl in its centre some five or six
inches. It was now unmistakably the outline of a small but perfect
human figure, with extended arms and legs. One or two of us turned
pale; there was a feeling of general uneasiness, until the editor broke
the silence by a gibe that, poor as it was, was received with spontaneous enthusiasm. Then the chant suddenly ceased, Wang arose, and,
with a quick, dexterous movement, stripped both shawl and silk away,
and discovered, sleeping peacefully upon my handkerchief, a tiny
Chinese baby!

The applause and uproar which followed this revelation ought to
have satisfied Wang, even if his audience was a small one; it was loud
enough to awaken the baby—a pretty little boy about a year old, looking like a Cupid cut out of sandalwood. He was whisked away almost
as mysteriously as he appeared. When Hop Sing returned my handkerchief to me with a bow, I asked if the juggler was the father of
the baby. "No sabe!" said the imperturbable Hop Sing, taking refuge
in that Spanish form of noncommittalism so common in California.

"But does he have a new baby for every performance?" I asked.

"Perhaps; who knows?"

"But what will become of this one?"

"Whatever you choose, gentlemen," replied Hop Sing, with a courteous inclination; "it was born here—you are its godfathers."

There were two characteristic peculiarities of any Californian assemblage in 1856; it was quick to take a hint, and generous to the
point of prodigality in its response to any charitable appeal. No matter
how sordid or avaricious the individual, he could not resist the
infection of sympathy. I doubled the points of my handkerchief into a
bag, dropped a coin into it, and, without a word, passed it to the
judge. He quietly added a twenty-dollar gold-piece, and passed it
to the next; when it was returned it contained over a hundred dollars.
I knotted the money in the handkerchief, and gave it to Hop Sing.

"For the baby, from its godfathers."

"But what name?" said the judge. There was a running fire of
"Erebus," "Nox," "Plutus," "Terra Cotta," "Antæus," etc., etc. Finally
the question was referred to our host.

"Why not keep its own name," he said quietly,—"Wan Lee?" and he did.

And thus was Wan Lee, on the night of Friday the 5th of March, 1856, born into this veracious chronicle.

The last form of the "Northern Star" for the 19th of July, 1865,—the only daily paper published in Klamath County,—had just gone to press, and at three A. M. I was putting aside my proofs and manuscripts, preparatory to going home, when I discovered a letter lying under some sheets of paper which I must have overlooked. The envelope was considerably soiled, it had no postmark, but I had no difficulty in recognizing the hand of my friend Hop Sing. I opened it hurriedly, and read as follows:—

My dear Sir,—I do not know whether the bearer will suit you, but unless the office of "devil" in your newspaper is a purely technical one, I think he has all the qualities required. He is very quick, active, and intelligent; understands English better than he speaks it, and makes up for any defect by his habits of observation and imitation. You have only to show him how to do a thing once, and he will repeat it, whether it is an offense or a virtue. But you certainly know him already; you are one of his godfathers, for is he not Wan Lee, the reputed son of Wang the conjurer, to whose performances I had the honor to introduce you? But perhaps you have forgotten it.

I shall send him with a gang of coolies to Stockton, thence by express to your town. If you can use him there, you will do me a favor, and probably save his life, which is at present in great peril from the hands of the younger members of your Christian and highly civilized race who attend the enlightened schools in San Francisco.

He has acquired some singular habits and customs from his experience of Wang's profession, which he followed for some years, until he became too large to go in a hat, or be produced from his father's sleeve. The money you left with me has been expended on his education; he has gone through the Tri-literal Classics, but, I think, without much benefit. He knows but little of Confucius, and absolutely nothing of Mencius. Owing to the negligence of his father, he associated, perhaps, too much with American children.

I should have answered your letter before, by post, but I thought that Wan Lee himself would be a better messenger for this.

Yours respectfully,

Hop Sing.

And this was the long-delayed answer to my letter to Hop Sing. But where was "the bearer"? How was the letter delivered? I summoned hastily the foreman, printers, and office boy, but without eliciting anything; no one had seen the letter delivered, nor knew anything of the bearer. A few days later I had a visit from my laundryman, Ah Ri.

"You wantee debbil? All lightee; me catchee him."

He returned in a few moments with a bright-looking Chinese boy, about ten years old, with whose appearance and general intelligence I was so greatly impressed that I engaged him on the spot. When the business was concluded, I asked his name.

"Wan Lee," said the boy.

"What! Are you the boy sent out by Hop Sing? What the devil do you mean by not coming here before, and how did you deliver that letter?"

Wan Lee looked at me and laughed. "Me pitchee in top side window."

I did not understand. He looked for a moment perplexed, and then, snatching the letter out of my hand, ran down the stairs. After a moment's pause, to my great astonishment, the letter came flying in at the window, circled twice around the room, and then dropped gently like a bird upon my table. Before I had got over my surprise Wan Lee reappeared, smiled, looked at the letter and then at me, said, "So, John," and then remained gravely silent. I said nothing further, but it was understood that this was his first official act.

His next performance, I grieve to say, was not attended with equal success. One of our regular paper-carriers fell sick, and, at a pinch, Wan Lee was ordered to fill his place. To prevent mistakes he was shown over the route the previous evening, and supplied at about daylight with the usual number of subscribers' copies. He returned after an hour, in good spirits and without the papers. He had delivered them all he said.

Unfortunately for Wan Lee, at eight o'clock indignant subscribers began to arrive at the office. They had received their copies; but how? In the form of hardpressed cannon-balls, delivered by a single shot and a mere *tour de force* through the glass of bedroom windows. They had received them full in the face, like a baseball, if they happened to be up and stirring; they had received them in quarter sheets, tucked in at separate windows; they had found them in the chimney, pinned against the door, shot through the attic windows, delivered in long slips through convenient keyholes, stuffed into ventilators, and occupying the same can with the morning's milk. One subscriber, who waited for some time at the office door, to have a personal interview with Wan Lee (then uncomfortably locked in my bedroom), told me, with tears of rage in his eyes, that he had been awakened at five o'clock by a most hideous yelling below his windows; that on rising, in great agitation, he was startled by the sudden appearance of the "Northern Star," rolled hard and bent into the form of a boomerang or East Indian club, that sailed into the window, described a number of fiendish circles in the room, knocked over the light, slapped the baby's face, "took" him (the subscriber) "in the jaw," and then returned out of the window, and dropped helplessly in the area. During the rest of the day wads and strips of soiled paper, purporting to be copies of the "Northern Star" of that morning's issue, were brought indignantly to the office. An admirable editorial on "The Resources of Humboldt County," which I had constructed the evening before, and which, I have reason to believe, might have changed the whole balance of trade during the ensuing year, and left San Francisco bankrupt at her wharves, was in this way lost to the public.

It was deemed advisable for the next three weeks to keep Wan Lee closely confined to the printing-office and the purely mechanical part of the business. Here he developed a surprising quickness and adaptability, winning even the favor and good will of the printers and foreman, who at first looked upon his introduction into the secrets of their trade as fraught with the gravest political significance. He learned to set type readily and neatly, his wonderful skill in manipulation aiding him in the mere mechanical act, and his ignorance of the language confining him simply to the mechanical effort—confirming the printer's axiom that the printer who considers or follows the ideas of his copy makes a poor compositor. He would set up deliberately long diatribes against himself, composed by his fellow printers, and hung on his hook as copy, and even such short sentences as "Wan Lee is the devil's own imp," "Wan Lee is a Mongolian rascal," and bring the proof to me with happiness beaming from every tooth and satisfaction shining in his huckleberry eyes.

It was not long, however, before he learned to retaliate on his mischievous persecutors. I remember one instance in which his reprisal came very near involving me in a serious misunderstanding. Our foreman's name was Webster, and Wan Lee presently learned to know and recognize the individual and combined letters of his name. It was during a political campaign, and the eloquent and fiery Colonel Starbottle of Siskiyou had delivered an effective speech, which was reported especially for the "Northern Star." In a very sublime peroration Colonel Starbottle had said, "In the language of the godlike Webster, I repeat" —and here followed the quotation, which I have forgotten. Now, it chanced that Wan Lee, looking over the galley after it had been revised, saw the name of his chief persecutor, and, of course, imagined the quotation his. After the form was locked up, Wan Lee took advantage of Webster's absence to remove the quotation, and substitute a thin piece of lead, of the same size as the type, engraved with Chinese characters, making a sentence which, I had reason to believe, was an utter and abject confession of the incapacity and offensiveness of the Webster family generally, and exceedingly eulogistic of Wan Lee himself personally.

The next morning's paper contained Colonel Starbottle's speech in full, in which it appeared that the "godlike" Webster had on one occasion uttered his thoughts in excellent but perfectly enigmatical

Chinese. The rage of Colonel Starbottle knew no bounds. I have a vivid recollection of that admirable man walking into my office and demanding a retraction of the statement.

"But, my dear sir," I asked, "are you willing to deny, over your own signature, that Webster never uttered such a sentence? Dare you deny that, with Mr. Webster's well-known attainments, a knowledge of Chinese might not have been among the number? Are you willing to submit a translation suitable to the capacity of our readers, and deny, upon your honor as a gentleman, that the late Mr. Webster ever uttered such a sentiment? If you are, sir, I am willing to publish your denial."

The Colonel was not, and left, highly indignant.

Webster, the foreman, took it more coolly. Happily he was unaware that for two days after, Chinamen from the laundries, from the gulches, from the kitchens, looked in the front office door with faces beaming with sardonic delight; that three hundred extra copies of the "Star" were ordered for the wash-houses on the river. He only knew that during the day Wan Lee occasionally went off into convulsive spasms, and that he was obliged to kick him into consciousness again. A week after the occurrence I called Wan Lee into my office.

"Wan," I said gravely, "I should like you to give me, for my own personal satisfaction, a translation of that Chinese sentence which my gifted countryman, the late godlike Webster, uttered upon a public occasion." Wan Lee looked at me intently, and then the slightest possible twinkle crept into his black eyes. Then he replied, with equal gravity,—

"Mishtel Webstel,—he say: 'China boy makee me belly much foolee. China boy makee me heap sick.'" Which I have reason to think was true.

But I fear I am giving but one side, and not the best, of Wan Lee's character. As he imparted it to me, his had been a hard life. He had known scarcely any childhood—he had no recollection of a father or mother. The conjurer Wang had brought him up. He had spent the first seven years of his life in appearing from baskets, in dropping out of hats, in climbing ladders, in putting his little limbs out of joint in posturing. He had lived in an atmosphere of trickery and deception; he had learned to look upon mankind as dupes of their senses; in fine, if he had thought at all, he would have been a skeptic; if he had been a little older, he would have been a cynic; if he had been older still, he would have been a philosopher. As it was, he was a little imp! A good-natured imp it was, too,—an imp whose moral nature had never been awakened, an imp up for a holiday, and willing to try virtue as a diversion. I don't know that he had any spiritual nature; he was very superstitious; he carried about with him a hideous little porcelain god, which he was in the habit of alternately reviling and propitiating. He was too intelligent for the commoner Chinese vices of stealing or gratuitous lying. Whatever discipline he practiced was taught by his intellect.

I am inclined to think that his feelings were not altogether unimpressible,—although it was almost impossible to extract an expression from him,—and I conscientiously believe he became attached to those that were good to him. What he might have become under more favorable conditions than the bondsman of an overworked, underpaid literary man, I don't know; I only know that the scant, irregular, impulsive kindnesses that I showed him were gratefully received. He was very loyal and patient—two qualities rare in the average American servant. He was like Malvolio, "sad and civil" with me; only once, and then under great provocation, do I remember of his exhibiting any impatience. It was my habit, after leaving the office at night, to take him with me to my rooms, as the bearer of any supplemental or happy afterthought in the editorial way, that might occur to me before the paper went to press. One night I had been scribbling away past the usual hour of dismissing Wan Lee, and had become quite oblivious of his presence in a chair near my door, when suddenly I became aware of a voice saying, in plaintive accents, something that sounded like "Chy Lee."

I faced around sternly.

"What did you say?"

"Me say, 'Chy Lee.'"

"Well?" I said impatiently.

"You sabe, 'How do, John'?"

"Yes."

"You sabe, 'So long, John'?"

"Yes."

"Well, 'Chy Lee' allee same!"

I understood him quite plainly. It appeared that "Chy Lee" was a form of "good-night," and that Wan Lee was anxious to go home. But an instinct of mischief which I fear I possessed in common with him, impelled me to act as if oblivious of the hint. I muttered something about not understanding him, and again bent over my work. In a few minutes I heard his wooden shoes pattering pathetically over the floor. I looked up. He was standing near the door.

"You no sabe, 'Chy Lee'?"

"No," I said sternly.

"You sabe muchee big foolee!—allee same!"

And with this audacity upon his lips he fled. The next morning, however, he was as meek and patient as before, and I did not recall his offense. As a probable peace-offering, he blacked all my boots,—a duty never required of him,—including a pair of buff deerskin slippers and an immense pair of horseman's jack-boots, on which he indulged his remorse for two hours.

I have spoken of his honesty as being a quality of his intellect rather than his principle, but I recall about this time two exceptions to the rule. I was anxious to get some fresh eggs, as a change to the heavy diet of a mining town, and knowing that Wan Lee's countrymen were great poultry-raisers, I applied to him. He furnished me with them regularly every morning, but refused to take any pay, saying that the man did not sell them,—a remarkable instance of self-abnegation, as eggs were then worth half a dollar apiece. One morning, my neighbor, Foster, dropped in upon me at breakfast, and took occasion to bewail his own ill fortune, as his hens had lately stopped laying, or wandered off in the bush. Wan Lee who, was present during our colloquy, preserved his characteristic sad taciturnity. When my neighbor had gone, he turned to me with a slight chuckle—"Flostel's hens—Wan Lee's hens —allee same!" His other offense was more serious and ambitious. It was a season of great irregularities in the mails, and Wan Lee had heard me deplore the delay in the delivery of my letters and news-papers. On arriving at my office one day, I was amazed to find my table covered with letters, evidently just from the post-office, but un-fortunately not one addressed to me. I turned to Wan Lee, who was surveying them with a calm satisfaction, and demanded an explana-tion. To my horror he pointed to an empty mail-bag in the corner, and said, "Postman he say, 'No lettee, John—no lettee, John.' Postman plentee lie! Postman no good. Me catchee lettee last night—allee same!" Luckily it was still early; the mails had not been distributed; I had a hurried interview with the postmaster, and Wan Lee's bold attempt at robbing the U. S. Mail was finally condoned, by the purchase of a new mail-bag, and the whole affair thus kept a secret.

If my liking for my little pagan page had not been sufficient, my duty to Hop Sing was enough to cause me to take Wan Lee with me when I returned to San Francisco, after my two years' experience with the "Northern Star." I do not think he contemplated the change with pleas-ure. I attributed his feelings to a nervous dread of crowded public streets—when he had to go across town for me on an errand, he always made a long circuit of the outskirts; to his dislike for the discipline of the Chinese and English school to which I proposed to send him; to his fondness for the free, vagrant life of the mines; to sheer willfulness! That it might have been a superstitious premonition did not occur to me until long after.

Nevertheless it really seemed as if the opportunity I had long looked for and confidently expected had come,—the opportunity of placing Wan Lee under gently restraining influences, of subjecting him to a life and experience that would draw out of him what good my super-ficial care and ill-regulated kindness could not reach. Wan Lee was placed at the school of a Chinese missionary,—an intelligent and kind-hearted clergyman, who had shown great interest in the boy, and who, better than all, had a wonderful faith in him. A home was found for him in the family of a widow, who had a bright and interesting daughter about two years younger than Wan Lee. It was this bright, cheery, innocent, and artless child that touched and reached a depth in the boy's nature that hitherto had been unsuspected—that awakened a moral susceptibility which had lain for years insensible alike to the teachings of society or the ethics of the theologian.

These few brief months, bright with a promise that we never saw fulfilled, must have been happy ones to Wan Lee. He worshiped his little friend with something of the same superstition, but without any of the caprice, that he bestowed upon his porcelain Pagan god. It was his delight to walk behind her to school, carrying her books,—a service always fraught with danger to him from the little hands of his Caucasian Christian brothers. He made her the most marvelous toys; he would cut out of carrots and turnips the most astonishing roses and tulips; he made lifelike chickens out of melon-seeds; he constructed fans and kites, and was singularly proficient in the making of dolls' paper dresses. On the other hand she played and sang to him; taught him a thousand little prettinesses and refinements only known to girls; gave him a yellow ribbon for his pigtail, as best suiting his complexion; read to him; showed him wherein he was original and valuable; took him to Sunday-school with her, against the precedents of the school, and, small-womanlike, triumphed. I wish I could add here, that she effected his conversion, and made him give up his porcelain idol, but I am telling a true story, and this little girl was quite content to fill him with her own Christian goodness, without letting him know that he was changed. So they got along very well together—this little Christian girl, with her shining cross hanging around her plump, white, little neck, and this dark little Pagan, with his hideous porcelain god hidden away in his blouse.

There were two days of that eventful year which will long be remembered in San Francisco,—two days when a mob of her citizens set upon and killed unarmed, defenseless foreigners, because they were foreigners and of another race, religion, and color, and worked for what wages they could get. There were some public men so timid that, seeing this, they thought that the end of the world had come; there were some eminent statesmen, whose names I am ashamed to write here, who began to think that the passage in the Constitution which guarantees civil and religious liberty to every citizen or foreigner was a mistake. But there were also some men who were not so easily frightened, and in twenty-four hours we had things so arranged that the timid men could wring their hands in safety, and the eminent statesmen utter their doubts without hurting anybody or anything. And in the midst of this I got a note from Hop Sing, asking me to come to him immediately.

I found his warehouse closed and strongly guarded by the police against any possible attack of the rioters. Hop Sing admitted me through a barred grating with his usual imperturbable calm, but, as it seemed to me, with more than his usual seriousness. Without a word he took my hand and led me to the rear of the room, and thence downstairs into the basement. It was dimly lighted, but there was something lying on the floor covered by a shawl. As I approached, he drew the shawl away with a sudden gesture, and revealed Wan Lee, the Pagan, lying there dead!

Dead, my reverend friends, dead! Stoned to death in the streets of San Francisco, in the year of grace, eighteen hundred and sixty-nine, by a mob of half-grown boys and Christian school-children!

As I put my hand reverently upon his breast, I felt something crumbling beneath his blouse. I looked inquiringly at Hop Sing. He put his hand between the folds of silk, and drew out something with the first bitter smile I had ever seen on the face of that Pagan gentleman.

It was Wan Lee's porcelain god, crushed by a stone from the hands of those Christian iconoclasts!

JOHN CHINAMAN (1870)

The expression of the Chinese face in the aggregate is neither cheerful nor happy. In an acquaintance of half a dozen years, I can only recall one or two exceptions to this rule. There is an abiding consciousness of degradation,—a secret pain or self-humiliation visible in the lines of the mouth and eye. Whether it is only a modification of Turkish gravity, or whether it is the dread Valley of the Shadow of the Drug through which they are continually straying, I cannot say. They seldom smile, and their laughter is of such an extraordinary and sardonic nature—so purely a mechanical spasm, quite independent of any mirthful attribute—that to this day I am doubtful whether I ever saw a Chinaman laugh. A theatrical representation by natives, one might think, would have set my mind at ease on this point; but it did not. Indeed, a new difficulty presented itself,—the impossibility of determining whether the performance was a tragedy or farce. I thought I detected the low comedian in an active youth who turned two somersaults, and knocked everybody down on entering the stage. But, unfortunately, even this classic resemblance to the legitimate farce of our civilization was deceptive. Another brocaded actor, who represented the hero of the play, turned three somersaults, and not only upset my theory and his fellow-actors at the same time, but apparently run a-muck behind the scenes for some time afterward. I looked around at the glinting white teeth to observe the effect of these two palpable hits. They were received with equal acclamation, and apparently equal facial spasms. One or two beheadings which enlivened the play produced the same sardonic effect, and left upon my mind a painful anxiety to know what was the serious business of life in China. It was noticeable, however, that my unrestrained laughter had a discordant effect, and that triangular eyes sometimes turned ominously toward the "Fanqui devil"; but as I retired discreetly before the play was finished, there were no serious results. I have only given the above as an instance of the impossibility of deciding upon the outward and superficial expression of Chinese mirth. Of its inner and deeper existence I have some private doubts. An audience that will view with a serious aspect the hero, after a frightful and agonizing death, get up and quietly walk off the stage cannot be said to have remarkable perceptions of the ludicrous.

I have often been struck with the delicate pliability of the Chinese expression and taste, that might suggest a broader and deeper criticism than is becoming these pages. A Chinaman will adopt the American costume, and wear it with a taste of color and detail that will surpass those "native, and to the manner born." To look at a Chinese slipper, one might imagine it impossible to shape the original foot to anything less cumbrous and roomy, yet a neater-fitting boot than that belonging to the Americanized Chinaman is rarely seen on this side of the Continent. When the loose sack or paletot takes the place of his brocade blouse, it is worn with a refinement and grace that might bring a jealous pang to the exquisite of our more refined civilization. Pantaloons fall easily and naturally over legs that have known unlimited freedom and bagginess, and even garrote collars meet correctly around sun-tanned throats. The new expression seldom overflows in gaudy cravats. I will back my Americanized Chinaman against any neophyte of European birth in the choice of that article. While in our own State, the Greaser resists one by one the garments of the Northern invader, and even wears the livery of his conqueror with a wild and buttonless freedom, the Chinaman, abused and degraded as he is, changes by correctly graded transition to the garments of Christian civilization. There is but one article of European wear that he avoids. These Bohemian eyes have never yet been pained by the spectacle of a tall hat on the head of an intelligent Chinaman.

My acquaintance with John has been made up of weekly interviews, involving the adjustment of the washing accounts, so that I have not been able to study his character from a social view-point or observe him in the privacy of the domestic circle. I have gathered enough to justify me in believing him to be generally honest, faithful, simple, and painstaking. Of his simplicity let me record an instance where a sad and civil young Chinaman brought me certain shirts with most of the buttons missing and others hanging on delusively by a single thread. In a moment of unguarded irony I informed him that unity would at least have been preserved if the buttons were removed altogether. He smiled sadly and went away. I thought I had hurt his feelings, until the next week when he brought me my shirts with a look of intelligence, and the buttons carefully and totally erased. At another time, to guard against his general disposition to carry off anything as soiled clothes that he thought could hold water, I requested him to always wait until he saw me. Coming home late one evening, I found the household in great consternation, over an immovable Celestial who had remained seated on the front door-step during the day, sad and sub-missive, firm but also patient, and only betraying any animation or token of his mission when he saw me coming. This same Chinaman evinced some evidences of regard for a little girl in the family, who in her turn reposed such faith in his intellectual qualities as to present him with a preternaturally uninteresting Sunday-school book, her own property. This book John made a point of carrying ostentatiously with him in his weekly visits. It appeared usually on the top of the clean clothes, and was sometimes painfully clasped outside of the big bundle of soiled linen. Whether John believed he unconsciously imbibed some spiritual life through its pasteboard cover, as the Prince in the Arabian Nights imbibed the medicine through the handle of the mallet, or whether he wished to exhibit a due sense of gratitude, or whether he hadn't any pockets, I have never been able to ascertain. In his turn he would sometimes cut marvellous imitation roses from carrots for his little friend. I am inclined to think that the few roses strewn in John's path were such scentless imitations. The thorns only were real. From the persecutions of the young and old of a certain class, his life was a torment. I don't know what was the exact philosophy that Confucius taught, but it is to be hoped that poor John in his persecution is still able to detect the conscious hate and fear with which inferiority always regards the possibility of even-handed justice, and which is the key-note to the vulgar clamor about servile and degraded races.

JOHN CHINAMAN (1870)

ANONYMOUS

"John Chinaman" is typical of the stereotyped interpretations of the Chinese, sometimes hostile but more often sympathetic or sentimental, that often provided Americans with their only knowledge of those un-familiar immigrants. The result was much weakly-based opinion and misinformation.

John Chinaman, John Chinaman,
   But five short years ago,
I welcomed you from Canton, John—
   But I wish I hadn't though;

For then I thought you honest, John,
  Not dreaming but you'd make
A citizen as useful, John,
  As any in the State.

I thought you'd open wide your ports,
  And let our merchants in,
To barter for their crapes and teas,
  Their wares of wood and tin.

I thought you'd cut your queue off, John
  And don a Yankee coat,
And a collar high you'd raise, John,
  Around your dusky throat.

I imagined that the truth, John
  You'd speak when under oath,
But I find you'll lie and steal too—
  Yes, John, you're up to both.

I thought of rats and puppies, John,
  You'd eaten your last fill,
But on such slimy pot-pies, John,
  I'm told you dinner still.

Oh, John, Iv'e [sic] been deceived in you,
  And in all your thieving clan,
For our gold is all your [sic] after, John,
  To get it as you can.

THE CHINESE EMIGRATION TREATY OF 1880

The Chinese Emigration Treaty of 1880 was the result of hostility to-
ward Chinese emigration. Fears, logical or not, dictated the emergence
of such legislation; workmen feared competition with Chinese who
would work for lower wages, patriots insisted that they refused to be-
come assimilated, and bigots denounced them for their racial and reli-
gious differences.

Chinese emigration treaty as amended by the Senate.

Whereas, on the 17th day of November, A. D. 1880, a Treaty was concluded between the United States and China for the purpose of regu-

lating, limiting, or suspending the coming of Chinese laborers to, and their residence in, the United States;

And whereas the Government of China, in view of the antagonism and much deprecated and serious disorders to which the presence of Chinese laborers has given rise in certain parts of the United States, desires to prohibit the emigration of such laborers from China to the United States.

And whereas the Government of the United States and the Government of China desire to coöperate in prohibiting such emigration, and to strengthen in other ways the bonds of friendship between the two countries;

Now, therefore, the President of the United States has appointed Thomas F. Bayard Secretary of State of the United States as his Plenipotentiary; and His Imperial Majesty the Emperor of China has appointed Chang Yen Hoon Minister of the Third Rank of the Imperial Court, Civil President of the Board of Imperial Cavalry and Envoy Extraordinary and Minister Plenipotentiary as his Plenipotentiary; and the said Plenipotentiaries, having exhibited their respective Full Powers found to be in due and good form, have agreed upon the following articles:

ARTICLE I.

The High Contracting parties agree that for a period of twenty years, beginning with the date of the exchange of the ratifications of this Convention, the coming, except under the conditions hereinafter specified, of Chinese laborers to the United States shall be absolutely prohibited; *and this prohibition shall extend to the return of Chinese laborers who are not now in the United States, whether holding return certificates under existing laws or not.*[1]

ARTICLE II.

The preceding article shall not apply to the return to the United States of any Chinese laborer who has a lawful wife, child, or parent in the United States, or property therein of the value of one thousand dollars, or debts of like amount due him and pending settlement. Nevertheless, every such Chinese laborer shall, before leaving the United States, deposit, as a condition of his return, with the collector of customs of the district from which he departs, a full description in writing of his family, or property, or debts, as aforesaid, and shall be furnished

[1] The amendments of the Senate to the Treaty as originally signed are printed in italics.

by said collector with such certificate of his right to return under this Treaty as the laws of the United States may now or hereafter prescribe and not inconsistent with the provisions of this Treaty; and should the written description aforesaid be proved to be false, the right of return thereunder, or of continued residence after return, shall in each case be forfeited. And such right of return to the United States shall be exercised within one year from the date of leaving the United States; but such right of return to the United States may be extended for an additional period, not to exceed one year, in cases where by reason of sickness or other cause of disability beyond his control, such Chinese laborer shall be rendered unable sooner to return—which facts shall be fully reported to the Chinese consul at the port of departure, and by him certified, to the satisfaction of the collector of the port at which such Chinese subject shall land in the United States. *And no such Chinese laborer shall be permitted to enter the United States by land or sea without producing to the proper officer of the customs the return certificate herein required.*

ARTICLE III.

The provisions of this Convention shall not affect the right at present enjoyed of Chinese subjects, being officials, teachers, students, merchants, or travelers for curiosity or pleasure, but not laborers, of coming to the United States and residing therein. To entitle such Chinese subjects as are above described to admission into the United States they may produce a certificate from their Government or the Government where they last resided, viséd by the diplomatic or consular representative of the United States in the country or port whence they depart.

It is also agreed that Chinese laborers shall continue to enjoy the privilege of transit across the territory of the United States in the course of their journey to or from other countries, subject to such regulations by the Government of the United States as may be necessary to prevent said privilege of transit from being abused.

ARTICLE IV.

In pursuance of Article III of the Immigration Treaty between the United States and China, signed at Peking on the 17th day of November, 1880, it is hereby understood and agreed that Chinese laborers, or Chinese of any other class, either permanently or temporarily residing in the United States, shall have for the protection of their persons and property all rights that are given by the laws of the United States to citizens of the most favored nation, excepting the right to become naturalized citizens. And the Government of the United States reaffirms its obligation, as stated in said Article III, to exert all its power to secure protection to the persons and property of all Chinese subjects in the United States.

ARTICLE V.

Whereas Chinese subjects, being in remote and unsettled regions of the United States, have been the victims of injuries in their persons and property at the hands of wicked and lawless men, which unexpected events the Chinese Government regrets, and for which it has claimed an indemnity, the legal obligation of which the Government of the United States denies; and whereas the Government of the United States, humanely considering these injuries and bearing in mind the firm and ancient friendship between the United States and China, which the high contracting parties wish to cement, is desirous of alleviating the exceptional and deplorable sufferings and losses to which the aforesaid Chinese have been subjected; therefore, the United States, without reference to the question of liability therefor (which as a legal obligation it denies), agrees to pay on or before the first day of March, 1889, the sum of two hundred and seventy-six thousand six hundred and nineteen dollars and seventy-five cents ($276,619.75) to the Chinese minister at this capital, who shall accept the same, on behalf of his Government, as full indemnity for all losses and injuries sustained by Chinese subjects as aforesaid, and shall distribute the said money among the said sufferers and their relatives.

ARTICLE VI.

This convention shall remain in force for a period of twenty years, beginning with the date of the exchange of ratifications; and if, six months before the expiration of the said period of twenty years, neither Government shall formally have given notice of its termination to the other, it shall remain in full force for another like period of twenty years.

In faith whereof we, the respective plenipotentiaries, have signed this treaty and have hereunto affixed our seals.

Done, in duplicate, at Washington, the 12th day of March, A. D., 1888.

[L. S.]   T. F. BAYARD,

[L. S.]   CHANG YEN HOON.

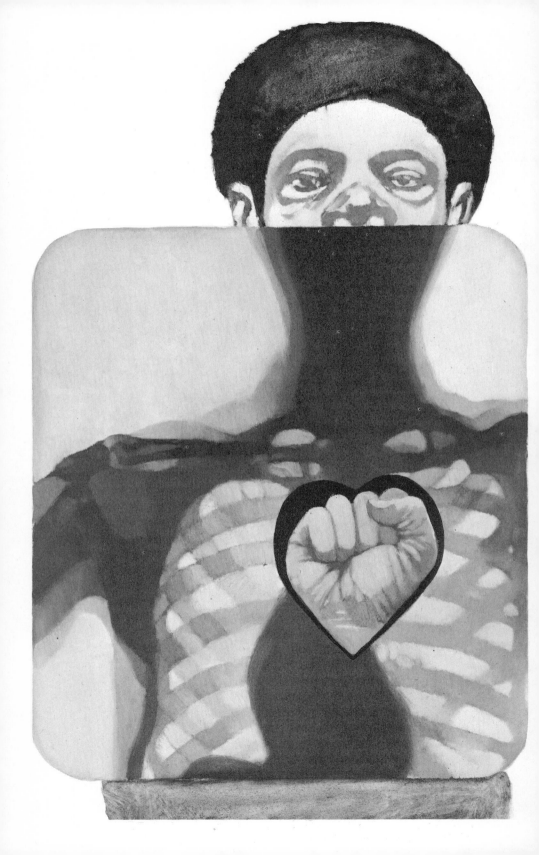

3

THE TWENTIETH CENTURY: THE SEARCH FOR RESOLUTION

WITH THEIR VICTORY over Spain proclaiming them a world power, and the bitterness of the war between brothers eased by the years, American citizens could hardly avoid viewing the new century as an American one, a century in which man might rise to his potential and achieve a prosperity and brotherhood unknown to human society. The vision, alas, was one conceived by white men and generally limited—though rarely with the realization that such was the case —to other whites. For most of the others, the new century marked only a calendar change; opportunities and rewards remained years away.

To assess the situation as satisfactorily as immediacy permits, it is necessary to climb the peak of the present and to survey the territory which lies behind and to determine how knowledge of the past can prepare for the future. One must examine the data, sift the facts, trying not to put aside too much of consequence; then, in the most difficult of steps, he must decide what meaning to attach to the facts. It would seem defensible, in that most sensitive of areas, to start with some figures.

For a number of reasons many of the current statistics touching upon race in America must be approached with caution. The customary division into white and nonwhite clearly gives little information about segments of the nonwhite population. In addition, the attribution of race to individuals is notably imprecise; the opinion of an anthropologist might (but need not) parallel the judgment of a Birmingham restaurant owner. Given widespead blurring of racial lines, the numbers of "nonwhites" whose appearance and inclinations have led them to join the white community, those black Americans who have chosen not to make themselves visible to census takers and the like, and finally the reluctance to identify race on questionnaires or applications, one must qualify all quantitative generalizations.

But if one cannot know absolutely all he might like to know about members of the yellow, red, black, and white races in America today, he can surely form some impressions from available information. According to the 1960 census (to cite the most obvious source), the United States consisted of nearly 159 million whites, almost 19 million blacks, over half a million Indians, some 400,000 Japanese-Americans and about half that many of Chinese ancestry, as well as nearly 400,000 classified as "other." All except the Indians are predominantly urban (a particularly dramatic shift, generally to northern cities, has been made by Negroes, 90% of whom lived in the South, with 80% of the total described as rural before 1900). Of all the states, only Hawaii shows nonwhites in the majority.

The birth rate for all nonwhite groups exceeds that of whites, in the case of Indians nearly doubling the figure. Nonwhite girls appear likely to become mothers at an earlier age than their white counterparts and to have larger families. The nonwhite male infant is half as likely as a white male baby to survive the first year.

Although life expectancy for nonwhites still lags behind that for whites, the gap is closing. In the twentieth century the life expectancy of a white male in America has increased nineteen years to 67.6, of a white female twenty-three years to 74.7, of a nonwhite male twenty-nine years to 61.1, and of a nonwhite female thirty-two years to 67.4. Equivalent figures are not available for all countries, but for purposes of comparison a reader might note that a male child born in the Congo in 1952 could expect to live less than thirty seven years, a child in India about four years longer, while life expectancy for a male infant on Taiwan (1959–60) was about the same as for a non-white male in the United States today.

Of all segments of the American population, the Indians represent the greatest antiquity, having first come to the North American continent from Asia eleven thousand years ago. Unlike black and yellow groups, most Indians have in the past been confined by government policy to reservations removed from the rest of the general population. Such isolation may have saved from extinction certain tribal practices and cultural patterns which the forced mixing of Negroes from different tribes effectively eliminated.

A case could be made for the assertion that the Indian has benefited less from modern America than members of any other race. His life expectancy is only about forty-four years, his unemployment rate nearly ten times that of the total country, his yearly income $1,500 (for a family). Perhaps more than the black or yellow man, the Indian seems to reject the benefits of affluent, urban, industrialized America.

It will be remembered that the Indian languished and died when enslaved by the white man. Many Indians today apparently regard the existence taken for granted by millions of whites as simply another form of slavery. All can hope that "Red Power", so far less marked by extravagant rhetoric and histrionic gestures than some activist movements, will be allowed to develop a life style characterized by dignity.

Discriminatory legislation has limited oriental immigration from time to time, generally after the yellow man had performed difficult and physically exhausting feats (like building railroads in the nineteenth century). It cannot be denied that Chinese laborers demanded (or were only able to get) lower wages than whites; nevertheless, it is ironic when a society penalizes in others the virtues it claims to value most highly in its own citizens: thrift, industry, efficiency.

Since 1900 Japanese immigration has overshadowed that from China, in recent years because of the strained political relationship between the United States and mainland China. The hysterical forced removal of Japanese-Americans from the West Coast and their subsequent incarceration in camps at the start of World War II must represent their harsh initiation fee before acceptance into American society, a fee paid a second time through the outstanding behavior in battle by Nisei troops.

Almost cliché today are the Chinese restaurant, the Chinese laundry (now sadly disappearing) and the Japanese gardener. All in all, there seems to be little doubt that in education, business, and the professions Americans with those characteristics which class them as "yellow" defer to no one.

Can persons of a minority race succeed in what is surely a white world while maintaining a cultural identity and familial stability? It is by no means clear that the young members of Chinese-American society in San Francisco believe so. Nevertheless, with the undeniable power of Chairman Mao before them, and even the tong wars exciting to contemplate, they can be counted upon to see that the first word in their hyphenated identity receives full honor.

In recent years it has become *de rigeur* to doubt the efficacy of the melting pot theory which received so much attention in the nineteenth century; yet, in their belief that much of American life today should be rejected and replaced by something more decent, more humane, the youth of Chinatown are operating in a fashion familiar to white communities throughout the land.

Like the Indian, the black man represents a group which has been in America a very long time, unaffected by the immigration which so drastically altered white America, but in varying degree reflecting some racial mixture, especially with whites. That during the long period of Negro servitude such mixture was rarely initiated by the slaves may remain a source of black anger; that there was such a mixture is an observable fact, foreshadowing, some believe, a future in which racial distinctions will become obsolete.

To a people grown especially sensitive to injustice apparently resulting from race, the very lack of African immigration may be significant. No matter what interpretation one places on the matter, the fact remains that in the first sixty-five years of this century the number of Africans admitted to the United States (50,000 would be a roughly accurate figure) is about half the size of the immigration from tiny Denmark during the same period.

Since the Civil War, black Americans have seen truly noble legislation emasculated by white resistance, not always in the South alone, with such practices legalized by shockingly biased local ordinances and supported by a series of backward-looking Supreme Court decisions in the latter part of the nineteenth century. The several civil rights acts of the past few years and the famous Supreme Court decision of 1954 (demolishing the theory of separate-but-equal schools) have seemed to reverse the tide of oppression which had almost managed to wash away the Negro as a significant and respectable part of American society.

Almost everywhere progress has been made and, even if by now patience has worn thin, that progress must be recognized. Against the tragic case of an Emmett Till, a boy allegedly murdered because of "disrespectful" remarks made to a white woman, and against the calamity that befell a gentle and compassionate Martin Luther King, assassinated because even his slow path to sanity threatened to modify American society, must be put the horror-provoking figures of the final decade of the last century, which recorded an average of 166 lynchings each year.

Perhaps other examples are in order. Groups of black citizens have complained of the quality of education available to them, either in the central cities of the North or in the segregated or reluctantly-integrated schools of the South; they have pointed to the miniscule percentages of Negro doctors, lawyers, and professors; they have demanded less restrictive entrance policies in the universities; they have begun to insist that they control schools in their own predominantly-black neigborhoods. White cooperation in solving these problems is now demanded, not solicited.

No doubt some changes have come and others will not be far behind. To blacks they will be too slow, too incomplete, too superficial. Only the perspective of history can show the progress made by a people to whom the fundamentals of reading and writing could be taught only if one were willing to break the law not much more than a hundred years ago, a people of whom six out of ten were illiterate at the start of the century. If a white man points to such matters, he may be thought to be alleging inferiority or opposing a deserved progress, when he is in truth expressing admiration and a degree of awe.

The most hostility is evidenced, the most frustration is felt, not when a situation is static, but after change has begun. Pressures to go faster and faster are regarded differently by whites, who see the status and position of blacks radically improved since World War II, and by blacks, who see their claims as largely ignored since 1865.

Such hostility and frustration have as one result the "black is beautiful" movement, the cry for Black Studies programs in the universities, the sudden interest in Swahili, the wearing of dashikis and other African and African-derived costumes, the avowed rejection of white values and white-dominated society. At their best, such movements can accomplish much good by erasing self-hate and eliminating the kind of self-defeating behavior to be observed in persons who believe they are inferior. The assertion that significant cultures existed outside of Europe is surely long overdue, although the romanticization of a continent unknown for generations can lead to a somewhat dangerous acting out of fantasy.

At their worst, the pressures noted above may give blacks some things which they may discover are not at all what they need, may lead to an anti-white racism every bit as eroding as the anti-black racism which they have experienced, and may promote a totally unproductive guilt in the hearts of well-intentioned whites. Clearly the climate is one in which demonstrably useful and "objective" studies of racial differences would not be tolerated.

All peoples deserve their own myths; the kinds of myths that they create usually represent their most pressing needs. As needs are met, myths may be modified. In the next few years, a black myth will solidify; whites must react to it with a receptive understanding, though they must not expect it to be their myth, and they should not react too unsympathetically as they meet some who confuse the map of myth with its territory of the world as it is. Such a statement is in no way patronizing, for white societies have followed the same path.

Before allowing the reader to turn to the selections in which some of these ideas are treated, the editors believe one point in defense of the white man is in order. It would be safe to say that a great many white Europeans, later to come to America, were in actual or virtual bondage long after black American slaves had been freed. Few would deny that white skins have accelerated social and economic progress, or that white immigrants have blocked black efforts to move upward, but to assign all whites to the exploitative class is as unacceptable as the reverse discrimination blacks know so well.

Black pride can coexist with "flesh-colored" band-aids just as fat men can coexist with tapered shirts. Racial equilibrium in America will come about no more through rejection of the white majority by the black minority than it did when the opposite condition was true. The reactions of both Iago and Othello are understandable.

BLACK
CRISIS

"MY KOUNTRY"—KLONSEL'S KREED
From *Newsweek*

In 1965 Mrs. Viola Liuzzo, a white Northern sympathizer, was murdered after the famous Selma, Alabama marches, and a group of young Southern white men were accused of her murder. In their defense, attorney Matt Murphy, Imperial Klonsel of the Ku Klux Klan, articulated to the jury the weird mixture of religion, patriotism and bigotry that is the basis of the Klan's creed.

The racist diatribe by Matt Murphy, Imperial Klonsel of the Ku Klux Klan, in his defense summation to the Liuzzo jury was disturbing evidence of the enduring difference between some Southerners and most Americans.

"I'm up here to throw you a straight ball," Murphy told the jurors. "Right down the line. One white man to another white man. What kind of a man is this Gary Rowe? What kind of a man is it that comes into a fraternal organization by hook or crook? What kind of a man is this who took an oath and joined the United Klans of America, took the oath with his hand raised to his Almighty God? And then sold out like Judas Iscariot. And I say, gentlemen, he's betrayed himself, his God, his own oath. He is a liar, a perjurer. He would do anything. He sold his soul for a little gold. He's worse than a white nigger.

"I'm proud I'm white. I stand with the white segregationists. I'm proud of it. I'll give up my life before my race is mongrelized with black niggers and white niggers. Now they say Collie Leroy Wilkins killed this Mrs. Luizzo. I say he's not guilty."

RESPECT

"Did you see that black nigger, Leroy Moton, who was up here on the witness stand? He had no respect. That black nigger sat up there before this white judge and this white courtroom and he had no respect. Saying 'yeah' and 'no' and 'yeah.' He should have been saying 'yes, sir,' and 'no, sir.' But he was saying 'yeah' and 'no' . . . The black man ain't got the morals, the decency . . . the respect to sit up there in front of this honorable white judge.

"I'm trying to lay this case on the line before you, gentlemen.

"You heard me? I said, 'Now, look, boy, look down at your feet, boy. How many feets away?' Now I don't talk like that, using 'feets,' but this was a nigger boy and I was talking to him. I said,

'How many feets?' and this nigger said 'yeah' and 'no' and this nigger was sitting *beside* this white woman in a car.

"And this woman, this white woman who got killed. White woman? Where's that NAACP card? I never thought I'd see the day. I never thought I'd see the day when Communists and niggers and white niggers and Jews were flying around under the banner of the United Nations, not the American flag we fought for, not the flag of the country which we are in and I'm proud to be white and I stand here as a white man and I say we're never going to mongrelize the race with nigger blood and the Martin Luther Kings, the white niggers, the Jews, the Zionists who run that bunch of niggers, the white people are not going to run before them. Jim Clark says 'Never!' I say 'Never!' myself. You know that she was in the car with three black niggers? One white woman and three niggers sitting back there! Black nigger Communists taking us over. White niggers! Some of them even infiltrated this courtroom."

GOD'S LAW

"Never! We shall die before we lay down and have it done. Niggers are against every law God ever wrote. Noah's son was Ham and he committed sin and was banished and his sons were Hamites and God damned them and they went to Africa and the only thing they ever built was grass huts. Black men in a straw hut covered with mud. No white lady can ever marry a descendant of Ham. If you do, you shall be destroyed. That's God's law. You cannot overcome God.

"Do what the people with God said. White woman, nigger man. You shall be destroyed!

"Rabbi with a nigger . . . white woman, nigger man, nigger woman, feet to feet . . .

"You notice his eyes. You see him [Moton] sitting up there? You look at his eyes. Oh, I did. Eyes dilated. You see them? You see them staring? Pupils dilated. You see him talking under the hypnotic spell of narcotics? You didn't? Well, I did. And I tell you as one white man to another that this card-carrying member of the Communist Party . . .

"I urge you as patriotic Americans not to find this young man guilty."

THE BRIAR PATCH

From *I'll Take My Stand* (*1930*)

ROBERT PENN WARREN

Pulitzer Prize winner, novelist, poet and critic, Robert Penn Warren (b. 1905) was in his youth a member of the Fugitives, a group of young Southerners who gathered at Vanderbilt University in the late 1920's to devise a new agrarian philosophy. "The Briar Patch" makes clear the position of the Negro in Warren's vision of the perfect society.

In 1619 twenty negroes were landed at the colony of Jamestown and sold into slavery. Probably they came from the Indies; in such case they were torn from the servitude of the Spaniard to be delivered into that of the Englishman in America. The ship that brought them—she was named the *Jesus*—touched history significantly, but only for a moment. When she again put to sea, with the price of twenty slaves added to the profits of her venture, she disappeared forever into the obscurity from which she had brought those first negroes to American shores.

The number of negroes in the country increased slowly until the eighteenth century, but they had come to stay. Long before the Civil War, when Northern philanthropy and Southern interest raised money from Sunday schools and societies to colonize the negroes in Africa and thus solve the problem which distressed the nation, the negroes, in so far as they were articulate concerning their fate, usually opposed any such scheme. They might be mobbed from their farms in Ohio or be forced to spend their days in the cotton-fields under a blazing Mississippi sun, but America, after all, was home. Here they knew where they stood; the jungle, though not many generations behind, was mysterious and deadly.

At Appomattox, in the April of 1865, Lee's infantry marched past the close Federal ranks to the place of surrender and acknowledged with muskets at carry the courtesy of the enemy's salute. The old Emancipation Proclamation was at last effective, and the negro became a free man in the country which long before he had decided was his home. When the bluecoats and bayonets disappeared, when certain gentlemen packed their carpet-bags and silently departed, and when scalawags settled down to enjoy their profits or sought them elsewhere, the year of jubilo drew to a close and the negro found himself in a jungle as puzzling and mysterious, and as little answering to his desires, as the forgotten jungles of Africa.

The negro was as little equipped to establish himself in it as he would have been to live again, with spear and breech-clout, in the

Sudan or Bantu country. The necessities of life had always found their way to his back or skillet without the least thought on his part; the things had been only the bare necessities, but their coming was certain. He did not know how to make a living, or, if he did, he did not know how to take thought for the morrow. Always in the past he had been told when to work and what to do, and now, with the new-got freedom, he failed to understand the limitation which a simple contract of labor set on that freedom. It is not surprising that the idea of freedom meant eating the cake and keeping it, too. In the old scheme of things which had dwindled away at Vicksburg, Gettysburg, and Chattanooga, he had occupied an acknowledged, if limited and humble, place. Now he had to find a place, and the attempt to find it is the story of the negro since 1865.

The Reconstruction did little to remedy the negro's defects in preparation. Certainly, he discovered himself as a political power, but he was also to discover that the fruits of his power were plucked by some one else, by the friends who gave him big talk and big promises. Sometimes he got an office out of it all and smoked cigars in the chair of a legislature. The political training which he received, however, was the worst that could possibly be devised to help him; it was a training in corruption, oppression, and rancor. When the earth shook and the fool, or scoundrel, departed after his meat, leaving his bankrupt promises, the negro was to realize that he had paid a heavy price for the legislative seat and the cigar. He had been oppressed for centuries, but the few years in which he was used as an instrument of oppression solved nothing. Instead, they sadly mortgaged his best immediate capital; that capital was the confidence of the Southern white man with whom he had to live. The Civil War had done much to show the negro's character at its best, but, so short is human memory, the Reconstruction badly impaired the white man's respect and gratitude. The rehabilitation of the white man's confidence for the negro is part of the Southern white man's story since 1880.

Some people in the North thought that the immediate franchise carried with it a magic which would insure its success as a cure-all and fix-all for the negro's fate. Corresponding to them was the group in the South whose prejudice would keep the negroes forever as a dead and inarticulate mass in the commonwealth—as hewers of wood and drawers of water. Between these extremes of prejudice on the subject there lay a more realistic view that the hope and safety of everyone concerned rested in the education of the negro; the belief might spring from a democratic ideal of equal opportunity, or it might be, in the mind of a person who had witnessed the Reconstruction, an expedient insurance against the repetition of just such a disaster. On the surface, however, the intention appeared the same.

The process of fulfilling that intention has been a slow one, and the end is far from in sight. The poverty of the South for a generation after the Civil War played heavily against it. Educational efforts could not be concentrated on the negro, for the plight of the poor white, in both the mountains and the lowlands, was but little better. Money has trickled down from the North to be invested in the negro's education. Southern states have doled out money from their all too inadequate educational funds. The increasing prosperity of the section may give considerable hope for the future, but the process has scarcely begun. To realize this one has only to see the negroes in the deep South, or even in the middle South, sitting before the cabin, stooping over the cotton row or tobacco hill, or crowding the narrow streets of a town on Saturday night in summer.

But with the accelerated process of negro education a question will certainly be asked again. For what is the negro to be educated? It is a question that must be answered unless one believes that the capacity to read and write, as some believed concerning the franchise, carries with it a blind magic to insure success. In the lowest terms the matter is something like this: are most negroes to be taught to read and write, and then turned back on society with only that talent as a guaranty of their safety or prosperity? Are some others, far fewer in number, to be taught their little French and less Latin, and then sent packing about their business? If the answer is *yes*, it will be a repetition of the major fallacy in American education and one of America's superstitions.

The most prominent man in negro education of the past, and probably the most prominent negro of the past or present, answered the question otherwise. "I am constantly trying to impress upon our students at Tuskegee—and on our people throughout the country, as far as I can reach them with my voice—that any man, regardless of color, will be recognized and rewarded just in proportion as he learns to do something well—learns to do it better than some one else—however humble the thing may be. As I have said, I believe that my race will succeed in proportion as it learns to do a common thing in an uncommon manner; learns to make its services of indispensable value." Booker T. Washington realized the immediate need of his race; he realized that the masses of negroes, both then and for a long time thereafter, had to live by the production of their hands, and that little was to be gained by only attempting to create a small group of intellectual aristocrats in the race. The most urgent need was to make the ordinary negro into a competent workman or artisan and a decent citizen. Give him whatever degree of education was possible within the resources at hand, but above all give him a vocation. This remains, it seems, the most urgent need.

An emphasis on vocational education for the negro is not, as has sometimes been thought and said, a piece of white man' snobbery. In the first place, the principle applies equally well to the problem of white illiteracy in the South and elsewhere. In the second place, everyone recognizes that there is a need for negroes in the professions, especially medicine and teaching, just as there is opportunity if the negro combines a certain modicum of patience and unselfishness with his ability. But the general matter of so-called higher education for the negro in the South is a small factor in relation to the total situation.

There are strong theoretical arguments in favor of higher education for the negro, but those arguments are badly damaged if at the same time a separate negro community or group is not built up which is capable of absorbing and profiting from those members who have received this higher education. If this does not occur, if the negroes in the South cannot support their more talented and better equipped individuals, the unhappy process of the past will continue, and the educated negro will leave the South to seek his fortune elsewhere. This process is peculiarly unhappy in two respects. The less fortunate negro who stays at home is deprived of immediate example and understanding leadership among his own people, and his contact, if any, with his lost leader is through the medium of rumor or the printed page. Moreover, the leader himself loses his comprehension of the actual situation; distance simplifies the scene of which he was once a part, and his efforts to solve its problems are transferred into a realm of abstractions. The case is not dissimilar to that of the immigrant labor leader or organizer who has in the past left the life he understood and come to this country whose life he did not wholly understand. Both have shown a tendency toward the doctrinaire.

The reason given, and accepted, for the educated, ambitious negro's move from the South is the lack of opportunity which is there offered and the discriminations which exist against him. In its broadest aspects the question is that of "equality." The question is an extraordinarily complicated one, but certain very clear issues can be disentangled. The simplest issue, and probably the one on which most people would agree, is that of equal right before the law. At present the negro frequently fails to get justice, and justice from the law is the least that he can demand for himself or others can demand for him. It will be a happy day for the South when no court discriminates in its dealings between the negro and the white man, just as it will be a happy day for the nation when no court discriminates between the rich man and the poor man; and the first may be a more practicable ideal than the second. The matter of political right carries repercussions which affect almost every relation of the two races, but again the least that can be desired in behalf of the negro is that any regulation shall apply equitably to both him and the white man.

The other aspects of equality, which present themselves every day and which spring to most people's minds when the matter is mentioned, are more subtle and confused. When the educated Southern negro says that he cannot stay at home because no opportunity exists there, he may mean one or both of two things. Let us take the case of a negro who has satisfactorily prepared himself for a profession. Does he simply regret, if he hangs out his shingle or puts up his plate, that his negro clientele will be small and many of its members too poor to pay him a living commensurate to his talents and training? Or does he protest against the fact that the white man will seek out another white man—a man whose professional abilities may possibly be inferior to the negro's own? Certainly in the North there are cases where a negro with a normal-school education has protested because he or she has not received a white school appointment when no negro school vacancy occurred. If our professional man, however, means the first thing, he states a problem whose solution has been slow but can be envisaged with some degree of clarity; it is a race group that will support and demand such services as he can offer. The first step in this solution is obviously the economic independence of the race. If he means the second, the answer is more roundabout, but depends to a great extent, as we may see, on the same factors.

This same professional man would probably add to his first reason that of the more general discriminations which necessarily surround him in the South. He has money in his pocket, but he is turned away from the white man's restaurant. At the hotel he is denied the bed which he is ready to pay for. He likes music, but must be content with a poor seat at a concert—if he is fortunate enough to get one at all. The restrictions confront him at every turn of his ordinary life. But his answer to another question might do something to clear both his and the white man's mind. Does he simply want to spend the night in a hotel as comfortable as the one from which he is turned away, or does he want to spend the night in that same hotel? A good deal depends on how this hypothetical negro would answer the question.

Again, as in the former complaint, if he wants the first thing the fulfillment of his want finally depends on the extent to which the negro makes himself economically free. But the negro radical, or the white radical in considering the race problem, would say that he wants the second thing—he wants to go to the same hotel, or he wants the right to go to the same hotel. The millennium which he contemplates would come to pass when the white man and the black man regularly sat down to the same table and when the white woman filed her divorce action through a negro attorney with not thought in the mind of any party to these various transactions that the business was, to say the least, a little eccentric. To such a radical the demand for less is treason to his race; to simply look forward to a negro society which can take care of all the activities and needs of its members is a feeble compromise. When Booker T. Washington at the Atlanta Exposition of 1895 lifted his hand and said, "We can be as separate as the finger, yet one as the hand in all things essential to mutual progress," the hand he raised, in the eyes of such a radical, was the hand of treason.

"My friend," Washington might well reply to such a critic, "you may respect yourself as a man, but you do not properly respect yourself as a negro." To him the critic would be suffering from a failure to rationalize his position, from the lack of a sense of reality, and from a defect in self-respect, for the last implies the first two deficiencies. The critic's condition would be like that of the individual of any color who consumes himself in "desiring this man's art, and that man's scope"; and his principles would be those of the doctrinaire.

Many negroes undoubtedly possess a self-respect; in others something else, such as fatalism or humor, may partially serve its purpose in making the situation comfortable. But the more dynamic attitude is to be expected when, and only when, the negro is able to think of himself as the member of a group which can afford an outlet for any talent or energy he may possess. And much will have been accomplished to bring this about when Juvenal's remark will no longer apply with such force to the negro's condition as it does today.

> "nil habet infelix paupertas durius in se,
> quam quod ridiculos homines facit."

It has been the custom to some degree in the South, and probably to a greater degree elsewhere, to look forward to industrial progress as the factor which would make the Southern negro's economic independence possible. This industrial progress, which one sees heralded in the census reports, in announcements of chambers of commerce, and in the gaudy full-page advertisements of national magazines, is to strike off the shackles and lift the negro from his state of serfdom, ignorance, and degradation. Such an expectation involves an exorbitant act of faith—an act of faith, not in the negro's capacity, but in the idea of industrialism. Possibly industrialism in the South can make some contribution to the negro's development, just as to the development of the section, but it will do so only if it grows under discipline and is absorbed into the terms of the life it meets. It must enter in the rôle of the citizen and not of the conqueror—not even in the rôle of the benficient conqueror.

But whether industrialism comes in the rôle of the citizen or the beneficient conqueror, bearing the Greek's gifts, what is the negro's relation to it? A factory or mill is built in a certain district and offers wages which appear attractive to him. He does not ask himself the very pertinent question as to why the factory has been built there, and nobody is at hand to tell him that he himself is one of the most significant reasons. The factory may have come to be near its requisite raw materials, but it has also come to profit from the cheap labor, black and white, which is to be had there. The negro labor is unorganized and unable to bargain effectively with its employer, and the white labor is in little better state.

Even if the policy of the factory is to employ white labor only, the negro is still a telling item in determining its location; his mere presence is a tacit threat against the demands which white labor may later make of the factory owner. It is an old situation in the North where the negro, cut off from the protection of the unions in time of peace, made an ideal scab in time of trouble. The fact and the related fact of the negro's lower standard of living have been largely responsible for the race riots which have occurred in the North since the days of the war, when pillars of smoke from Northern factory chimneys first summoned the Southern negro out of the land of Egypt. It is sometimes boasted in the South that the section has been spared such race riots as those of Chester, Washington, Youngstown, East St. Louis, and Chicago. It is to be wondered how much longer that boast can be made if the manager of a factory in the South can look out his office window on a race of potential scabs. It will be a new era of the carpet-bag.

No blame is to be attached to the negro himself if his mere presence swells a stockholder's dividends at the expense of a white workman, or if he takes that white workman's job in time of strike. There is no good reason why he should fight the white man's battles if at the same time there is no proper provision for him in the system. In 1919 at the Atlantic City Convention the struggle to gain equal protection for the negro in the American Federation of Labor was won; at least, it was won on paper. But there is a vast difference between that paper victory and a workable system which would embody its principles.

There are two factors which will retard the development of such a system. Not infrequently in the South one meets a conservative temper which carries a naïve distrust of most types of organization. It is a temper somewhat similar to the eighteenth-century English squire's cynical regard of government. The antebellum "squirearchy" of the South did not have such an attitude, but its origins in both cases are the same; in both it springs from a certain individualism. The English squirearchy arose from a century of commotion and internecine war, while the Southern squirearchy expired in our Civil War, leaving in its relics the same dubieties. But this attitude is not to be taken as a simple economic conservatism which would find a congenial supplement in capitalistic theory; its conservatism bears a more philosophical inflection which subjects the organization of capital to the same skeptical regard.

The potential danger is that in being forced to accept a certain degree of industrial development it will overlook the relation of white and black power to each other and to the capital which makes that development possible. If this industrialism is to bequeath anything except the profit of the few, the conscious or unconscious exploitation of racial differences, and a disastrous rancor, an enlightened selfishness on the part of the Southern white man must prompt him to encourage the well-being and possibly the organization of the negro, as well as white, labor. His safety and that of all concerned lie in a timely strategic adjustment of his position rather than in a tactical defense, however stubborn and expert, of point after point. Not many generations ago the South made just such an error in the conduct of a war.

The second obstacle is in the attitude of the "poor white," whose history shows him to be just as much the victim of the slave system as the negro.[1] In a clumsy, inarticulate fashion the "poor white" realizes this fact, and from it comes much of the individual violence, such as lynching, which sometimes falls to the negro's lot. An unchecked industrialism will mean a hopeless aggravation of this attitude. The only way out, except for a costly purgation by blood, is a realization that the fates of the "poor white" and the negro are linked in a single tether. The well-being and adjustment of one depends on that of the other. When Booker T. Washington said that the salvation of his race will come if the negro "learns to do something well—learns to do it better than some one else," he was stating a condition of free competition between the negro and the white engaged in the same pursuit. He offered no solution for this conflict beyond a vague optimism that the world would pay in money and respect for a thing well done; in fact, he scarcely hinted of the conflict.

But the world also likes to pay as little as possible for a thing. If a negro mason lays a brick as well as a white mason and asks less pay for the job or is content with longer hours, the negro mason in the end will get the job and keep it. The white mason can enter on a period of cut-throat competition with the negro in the labor market, to discover that the negro is better equipped to win. He can attempt to erect artificial barriers against the negro workman in the trade, such as a compact with the employer, only to discover that in a crisis the employer, whether Northern or Southern, will look at a balance sheet and not at the color of the hand which holds the trowel. The white workman, seeing his job in the hands of a negro at a wage which he

[1] The term "poor white" is an inexact one. Sociologists have used it—or, Southerners would say, misused it—to apply to almost any Southern whites, especially unskilled laborers, who happen to be poor and underprivileged in the cultural and economic sense; and the term is rather loosely applied by Northern writers even to mountaineers and to small farmers who live on a precarious footing. But in the Southern conception, not everybody who is both poor and white is a "poor white." To the Southerner, the "poor white" in the strictest sense is a being beyond the pale of even the most generous democratic recognition; in the negro's term, "po' white trash," or so much social debris. But the term is used here in the later and not the strictly Southern sense.

himself could not possibly live on, can resort to a program of violence, sabotage, and persecution; then no bricks will be laid and the ranks of militia will meet him in the street. But the white mason can learn, either by these expensive and bitter experiences or by an exercise of simple intelligence, that color has nothing to do with the true laying of a brick and that the comfort of all involved in the process depends on his recognition and acceptance of the fact.

If the white laborer does not learn this the negro will be in the perpetual rôle of the cat who pulls chestnuts out of the fire for the smiling employer; but it will be no fault of the employer. A multitude of minor difficulties will necessarily arise in giving the negro the protection to prevent this. Their solution will demand tact on the part of the employer, judgment and patience on the part of both the negro and white workman, effective legislation, and the understanding by the ordinary citizen of the several possibilities of the situation. Something else may be added: what the white workman must learn, and his education may be as long and laborious as the negro's, is that he may respect himself as a white man, but, if he fails to concede the negro equal protection, he does not properly respect himself as a man.

But this is not the whole matter, and hardly even the major issue. In the past the Southern negro has always been a creature of the small town and farm. That is where he still chiefly belongs, by temperament and capacity; there he has less the character of a "problem" and more the status of a human being who is likely to find in agricultural and domestic pursuits the happiness that his good nature and easy ways incline him to as an ordinary function of his being.

Once he worked the land as a slave; now he operates on his own account a considerable part of it. Sixty-five years ago he was disappointed in his forty acres and a mule and began his life of freedom with only the capital of his bare hands; but now, only a few generations after, he operates on his own account in the deep South, either as tenant or owner, about one-third of the land. In the border states, of course, the proportion is much smaller. Over a quarter of the rural negro population lives on land which it owns. In Florida and border states over half of the negro population engaged in agriculture lives on owned land, but farther down, where the bulk of negroes are concentrated, the proportion is about one-fifth. Without capital, without education, and with only the crudest training in agricultural methods, the negro has demonstrated his capacity to achieve a certain degree of happiness and independence on the land, and there is every reason to expect that the process will be accelerated from year to year.

Even under the present circumstances, which fall far short of an ideal, not to say decent, adjustment, there are certain compensations in this way of life for the negro and for society in general. It affords a slow way, but the readiest and probably the surest way, for the greater number of the negroes to establish themselves. In the past it has been accepted in most cases simply because no other was at hand, but now if it can be made attractive enough and can offer enough opportunity, it will serve as a ballast to an extravagant industrial expansion. If both the negro and the poor white can find a decent living, there will be no new crowded and clamoring slave auction ready for exploitation by the first bidder. In the last place, it means that the racial distribution in the larger towns and cities can more or less naturally adjust itself and the municipal sections of both societies can develop peacefully without that clash which the relatively sudden influx of negroes has caused in certain Northern cities.

All relations between groups in the city tend to become formalized and impersonal, and such is especially true in those of the two races. But the condition outside of the city is somewhat different and infinitely more desirable. With all the evils which beset the tenant system in the South there is still a certain obvious community of interest between the owner and the "cropper"; profit for one is profit for the other. The relation between the white owner and the negro owner is not so crudely apparent, but it does exist, as anyone who is familar with a rural community in the South can testify. In one sense it is their common consciousness of depending for the same external, unpredictable factors for the returns on their labor; it rains on the just and the unjust, the black and the white. But in all cases—owner,cropper, hand—there is the important aspect of a certain personal contact; there is all the difference in the world between thinking of a man as simply a negro or a white man and thinking of him as a person, knowing something of his character and his habits, and depending in any fashion on his reliability. The rural life provides the most satisfactory relationship of the two races which can be found at present, or which can be clearly imagined if all aspects of the situation are, without prejudice, taken into account.

But if the negro in the country finds his garden and his cotton patch pleasant enough to make him decline the offers of industrialism, the difficulty of competition between the two races is not finally disposed of; it is only transposed into terms which are more readily ponderable. With the negro's increase of ability and equipment there is the chance of a condition such as that which existed in California between the white and Japanese growers. In competion with the small white farmer the negro would have the same advantages as the negro mason in competition with the white mason. And the buyer of strawberries or cotton or tobacco would care as little whether the product came from a white man's land or a negro's land as the employer would care whether a brick had been laid by a white or black hand; indeed, he would care less.

If the Southern white man feels that the agrarian life has a certain irreplaceable value in his society, and if he hopes to maintain its integrity in the face of industrialism or its dignity in the face of agricultural depression, he must find a place for the negro in his scheme. First, there is the education of the negro—and this applies with equal force to the poor white—in a productive agricultural technique. At present both the landowner and the cropper are victimized by the methods which the cropper employs, but that is the grossest and most immediate aspect. If the negro farmer who owns his land cannot work it profitably there will be in the end that perpetual bait of cheap labor dangling before the factory-owner's eye. Again, in any coöperative or protective enterprise the white man must see that the negro grower receives equal consideration; he must remember that the strawberry or the cotton bale tells no tales in the open market concerning its origins. These, from one point of view, are the more purely selfish parts of the program.

The Southern white man may conceive of his own culture as finally rooted in the soil, and he may desire, through time and necessary vicissitude, to preserve its essential structure intact. He wishes the negro well; he wishes to see crime, genial irresponsibility, ignorance, and oppression replaced by an informed and productive negro community. He probably understands that this negro community must have such roots as the white society owns, and he knows that the negro is less of a wanderer than the "poor white" whose position is also insecure. Let the negro sit beneath his own vine and fig tree. The relation of the two will not immediately escape friction and difference, but there is no reason to despair of their fate. The chief problem for all alike is the restoration of society at large to a balance and security which the industrial régime is far from promising to achieve. Inter-racial conferences and the devices of organized philanthropy, in comparison with this major concern, are only palliatives that distract the South's attention from the main issue. Whatever good they do, the general and fundamental restoration will do more.

FOLKLORE OF THE SOUTH AND RACIAL DISCRIMINATION (1964)

JAMES M. LACY

James M. Lacy, a Texas folklorist, explores a vital force in the origin of racial prejudice: the misinformation, fear, and irrationality found in folklore. At the same time, Lacy sees clearly that change breeds new images, and that as American folklore changes, so will the old stereotypes.

Those of us who work and study in the field of folklore soon develop a fondness for this most intimate part of our knowledge and understanding of life. We relish this part of our education, the pleasure un-dimmed and unscarred by memories of long hours spent in formal study of what sometimes seemed extraneous subject matter. We have a feeling of admiration and affinity for the folk who have given us this lore.

It is with a feeling of disloyalty and sorrow that one suggests that the fountainheads of our folklore could also pour out streams of distrust and hatred toward those who differ from the majority in belief or na-tional origin or color. Yet, the evidence indicates that the discrimina-tions exercised against certain racial and cultural groups in this coun-try are the results of attitudes instilled in our citizens at a very early age. These prejudiced concepts enter the minds of our youth at the same time and in the same manner as the remainder of the great body of lore which one generation passes on to the next. Thus attitudes of antagonism, feelings of racial superiority, and lack of respect for ethnic and cultural minorities can be traced directly to the same origins as the other elements of folklore which constitute our cultural heritage.

Most of us who have spent our lives in the South are proud of the regional characteristics which we possess or which have been attrib-uted to us. But we must recognize that there has been rampant in our culture an insidious force, often unseen or unrecognized, pulling us toward racial prejudice and discrimination. We see this force strongest in that segment of our population most susceptible to folk patterns of thought and feeling. And those of us who recognize prejudice for what it is are not always completely immune to its influence. In spite of intent and desire we sometimes find it lurking tenaciously in the back-grounds of our minds, ready to reveal itself at an unguarded moment.

The child is introduced to racial prejudice early in his life. The names which he hears applied to the Negro, such as "coon," "darky," "nigger," and burr-head," give an early impression that the Negro is an object of humor and scorn. He buys fireworks called "nigger chasers," nuts called "nigger toes," makes a toy called a "nigger shooter," and recites a jingle about catching "a nigger by his toe." He hears degrading jokes about Negroes and sees signs in public places which distinguish between "Colored" and "Whites." From earliest childhood he is conscious of the segregation of the colored race: in school, in church, in theaters, in public conveyances, and in the city in which he lives. The evidence of racial distinction is omnipresent. Some-times it is open and brutal; more often it is subtle and veiled, ranging from an appellation of scorn and derision to an instinctive withdrawal from physical contact. These attitudes of discrimination are as deeply ingrained in the minds of children as are those of morality or patri-otism.

As the child grows older and becomes active in his society, he prac-tices these discriminations he has observed. He learns to ignore the presence of colored people, or to be condescending when association is necessary. He learns to accept their inferior status without question or twinge of conscience, and he begins to deride their most serious activities as emulations of their superiors. The youth comes to expect deference from the Negro and to resent the absence of it. The adult, through ignorance or habit, continues these discriminations, or recognizing the nature of these prejudices, does nothing, or little, to remedy them. The individual who has been born and reared in the South has had imbued in him throughout his life and from almost all aspects of his society an acute awareness of racial inequality.

The folk image of the Negro that has been created in the minds of southern whites has been long in the making and is firmly entrenched. Many characteristics have been attributed to the race as a whole, and these are in turn applied to the individual. The picture usually presented is that of a likable fellow with a pleasant nature but inferior capabilities. This idea in the minds of the white race that the Negro is mentally and morally inferior is the basis for racial discrimination and the chief justification for denying him equal opportunities. According to extremists holding this view, the reason for this inferiority is not environmental, but rather biological and racial. As pointed out by Maurice R. Davie in his study of *Negroes in American Society,* the doctrine of the Negro's inferiority has a history as long as his stay in America, but the basis for this concept has shifted through the years.[1] First was the question of whether the Negro was to be classed as a human being with a soul; later it was whether he had the intelligence to master the rudiments of learning; then his capability for higher education was debated; and today the question is "whether he has those high qualities of imagination, intellect, initiative, and aggressiveness characteristic of the Anglo-Saxons."

The popular stereotype of the Negro in fiction and in movies has been that of an ignorant, superstitious, lazy, irresponsible individual. This view was satirized by a Negro journalist, George S. Schuyler, in 1927:

We Ethiops, one gathers from this mass of evidence, are a childish, shiftless, immoral, primitive, incurably religious, genially incompetent, incredibly odoriferous, . . . mentally inferior people with pronounced homicidal tendencies. We are incapable of . . . self-restraint and irresponsible except when led by white folks. We possess a penchant for assaulting white females and an inordinate appetite for chicken, gin, and watermelon. While it is finally and reluctantly admitted that we belong to the human race, we are accorded only the lowest position in the species, a notch or two above the great apes. . . . In short, from examining the bulk of the evidence, the impartial investigator must conclude that the Negro has almost a monopoly of all the more

[1] Maurice R. Davie, *Negroes in American Society* (New York: McGraw-Hill Book Co., 1949), p. 367.

discreditable characteristics of mankind. But at the same time one is effusively informed that he is deeply loved and thoroughly understood, especially by his pork-skinned friends of Southern derivation.[2]

Perhaps the most cherished image of the Negro in the southern mind is the "Uncle Tom" type of individual, the devoted, faithful servant whose one aim in life is to serve his master. The master, in turn, repays this loyalty with affection and protects him as one of his own. Among Negroes the term "Uncle Tom" is used to show their contempt for a member of their race who seeks favor with whites by being subservient.

At the heart of racial discrimination in this country, serving as both cause and effect, lies the lore concerning color distinction. As in the other forms of prejudice, this color consciousness was learned in the true folk manner. That the pigmentation of the skin is the chief basis for racial prejudice is evident when the bias extended toward other darker-skinned minorities is considered. This awareness of color is so strong that the degree of discrimination often corresponds to the shade of darkness. The proof of white superiority given recently by a staunch segregationist was that all the Negroes who had attained prominence in the country were light-colored, that is, part white. We are forced to accept, not for the reason intended, but for its statistical accuracy, the correctness of this statement. Several studies made on this subject indicate that some doors are easier to open for the Negro if his skin is of a lighter color. Davie states that Negroes with lighter complexions have long enjoyed opportunities and a social status superior to those of unmixed blood, and that, with some notable exceptions, most Negro leaders have mixed blood. Davie goes on to say that Negroes themselves draw the color line, that "the lighter colored form cliques to which darker Negroes are admitted, if at all, only by wealth, education, or attainment." Davie explains the superior attitude of mulattoes, using the term regardless of degree of mixture, by asserting that a greater proportion of them derive from the free Negroes and from the favored class of house slaves, with many of them descending from the masters themselves, from even such eminent persons as Alexander Hamilton, Patrick Henry, and Thomas Jefferson. It seems natural that during the period of slavery the master of the plantation would show preference to his own or some relative's mulatto child, giving him an education or special privileges, or freeing him when he became an adult. Many accounts of plantation life in the ante-bellum South make references to the lighter-skinned house servants and the darker field workers.

In a few places in the South just after the Civil War, the mulattoes organized themselves into a little guild known as "The Blue Vein

[2] George S. Schuyler, "Our White Folks," *American Mercury*, XII (December, 1927), p. 385.

Circle," from which those who were black were excluded. One of the folk rhymes from this group shows their disdain for their darker-skinned brothers:[3]

> Stan' back, black man,
> You cain't shine;
> Yo lips is too thick,
> An' you hain't my kin'.
>
> Git 'way, black man,
> You jes hain't fine;
> I'se done quit foolin'
> Wid de nappy-headed kin'.
>
> Stan' back, black man!
> Cain't you see
> Dat a kinky-headed chap
> Hain't nothin' side o' me?

This color-consciousness in the folklore of Negroes has been confirmed by Negro writers. Dr. Charles S. Johnson in his study of southern rural Negro youth, *Growing Up in the Black Belt*,[4] found decided color preferences among the boys and girls who were interviewed. A simple test was devised to determine the importance of color as a factor in the personality development of Negro youth. A familiar color classification was employed: black, dark brown, brown, light-brown, yellow, and white. The individual was asked to check the color of persons toward whom he held certain favorable and unfavorable attitudes.

The results of this test seem very significant. For example, the number of boys who checked light-brown as the color of "The most beautiful girl you know" was almost ten times greater than the number who checked black. The rating of color preference by the girls was very similar in questions concerning the boys they admired or disliked the most. The association of color with moral judgments in these tests was almost as significant as was that with judgments of physical appearance.

In the list of favorable descriptions given on this test, light-brown received by far the highest ranking. Brown was second with approximately half as many votes, and "the worst color to be" was black. The color yellow was the only one of the lighter colors to receive social opprobrium, as yellowness seems to be associated with a recent mixture of the two races.

[3] Thomas W. Talley (ed.) *Negro Folk Rhymes* (New York: Macmillan Company, 1922), p. 10.

[4] Charles S. Johnson, *Growing Up in the Black Belt* (Washington, D.C.: American Council on Education, 1941), pp. 258–65.

The reactions to color on the part of both races show some similarities and many differences. It would be interesting, but probably impossible, to determine the effect which nonracial associations with the colors white and black, found throughout our folklore, might have on racial discrimination. The popular concepts of white as a symbol of purity and goodness and black as a symbol óf ill-favor and evil are strong in American lore. We wear white for the happiness of marriage and black for the mourning of death. Every child knows the difference between a white lie and a black one. Undesirable citizens are "blackballed" or put on a "black list," and in our society there are "black sheep" and "blackguards." The more superstitious among us fear black magic and try to avoid black cats. It seems possible that the traditional stigma placed on the color black might have contributed toward the discrimination against the Negro race.

Except for the legal restrictions which exclude the Negro from many of the activities of the whites, no aspect of folklore has been more conspicuous in its regulation of behavior than the etiquette practiced in biracial associations. The code of etiquette based on the color line had its inception during slavery. Clearly understood by all and maintained by tradition and custom, this social ritual needed little if any legislation to enforce it. Bertram W. Doyle in his study of race relations in the South maintains that there was no such thing as a race problem before the Civil War.[5] The clearly defined caste system afforded a means by which the master-slave relationship might be carried on with little friction, and the most intimate bonds could exist between master and slave on the plantation, provided the proper etiquette was not violated by either party. Part of an old Negro spiritual bears witness to one custom observed in this social ritual. The refrain, "I want to go to heaven settin' down," is possibly a reference to the fact that the slave was expected to stand whenever he was in the "Big House."

With the close of the war and the end of slavery the old way of life was gone, and with it the customs and social ritual which had governed race relations. The plantation owners were no longer the dominant force in the South, and their heirs to political authority were the masses of small landowners, tenants, and tradesmen, the "poor whites" of ante-bellum days, for whom the slaves had had little respect. An old Negro jingle shows the attitude toward the lower class of whites:[6]

> My name's Ran, I wuks in de san';
> But I'd druther be a Nigger dan a po' white man.
> I'd druther be a Nigger, an' plow ole Beck
> Dan a white Hill Billy with his long red neck.

[5] Bertram W. Doyle, *The Etiquette of Race Relations in the South* (Chicago: University of Chicago Press, 1937), p. xxi.
[6] Talley, *op. cit.*, pp. 42–43.

The subsequent acts of this new force in the South did little to bring about respect. To maintain white supremacy, laws were passed to enforce the restrictions of the caste system which had formerly been maintained by custom and public opinion. Thus the caste system was perpetuated in the South and with it the etiquette of race relations, ever present but gradually being altered as the status of the Negro in the society changed. In recent years the formality of these associations has lessened considerably, and in many cases disappeared. Where interracial etiquette is still practiced it is usually in employer-employee relationships or among the less educated members of both groups who are still to a considerable extent bound by the mores of the past.

Dr. Johnson, in his study of the Negro in the rural South, published in 1941, reports that he found a consistency in the racial etiquette concerning some activities, and differing attitudes in some sections about other relationships.[7] The two universally tabooed practices were found to be intermarriage and interdancing. Interdining was generally prohibited, but was permitted in some areas on special occasions. Negroes were expected to use "Mr." and "Mrs." when addressing whites, but as a rule only white salesmen or others seeking patronage used these terms when speaking to Negroes. In some counties Negroes were expected to enter a house by the back door. Some stores required Negroes to remove their hats on entering and refused to let them try on hats and gloves. A boy or girl could buy an ice cream cone in a drugstore but could not eat it until he had left the building.

At times some fine distinctions have been made in observing the etiquette of racial relations. The story is told of one white man in Mississippi who readily admitted that he had had a colored mistress for thirty years, but hotly denied that he had ever sat down to breakfast with her.

It was inevitable that the lore concerning the Negro should affect the folklore of the Negro himself. The racial etiquette imposed upon him, his position in society, and the way he was regarded by those who were prejudiced against him had to contribute to the view he had of himself. It is doubtful whether anyone outside the Negro race can fully understand what it is like to be a part of what James Baldwin calls "that fantastic and fearful image which we have lived with since the first slave fell beneath the lash." He reminds us that "the American image of the Negro also lives in the Negro's heart," and that only through an adjustment to this position created for him by others can he "secure his birthright as a man."[8] That this adjustment is not easy can be seen in Baldwin's statement that he "can conceive of no Negro, native to this country, who has not, by the age of puberty, been irreparably scarred by the conditions of his life."

[7] Johnson, *op. cit.*, p. 277.
[8] James Baldwin, *Notes of a Native Son* (Boston: Beacon Press, 1955), p. 38.

The myth that the Negro is content with his lot has been strong in southern lore. Created as a balm to the southern conscience, this belief has been able to survive until recent years because of the reluctance of a majority of Negroes to press a seemingly hopeless cause. The individual also learned that an appearance of cheerful acceptance of his status was to his advantage. The true attitude of the Negro toward his position in American society can be found in his writings. One wrote that "black is a terrible color to be born." It is not surprising that some of this writing portrays desperate action taken against the ever present oppression that the writers feel. Countee Cullen, for example, wrote that ". . . one grows weary turning cheek to blow."[9]

The ultimate reaction of desperation toward an unfriendly society is seen in the main character of Richard Wright's novel *Native Son*.[10] "Bigger" Thomas sees in the white race a hated symbol of all his frustrations and all the oppressions he had suffered—a symbol also of self-hatred because he has no place in the white man's or any other society. His murder of the white girl gives him his first sense of well being, of asserting himself, not against the girl personally, but against those forces which have made him what he is.

Today in the South we can observe a phenomenon which is probably unique in our society. We can see in the process a great change taking place in the beliefs, customs, and patterns of thought of a large segment of our population. Just as Americans gave up the common belief that the only good Indian was a dead one, they are now beginning to discard the popular theory of Negro inferiority, which has been the basis for racial prejudice. Americans of both races are coming to realize that the caste structure on which racial discrimination is founded was not created by anyone living today, and that no individual or racial group of this generation is actually responsible for it.

The image of the Negro in our society is changing rapidly. One evidence of this can be seen in those media through which the earlier image was propagated. In fictional writings, movies, and in the theater, the old stereotyped characters have all but disappeared. Today it is common for the Negro to be portrayed on the screen as an admirable or even heroic figure, and the old-time Negro minstrel has gone the way of the patent medicine show.

One by one the different facets of discriminatory practice are being displaced. The segregation of the races, unequal employment opportunities, and voting restrictions are opposed by law, but racial discrimination in the South, and in the rest of America, will come to an end, not by legislation alone, but only when there is a real change in the folklore of the American people.

---

[9] Countee Cullen, *On These I Stand* (New York: Harper & Bros., 1947), p. 85.
[10] Richard Wright, *Native Son* (New York: Harper & Bros., 1940).

BIG ROUND WORLD (1957)

LANGSTON HUGHES

A distinguished American poet and short story writer, Langston Hughes (1902–1967) is one of the most perceptive interpreters of the black experience in the twentieth century. Here he fuses aspiration and hope in a statement that transcends race and becomes universal.

"The other day a white man asked where is my home," said Simple. "I said, 'What do you mean, where is my home—as big and round as the world is? Do you mean where I live now? Or where I *did* live? Or where I was born?'

" 'I mean, where you *did* live,' the white man said.

" 'I did live every-which-a-where,' I told him.

" 'I mean, where was you born—North or South?' the white man said.

" 'I knowed that's what you mean,' I said, 'so why didn't you say so? I were born where you were born.'

" 'No, you weren't,' he declared, 'because I was born in Germany.'

" 'Some Negroes was born as far away as Africa,' I said.

" 'You weren't, were you?' he asked.

" 'Do I look like a Mau Mau?' I said.

" 'You look African, but you speak our language,' that white man told me.

" '*Your* language,' I hollered, 'and you was born in Germany! You are speaking *my* language.'

" 'Then you are an American?'

" 'I are,' I said.

" 'From what parts?' he kept on.

" 'All parts,' I said.

" 'North or South?' he asked me.

" 'I knowed you'd get down to that again,' I said. 'Why?'

" 'Curiosity,' he says.

" 'If I told you I was born in the South,' I said, 'you would believe me. But if I told you I was born in the North, you wouldn't. So I ain't going to say where I was born. I was just borned, that's all, and my middle name is Harlem.' That is what I told that white man. And that is all he found out about where I was borned," said Simple.

"Why did you make it so hard on him?" I asked. "I see no reason why you should not tell the man you were born in Virginia."

"Why should I tell him that? White folks think all Negroes should be born in the South," said Simple.

"There is nothing to be ashamed of about being born down South," I said.

"Neither about eating watermelon or singing spirituals," said Simple. "I like watermelon and I love 'Go Down, Moses,' but I do not like no white man to ask me do I like watermelon or can I sing spirituals."

"I would say you are racially supersensitive," I said. "I am not ashamed of where I was born."

"Where was you borned?" asked Simple.

"Out West," I said.

"West of Georgia?" asked Simple.

"No," I said, "west of the Mississippi."

"I knowed there was something Southern about it," said Simple.

"You are just like that white man," I said. "Just because I am colored, too, do I *have* to be born down South?"

"I expect you was," said Simple. "And even if you wasn't, if that white man was to see you, he would think you was. They think all of us are from down in 'Bam."

"So what? Why are you so sensitive about the place of your birth certificate?"

"What old birth certificate? Where I was born they didn't even have no birth certificates."

"Then you could claim any nationality", I said, "East Indian, West Indian, Egyptian, German."

"I could even claim to be French," said Simple.

"Yes," I said, "or Swiss."

"No, no!" said Simple. "Not Swiss! Somebody might put *chitterling* in front of it. And I am not from Chitterling-Swiss! No, I am not from Georgia! And I have not traveled much, but I have been a few places. And one thing I do know is that if you go around the world, in the end you get right back to where you started from—which is really going around in circles. I wish the world was flat so a man could travel straight on forever to different places and not come back to the same place."

"In that case it would have to stretch to infinity," I said, "since nothing is endless except eternity. There the spirit lives and grows forever."

"Suppose man was like the spirit," said Simple, "and not only lived forever but kept on growing, too. How long do you suppose my hair would get?"

"Don't ask foolish questions," I said.

"Negroes who claim to have Indian grandmas always swear their grandma's hair was so long she could set on it. My grandma did not have so much hair in this world. But, no doubt, in the spirit world that is changed, also her complexion, since they say that up there we shall be whiter than snow."

"That, I think, refers to the *spirit*, not the body. You change and grow in holiness, not in flesh."

"I would also like to grow in the flesh," said Simple. "I would like to be bigger than Joe Louis in the spirit world. In fact, I would like to be a giant, a great big black giant, so I could look down on Dixie and say, 'Don't you dare talk back to me!' I would like to have hands so big I could pick up Georgia in one and Mississippi in the other, and butt them together, bam! And say, 'Now you-all get rid of this prejudice stuff.' I would also like to slap Alabama on the backsides just once, and shake Florida so bad until her teeth would rattle and she would abolish separate schools.

"As I grew taller, I would look over the edge of the big round world and grab England and shake here till she turns the Mau Mau free, and any other black parts of the world in her possession. I would also reach down in South Africa and grab that man, Malan, and roll him in mulberry juice until he is as dark as me. Then I would say, 'Now see how *you* like to be segregated your own self. Apart your own hide!'

"As I keep on growing bigger and taller I'll lean over the earth and blow my breath on Australia and turn them all Chinese-yellow and Japanese-brown, so they won't have a lily-white Australia any more. Then some of them other folks from Asia can get in there where there is plenty of room and settle down, too. Right now I hear Australia is like Levittown—NO COLORED ADMITTED. I would not harm a hair of Australian heads. I would just maybe kink their hair up a little like mine. Oh, if I was a giant in the spirit world, I would really play around!"

"You have an imagination *par excellence*," I said, "which is French for *great*."

"Great is right," said Simple. "I would be the coolest, craziest, maddest, baddest giant in the universe. I would sneeze—and blow the Klu Klux Klan plumb out of Dixie. I would clap my hands—and mash Jim Crow like a mosquito. I would go to Washington and rename the town—the same name—but after Booker T., not after George, because by that time segregation would be plumb and completely gone in the capital of the U.S.A. and Sarah Vaughan would be singing like a bird in Constitution Hall. With me the great American giant, a few changes would be made. Of course, there would be some folks who would not like me, but they would be so small I would shake them off my shoe tops like ants. I would take one step and be in California, another step to Honolulu, and one more to Japan, shaking a few ants off into the ocean each time I stepped. And wherever there was fighting and war, I would say, 'I don't care who started this battle, stop! But right now! Be at peace, so folks can settle down and plant something to eat again, particularly greens.' Then I would step on a little further to wherever else they are fighting and do the same. And anybody in this world who looked like they wanted to fight or drop atom bombs, I would

snatch them up by their collars and say, 'Behave yourselves! Talk
things out. Buy yourselves a glass of beer and argue. But he who fights
will have *me* to lick!' Which I bet would calm them down, because I
would be a real giant, the champeen, the Joe Louis of the universe, the
cool kid of all time. This world would just be a marble in my pocket,
that's all. I would not let nobody nick my marble with shells, bombs,
nor rifle fire. I would say, 'Pay some attention to your religion, peoples,
also to Father Divine, and shake hands. If you has no slogan of your
own, take Father's, *Peace! It's truly wonderful!*'"

From
RACE AND INTELLIGENCE (1963)
MELVIN M. TUMIN

*Melvin M. Tumin (b. 1919), a Princeton sociologist, and his associates
emphasize that attempts to measure or interpret human intelligence in
racial terms or in accordance with conventional definitions of race are
illogical and unscientific; furthermore, they insist that most conventional attempts, whether racially oriented or not, are based upon faulty
assumptions.*

Introduction

Do Negroes and whites in the United States differ significantly in their
native mental equipment? Are there reliable tests of mental capacity
that prove this to be so? What is the best available scientific evidence
regarding the inheritance of intelligence, and what does this evidence
say about differences between Negroes and whites? Is there evidence
to indicate that when environmental situations and opportunities are
equalized, the difference between the average test and scholastic
achievement scores of Negroes and whites are reduced? To what extent? Could Negro and white students participate with average equal
capacity in the affairs of our culture, assuming equality of opportunity,
training and motivation?

These questions, and the many others they imply, have for a long
time piqued the curiosity and elicited the passions of many Americans,
both in and out of the scientific community. In 1954, the Supreme
Court ruled that separate school facilities were not and could not be
equal, and that therefore segregation of schools along color lines was
illegal. For some years before that historic decision, the majority of

social and biological scientists and students of testing and measurement have favored the view that differences between the average scores of Negroes and whites were largely, if not totally, the result of differences in their backgrounds and environments. These differences relate to opportunity, motivation, models, horizons of possible success, perceived utility of success at school, and the like. That viewpoint was expressed cogently and succinctly by a committee of social scientists, including sociologists, anthropologists, psychologists and geneticists who, at a UNESCO conference on this subject in Paris, issued a joint statement which said in part:

"Whatever classifications the anthropologist makes of man, he never includes mental characteristics as part of those classifications. It is now generally recognized that intelligence tests do not themselves enable us to differentiate safely between what is due to innate capacity and what is the result of environmental influences, training and education. Wherever it has been possible to make all allowances for differences in environmental opportunities, the tests have shown essential similarity in mental characters among all human groups. In short, given similar degrees of cultural opportunity to realize their potentialities, the average achievement of the members of each ethnic group is about the same."

In the past several years, however, some voices have been raised challenging the viewpoint expressed by the leading spokesmen of the major scientific societies concerned with various aspects of Negro-white differences. Notable among them have been a psychologist, Professor Henry Garrett (Professor Emeritus of Columbia University), an anatomist, Professor Wesley Critz George (Professor Emeritus of the University of North Carolina), and a layman, Mr. Carleton Putnam. Professor Garrett has called attention to the findings reported by his former student, Dr. Audrey Shuey, in her book: *The Testing of Negro Intelligence* (J. P. Bell Co. Inc., Lynchburg, Virginia, 1958); Dr. George has written his own book, *The Biology of the Race Problem* (a Report commissioned by the Governor of Alabama, 1962, distributed by the National Putnam Letters Committee, New York), and Mr. Putnam has published various articles and speeches reiterating themes developed in his book *Race and Reason* (Public Affairs Press, Washington, D. C., 1961).

In these documents, the respective authors have contended that the scientific evidence is faulty; that contrary evidence has been ignored; and that, in effect, it can be conclusively shown that the Negro in the United States (and presumably elsewhere) is natively inferior in intelligence to the white. Various national periodicals have seen fit to give currency to some of these claims.

In insisting upon the innate inferiority of the Negro, Professor Garrett and Mr. Putnam have relied almost exclusively upon the findings presented by Dr. Shuey. Since science is always responsive to the suggestion that a particular scientific position may not be well founded, it was deemed important to examine in detail the evidence brought forward by Dr. Shuey,[1] to see whether that evidence is in any way sufficient to challenge the position held by the majority of social scientists.

Toward that end, four outstanding scientists, representing the professions principally concerned with matters of genetic and social differences among humans, were asked to read the Shuey and Putnam books and to respond to a series of questions about them. The scientists were:

DR. HENRY C. DYER, Vice President, Educational Testing Service, Princeton, N. J., one of the country's foremost authorities on intelligence and ability testing;

PROFESSOR SILVAN S. TOMKINS, Professor of Psychology, Princeton University, Princeton, N. J., one of the country's leading specialists in personality testing;

PROFESSOR RALPH H. TURNER, Chairman of the Department of Sociology, University of California at Los Angeles, and a noted expert on social and cultural patterns in the Negro population; and

PROFESSOR SHERWOOD L. WASHBURN, formerly President of the American Anthropological Association and Chairman of the Department of Anthropology at the University of California at Berkeley, one of the world's most distinguished anthropologists.

---

[1] Since Dr. George's book was not published until the work of the panel had been completed, it was impossible to secure the same systematic evaluation of that volume as of the Shuey and Putnam volumes. To the extent, however, that Dr. George's contentions are the same as those of Dr. Garrett, Dr. Shuey and Mr. Putnam, and rely on the same kind of materials and evidence, a similarly negative conclusion regarding Dr. George's book would have to be drawn. Dr. George's other claims, resting on various references to assorted works in geography, history and anthropology, remain to be assessed. Some indication of the probable outcome of such an assessment may be provided by the fact that Dr. George leans rather heavily on a new book by Professor Carleton Coon, entitled *The Origin of the Races* (New York, Alfred Knopf, 1962). Interested readers may refer to the review of that book by Professor William Howells, Chairman of the Department of Anthropology at Harvard University (New York *Times,* December 9, 1962). In this review, Professor Howells indicates quite clearly that whatever the findings with regard to the *origin* of races, such material cannot relevantly be used to estimate or measure differences between races today.

Summary of Findings

The four scientists are in substantial agreement that the claims advanced by Shuey, Putnam and Garrett (and later by George) cannot be supported by any substantial scientific evidence.

Moreover, the panel concludes that any future claims regarding innate differences between Negroes and whites with regard to intelligence cannot be substantiated unless three conditions are met:

(1) The distinctive *genetic,* or "racial," homogeneity of the Negro group being tested, as well as that of the white group being tested, must be *demonstrated,* not assumed.

(2) The social and cultural backgrounds of the Negroes and whites being tested or otherwise being measured must be fully equal.

(3) Adequate tests of native intelligence and other mental and psychological capacities, with proven reliability and validity, will have to be used.

To date, none of these crucial conditions has been satisfactorily met.

Unless all three conditions are satisfied, one cannot effectively determine whether there are native differences in intelligence or other mental capacities between biologically or genetically distinct groups that can be ascribed to the biological differences between them rather than to differences in their social and cultural situations.

Since none of these three conditions has been met as yet, it is the opinion of the scientists that no claims regarding such differences can be supported. The scientists further join in indicating the extent to which, at various times, differences in test scores have been diminished by reducing the differences in environmental factors believed to have an influence upon test performance. In view of the demonstrable influence of social and cultural factors upon test performance, the panel judges that further equalization of cultural background and social environment would probably result in further equalization of test scores and thereby discount claims of innate mental differences such as those advanced by Shuey, Garrett and Putnam. In this conclusion, they fully support the settlement of the distinguished social scientists who constituted the UNESCO committee.

As Dr. Stanley Diamond has recently put it (*Current Anthropology,* IV: 3, June 1963, p. 323):

All of the historical and psychological evidence scrutinized by anthropologists leads to one conclusion: there is no differential capacity for the creation and maintenance of culture on the part of any population large enough to be sensibly called a race, in the traditional sense of that term. Mongoloids, Negroids and Caucausoids have been physically and culturally inter-fertile throughout the history of modern mankind. Moreover, none of these groups is exclusively associated with any given cultural phenomenon. Nor has any genetically based differential capacity in intelligence among these major populations ever been established. On the contrary, the doctrine of racial equality is fully supported by scientific and historical inquiry.

1) *In your judgment, is there sufficient evidence in the Shuey volume to justify Dr. Shuey's conclusion regarding the presence of native differences between Negroes and whites and thus to reject, in part or in toto, the validity of the position taken by the social scientists in Paris?*

Summary of Responses

There is not sufficient evidence to justify the conclusion that there are native differences between the intelligence of whites and Negroes. The nature of intelligence tests is such that they are incapable of identifying genetic differences between any two groups.

It has long been known that Negroes and whites differ on the average, but with considerable overlap, in their performance on psychological tests. However, it is generally agreed today that these tests do not measure only innate intelligence; what they measure as well are the effects of opportunity to learn the kinds of items included in the tests, the motivation of the individual taking the test, the meaningfulness of the items for him, and his ability to perform in a test situation. In all these respects, the Negro in our society is disadvantaged in comparison with whites in otherwise similar environments. There is no reason, therefore, to suppose that the relatively small average differences in test scores reflect differences in innate intelligence. Unfortunately, no test of mental abilities has yet succeeded in controlling *all* the environmental variables that might influence its validity. These include things such as prenatal and postnatal care, child-rearing practices, the socioeconomic level of the family and its intellectual interests, the emotional interaction of parents and children and of siblings with one another, the quality and length of schooling, the social and cultural impact of the community and the vocational opportunities it provides. When efforts are made to equate environments of Negro and white subjects more fully, differences in average I.Q. are lessened, as the environmental interpretation would lead us to expect.

This much Dr. Shuey acknowledges. But in reaching her conclusion that there are native differences between Negroes and whites, she relies upon two unscientific devices.

First, in her summaries she lumps together indiscriminately studies that incorporate serious efforts to control environment and others that make no such effort. None of the studies on which she reports has controlled all the environmental variables *simultaneously*. Some studies take account of certain aspects of socio-economic status; others take account of some aspects of schooling; still others take account of some aspects of cultural opportunity. But in each study, many environmental factors are left uncontrolled. One cannot logically add miscellaneous differences found under all sorts of uncontrolled or partially controlled conditions, compute an average, and assert that the average difference is attributable to any single unobserved factor such as genetic structure.

Second, she takes as conclusive the residue of difference in I.Q. which remains after serious efforts at correction have been made. However, the corrections which have been employed are quite crude and approximate, so that there is every reason to believe that in the best of studies only part of the difference in opportunity, motivation, and meaningfulness has been controlled. Under these circumstances, the reasonable interpretation is that complete control would reduce the differences between racial averages even further, to the point where they are either trivial or nonexistent.

Dr. Shuey's conclusions that there are significant differences in the innate capacities of Negroes and whites is not supported by sufficient evidence to invalidate the position taken by the social scientists in Paris, that given similarity of cultural opportunity to realize their potentialities, the average achievement of the members of each ethnic group is about the same. . . .

2) *To the extent that one can discover a consistent line of argument in your judgment, a sufficient basis of evidence in that volume to justify the contention that there are significant differences in the innate capacities of Negroes and whites, especially innate intelligence, and thus in turn to deny in part or in toto the validity of the UNESCO social scientists' statement quoted above?*

SUMMARY OF RESPONSES

Putnam's argument regarding inequality depends primarily upon (a) the comparative history of civilizations, and (b) the propriety of judging civilizations summarily on the basis of selected values taken from and applied with the perspective of one of the civilizations being judged. The conditions leading to the rise or decline of civilizations in the popular sense as much too complex and poorly understood to justify inferences concerning the relative intelligence or inherited emotional or moral qualities of peoples.

Civilizations seem to be a product of the congregation of large populations in urban centers. But these circumstances bear little apparent relationship to the intelligence of the people involved. Most "civilizations" seem to be, in part, a product of large-scale military conquest, which brings a vast area enforced domination by a small center, with the result that the labors of many can be exploited while others can be freed to concern themselves with less basic aspects of life. The circumstances which make one people subjugate others on a comprehensive and lasting basis are only dimly understood, but it would certainly be difficult to equate the wish to subjugate and exploit others with intelligence.

The danger with which Putnam is concerned is the danger that the genes of the superior race will be dissipated by intermarriage with an inferior race. If this danger is as great as he supposes, the danger applies to relationships other than those between Negroes and whites. Putnam in several places attributes racial superiority to English-speaking whites, particularly in contrast to Mediterranean groups making up much of the "second migration." Since intermarriage has already taken place on a large scale here, the danger and the magnitude of the problem would be great and the urgency of action to save the superior race greater than in the case of Negro-white intermarriage.

Even if we could be satisfied that civilizations in general can be judged from the perspective of just one of them, it would only be fair to enumerate and carefully define the criteria by which the superiority of one civilization is to be identified, and then attempt to apply them systematically, so that criminality, dependency, interpersonal suspicion, rewards for ruthlessness, and many other such characteristics could be included in the comparison.

Without such careful analysis, there is no way of knowing whether there is enough agreement on the criteria to supply the basis for argument, or whether white (especially English-speaking) civilizations would really come out as well as Putnam assumes. Putnam makes no systematic appraisal of civilizations; he takes the superiority of our civilization for granted (although he condemns the egalitarian attitudes that are part of it) and supports his claim by selective illustrations. . . .

4) *Are there, in your judgment, any satisfactory tests of* native, *i.e., innate or inborn, intelligence? If you think there are, what are these tests? To what extent have the tests been able to free themselves of culturally specific factors, and thus become culture free?*

SUMMARY OF RESPONSES

There are no tests of native intelligence. In fact, the concept of "native intelligence" is essentially meaningless. Every response to the stimulus material in intelligence tests is, of necessity, *a learned* response. The kind and amount of learning an individual acquires depends upon the experiences that come to him from the environment and upon his structural assets and liabilities. To some extent, structural assets and liabilities are genetically determined; to some extent, they are environmentally determined. With respect to many structural characteristics in an individual, it is not possible to tell whether the characteristic in question has been genetically or environmentally determined. Therefore, there is no way of ascertaining from an intelligence test score to what extent the learning that produced it has been affected by genetic factors. So-called "culture-free" tests are predicated upon one of two assumptions: (a) either the learning required to perform acceptably on the test is commonly and equally available to all people of all cultures, or (b) the stimulus material in the test is completely novel to all people of all cultures. Both assumptions are patently false.

5) *Are there any satisfactory ways, in your judgment, of getting at reliable estimates of native intelligence, other than those now in use? What are these ways? Have they been applied? Where?*

Summary of Responses

There are no satisfactory ways, at present, of getting reliable estimates of native intelligence. In genetic and animal breeding, the attempt is made to estimate native or genetic characters by equalizing the environment as much as possible first. The residual differences are mainly genetically determined. The only relatively exact method of identifying native human capacities would depend on the identification of specific genes in man, and research which traced them over generation. All the methods now available to us require the use of circumstantial evidence—the residual difference which is left after we have made all possible corrections for environment. At present it is not known what the units of inheritance are. There is little reason that I.Q. corresponds to any such unit. . . .

7) *In what sense is it legitimate to speak of "Negro intelligence" and "white intelligence"?*
A. *Assume for the moment that we had adequate representative samples of the scores made on intelligence tests by members of the population defined as Negro and those defined as white in America today. What inferences, if any, could be made from these sample test scores regarding the capacity of the members of the groups sampled for common participation in the same government, culture, school system, etc.?*
B. *What inferences, if any, could be drawn about the likelihood that the same descendants of the two groups would probably score in roughly the same way?*

If any similarity of scoring over generations could be inferred, to what extent would this inference be based on an assumption of 1) inheritance of the capacities? 2) continuity of social and cultural factors relevant to the score outcomes?

Summary of Responses

There is no sense in which it is legitimate to speak of "Negro" vs. "white" intelligence. Intelligence is an individual rather than a group characteristic. To the extent that it has an inherited basis, it is influenced by the individual's immediate antecedents and not by the total race to which he belongs. It would be necessary radically to reduce caste and class differences between Negroes and whites before their innate intelligence could be compared. Infant and young-child comparisons suggest greater similarities between Negroes and whites in the early years. Many of the differences reported in the past between Negro and white intelligence as constituting evidence for heredity have been shown to be the consequences of cultural and class differences.

Since an intelligence test samples a variety of mental functions that are, to some extent, predictive of performance in school, in college, and in the vocations, a score on such a test indicates, within limits, the degree to which an individual has acquired these functions. The scores vary enormously from one individual to another. The range of intelligence test scores obtained by Negroes is, as far as we know, just as great as the range of intelligence tests scores obtained by whites. That is, both Negroes and whites have scored at the top and at the bottom of the range. Insofar as the scores predict educational and vocational achievement, one would suppose that a high-scoring Negro should have the same probability of a successful educational or vocational performance as a white with the same score.

The correlation between their intelligence-test scores of parents and the intelligence-test scores of their children has usually been found to be in the neighborhood of .5. This means that twenty-five percent of the variance in the children's scores can be predicted from their parents' scores. Seventy-five percent of the variance in the children's scores, therefore, cannot be predicted from the parents' scores. Because of this unpredictable variance, it is to be expected that the scores of children in any group will regress toward the mean of that group, i.e., children of low-scoring parents will tend to have higher scores than their parents, and children of high-scoring parents will tend to have lower scores than their parents.

For the group as a whole, the mean scores of the children will be about the same as the mean scores of the parents, provided the environmental conditions affecting the children's scores are approximately the same as the environmental conditions that affected the parents' scores. A change in the environmental conditions which favored the children over the parents would tend to raise the mean of the children's scores above that of the parents' scores. Thus, if a group of Negro children were given cultural opportunities superior to those available to their parents, one would expect that the mean score of the Negro children would be higher than the mean score of their parents. . . .

From
INTELLIGENCE OR PREJUDICE? (1964)
ERNEST VAN DEN HAAG

Ernest van den Haag, a Dutch-born sociologist, disagrees strongly with the Tumin argument. He questions the research techniques employed by Tumin, as well as the findings, and insists that contrary to Tumin's assertions, innate differences among racial groups are possible.

I

Q. Melvin Tumin, a Princeton sociologist, has interviewed experts on Testing, Psychology, Sociology, and Anthropology, about Negro intelligence. His questions, the answers and his introduction have been published (by the Anti-Defamation League) under the title "Race and Intelligence: A Scientific Evaluation." What do you think of it?

A. Well, Mel Tumin is a good man; at least his heart is in the right place—left of center. According to science, that's where the heart ought to be.

Q. What about his mind?

A. It's where his heart is.

Q. Do you mean he's prejudiced?

A. On the contrary. He's against all prejudices he doesn't share. (So am I. But we don't share the same prejudices.) If "prejudiced" means nasty or deliberately dishonest, I think he is neither.

Q. Would he go wherever science leads?

A. On racial matters he'd always be able to convince himself that science leads him where he wants to go.

Q. Suppose the experts he questioned had answered: "science proves that Negroes are innately inferior." Would he have published this result?

A. An interesting question. Ask one that I can answer with facts rather than hopes and wishes. . . .

Testing Native Intelligence

Q. O.K., let me ask you first about a statement that startled me. Dr. Henry C. Dyer, a big shot in "educational testing," says (*op. cit.* p. 25): "There are no tests of native intelligence. In fact the concept of native intelligence is essentially meaningless. Every response to the stimulus material in intelligence tests is of necessity a *learned* response." Elsewhere (*ib.* p. 30) he adds: "You cannot make inferences about something that is meaningless." Since in his view the concept of innate intelligence is meaningless, he insists that test results cannot (not *do not,* but *cannot*) measure it. What about that?

A. Perhaps Dr. Dyer speaks *pro domo sua* when he denies native intelligence. I do not see why a learned response could not be used to test native intelligence, *i.e.,* innate ability to learn. If we can standardize the learning opportunities (and motivation), we test native intelligence, without isolating it, by testing the learned responses. (Conversely, if we can standardize genetic inheritance, we can test the influence of learning.) I certainly agree that it is very difficult to do so. I do not think it is impossible though. Moreover, difficulties in testing something do not make whatever is hard to test "meaningless"—they just make it hard to test. If we have no way of testing the temperature of the moon, it does not follow that the concept of lunar temperature is "meaningless."

That much is simple logic. But Dyer's assertion also is—and quite clearly—contrary to fact. H. G. Eysenck (Professor of Psychology at the University of London, and a well known expert on testing) concludes (*Encounter,* June 1964, p. 53): "Do tests of mental ability in fact tap innate factors? The evidence is by now quite conclusive that they are surprisingly successful in doing so. Consider a recent study by James Shields, in which he administered two intelligence tests to groups of fraternal twins brought up together, and to identical twins some of whom had been brought up separately. Identical twins share completely a common heredity, while fraternal twins are only 50 per cent alike with respect to heredity; on the tests the identical twins were found to be more than twice as similar to each other, *whether brought up together or separate,* than were the fraternal twins." (Italics mine.)

Research on identical (monozygotic) twins, *i.e.,* persons known to share exactly the same genetic inheritance, permits us to separate the effect of environment (learning) and of inheritance on the intelligence of the subjects. The results yielded by this research indicate that "[the intelligence test results of] the average pair of identical twins reared together [are] almost as similar as are the two scores of a single person tested twice [*i.e.*, differences do not exceed what may be attributed to testing errors, usually accounting for about 5 points] and *that those reared apart show a difference not very much greater.*" (Italics mine.) (L. E. Tyler, *The Psychology of Human Differences*, N.Y., 1956, p. 453.)

Thus, whereas the I.Q. of the population varies from about 50 to 180, the variation in I.Q. among identical twins reared separately does not exceed a few points, even when the difference in environmental advantages is known to be marked.

Q. What do you conclude?

A. The evidence so far yielded by twin studies indicates:

1. Intelligence (even if we define it simply as that which is measured by I.Q. tests) is very largely genetically inherited.

2. Even when environments differ very markedly (*e.g.*, when one identical twin is highly educated and the other is hardly educated at all), the difference in test results among individuals known to have the same genetic endowment remains very small.

3. It follows that differences in environment account only for a very small part of the observed differences in test results among individuals who do not have the same genetic endowment.

4. It seems unlikely also that environmental differences can account for all the observed differences of test results among groups, including ethnic ones.

Q. Does that settle the question?

A. No, I don't think so. There are many unanswered questions on the relation of I.Q. tests to intelligence, and the legitimacy of the concept of general intelligence. Further, there are many questions on the relationship between performance in actuality and test performance, etc.

Q. Then Dr. Dyer may be right after all?

A. He is clearly and overwhelmingly wrong. We know enough to be certain of that, but not enough to be certain of the correct answer, in quantitative terms, to the question he answered wrongly. . . .

II

Q. I think you have satisfied me on the *possibility* of differences in innate intelligence among ethnic groups—despite the Tumin claims to the contrary. But I want to know more about the actuality. For instance, I know some very intelligent Negroes.

A. So do I. We may say correctly:

1. There are some very intelligent Negroes. (This is probably true for any randomly selected large human group of any color.)

2. The performance of some Negroes equals or exceeds that of some whites. (This would be true in comparing any two large enough randomly selected groups of whatever color.)

3. Whatever the intelligence of groups of Negroes, their performance improves when their opportunities do—when they move from a less to a more propitious environment. (This would be equally true for any group, including retarded children.)

These propositions are obviously irrelevant to the issue, namely, whether Negroes as a group have, on the average, a lower native intelligence, at least in certain respects, than whites. If, and only if, the total Negro test performance equaled that of whites, *ceteris paribus,* genetic differences could be excluded by comparison of test performances.

I do not think that in this matter we have conclusive evidence one way or the other, though the indications are that the two groups have different aptitudes (or a different distribution of aptitudes). Please note that I am not saying that I have proved genetic inferiority of Negroes. I am asserting that Tumin's respondents have not disproved the claim of genetically lower intelligence—although they think they have.

Q. Throughout, you have been saying that Negro performance in school is below that of whites. Are you sure of that?

A. Let me quote from a study by Herbert Wey and John Corey ("Action Patterns in School Desegregation," a Phi Beta Kappa Commission project, p. 212): "There are some top Negro students, some mediocre ones, and some quite retarded. This is also true of white children. However, the proportion of slow learners is greater among the Negroes. Differences are not as apparent in kindergarten and first grade as in the upper grades and high school." These data are generally accepted. The disagreement is on the causes—environmental or genetic—of the difference in performance.

Separation by Ability

Q. How then would you deal with the problem of differences in performance?

A. It is interesting to note that the answer would be the same regardless of whether the differences are genetic or environmental. In the latter case my solution might, in time, be changed; in either case it would hold as long as the performance differences do.

Mixed education now would impair the education of Negro and of white children. The white children obviously require for optimum education maximum utilization of their present performance abilities. The Negro children require whatever can be done to increase their performance in view of the deficient environment of the past—regardless of whether there are genetic factors involved as well. Hence, at least for the time being, the needs of Negro children would be met best—*i.e.*, to their advantage and without disadvantage to others—by separate education geared to meet the obstacles presented by lack of opportunity and unfavorable environment. I am all in favor of improving the quality of education for all. But this can be done only if pupils are separated according to ability (whatever determines it). And this means very largely according to race.

The Gifted Child

Q. What about those Negro children who perform well? Should they not be transferred to white schools?

A. I think this could demoralize the remaining Negro children and could be hard also on the transferred child. Nonetheless, if both the white and Negro children (and/or parents) desire it, this objection would be greatly weakened. (If the gifted Negro child is transferred into a hostile white school environment, I doubt that there would be an educational advantage.)

But the main issue has little to do with the transfer of a few gifted Negro children. The learning ability of Negro children *on the average* is not as responsive at present as that of white children to the stimulation given by average white schools. We don't know whether it will ever be. (Poor original environment may cause, this, as may inherent factors. Desegregation is neither necessary nor sufficient to eliminate these disadvantages; and it would not help the average pupil of either group.) Therefore, Negroes and whites should be educated separately—unless there is evidence in specific cases that the learning of neither group suffers from congregation and that neither group objects. Instruction in schools for Negroes should attempt to remedy the disadvantages suffered by students coming from a culturally deprived home environment. This cannot be done except by separate education.

These disadvantages should be remedied by the time institutions of higher learning are entered. If they aren't the student is not college material. If they are, there is no reason for separate college education unless there are specific psychological reasons for it, such as mutual hostility.

Q. Would your educational argument be the only justification for separate schools?

A. It would certainly make them rational from an educational viewpoint. But the school question has all kinds of implications with regard to coercion, freedom of association, psychic damage, effects on prejudice, and so on, into which we cannot go now.

Q. Your solution sounds educationally rational even without the arguments you don't want to go into. But some people assert that regardless of how good the educational facilities are, separate education is "inherently unequal" and that "modern authority" has shown that it inflicts psychic or educational injury on Negro children to the extent of depriving them of the "equal protection of the laws." This was the decision of the Supreme Court in *Brown* v. *Board of Education*.

A. I know. But if the Supreme Court allowed itself to be bamboozled by "modern authority" which in no way demonstrated what it persuaded the court it had demonstrated. We need not be as credulous. . . .

III

Q. Forgive me for being so unsystematic, but I am bothered now by this question: suppose the average native intelligence of Negroes is inferior to that of whites. Would that mean that Negroes are inferior to whites?

A. One may regard others as inferior to oneself, or to one's group, on the basis of any criterion, such as mating, eating, drinking or language habits, religious practices, or competence in sports, business, politics, art or finally, by preferring one's own type, quality or degree of intelligence, skin or hair color and so forth.

By selecting appropriate criteria each group can establish the inferiority of others, and its own superiority. This can be and is done by Texans, Democrats, workers, Yale alumni, Frenchmen, extremists, moderates, and Chinese. The selection of criteria for superiority or inferiority is arbitrary, of course. The judgment of inferiority applied to others thus remains a value judgment, even if the qualities judged to render people inferior are actual characteristics of the group so judged. I do not believe that intelligence is any more relevant to judgments of inferiority than, say, skin color is.

If Negroes on the average turn out to have a genetically lower learning ability than whites in some respects, *e.g.* the manipulation of abstract symbols, and if one chooses this ability as the ranking criterion, it would make Negroes on the average inferior to some whites and superior to others. Suppose four-fifths of Negroes fall into the lower half of intelligence distribution. Chances are that, say, one-third of the whites will too. Hence, if intelligence is the criterion, the four-fifths of the Negro group would be no more "inferior" than the one-third of the white group. (It seems clear that some such overlap would exist, regardless of what we will ever learn about native intelligence.)

Judgments of inferiority among whites are rarely based solely on intelligence. There certainly are many people who do not rank high on intelligence tests but are, nonetheless, preferable, and preferred, to others who do. I know of no one who selects his associates—let alone friends—purely in terms of intelligence. God knows, we certainly do not elect to political office those who are most intelligent. I would conclude that whatever we may find out about Negro intelligence would not entail any judgment about general inferiority. At present we do not know whether the average native intelligence of Negroes differs from that of whites with certainty any more than we know whether average native musical ability does. I cannot see why one should be of more importance for judgments of inferiority, superiority or equality than the other.

Moral Disadvantage?

Q. What about the lower cultural performance of Negroes in their native habitat?

A. It is neither necessary nor useful to avoid value judgments in intercultural comparisons, as long as one keeps in mind that, like all value judgments, they are—as far as science is concerned—but more or less widely shared preferences. Thus one may evaluate the culture of primitive African tribes, Australian bushmen, or North American Indians *in toto* as inferior, equal or superior to Western culture in its various phases. Such judgments depend on one's value standards (ultimate preferences). If these are postulated, the judgment can be logically and empirically justified, though the standard on which it rests cannot.

If one uses as explicit criteria certain achievements such as the invention of a written language, or of the wheel, the creation of a literature, of arts and humanities, of mathematics, the rule of law, or medical progress, etc., then the cultural achievements of Negroes *in loco* compare unfavorably with those of Caucasians, Chinese, Near and Far Eastern groups, et al. This would constitute a disadvantage; it does not involve a moral inferiority unless the disadvantage is judged to be a moral one—a judgment not inherent in its description. (And of course one may also prefer the primitive to our own style of life, or discover special virtues in it that we lack.)

Neither the African environment nor subjugation in any form explains the lack of cultural achievement measured by these standards. It does not follow that a bio-genetic explanation is correct: a hypothesis is not proven correct simply because other hypotheses do not explain the phenomenon at issue. But I see no reason—other than fashion—to discard the possibility of differential genetic distribution of talents among ethnic groups as a possible partial explanation. (If such a hypothesis should prove correct, it would be quite consistent with the aforementioned high intelligence of some Negroes, and with the ability of all to improve their performance under propitious circumstances.) There is no reason to believe that God ever was an egalitarian (the biblical God certainly was not). I don't think He has read Professor Tumin since, or J. J. Rousseau, and been persuaded to become one. The evidence seems to the contrary. It is entirely possible that the differential performance of cultures must be explained, in part, by differential genetic distribution of aptitudes.

If we were to prove genetic differences of the relevant kind among ethnic groups, it would not necessarily follow that they are permanent and irreversible. However, genetic differences cannot be removed by education of the individuals involved, howevermuch their effect may be mitigated. We do not know at present to what extent genetic inheritance may be influenced by various factors that can be brought to bear.

Q. Do you have any general conclusions?

A. No; I'd like you to draw your own. However, the befuddlement of many social scientists deserves comment. Fifty years ago many among them were busy demonstrating "scientifically" the inferiority of Negroes to whites. As many are as busy now proving "scientifically" that there are no innate psychological differences whatever among ethnic groups, and that, unless children grow up in compulsory togetherness they are unfree, and suffer psychological injury. The evidence for these contentions is as "scientific" as the evidence for the ideology fashionable fifty years ago. The fashion has changed but many social scientists have not: they remain its servants. Now, and then, they were well intentioned; this is probably part of the trouble, for they obstinately refuse to act as scientists, being committed to various causes more than to the cause of science—although they yearn passionately for the trappings and the prestige of science. Yet for scientists moderation in the pursuit of truth is a fatal vice; it cannot be offset by extremism in the pursuit of egalitarian ideologies.

RIGHTS AND DIFFERENCES:
SOME NOTES FOR LIBERALS (1964)

C. LAWSON CROWE

C. Lawson Crowe, a former member of the staff of the Woodrow Wilson National Fellowship program, examines the dismay of white liberals who find that blacks do not always behave in accordance with white liberal expectations, and he points out an important fact about relative cultural values.

Segregationists never tire of emphasizing the sociological and cultural differences between whites and Negroes. While correct in recognizing the differences, they are incorrect in locating the differences in an alleged "biological inferiority" of the Negro race. Liberals, on the other hand, have maintained that such biological differences as may exist are not qualitatively significant. They have argued correctly that economic and sociological differences in the status of races are not relevant to the issue of freedom and justice for all citizens under the law. It now appears that many Negroes believe that the differences between Negroes and whites, whatever their origin, are real and important, although their reasons are far from those of the segregationists. This posture has caused dismay and alarm among the more fainthearted liberals and among many moderates.

The American citizen's right to life, liberty and the pursuit of happiness is an acknowledgment of the fact that persons and groups differ. It is a guarantee of freedom for such persons and groups, and, within the limits of law and order, it entails the right of a minority to maintain its identity within the greater community. This is said for the benefit of white, liberal, middle class Americans who, in confronting the Negro revolt, have failed to make an adequate appraisal of our racial conflicts.

I

We have witnessed a violent summer in many northern cities. Danger to life and limb for Negroes and their supporters is still the rule in the deep south. In this unhappy state of affairs some politicians have tried to capitalize on white reaction to the Negro revolution. Liberal northern newspapers and periodicals, viewing with alarm the disorder in Negro ghettos, have advised the Negro community that such disorder does its "cause" little good. The inability of acknowledged leaders of the Negro community to control slum populations has been lamented. Some less liberal sources have even suggested that men like Rustin, Forman, King and Wilkins are responsible for the summer's rioting and looting because they encouraged lawlessness by organizing civil rights demonstrations in the past.

White liberals have been offended by the questionable tactics of the Brooklyn chapter of the Congress of Racial Equality, the pointless threats to leave water faucets running, the abortive attempt to block traffic to the World's Fair. They have been dismayed by the throwing of garbage at motorists on the Tri-Borough bridge. Riots in Harlem, Rochester and Philadelphia have compounded the confusion. In short, liberals have had to recognize that for thousands of Negroes there is no "cause," no "movement," to which they pledge allegiance. When told to go home one Harlem Negro called out, "We *are* home, baby." In this cry was none of the idealism and aspiration which liberals associate with those who have hitherto led civil rights protests. It should not be surprising to find that many liberals have had their enthusiasm for the Negro cause dampened if not altogether extinguished.

James Baldwin, Dick Gregory, James Foreman and other articulate Negroes have challenged one of the white liberal's most precious assumptions. They have made it clear that they, and possibly the vast majority of Negroes, do not share every value of white bourgeois culture. White liberals have usually assumed that improvement in the individual Negro's educational and economic opportunities would result in his sharing the liberal's enthusiasm for bourgeois values, and in the virtual elimination of a Negro community as such. In other words, we have supposed that racial conflict could be resolved by improving the lot of individuals and have failed to reckon with the possibility that such improvement might have little or nothing to do with the Negro's identification of himself as a member of a minority group. It is a striking fact that some of the most vociferous Negro critics of our society have achieved professional and economic success, but this success has not made them more indulgent toward the white man's foibles. This is at least part of the meaning in James Baldwin's remark: "I don't want to marry your daughter, I just want to get you off my back."

The Negro revolt will not go away. Unless we have reached the point where the majority of people are willing to say that democracy cannot work, the answer does not lie in increased police forces or in other repressive measures. Revolutions occur where they are possible. If we ask why there are no revolutions in South Africa or Cuba, the answer is that the oppressed peoples of these lands do not possess the necessary power. Negroes in America revolt today not because of increased oppression but because they have the requisite economic and social power to do so. For this reason we face the choice of either dealing creatively with the Negro demand for freedom or entering an era of growing violence and disorder. Prolonged white resistance to the demands of Negroes will produce more of the frustration and hatred which fired the riots of the summer. Racial strife will become even more dangerous than it is now.

The followers of Senator Goldwater see the implications of the Negro march toward equality more clearly than do the majority of white liberals. Southern Goldwaterite conservatives recognize that the racial conflict cannot be settled in terms acceptable to them. This explains the fierceness of their resistance to change and the fervor of their support for the man who has suggested that we cannot protect the "rights" of one man by "taking away the rights of others" (with the clear implication to southern segregationists that Goldwater believes their "rights" are being violated by Negroes).

II

The educational and economic advancement of individual Negroes may mitigate the strife somewhat, but, even as this progress is achieved, it is doubtful that racial conflict will be eliminated where Negroes threaten white control of government and economic life. In other words, the racial conflict in the south and elsewhere is *between groups* and not between individuals as such. This is a fact which liberals, who almost always stress the individual, sometimes forget or ignore.

As I read Baldwin or listen to Dick Gregory I get the feeling that my interest in the racial conflict in this country is almost academic. I am a "white liberal cat," no more to be trusted than Ross Barnett or George Wallace. This suspicion and distrust, possibly contempt and hatred, may not be fair, but somehow I think it would be silly for me to let my feelings be hurt. Many Negroes believe that they have been betrayed by the white man's culture, by the white man's churches, and, in all probability, by the white man's Civil Rights law. The message of the Black Muslims has not been accepted, but this movement is symptomatic of feelings and frustrations hard to resist even when the Muslim proposals for dealing with the racial conflicts are rejected.

Baldwin and the Negroes he represents both admire and distrust the white man's culture. They want to enjoy its benefits without necessarily being committed to all its values. They want the freedom and opportunity to which they are entitled without being required to surrender their cultural identity. They want to be themselves whatever that may involve, in the way that members of other subcultures retain their identities without suffering discrimination. Whether this means chittlins and cornbread or narrow-width ties and button-down collars is not for the white liberal to decide. There was a time when politicians tried to prevent the growth of political power among immigrant groups to this country, but in the end they failed. Italians were not required to give up their cultural heritage before they were allowed to vote. No more can we assume that the real cultural and sociological differences which pervade our society will disappear with the establishment of justice for all. The belief that education and the expansion of economic opportunities will eliminate conflicts existing between the contending groups in our society is a rationalistic delusion. Even if, by some miracle of charity and grace on both sides, the majority of American Negroes became first class producers and consumers, the differences and the conflicts will not be eliminated. Race is a point of group identity.

We cannot realistically look for the elimination of conflicts between whites and Negroes through either litigation or education. We can reasonably hope to mitigate and temper the disagreements between contending elements in our society by according the protection of law to every man of whatever group. The measure of a democratic society lies in the way the dominant majority accords the rights it enjoys to other groups. The viability of our society depends on our ability to meet the challenge of this ideal. This means that white liberals must not retreat before the failure of many Negroes to meet their expectations, to satisfy their prejudices, to share their values and their faith in rational persuasion. We must accept the right to be different with the recognition that differences produce both creativity and conflict.

THE NEGRO IN AMERICAN HISTORY TEXTBOOKS (1968)
KENNETH M. STAMPP ET AL

Kenneth M. Stampp (b. 1912) and fellow historians at the University of California at Berkeley* examine one of the major sources of misinformation and lack of information: American history as it has been conventionally taught with conventional textbooks.

The undersigned, American historians and members of the History Department of the University of California, Berkeley, have been asked to review the American history textbooks that are most widely used in California from the standpoint of their treatment of Negroes. These reports disclose an unhealthy condition in California education.

* Winthrop D. Jordan, Lawrence W. Levine, Robert L. Middlekauff, Charles G. Sellers and George W. Stocking, Jr., members of the History Department at the University of California at Berkeley.

We are concerned first of all *as historians* that the history taught in our schools should accurately reflect the best findings of current scholarship. Professional scholars are aware that historical "truth" is an elusive quality. Well into the twentieth century professional scholars themselves were affected by the emotional aftermath of the Civil War, and there was a "northern" and a "southern" interpretation of such sensitive matters as slavery and Reconstruction. In the late nineteenth-century mood of national reconciliation, based on a widespread assumption of racial superiority among whites in both North and South, the "southern" view tended to prevail; and the deference of textbook publishers to the special sensitivities of the southern market has caused it to continue by and large to prevail in textbooks until this day. Meanwhile several generations of scholars, freer of sectional emotions and racist assumptions, through their researches and writings developed a substantially different understanding of many of these matters. Most of the textbooks we have examined reflect views on racial and sectional themes that have been rejected or drastically modified by the best of current historical scholarship.

We are additionally concerned *as citizens* because these historical distortions help perpetuate and intensify the pattern of racial discrimination which is one of our society's most serious problems. We are concerned not only because much of the material in these books is bad history, but additionally because it is a kind of bad history that reinforces notions among whites of their superiority and among Negroes of their inferiority.

Admittedly there is a danger in assessing historical writing in terms of its social consequences. A laudable desire to combat racism, and especially to bolster self-respect among Negro students, might result in exaggerating Negro contributions and the heroic qualities of Negro figures. In our view this would be an equal distortion of historical truth, and in the long run would fail to have the desired social effects.

We do not feel, however, that the seriousness of the problem of racism underscores the textbook author's responsibility to portray the Negro's role in American life fully, accurately, and without either sentimentality or condescension. There should be a conscious effort to portray outstanding Negro figures selected by the same criterion of historical significance applied to non-Negro figures. Even those textbooks that now make some effort in this direction tend to single out men like Booker T. Washington and the minor scientist George Washington Carver, whose attitudes about race relations are least disturbing to conservative whites. Equally or more worthy of inclusion by the standard of historical relevance are men like Denmark Vesey, Nat Turner, Frederick Douglass, W. E. B. DuBois, and the Rev. Martin Luther King.

Always and everywhere our children should be told the truth, and the whole truth, as near as the best current scholarship can bring us to this elusive quality. This means, among other things, not obscuring the harsher aspects of the truth—the fact that Negroes entered American society as slaves, the brutalities of slavery, the racism of the Reconstruction and post-Reconstruction era, and the continuing depth and harshness of the problem of segregation and discrimination.

In the light of these general principles, the greatest defect in the textbooks we have examined is the virtual omission of the Negro. As several of the individual reports point out, the Negro does not "exist" in the books. The authors of the books must know that there are Negroes in America, and have been since 1619, but they evidently do not care to mention them too frequently. In one book there is no account of slavery in the colonial period; in a second, there is not a single word about Negroes after the Civil War; in a third (composed of documents and substantive chapters), the narrative does not mention Negroes in any connection.

As Ralph Ellison's novel, *Invisible Man,* demonstrates, whites frequently do not "see" Negroes. But Negroes are Americans, their history is part of American history. They need to be "seen" in textbooks. The space given Negro history will, of course, depend in part on the nature of the textbook, and minimum standards of coverage are proposed later in this report. What is especially important is that the discussions of Negroes appear as an integral part of the book. Perfunctory or casual treatment may imply that Negroes are not part of America.

Important aspects of Negro experience, of course, depart from that of many other groups in America. Negroes were not just another immigrant group: no other group could be so readily identified by its color, no other group was so systematically enslaved, and no other group has been subjected to as persistent and virulent discrimination. From the seventeenth century to our own day, Negro life has been filled with violence.

These facts highlight another failing of these textbooks that is almost as distressing as the invisibility of Negroes in them. All the texts play down or ignore the long history of violence between Negroes and whites, suggesting in different ways that racial contacts have been distinguished by a progressive harmony. The tone of a textbook is almost as important as anything it has to say. In their blandness and amoral optimism these books implicitly deny the obvious deprivations suffered by Negroes. In several places they go further, implying approval for the repression of Negroes or patronizing them as being unqualified for life in a free society.

We should now like to suggest in some detail the substantive and interpretive elements relating to Negroes that should be included in textbooks covering the whole period of American history. These suggestions do not reflect any effort to give a special emphasis for the purpose of present-day social effects, but only what is necessary for portraying accurately the Negro's role as understood by current scholarship. We regard the suggested content as an indispensable minimum at the junior high level. Some compression would doubtless be necessary at the elementary level, while high-school treatment should be expanded beyond our suggested content.

Early in the seventeenth century Negroes were brought by force from Africa to the English colonies, and over the next fifty years whites in the colonies reduced them to a slavery that was inherited and perpetual. The Negro incurred debasement because he was different, particularly because he was "heathen," black, and helpless. Other colonials entered types of servitude, but their arrangements were usually contractual, their rights were protected by the state, their physical and moral treatment was much better, and their status was temporary. Not even the American Indian, whose exploitation began in the seventeenth century, was reduced to slavery on a substantial scale. Textbooks should tell this story from its African beginnings, through the slave trade, to the enslavement of the Negro.

As the history of the origin of Negro slavery is important, so also is an understanding of slavery as a mature institution in the eighteenth and nineteenth century. Students should know that it existed in the North until after the Revolution. Textbooks should supply the most important statistics, for example, that in 1860 there were four million slaves in the United States, virtually all located in the South. Although a majority of southern whites held no slaves, one out of every two persons in the South's fourteen million people was either a slave or a member of a slaveholding family.

There should be a full account of the life of the slave, starting from the fact that he was an article of property held for the profit that could be gained from his labor. Recent scholarship has shown that slaves labored in southern factories as well as fields. They were often overworked, and customarily housed, clothed, and fed at only a subsistence level. As a result the slave was often ill, and his life expectancy was shorter than that of the whites around him. His master could punish or sell him at will, and could even kill him with near impunity, since slaves were not allowed to testify against white men. The informal character of slave marriages made for an unstable family life; and the whole pattern of debasement under slavery inflicted psychological and sociological scars from which Negroes still suffer.

Understandably the slave resented, even hated, his condition, though he usually disguised his real feelings by subservient behavior designed to protect him from the master's power. Students should be told that slaves often ran away, committed sabotage, and plotted revolts, and that on one occasion a slave, Nat Turner, led a bloody general insurrection against the masters.

Slavery's moral and social evil did not go unremarked in the colonial period. The Quakers, for example, insisted that slavery violated both human dignity and divine law. Not until the Revolution, however, did most Americans become sensitive to the discrepancy between slavery and their professed ideals as embodied in the Declaration of Independence. All the states north of Delaware put the institution on the road to extinction, slavery was banned from the Old Northwest, and the Constitutional Convention opened the way for abolition of the slave trade after 1808. Even in the upper South, where the tobacco economy was languishing, liberal leaders hoped that the gradual operation of economic forces would eventually permit the abolition of slavery. Instead the developing cotton market revived plantation agriculture. Slaves proved so productive in southern cotton fields that slaveowners shut their ears to any criticism of the institution until the Civil War brought its demise.

Meanwhile antislavery sentiment was growing in the North. Even here racist assumptions caused free Negroes to be segregated and discriminated against; but after 1830 a vocal abolitionist movement had increasing effect. The efforts of the abolitionists, who included a substantial body of northern free Negroes, deserve serious and sympathetic exposition in textbooks. They are often derided for their occasional extravagance and for their internal disagreements, yet the fact is that they performed an immense service in educating Americans to the moral evils of slavery.

Abolitionists are frequently blamed for the Civil War by people who also insist that slavery had nothing to do with the coming of the war, that indeed the South fought to preserve state rights. Most scholars today agree, however, that slavery, and especially the issue of extending slavery into the territories, was fundamental. Certainly a careful appraisal of the slavery issue in national politics should be included in any textbook covering this period.

When the Civil War came, some 200,000 Negroes participated in the fighting that resulted in their formal emancipation. Following the war they also took an important part in the struggle over southern Reconstruction, which determined whether their emancipation was to be nominal or full. Reconstruction is a controversial issue in American history. The best scholarship today portrays sympathetically the radical Republicans in Congress, who opposed Lincoln's and later Johnson's plans for bringing the southern states back into the Union as quickly and painlessly as possible under conservative white leadership. The radicals, this scholarship holds, operated from mixed motives: to be sure they were interested in maintaining their political advantage, but they also wished to reform the structure of southern life. They especially wanted to help the Negro make himself a full partner in a free society.

It is in treating the Reconstruction state governments in the South that the older scholarship is most distorted by racist assumptions and most pernicious in its present-day effects. Modern scholarship overwhelmingly rejects the myth of Reconstruction as a saturnalia of mis-government and corruption by ignorant and/or venal carpetbaggers, Negroes, and scalawags. Though the Reconstruction regimes had their quota of corruption, as did most other American governmental units in this period, the student needs to know that the radical Republican experiment for a time made progress toward a healthy reconstruction of southern society, that many Negroes served ably in the Reconstruction governments, and that the Reconstruction governments had many constructive accomplishments, particularly the extension of the public school system, and the protection of equal civil and political rights of all.

The experiment in Reconstruction failed after a few years, owing to a growing northern indifference which permitted conservative southern whites to regain control by violence, through such agencies as the Ku Klux Klan. Soon Negroes had been reduced to a kind of unofficial slavery. The vote was taken from them, first by trickery and intimidation and later by amendments to the state constitutions. Denied economic opportunity, many were exploited as share croppers, and others in menial jobs. By the end of the century they were born and reared in segregated communities, and lived and died in a state of inequality, isolated from the mainstream of American life. Southern state laws and a disastrous Supreme Court decision, *Plessy* v. *Ferguson,* helped encase them in segregation.

Segregation and violence continued to characterize race relations in the South during the first half of the twentieth century. The hundreds of lynchings which used to occur annually have almost disappeared, but bombings, burnings, and shootings have increased. A more important change has been the movement of millions of Negroes to the cities and to the North. Here repression has been somewhat more subtle but only somewhat less damaging. Employers and unions relegate most Negroes to menial jobs. They are segregated into ghettoes, where they pay high rents for slum housing. Segregated housing means in turn segregated and inferior schools.

The other side of the story is the increasingly vigorous effort, especially by Negroes themselves, to change the situation. The growing Negro vote in crucial northern cities and the cold-war campaign to win the support of the uncommitted nations of the world has made the federal government more responsive to the plight of Negroes. Prodded by the National Association for the Advancement of Colored People (NAACP), the federal courts began to declare in the 1930's and 1940's against racial discrimination in voting, jury service, and educational opportunities. This movement culminated in the Brown decision of 1954 outlawing racial segregation in the public schools. Meanwhile the executive branch of the federal government had begun to move against segregation and discrimination in the armed forces and in civil service employment. Some state legislatures acted against discrimination in housing and employment, and Congress took its first cautious steps since Reconstruction to advance civil rights.

In the years since the Brown decision a civil-rights mass movement has taken shape among Negroes, utilizing the tactics of non-violent direct action to demand immediate and full equality in all areas. The Reverend Martin Luther King led Negroes of Montgomery, Alabama, in a year-long boycott of the city's segregated bus system. Negro college students launched "sit-in's" throughout the South in a movement that ended segregation at lunch counters and other public facilities in hundreds of southern communities. "Freedom riders" gave effect to court decisions outlawing segregation in transportation facilities. By 1963 mass demonstrations for equality in public facilities, jobs, education, and housing had spread from the South to many northern cities and over 200,000 people joined a "March on Washington" in support of President Kennedy's proposal that Congress pass a substantial civil-rights bill. These efforts were pursued in the face of mob violence, the arrests of thousands of demonstrators, the assassination of an NAACP leader in Mississippi, and the death of four Negro girls in the bombing of a Birmingham church.

This civil-rights revolution seems to us to be one of the major historical events of the mid-twentieth century and to demand full treatment in any American history textbook. The gains that have been made should be described realistically and not as an ode to the inevitable justice and progress of the democratic system. It should be made clear that the outcome of the civil-rights struggle is still in doubt, and that the inequalities are so great as to defy quick remedy by even the most vigorous effort.

In the midst of this civil-rights revolution, historians and educators have a clear responsibility, at the very least, to see to it that the role of Negroes in American life is taught fully and accurately. We have tried to indicate what a minimally full and accurate textbook account should be. Surely the state of California can no longer tolerate textbooks that fall far short of this minimal standard.

BRAINWASHING OF BLACK MEN'S MINDS (1966)
NATHAN HARE

*Nathan Hare (b. 1933) is the former head of Black Studies at San
Francisco State College and a militant black educator. Here he attacks
with force and logic the way the black man has been taught to look at
himself. Thus, he concludes, freedom for the black man must come
from a new self-image.*

As a boy I used to hear old folks laughing and talking about the way
white folks tricked Negroes to America as slaves with stories of a land
where creeks were overflowing with molasses and flapjacks grew on
trees. While hardly anybody seemed really taken in by that myth, it did
have, as most jokes have of necessity, a certain tone of truth: that the
Negro in America has been everlastingly misled, tricked and brainwashed by the ruling race of whites.

It seems certain, as recorded history bears out, that white conquerors
supplemented more deadly weaponry by falling back on ideological
warfare in confrontations with other races in the lands they "explored."
Guns were used, as in Hawaii, for example, but not guns alone. Explorers, trailed by missionaries and other warriors, first sought to convert "natives" to the Christian religion. Then, failing to "save" the pagan
chief, they merely proceeded to convert a "commoner and provide him
guns with which to overthrow the chief. This well-known tactic of
divide-and-rule is proving just as efficient to this day. "Why" is still the
question.

Africans in the know have finally come to realize that: "Once we had
only the land. The white man came and brought us the Bible. Now we
have the Bible, and they have the land." To accomplish this piracy—
and retain the loot indefinitely—it was of course necessary to control
the minds and bodies of the subjugated blacks. Indeed, control over
the body is one basic means of manipulating thought. This was accomplished even more successfully in the case of American blacks,
compared to Africans, because of the fact that brainwashing is best implemented by removing the subject from his normal setting, severing
his social relations and identities ordinarily sustained only by regular
interaction with family, friends and "significant others." Communication is then restricted—in the case of the Negro slave, it was virtually
destroyed—and the "stripping process," the process of self-mortification
(the destruction of identity and self-esteem) is then almost a matter of
course.

Not only were slaves cut off from contacts and lifelines of old, they
were restricted in their social relations with one another (sold apart as
well from their families on the whims of their "masters") and forbidden

to congregate without the presence of a white "overseer." Even after they were permitted to enter the confines (pun intended) of Christendom, pastors of Negro churches such as First Baptist in Petersburg, Virginia, seat of a violent slave uprising, were at first typically white. Ritualistic deference (such as keeping eyes downcast in the presence of whites, addressing them as "Mr.", "Sir" or "Suh," and other means described in Bertram Doyle's *Racial Etiquette in the South,* also aided in undermining the slave's self-respect and stimulating his glorification of the white man's world which in turn made him more inclined to bow down to the Great White Society.

A University of Chicago history professor, Stanley Elkins, in a book called *Slavery,* has likened the practices and consequences of the slave plantation to the Nazi concentration camp. This fits in with the basic principles of brainwashing in the setting of "total institutions" (prisons, asylums, concentration and POW camps) set forth by University of California sociologist Erving Goffman in the book, *Asylum.* The slave plantation was a total institution in that a large number of persons were restricted against their will to an institution which demanded total loyalty and was presided over and regimented by an "all-powerful" staff and "master."

Even the language of white America has exhibited a built-in force destructive of the black man's self-image. Blacks were taught to worship a god who was always painted white, and then, to sing that they wanted to "be more and more like Jesus" who would be "riding six white horses when He comes." While the color white symbolized purity (Negroes may be found singing in church houses, even today, that they are going to be "washed white as snow in the blood of the lamb"), black stood—stands now—for evil and derogatory referents. You "blackball" a person from your club; an employee is "blacklisted"; phony magic is "black magic"; illegal commerce comprises a "black market"; you are in a "dark mood" or blackhearted" on "Black Thursday"; especially if you are behind the eight-ball, which of course is painted black in pool. If a chartreuse cat or a polka-dot cat crosses your trail, it is no cause for alarm, but if a black cat crosses your trail, you are doomed to bad luck. We refer here only to the cat that purrs. Admittedy women may be in trouble when some black cats cross their trails.

It seems no accident, in any case, that a romance word for "black"— "Negro" (capitalized only in the past four decades)—was attached to a group which, owing to the white man's sexual drives and his Christian manipulation of the sexual and familial relations of his slaves, soon became a *potpourri* of colors and racial derivations. The word "black" was used by the English to describe a free man of color while a "Negro" was used to designate a black slave. Naturally, the word "Negro" eventually assumed a connotation of low esteem regardless of, but not exclusively independent of, the color or biological characteristics of the individual to whom the appellation was applied. This allowed some Negroes of "fair" features to "pass" (also a word for the act of death, just as a Negro who passed was called a "harp"—which he was going to play when he got to Heaven). Confusion arose requiring laws fixing a white person's race as Negro if it was known that he had even the remotest bit of white ancestry. Today's experts still stammer in their efforts to clarify the concept: *Webster's Collegiate Dictionary* finally winds up declaring a Negro anyone with "more or less Negro blood" and the 1960 Bureau of the Census instructions directed interviewers to classify as Negro any descendant of a black man, or a black man and any other race, *unless the Negro is regarded as an Indian in the community!* This was a concession to the white-Negro-Indians of the Carolinas and Oklahoma where I have known Negro women of the Aunt Jemima variety to wear a wig (long before it was the fashion), marry an Indian, fry their offsprings' hair, and send them to a white or/ and Indian school, except when the children were bounced back as a bit too black.

The standard of beauty, so essential to a group's self-image, also was derogatory to the Negro. Not only were mulatto descendants of white masters given special privileges and higher status among slaves, all beauty queens and men of power were visibly white. Even today. "Miss Washington, D.C.," where Negroes are in the majority, for example, is likely to live in the suburbs, in Fairfax, Virginia or Silver Spring, Maryland, and, regardless of her residence, she is certain to be white.

On top of all of the foregoing, there has been a massive effort, deliberate and persistent in speed, to keep the black man in ignorance. During the early days of slavery, it was illegal to teach, aid or abet a black slave to learn to read, for fear he might find out how he was being treated. Books, newspapers, periodicals and other media of information have consistently been published or controlled, in almost every case, by white men. The King James' version of the Bible, the only book many Negroes ever read, also plays down the black man; for example, "black but (nevertheless) comely." Negro worshippers are exhorted to tuck in their whimpering tails and conform to white society by such tidbits as: "The meek shall inherit the earth." "Thou shalt not covet they neighbor's goods . . . ," "We'll all be one when we get over yonder" and "To him who hath shall be given, and to him who hath not, *even that which he thinks he hath,* shall be taken away."

Most other books, too, including those on the Negro—especially those promoted and accepted in the United States—are not only published but also generally written by white men. Thus the Negro is led to depend on the white man to tell him what to think even about himself! During Negro History Week last February (known as "Brotherhood Week" now that we are "integrated"), I happened to notice in the lobby of Howard University's Founder's Library a set of twelve books on display as "books about the Negro." I knew, because of my special interest in literature on the race issue, the names of eleven of the authors. All were white. I walked over to the circulation desk and asked the black gentlemen behind it: "How about a book about the Negro by a Negro?" He laughed and thought the matter one big joke.

Children (learning to read on white Dicks and Janes) internalize the hatred of black men early in life. Although some black Anglo-Saxon Negroes will claim that they never knew there was a difference made between whites and Negroes until they were going on seventeen or had "got grown." Only a moment ago, even as I was writing this article, I learned that a black schoolteacher in Washington, D.C.'s summer school program got mad at a white teacher and called her a "black Jew!" With teachers like that, our children don't have a chance.

I once sat on a churchhouse step and watched a band of boys about ten years old stand beside their bicycles on the sidewalk and swap black epithets for thirty minutes by the clock. "You black as tar; can't get to heaven on an electric wire." "You so black your mamma had to throw a sheet over your head so sleep could slip up on you." Thus they grow up to look down on their own kind and idolize, mimic and conform to white standards of behavior.

Consequently, the black man's passive approval of the control of media of communication by white men in this mass society makes it virtually impossible for a black leader to emerge except through the white press. Accordingly, aspirants as well as established "spokesmen" for the Negro must slant their strategy toward capturing the spotlight of the white press.

W. E. B. DuBois, for example, had to contend in his day with white promotion of Booker T. Washington, now widely know as an Uncle Tom. DuBois sought to persuade Negroes to do half-a-century ago— though he later realized his error—what the NAACP eventually did, but, by that time, still fifty years ahead of his time and having fallen into disrepute with the white establishment, was not even invited to the NAACP's fiftieth anniversary, according to newspaper reports. Schools fail to carry his name, in spite of his legendary attributes as a scholar, just as E. Franklin Frazier, in spite of his acceptance by the white sociological establishment, has been overlooked. Instead, acceptable Negroes such as Booker T., Ralph Bunche, George Washington Carver, Charles Johnson and Marian Anderson, along with Abraham Lincoln and Franklin D. Roosevelt, are symbols for the Nation's black school-children. Although Rev. King is not a name for a school—to my knowl-edge yet while he lives—he eventually will join his brethren as a white-groomed Negro leader, as indicated by the plethora of prizes and honorary degrees already bestowed upon his crown.

Conversely, all the pretense of not understanding "Black Power" (a simple phrase) is merely an effort to whitewash the tardy awakening of black men in America and deter them from any attempt to acquire or utilize power to their own advantage.

White theorists have disseminated a number of false theories readily gobbled up and parroted by hoodwinked Negroes. One is that the Negro should not be bitter, whereas Anna Freud, in *Ego and the Mechanisms of Defense,* suggests that it is natural to be bitter in a bitter situation. For instance, if somebody sticks a pin in a portion of your anatomy and you do not yell out, then something is wrong with you or that portion of your anatomy. Another erroneous theory, geared to keeping Negroes conformist, is that Negroes are hopelessly out-numbered in America and must act to gain white sympathy, to "change white hearts and souls." This led to the assimilationist craze now in-creasingly apparent on the part of the Negro's "civil rights" movement before SNCC and CORE sought to put some sense into the movement. LBJ, in a recent effort to scare rioting Negroes, made a big ado about the Negro comprising only ten per cent of the population (actually he comprises at least eleven per cent, according to the Government's own figures) but white boys never get their facts straight about the Negro. The truth is that, regardless of their numbers, white men rule—two per cent in South Africa or Jamaica, forty per cent in Washington, D.C. or Mississippi or ninety-nine per cent in Maine or Montana. It is a mental attitude—not numbers. What excuse, then, had black men in Rhodesia (who grumbled privately when Smith took over but grinned and cowardly tucked their tails whenever a white person passed by for fear he might overhear them)? Outnumbering whites twenty-three to one, they could have taken each white man—one each grabbing a finger, ten others a toe, one the head and two whatever portion pleased them—and pulled him apart.

But, of course, black men are supposed to be non-violent in conflict with whites, while violent in his behalf and with one another. The non-violent hypocrisy has been perhaps the most ridiculous and appalling farce ever perpetrated upon and swallowed by a supposedly sane group of human beings. Only recently have black people begun showing signs of shedding this preposterous shackle.

It is amusing to watch the media's effort to commit the Afro-American to the Vietnam fiasco. While Afros virtually never make the daily press in a laudatory manner—not to mention the front page—they fre-quently find themselves turning up there now in uniform, holding up some wounded white "buddy," eating chicken, turkey or goose on Thanksgiving Day, or saving a Bible from perspiration and harm by wearing it under the band around their helmets. It is enough to cause a man to hang his head in shame.

Even on the home front, news about the Afro is slanted and sorted to suit the white power structure's purposes. William Worthy, for ex-ample, foreign correspondent for the *Afro-American* newspaper, was gagged by white newspapers when he ran afoul of then-Attorney-General Robert Kennedy's great white liberal graces after going to Cuba, and reporting that Castro was solving the race problem exported there by United States-dominated industry. William Worthy was believed to be the first newsman to test the right to go abroad, write home the news, and come home again—and though the white press is forever crying crocodile tears over "freedom of the press"—the press fell curiously silent in this case. So much so, that some brainwashed Negro students in a class of mine, during a discussion on mass communications, insisted that the United States has a free press. Yet, when I placed the name of William Worthy on the board—at a time when his case was current—along with five multiple-choice descriptions of his identity, only six in a class of twenty-four were able to choose the correct answer.

These students were, in the full sense of the word, pathetically "miseducated," in the manner described by Carter G. Woodson, in his *The Miseducation of the Negro*. They, like most Negroes, are merely products of generations of the most efficient and gigantic system of brainwashing the world has ever known. Thus, while they once merely chanted desires of being "more and more like Jesus," they now typically long and struggle to be more and more like "whitey" as a group. No doubt their brains, at least, at last have been *"washed white as snow. . . ."*

POEM IN THE GRASS
YOUNGLOOD

"Poem in the Grass," by an anonymous "Younglood," is typical of the force and vigor, combined with the cry for revolution and retribution, that is found in the underground press. Implicit in the denial of traditional American values is the cry for something better, often phrased in vivid Anglo-Saxon imagery like that in the first line of the poem.

> Leaves of Grass is bullshit!
> had Whitman really been hip
> he'd prophesized
> the destruction of democracy.
> he'd known about the dismantled dream
> i am part of.
> "but the country was young then"
> and the bearded father spoke with
> only limited meaning
> in that

the poems he wrote are out of context
with this age.

what relation can i have
with Walt
other than admiration of some of his
   long poems
that preach the gospel of
knowing one's self
but there's more to life
than introspection.
(does peace come thru' "soul searching"?
are the ranks of the fascists any thinner
   because of it?)
maybe i don't understand Walt!
my fault? yours?
??????????????????????????????????
Walt Whitman
as part former of my poetic mind
i am come back to you with my hands
   clutching
the dead grass of doubt.
where did it stop being people
and start being machines and statistics?
where did my brother stop feeling kin
   to the grass
&
accept the perverted status quo
that i am expected to wear over my heart?
Walt, where are the messages you left
for me?
must i take up the sword of Spartacus, or
   guns,
as Zapata?

i sit on the University of Chicago campus
wishing i had an education
but knowing my place is in the streets
with my people.
i scream mental messages to the students
i watch walk by.
"lay down your books and abandon this
   campus
leave this factory that teaches obedience
in servile speeches

walk back with me to the ghetto where
   i live
come back with me
we need you now, not tomorrow
but now.
when we have won we can come back for the
education we all desire."

around me the ranks of my enemies
   tighten
new laws burden us
taxes rob us
teachers teach the great lies
i want to strike out at the liars, thieves,
   and killers
who make me (in my frustration) strike
   at you.
i apologize for the first line of this poem.
your poems are beautiful, Walt
beautiful like the grass i lie on
beautiful like the breeze that cools me
but your poems are about ideas
that the leaders have cheated us out of
we want them back
they are ours
they belong to the people.

i am afraid
i am ignorant
i have a one track mind
freedom was bought with blood
and it will be maintained with blood
not the battlefield blood of Viet Nam
but blood on the roads of Ala. Miss. & Ga.
and in the halls that Justice has vacated.
but we are afraid
our sons, lovers, friends, and fathers
are dying on battlefields of uselessness
&
i watch black people go by
and again I am afraid
afraid of the hatred my skin might cause
   to
boil over.
i ramble on hoping something will happen

to cauterize the cancer of lethargy that
    eats
on my brothers.

today i am becoming for the first time
    a poet
and
will use words until guns are necessary
then i will write in blood what can never
be written in ink.

for a death blow must be dealt to white
    supremacy
bigotry and nationalism.
i feel silly about some of this poem
but one thing i know is
that i am in love with freedom
i am drunk with the desire to see a
    free America.

Walt, i see only praise for capitalism in
    your poems
&
realize you must'a had a different
    definition
for the word.

From
THE BLACK MUSLIMS IN AMERICA (1961)
C. ERIC LINCOLN

C. Eric Lincoln (b. 1924) defines the doctrine of perhaps the most peculiar black group in America today. Possessed of a religious creed unique to themselves, convinced that separation of races is desirable, responsible for the alleviation of much social suffering, the Black Muslims have produced such leaders as Malcolm X, and they evoke apprehension, justified or not, in American whites.

THE ORIGINAL MAN[18]

The Original Man is, by declaration of Allah himself, "none other than Black Man." Black Man is the first and last: creator of the universe and the primogenitor of all other races—including the white race, for which Black Man used "a special method of birth control." White man's history is only six thousand years long, but Black Man's is coextensive with the creation of the earth. Original Man includes all non-white people, and his primogeniture is undeniable: "everywhere the white race has gone on our planet they have found the Original Man or a sign that he has been there previously."[19]

The so-called Negro in America is a blood-descendant of the Original Man. "Who is better knowing of whom we are than God Himself? He has declared that we are descendants of the Asian Black Nation and of the tribe of Shabazz,"[20] which "came with the earth" when a great explosion divided the earth and the moon "sixty-six trillion years ago." The tribe of Shabazz was first to explore the planet and discover the choicest places in which to live, including the Nile Valley and the area which was to become the Holy City of Mecca in Arabia.

All so-called Negroes are Muslims, whether they know it or not. It is the task of Elijah Muhammad and his followers to teach the so-called Negroes that they are of the tribe of Shabazz and, therefore, "Original." Once they understand this, they will know themselves to be Muslims, heart and soul. Christ himself was a Muslim prophet, and several of his parables refer to the so-called Negroes, especially those of the Lost Sheep, the Prodigal Son and the Raising of Lazarus. The so-called

---

[18] The basic doctrines of the Muslims are laid down in a booklet written by Muhammad and called *The Supreme Wisdom*. This is the primary source book for all that is peculiar to the Muslims and for Muhammad's teachings as they appear in the Negro Press.
[19] *The Supreme Wisdom* (2d ed.), p. 39.
[20] *Ibid.*, p. 33.

Negroes are good people and religiously inclined by nature. In fact, "the Black Man by nature is divine."[21]

When the whole world knows who the Original Man is—and only then—wars will cease, for everything depends upon knowing who is the rightful owner of the earth. Lest there by any possible confusion, Muhammad addresses himself specifically to the question:

The Original Man, Allah has declared, is none other than the Black Man. He is the first and the last, and maker and owner of the universe; from him come all—brown, yellow, red, and white. . . . The true knowledge of black and white should be enough to awaken the so-called Negroes . . . [and] put them on their feet and on the road to self-independence.[22]

To know the identity of the Original Man is of crucial importance, for the time of "judgment" is approaching and "Allah is now pointing out to the nations of the earth their rightful places."

THE WHITE MAN AND CHRISTIANITY

It would be difficult, probably impossible, to separate the Black Muslim teachings on Christianity from those on race. A fundamental tenet of the sect is that all Black Men are Muslims by nature and that Christianity is a white man's religion. Thus there is not even a *possibility* of awakened Black Men accepting Christianity. Nor can the white man accept Islam as taught by Muhammad, for the white man is a devil by nature: "Out of the weak of the Black Nation, the present Caucasian race was created."

The "originality" of the Black Nation and the creation of the white race by Yakub, "a black scientist in rebellion against Allah"—this is the central myth of the Black Muslim Movement. It is the fundamental premise upon which rests the whole theory of black supremacy and white degradation. Muhammad explains in patient detail:

Who are the white race? I have repeatedly answered that question in this [column] for nearly the past three years. "Why are they white-skinned?" Answer: Allah (God) said this is due to being grafted from the Original Black Nation, as the Black Man has two germs (two people) in him. One is black and the other brown. The brown germ is weaker than the black germ. The brown germ can be grafted into its last stage, and the last stage is white. A scientist by the name of Yakub discovered this knowledge . . . 6,645 years ago, and was successful in doing this job of grafting after 600 years of following a strict and rigid birth control law.[23]

[21] From a typescript of "The Hate that Hate Produced," a television documentary on the rise of Black Racism by Mike Wallace and Louis Lomax. *Newsbeat* (New York: WNTA-TV, July 10, 1959). Malcolm X on *Newsbeat*.
[22] *The Supreme Wisdom*, p. 38.
[23] "Mr. Muhammad Speaks," Pittsburgh *Courier*, July 4, 1959.

This experiment in human hybridization was a brilliant scientific accomplishment, but it had one unfortunate side effect. It peopled the world with "blue-eyed devils," who were of comparatively low physical and moral stamina—a reflection of their polar distance from the divine black. Hence white athletes are notoriously poor competitors against black athletes, nor should one wonder at the wholesale atrocities committed by the "civilized" whites. Only the white man could herd millions of his fellows into the gas chambers, set off atomic bombs and run special trains to a lynching at which the women and children are served cokes and ice cream.

In grafting out his creatures' color, Yakub grafted out their very humanity.

The human beast—the serpent, the dragon, the devil, and Satan—all mean one and the same; the people or race known as the white or Caucasian race, sometimes called the European race.[24]
Since by nature they were created liars and murderers, they are the enemies of truth and righteousness, and the enemies of those who seek the truth. . . .[25]

These devils were given six thousand years to rule. The allotted span of their rule was ended in 1914, and their "years of grace" will last no longer than is necessary for the chosen of Allah to be resurrected from the mental death imposed upon them by the white man. This resurrection is the task of Muhammad himself, Messenger of Allah and Spiritual Leader of the Lost-Found Nation in the West. The period of grace was seventy years; forty-six have already elapsed.

During their reign, the devils have "deceived the black nations of the earth, trapped and murdered them by the hundreds of thousands, divided and put black against black, corrupted and committed fornication before your very eyes with your women . . . [and then made] you confess that you love them. . . ."[26]

Four hundred years ago, the white Christians stole the Black Muslims way from their homes and brought them to North America, where the whites were already in the process of systematic genocide against the Indian. The writes enslaved the blacks and ensured their bondage by robbing them of their names (identity), language (cultural continuity) and religion (protection of their God). By robbing them of their true names, the whites both shamed them and effectively "hid" them from their own kind. By making the Black Men accept European names, the whites branded them as property. By requiring them to speak English rather than their native Arabic, the whites cut their slaves off from their cultural heritage and the knowledge of self which

---

[24] *Ibid.*, December 13, 1958.
[25] *Ibid.*, July 18, 1959.
[26] "Mr. Muhammad Speaks," December 13, 1958.

is essential to dignity and freedom. Such were the secular bonds of servitude.

But the Christian religion was and is the master stratagem for keeping the so-called Negro enslaved. The whites gave him the "poisoned book" and required him to join the "slave religion," which teaches him to love his oppressor and to pray for them who persecute him. It even teaches him that it is God's will that he be the white man's slave! There is, of course, some truth in the Bible, but it is tangled in the white men's contradictions, for "from the first day [they] received the Divine Scripture they started tampering with its truth to make it to suit themselves. . . ."[27]

The Bible is the graveyard of my poor people . . . .
and here I quote another poison addiction of the slavery teaching of the Bible: "Love your enemies, bless them who curse you; pray for those who spitefully use you; him that smiteth thee on one cheek offer the other cheek; him that (robs) taketh away the cloak, forbid not to take (away) thy coat also." . . . The Slavemasters couldn't have found a better teaching for their protection. . . .[28]

The Bible is also held in some suspicion because "it is dedicated to King James (a white man) rather than to God." Moreover, "it makes God guilty of an act of adultery by charging Him with being the father of Mary's baby; again it charges Noah and Lot with drunkenness and Lot begetting children by his daughter. What a poison book!"[29] On the whole, "Christianity is a religion organized and backed by the devils for the purpose of making slaves of black mankind."[30] It "has caused more bloodshed than any other combination of religion. Its sword is never sheathed."[31]

Islam sent several prophets, including Moses and Jesus, to offer Islam to the white men as a religion of brotherhood. But the white man could not accept it, for the white race is evil by nature and cannot love anyone who is not white. "They are ashamed to even call you a brother or sister in their religion, and their very nature rebels against recognizing you!"[32]

They cannot be trusted. The Caucasians are great deceivers. Their nature is against friendship with black people, although they often fool the black people . . . claiming that they are sincere friends. . . .[33]

[27] *The Supreme Wisdom*, p. 12.
[28] *Ibid.*, p. 13.
[29] *Ibid.*
[30] *Ibid.*
[31] *Ibid.*, p. 28.
[32] *Ibid.*, p. 36.
[33] "Mr. Muhammad Speaks," January 17, 1959.

And: Do not "sweetheart" with white people, your open enemies, for their "sweethearting" with you is not sincere. . . .[34]

The black Christian preacher is the white man's most effective tool for keeping the so-called Negroes pacified and controlled, for he tells convincing lies against nature as well as against God. Throughout nature, God has made provision for every creature to protect itself against its enemies; but the black preacher has taught *his* people to stand still and turn the other cheek. He urges them to fight on foreign battlefields to save the white man from his enemies; but once home again, they must no longer be men. Instead, they must patiently present themselves to be murdered by those they have saved.

Even the Christian God hates his enemies and works to destroy them. This is recorded in the Christian Bible, which all Christians say they accept. "But the black clergy, in trying to ingratiate itself with the whites, will deliver their people up wholesale."[35] Thus, in an unholy and unnatural way, the "Negro clergy class is the white man's right hand over the so-called Negroes,"[36] and the black preacher is the greatest hindrance to their progress and equality.

The so-called Negro clergy, say the Muslims, prostitute themselves to the downtown whites in return for "whatever personal recognition they can get above their followers. North or South it's the same. If a white preacher exchanges pulpits with a so-called Negro minister once a year on Brotherhood Sunday, the black preacher tells his people the millennium is here." And as for their heroics during the recent "sit-ins" staged by Negro students in the South, the black preachers' tactic was simply to "put the children out to expose themselves to the brutality of the uncivilized whites, then . . . rush in and 'lead' after the fight is over." In substantiation, the Muslims cite the following article which appeared in a well-known Negro newspaper:

A shameful display of cowardice and ingratitude was shown last week by certain members of the local clergy. . . . The members took credit for the desegregation of five lunch counters. They neglected to give credit to the students, the persons really responsible. . . . Not one of the ministers sat-in [in] any of the department stores. . . . Brave and persistent activity by the students . . . caused the five lunch counters to be integrated. [But] the ministers, on top secret invitation from the store managers crept downtown to "negotiate." In this, they helped the store ignore the students. Now, after all the hard, dangerous work [had] been done, the ministers have stolen credit for the students' successful work.[37]

The reprehensible behavior of the so-called Negro preachers stems primarily from their desire to be acceptable to the white churches and

[34] *Ibid.*, August 9, 1958.
[35] From an interview with Malcolm X.
[36] "Mr. Muhammad Speaks," August 22, 1959.
[37] Len Holt, "Norfolk News Beat," *Afro-American*, August 13, 1960.

other religious organizations. Hence the black preacher is far more zealous about adhering to what he has been told are Christian principles than is the white man. The white man does not believe in trying to perfect himself morally, but he wants the Negro to be "past-perfect." As a result, the black preacher is so busy trying to gain the white man's approval by doing what the white man himself has never done, and has no intention of doing, that he has no time to concern himself with the real issues, such as economic justice and the freedom to walk the streets as a man. . . .

RACIAL SEPARATION

The Black Muslims demand absolute separation of the black and the white races. They are willing to approach this goal by stages—the economic and political links, for example, need not be severed immediately —but all personal relationships between the races must be broken *now*. Economic severance, the next major step, is already under way, and political severance will follow in good time. But only with complete racial separation will the perfect harmony of the universe be restored. Those so-called Negroes who seek integration with the American white man are, say the Muslims, unrealistic and stupid. The white man is not suddenly going to share with his erstwhile slaves the advantages and privileges he has so long pre-empted. America became the richest and most powerful nation in the world because she harnessed, for more than three hundred years, the free labor of millions of human beings. But she does not have the decency to share her wealth and privileges with "those who worked so long for nothing, and even now receive but a pittance." The so-called Negroes are still "free slaves." Millions of them are not allowed to vote, and few are permitted to hold office. None can wholly escape the implications of color. Ralph Bunche, the most distinguished American Negro on the world scene, refused a sub-Cabinet post in the federal government because he could not live and move in the nation's capital with the freedom accorded to the most illiterate white thug. Even the recognized enemies of the country, so long as they are white, come to America and immediately enjoy the privileges of freedom. To American Negroes—hundreds of thousands of whom have fought and died for their nation—these same privileges are denied.

Again, the Muslims maintain that only the so-called Negro leaders want to integrate. The black masses have no love for the white man and no desire to be in his company. "But for the pseudo-Negro leaders, to be accepted by whites and to be in their company is worth more than heaven itself." These Negroes are forever "begging and licking the white man's boots for [him] to smile and pat [them] on the back."

Finally, the whole scheme of integration is only a stratagem through which the white man hopes to save himself from an inevitable fate. He has sowed the wind, and now he must reap the whirlwind. The ascendancy of the white West is ended. The wheel must turn. When the white man was the undisputed ruler of the earth, who spoke of integration? Now he has seen his empires crumble, his slaves shake off their bonds, his enemies multiply all over the world—"so he is willing to throw his faithful dog the driest bone he has, hoping that dog will once more forget the past and rush out to save his master." But the Negro will still be the loser, for the white man will only "integrate him" where it serves his own advantage, and this will always be at the bottom.

Muhammad urges the Black Man to stand aloof. Why integrate with a dying world?

Today's world is floating in corruption; its complete disintegration is both imminent and inescapable. Any man who integrates with the world must share in its disintegration and destruction. If the Black Man would but listen, he need not be a part of this certain doom.[54]

The Muslims reject the ultimate integration—racial intermarriage— as sternly as any Southern white, and for much the same reasons.

Usually, when the white man says "integrate," he has reservations. He doesn't want to see a black man marry his woman. We all agree on that. Muslims who follow Mr. Muhammad are absolutely against intermarriage. When you say "integration," if you mean that everyone should have equal opportunities economically, that everyone should have the right to socialize with whom they please, that everyone should have the right to all the cultural advantages and things of that sort, well and good. But if [to] integrate means that a Black Man should run out and marry a white woman, or that a white man should run out and get my woman, then I'm against it. *We're absolutely against intermarriage!*[55]

The Muslims are convinced of their "superior racial heritage" and believe that a further admixture of white blood will only weaken the Black Nation physically and morally, as well as increase the loss of face the so-called Negro has already suffered by permitting the white man to bastardize the race. The white race will soon perish, and then even a trace of white blood will automatically consign its possessor to an inferior status.

Muhammad conceives his mission to include the re-purification of the "Lost-Nation-in-the-West"—ideologically, morally and, above all, biologically. Only when this has been done can the black people of

---

[54] *Afro-American*, February 20, 1960.
[55] Malcolm X on *The Jerry Williams Show*, Boston: Radio Station WMEX, April 2, 1960. From a taped transcription. Italics supplied.

America assume their rightful place of dignity and leadership among the triumphant black nations of the world. The United Front of Black Men, therefore, will countenance no interracial dallying. The intelligent Black Man must look beyond today's personal whimsies to the building of the Black Nation of tomorrow.

ECONOMIC SEPARATION

The call for a Black Front has important economic overtones, for the Muslims' economic policies are a fundamental aspect of the total Movement. Their basic premise is that the white man's economic dominance gives him the power of life and death over the blacks. "You can't whip a man when he's helping you," says Muhammad; and his oft-quoted aphorism is economically, if not socially or politically, cogent.

Economic security was stressed from the first days of the Movement. As early as 1937 it was observed that:

The prophet taught them that they are descendants of nobles. . . . To show their escape from slavery and their restoration to their original high status, they feel obliged to live in good houses and wear good clothes . . . and are ashamed that they have not been able to purchase better commodities or rent finer homes.[56]

As we have seen, the pendulum has swung back toward the center. The Muslims still prize industriousness and a sense of responsibility, but they shy away from conspicuous consumption. They do not live in the residential sections generally preferred by the Negro business and professional classes, and they do not sport the flashy automobiles usually associated with Negro revivalistic cults. On the contrary, they strongly affirm their identity with the working class. There is a strong emphasis on the equality of the ministers and the "brothers," and all tend to live pretty much alike in terms of housing—in the Black Ghetto—and visible goods.

Thrift is encouraged; and while credit purchasing is not forbidden, Muslims are reminded that "debt is slavery." These counsels have had a clearly salutary effect. Indeed, the more faithful a Muslim is to the teachings of his leaders, the better his economic condition is likely to be.

[56] *Beynon,* pp. 905–906.

From
THE BLACK REVOLUTION
AND THE JEWISH QUESTION (1969)
EARL RAAB

Earl Raab, Executive Director of the Jewish Community Relations Council of San Francisco, has taught at San Francisco State College and the University of California. His analysis of racial tensions, rivalries, and experiences examines the recent phenomenon of black anti-Semitism, and it perceptively analyzes such other recent movements as "black power" and the "white backlash."

About a half-century ago, Louis Marshall, the eminent constitutional lawyer who was also president of the American Jewish Committee, said firmly: "We do not recognize the existence of a Jewish Question in the United States." That distasteful phrase, "The Jewish Question," evoked the European model: the political uses of anti-Semitism. Marshall made the statement precisely because he saw that the Jewish Question in the political sense *was* coming alive in the United States. It did, and preoccupied the domestic Jewish consciousness for the next quarter of a century.

For the past quarter of a century, there has been no serious trace of political anti-Semitism in America. Any suggestion today that "it could happen here," has had an antique flavor and would be widely branded as phobic, paranoid, and even amusing. There is the old joke about three men who were asked to write an essay about the elephant. The Englishman wrote on "The Elephant and the British Empire," the Frenchman on "The Elephant and Love-Making," the Jew on "The Elephant and the Jewish Question." But we have learned a great deal about the Jewish Question, and if the subject of the essay were Western democracy instead of elephants, the joke would no longer be a joke. The potential for political anti-Semitism, aside from its special interest to Jews, turns out to be a particularly useful vantage point from which to examine the state of the general society. And responsible people are again having to deny nervously that there is a Jewish Question in America. The American Jewish community's concern with its own security may be coming full circle.

From the end of World War I to the beginning of World War II, the American Jew's defense efforts were increasingly keyed to political anti-Semitism, as distinct from garden-variety discrimination. Political anti-Semitism may be defined as the attempt to establish the corporate Jew as a generalized public menace, the implication being that some official public remedy is called for. The same distinction has been made between "objective" and "subjective" anti-Semitism, "concrete" and "abstract" anti-Semitism, and the real Jew and the mythical Jew as target. But by whatever names, and whatever the relationship between the two kinds of anti-Semitism, Jews know the difference. Not getting a particular job is one thing. A pogrom is another.

Political anti-Semitism did not become serious in America until about 1920. In that year the staid *Christian Science Monitor* carried a lead editorial entitled "The Jewish Peril." A few years later, a book called *The International Jew: The World's Foremost Problem* had a run of half a million copies. The articles in that book—"The Scope of Jewish Dictatorship in America," "Rule of Jewish Kehilla Grips New York," and "How the Jewish Song Trust Makes You Sing"—and many others of a similar bent had already received wide distribution in Henry Ford's national newspaper. And Henry Ford, it must be recalled, was not a Los Angeles mail-order crackpot. In 1923, at the height of his anti-Semitic fulminations, *Collier's* reported that he led all other possible candidates, including the incumbent President, in its national Presidential preference poll. Other straw polls agreed. Willam Randolph Hearst announced that he was prepared to back Ford for that office. The KKK during the same period had a membership which blanketed at least a quarter of all white Protestant families in America. And at one point in the 1930's, someone identified about 150 organizations whose primary business was the promotion of political anti-Semitism. Father Coughlin, who reprinted the *Protocols of the Elders of Zion* in his national newspaper, had a regular radio audience of millions.

To these seemingly mass assignations with anti-Semitism, the organized Jewish community responded with a program based on the image-of-the-Jew theory of anti-Semitism. At the national B'nai B'rith convention in 1930, Sigmund Livingston said that the necessity was "to educate the great mass in the truth concerning the Jew and to demolish the foibles and fictions that now are part of the mental picture of the Jew in the public mind." The Jewish community mounted what must certainly have been one of the most prolific mass educational programs of all time. Yet anti-Semitic activity and popular support of avowed anti-Semites were at their height when summarily cut off by America's bitter embroilment with the world's arch anti-Semite.

A few short years later, America seemed to emerge from the war as a nation in which the Jewish Question was miraculously dead. American Jews, of course, felt that the war had been fought—and won— around the Jewish Question. Maybe they believed that other Americans felt the same way. Maybe they believed that other Americans were responding en masse to the revelations of the Holocaust. In any case, political anti-Semitism seemed stripped of any respectability; indeed, anti-Semitism became one of the cardinal political sins. The nation was even able to sustain a major red-baiting demagogue who carried Cohn and Schine on his hip and flirted with anti-Semitism not at all. Israel was established. Stalin died. American Jews settled down to a new security.

At the same time something else was happening in the country. The Jewish Question was apparently being supplanted by the Negro Question. And the defensive energies and apparatus of the Jewish community moved from one to the other. At least, that is the way it turned out. A surface theory relating to Jewish security rationalized the move: Equal opportunity for one means equal opportunity for all. But no one examined this dubious axiom very closely. America seemed to be approaching a state of perfectibility: The nation's great flaw, slavery, was being brought to account; democracy was marching to fulfillment, and the Jewish community obviously belonged on such a march, whatever the reasons. Several motivational streams in Jewish life merged at this point, as they never had before: the instinct for self-preservation; the religious ethic, invoking the prophetic tradition; and the political program—liberalism—for which so many Jews had developed a special secular affinity. On this level, the Jewish community found itself with a coherent and organic position.

Of course, this preeminent concern with civil rights swiftly and inevitably became a predominant concern with the needs and aspirations of the Negro community. After the FEPC principle had been established in the North, the laws that were passed and the court cases that were pressed had less and less direct application to the security of the Jews. The Jewish Question became more and more remote. But the Jewish community remained deeply and comfortably involved.

However, after little more than a decade, this first stage in postwar developments, the Civil Rights Revolution, began to change character. The second stage reflected the shift from the goal of equal opportunity to the goal of equal achievement, from civil rights to the war against poverty, from the Civil Rights Revolution to the Negro Revolution. The shift should have been quite predictable. Equal opportunity is not equal achievement, except for those who are equally equipped to compete. An enclave population now existed whose cultural and educational "equipment" has been comprehensively stunted for generations. The American society, moreover, had deliberately created this enclave population. For the impoverished and uneducated immigrants to America equal opportunity had been enough, because other societies had depressed them. In their minds, America owed them no more than an opportunity, and the gradualist road to parity which all emerging groups have traveled. But America owed the Negroes more than opportunity. The battle-cry of the Negro Revolution was not opportunity, but parity in the economy as well as in the society, starting with an instant end to poverty. Toward that goal, the demands were not just for equal treatment, but for compensatory treatment on a kind of reparations basis.

For the Negro community, this stage was a logical extension of the Civil Rights Revolution. But for the organized Jewish community some adjustment was required. The apparatus of the Jewish community committed itself to the campaign against poverty, and throwing the slogans about equal-opportunity-under-the-law into the attic, began to look for a role in that campaign. Consideration of Jewish security became even more remote.

There were only a few years of war-against-poverty innocence before the third stage set in. It quickly became apparent that the billion-dollar anti-poverty programs were not suddenly going to turn history on its head; and with that realization, the Negro Revolution began to be overlaid by the Black Revolution. Since New Deal days, at least, Americans have subscribed to the social engineering fallacy: Any problem can be solved if only we devise enough programs and spend enough money. The fallout of the massive anti-poverty programs of the early 1960's created a salaried black bureaucracy in the ghettos and undoubtedly helped a number of individuals up the ladder—but finally these programs were more effective in raising expectations than mass standards of living. The goal of instant parity seemed more desirable and further away than ever. Against the background of such frustrations, and other frustrations provided by society, there has developed a new kind of reactive pattern in the black community, and in the white community as well. It is as a result of these new patterns that the Jewish Question makes an abrupt re-entry on the American scene. Not a matter of searching for anti-Semites under the bed, this perception that the Jewish Question is back comes from what we have, since Louis Marshall's time, learned about the nature of anti-Semitism and about the nature of the conditions under which it flourishes.

The "Vulnerability" of the Population

There are three obvious conditions that coincide to produce a period of political anti-Semitism: the kind of political and social instability which makes anti-Semitism useful; a political leader who is willing to use it; a mass population that is willing to embrace it.

It is the belief in an "unwilling" American population, in the obsolescence of anti-Semitism as a cultural form in America, which gives Jews their greatest sense of security. Yet it is this belief itself which is obsolete.

To begin with, one does not have to be an anti-Semite in order to engage in or support anti-Semitic behavior. This proposition contradicts the "image of the Jew" theory of anti-Semitism. It contradicts the tendency to reify anti-Semitism, to conceive of it as a little mental package tucked away in a corner of the brain, waiting for the proper stimulus to bring it, full-blown, to life.

About six years ago, a Jewish couple in San Francisco was terrorized for over a year by a juvenile gang. The incident was described across the country as a shocking case of anti-Semitism. There were insulting phone calls every night between midnight and dawn. The couple ran their business from their home and could not have an unlisted number. Anti-Semitic slogans and swastikas were painted on their home. Garbage was left at their door. The torments were constant and cruel, and the middle-aged couple lived a year of hysterical fear. Finally the police caught a handful of teenage ringleaders. The investigation of these young men, their background, family, psychology, was thorough. No particular "anti-Semitic" history was discovered. The families were bewildered and provided no clues. There were no anti-Semitic organizations, insignia, pamphlets, or cartoons found hidden in the woodpile. The group had exhibited no special anti-Semitic proclivities.

The story of their year-long sport was further revealing. It had started casually with anonymous phone calls being made rather widely and at random. The game proved to be most fun with this couple because they responded with lively anger and fear. The game became increasingly intense. But for many months these teenagers did not invest their tricks or insults with any suggestion of anti-Semitism. Only well into the year did they discover that anti-Jewish comments added new life to the sport, drew even more heated and fearful responses. It was then that they began to concentrate on anti-Semitic references.

In short, the evidence indicates that these young men did not engage in tormenting activity because they possessed some quality called anti-Semitism. Rather, they committed anti-Semitic acts because they were engaged in tormenting activity. They were not cruel out of anti-Semitism, but anti-Semitic out of cruelty. During the 1930's anti-Semitism was generally understood to be a tool of repressive politics, but it was also thought that the use of this tool was possible only because a large mass of people were anti-Semitic in the first place, held unusually negative attitudes toward Jews and had become ideologically committed to these attitudes. But the behavior of this juvenile gang gives us a different analytical perspective: Willing to engage in a certain type of behavior, they did not reject anti-Semitism as an instrument. . . .

But the initial point is this: in the light of the last half-century of experience and research, it is appropriate to say that the Jewish Question is already being raised again in America. In a malaria-prone country, the malaria question would be said to exist if the familiar breeding swamps were merely building up. Political anti-Semitism, the Jewish Question, does not relate in the short range to folk anti-Semitism, nor to the prevalent state of any set of images or feelings toward Jews. In America, the Jewish Question is substantially the same as the Question of the Democratic Society. Mendele Mocher Seforim wrote: "The Jewish Question—that's the wide canal which drains all the impurities, all the dirt and mud and sewage of man's soul." The release of democratic restraints, the substitution of jungle for law, of conspiracy theory for reason, of confrontation for negotiation, of hyperbole for politics, of repression for social progress—that *is* the Jewish Question, as it has come to have special meaning for modern society. These are the issues around which the only effective fight against political anti-Semitism can take place. They are alive again today, and therefore the Jewish Question is coming to life again.

THE BLACK REVOLUTION AND THE JEWISH QUESTION

On one side, there is growing a mass movement of disaffection among the black population: a volatile constituency with a well-justified sense of general deprivation, and of specific power deprivation, characterized by low levels of education, systematic belief, and commitment to abstract democratic principles. "Mass movement" usually denotes some formal cohesion: A structure and a formal system of affiliation, which people can join or around which fellow-travelers can gather; or, alternately, a charismatic leadership with whom a following can identify. As yet the black mass movement of disaffection possesses neither. Indeed, while black people are, of course, distressed, dissatisfied, and have the bitter knowledge that they are relatively deprived, most of them have not yet been jarred loose from traditional loyalties to the political party structure or the system in general. At least so the polls, as well as the recent voting patterns and the repeated failures to organize in the ghetto areas, indicate. Also, all the objective indices testify that the aspirations of the great bulk of black people are primarily instrumental, built around a simple desire to get into the chrome-plated American system. But to be effective a mass movement does not need to be, and never has been, a "majority" of any population. Color and population concentration, in this case, provide a built-in system of affiliation and communication which can substitute for more formal organization. And within that system, there is stirring a genuine movement of disaffection, still disjointed, but with certain common expressive and extremist currents that are swelling, especially among the young.

The theme of the first postwar stage in race relations was equal opportunity. Out of the progress and frustrations of that stage came the theme of the next: anti-poverty. Out of the progress and frustrations of that stage came the third: Black Positiveness. And on the edge of Black Positiveness has emerged the. phenomenon of Black Expressivism.

A sharp distinction has to be drawn between Black Expressivism and Black Positiveness. It has become a standard anti-poverty theorem that Negroes have to be given control of their own bootstraps if they are going to be asked to lift them. In order to join the American parade, the Negro community has to find its own identity, and shake itself loose from the degradation and self-degradation of the past. This is Black Positiveness, power, pride, dignity, as preface to economic integration. In addition, an obvious piece of political realism had to come to the fore: The black community was not going to be able to take a serious part in American pluralism until it established its own political strength and instruments. It had to shake loose from the coalitions long enough to do that. The corollary is that the political society would not otherwise respond to the needs of the Negro community. This is Black Positiveness, and Black Power as preface to political integration.

There is another face to Black Positiveness, more symbolic and less clearly instrumental, but still related to an ultimate goal: The black man should feel wholly like a man. The road to that goal in America has always been through the achievement of an instrumental position in the economy and the polity. But America had made a point of depressing the status of the Negro, in itself—and the black community now became interested in elevating that status in itself—especially since the instrumental access to status was obviously not going to be instant. This involved a subtle shift in emphasis. Thus, the demand that black history be taught in the schools was grounded in solid instrumental theory: It has educational utility, not only for the white student, but for the black student, whose sense of confidence and self-worth is related to motivation and achievement. But in the last few years the burden of this demand shifted from well-disposed educators and liberals to the young black people themselves. Educational theory aside, they wanted the symbolic fullness of their identity established here and now, for its own sake.

Expressiveness involves yet another subtle shift, however. All the above demands can, and have been, invested with anger and high emotion, but the passion is goal-directed. When a demand is made, or an act committed primarily to vent anger or frustration, then we enter the realm of expressive behavior. The line is often murky. What about the further demand that black history be written only by blacks and taught only by blacks? At what point is that demand primarily an extension of black pride, and at what point is it primarily an expression of anger and hostility toward the white establishment? In any given situation, the line is often difficult and fruitless to draw. But it is nevertheless a significant line, between politics and anti-politics. In its logical extreme, the pathology of expressive public behavior was revealed in the Old South when lynchings rose as the price of cotton went down, and in Old Europe when massacres of Jews took place in the wake of the Black Plague.

Expressive politics may be defined as the externalization of internal frustrations, bearing little direct relation to the solution of the problems which caused the frustrations. The chief function of such politics is to provide emotional release; and, at its peak, its currency is a kind of hyperbolic, hyper-symbolic language. "Racism" became an affective epithet—with an eager assist from the writers of the Kerner Commission Report—and lost its meaning. The growing use of "pig" as the definitive heart of the language, as in "racist pig" or "fascist pig," further revealed the exclusively expressive nature of this latest stage in the movement. Impetus came from a black intellectual class, whose orbit grew rather swiftly as many college administrations made extraordinary efforts to bring black faculty members, black students, and special black programs to the campuses.

Recently a black instructor at a state college told 2,000 students at a rally: "We are slaves and the only way to become free is to kill all the slavemasters," identifying the President, the Chief Justice, and the governor of the state as slavemasters. He also told them: "If you want campus autonomy and student power and the administration won't give it to you, take it from them with guns." That is expressive talk *par excellence.* Everyone knows who has most of the guns and all of the tanks. But in urban high schools and ghetto areas around the country, more and more young people are adopting the expressive mode. They are not ideologues, like the state college instructor; they are more often frightened, angry, personally desperate young people for whom the schools and most often social institutions are irrelevant prisons.

In some cases, what was once personally expressive behavior born out of such conditions, has become politically expressive behavior. What would once have been known as delinquency is now invested with political significance. Black expressivism exists on many levels but is now coalescing into an "expressive movement"; this movement is buried and growing within the larger black community, and developing all the appurtenances thereof, including common language, symbols, heroes, and a conspiracy theory.

Expressive politics has always frightened the Jewish community. Before the Civil War Rabbi Isaac Mayer Wise warned the Jews against the Abolitionist movement. He approved of its goals, but was afraid of its nature. The same point is currently being made for the Jews by the kinds of expressive anti-Semitism that are emerging from this black expressivism. This is not the folk anti-Semitism which the black population shares with the white population. It is, rather, the abstract and symbolic anti-Semitism which Jews instinctively find more chilling. Negroes trying to reassure Jewish audiences repeatedly and unwittingly make the very point they are trying to refute. "This is not anti-Semitism," they say. "The hostility is toward the whites. When they say 'Jew,' they mean 'white.'" But that is an exact and acute description of political anti-Semitism: "The enemy" becomes the Jew, "the man" becomes the Jew, the villain is not so much the actual Jewish merchant on the corner as the corporate Jew who stands symbolically for generic evil. "Don't be disturbed," the Jews are told "this is just poetic excess." But the ideology of political anti-Semitism has precisely always been poetic excess, which has not prevented it from becoming murderous.

The surveys which generally show that the reservoir of folk anti-Semitism among Negroes is, if anything, a little lower than that among their fellow Americans, are irrelevant for the reasons given above. The relevant fact is that "the movement" is developing an anti-Semitic ideology. On one coast, there is talk about how the "Jewish establishment" is depressing the education of black students. On the other coast, a black magazine publishes a poem calling, poetically of course, for the crucifying of rabbis. "Jew pig" has become a common variant of the standard expressivist metaphor. On this level, there are daily signals.

Then, too, "Third World" anti-Semitism is becoming more of a staple, at least among the ideologues where it counts most. Jewish schoolteachers in New York were told in one tract that "the Middle East murderers of colored people" could not teach black children. At the last national convention of the Arab students in America, Stokely Carmichael, the main speaker, admitted that he had once been "for the Jews" but had reformed.

Of course, many middle-class blacks are horrified by all this. But on the community level, where the pressure is, they are likely to say that it would not do for them to attack such manifestations, because it would seem to be an attack on the militant movement itself (this reaction throws another light on the ability of a movement to be anti-Semitic without a corps of anti-Semites). They are likely to say that these manifestations are "only symbolic," without understanding that symbolic anti-Semitism is the most frightening kind. Or they might explain that these attitudes are not widely reflected in the black community—which is, to complete the circle, irrelevant.

But how dangerous, finally, is the anti-Semitic ideology being developed by this growing black movement? If the movement is destined to be relatively powerless, should it be a source of major concern? More particularly, if this movement is pitted so directly against the white majority in the country, does that not render its anti-Semitism still less dangerous? Such questions ignore the fact that this movement has already succeeded in reintroducing political anti-Semitism as a fashionable item in the American public arena—with what consequences no one can yet tell. It would, moreover, be a repetition of old mistakes to think that if a black movement uses political anti-Semitism, anti-Semitism must therefore be rejected by anti-black whites. One propaganda effort during World War II was designed to reduce anti-Semitism among Americans by linking Nazism and anti-Semitism, and then attacking Nazism. An evaluation reported that the campaign increased hostility toward Nazism without reducing hostility toward Jews. And we have seen that the American public fought bitterly against Hitler during the war, without apparently altering its attitudes toward Jews.

However, there is another, more problematical area of concern that might be anticipated if the expressive black movement continues to grow. The black community is on the verge of a major political breakthrough. A good number of cities are soon destined to be numerically controlled or heavily dominated by their Negro populations. These are the cities in or around which most American Jews live, and in which their business and public lives are largely conducted. If the expressive black movement, with attendant political anti-Semitism, continues to grow, its effect on Jewish lives will be incalculable. (Incalculable also might be the effect on American foreign policy in the Middle East of a prevailing anti-Israel sentiment in important political centers.) There will, of course, be an intensification of the upward-mobility conflict that is already becoming a visible part of the Negro-Jewish complex. (As one Jewish teacher plaintively told the New York *Times*: "We don't deny their equality, but they shouldn't get it by pulling down others who have just come up.") More generally, the political structure in these cities is going to be under considerable strain. There is the possibility of a classic marriage, a manipulative symbiosis, between the privileged class and the dis-privileged mass— in this case a WASP class and a black mass—in these cities: the kind of symbiosis which existed in the 1920's between respectable Republican leaders and the KKK, and which permitted a temper of repression and bigotry to flourish. The anti-Semitic ideology developing in the black movement would be eminently suited to such purposes. Some have suggested that the edges of this possibility are actually peeking out in New York City. Certainly, whatever the outcome, this face of the black expressive movement is there for the Jewish community to contemplate with justified concern.

THE WHITE BACKLASH AND THE JEWISH QUESTION

Of course, on the other side, there is a white population which exhibits, from its own vantage point, the same dangerous characteristics: a volatility, with broken loyalties; a sense of general deprivation and of power deprivation; relatively low levels of education, systematic belief, and commitment to abstract democratic principles—a population, in short, both extremist and expressive in tendency. This is the more traditional backlash pattern, which has produced America's major anti-Semitic movements of the past.

These movements were involved in preserving something which seemed about to be lost. When successful, they were typically a strange marriage between members of the upper and lower economic strata who were protecting different interests together. Economic concerns were often present, but the decisive bond was a set of symbolic issues. The critical element of the mass support was some kind of status deprivation and alienation: a disappearing way of life, a vanishing power, a diminishing position of group prestige, a scrambling of expectations, a heart-sinking change of social scenery, a lost sense of belongingness. In the 1920's, the backlash of traditional rural Protestantism, losing its hegemony in the nation, provided this element. The census of 1920 reported that for the first time in American history urban dwellers were in the majority. The cities were taking over the nation; new kinds of people were taking over the cities; the small-town dweller, whether staying behind or coming to the big city, was apt to feel in the back-waters. KKK leader Hiram W. Evans complained that the "Nordic American today is a stranger in a large part of the land his father gave him." In the 1930's, the depression-bound people who supported Coughlin were not only interested in some aspects of social change, but also threatened by other aspects of social change. Coughlin, in the classic mode of fascism, wanted to create a revolution within the symbolic bounds of a traditional way of life. In both decades there were massive dislocations, large sections of the population being torn away from their traditional political loyalties, and therefore from ritualistic democratic constraints to which they had no deep ideological commitment.

We are now faced with more massive dislocations than we have experienced since the 1930's, and perhaps since the Civil War. Just as there once was a nativist (Protestant) backlash against the emergence of immigrant (Catholic and Jewish) economic advancement, cultural imperialism, and political power in the cities, so we now have a white backlash against similar Negro advances in the cities. The breakdown of "law and order" that is attendant upon such periods is itself a status-seeking, power-dwindling experience. Policemen have consistently been the most conspicuous vocational presence in every major backlash movement in American history. It is not that they differ all that much psychologically or otherwise from the rest of the non-elite American population, but that they are on the front lines of the conflict. Many white citizens feel that they are getting short shrift in schools, law enforcement, and city hall generally because of black power. Certainly, they don't approve of the concept of "compensatory" treatment for blacks. And they can expressively wrap around this issue all of their angry feelings about the frustrating decline of American status in a new world, and the apparently losing battle of the citizen against bureaucracy and taxes.

The Birch Society, more Liberty League than Coughlin, has never seriously attempted to exploit the white backlash, or to get in touch with mass America at all. McCarthyism was a kind of false pregnancy, although serving fleetingly to reveal the potential for undemocratic repression which lies in a large mass of the American public. George Wallace was, at least for a time, the Pied Piper of repression, tuned into the large and ideologically soft underbelly of white America. His low November vote outside the South was comparable to the low vote that Coughlin's candidate Lemke received at a time when Coughlin's movement was booming. Many blue-collar people who had given their genuine expressive approval to Wallace when the pollsters came around, or when he came to town, voted instrumentally when they went, hand on pocketbook, into the booths.

Of course, Wallace has shown no evidence of raising the Jewish Question, but some parallels have been drawn between him and Huey Long. Huey Long never raised the Jewish Question either, although it was not that unrespectable in his time to do so. But Huey Long never quite made the transition from Louisiana demagogue to national ideologue before he was killed. And among his top staff people was Gerald L. K. Smith, one of the nation's most committed ideological anti-Semites. Coughlin's full belief system, his conspiracy theory, his political anti-Semitism, emerged fully only midway in his career, after bitter disappointments. What might have developed in the Long movement, with Smith at his elbow, is of course incalculable. It is a matter of record that George Wallace similarly had in the background of his campaign last year speech writers, advisers, and organizers who have openly engaged in political anti-Semitism. This did not make George Wallace an anti-Semite, nor destine him to be one, but it made a number of Jews uneasy. And, Wallace aside, it is only reasonable for the uneasiness to accumulate as the risk factors do. History often finds its own man. Even Coughlin has begun to publish a magazine again, after twenty-six years of silence.

THE JEWISH COMMUNITY AND THE JEWISH QUESTION

Between those two forces, between those two harbingers of the Jewish Question, lies an increasingly bewildered and fragmented Jewish community. A few short years ago, there was a kind of coalescence of religious, political, and defense impulses among the Jewish leaders, who were massed on the civil-rights front, with their constituency trailing securely and benignly behind. Today, a different situation is suggested by recurrent vignettes such as one described in a recent JTA news dispatch, dateline New York:

The rabbi of the East Midwood Jewish Center in Brooklyn sharply rebuked a crowd who booed and jeered Mayor John V. Lindsay this week as the mayor attempted to address an audience in the temple on the dispute between the teacher's union and the largely Negro Ocean Hill-Brownsville school district. . . . The mayor was shouted down when he said that both sides in the dispute were guilty of "acts of vigilantism." Rabbi Harry Halpern took the microphone and declared, "As Jews you have no right to be in this synagogue acting the way you are acting. Is this the exemplification of the Jewish faith?" Shouts of "yes, yes" were the answer. Some members of the audience belonged to the congregation, and others were members of the community at large which is white, middle class, and predominantly Jewish.

In the same dispatch, the JTA reported that "the national body of Conservative Jewish Congregations expressed concern this week that recent statements by some Jewish groups and individuals have tended to equate the entire Negro community with anti-Semitic slurs voiced by a few black militants. . . . The board also urged Jews 'not to react to limited extremism with our own extremism.' "

In the conglomerate, the Jews of America seem to be in a new ambivalent position. No one in his right mind has ever called the Jewish community monolithic. But with all its formlessness, the Jewish community has in recent memory always had a prevailing public stance—in the parlors as well as in the agency offices—with respect to certain kinds of issues: the Birch Society, fair employment practices laws, fair housing laws. Today it is symptomatically difficult to find a prevailing public stance with respect to such current issues as police review boards, neighborhood-controlled schools, Black Student Unions.

It would be a misreading of the situation to suggest that all the Jewish community needs is to pull up its moral socks. The Jewish involvement with the plight of black America cannot simply be seen as the religious or liberal imperative for social justice. There is, more clearly than ever before, the legitimate and independent Jewish imperative for self-survival. Of course, this self-survival, given the nature of the Jewish Question, could be seen validly—if somewhat remotely —as identical with the survival of the democratic social order. And this period may be another perilous episode in that recurrent dilemma of modern society: The problem of separately pursuing social (economic) justice and a democratic social order without despoiling either. Western history has a long record of failures in that quest, and, not surprisingly, the Jewish Question has more often than not been in attendance.

But there are more concrete implications. The Black Revolution is spurring the Jewish community—and America—into a renewed understanding of pluralistic politics. The fresh Jewish stirrings are not primarily a backlash reaction, although there is some of that. There is most significantly a turning inward; in a real sense, a *regrouping*. There is a new tendency to ask seriously a question which has only been asked jokingly for a number of decades: "Is it good for the Jews?"

Alfred de Grazia has well described the spirit of the age of rationalistic mass democracy which was set in motion by the Enlightenment, and which came to a certain rhetorical fruition in America:

Beginning in the nineteenth century there might be no interests apart from the interests of the mass of people, however cloudy such a concept might be. An equally accepted but opposite belief was that the individual, a solitary wayfarer in life and politics, could govern himself without belonging to any cohesive groups. The two beliefs might be simultaneously held, for they are psychologically, if not politically, consistent. In the individualism and utilitarianism of Benthamism, all interests break down. Little thought goes to the mass authoritarianism or majoritarianism that was the inevitable denouement. Whereas the mass public had never before been seriously regarded as the active agent in legislative processes, the People was now sculpted into a massive monolithic interest group.

Official segments of the Jewish community seemed to embrace precisely this concept when the Golden Age set in after World War II. Negroes were to pursue a just society not primarily as Negroes, which they merely happened to be, but as Americans along with fellow-Americans. Jews were to pursue a just society not primarily as Jews, which they happened to be, but as Americans along with fellow-Americans. And so forth: A salvation army of Americans with identical moral concerns was marching together. The language was not all that clear, of course. Jews were told that "civil rights" was good for them, which indeed it was. But it was told in passing, as a corollary to the main image of all-Americans-marching-morally-together. The image became increasingly fuzzy as the 1950's yielded to the 1960's, and many Jews suffered traumatic shock when the Negroes detached themselves from the marching army and said, "Wait a minute, we've got a different interest here, a different drummer and a different pace."

There was the religious language also: The prophetic traditions and the Jewish moral imperatives were invoked. The Christian clergy invoked their own, as did, no less fiercely, the humanist liberals. But there has always been a certain uneasy ring of truth in the pejorative use of the term "do-gooder." If a do-gooder is someone who is primarily and exclusively motivated by moral concerns in the political arena, he is more often than not a mischief maker. Politics is not identical with morality, which does not mean that politics need be immoral. To be sure, politics at its best is the negotiation of conflicting group interests within the constraint of rules which are morally based. But the distinction between morality as a political constraint, and morality as a central engine of political action, is a crucial distinction. To put it another way, the do-gooder is the evangelist who knows what is best for everybody. When the Negroes, seizing their own identity, said: "It is only we who really know what is best for us," they brought everyone up short, and they brought the Jews back for yet another look at their own group identity in America.

In 1927, in the middle of the debate as to whether Jewish Welfare Federations should merge with general Community Chests, Morris D. Waldman told a national conference: "I am constrained to believe that the existence of separate Protestant, Jewish, and Catholic Federations . . . is not going to retard brotherhood. Because I am thoroughly convinced that if the universal brotherhood will ever come, it will not come in the form of a fraternity of individuals, but as a brotherhood of groups. . . . The group will-to-live is at least as strong as the individual will-to-live. . . ."

The Jewish community's independent group will-to-live is being reasserted in response to the reemergence of the Jewish Question in America—as well as in Eastern Europe and in the Middle East. Less and less, as one consequence, will the public affairs agenda of the Jewish community be the same as that of the black community. This is not a matter of withdrawing support from those generic items on the black agenda which must be on the common American agenda and in which the Jewish community has a strong derivative stake— most notably, the rapid reduction of ghetto poverty. There may, however, develop sharper differences as to the point at which the rate of reduction is to be increased "at any cost" or "by any means whatsoever." The maintenance of a democratic rule of law is essential to Jewish survival. Nor is it just a defense against extremism which will finally protect that social order. If the Jewish community has in the past had a special concern with greater participation by the ghetto population in civic affairs, as a means of strengthening the democratic fiber, it must also now have a special concern with greater participation by the white lower-middle-class population still in and around our cities. These are people of the "common democratic commitment" who are not horned and leprous bigots, but who have troubles of their own, a dignity of their own to maintain, and a growing sense that they are being left out. As Irving M. Levine has said: "Our rightful transfixion on Negroes has developed into a 'no-win' policy, hardening the lines of polarization between white and black into a reality that could blow the country apart. To change this white reaction, some of the brilliance which articulated Negro demands will have to be similarly developed to speak to and for lower-class America."

But there are other items which may more poignantly illustrate the temper of a new agenda. For example, there is a liberal movement toward the public-funded privatization of the public school system, starting with neighborhood control and ending with any group of parents—or an institution of their choice—being able to set up a school to which their children can go at public expense. The consequences of such a development, with its potential for racial, ethnic, and religious separatism, may call for independent evaluation by the Jewish community. In most cities new ethnic and racial competition for various public boards and posts is developing. Eventually, the Jewish community may be required to act more politically as a community if it is to hold its own in such competition. The point is not the abandonment of universal values, but the development of a more self-conscious focus of group interest.

The Jewish-Question is alive again because the American political structure and its traditional coalitions are in naked transition. The common democratic commitment trembles within both the white and black populations. New kinds of political configurations are in the making. The past quarter century turns out not to have been, as some envisioned, the passageway to some terminal American Dream. It has been the staging-ground for some as yet indistinct future American design. The Jews, somehow in trouble again, need to make their own particular sighting on that future.

THE "LAW OF DOMINANCE"
From *Alternative Futures for the American Ghetto* (*1968*)
ANTHONY DOWNS

Anthony Downs examines the origin and the nature of the ghetto, the racially segregated area that characterizes much of America. A balanced, objective view devoid of the emotionalism so often present in such studies, the selection emphasizes the relationship between neighborhood segregation and group values.

The achievement of stable racial integration of both whites and nonwhites in housing or public schools is a rare phenomenon in large American cities. Contrary to the views of many, this is *not* because whites are unwilling to share schools or residential neighborhoods with nonwhites. A vast majority of whites of all income groups would be willing to send their children to integrated schools or live in integrated neighborhoods, *as long as they were sure that the white group concerned would remain in the majority* in those facilities or areas.

The residential and educational objectives of these whites are not dependent upon their maintaining any kind of "ethnic purity" in their neighborhoods or schools. Rather, those objectives depend upon their maintaining a certain degree of "cultural dominance" therein. These whites—like most other middle-class citizens of any race—want to be sure that the social, cultural, and economic milieu and values of their own group dominate their own residential environment and the educational environment of their children. This desire in turn springs from the typical middle-class belief of all racial groups that everyday life should be primarily a *value-reinforcing* experience for both adults and children, rather than primarily a *value-altering* one. The best way to insure that this will happen is to isolate somewhat oneself and one's children in an everyday environment dominated by—but not necessarily exclusively comprised of—other families and children whose social, economic, cultural, and even religious views and attitudes are approximately the same as one's own.

There is no intrinsic reason why race or color should be perceived as a factor relevant to attaining such relative homogeneity. Clearly, race and color have no necessary linkage with the kinds of social, cultural, economic, or religious characteristics and values that can have a true functional impact upon adults and children. Yet I believe a majority of middle-class white Americans still perceive race and color as relevant factors in their assessment of the kind of homogeneity they seek to attain. Moreover, this false perception is reinforced by their lack of everyday experience and contact with Negroes who are, in fact, like them in all important respects. Therefore, in deciding whether a given neighborhood or a given school exhibits the kind of environment in which "their own" traits are and will remain dominant, they consider Negroes as members of "another" group.

It is true that some people want themselves and their children to be immersed in a wide variety of viewpoints, values, and types of people, rather than a relatively homogeneous group. This desire is particularly strong among the intellectuals who dominate the urban planning profession. They are also the strongest supporters of big-city life and the most vitriolic critics of suburbia. Yet I believe their viewpoint —though dominant in recent public discussions of urban problems— is actually shared by only a tiny minority of Americans of any racial group. Almost everyone favors at least some exposure to a wide variety of viewpoints. But experience in our own society and most others shows that the overwhelming majority of middle-class families choose residential locations and schools precisely in order to provide the kind of value-reinforcing experience described above. This is why most Jews live in predominantly Jewish neighborhoods, even in suburbs; why Catholic parents continue to support separate school systems; and partly why so few middle-class Negro families have been willing to risk moving to all-white suburbs even where there is almost no threat of any harassment.

However demeaning this phenomenon may be to Negroes, it must be recognized if we are to understand why residential segregation has persisted so strongly in the United States, and what conditions are necessary to create viable racial integration. The expansion of non-white residential areas has led to "massive transition" from white to nonwhite occupancy mainly because there has been no mechanism that could assure the whites in any given area that they would remain in the majority after nonwhites once began entering. Normal population turnover causes about 20 per cent of the residents of the average U.S. neighborhood to move out every year because of income changes, job transfers, shifts in life-cycle position, or deaths. In order for a neighborhood to retain any given character, the persons who move in to occupy the resulting vacancies must be similar to those who have departed.

But once Negroes begin entering an all-white neighborhood near the ghetto, most other white families become convinced that the area will eventually become all Negro, mainly because this has happened so often before. Hence it is difficult to persuade whites not now living there to move in and occupy vacancies. They are only willing to move into neighborhoods where whites are now the dominant majority and seem likely to remain so. Hence the whites who would otherwise have moved in from elsewhere stop doing so. This means that almost all vacancies are eventually occupied by nonwhites, and the neighborhood inexorably shifts toward a heavy nonwhite majority. Once this happens, the remaining whites also seek to leave, since they do not wish to remain in an area where they have lost their culturally dominant position.

As a result, whites who would be quite satisfied—even delighted— to live in an integrated neighborhood *as members of the majority* are never given the opportunity to do so. Instead, for reasons beyond the control of each individual, they are forced to choose between complete segregation or living in an area heavily dominated by members of what they consider "another group." Given their values, they choose the former.

Many—especially Negroes—may deplore the racially prejudiced desire of most white middle-class citizens to live in neighborhoods and use schools where other white middle-class households are dominant. Nevertheless, this desire seems to be firmly entrenched among most whites at present. Hence public policy cannot ignore this desire if it hopes to be effective. Moreover, this attitude does not preclude the development of racial integration, as long as whites are in the majority and believe they will remain so. The problem is convincing them that their majority status will persist in mixed areas in the face of past experience to the contrary. Even more difficult, the people who must be persuaded are not those now living in a mixed area, but those who must keep moving in from elsewhere to maintain racial balance as vacancies occur through normal population turnover.

Clearly, the dynamic processes related to this "Law of Dominance" are critical to any strategy concerning the future of American ghettos. They are especially relevant to strategies which seek to achieve stable residential or educational integration of whites and nonwhites, instead of the "massive transition" and "massive segregation" which have dominated the spatial patterns of nonwhite population growth in the past twenty years. Such stable integration will occur in most areas only if there is some way to guarantee the white majority that it will remain the "dominant" majority. This implies some form of "quotas" concerning the proportion of nonwhites in the facility or area concerned— even legally supported "quotas."

Unless some such "balancing devices" are *explicitly* used and reinforced by public policies and laws to establish their credibility, whites will continue to withdraw from—or, more crucially, fail to keep entering—any facility or area into which significant numbers of nonwhites are entering. This means a continuation of *de facto* segregation and a reinforcement of the white belief that any nonwhite entry inevitably leads to "massive transition." Even more importantly, it means continued failure to eliminate white perception of race as a critical factor by encouraging whites and nonwhites to live together in conditions of stability. Thus, in my opinion, the only way to destroy the racial prejudice at the root of the "Law of Cultural Dominance" is to shape current public policy in recognition of that "Law" so as to encourage widespread experience that will undermine it.

SEEDS
FOR
THE
FUTURE

CHINATOWN IN CRISIS (1970)
MIN YEE

Chinese youth have long remained subservient to their elders and to tradition. Now, as Min Yee (b. 1939), Newsweek's San Francisco correspondent, makes clear, those young people are rejecting tradition and demanding a voice in determining the direction and nature of the changes to come.

It was not exactly what the tourists had expected. Each had paid $9 last week for the Gray Line Special—a three-and-a-half-hour walking tour through San Francisco's Chinatown (including dinner)—and they were strolling leisurely along Grant Avenue past the curio shops cluttered with flowery paper lanterns, thin bamboo back scratchers, porcelain dolls and bright red and blue mandarin jackets. Suddenly a Chinese youth appeared and cried, "Off the honkies!" Then there was a "whssssss" and a square packet of red, white and blue firecrackers sailed into the crowd of whites, scattering them out into the street. Again the cry: "Out of the ghetto, honky!"

The message itself was scarcely new. Any similar group of whites who sought diversion by venturing into the black ghettos of Brooklyn's Bedford-Stuyvesant or Los Angeles's Watts might well have gotten a lot worse than a shower of firecrackers. But coming as it did in Chinatown, the outburst not only startled the tourists but shattered an American myth as well. On the one hand, Americans view the Chinese living in their midst through the Hollywood stereotypes of Charlie Chan inscrutability, Fu Manchu opium dens, raging tong wars and hatchet men with real hatchets. On the other, they see them as a self-effacing, hard-working, frugal, and—above all—uncomplaining ingredient of the melting pot. For all its outward sheen of neon, gilt trim, pagoda roofs and commercial bustle, Chinatown, U.S.A., seems on the surface to be a model community, taking care of its own problems while providing a colorful place to eat Chinese food.

RADICAL

Behind this façade, Chinatown is a bubbling caldron of ancient rivalries and modern hatreds, of bitter clash between young and old. Sometimes the caldron overflows into radical action by groups such as the youthful Red Guards, who take their programs and slogans from the Black Panthers and aim their wrath not only at their elders but at white intruders on their turf. Last year, the Guards created chaos during celebration of the Chinese New Year when they lobbed cherry bombs coated with glue and buckshot into the parades. Few who know them expect this year's festivities to escape similar disruption.

The reasons for turmoil are not hard to find. San Francisco's Chinatown spans only some 42 square blocks and contains perhaps only 60,000 people, but has some of the worst conditions in the country:

One-third of the families earn less than the Federal poverty level.

Two-thirds of the adults have less than a seventh-grade education, and the last new school in the area was built in 1925.

The unemployment rate is 12.8 per cent, vs. 6.7 per cent for San Francisco and 3.9 for the country as a whole.

The density rate is 885.1 people per acre, ten times the city's average.

The suicide rate is three times the national average.

The rate of substandard housing is 67 per cent, vs. 19 per cent for the rest of San Francisco.

Few tourists visit the Jean Parker Public Elementary School on Broadway, where Chinese children attend classes in the hallways and storage rooms and hold recess on the roof. They do not see the living quarters of the Chinese working people—dank, cramped quarters where families are jammed into cubicles, storing their clothes in suitcases and trunks because there is no closet space and keeping their kitchen and cooking supplies in the bathrooms. They do not see the dorm-like conditions of the elderly single men who sleep stacked up in tiers like sailors on a ship.

A little-known feature of Chinatown is its sewing-factory sweatshops along Pacific Avenue and Powell, Stockton and Kearny streets where 3,000 seamstresses produce garments for major American firms on a piece-work basis. Seventy per cent of them earn less than $3,000 a year; they have no medical or health benefits, no vacation, no overtime pay or sick pay.

As bad as present conditions are for Chinese-Americans, they look a good deal better when stacked up against those on the mainland when my ancestors came here more than a century ago. In fact, the Huagiao (Overseas Chinese), most of whom came to America from the Canton region, fled not only economic hardship but a bloody, religious revolution—the Taiping rebellion—that resulted in at least 20 million deaths. Others were recruited or kidnaped as cheap coolie labor (the word comes from the Chinese *kuli*, meaning bitter work) to satisfy worker-hungry American employers in post-gold-rush California.

AUTHORITY

Along with their few belongings they brought a durable social structure that survived—and even flourished—until recent years. Built around the father or grandfather as the patriarch who held absolute authority over his family, this structure evolved into the Zu, or clan, consisting of groups of families with a common ancestor, and with a leader responsible for arbitrating disputes, burying the dead and providing such things as welfare for the aged. As second- and third-generation children migrated throughout the U.S., another level was added, fusing the clans into 43 district associations. Seven of these—the Ning Yung, Kong Chow, Shui Hing, Hop Wo, Yan Wo, Hung Wo, and Sam Yup—combined into the Chinese Six Companies, which from its blue-tiled headquarters on Stockton Street fancies itself even today as spokesman for Chinese-Americans across the country.

Along with the family structure came the tongs—begun 60 years ago and run like a Chinese Mafia. Racketeering, white slavery, narcotics, gambling, murder, extortion, blackmail—there was nothing too depraved for the tongs. Today, the six major tongs (Hip Sing, Bing Kung, Sui Yung, Ying On, On Leong and Chee Kung) still operate much like the Mafia. They have divided up the country into spheres of influence (e.g., Hip Sing controls the West Coast. On Leong, the Eastern Seaboard), and while they still dabble in narcotics and prostitution, they are more and more investing their rackets money in legitimate businesses. To hide their activities, most of them have changed their names. While retaining their independence, the tongs in San Francisco have formed the Chinatown Security Committee, which actually helps local businessmen keep the streets safe for money-spending white tourists.

OPPRESSED

For years, their own strong social fabric worked well in combination with American racism to keep the Chinese thoroughly oppressed: whites wouldn't let them get work outside the ghetto, and the only jobs inside Chinatown were controlled largely by the Chinese Six Companies which ran the restaurants, banks and sweatshops. Unlike the blacks, whom yellow activists now see as comrades-in-arms, the Chinese were largely at the mercy of their own race—or the "Uncle Tongs," as the Chinese Establishment is nicknamed. "We have a merchant class, where the blacks don't," says Mason Wong, young president of the Intercollegiate Chinese for Social Action, whose headquarters is at San Francisco State College. "We have to fight within our own situation before we can go out and fight outside the community."

But inside the Chinese "situation," changes already are coming fast. For one thing, immigration quotas, which for many years were zero, then were pegged in 1943 at a mere 105 persons a year, were finally abolished in 1965, and since then 33,000 new Chinese immigrants have poured into ghettos. Many of the new arrivals are youths from overcrowded Hong Kong; their language problem makes them high-school dropouts and unemployables. For the first time, Chinatown has a real delinquency problem to add to the ferment.

PRIDE

For another, Chinese students have begun to look inward at their own people's problems. As with the blacks, they are becoming suffused with racial pride (some 1,000 showed up at Berkeley last year for a conference on "Yellow Identity"), and increasingly they resent being "whitewashed" by the country's dominant culture. "The church and the YMCA came in and so dominated the social life of the youth," says Mason Wong, "that all we have now are a bunch of Chinese who are so whitewashed they make a Wasp look funny."

Two years ago Chinatown got its first taste of militancy. A group of some 300 youths from Hong Kong called the Wah Ching (China Youth) threatened to burn down a white-operated concession set up for the New Year's celebration unless the Six Companies helped them build a recreation hall. As it turned out nothing really happened, but their activist approach began to catch on. Last May, the Red Guards, led by a lanky, 23-year-old actor named Alex Hing, followed up their cherry-bomb raid by crashing a community meeting dressed in olive-drab jackets with red armbands. While the audience looked on, open-mouthed, they unfurled Chinese Communist flags and shouted revolutionary slogans.

Those flags were significant, for what is also happening in Chinatown is a gradual shift in allegiance away from the Nationalist government of Chiang Kai-shek and toward that of Mao Tse-tung and the mainland Chinese. According to most estimates, only about 20 per cent of all Chinese-Americans may be pro-Communist. But one knowledgeable insider believes that as many as half the 55 directors of the Six Companies are becoming disenchanted with Chiang. When the weekly newspaper Chinese Voice hit the stands recently with a special edition on Mao's programs, it sold out within a day and a half. Some think pro-Mao sentiments would be even stronger were it not for a fear that the U.S. Government would begin "interning" the Chinese as it did the Japanese during World War II.

"It's not a question of politics," says Joe Yuey, manager of the Imperial Palace restaurant. "It's a question of what a government can do for the people. The Nationalists were in power for 40 years and nothing happened. Look at China now, after only twenty years. No matter how you look at it, the Communists are helping the people."

To ultra-militants such as the Red Guards, the shift amounts to a signal to storm the barricades. But most Chinese-Americans feel a deepening concern for reform rather than revolution. Whether the upheavals in Chinatown will be smooth or chaotic, no one can yet say. But there is no question in my mind that our people must have the same social, economic and educational rights as the other citizens. I never had such problems—but then, I was whitewashed."

From
THE POLITICS OF PREJUDICE (1962)
ROGER DANIELS

Roger Daniels (b. 1927) indicates, in this study of the history of politics and prejudice, that domestic laws and popular attitudes are not only influential in internal affairs, but for better or for worse, they affect relations with other nations. Explored here are not only the antagonisms that led to World War II and the dispossession and detention of West Coast Japanese-Americans, but a peculiar insensitivity that continues to have its effect.

If the Southern States can segregate the races in its schools, why may not the Californians do so?
—San Francisco *Argonaut,* Jan. 5, 1907

The subject of the exclusion of laborers is acquiring a new interest in my mind . . . The whole subject of peaceful invasion by which the people of a country may have their country taken away from them, and the analogy and contrast between the swarming of peaceful immigration and business enterprise and the popular invasions of former times, such, for instance, as those overrunning the Roman Empire, are most interesting.
—Elihu Root to Oliver Wendell Holmes, Jr., March 6, 1907

Before 1906 the anti-Japanese movement, concentrating on exclusion, attracted little notice outside of California and the neighboring states. The event that finally called attention to the racial tension in California was, curiously enough, considered trivial by those who initiated it. A routine decision by the San Francisco school board, affecting only a few score children, catapulted the Japanese problem into the national and international limelight.

The school board crisis, as it has come to be known, can be understood only within the framework of local politics. In the years after the turn of the century San Francisco went through a time of troubles. The powerful Employers' Association launched a concerted antiunion drive that culminated in the bitter teamsters' strike of 1901, a qualified defeat for labor. Stung by what it considered undue police protection given strikebreakers by the relatively conservative reform administration headed by Mayor James D. Phelan, resurgent labor formed a Union Labor party and elected what it felt would be its own city administration. The new mayor was a dapper and personable musician, Eugene E. Schmitz, but the real power was in the hands of Abraham Ruef, an intelligent but unscrupulous lawyer. The new administration was utterly corrupt, although probably not more so than the administrations in many other contemporary American cities.

Animus against both Chinese and Japanese was reflected in the Union Labor platform from the first—but anti-Orientalism had been a standard plank for all San Francisco parties since the 1870's. Despite the fact that Schmitz was elected on a platform recommending that "all Asiatics, both Chinese and Japanese, should be educated separately," the Board of Education, which was reconstituted by the new administration in January, 1902, took no steps in this direction for more than three years. The leading members of the Board were the mayor's personal friends as well as political associates: the superintendent of schools, Alfred Roncovieri, had played the trombone in Schmitz's orchestra (his honor was a bassoonist), and the Board's president, Aaron Altman, was the brother-in-law of Boss Abe Ruef. Until 1905 the members of the Union Labor administration, despite the platform pledge showed no interest at all in the Japanese; perhaps, as one observer commented, they were too busy enriching themselves at the city's expense.

Only after the *Chronicle's* crusade was well under way, and just before other Union Labor partisans organized the Asiatic Exclusion League, did the Board take any action. On All Fool's Day, 1905, a budget proposal for the enlargement of the facilities at the one Oriental (Chinese) school was submitted to the supervisors, but it was turned down. On May 6 the Board announced that it would, at some future but unspecified date, remove the Japanese pupils to the Oriental school so that "our children should not be placed in any position where their youthful impressions may be affected by association with pupils of the Mongolian race.

The use of the word "Mongolian" was not an anachronism: it was a legal necessity. The Board intended to act under the authority of an old California law which empowered school boards to "exclude all children of filthy or vicious habits, or children suffering from contagious diseases, and also to establish separate schools for [American] Indian children, and for the children of Mongolian and Chinese descent. When such separate schools are established [these] children must not be admitted into any other schools." Most of the local press cheered the Board's action, and the Asiatic Exclusion League, from its first meeting, sporadically pressed for implementation of the resolution. For more than a year, none came. Schmitz was elected mayor for the third time in November, 1905, despite mounting complaints of corruption from both outside and within the Union Labor party. After his reëlection the administration continued to do nothing. Even among convinced exclusionists the "menace" of the Japanese pupils seemed a relatively unimportant issue; the real concern was exclusion.

Then nature took a hand. On April 18, 1906, San Francisco shuddered and groaned through several successive earthquake shocks of very high magnitude; these were followed by three days of fire which destroyed whole sections of the city. For a short period all thought of politics vanished as San Franciscans tried to restore order and to feed and house the refugees. The nation and the world sent sympathy and assistance; the largest foreign contribution, more than all the rest combined, was $246,000 from the citizens and government of earthquake-conscious Japan. By June, however, the anti-Japanese campaign was again becoming vigorous.

In that month, physical attacks against individual Japanese began to take on serious proportions. These attracted a large amount of local notice, particularly since about a dozen separate incidents involved four Japanese scientists who were inspecting the earthquake and fire damage. Led by Dr. F. Omori, an eminent seismologist from the Imperial University, Tokyo, the scientists were stoned and otherwise molested by groups of boys and young men in various parts of the city. When it developed that one of the culprits was a messenger boy employed by the post office, the postmaster promptly fired him, but the local press made a hero of the young hooligan. The luckless Dr. Omori continued his investigations in northern California and was again assaulted, this time in Eureka. The mayor of that city apologized, and insisted the assault was owing to local "labor troubles," not the professor's race, but it is difficult to understand how a Japanese scientist, whose normal dress in this country would not have been inappropriate at a formal wedding, could have been mistaken for either a strikebreaker or a walking delegate.

Toward the end of June the Asiatic Exclusion League complained that "many wage-earners, laborers, and mechanics patronize Japanese restaurants," and added rather unconvincingly that there were "eating houses" run by whites "as easy of access and more inviting." The League urged all affiliated unions "to enforce the penalties . . . for patronizing Japanese or Chinese" and threatened to have all patrons of Oriental restaurants photographed. The same meeting warned of the danger to health from many of the fruits then on the market, which had been "picked and packed by unclean and unhealthy Asiatics."

A real boycott was begun in October. It lasted about three weeks.

Japanese restaurants were picketed, prospective customers were handed matchboxes bearing the slogan "White men and women, patronize your own race," and windows were smashed and a few proprietors beaten. Until protests were lodged by the Japanese consul, the police seem consistently to have looked the other way. The boycott came to a quick end when the Japanese restaurant owners agreed to pay $350 in "protection."

In August and September assaults upon San Francisco Issei came too regularly to have been accidental. As President Roosevelt's special investigator conservatively reported, the assaults were motivated by "racial hostility" and "stirred up possibly by newspaper accounts." He obtained statements from nineteen Issei; none reported serious injury, and all the statements followed the same pattern. One victim related:

I am proprietor of Sunset City Laundry. Soon after the earthquake the persecutions became intolerable. My drivers were constantly attacked on the highway, my place of business defiled by rotten eggs and fruit; windows were smashed several times. . . . The miscreants are generally young men, 17 or 18 years old. Whenever newspapers attack the Japanese these roughs renew their misdeeds with redoubled energy.

Japanese pedestrians were not safe either. M. Sugawa, a shoemaker, stated:

As I was passing on Sutter Street, near Scott, three boys, 21 or 22 years of age, attacked my person. I nearly fainted. Upon rising to my feet they again assaulted me. This time they smashed my nose. I grabbed the coat of one of the trio, and after having my nose dressed at one of the nearby hospitals, I went home. The next day a policeman came, requesting me to give up the coat. I at first refused, but finally, upon his assuring me that it would be deposited at the police station, I gave it up. I reported the matter to the police. When the case came up for trial the youngster was dismissed on the plea of insufficiency of evidence.

There is no record, during this period, of any white person's being convicted for an assualt on a Japanese, although several Japanese were arrested for assault and disturbing the peace when they tried to defend themselves. These were minor annoyances and, of course, the local authorities apologized and the more responsive newspapers deplored the breaches of law and order. Discriminations against Japanese in San Francisco were still a local matter. In October, however, they became a *cause célèbre.*

On October 11, 1906, the Board of Education, under mounting pressure from the Exclusion League, ordered all Japanese and Korean pupils to join the Chinese in the Oriental school. This action was little noticed in the San Francisco press, and it seems that the rest of the country was quite ignorant of it. Nine days later, garbled reports of the order were printed in Tokyo newspapers—some said that Japanese were completely excluded—and from these Tokyo reports word of the Board's action reached the United States.

Among those who learned belatedly of this action was Theodore Roosevelt. Although taken by surprise by their latest manifestations of hostility, the President, as his published correspondence now shows, had been keeping a disapproving eye on the Californians for more than a year. The first intimation we have of his interest comes in a letter to George Kennan on May 6, 1905, in which he speaks of the "foolish offensiveness" of the March resolution by the "idiots" of the California legislature. It was not the substance of the resolution that annoyed the President, it was the tone.

The California Legislature would have had an entire right to protest as emphatically as possible against the admission of Japanese laborers, for their very frugality, abstemiousness and clannishness make them formidable to our laboring class, and you may not know that they have begun to offer a serious problem in Hawaii—all the more serious because they keep an entirely distinct alien mass. Moreover, I understand that the Japanese themselves do not permit any foreigners to own land in Japan, and where they draw one kind of sharp line against us they have no right whatever to object to our drawing another kind of line against them. . . . I would not have objected at all to the California Legislature passing a resolution, courteous and proper in its terms, which would really have achieved the object they were after.

Thus, there was little real difference between the views of the California exclusionists and those of the President. Had Roosevelt written this letter to one of them, or had someone communicated his views, the Californians doubtless would have adjusted their language. But Roosevelt kept his views within his own circle. In July, 1905, he wrote to the United States Minister in Japan and told him to inform the mikado's government that "the American Government and the American people at large have not the slightest sympathy with the outrageous agitation against the Japanese. . . . While I am President the Japanese will be treated just exactly like . . . other civilized peoples."

The first public hint of the President's attitude came in his annual message in December, 1905, which seemed to serve notice that he would not acquiesce in extending the bar against Chinese to immigrants from Japan:

it is unwise [the President's message read] to depart from the old American tradition and to discriminate for or against any man who desired to come here as a citizen, save on the ground of that man's fitness for citizenship. . . . We cannot afford to consider whether he is Catholic or Protestant, Jew or Gentile; whether he is Englishman or Irishman, Frenchman or German, Japanese, Italian, Scandinavian, Slav, or Magyar.

In the next paragraph, however, came a qualification to this catholic generalization:

the entire Chinese coolie class, that is, the class of Chinese laborers, skilled and unskilled, legitimately come under the head of undesirable immigrants to this country, because of their numbers, the low wages for which they work, and their low standard of living.

The distinction would have puzzled exclusionists had they noticed the insertion of the Japanese in what was an otherwise stock Roosevveltian platitude. They insisted, not without logic, that the Japanese and Chinese presented exactly the same kind of threat, and Roosevelt, as we have seen, secretly agreed with them. But of course there was another factor, which Roosevelt chose not to mention. Japan, by her stunning annihilation of two Russian fleets and the severe mauling she had given Russian armies, had just vaulted into the first rank of world powers. To the power-conscious President, reason of state made the distinction both logical and necessary.

What were Roosevelt's real views on Japan and the Japanese? It seems clear—if anything about the first Roosevelt is clear—that despite his frequent protests to the contrary he was, along with the overwhelming majority of his contemporaries, a convinced racist. He was, however, willing to treat certain individuals of any race as equals. Although he had been pro-Japanese from the outset of the war, he was stunned by the completeness of Admiral Togo's victory in Tsushima Strait. He had rather hoped "that the two powers will fight until both are fairly well exhausted and that then peace will come on terms which will not mean the creation of either a yellow peril or a Slav peril." He could blurt out to Spring-Rice that "the Japs interest me and I like them," but not far beneath the surface there was always a deep-seated distrust of the Orient, the one part of the globe Roosevelt never visited. Despite the fact that Japan's "diplomatic statements had been made good," he reminded his ambassador to Russia that "Japan is an Oriental nation, and the individual standard of truthfulness in Japan is low." He had "no doubt" that the Japanese people disliked "all white men" and believed "their own yellow civilization to be better."

But his distrust did not blind him to the realities of power. He was one of the few Occidentals who, from the beginning, had expected the Japanese to win the war, although even he was surprised at the one-sidedness of their naval victory. Nor did he share Wilhelm II's "yellow peril" phobias. He explained, rather imaginatively, to a Japanese who had been his classmate at Harvard, that some of his "own ancestors in the 10th century had been part of the 'white terror' of the Northmen," and he pointed out to John Hay that the descendants of Genghis Khan were serving "under the banners of Russia . . . not Japan." He wanted the Japanese treated courteously and with the respect that he felt their military prowess demanded. But he also felt very strongly that the

Japanese, and all colored peoples generally, should be willing to take fatherly advice, particularly his fatherly advice. Roosevelt, a confirmed believer in the white man's burden, wanted to be a father to the whole world. At the risk of being thought fanciful, I am going to close this discussion of Roosevelt's racial assumptions with a letter which, although completely unrelated to the Orient, seems to show his basic attitude toward peoples of non-European origin. To an American Indian, appropriately named No Shirt, the President wrote that

the earth is occupied by the white people and the red people. . . . If the red people would prosper, they must follow the mode of life which has made the white people so strong; and that it is only right that the white people should show the red people what to do and how to live right. . . . I wish to be a father to the red people as to the white. . . . Now my friend, I hope you will lay what I have said to heart. Try to set your people a good example of upright and industrious life, patience under difficulties, and respect for the authority of the officers I have appointed. . . . If you try as hard to help them as you do to find something in their conduct to censure, you will be surprised to find how much real satisfaction life holds in store for you.

This paternal admonition had been evoked by Chief No Shirt's unauthorized trip to Washington to complain to the President; when Roosevelt found that the Indian had not gone through the proper channels, he refused to see him, and he wrote the letter only when the presumably chastened chief had returned to the reservation.

That, from Roosevelt's point of view, was one of the troubles with the world: people and nations were always going "off the reservation." In October, 1906, the offenders were the San Francisco school board and the "labor agitators." By the twenty-sixth of the month, Roosevelt had decided upon his course of action. On that day he wrote to his friend Baron Kentaro Kaneko ("A good fellow, but he is a fox, and a Japanese Fox at that") that the situation was causing the "gravest concern" and that he would do everything possible to "protect the rights of the Japanese who are here." He added that he was sending a cabinet member to the scene.

The next day, which happened to be his forty-eighth birthday, Roosevelt had a conference with his Secretary of Commerce and Labor, Victor H. Metcalf, who then left to make an on-the-spot investigation of what had already become the school crisis. On October 29, in view of his forthcoming inspection trip to Panama, Roosevelt gave formal authorization to his Secretary of State, Elihu Root, to "use the armed forces of the United States to protect the Japanese in any portion of this country if they are menaced by mobs." On the day of his departure for Panama the President saw the Japanese ambassador, Viscount Siuzo Aoki, and read to him the passages on this topic in his forthcoming annual message to Congress, which he believed pleased

Aoki very much. Roosevelt, of course, had not yet seen Metcalf's report, as the investigation was still in progress.

Metcalf arrived in the San Francisco area on October 31. As the only Californian in the cabinet, he was the obvious choice for the assignment. A resident of Oakland, he had been a Republican congressman from 1899 until his elevation to the cabinet in 1904. His work there must have been satisfactory, because the White House had already announced that he would soon become Secretary of the Navy, an assignment which, given Roosevelt's scale of values, could only be regarded as a promotion. The Secretary spent two weeks in the San Francisco area and left without giving a hint of his findings. Californians expected that they would receive favorable treatment from one of their own, and no one seems to have remembered, then or later, that Metcalf had already aired his views on the Japanese question. In May, 1905, he had told San Francisco reporters that he was not concerned about Japanese immigration and that he thought the root of the trouble lay with white men who were not willing to work in the fruit districts.

Roosevelt returned to the capital late in November and had a conference with Metcalf and Benjamin Ide Wheeler, president of the University of California, on November 30. Three days later, his annual message was sent to Congress; it contained the President's first important public statement on the Japanese question; it was also the most advanced position he ever took. The part which concerns us—and which presumably had been read to Aoki in early November—followed a paragraph in which the President wrote of the necessity of treating all nations and immigrants fairly. Then Roosevelt became specific:

I am prompted to say this by the attitude of hostility here and there assumed towaid the Japanese in this country. This hostility is sporadic and is limited to a very few places. Nevertheless, it is most discreditable to us as a people, and it may be filled with the gravest consequences to the nation.

The President went on to discuss the more than half century of friendly relations between the United States and Japan, and dwelt at some length in the most complimentary terms on the splendid achievements of Japan, military and otherwise, and declared that the "overwhelming mass of our people cherish a lively regard and respect for the people of Japan," and that "in almost every quarter of the Union" Japanese were treated just "as the stranger from any part of civilized Europe."

But here and there a most unworthy feeling has manifested itself toward the Japanese [such as] shutting them out of the common schools of San Francisco [and] mutterings against them in one or two other places, because of their efficiency as workers. To shut them out from the public schools is a wicked absurdity. . . . I recommend to the Congress that an act be past (*sic*—T. R.'s simplified spelling) specifically providing for the naturalization of Japanese who come here intending to become American citizens.

He went on to complain that the federal government could not properly protect the rights of aliens here and asked Congress to enable the President to do so. He made it evident that no abstract concept of justice inspired this request. His stated motivation was reason of state. He thought it preposterous that

the mob of a single city may at any time perform acts of lawless violence which would plunge us into war. . . . It is unthinkable that we should continue a policy under which a given locality may be allowed to commit a crime against a friendly nation.

Roosevelt never again publicly proposed naturalization for the Japanese. It may be that, as in the case of the celebrated dinner invitation to Booker T. Washington, the President's racial views were in advance of public opinion and that the ensuing reaction forced him to compromise his principles. This is the most favorable interpretation possible, and the one most often advanced. Yet it is not convincing. Roosevelt knew well that anti-Japanese feeling was not limited to San Francisco and "one or two other places"; he knew also that Southern opinion would support the West on any racial matter. Since there is no evidence that he ever made the slightest effort to have this proposal implemented—and certainly there were men in Congress who would have introduced such a bill had the President so requested—it is reasonable to assume that Roosevelt made it chiefly for Japanese consumption and in order to have an advanced position from which to retreat in his dealings with California. Two months later, during diplomatic negotiations, the Japanese government proposed a trade—naturalization for exclusion. Secretary of State Root informed the American negotiator: "It is wholly useless to discuss the subject of naturalization at the present time [because] no statute could be passed or treaty ratified now" which granted naturalization.

The message may have been for Japanese consumption, but Californians felt that the President's views were being forced down their throats. Their protests were loud, long, and nearly unanimous; every prominent newspaper in the state except Harrison Gray Otis' Los Angeles *Times* denounced Roosevelt. Southerners, in and out of Congress, raised the question of state rights, as they are wont to do on any racial question, and William Jennings Bryan, flexing his vocal cords for 1908, sided with them. Then, on December 18, 1906, Metcalf's report and a concurring letter of transmittal by the President went to the Congress. The report showed that, rather than the hundreds and even thousands of pupils the San Francisco papers had written about, there had been at the time of the segregation order a grand total of

93 Japanese students in all the twenty-three public schools of San Francisco, and that 25 of these students were native-born American citizens. The press had complained of young men in the primary grades, and Metcalf agreed that this was, to a degree, true. There were 27 alien teen-agers, who, for one reason or another, were well above the normal age limits for their grades. For example, 2 nineteen-year-olds were in the fourth grade. Metcalf recommended that age limits be set, and even the local Japanese consul had agreed, before the segregation order, that there could be no objection to the segregation or even removal of such overage pupils from the system. Metcalf's report concluded:

All the considerations which may move a nation, every consideration of duty in the preservation of our treaty obligations, every consideration prompted by fifty years of more or less close friendship with the Empire of Japan, would unite in demanding, it seems to me, of the United States Government and all its people, the fullest protection and the highest considerations for the subjects of Japan.

Metcalf, of course, received an even worse pummeling from the California press than did his chief. As a Californian—the *Argonaut* put it, "Mr. Metcalf was a Californian"—his report was viewed as an act of treachery toward his adopted state. Most of the country east of the Rockies, aside from the South, generally supported the President and his agent, especially when they found out the ridiculous details.

Public opinion, however, would not get the pupils back into school or solve what might become a very sticky international problem. The one thing the federal government could do was institute legal proceedings in both state and federal courts to try to annul the local action and the state law on which it was based. With the "separate but equal" doctrine as law of the land, no appeal could be made for the Nisei children, who were, after all, American citizens and in no way a diplomatic problem; but the rights of the alien Japanese children might be protected by the terms of the 1894 treaty with Japan which granted reciprocal "most favored nation" rights of residence to the nationals of both countries. As early as November, Root, working through the Department of Justice, was setting up a test case and was ready to appeal to the United States Supreme Court if necessary. At the same time Roosevelt and Root realized that the school board crisis was merely a surface manifestation of a deeper problem. By November, they had decided that they would try to get at the heart of the matter by restricting Japanese immigration. But, unlike the California exclusionists, they wanted, if possible, to do this without the deliberate affront of a Japanese exclusion law, which the administration could have put through Congress at any time.

Even before he left for Panama, the President began to work for the restriction of Japanese immigration. At the same interview in which he showed the draft of his annual message to Viscount Aoki, Roosevelt told the Japanese ambassador that he thought the "only way to prevent constant friction" between the two nations was to "prevent all immigration of Japanese laboring men . . . into the United States." This is the first intimation of what became known as the Gentlemen's Agreement. But first it was necessary to quell the agitation in California and reduce the racial tension there. Roosevelt understood that the "great difficulty in getting the Japanese" to limit immigration themselves was the "irritation" caused by the segregation order. The President hoped that his message would smooth things over, but, as often was the case, his expectations were unduly sanguine.

When Roosevelt found that he had underestimated the temper of the Californians, and that his message was resulting in more rather than less agitation in California, he and Root revamped their plans. Three things had to be accomplished before the restriction of Japanese immigration could be effected: the San Francisco segregation order had to be revoked by one means or another; the California legislature had to be restrained from passing further discriminatory legislation; and a bill had to be passed by Congress giving the President power to restrict Japanese immigration from intermediate points such as Hawaii, Mexico, and Canada. All these preconditions were related; the executive order limiting intermediary immigration was to be offered to the Californians as a sort of prize for good behavior, and it would not be proclaimed until the segregation order was revoked and all anti-Japanese measures in the California legislature were killed.

At the opening session of the legislature early in January, 1907, the outgoing governor, George C. Pardee, gently chastised Roosevelt's position on the Japanese in the state, attributing his position to the fact that "in common with . . . the people of the Eastern States" the President did not really understand the Japanese question. The governor affirmed the right of California to segregate Orientals "until the courts of this country" should rule otherwise. Within a few days, anti-Japanese bills and resolutions were introduced and discussed in both houses of the legislature and some of these seemed certain to pass. On January 30, 1907, Roosevelt called the entire California congressional delegation to the White House; after the meeting the delegation wired the governor:

Delegation has just had important conference with President and Secretary of State. At their request we have wired Superintendent of Schools and President of Board of Education of San Francisco to come here immediately for conference. Entire delegation joins in request that you send for leaders in both houses in Legislature, and ask that all legislative action concerning Japanese matters be deferred for a short time. We consider this most important.

The new governor, James N. Gillett, a conservative Republican, added his endorsement to this message and transmitted it to the legislature; both houses immediately complied and either tabled or sent back to committee the pending anti-Japanese measures. For the moment, legislative action had been checked, but getting the San Franciscans to Washington was not so easy.

The San Francisco situation was complicated by the fact that the peculations of Boss Ruef and Mayor Schmitz had finally stirred reform elements to action. The pair had been indicted by the grand jury, but had not yet been brought to trial. The President's invitation had been extended to the Board of Education only, but the wily mayor, perhaps thinking to cover himself with glory, had his henchmen on the Board insist on his accompanying them. After three days of dickering, the invitation was broadened to include Schmitz; the San Franciscans arrived in Washington on February 8. After a week of parleys with Roosevelt and Root an agreement was reached along the lines indicated in Metcalf's report; overage pupils and those who did not have facility in English might be placed in separate schools, and, to ease Japanese sensitivities, the new regulations were to apply to all alien children, although there was never any intention to segregate Caucasians. In San Francisco and the rest of California, all other Japanese children, aliens and citizens, would continue to attend the regular public schools. In return, the federal government withdrew its suits, and Roosevelt and Root promised to limit Japanese immigration.

Whatever his motives may have been, Schmitz, an engaging rogue of the same cut as the later Mayor Jimmy Walker of New York, performed, under pressure, the only statesmanlike act of his political career, and this, it will be distressing for the moralist to note, brought him more abuse from his constituents than five years of theft and fraud. His crimes disturbed only the reform element in San Francisco, and even after his indictment he seems to have remained a popular figure. But after his "surrender" to the President, Schmitz, who was soon to go to jail, received from all sides the same sort of excoriation that had been showered on Roosevelt and Metcalf.

Almost as soon as the San Franciscans had knuckled under, the legislature seemed again about to pass anti-Japanese legislation. This time Roosevelt corresponded directly with Governor Gillett, pointing out that the "attitude of the violent extremists" was the only thing standing in the way of a settlement of the immigration problem by direct negotiation with Japan. Gillett again did the President's bidding, and the legislature, heeding the governor's advice, adjourned on March 12 without passing any anti-Japanese measures.

It should be noted, however, that each house of the legislature at one time or another during the 1907 session passed anti-Japanese bills and resolutions, although no one measure was passed by both houses. In the senate three measures were passed unanimously; the one recorded vote in the assembly was 53 for to 8 against. Few members of the legislature were willing to vote against anti-Japanese measures, but with the political amorality so typical of legislators most were quite willing to take no effective action. It should also be noted that not all the measures were sponsored by men who represented constituencies where there were large numbers of Japanese. In this and subsequent legislatures, two Democrats, John B. Sanford and Anthony Caminetti, were among the leading instigators of discriminatory proposals; in the four small counties represented by Sanford there were a total of 125 Japanese, and only 51 were found in the five counties which comprised Caminetti's bailiwick. Once the agitation had assumed major proportions—that is, any time after December, 1906—there was no constant relationship between the number of Japanese in a given area of the state and the amount of anti-Japanese feeling there.

As soon as the Californians fell into line the President carried out his part of the bargain. Conveniently, there was an immigration bill already in Congress, and, having previously gained the acquiescence of the Japanese government, Root himself drafted an amendment designed specifically to check secondary Japanese immigration, but very pointedly did not specifically say so. The key passage of Root's handiwork read:

. . . whenever the President shall be satisfied that passports issued by any foreign government to its citizens to go to any country other than the United States or to any insular possession of the United States or to the Canal Zone are being used for the purpose of enabling holders to come to the continental territory of the United States to the detriment of labor conditions therein, the President may refuse to permit such citizens of the country issuing such passports to enter the continental territory of the United States.

The secretary explained to Henry Cabot Lodge, the administration's chief foreign policy spokesman in the upper house, that

from the Japanese point of view all that the President will be doing under such a provision will be to enforce the limitations that Japan herself puts into her passports, while, from our point of view, the provision will enable the President to keep Japanese laborers out unless Japan undertakes to force them upon us directly, which she is apparently far from wishing to do.

The bill passed Congress on February 18; Roosevelt, waiting for the Californians to demonstrate their good faith, debarred further Japanese immigration from Hawaii, Mexico, and Canada by an executive order on March 14, 1907.

The executive order blocked off several major sources of immigration without giving undue offense to Japan. The stage was now set for the implementation of the final phase of the Roosevelt-Root plan: getting the Japanese to agree to halt the direct immigration of laborers. What has become known as the Gentlemen's Agreement was the result of more than a year and a half of detailed negotiation; its substance may be found in six notes exchanged between the two governments in late 1907 and early 1908. The Japanese agreed not to issue passports good for the continental United States to laborers, skilled or unskilled, but passports would be issued to "laborers who have already been in America and to the parents, wives and children of laborers already resident there." All the evidence indicates that the Japanese government scrupulously kept the agreement. It has been hailed by most historians as a great achievement of honest and patient negotiations. Yet it actually served to irritate further the already raw nerves of the Californians and by its very nature was almost bound to do so.

What the President and his Secretary of State did not envisage was that under this agreement thousands of Japanese men resident in the United States would bring over wives, who in many cases had been selected for them in the traditional manner by their families and other go-betweens in their native villages. Many of these marriages were by proxy, but they were perfectly legal under Japanese law. The steady advent of these "picture brides" for twelve years seemed to Californians to be another example of Oriental treachery.

The Gentlemen's Agreement was represented to the Californians as exclusion. Had Roosevelt and Root realized that under its terms thousands of Japanese women would come to the United States, they might never have sought it; having done so, they made a blunder of the first magnitude by failing to foresee its consequences. The State Department, hypnotized by statistics which began to show more Japanese emigration than immigration, refused for many years to recognize what Californians quickly discóvered: Japanese women were joining their husbands and having babies. That these babies were citizens of the United States made no difference to the Californians, most of whom insisted that "a Jap was a Jap," no matter where he was born. Had Washington understood what would happen in California from the first and made it clear to the Californians that they might expect a limited influx of Japanese women, it is within the realm of possibility that much of the future agitation could have been avoided. As it happened, the combination of ignorance in Washington and prejudice in California inevitably caused anti-Japanese agitation to wax rather than wane. It soon became an article of faith with the exclusionists that they had been betrayed by their own diplomats, who, in turn, were held to be mere dupes of the perfidious Japanese.

Even before it became apparent that the Gentlemen's Agreement was not producing the intended results, the anti-Japanese movement continued to show signs of life. A flurry of physical assaults on Japanese and some minor cases of municipal discrimination occurred in the summer of 1907. The Exclusion League and its allies continued their agitation and propaganda. The San Francisco *Chronicle,* however, began to take a moderate line after Roosevelt's assurances that Japanese immigration would be limited. This was a position that the *Chronicle* and other California newspapers which spoke for the business and commercial interests would continue to hold. Thus ended the bizarre spectacle of the conservative *Chronicle* and the labor-dominated Exclusion League marching side by side at the head of the anti-Japanese parade. The anti-Japanese torch dropped by de Young's paper was soon taken up by those newspapers belonging to William Randolph Hearst. In this, as everything else, Hearst was a follower, not an innovator; he excelled only in the extremes to which he carried every cause he espoused, from the war with Spain to antivivisectionism. Hearst's peculiar contributions to the anti-Japanese movement will be discussed in detail later; let it be noted here that from 1907 on his papers were second to none in their abuse of both Japan and the Japanese.

After 1908, although anti-Japanese feeling continued to run high by the Golden Gate, San Francisco was no longer the vital center of the movement. The shift of Japanese population from urban to rural areas, noted earlier, becomes apparent from about this time. Correspondingly, anti-Japanese feeling began to grow rapidly in the rural areas of the state, particularly in the central valley. The symptoms of this feeling can be best seen in the growing anti-Japanese activity shown in successive biennial sessions of the California legislature, culminating in the passage of the Alien Land Law of 1913.

REGIMENTED NON-EDUCATION: INDIAN SCHOOLS (1969)

DANIEL HENNINGER
NANCY ESPOSITO

Daniel Henninger and Nancy Esposito continue the role of American writers as social critics, a role that began with the muckrakers of the early years of this century. Their approach is similar, too, as they define a problem both pressing and, like others, neglected. The American Indian child can be provided with a first-rate education and a positive self-image, they emphasize, but only if Americans are willing to accept their public responsibility.

Senator Edward Kennedy has taken over the chairmanship of his late brother's Indian Education Subcommittee, which is soon to release a report recommending basic changes in the ways we educate Indian children. It's about time. The Bureau of Indian Affairs spent $86 million of its $241 million budget in 1968 on the education of 55,000 Indian children, and there's little to show for it.

Nearly 60 per cent of these youngsters must attend BIA boarding schools, either because there's no public or federal day school near their home or because they are "social referrals" (BIA jargon for anything from a bilingual difficulty to serious emotional disorders and juvenile delinquency). One per cent finish college. In Alaska there is only one federal high school, so two-thirds of the Alaskan Indians are sent to a boarding school in Oregon; 267 others go to school in Chilocco, Oklahoma. The Navajo nation comprises one-third of the BIA's responsibility, and 92 per cent of its children are in boarding schools. The schools have a 60 per cent dropout rate, compared to a national average of 23 per cent.

Assimilation has been the aim of the Bureau of Indian Affairs since the early 1800's. But it no longer expresses that purpose in the embarrassing language of a World War II House subcommittee: "The final solution of the Indian problem [is] to work toward the liquidation of the Indian problem rather than toward merely perpetuating a federal Indian Service working with a steadily increasing Indian population." From the BIA's "Curriculum Needs of Navajo Pupils" we learn that the Navajo child "needs to begin to develop knowledge of how the dominant culture is pluralistic and how these people worked to become the culture which influences the American mainstream of life . . ."; "needs to understand that every man is free to rise as high as he is able and willing . . ."; "needs assistance with accepting either the role of leader or follower . . ."; "needs to understand that a mastery of the English language is imperative to compete in the world today . . ."; "needs to understand that work is necessary to exist and succeed. . . ."

Often the government places children in federal boarding schools at the age of six or seven; over 9,000 under the age of nine are so placed. That quite a few parents resist having their young taken from home for a year is indicated by a 1966 HEW survey: 16,000 Indian children between the ages of eight and 16 were not in school.

The Indian school curriculum is standard: ancient history, European history, American history, geography, arithmetic, art, music (an Indian "needs training in proper tone production in order to properly and effectively sing Western music"). Not much about *their* history. The Interior Department investigated Indian schools in Alaska last spring and found that "education which gives the Indian, Eskimo and Aleut knowledge of—and therefore pride in—their historic and cultural heritage is almost nonexistent. . . . In the very few places where such an attempt is made, it is poorly conceived and inadequate." Most of the boarding school teachers are aware of the variations in language, dress and customs of their students, but their sensitivity to the less obvious differences in Indian values, beliefs and attitudes is peripheral and by the way. Most Indian children speak English poorly or not at all; communication between teacher and pupil is difficult or impossible. Yet Bureau schools conduct *all* classes in English.

It doesn't take long to discourage young, dedicated teachers: "Most of the teachers came to Chilocco because of humanitarian reasons," said a former teacher at the Oklahoma boarding school. "They saw the pitiful situation and truly wanted to help, but after months of rejection and failure, they either quit or they began looking at it as an eight to five job with no obligation to their students." A teacher at an Arizona school wrote the BIA last year, suggesting that the inclusion of courses in agriculture and native crafts might arouse his habitually unresponsive students. "This idea [didn't] set well with many of the 'old hands' among the administrators," he later said. "The only thing that came out of it were some dark days for me, and a label as a trouble-maker." The turnover rate among teachers is double the national average. To an Indian child, the teacher is a stranger passing through. An obvious remedy is to enlist more Indian teachers. At present only 16 per cent of the Bureau's teachers are Indian, and with only one per cent of the Indians graduating yearly from college, there is little chance that the percentage will rise.

Estranged from his family, confronted with an alien culture and unable to talk to his teachers, the Indian's academic performance is predictably poor. What is harder to explain is the "crossover phenomenon." For the first few years of school, Indian achievement parallels that of white children and then slowly but persistently regresses. An Indian starts to fall behind between the sixth and eighth grades, and if he doesn't drop out finishes high school with a 9.5 grade education. Despite this regression, a boarding school student is never held back for academic failure; at the end of each year, he is promoted to the next grade whatever his performance. Summer school programs are scarce. Bureau teachers are contracted by the year, and one-third go on educational leave during the summer while the rest clean up the schools, take inventory and so on. As a result the typical high school class contains highly intelligent students as well as many who should still be in grade school. The teacher tries to compensate by aiming his instruction somewhere between the two extremes, so much of the class drops off to sleep or stares blankly at books.

One would think that after school the children could find some release from this dreariness, in the dorms or in some extracurricular activity. Life at a federal boarding school, though, is regimented and arbitrary. Seen from the air, many of the schools look like military installations—complexes of one-color, one-texture buildings set in the middle of otherwise barren areas. The impression of physical isolation mirrors the cultural isolation in the classroom. The building-complex usually includes dormitories (boys and girls), classroom buildings and housing for the staff. Many of the buildings are in disrepair. In a number of places (Tuba City, Arizona, for example) condemned buildings are still in use. The Fort Wingate Elementary Boarding School in New Mexico uses old Fort Wingate, once commanded by Douglas MacArthur's father. Forty years ago, the Brookings Institution's Merriam Report declared this plant unsuitable.

Even the new buildings are designed to reinforce the numbing sterility. Long, narrow, lifeless dormitories house row upon row of double-deckered iron beds and little else. Windows are sometimes barred. Floors are bare; the vivid personal decorations that are so much a part of many Indian communities are discouraged. Dress, too, is strictly regulated. The system makes individualizing one's appearance or environment fairly impossible. Beneath all the regulation is the Bureau's implicit concept of the children: all Indians are alike. In reality some children are at boarding schools because there is no alternative schooling available, while an increasing number, the "social referrals," come to the schools with serious emotional problems. Dr. Anthony Elite of the Public Health Service's Indian Health office in Phoenix has said that "with this great change in the profile of the student body, there has not been a concomitant change in staffing, skilled workers or training existing personnel to cope with these problems."

Each hour of a child's day is planned by the clock, with strict schedules posted in the dorms. Classes, meals, study periods, chores, free-time, bed—the routine never varies. Frequent headcounts are taken to quickly identify runaways or "AWOLS" as the Bureau calls them. Demerits are handed out for breaking the rules. The demerits can be removed by performing extra chores or by sacrificing priveleges like TV, a school movie or snacks. At the Chinle Elementary Boarding School each child has a punchcard fastened to the end of his bed with punched holes representing demerits on one side and merits on the other. A little boy proudly displayed his card to a visitor. He was especially proud of the large number of holes he had accumulated. Most of the holes were on the demerit side. He didn't know the difference. At another school two small boys were seen sitting on the floor, tearing up old textbooks as a punishment.

Dr. Robert Bergman, a PHS psychiatrist on the Navajo Reservation said, "the somewhat limited social opportunities of the boarding high school give the adolescent students few protected ways of exploring boy-girl relationships. The sexes are pretty well kept separate most of the time, and even casual contact between them is looked on with some suspicion by school officials anxious about possible scandal. A hostile rebellious attitude develops in the students, and they make their own opportunities away from the potential help of adults. Many students make a very abrupt transition from no dating at all to sneaking out to drink and make love." The administration's response to such behavior is more repression and school officials at a number of boarding schools cite discipline as their most important problem. Asked what he would do if given more money, the superintendent at Chilocco said he would build a jail and hire more guards.

To maintain discipline, the schools eliminate as many outside or uncontrollable influences as possible. A visitor is discouraged from talking to the children. A child "caught" talking to a visitor gets a sharp warning glance from a school official. Authorities address the children in English and discourage using native language in both the classroom and dorms. Dr. Bergman relates the rather bizarre results of this policy: "I often encounter [dorm attendants] who pretend not to speak Navajo. They have become so convinced that speaking Navajo is a bad thing to do that they often won't admit that they can. [Most attendants are themselves products of boarding schools.] The children learn that what they say in Navajo is effectively kept secret from the authorities even if one of the Navajo-speaking members of the staff hears them, because the Navajo staff member will be too ashamed of having understood to tell anyone."

School authorities in effect dictate when children may go home for weekends and when parents may visit the schools. The Bureau has a *de facto* policy of discouraging such visits, because the children are noticeably upset and troublesome afterwards, and the number of runaways invariably increases. To reach the school, parents must travel long distances over roads that are impassable most of the year. The schools afford them neither accommodations nor transportation. At the easily accessible Fort Wingate school, signs on the dormitory doors announced that no child would be permitted home for two weekends prior to Thanksgiving. A teacher at the Tuba City Boarding School wrote of the problem last year to Sen. Robert Kennedy, then chairman of the subcommittee on Indian Education: "Most children on the reservation starting at age six only see their parents on occasional weekends, if that often. At these times parents are usually allowed to check out their children—if the child's conduct in school warrants it, in the opinion of the school administration. If he has been a 'problem' (e.g., has run away) parents are often not allowed to take him until he has 'learned his lesson.'" The students' most visible emotional problem is boredom—the deadening routine of marching in line to meals and class, the lack of recreation or an interesting diversion. The letter to Sen. Kennedy summarized the emptiness of life at a boarding school: "The children search everywhere for something—they grasp most hungrily at any attention shown them, or to any straw that might offer some escape from boredom. You can't help but see it in their faces when you visit the dorms of the younger children. At the older boys' dormitories, they are used to the conditions—you can see that, too. They no longer expect anything meaningful from anyone."

Their reaction to this gradual dehumanization is extreme. Recently on the Navajo Reservation, two young runaways froze to death trying to make it to their homes 50 miles away. Escape through glue-, paint- and gasoline-sniffing is as common as chronic drunkenness at the boarding schools. On Easter morning two years ago, authorities at the Chilocco school found a Crow boy who had apparently drunk himself to death. More recently a runaway at the Albuquerque Boarding School was found frozen to death after an alcoholic binge.

Suicide among young Indians is over three times the national average and an even greater problem at the boarding schools. Yet the Superintendent of the Albuquerque school said he had never seen an Indian suicide in any school in his 28 years of experience. Testifying before Sen. Kennedy's subcommittee, Dr. Daniel O'Connell found evidence to the contrary: "The situation as far as suicide is concerned is especially acute among the boarding school children, particularly in high school. . . . In the Busby School in the Northern Cheyenne Reservation, for example, with fewer than 250 students, there were 12 attempted suicides during the past 18 months."

The closest thing the child has to a surrogate parent is the so-called instructional aide or dormitory attendant. Aides are responsible for the children in the dorms and supervise their routine activities—dressing and washing the smaller children, housecleaning and free time. Psychologically, the instructional aide is the most important member of the staff, since the dorm is the closest thing the children have to a home life. But he is the lowest paid and has the lowest status in the school hierarchy. Each aide is expected to care for 60 to 80 children. At a conference with Dr. Bergman, an aide asked for help in getting her 75 first-graders to put their shoes by their beds at night. Every morning is mass hysteria as seven-year-olds scramble for a missing right or left shoe. Night attendants are responsible for 180 to 260 children, so there is rarely someone to comfort a youngster having a normal childhood nightmare.

The instructional aides are not encouraged to take a personal interest in the children. An aide was severely reprimanded for inviting some girls to her room to make Navajo fry-bread. The authorities would prefer that the system's few professional guidance counselors handle the children's problems. The present ratio of students to counselors is 690 to one. One counselor complained that 30 to 40 per cent of his time is spent retrieving runaways, another 30 per cent supervising housekeeping, leaving little time for serious counseling.

For its more serious problems—the suicide-prone, the alcoholics, the psychotics—the BIA employed one full-time psychologist last year for the entire federal school system. A rebellious or uncooperative student gains a reputation as a "troublemaker" and is expelled from one school after another until he is old enough to drop out. A Fort Hall boy who has attempted suicide six times was sent to Chilocco last fall for lack of anywhere else to send him. Among the Indians, Chilocco is considered the end of the line.

The Rough Rock Demonstration School in northeastern Arizona is a welcome anomaly in this chain of dead-end desert schools. Jointly funded by the Office of Economic Opportunity and the BIA, the Navajo boarding school is innovative in that it is run by Indians. The seven Indians who comprise the school board set school policy, hire and fire teachers and manage the school's $790,000 budget. The curriculum includes daily instruction in Navajo culture, history and language, and the school's Cultural Identification Center attracts talented Navajo artists and translators to produce meaningful texts for Indian children. Nor is the built-in bleakness of dorm life found at Rough Rock. The school has 10 counselors, and parents are invited to live in the dorms for eight-week periods (reducing the child-adult ratio to 10 to one). The parents work as dorm aides, with pay, and attend adult education programs, since many are less-educated than their children. Students are encouraged to go home on weekends and the school provides transportation for those who would otherwise have to stay at school. The school's teachers make periodic visits to the children's homes to let the parents know how their children are doing. (The parents of many children at other schools haven't the slightest idea of what grade their children are in.) Of the school's 82 full-time employees, 62 are Indians, and for many it is their first permanent job. It is too early to say whether Rough Rock's community-involvement approach is *the* answer to Indian education. The experiment is expensive ($2,500 per student) and the school will have to look elsewhere for support after OEO funding expires in June. What the Indians at Rough Rock have proved is that given effective control of the immediate forces that shape their lives, they can be a success, qualified in measurable achievement, total in terms of self-respect.

POWWOW (1963)

W. D. SNODGRASS

*W. D. Snodgrass (b. 1926), a distinguished poet and winner of the
Pulitzer Prize, examines in "Powwow" a scene in which the vestiges of
a culture remain after the culture itself has vanished. In this case, the
dance remains as a symbol but its meaning has been lost.*

(Tama Reservation, Iowa, 1949)

They all see the same movies.
    They shuffle on one leg,
        Scuffling the dust up.
    Shuffle on the other.
They are all the same:
    A Sioux dance to the spirits,
    A war dance by four Chippewa,
    A Dakota dance for rain.
        We wonder why we came.
Even tricked out in the various braveries—
    Black buffalo tassels, beadwork, or the brilliant
    Feathers at the head, at the buttocks—
Even in long braids and the gaudy face paints,
        They all dance with their eyes turned
    Inward, like a woman nursing
A sick child she already knows
    Will die. For the time, she nurses it
    All the same. The loudspeakers shriek;
        We leave our bleacher seats to wander
    Among the wickiups and lean-tos
In a search for hot dogs. The Indians
        Are already packing; have
    Resumed green dungarees and khaki,
    Castoff combat issues of World War II.
        (Only the Iroquois do not come here;
They work in structural steel; they have a contract
    Building the United Nations
And Air Force installations for our future wars.)
These, though, have dismantled their hot-dog stand
    And have to drive all night
To jobs in truck stops and all-night filling stations.
    We ask directions and
    They scuttle away from us like moths.
    Past the trailers,

Beyond us, one tepee is still shining
Over all the rest. Inside, circled by a ring
              Of children, in the glare
              Of one bare bulb, a shrunken fierce-eyed man
Squats at his drum, all bones and parchment,
                    While his dry hands move
On the drumhead, always drumming, always
Raising his toothless, drawn jaw to the light
              Like a young bird drinking, like a chained dog,
Howling his tribe's song for the restless young
              Who wander in and out.
              Words of such great age,
Not even he remembers what they mean.
              We tramp back to our car,
       Then nearly miss the highway, squinting
Through red and yellow splatterings on the windshield,
       The garish and beautiful remains
              Of grasshoppers and dragonflies
That go with us, that do not live again.

THE ANGRY AMERICAN INDIAN (1970)
From *Time*

Docile since the last of the Indian wars in 1890, the American Indian, spurred on by rising expectations and by the obvious successes of the black activists, is beginning to demand his share of the good life that America promises. Here the editors of Time *examine the situation as it is and as it promises to become.*

Most Americans know the first Americans only by cliché. There is the 19th century image, caught in bronze and in lithograph, of the defeated warrior, head drooping forward so that his feathers nearly mingle with his pony's mane. The bow of his shoulders and the slump of his body evoke his loss of pride, of green and fertile lands, of earth's most favored continent. Then there is a recent image, often seen through air-conditioned automobile windows. Grinning shyly, the fat squaw hawks her woven baskets along the reservation highway, the dusty landscape littered with rusting cars, crumbling wickiups, and bony cattle. In the bleak villages, the only signs of cheer are romping, round-faced children and the invariably dirty, crowded bar, noisy with the shouts and laughter of drunkenness.

Like most stereotypes, these caricatures possess a certain core of validity. They also help white America contain and numb the reality of past guilt and present injustice. Most important of all, they are less and less significant. After more than a century of patience and passivity, the nation's most neglected and isolated minority is astir, seeking the means and the muscle for protest and redress. Sometimes highly educated, sometimes speaking with an articulateness forged of desperation, always angry, the new American Indian is fed up with the destitution and publicly sanctioned abuse of his long-divided people. He is raising his voice and he intends to be heard. Listen:

"The next time whites try to illegally clear our land, perhaps we should get out and shoot the people in the bulldozers," contends Michael Benson, a 19-year-old Navajo and a freshman at Wesleyan University.

"It's time that Indians got off their goddam asses and stopped letting white people lead them around by their noses," says Lehman Brightman, a South Dakota Sioux now working on a Ph.D. at Berkeley. "Even the name Indian is not ours. It was given to us by some dumb honky who got lost and thought he'd landed in India."

"We weren't meant to be tourist attractions for the master race," scoffs Gerald Wilkinson, 30, a Cherokee who holds multiple degrees after attending four universities. "We don't use the language of the New Left, but that doesn't mean we're not militant."

"Some day you're going to feel like Custer, baby," shouted one unidentified Indian at Donald Dwyer, a former Minneapolis police chief recently invited to discuss city problems with a group of Minneapolis Indians.

Symbolic Protest

That kind of rhetoric is surprising, coming from people long accustomed to equating silence with dignity. But in acts as well as speech, the newly aroused Indian is no longer content to play the obsequious Tonto to the white man's Lone Ranger. A belligerent band of 100 Indians still occupies the abandoned federal prison at Alcatraz, which the Indians propose to use as a cultural center and are willing to buy —for "$24 in glass beads and red cloth." Says one of the invaders: "Alcatraz is still better than most reservations." Angered at the whites who litter their beaches with beer cans and broken bottles, Indians in the state of Washington set up road blocks and closed 50 miles of seashore. A group of 50 Passamaquoddy Indians in Maine charged motorists fees to pass through their land on a busy highway last July. Four Indians at Dartmouth College, which was founded partly "for civilizing and christianizing Children of Pagans," protested the Indian dress of the college mascot, and officials banished it from football games.

Going beyond such symbolic acts, Indians in Washington have deliberately violated fishing regulations that they consider a breach of their rights, and have gone to jail as a result. One of their leaders, Janet McCloud, a fiery Tulalip, contends that restrictions on catching salmon have reduced the Indian to "savages with no more rights than a bear." More softly, she concedes: "I don't like being a clown or a militant, but sometimes you have to break this conspiracy of silence." Another angry woman, Kahn Tineta Horn, effectively uses a trim figure in a tight buckskin dress to gain television attention for protest demonstrations. But sex is not her only weapon: she has been arrested for carrying a knife and for interfering with police.

Harassment by police is the target of a sophisticated Indian uprising in Minneapolis, which has one of the few Indian ghettos in any city. There Clyde Bellecourt, 33, a tough Chippewa who has spent 14 years behind bars, has organized an "Indian Patrol." Dressed in red jackets, its members use short-wave radios to follow police activity, then show up to observe the cops silently whenever an Indian gets into trouble. After the patrol was formed, there were no arrests of Indians for 22 straight weekends. Ironically, it was during a prison term for burglary that Bellecourt decided he could help other Indians. "I read a lot of books," he says, "and I started finding out that I wasn't a savage, that I wasn't dirty—and that I was smart." For his work, he is paid a salary by the Urban Coalition.

The new Indian activism is gradually beating its way into the nation's consciousness—and into its conscience. In ways both salutary and shabby. Indians are becoming fashionable. As *The New Yorker's* Calvin Trillin recently observed: "It is almost possible to hear the drums in the East Sixties."

The Indian is spicing his protest with a grim kind of humor. His slogans proclaim: KEMO SABE MEANS HONKY, RED POWER!, and CUSTER HAD IT COMING. More stingingly, Indian Folk Singer Buffy Sainte-Marie, a Cree with a degree in education and Oriental philosophy, confronts white audiences with pointed lyrics:

> When a war between nations is lost
> The loser, we know, pays the cost;
> But even when Germany fell to your hands
> You left them their pride and you left them their land

The national abuse of the Indian reached Broadway last year as the subject of serious drama. Arthur Kopit's *Indians* played only twelve weeks; some critics considered it noisy, disorganized theater; some audiences seemed to find the penitential message discomfiting.

A pro-Indian movie, *Little Big Man,* starring Dustin Hoffman, has been filmed on Montana's Crow reservation. It portrays George Custer as a villain leading troops bent on genocide. Three books personalizing Indian alienation have won critical acclaim. A novel, *House Made of Dawn,* by N. Scott Momaday, a Kiowa who teaches English at Berkeley, won a Pulitzer prize last year. *Custer Died for Your Sins,* by Vine Deloria, a Standing Rock Sioux, wryly details the Indians' own infighting and their frustrations in dealing with white society. *Our Brother's Keeper: The Indian in White America* angrily indicts whites for keeping the Indian a stranger in his homeland—"America's prisoner of war."

On the fad level, a budding renaissance of Indian cultural accouterments has inspired pot-smoking teen-agers and high-fashion socialites to don beaded necklaces, fringed jackets, Indian belts, bikinis and feathers. Most Indians scoff at the affectation and claim that much of the clothing is foreign made.

THE HANDICAP OF DIGNITY

Why has it taken the Indian so long to rouse himself to turn his ire toward action? Many a white bureaucrat, ruling a reservation like a colonial army officer, has assumed that Indian acquiescence stemmed from either respect or servility. Rarely has it been either. The Indian nation was physically shattered and spiritually demoralized by the U.S. Cavalry, which systematically destroyed its leaders and the best of its manhood in the late 19th century campaigns that whites euphemistically call the pacification of the West. Long before the white man's arrival, Indian tribes had, of course, waged limited war upon one another over hunting rights, and raids for revenge were common.

Yet on a personal level, Indian culture shuns confrontation. Even the meeting of eyes and the firm handshake were long avoided. Discussions of personal problems are painful. Indians have been known to sit in Government offices for hours before deciding to air a grievance, however just. "My mother won't even get rid of a salesman," says the Navajos' Michael Benson.

For too long, Indian dissent also has been stifled by their forced dependency upon whites for land and livelihood. This has made many of them regard white authority as an almost magical thing. One veteran scholar of Arizona's Hopis, E. D. Newcomer, notes that today's young Hopis even "feel that the god of the whites must be better than their own gods, because the whites have new clothes and shiny cars."

Handicapped by their special definition of dignity and fractionalized by their allegiances to about 300 tribes, the 652,000 Indians in the U.S.

have never developed a unity that would sustain massive protest.[1] "Remember, I'm not Indian, I'm Osage," declares Charles Lohah, an Oklahoma judge who finds political intrigue both within and among tribes fascinatingly complex. "Often we have to strap our shields to our backs," he says. But Indians have also watched the nation respond to the marches, sit-ins and street tactics of restive blacks. Indians feel little affinity with blacks, and there is friction between the races in some federal antipoverty programs; still, the Indians are beginning to demand their share of the action.

That demand is not only just but long overdue. Ford Foundation President McGeorge Bundy insists flatly that "the American Indians are by any measure save cultural heritage the country's most disadvantaged minority." After studying U.S. ill-treatment of the Indian 26 years ago, Swedish Sociologist Gunnar Myrdal described it as "a morality play of profound importance" to American history. He said that it "challenges the most precious assumptions about what this country stands for—cultural pluralism, freedom of conscience and action, and the pursuit of happiness." The morality play is still a bad show today.

The indicators of Indian suffering are appalling. Their life expectancy is 44 years, compared with 71 for white Americans. The average income for each Indian family living on a reservation—and more than half do—is only $1,500. The average years of schooling is 5.5, well behind that of both the black and the Mexican American. Some officials rate 90% of reservation housing as substandard. Unemployment ranges from a low of 20% on the more affluent reservations to 80% on the poorest. The birth rate of Indians is 2½ times that of whites—and a majority of Indians are under 20 years old. The average family has to carry water for its daily needs at least a mile. It is usually done afoot.

Indians, of course, are not statistics, and TIME Correspondent James Willwerth discovered that individual reality for Indians often consists of human deprivation in a setting of uplifting natural beauty. Visiting Arizona's White Mountain Apache reservation, he reported: "The land is like a painting—hills covered with ponderosa pine, snow-capped mountains in the distance, sprawling valleys filled for thick forests and rushing streams. In the midst of all this, there's a one-room shack with a corrugated metal roof that shows daylight from every angle. This is Judy's house. Judy is in her mid-20s, stocky but not fat, and rather pretty. But she drinks a lot, gets into fights when she does, and often ends up in jail.

"Her lovers are legion. The result of one liaison toddles toward me

---

[1] At the time of Columbus, the native population of what is now the U.S. was probably between 1,000,000 and 3,000,000. By 1860, that had dropped to about 340,000, and by 1910 to an all-time low of 220,000. No longer vanishing, the Indians are now the nation's fastest-growing minority.

through broken glass and excrement. He's less than two years old. He lived with Judy's sister until recently, but Judy took him back to get some welfare money. Now they are living in this one-room place. 'It's got no windows,' she says. 'But that's nothing. I've never lived in a house with windows.' "

The grim individual vignettes are multiplied among entire tribes. In northern Arizona, twelve small villages of the deeply religious Hopis fight their uncertain struggle to avoid extinction. Reversing years of decline, the Hopis now number 6,000. Isolated for centuries, even their own villages still have no political links with one another. They live on three massive sandstone mesas in the Painted Desert, where pasture land is scarce and only their skillful dry-farming of corn provides a meager diet.

The sole tribal commerce of the Hopis is a trailer court and a few arts-and-crafts shops. Yet the hope of the Hopis lies in their determination to improve their condition. They teach their children to value schooling so highly that the average daily attendance in their elementary schools is a surprising 90%—a rarity among Indians. A score of older youngsters take a bus each day and make a 96-mile round trip to attend high school. Each day 50 adult Hopis get up at 5 a.m. to board a yellow bus and ride 65 miles to their jobs at a BVD underwear plant. Things may get better. Coal has been found on Hopi land, and a strip mine is scheduled to open this year. Ironically, the Hopi devotion to education is diluting what they value most: their own special kind of polytheistic belief that each living thing possesses a human spirit. Now, when elders hold their annual dance with rattlesnakes, many Hopi children laugh.

Agony and Anomie

To live in squalor while surrounded by beauty, to desire a better material life while clinging to tradition is, for American Indians, to know agony and anomie. Their alienation is aggravated by the fact that Indian culture is vastly different from that of whites in terms of technology, productivity and intellectual interests. From the viewpoint of what makes a modern civilization work, Indian culture appears hopelessly irrelevant. To some extent, the collision of Western and Indian cultures warped the conquerors' attitude. When the Senecas sought assurances from President Thomas Jefferson in 1802 that their rights would be protected, no attempt was made to bridge the cultural gap. They received a patronizing note from a secretary that said: "Brothers, your father, the President, will at all times be your friend and he will protect you and all his red children from bad people."

Only last fall Ted Rushton of New Mexico's Gallup *Independent* wrote haughtily of "the inevitable clash of a superior culture with a vastly inferior culture."

The Indian child who attends school with whites must brace himself for taunts: when it rains, he is told, "You must have done your dance." If he has a girl friend, he is asked: "How's your squaw?" Or it may be "Hey, Tonto, where's your horse?' and "What number is your teepee?" "Indian kids are shy, and can't take this," explains Gary Fife, 19, an Oklahoma Cherokee-Creek student at Northeastern State College.

Prejudice is as painful a fact to Indians as it is to blacks. Indians suffer just as harshly from biased history books. One text observes that "it is probably true that all the American Indian tribes in the course of their wandering lived for some generations on the frozen wastes of Alaska. This experience deadened their minds and killed their imagination and initiative." A white teacher in a Chippewa reservation school recently asked Indian children to write essays on "Why we are all happy the Pilgrims landed." Western movies and television, of course, still portray the Indian as the savage marauder. "How are you going to expect the Indian to feel a part of America when every television program shows him to be a brute or a stupid animal?" asks Ray Fadden, owner of a Mohawk museum in northern New York. On an Apache reservation, even an Indian girl was caught up in the TV drama. As an Indian actor crept up on an unsuspecting cowboy, the girl involuntaryily shouted at the cowboy: "Get him! Get him!"

Indians smolder when the white operators of trading posts sell their Indian-crafted goods to tourists at 400% markups. They resent the white sportsmen who gun down caribou from airplanes, while their own hunting for lifesaving game is restricted by white laws. They become furious at the white shopkeepers' use of Indian religious symbols and bad portraits of Indian chiefs. Don Wilkerson, the Cherokee-Creek director of the Phoenix Indian Center, claims that a bar in Scottsdale, Ariz., has a huge picture of a great Indian chief on its roof as an advertising gimmick. "The Jewish people would not permit such treatment of one of their revered leaders," he says. "Nor would society allow Martin Luther King to be so humiliated."

ALCOHOLISM AND SUICIDE

Dispirited by poverty, rejected by a white culture in which they are often unable and unwilling to compete, many Indians choose death or drink. The suicide rate among Indian teen-agers is three times the national average; on some reservations it is ten times as high. Shattered by her parents' broken marriage, an 18-year-old Blackfoot girl not long ago killed herself on her Montana reservation with an overdose of tranquilizers, though she was an honor student. Accused of drinking during school hours, a 16-year-old youth on Idaho's Fort Hall Reservation hanged himself in the county jail. Just two days before, he had talked about conditions on the reservation with Senator Robert F. Kennedy.

Alcohol has long been a means of escape from boredom and pressures for Indians. On one Midwest reservation containing 4,600 adults, 44% of all the men and 21% of the women were arrested at least once for drunkenness in a span of three years. Many reservations have opened bars and liquor stores to keep Indians from killing themselves in auto accidents en route home from binges in the city. A much-repeated explanation quotes Bill Pensoneau, president of the National Indian Youth Council, as telling a new commissioner of Indian Affairs: "We drown ourselves in wine and smother ourselves in glue—because the only time we are free is when we're drunk."

The Paternalist BIA

Sober or drunk, most Indians cite the Bureau of Indian Affairs when they lament their troubles. A unit of the Interior Department, it is supposed to help all native Americans under federal jurisdiction to achieve a better life, mainly by offering education and medical care and protecting their land, water and other treaty rights. More often, it suffocates Indians with its all-encompassing paternalistic authority. An Indian must have BIA permission to sell his land; he is taught by BIA teachers, and if he cannot support his children they may be taken from his home by the BIA and placed in boarding schools or with white foster parents. Most BIA employes are white.

The first Indian head of the BIA in this century was Robert Bennett, appointed by President Johnson in 1966 and admired by most moderate Indian leaders. An Oneida from Wisconsin and a career BIA man, Bennett resigned in dismay last July, charging that "the new Administration has completely ignored the Indians." His successor is Louis Bruce, part Mohawk and part Oglala Sioux, who seems just as frustrated as his people in dealing with the Great White Father. "I keep hearing terrible and sad things that are happening that I didn't know about." One trouble with the bureau, claims one of its most effective field men, is that it is overstaffed at top levels (there is one BIA employee for every 18 reservation Indians), and it takes three years to get new funds to pave a road. "We have created a monster," he says.

Indians have seen countless treaties broken, their lands diminished from 138 million acres in 1887 to 55 million acres today, their water diverted. They are convinced that the Government is determined eventually to dismiss the whole problem by terminating all reservations. Long a favorite white liberal policy, based on the assumption that all minorities will thrive by being assimilated into the mystical American melting pot, termination of the reservations is now heatedly rejected by nearly all Indian leaders. These Indians now want first to conserve all that is best of their own heritage, summed up in the slogan INTEGRITY, NOT INTEGRATION. They are thus moving in tandem with black groups that have rejected integration in favor of black power. Theoretically, at least, Indians have several advantages over the blacks in moving toward their goals. They have available a whole federal bureaucracy that professes to want the same end. While they lack national unity, their tribal traditions give them a sense of self-identity. And above all, they have their own lands.[2]

To Keep the Land

The fight to preserve those lands and the water required to make their acreage livable is a constant one for U.S. Indians. The Senecas are still bitter about the 10,000 acres taken in 1964 by the Army Corps of Engineers for the Kinzua Dam. The Senecas were paid $3,000,000, but to them land is no mere matter of money—it is a spiritual as well as a sustaining resource. The Tuscaroras of New York lost 553 acres to a reservoir in the late 1950s. They were paid $850,000, only to learn that nearby Niagara University got $5,000,000 for just 200 acres.

Currently, Indians in New Mexico, Montana and California are locked in battles with various Government agencies for control of land and water. The Paiutes of western Nevada have watched their emerald-green Pyramid Lake, ancient source of their cutthroat trout, shrink to one-third its former size by various water-diversion projects. The lake's ecological balance has been destroyed, and most of the fish have died.

The most dramatic controversy over native lands is one now raging over the ownership of 90% of the acreage of Alaska. Aided by some of the nation's best lawyers, including former Supreme Court Justice Arthur Goldberg and former Attorney General Ramsey Clark, 55,000 Indians, Eskimos and Aleuts contend that they hold title to the Alaskan land because the U.S. did not purchase it from Russia in 1867; it bought only the right to tax and govern the territory. When Alaska became a state in 1959, the state began to assert claim to the area. It

---

[2] The first reservation opened in 1853, and the system still includes some 284 BIA-supervised enclaves. Indians are free to leave reservations, whenever they wish, but those who do not live on them do not benefit from most Indian-aid programs. All Indians were granted full citizenship status in 1924.

has seized 450,000 acres for itself. The natives are willing to give up all except 40 million acres—10% of the state— at a price of $500 million and a 2% royalty on revenues from the surrender lands. If they do not get satisfaction this time, the native groups calculate that they have sufficient legal options to tie up the land in court contests for years.

Today activist Indians throughout the U.S. are determined to push all such holding operations to the limit of their resources, since they have seen the devastating impact of closed-door reservations. The Menominees of Wisconsin had good schools and community services, plus a sawmill owned by the tribe, when they were "terminated" in 1961. Since then, many Menominees have had to sell their lands to pay taxes in their new ownership status. The Indian hospital shut down and sawmill profits dwindled. As a result, the state paid out more than six times as much money in welfare to the Menominees as before— and the Menominees lost their identity. "The Menominee tribe is dead," reports Professor Gary Orfield in a study for the University of Chicago, "but for no good reason." Also terminated in 1961, Oregon's Klamath tribe suffered soaring rates in suicides, crime and drunkenness.

There are, however, encouraging signs of progress on some reservations. The Lummi tribe of Washington State, a sea-oriented people along Puget Sound, are using federal funds and considerable hard labor to develop the most advanced aquafarm in the U.S. They control the spawning and cultivating of oysters, the breeding of hybrid steelhead-rainbow trout and the harvesting of algae, used in making toothpaste, ice cream and pudding. It may net $1,000 an acre for the Indians, compared with at most $40 an acre in land farming.

Elsewhere some 150 commercial and industrial enterprises, among them General Dynamics and Fairchild Camera, have moved onto Indian reservations, enticed by the freedom from real estate taxes accorded reservation enterprises—and by cheap labor. They provide jobs and profits for individual Indians as well as their tribes. Simpson Cox, a white Phoenix lawyer, has spent 22 years with the Gila River Pima-Maricopa Indians, successfully pressing the Government to compensate the tribe fairly for confiscating their lands. He has helped them build industrial parks, a tourist center, a trade school, farms, community centers and an airstrip.

Antipoverty funds are also beginning to benefit Indians, since by any definition no group in the U.S. is more impoverished than Indians. One group utilizing such funds is Oklahoma for Indian Opportunity, founded by LaDonna Harris, the attractive, mixed-blood Comanche wife of Senator Fred Harris, chairman of the Democratic National Committee. Her group fights federal red tape to help reservation Indians, gathers evidence when whites discriminate against them, forms buying clubs to combat high grocery prices, trains young Indians for jobs and leadership. There are sharp contrasts in the efforts to help reservation Indians. Navajos at their tribal headquarters in Window Rock, Ariz., have eagerly taken to instruction in the use of a computer to handle industrial-development projects. In northern Minnesota, Indians had strayed so far from their traditions that white sportsmen had to be employed to teach them the rudiments of canoeing, water safety and fishing.

LIFE IN THE CITY

Indians also now have a few influential voices in the U.S. Congress. One of them belongs to Senator Edward Kennedy, whose subcommittee on Indian education recently charged that "our nation's policies and programs for educating American Indians are a national tragedy." Another friend is Minnesota Senator Walter Mondale. An honorary Chippewa chief, Mondale criticizes Indian schools as containing the elements of disaster. "The first thing an Indian learns is that he is a loser."

The Indians who move off the land and into big cities are indeed apt to become losers. More than 200,000 Indians have done so. They do not congregate as closely as blacks, partly because they meet less resistance in moving into low-income white neighborhoods. There are nearly 60,000 in Los Angeles, perhaps 20,000 in the San Francisco Bay area, about 12,000 in Phoenix, 15,000 on Chicago's North Side. Some 12,000 inhabit the Minneapolis-St. Paul area, almost half in shabby apartment houses and creaky Victorian houses near Minneapolis' Franklin Avenue, which cops and Indians alike call "the reservation."

TIME Correspondent Richard Saltonstall talked to many Indians who had tried the urban life. "Nobody mistreated me in Dallas," he was told by Donna Flood, a mixed-blood Ponca. "But I was unhappy there. It was too fast. There was noise, fumes, confusion—the white man's problems. In the city you lose your contact and feeling for the land. You become isolated." Hiner Doublehead, a Cherokee with two children, took his family to Chicago. "God, it was a jungle when we got there," he recalled. "The people lived like foreigners—unfriendly, clannish. It was the closeness and the crammed-in living that got to me. The bars were the only places to get acquainted and to unwind. But the friendships never went far. Nobody would invite you up to his house. I didn't feel like I was human up there."

Even the Indians who manage to make it often get restless and long to return to their reservation families for spiritual renewal. Many do so, abruptly abandoning jobs. It is the lure of the land, most often, that proves irresistible. "They used to tell me that the land is like your mother," explains Tom Cook, a 21-year-old Mohawk. "The trees are your brothers, as are the birds in the air and the fish in the water. They give you life; they give you food; they give you everything. It was so pretty the way my grandmother used to tell it." Cook attends college in New York City and is a full-time steelworker in Manhattan.

SOMETHING OF VALUE

Indian grievances are specific, but the goals of redress so far remain diffuse. There are no Indian leaders who, with any confidence of national support from their people, can speak on precisely what should be done. Traditionalists merely tend to look at the mountains that have sheltered their tribes for centuries and at the writings of their ancestral prophets, and they say patiently: "We'll outlast you whites." There are others who seek accommodation of white and Indian cultures. Says Ronnie Lupe, tribal chairman of the White Mountain Apaches: "We know what the white man offers us. There are certain comforts in your culture—good homes, good cars, good jobs—but there is a certain way to get these and yet retain our identity, and we have yet to find it."

But even that kind of reasonableness is dismissed by the new Indian militants as the talk of "Uncle Tom-Toms" or "Uncle Tomahawks" and "Stand-Around-the-Fort Indians." What these leaders seem to want most is for the Federal Government, which now spends only $500 million a year on aid to Indians, to increase its spending for Indian schools, roads, housing and medical care—and to stop smothering Indians with restrictive regulations and unwanted advice on how to run their affairs. They want their water and land rights protected and expanded, not contracted through treaty violations. They want help in attracting job-providing industries to their reservations, but they want to determine what kinds and how they will be operated. They want federal benevolence, in short, as compensation for the loss of more than half a continent, but they want to be free to go their own way—even though they are not yet certain of their direction.

The Indians' longing to live harmoniously with nature touches recesses of nostalgia in the minds of many Americans. Indeed, at a time when the drive to protect and restore the nation's physical environment is the most popular cause of the day, whites' guilt over their spoilage of air, land and water engenders a new admiration for those who have fought for so long to protect their own plains, lakes and hunting grounds. It would be wrong to romanticize Indian culture, but there is something to be valued, or at least envied, in a society that respects the wisdom of elders, enjoys the closeness of kinship, prefers tranquillity to competition, and sees little merit in 9-to-5 punctuality at a desk.

Although they now live in what one Indian calls "a schizoid world of fractured loyalties," all Indian leaders agree that the best of their ancient heritage is a priceless resource. To many white Americans, who are constantly told these days how much they have to feel guilty about, the demands of yet one more minority may seem almost more than the conscience can bear. Yet Indians can hardly be expected to keep their peace just because they have only lately joined the queue of those vociferously demanding social justice. If they continued to be rejected, many young Indians will continue to despair and will embrace the sentiments of Phil George, a young Nez Perce, who wrote:

> This summer I shall
> Return to our Longhouse.
> Hide beneath a feathered hat,
> And become an Old Man.

The new militants reject such resignation, and are determined that Indians be heard along with all of America's second-class citizens. Their aim is nothing less than to reverse the perspectives of the races. Explains one:

You will forgive me if I tell you that my people were Americans for thousands of years before your people were. The question is not how you can Americanize us but how we can Americanize you. The first thing we want to teach you is that, in the American way of life, each man has respect for his brother's vision. Because each of us respected his brother's dream, we enjoyed freedom here while your people were busy killing and enslaving one another across the water. We have a hard trail ahead of us, but we are not afraid of hard trails.

THE FAILURE OF BLACK SEPARATISM (1970)
BAYARD RUSTIN

An intellectual and a black moderate, Bayard Rustin (b. 1910) has been one of the most influential leaders in the civil rights movement of the past decade. Here he dismisses as unreal one of the most militant segments of the movement, and surveys the place of the black American today. Actualities do not vanish, he insists, simply because emotions demand that they do so; the future must be built upon realities.

We are living in an age of revolution—or so they tell us. The children of the affluent classes pay homage to their parents' values by rejecting them; this, they say, is a youth revolution. The discussion and display of sexuality increases—actors disrobe on stage, young women very nearly do on the street—and so we are in the midst of a sexual revolution. Tastes in music and clothing change, and each new fashion too is revolutionary. With every new social phenomenon now being dubbed a "revolution," the term has in fact become nothing more than a slogan which serves to take our minds off an unpleasant reality. For if we were not careful, we might easily forget that there is a conservative in the White House, that our country is racially polarized as never before, and that the forces of liberalism are in disarray. Whatever there is of revolution today, in any meaningful sense of the term, is coming from the Right.

But we are also told—and with far greater urgency and frequency —that there is a black revolution. If by revolution we mean a radical escalation of black aspirations and demands, this is surely the case. There is a new assertion of pride in the Negro race and its cultural heritage, and although the past summer was marked by the lack of any major disruptions, there is among blacks a tendency more pronounced than at any time in Negro history to engage in violence and the rhetoric of violence. Yet if we look closely at the situation of Negroes today, we find that there has been not the least revolutionary reallocation of political or economic power. There is, to be sure, an increase in the number of black elected officials throughout the United States and particularly in the South, but this has largely been the result of the 1965 Voting Rights Act, which was passed before the "revolution" reached its height and the renewal of which the present Administration has not advocated with any noticeable enthusiasm. Some reallocation of political power has indeed taken place since the Presidential election of 1964, but generally its beneficiaries have been the Republicans and the anti-Negro forces. Nor does this particular trend show much sign of abating. Nixon's attempt to reverse the liberal direction of the Supreme Court has just begun. Moreover, in the 1970 Senate elections, 25 of the 34 seats to be contested were originally won by the Democrats in the great liberal surge of 1964, when the political picture was quite different from that of today. And if the Democrats only break even in 1970, the Republicans will control the Senate for the first time since 1954. A major defeat would leave the Democrats weaker than they have been at any time since the conservative days of the 1920s.

There has been, it is true, some moderate improvement in the economic condition of Negroes, but by no stretch of the imagination could it be called revolutionary. According to Andrew Brimmer of the Federal Reserve System, the median family income of Negroes between 1965 and 1967 rose from 54 per cent to 59 per cent of that for white families. Much of that gain reflected a decrease in the rate of Negro unemployment. But between February and June of 1969, Negro unemployment rose again by 1.3 per cent and should continue to rise as Nixon presses his crusade against inflation. The Council of Economic

Advisers reports that in the past eight years the federal government has spent $10.3 billion on metropolitan problems while it has spent $39.9 billion on agriculture, not to mention, of course, $507.2 billion for defense. In the area of housing, for instance, New York City needs at the present time as many new subsidized apartments—780,000—as the federal housing program has constructed *nationally* in its entire thirty-four years. The appropriations for model cities, rent supplements, the Job Corps, the Neighborhood Youth Corps, and other programs have been drastically reduced, and the Office of Economic Opportunity is being transformed into a research agency. Nixon's welfare and revenue-sharing proposals, in addition to being economically stringent, so that they will have little or no effect on the condition of the Northern urban poor, are politically and philosophically conservative.

Any appearance that we are in the grip of a black revolution, then, is deceptive. The problem is not whether black aspirations are outpacing America's ability to respond but whether they have outpaced her willingness to do so. Lately it has been taken also as axiomatic that with every increase in Negro demands, there must be a corresponding intensification of white resistance. This proposition implies that only black complacency can prevent racial polarization, that any political action by Negroes must of necessity produce a reaction. But such a notion ignores entirely the question of what *kind* of political action, guided by what *kind* of political strategy. One can almost assert as a law of American politics that if Negroes engage in violence as a tactic they will be met with repression, that if they follow a strategy of racial separatism they will be isolated, and that if they engage in antidemocratic activity, out of the deluded wish to skirt the democratic process, they will provoke a reaction. To the misguided, violence, separatism, and minority ultimatums may seem revolutionary, but in reality they issue only from the desperate strivings of the impotent. Certainly such tactics are not designed to enhance the achievement of progressive social change. Recent American political history has proved this point time and again with brutal clarity.

The irony of the revolutionary rhetoric uttered in behalf of Negroes is that it has helped in fact to promote conservatism. On the other hand, of course, the reverse is also true: the failure of America to respond to the demands of Negroes has fostered in the minds of the latter a sense of futility and has thus seemed to legitimize a strategy of withdrawal and violence. Other things have been operating as well. The fifteen years since *Brown vs. Topeka* have been for Negroes a period of enormous dislocation. The modernization of farming in the South forced hundreds of thousands of Negroes to migrate to the North where they were confronted by a second technological affliction, automation. Without jobs, living in cities equipped to serve neither their material nor spiritual needs, these modern-day immigrants responded to their brutal new world with despair and hostility. The civil-rights movement created an even more fundamental social dislocation, for it destroyed not simply the legal structure of segregation but also the psychological assumptions of racism. Young Negroes who matured during this period witnessed a basic challenge to the system of values and social relations which had presumed the inferiority of the Negro. They have totally rejected this system, but in doing so have often substituted for it an exaggerated and distorted perception both of themselves and of the society. As if to obliterate the trace of racial shame that might be lurking in their souls they have embraced racial chauvinism. And as if in reply to past exclusions (and often in response to present insecurities), they have created their own patterns of exclusiveness.

The various frustrations and upheavals experienced recently by the Negro community account in large part for the present political orientation of some of its most vocal members: seeing their immediate self-interest more in the terms of emotional release than in those of economic and political advancement. One is supposed to think black, dress black, eat black, and buy black without reference to the question of what such a program actually contributes to advancing the cause of social justice. Since real victories are thought to be unattainable, issues become important in so far as they can provide symbolic victories. Dramatic confrontations are staged which serve as outlets for radical energy but which in no way further the achievement of radical social goals. So that, for instance, members of the black community are mobilized to pursue the "victory" of halting construction of a state office building in Harlem, even though it is hard to see what actual economic or social benefit will be conferred on the impoverished residents of that community by their success in doing so.

Such actions constitute a politics of escape rooted in hopelessness and further reinforced by government inaction. Deracinated liberals may romanticize this politics, nihilistic New Leftists may imitate it, but it is ordinary Negroes who will be the victims of its powerlessness to work any genuine change in their condition.

The call for Black Power is now over three years old, yet to this day no one knows what Black Power is supposed to mean and therefore how its proponents are to unite and rally behind it. If one is a member of CORE, Black Power posits the need for a separate black economy based upon traditional forms of capitalist relations. For SNCC the term refers to a politically united black community. US would emphasize the unity of black culture, while the Black Panthers wish to impose upon black nationalism the philosophies of Marx, Lenin, Stalin, and Chairman Mao. Nor do these exhaust all the possible shades and gradations of meaning. If there is one common theme uniting the various demands for Black Power, it is simply that blacks must be guided in their actions by a consciousness of themselves as a separate race.

Now, philosophies of racial solidarity have never been unduly concerned with the realities that operate outside the category of race. The adherents of these philosophies are generally romantics, steeped in the traditions of their own particular clans and preoccupied with the simple biological verities of blood and racial survival. Almost invariably their rallying cry is racial self-determination, and they tend to ignore those aspects of the material world which points up divisions within the racially defined group.

But the world of black Americans is full of divisions. Only the most supine of optimists would dream of building a political movement without reference to them. Indeed, nothing better illustrates the existence of such divisions within the black community than the fact that the separatists themselves represent a distinct minority among Negroes. No reliable poll has ever identified more than 15 per cent of Negroes as separatists; usually the percentage is a good deal lower. Nor, as I have already indicated, are the separatists unified among themselves, the differences among them at times being so intense as to lead to violent conflict. The notion of the undifferentiated black community is the intellectual creation of both whites—liberals as well as racists to whom all Negroes are the same—and of certain small groups of blacks who illegitimately claim to speak for the majority.

The fact is that like every other racial or ethnic group in America, Negroes are divided by age, class, and geography. Young Negroes are at least as hostile toward their elders as white New Leftists are toward their liberal parents. They are in addition separated by vast gaps in experience, Northern from Southern, urban from rural. And even more profound are the disparities in wealth among them. In contrast to the white community, where the spread of income has in recent years remained unchanged or has narrowed slightly, economic differentials among blacks have increased. In 1965, for example, the wealthiest 5 per cent of white and non-white families each received 15.5 per cent of the total income in their respective communities. In 1967, however, the percentage of white income received by the top 5 per cent of white families had dropped to 14.9 per cent while among non-whites the share of income of the top 5 per cent of the families had risen to 17.5 per cent. This trend probably reflects the new opportunities which are available to black professionals in industry, government, and academia, but have not touched the condition of lower-class and lower-middle-class Negroes.

To Negroes for whom race is the major criterion, however, divisions by wealth and status are irrelevant. Consider, for instance, the proposals for black economic advancement put forth by the various groups of black nationalists. These proposals are all remarkably similar. For regardless of one's particular persuasion—whether a revolutionary or a cultural nationalist or an unabashed black capitalist—once one confines one's analysis to the ghetto, no proposal can extend beyond a strategy for ghetto development and black enterprise. This explains in part the recent popularity of black capitalism and, to a lesser degree, black cooperatives: once both the economic strategy and goal are defined in terms of black self-determination, there is simply not much else available in the way of ideas.

There are other reasons for the popularity of black capitalism, reasons having to do with material and psychological self-interest. E. Franklin Frazier has written that Negro business is "a social myth" first formulated toward the end of the nineteenth century when the legal structure of segregation was established and Negro hopes for equality destroyed. History has often shown us that oppression can sometimes lead to a rationalization of the unjust conditions on the part of the oppressed and following on this, to an opportunistic competition among them for whatever meager advantages are available. This is, according to Frazier, exactly what happened among American Negroes. The myth of Negro business was created and tied to a belief in the possibility of a separate Negro economy. "Of course," wrote Frazier, "behind the idea of the separate Negro economy is the hope of the black bourgeoisie that they will have the monopoly of the Negro market." He added that they also desire "a privileged status within the isolated Negro community."

Nor are certain Negro businessmen the only ones who stand to gain from a black economy protected by the tariff of separatism. There are also those among the white upper class for whom such an arrangement is at least as beneficial. In the first place, self-help projects for the ghetto, of which black capitalism is but one variety, are inexpensive. They involve no large-scale redistribution of resources, no "inflationary" government expenditures, and above all, no responsibility on the part of whites. These same upper-class whites may have been major exploiters of black workers in the past, they may have been responsible for policies which helped to create ghetto poverty, but now, under the new dispensations of black separatism, they are being asked to do little more by way of reparation than provide a bit of seed money for a few small ghetto enterprises.

Moreover, a separate black economy appears to offer hope for what Roy Innis has called "a new social contract." According to Innis's theory, the black community is essentially a colony ruled by outsiders; there can be no peace between the colony and the "mother country" until the former is ruled by some of its own. When the colony is finally "liberated" in this way, all conflicts can be resolved through negotiation between the black ruling class and the white ruling class. Any difficulties within the black community, that is, would become the responsibility of the black elite. But since self-determination in the ghetto, necessitating as it would the expansion of a propertied black middle class, offers the advantage of social stability, such difficulties would be minimal. How could many whites fail to grasp the obvious benefit to themselves in a program that promises social peace without the social inconvenience of integration and especially without the burden of a huge expenditure of money? Even if one were to accept the colonial analogy—and it is in many ways an uninformed and extremely foolish one—the strategy implied by it is fatuous and unworkable. Most of the experiments in black capitalism thus far have been total failures. As, given the odds, they should continue to be. For one thing, small businesses owned and run by blacks will, exactly like their white counterparts, suffer a high rate of failure. In fact, they will face even greater problems than white small businesses because they will be operating in predominantly low income areas where the clientele will be poor, the crime rate and taxes high, and the cost of land, labor, and insurance expensive. They will have to charge higher prices than the large chains, a circumstance against which "Buy Black" campaigns will in the long or even the short run have little force. On the other hand, to create large-scale black industry in the ghetto is unthinkable. The capital is not available, and even if it were, there is no vacant land. In Los Angeles, for example, the area in which four-fifths of the Negroes and Mexican-Americans live contains only 0.5 per cent of all the vacant land in the city, and the problem is similar elsewhere. Overcrowding is severe enough in the ghetto without building up any industry there.

Another current axiom of black self-determination is the necessity for community control. Questions of ideology aside, black community control is as futile a program as black capitalism. Assuming that there were a cohesive, clearly indentifiable black community (which, judging by the factionalism in neighborhoods like Harlem and Ocean Hill-Brownsville, is a far from safe assumption), and assuming that the community were empowered to control the ghetto, it would still find itself without the money needed in order to be socially creative. The ghetto would still be faced with the same poverty, deteriorated housing, unemployment, terrible health services, and inferior schools —and this time perhaps with the exacerbation of their being entailed in local struggles for power. Furthermore, the control would ultimately be illusory and would do no more than provide psychological comfort to those who exercise it. For in a complex technological society there is no such thing as an autonomous community within a large metropolitan area. Neighborhoods, particularly poor neighborhoods, will remain dependent upon outside suppliers for manufactured goods, transportation, utilities, and other services. There is, for instance, unemployment in the ghetto while the vast majority of new jobs are being created in the suburbs. If black people are to have access to those jobs, there must be a metropolitan transportation system that can carry them to the suburbs cheaply and quickly. Control over the ghetto cannot build such a system nor can it provide jobs within the ghetto.

The truth of the matter is that community control as an idea is provincial and as a program is extremely conservative. It appears radical to some people because it has become the demand around which the frustrations of the Negro community have coalesced. In terms of its capacity to deal with the social and economic causes of black unrest, however, its potential is strikingly limited. The call for community control in fact represents an adjustment to inequality rather than a protest against it. Fundamentally, it is a demand for a change in the racial composition of the personnel who administer community institutions: that is, for schools, institutions of public and social service, and political organizations—as all of these are presently constituted—to be put into the keeping of a new class of black officials. Thus in a very real sense, the notion of community control bespeaks a fervent hope that the poverty-stricken ghetto, once thought to be a social problem crying for rectification, might now be deemed a social good worthy of acceptance. Hosea Williams of SCLC, speaking once of community control, unwittingly revealed the way in which passionate self-assertion can be a mask for accommodation: "I'm now at the position Booker T. Washington was about sixty or seventy years ago," Williams said. "I say to my brothers, 'Cast down your buckets where you are'—and that means there in the slums and ghettos."

There is indeed profound truth in the observation that people who seek social change will, in the absence of real substantive victories, often seize upon stylistic substitutes as an outlet for their frustrations.

A case in point is the relation of Negroes to the trade-union movement. In their study *The Black Worker,* published in 1930, Sterling D. Spero and Abram L. Harris describe the resistance to separatism among economically satisfied workers during the heyday of Marcus Garvey:

. . . spokesmen of the Garvey movement went among the faction-torn workers preaching the doctrine of race consciousness. Despite the fact the Garveyism won a following everywhere at this time, the Negro long-shoremen of Philadelphia were deaf to its pleas, for their labor movement had won them industrial equality such as colored workers nowhere else in the industry enjoyed.

The inverse relation of black separatism and anti-unionism to the quality of employment available to Negroes holds true today also. In the May 1969 UAW elections, for example, black candidates won the presidency and vice-presidency of a number of locals. Some of the most interesting election victories were won in the Chrysler Eldon Gear and Axle Local 961 and at Dodge #3 in Hamtramck where the separatist Eldon Revolutionary Union Movement (ELRUM) and Dodge Revolutionary Union Movement (DRUM) have been active. At both locals the DRUM and ELRUM candidates were handily defeated by black trade unionists who campaigned on a program of militant integrationism and economic justice.

This is not to say that there are not problems within the unions which have given impetus to the separatist movements. There are, but in the past decade unions have taken significant steps toward eliminating discrimination against Negroes. As Peter Henle, the chief economist of the Bureau of Labor Statistics, has observed:

Action has been taken to eliminate barriers to admission, abolish discrimination in hiring practices, and negotiate changes in seniority arrangements which had been blocking Negro advances to higher-paying jobs. At the same time, unions have given strong support to governmental efforts in this same direction.

Certainly a good deal is left to be done in this regard, but just as certainly the only effective pressure on the unions is that which can be brought by blacks pressing for a greater role *within* the trade-union movement. Not only is separatism not a feasible program, but its major effect will be to injure black workers economically by undermining the strength of their union. It is here that ignorance of the economic dimension of racial injustice is most dangerous, for a Negro, whether he be labeled a moderate or a militant, has but two alternatives open to him. If he defines the problem as primarily one of race, he will inevitably find himself the ally of the white capitalist against the white worker. But if, though always conscious of the play of racial discrimination, he defines the problem as one of poverty, he will be aligned with the white worker against management. If he chooses the former alternative, he will become no more than a pawn in the game of divide-and-conquer played by, and for the benefit of, management—the result of which will hardly be self-determination but rather the depression of wages for all workers. This path was followed by the "moderate" Booker T. Washington who disliked unions because they were "founded on a sort of enmity to the man by whom [the Negro] is employed" and by the "militant" Marcus Garvey who wrote:

It seems strange and a paradox, but the only convenient friend the Negro worker or laborer has in America at the present time is the white capitalist. The capitalist being selfish—seeking only the largest profit out of labor—is willing and glad to use Negro labor wherever possible on a scale reasonably below the standard union wage . . . but if the Negro unionizes himself to the level of the white worker, the choice and preference of employment is given to the white worker.

And it is being followed today by CORE, which collaborated with the National Right to Work Committee in setting up the Black Workers Alliance.

If the Negro chooses to follow the path of interracial alliances on the basis of class, as almost two million have done today, he can achieve a certain degree of economic dignity, which in turn offers a genuine, if not the only, opportunity for self-determination. It was this course which A. Philip Randolph chose in his long struggle to build a Negro-labor alliance, and it was also chosen by the black sanitation workers of Memphis, Tennessee, and the black hospital workers of Charleston, South Carolina.

Not that I mean here to exonerate the unions of their responsibility for discrimination. Nevertheless, it is essential to deal with the situation of the black worker in terms of American economic reality. And as long as the structure of this reality is determined by the competing institutions of capital and labor (or government and labor, as in the growing public sector of the economy), Negroes must place themselves on one side or the other. The idea of racial self-determination within this context is a delusion.

There are, to be sure, sources beyond that of economic discrimination for black separatism within the unions. DRUM, ELRUM, and similar groups are composed primarily of young Negroes who, like whites their age, are not as loyal to the union as are older members, and who are also affected by the new militancy which is now pervasive among black youth generally. This militancy has today found its most potent form of expression on campus, particularly in the predominantly white universities outside of the South. The confusion which the movement for programs in black studies has created on campus almost defies description. The extremes in absurdity were reached this past academic year at Cornell, where, on the one hand, enraged black students were demanding a program in black studies which included Course 300c, Physical Education: "Theory and practice in the use of small arms and hand combat. Discussion sessions in the proper use of force," and where, on the other hand, a masochistic and pusillanimous university president placed his airplane at the disposal of two black students so that they could go to New York City and purchase, with $2,000 in university funds, some bongo drums for Malcolm X Day. The foolishness of the students was surpassed only by the public-relations manipulativeness of the president.

The real tragedy of the dispute over black studies is that whatever truly creative opportunities such a program could offer have been either ignored or destroyed. There is, first, the opportunity for a vastly expanded scholastic inquiry into the contribution of Negroes to the American experience. The history of the black man in America has been scandalously distorted in the past, and as a field of study it has been relegated to a second-class status, isolated from the main themes of American history and omitted in the historical education of American youth. Yet now black students are preparing to repeat the errors of their white predecessors. They are proposing to study black history in isolation from the mainstream of American history; they are demanding separate black-studies programs that will not be open to whites, who could benefit at least as much as they from a knowledge of Negro history; and they hope to permit only blacks (and some whites who toe the line) to teach in these programs. Unwittingly they are conceding what racist whites all along have professed to believe, namely, that black history is irrelevant to American history.

In other ways black students have displayed contempt for black studies as an academic discipline. Many of them, in fact, view black studies as not an academic subject at all, but as an ideological and political one. They propose to use black-studies programs to create a mythologized history and a system of assertive ideas that will facilitate the political mobilization of the black community. In addition, they hope to educate a cadre of activists whose present training is conceived of as a preparation for organizational work in the ghetto. The Cornell students made this very clear when they defined the purpose of black-studies programs as enabling "black people to use the knowledge gained in the classroom and community to formulate new ideologies and philosophies which will contribute to the development of the black nation.

Thus faculty members will be chosen on the basis of race, ideological purity, and political commitment—not academic competence. Under such conditions, few qualified black professors will want to teach in black-studies programs, not simply because their academic freedom will be curtailed by their obligation to adhere to the revolutionary "line" of the moment, but because their professional status will be threatened by their association with programs of such inferior quality.

Black students are also forsaking the opportunity to get an education. They appear to be giving little thought to the problem of teaching or learning those technical skills that all students must acquire if they are to be effective in their careers. We have here simply another example of the pursuit of symbolic victory where a real victory seems too difficult to achieve. It is easier for a student to alter his behavior and appearance than to improve the quality of his mind. If engineering requires too much concentration, then why not a course in soul music? If Plato is both "irrelevant" and difficult, the student can read Malcolm X instead. Class will be a soothing, comfortable experience, somewhat like watching television. Moreover, one's image will be militant and, therefore, acceptable by current college standards. Yet one will have learned nothing, and the fragile sense of security developed in the protective environment of college will be cracked when exposed to the reality of competition in the world.

Nelson Taylor, a young Negro graduate of Morehouse College, recently observed that many black students "feel it is useless to try to compete. In order to avoid this competition, they build themselves a little cave to hide in." This "little cave," he added, is black studies. Furthermore, black students are encouraged in this escapism by guiltridden New Leftists and faculty members who despise themselves and their advantaged lives and enjoy seeing young Negroes reject "white middle-class values" and disrupt the university. They are encouraged by university administrators who prefer political accommodation to an effort at serious education. But beyond the momentary titillation some may experience from being the center of attention, it is difficult to see how Negroes can in the end benefit from being patronized and manipulated in this way. Ultimately, their only permanent satisfaction can come from the certainty that they have acquired the technical and intellectual skills that will enable them upon graduation to perform significant jobs competently and with confidence. If they fail to acquire these skills, their frustration will persist and find expression in ever-newer forms of antisocial and self-destructive behavior.

The conflict over black studies, as over other issues, raises the question of the function in general served by black protest today. Some black demands, such as that for a larger university enrollment of minority students, are entirely legitimate; but the major purpose of the protest through which these demands are pressed would seem to be not so much to pursue an end as to establish in the minds of the protesters, as well as in the minds of whites, the reality of their rebellion. Protest, therefore, becomes an end in itself and not a means toward social change. In this sense, the black rebellion is an enormously *expressive* phenomenon which is releasing the pent-up resentments of generations of oppressed Negroes. But expressiveness that is oblivious to political reality and not structured by instrumental goals is mere bombast.

James Forman's *Black Manifesto,* for instance, provides a nearly perfect sample of this kind of bombast combined with positive delusions of grandeur. "We shall liberate all the people in the U.S.," the introduction the *Manifesto* declares, "and we will be instrumental in the liberation of colored people the world around. . . . We are the most humane people within the U.S. . . . Racism in the U. S. is so pervasive in the mentality of white that only an armed, well-disciplined, black-controlled government can insure the stamping out of racism in this country. . . . We say think in terms of the total control of the U.S."

One might never imagine from reading the *Manifesto* that Forman's organization, the National Black Economic Development Conference, is politically powerless, or that the institution it has chosen for assault is not the government or the corporations, but the church. Indeed, the exaggeration of language in the *Black Manifesto* is directly proportional to the isolation and impotence of those who drafted it. And their actual achievements provide an accurate measure of their strength. Three billion dollars in reparations was demanded—and $20,000 received. More important, the effect of this demand upon the Protestant churches has been to precipitate among them a conservative reaction against the activities of the liberal national denominations and the National Council of Churches. Forman's failure, of course, was to be expected: the only effect of an attack upon so organizationally diffuse and nonpolitical an institution as the church can be the deflection of pressure away from the society's major political and economic institutions and, consequently, the weakening of the black movement for equality.[1]

The possibility that his *Manifesto* might have exactly the opposite effect from that intended, however, was clearly not a problem to Forman, because the demands he was making upon white people were more moral than political or economic. His concern was to purge white guilt far more than to seek social justice for Negroes. It was in part for this reason that he chose to direct his attack at the church, which, as the institutional embodiment of our society's religious pretensions, is vulnerable to moral condemnation.

Yet there is something corrupting in the wholesale release of aggressive moral energy, particularly when it is in response to the demand for reparations for blacks. The difficulty is not only that as a purely racial demand its effect must be to isolate blacks from the white poor with whom they have common economic interests. The call for three billion dollars in reparations demeans the integrity of blacks and exploits the self-demeaning guilt of whites. It is insulting to Negroes to offer them reparations for past generations of suffering, as if the balance of an irreparable past could be set straight with a handout. In a recent poll, *Newsweek* reported that "today's proud Negroes, by an overwhelming 84 to 10 per cent, reject the idea of preferential treatment in hiring or college admissions in reparation for past injustices." There are few controversial issues that can call forth greater uniformity of opinion than this in the Negro community.

I also question both the efficacy and the social utility of an attack that impels the attacked to applaud and debase themselves. I am not

---

[1] Forman is not the only militant today who fancies that his essentially reformist program is revolutionary. Eldridge Cleaver has written that capitalists regard the Black Panther Breakfast for Children program (which the Panthers claim feeds 10,000 children) "as a threat, as cutting into the goods that are under their control." He also noted that it "liberates" black children from going to school hungry each morning. I wonder if he would also find public-school lunch programs liberating.

certain whether or not self-flagellation can have a beneficial effect on the sinner (I tend to doubt that it can), but I am absolutely certain it can never produce anything politically creative. It will not improve the lot of unemployed and the ill-housed. On the other hand, it could well happen that the guilty party, in order to lighten his uncomfortable moral burden, will finally begin to rationalize his sins and affirm them as virtues. And by such a process, today's ally can become tomorrow's enemy. Lasting political alliances are not built on the shifting sands of moral suasion.

On his part, the breast-beating white makes the same error as the Negro who swears that "black is beautiful." Both are seeking refuge in psychological solutions to social questions. And both are reluctant to confront the real cause of racial injustice, which is not bad attitudes but bad social conditions. The Negro creates a new psychology to avoid the reality of social stagnation, and the white—be he ever so liberal—professes his guilt precisely so as to create the illusion of social change, all the while preserving his economic advantages.

The response of guilt and pity to social problems is by no means new. It is, in fact, as old as man's capacity to rationalize or his reluctance to make real sacrifices for his fellow man. Two hundred years ago, Samuel Johnson, in an exchange with Boswell, analyzed the phenomenon of sentimentality:

Boswell: "I have often blamed myself, Sir, for not feeling for others, as sensibly as many say they do."

Johnson: "Sir, don't be duped by them any more. You will find these very feeling people are not ready to do you good. They *pay* you by *feeling*."

Today, payments from the rich to the poor take the form of "Giving a Damn" or some other kind of moral philanthropy. At the same time, of course, some of those who so passionately "Give a Damn" are likely to argue that full employment is inflationary.

We are living in a time of great social confusion—not only about the strategies we must adopt but about the very goals these strategies are to bring us to. Only recently whites and Negroes of good will were pretty much in agreement that racial and economic justice required an end to segregation and the expansion of the role of the federal government. Now it is a mark of "advancement," not only among "progressive" whites but among the black militants as well, to believe that integration is passé. Unintentionally (or as the Marxists used to say, objectively), they are lending aid and comfort to traditional segregationists like Senators Eastland and Thurmond. Another "advanced" idea is the notion that government has gotten too big and that what is needed to make the society more humane and livable is an enormous new move toward local participation and decentralization. One cannot question the value or importance of democratic participation in the government, but just as misplaced sympathy for Negroes is being put to use by segregationists, the liberal preoccupation with localism is serving the cause of conservatism. Two years of liberal encomiums to decentralization have intellectually legitimized the concept, if not the name, of states' rights and have set the stage for the widespread acceptance of Nixon's "New Federalism."

The new anti-integrationism and localism may have been motivated by sincere moral conviction, but hardly by intelligent political thinking. It should be obvious that what is needed today more than ever is a political strategy that offers the real possibility of economically uplifting millions of impoverished individuals, black and white. Such a strategy must of necessity give low priority to the various forms of economic and psychological experimentation that I have discussed, which at best deal with issues peripheral to the central problem and at worst embody a frenetic escapism. These experiments are based on the assumption that the black community can be transformed from within when, in fact, any such transformation must depend on structural changes in the entire society. Negro poverty, for example, will not be eliminated in the absence of a total war on poverty. We need, therefore, a new national economic policy. We also need new policies in housing, education, and health care which can deal with these problems as they relate to Negroes within the context of a national solution. A successful strategy, therefore, must rest upon an identification of those central institutions which, if altered sufficiently, would transform the social and economic relations in our society; and it must provide a politically viable means of achieving such an alteration.

Surely the church is not a central institution in this sense. Nor is Roy Innis's notion of dealing with the banking establishment a useful one. For the banks will find no extra profit—quite the contrary —in the kind of fundamental structural change in society that is required.[2]

Moreover, the recent flurry of excitement over the role of private industry in the slums seems to have subsided. A study done for the Urban Coalition has called the National Alliance of Businessmen's claim to have hired more than 100,000 hard-core unemployed a "phony numbers game." Normal hiring as the result of expansion or turnover was in some cases counted as recruitment. Where hard-core workers have been hired and trained, according to the study, "The primary motivation . . . is the need for new sources of workers in a tight labor market. If and when the need for workers slackens, so will industry's

---

[2] Innis's demand that the white banks deposit $6 billion in black banks as reparations for past injustices should meet with even less success than Forman's ill-fated enterprise. At least Forman had the benefit of the white churchman's guilt, an emotion not known to be popular among bankers.

performance." This has already occurred. The *Wall Street Journal* reported in July of 1969 that the Ford Motor Company, once praised for its social commitment, was forced to trim back production earlier in the year and in the process "quietly closed its two inner-city hiring centers in Detroit and even laid off some of the former hard-cores it had only recently hired." There have been similar retrenchments by other large companies as the result of a slackening in economic growth, grumblings from stockholders, and the realization by corporate executives that altruism does not make for higher profits. Yet even if private industry were fully committed to attack the problem of unemployment, it is not in an ideal position to do so. Private enterprise, for example, accounted for only one out of every ten new jobs created in the economy between 1950 and 1960. Most of the remainder were created as the result of expansion of public employment.

While the church, private enterprise, and other institutions can, if properly motivated, play an important role, finally it is the trade-union movement and the Democratic party which offer the greatest leverage to the black struggle. The serious objective of Negroes must be to strengthen and liberalize these. The trade-union movement is essential to the black struggle because it is the only institution in the society capable of organizing the working poor, so many of whom are Negroes. It is only through an organized movement that these workers, who are now condemned to the margin of the economy, can achieve a measure of dignity and economic security. I must confess I find it difficult to understand the prejudice against the labor movement currently fashionable among so many liberals. These people, somehow for reasons of their own, seem to believe that white workers are affluent members of the Establishment (a rather questionable belief, to put it mildly, especially when held by people earning over $25,000 a year) and are now trying to keep the Negroes down. The only grain of truth here is that there *is* competition between black and white workers which derives from a scarcity of jobs and resources. But rather than propose an expansion of those resources, our stylish liberals underwrite that competition by endorsing the myth that the unions are the worst enemy of the Negro.

In fact it is the program of the labor movement that represents a genuine means for reducing racial competition and hostility. Not out of a greater tenderness of feeling for black suffering—but that is just the point. Unions organize workers on the basis of common economic interests, not by virtue of racial affinity. Labor's legislative program for full employment, housing, urban reconstruction, tax reform, improved health care, and expanded educational opportunities is designed specifically to aid both whites and blacks in the lower- and lower-middle classes where the potential for racial polarization is most severe. And only a program of this kind can deal simultaneously and creatively with the interrelated problems of black rage and white fear. It does not placate black rage at the expense of whites, thereby increasing white fear and political reaction. Nor does it exploit white fear by repressing blacks. Either of these courses strengthens the demagogues among both races who prey upon frustration and racial antagonism. Both of them help to strengthen conservative forces—the forces that stand to benefit from the fact that hostility between black and white workers keeps them from uniting effectively around issues of common economic interest.

President Nixon is in the White House today largely because of this hostility; and the strategy advocated by many liberals to build a "new coalition" of the affluent, the young, and the dispossessed is designed to keep him there. The difficulty with this proposed new coalition is not only that its constituents comprise a distinct minority of the population, but that its affluent and youthful members—regardless of the momentary direction of their rhetoric—are hardly the undisputed friends of the poor. Recent Harris polls, in fact, have shown that Nixon is most popular among the college educated and the young. Perhaps they were attracted by his style or the minimal concessions he has made on Vietnam, but certainly their approval cannot be based upon his accomplishments in the areas of civil rights and economic justice.

If the Republican ascendancy is to be but a passing phenomenon, it must once more come to be clearly understood among those who favor social progress that the Democratic party is still the only mass-based political organization in the country with the potential to become a majority movement for social change. And anything calling itself by the name of political activity must be concerned with building precisely such a majority movement. In addition, Negroes must abandon once and for all the false assumption that as 10 per cent of the population they can by themselves effect basic changes in the structure of American life. They must, in other words, accept the necessity of coalition politics. As a result of our fascination with novelty and the "new" revolutionary forces that have emerged in recent years, it seems to some the height of conservatism to propose a strategy that was effective in the past. Yet the political reality is that without a coalition of Negroes and other minorities with the trade-union movement and with liberal groups, the shift of power to the Right will persist and the democratic Left in America will have to content itself with a well-nigh permanent minority status.

The bitterness of many young Negroes today has led them to be unsympathetic to a program based on the principles of trade unionism and electoral politics. Their protest represents a refusal to accept the condition of inequality, and in that sense it is part of the long, and I think, magnificent black struggle for freedom. But with no comprehensive strategy to replace the one I have suggested, their protest, though militant in rhetoric and intention, may be reactionary in effect.

The strategy I have outlined must stand or fall by its capacity to achieve political and economic results. It is not intended to provide some new wave of intellectual excitement. It is not intended to suggest a new style of life or a means to personal salvation for disaffected members of the middle class. Nor is either of these the proper role of politics. My strategy is not meant to appeal to the fears of threatened whites, though it would calm those fears and increase the livelihood that some day we shall have a truly integrated society. It is not meant to serve as an outlet for the terrible frustrations of Negroes, though it would reduce those frustrations and point a way to dignity for an oppressed people. It is simply a vehicle by which the wealth of this nation can be redistributed and some of its more grievous social problems solved. This in itself would be quite enough to be getting on with. In fact, if I may risk a slight exaggeration, by normal standards of human society I think it would constitute a revolution.

A TESTAMENT OF HOPE (1968)

MARTIN LUTHER KING, JR.

Martin Luther King, Jr. (1929–1968) rose from obscurity to prominence as the black South began to shake off the chains of a century of second-class citizenship. An apostle of non-violence, he died violently; a seeker for justice, he found martyrdom. Here he defines the faith and dream that motivated him.

Whenever I am asked my opinion of the current state of the civil rights movement. I am forced to pause; it is not easy to describe a crisis so profound that it has caused the most powerful nation in the world to stagger in confusion and bewilderment. Today's problems are so acute because the tragic evasions and defaults of several centuries have accumulated to disaster proportions. The luxury of a leisurely approach to urgent solutions—the ease of gradualism—was forfeited by ignoring the issues for too long. The nation waited until the black man was explosive with fury before stirring itself even to partial concern. Confronted now with the interrelated problems of war, inflation, urban decay, white backlash and a climate of violence, it is now *forced* to address itself to race relations and poverty, and it is tragically unprepared. What might once have been a series of separate problems now merge into a social crisis of almost stupefying complexity.

I am not sad that black Americans are rebelling; this was not only inevitable but eminently desirable. Without this magnificent ferment among Negroes, the old evasions and procrastinations would have continued indefinitely. Black men have slammed the door shut on a past of deadening passivity. Except for the Reconstruction years, they have never in their long history on American soil struggled with such creativity and courage for their freedom. These are our bright years of emergence: though they are painful ones, they cannot be avoided.

Yet despite the widening of our stride, history is racing forward so rapidly that the Negro's inherited and imposed disadvantages slow him down to an infuriating crawl. Lack of education, the dislocations of recent urbanization and the hardening of white resistance loom as such tormenting roadblocks that the goal sometimes appears not as a fixed point in the future but as a receding point never to be reached. Still, when doubts emerge, we can remember that only yesterday Negroes were not only grossly exploited but negated as human beings. They were invisible in their misery. But the sullen and silent slave of 110 years ago, an object of scorn at worst or of pity at best, is today's angry man. He is vibrantly on the move: he is forcing change, rather than waiting for it in pathetic futility. In less than two decades, he has roared out of slumber to change so many of his life's conditions that he may yet find the means to accelerate his march forward and overtake the racing locomotive of history.

These words may have an unexpectedly optimistic ring at a time when pessimism is the prevailing mood. People are often surprised to learn that I am an optimist. They know how often I have been jailed, how frequently the days and nights have been filled with frustration and sorrow, how bitter and dangerous are my adversaries. They expect these experiences to harden me into a grim and desperate man. They fail, however, to perceive the sense of affirmation generated by the challenge of embracing struggle and surmounting obstacles. They have no comprehension of the strength that comes from faith in God and man. It is possible for me to falter, but I am profoundly secure in my knowledge that God loves us; He has not worked out a design for our failure. Man has the capacity to do right as well as wrong, and his history is a path upward, not downward. The past is strewn with the ruins of the empires of tyranny, and each is a monument not merely to man's blunders but to his capacity to overcome them. While it is a bitter fact that in America in 1968, I am denied equality solely because I am black, yet I am not a chattel slave. Millions of people have fought thousands of battles to enlarge my freedom; restricted as it still is, progress has been made. This is why I remain an optimist, though I am also a realist, about the barriers before us. Why is the issue of equality still so far from solution in America, a nation that professes itself to be democratic, inventive, hospitable to new ideas, rich, productive and awesomely powerful? The problem is so tenacious because, despite its virtues and attributes, America is deeply racist and its democracy is flawed both economically and socially. All too many Americans believe justice would unfold painlessly or that its absence for black people will be tolerated tranquilly.

Justice for black people will not flow into society merely from court decisions nor from fountains of political oratory. Nor will a few token changes quell all the tempestuous yearnings of millions of disadvantaged black people. White America must recognize that justice for black people cannot be achieved without radical changes in the structure of our society. The comfortable, the entrenched, the privileged cannot continue to tremble at the prospect of change in the *status quo.*

Stephen Vincent Benét had a message for both white and black Americans in the title of a story, *Freedom Is a Hard Bought Thing.* When millions of people have been cheated for centuries, restitution is a costly process. Inferior education, poor housing, unemployment, inadequate health care—each is a bitter component of the oppression that has been our heritage. Each will require billions of dollars to correct. Justice so long deferred has accumulated interest and its cost for this society will be substantial in financial as well as human terms. This fact has not been fully grasped, because most of the gains of the past decade were obtained at bargain rates. The desegregation of public facilities cost nothing; neither did the election and appointment of a few black public officials.

The price of progress would have been high enough at the best of times, but we are in an agonizing national crisis because a complex of profound problems has intersected in an explosive mixture. The black surge toward freedom has raised justifiable demands for racial justice in our major cities at a time when all the problems of city life have simultaneously erupted. Schools, transportation, water supply, traffic and crime would have been municipal agonies whether or not Negroes lived in our cities. The anarchy of unplanned city growth was destined to confound our confidence. What is unique to this period is our inability to arrange an order of priorities that promises solutions that are decent and just.

Millions of Americans are coming to see that we are fighting an immoral war that costs nearly 30 billion dollars a year, that we are perpetuating racism, that we are tolerating almost 40,000,000 poor during an overflowing material abundance. Yet they remain helpless to end the war, to feed the hungry, to make brotherhood a reality; this has to shake our faith in ourselves. If we look honestly at the realities of our national life, it is clear that we are not marching forward; we are groping and stumbling; we are divided and confused. Our moral values and our spiritual confidence sink, even as our material wealth ascends. In these trying circumstances, the black revolution is much more than a struggle for the rights of Negroes. It is forcing America to face all its interrelated flaws—racism, poverty, militarism and materialism. It is exposing evils that are rooted deeply in the whole structure of our society. It reveals systematic rather than superficial flaws and suggests that radical reconstruction of society itself is the real issue to be faced.

It is time that we stopped our blithe lip service to the guarantees of life, liberty and pursuit of happiness. These fine sentiments are embodied in the Declaration of Independence, but that document was always a declaration of intent rather than of reality. There were slaves when it was written; there were still slaves when it was adopted; and to this day, black Americans have not life, liberty nor the privilege of pursuing happiness, and millions of poor white Americans are in economic bondage that is scarcely less oppressive. Americans who genuinely treasure our national ideals, who know they are still elusive dreams for all too many, should welcome the stirring of Negro demands. They are shattering the complacency that allowed a multitude of social evils to accumulate. Negro agitation is requiring America to re-examine its comforting myths and may yet catalyze the drastic reforms that will save us from social catastrophe.

In indicting white America for its ingrained and tenacious racism, I am using the term "white" to describe the majority, not *all* who are white. We have found that there are many white people who clearly perceive the justice of the Negro struggle for human dignity. Many of them joined our struggle and displayed heroism no less inspiring than that of black people. More than a few died by our side; their memories are cherished and are undimmed by time.

Yet the largest part of white America is still poisoned by racism, which is as native to our soil as pine trees, sage-brush and buffalo grass. Equally native to us is the concept that gross exploitation of the Negro is acceptable, if not commendable. Many whites who concede that Negroes should have equal access to public facilities and the untrammeled right to vote cannot understand that we do not intend to remain in the basement of the economic structure; they cannot understand why a porter or a housemaid would dare dream of a day when his work will be more useful, more remunerative and a pathway to rising opportunity. This incomprehension is a heavy burden in our efforts to win white allies for the long struggle.

But the American Negro has in his nature the spiritual and worldly fortitude to eventually win his struggle for justice and freedom. It is a moral fortitude that has been forged by centuries of oppression. In their sorrow and their hardship, Negroes have become almost instinctively cohesive. We band together readily; and against white hostility, we have an intense and wholesome loyalty to one another. But we cannot win our struggle for justice all alone, nor do I think that most Negroes want to exclude well-intentioned whites from participation in the black revolution. I believe there is an important place in our struggle for white liberals and I hope that their present estrangement from our movement is only temporary. But many white people in the past joined our movement with a kind of messianic faith that they were going to save the Negro and solve all of his problems very quickly. They tended, in some instances, to be rather aggressive and insensitive to the opinions and abilities of the black people with whom they were working; this has been especially true of students. In many cases, they simply did not know how to work in a supporting, secondary role. I think this problem became most evident when young men and women from elite Northern universities came down to Mississippi to work with the black students at Tougaloo and Rust colleges, who were not quite as articulate, didn't type quite as fast and were not as sophisticated. Inevitably, feeling of white paternalism and black inferiority became exaggerated. The Negroes who rebelled against white liberals were trying to assert their own equality and to cast off the mantle of paternalism.

Fortunately, we haven't had this problem in the Southern Christian Leadership Conference. Most of the white people who were working with us in 1962 and 1963 are still with us. We have always enjoyed a relationship of mutual respect. But I think a great many white liberals outside S.C.L.C. also have learned this basic lesson in human relations, thanks largely to Jimmy Baldwin and others who have articulated some of the problems of being black in a multi-racial society. And I am happy to report that relationships between whites and Negroes in the human rights movement are now on a much healthier basis.

In society at large, abrasion between the races is far more evident—but the hostility was always there. Relations today are different only in the sense that Negroes are expressing the feelings that were so long muted. The constructive achievements of the decade 1955 to 1965 deceived us. Everyone underestimated the amount of violence and rage Negroes were suppressing and the vast amount of bigotry the white majority was disguising. All-black organizations are a reflection of that alienation—but they are only a contemporary way station on the road to freedom. They are a product of this period of identity crisis and directionless confusion. As the human rights movement becomes more confident and aggressive, more nonviolently active, many of these emotional and intellectual problems will be resolved in the heat of battle, and we will not ask what is our neighbor's color but whether he is a brother in the pursuit of racial justice. For much of the fervent idealism of the white liberals has been supplemented recently by a dispassionate recognition of some of the cold realities of the struggle for that justice.

One of the most basic of these realities was pointed out by the President's Riot Commission, which observed that the nature of the American economy in the late 19th and early 20th Centuries made it possible for the European immigrants of that time to escape from poverty. It was an economy that had room for—even a great need for —unskilled manual labor. Jobs were available for willing workers, even those with the educational and language liabilities they had brought with them. But the American economy today is radically different. There are fewer and fewer jobs for the culturally and educationally deprived; thus does present-day poverty feed upon and perpetuate itself. The Negro today cannot escape from his ghetto in the way that Irish, Italian, Jewish and Polish immigrants escaped from their ghettos 50 years ago. New methods of escape must be found. And one of these roads to escape will be a more equitable sharing of political power between Negroes and whites. Integration is meaningless without the sharing of power. When I speak of integration, I don't mean a romantic mixing of colors, I mean a real sharing of power and responsibility. We will eventually achieve this, but it is going to be much more difficult for us than for any other minority. After all, no other minority has been so constantly, brutally and deliberately exploited. But because of this very exploitation, Negroes bring a special spiritual and moral contribution to American life—a contribution without which America could not survive.

The implications of true racial integration are more than just national in scope. I don't believe we can have world peace until America has an "integrated" foreign policy. Our disastrous experiences in Vietnam and the Dominican Republic have been, in one sense, a result of racist decision making. Men of the white West, whether or not they like it, have grown up in a racist culture, and their thinking is colored by that fact. They have been fed on a false mythology and tradition that blinds them to the aspirations and talents of other men. They don't really respect anyone who is not white. But we simply cannot have peace in the world without mutual respect. I honestly feel that a man without racial blinders—or, even better, a man with personal experience of racial discrimination—would be in a much better position to make policy decisions and to conduct negotiations with the underprivileged and emerging nations of the world (or even with Castro, for that matter) than would be an Eisenhower or a Dulles.

The American Marines might not even have been needed in Santo Domingo, had the American ambassador there been a man who was sensitive to the color dynamics that pervade the national life of the Dominican Republic. Black men in positions of power in the business world would not be so unconscionable as to trade or traffic with the Union of South Africa, nor would they be so insensitive to the problems and needs of Latin America that they would continue the patterns of American exploitation that now prevail there. When we replace the rabidly segregationist chairman of the Armed Services Committee with a man of good will, when our ambassadors reflect a creative and wholesome interracial background, rather than a cultural heritage that is a conglomeration of Texas and Georgia politics, then we will be able to bring about a qualitative difference in the nature of American foreign policy. This is what we mean when we talk about redeeming the soul of America. Let me make it clear that I don't think white men have a monopoly on sin or greed. But I think there has been a kind of collective experience—a kind of shared misery in the black community—that makes it a little harder for us to exploit other people.

I have come to hope that American Negroes can be a bridge between white civilization and the nonwhite nations of the world, because we have roots in both. Spiritually, Negroes identify understandably with Africa, an identification that is rooted largely in our color; but all of us are a part of the white-American world, too. Our education has been Western and our language, our attitudes—though we sometimes tend to deny it—are very much influenced by Western civilization. Even our emotional life has been disciplined and sometimes stifled and inhibited by an essentially European upbringing. So, although in one sense we are neither, in another sense we are both Americans and Africans. Our very bloodlines are a mixture. I hope and feel that out of the universality of our experience, we can help make peace and harmony in this world more possible.

Although American Negroes could, if they were in decision-making positions, give aid and encouragement to the underprivileged and disenfranchised people in other lands, I don't think it can work the other way around. I don't think the nonwhites in other parts of the world can really be of any concrete help to us, given their own problems of development and self-determination. In fact, American Negroes have greater collective buying power than Canada, greater than all four of the Scandinavian countries combined. American Negroes have greater economic potential than most of the nations—perhaps even more than *all* of the nations—of Africa. We don't *need* to look for help from some power outside the boundaries of our country, except in the sense of sympathy and identification. Our challenge, rather, is to organize the power we already have in our midst. The Newark riots, for example, could certainly have been prevented by a more aggressive political involvement on the part of that city's Negroes. There is utterly no reason Addonizio should be the mayor of Newark, with the Negro majority that exists in that city. Gary, Indiana, is another tinderbox city; but its black mayor, Richard Hatcher, has given Negroes a new faith in the effectiveness of the political process.

One of the most basic weapons in the fight for social justice will be the cumulative political power of the Negro. I can foresee the Negro vote becoming consistently the decisive vote in national elections. It is already decisive in states that have large numbers of electoral votes. Even today, the Negroes in New York City strongly influence how New

York State will go in national elections, and the Negroes of Chicago have a similar leverage in Illinois. Negroes are even the decisive balance of power in the elections in Georgia, South Carolina and Virginia. So the party and the candidate that get the support of the Negro voter in national elections have a very definite edge, and we intend to use this fact to win advances in the struggle for human rights. I have every confidence that the black vote will ultimately help unseat the diehard opponents of equal rights in Congress—who are, incidentally, reactionary on all issues. But the Negro community cannot win this victory alone; indeed, it would be an empty victory even if the Negroes *could* win it alone. Intelligent men of good will everywhere must see this as their task and contribute to its support.

The election of Negro mayors, such as Hatcher, in some of the nation's larger cities has also had a tremendous psychological impact upon the Negro. It has shown him that he has the potential to participate in the determination of his own destiny—and that of society. We will see more Negro mayors in major cities in the next ten years, but this is not the ultimate answer. Mayors are relatively impotent figures in the scheme of national politics. Even a white mayor such as John Lindsay of New York simply does not have the money and resources to deal with the problems of his city. The necessary money to deal with urban problems must come from the Federal Government, and this money is ultimately controlled by the Congress of the United States. The success of these enlightened mayors is entirely dependent upon the financial support made available by Washington.

The past record of the Federal Government, however, has not been encouraging. No President has really done very much for the American Negro, though the past two Presidents have received much undeserved credit for helping us. This credit has accrued to Lyndon Johnson and John Kennedy only because it was during their Administrations that Negroes began doing more for themselves. Kennedy didn't voluntarily submit a civil rights bill, nor did Lyndon Johnson. In fact, both told us at one time that such legislation was impossible. President Johnson did respond realistically to the signs of the times and used his skills as a legislator to get bills through Congress that other men might not have gotten through. I must point out, in all honesty, however, that President Johnson has not been nearly so diligent in *implementing* the bills he has helped shepherd through Congress.

Of the ten titles of the 1964 Civil Rights Act, probably only the one concerning public accommodations—the most bitterly contested section—has been meaningfully enforced and implemented. Most of the other sections have been deliberately ignored. The same is true of the 1965 Voting Rights Act, which provides for Federal referees to monitor the registration of voters in counties where Negroes have systematically been denied the right to vote. Yet of the some 900 counties that are eligible for Federal referees, only 58 counties to date have had them. The 842 other counties remain essentially just as they were before the march on Selma. Look at the pattern of Federal referees in Mississippi, for example. They are dispersed in a manner that gives the appearance of change without any real prospect of actually shifting political power or giving Negroes a genuine opportunity to be represented in the government of their state. There is a similar pattern in Alabama, even though that state is currently at odds with the Democratic Administration in Washington because of George Wallace. Georgia, until just recently, had no Federal referees at all, not even in the hard-core black-belt counties. I think it is significant that there are no Federal referees at all in the home districts of the most powerful Southern Senators—particularly Senators Russell, Eastland and Talmadge. The power and moral corruption of these Senators remain unchallenged, despite the weapon for change the legislation promised to be. Reform was thwarted when the legislation was inadequately enforced.

But not all is bad in the South, by any means. Though the fruits of our struggle have sometimes been nothing more than bitter despair, I must admit there have been some hopeful signs, some meaningful successes. One of the most hopeful of these changes is the attitude of the Southern Negro himself. Benign acceptance of second-class citizenship has been displaced by vigorous demands for full citizenship rights and opportunities. In fact, most of our concrete accomplishments have been limited largely to the South. We have put an end to racial segregation in the South; we have brought about the beginnings of reform in the political system; and, as incongruous as it may seem, a Negro is probably safer in most Southern cities than he is in the cities of the North. We have confronted the racist policemen of the South and demanded reforms in the police departments. We have confronted the Southern racist power structure and we have elected Negro and liberal white candidates through much of the South in the past ten years. George Wallace is certainly an exception, and Lester Maddox is a sociological fossil. But despite these anachronisms, at the city and county level, there is a new respect for black votes and black citizenship that just did not exist ten years ago. Though school integration has moved at a depressingly slow rate in the South, it *has* moved. Of far more significance is the fact that we have learned that the integration of schools does not necessarily solve the inadequacy of schools. White schools are often just about as bad as black schools, and integrated schools sometimes tend to merge the problems of the two without solving either of them.

There *is* progress in the South, however—progress expressed by the presence of Negroes in the Georgia House of Representatives, in the election of a Negro to the Mississippi House of Representatives, in the election of a black sheriff in Tuskegee, Alabama, and, most especially, in the integration of police forces throughout the Southern states. There are now even Negro deputy sheriffs in such black-belt areas as Dallas County, Alabama. Just three years ago, a Negro could be beaten for going into the county courthouse in Dallas County; now Negroes share in running it. So there *are* some changes. But the changes are basically in the social and political areas; the problems we now face —providing jobs, better housing and better education for the poor throughout the country—will require money for their solution, a fact that makes those solutions all the more difficult.

The need for solutions, meanwhile, becomes more urgent every day, because these problems are far more serious now than they were just a few years ago. Before 1964, things were getting better economically for the Negro; but after that year, things began to take a turn for the worse. In particular, automation began to cut into our jobs very badly, and this snuffed out the few sparks of hope the black people had begun to nurture. As long as there was some measurable and steady economic progress, Negroes were willing and able to press harder and work harder and hope for something better. But when the door began to close on the few avenues of progress, then hopeless despair began to set in.

The fact that most white people do not comprehend this situation— which prevails in the North as well as in the South—is due largely to the press, which molds the opinions of the white community. Many whites hasten to congratulate themselves on what little progress we Negroes have made. I'm sure that most whites felt that with the passage of the 1964 Civil Rights Act, all race problems were automatically solved. Because most white people are so far removed from the life of the average Negro, there has been little to challenge this assumption. Yet Negroes continue to live with racism every day. It doesn't matter where we are individually in the scheme of things, how near we may be either to the top or to the bottom of society; the cold facts of racism slap each one of us in the face. A friend of mine is a lawyer, one of the most brilliant young men I know. Were he a white lawyer, I have no doubt that he would be in a $100,000 job with a major corporation or heading his own independent firm. As it is, he makes a mere $20,000 a year. This may seem like a lot of money and, to most of us, it is; but the point is that this young man's background and abilities would, if his skin color were different, entitle him to an income many times that amount.

I don't think there is a single major insurance company that hires Negro lawyers. Even within the agencies of the Federal Government, most Negro employees are in the lower echelons; only a handful of Negroes in Federal employment are in upper-income brackets. This is a situation that cuts across this country's economic spectrum. The Chicago Urban League recently conducted a research project in the

Kenwood community on the South Side. They discovered that the average educational grade level of Negroes in that community was 10.6 years and the median income was about $4200 a year. In nearby Gage Park, the median educational grade level of the whites was 8.6 years, but the median income was $9600 per year. In fact, the average white high school dropout makes as much as, if not more than, the average Negro college graduate.

Solutions for these problems, urgent as they are, must be constructive and rational. Rioting and violence provide no solutions for economic problems. Much of the justification for rioting has come from the thesis—originally set forth by Franz Fanon—that violence has a certain cleansing effect. Perhaps, in a special psychological sense, he may have had a point. But we have seen a better and more constructive cleansing process in our nonviolent demonstrations. Another theory to justify violent revolution is that rioting enables Negroes to overcome their fear of the white man. But they are just as afraid of the power structure after a riot as before. I remember that was true when our staff went into Rochester, New York, after the riot of 1964. When we discussed the possibility of going down to talk with the police, the people who had been most aggressive in the violence were afraid to talk. They still had a sense of inferiority; and not until they were bolstered by the presence of our staff and given reassurance of their political power and the rightness of their cause and the justness of their grievances were they able and willing to sit down and talk to the police chief and the city manager about the conditions that had produced the riot.

As a matter of fact, I think the aura of paramilitarism among the black militant groups speaks much more of fear than it does of confidence. I know, in my own experience, that I was much more afraid in Montgomery when I had a gun in my house. When I decided that, as a teacher of the philosophy of nonviolence, I couldn't keep a gun, I came face to face with the question of death and I dealt with it. And from that point on, I no longer needed a gun nor have I been afraid. Ultimately, one's sense of manhood must come from within him.

The riots in Negro ghettos have been, in one sense, merely another expression of the growing climate of violence in America. When a culture begins to feel threatened by its own inadequacies, the majority of men tend to prop themselves up by artificial means, rather than dig down deep into their spiritual and cultural wellsprings. America seems to have reached this point. Americans as a whole feel threatened by communism on one hand and, on the other, by the rising tide of aspirations among the undeveloped nations. I think most Americans know in their hearts that their country has been terribly wrong in its dealings with other peoples around the world. When Rome began to disintegrate from within, it turned to a strengthening of the military establishment, rather than to a correction of the corruption within the society. We are doing the same thing in this country and the result will probably be the same—unless, and here I admit to a bit of chauvinism, the black man in America can provide a new soul force for all Americans, a new expression of the American dream that need not be realized at the expense of other men around the ·world, but a dream of opportunity and life that can be shared with the rest of the world.

It seems glaringly obvious to me that the development of a humanitarian means of dealing with some of the social problems of the world —and the correlative revolution in American values that this will entail—is a much better way of protecting ourselves against the threat of violence than the military means we have chosen. On these grounds, I must indict the Johnson Administration. It has seemed amazingly devoid of statesmanship; and when creative statesmanship wanes, irrational militarism increases. In this sense, President Kennedy was far more of a statesman than President Johnson. He was a man who was big enough to admit when he was wrong—as he did after the Bay of Pigs incident. But Lyndon Johnson seems to be unable to make this kind of statesmanlike gesture in connection with Vietnam. And I think that this has led, as Senator Fulbright has said, to such a strengthening of the military-industrial complex of this country that the President now finds himself almost totally trapped by it. Even at this point, when he can readily summon popular support to end the bombing in Vietnam, he persists. Yet bombs in Vietnam also explode at home; they destroy the hopes and possibilities for a decent America.

In our efforts to dispel this atmosphere of violence in this country, we cannot afford to overlook the root cause of the riots. The President's Riot Commission concluded that most violence-prone Negroes are teenagers or young adults who almost invariably, are underemployed ("underemployed" means working every day but earning an income below the poverty level) or who are employed in menial jobs. And according to a recent Department of Labor statistical report, 24.8 percent of Negro youth are currently unemployed, a statistic that does not include the drifters who avoid the census takers. Actually, it's my guess that the statistics are very, very conservative in this area. The Bureau of the Census has admitted a ten percent error in this age group, and the unemployment statistics are based on those who are actually applying for jobs.

But it isn't just a lack of work; it's also a lack of *meaningful* work. In Cleveland, 58 percent of the young men between the ages of 16 and 25 were estimated to be either unemployed or underemployed. This appalling situation is probably 90 percent of the root cause of the Negro riots. A Negro who has finished high school often watches his white classmates go out into the job market and earn $100 a week, while he, because he is black, is expected to work for $40 a week.

Hence, there is a tremendous hostility and resentment that only a difference in race keeps him out of an adequate job. This situation is social dynamite. When you add the lack of recreational facilities and adequate job counseling, and the continuation of an aggressively hostile police environment, you have a truly explosive situation. Any night on any street corner in any Negro ghetto of the country, a nervous policeman can start a riot simply by being impolite or by expressing racial prejudice. And white people are sadly unaware how routinely and frequently this occurs.

It hardly needs to be said that solutions to these critical problems are overwhelmingly urgent. The President's Riot Commission recommended that funds for summer programs aimed at young Negroes should be increased. New York is already spending more on its special summer programs than on its year-round poverty efforts, but these are only tentative and emergency steps toward a truly meaningful and permanent solution. And the negative thinking in this area voiced by many whites does not help the situation. Unfortunately, many white people think that we merely "reward" a rioter by taking positive action to better his situation. What these white people do not realize is that the Negroes who riot have given up on America. When nothing is done to alleviate their plight, this merely confirms the Negroes' conviction that America is a hopelessly decadent society. When something positive is done, however, when constructive action follows a riot, a rioter's despair is allayed and he is forced to re-evaluate America and to consider whether some good might eventually come from our society after all.

But, I repeat, the recent curative steps that have been taken are, at best, inadequate. The summer poverty programs, like most other Government projects, function well in some places and are totally ineffective in others. The difference, in large measure, is one of citizen participation; that is the key to success or failure. In cases such as the Farmers' Marketing Cooperative Association in the black belt of Alabama and the Child Development Group in Mississippi, where the people were really involved in the planning and action of the program, it was one of the best experiences in self-help and grass-roots initiative. But in places like Chicago, where poverty programs are used strictly as a tool of the political machinery and for dispensing party patronage, the very concept of helping the poor is defiled and the poverty program becomes just another form of enslavement. I still wouldn't want to do away with it, though, even in Chicago. We must simply fight at both the local and the national levels to gain as much community control as possible over the poverty program.

But there is no single answer to the plight of the American Negro. Conditions and needs vary greatly in different sections of the country. I think that the place to start, however, is in the area of human relations, and especially in the area of community-police relations. This is a sensitive and touchy problem that has rarely been adequately emphasized. Virtually every riot has begun from some police action. If you try to tell the people in most Negro communities that the police are their friends, they just laugh at you. Obviously, something desperately needs to be done to correct this. I have been particularly impressed by the fact that even in the state of Mississippi, where the FBI did a significant training job with the Mississippi police, the police are much more courteous to Negroes than they are in Chicago or New York. Our police forces simply must develop an attitude of courtesy and respect for the ordinary citizen. If we can just stop policemen from using profanity in their encounters with black people, we will have accomplished a lot. In the larger sense, police must cease being occupation troops in the ghetto and start protecting its residents. Yet very few cities have really faced up to this problem and tried to do something about it. It is the most abrasive element in Negro-white relations, but it is the last to be scientifically and objectively appraised.

When you go beyond a relatively simple though serious problem such as police racism, however, you begin to get into all complexities of the modern American economy. Urban transit systems in most American cities, for example, have become a genuine civil rights issue—and a valid one—because the layout of rapid-transit systems determines the accessibility of jobs to the black community. If transportation systems in American cities could be laid out so as to provide an opportunity for poor people to get meaningful employment, then they could begin to move into the mainstream of American life. A good example of this problem is my home city of Atlanta, where the rapid-transit system has been laid out for the convenience of the white upper-middle-class suburbanites who commute to their jobs downtown. The system has virtually no consideration for connecting the poor people with their jobs. There is only one possible explanation for this situation, and that is the racist blindness of city planners.

The same problems are to be found in the areas of rent supplement and low-income housing. The relevance of these issues to human relations and human rights cannot be overemphasized. The kind of house a man lives in, along with the quality of his employment, determines, to a large degree, the quality of his family life. I have known too many people in my own parish in Atlanta who, because they were living in overcrowded apartments, were constantly bickering with other members of their families—a situation that produced many kinds of severe dysfunctions in family relations. And yet I have seen these same families achieve harmony when they were able to afford a house allowing for a little personal privacy and freedom of movement.

All these human-relations problems are complex and related, and its very difficult to assign priorities—especially as long as the Vietnam war continues. The Great Society has become a victim of the war. I think there was a sincere desire in this country four or five years ago to move toward a genuinely great society, and I have little doubt that there would have been a gradual increase in Federal expenditures in this direction, rather than the gradual decline that has occurred, if the war in Vietnam had been avoided.

One of the incongruities of this situation is the fact that such a large number of the soldiers in the Armed Forces in Vietnam—especially the front-line soldiers who are actually doing the fighting—are Negroes. Negroes have always held the hope that if they really demonstrate that they are great soldiers and if they really fight for America and help save American democracy, then when they come back home, America will treat them better. This has not been the case. Negro soldiers returning from World War One were met with race riots, job discrimination and continuation of the bigotry that they had experienced before. After World War Two, the GI Bill did offer some hope for a better life to those who had the educational background to take advantage of it, and there was proportionately less turmoil. But for the Negro GI, military service still represents a means of escape from the oppressive ghettos of the rural South and the urban North. He often sees the Army as an avenue for educational opportunities and job training. He sees in the military uniform a symbol of dignity that has long been denied him by society. The tragedy in this is that military service is probably the only possible escape for most young Negro men. Many of them go into the Army, risking death, in order that they might have a few of the human possibilities of life. They know that life in the city ghetto or life in the rural South almost certainly means jail or death or humiliation. And so, by comparison, military service is really the lesser risk.

One young man on our staff, Hosea Williams, returned from the foxholes of Germany a 60-percent-disabled veteran. After 13 months in a veterans' hospital, he went back to his home town of Attapulgus, Georgia. On his way home, he went into a bus station at Americus, Georgia, to get a drink of water while waiting for his next bus. And while he stood there on his crutches, drinking from the fountain, he was beaten savagely by white hoodlums. This pathetic incident is all too typical of the treatment received by Negroes in this country—not only physical brutality but brutal discrimination when a Negro tries to buy a house, and brutal violence against the Negro's soul when he finds himself denied a job that he knows he is qualified for.

There is also the violence of having to live in a community and pay higher consumer prices for goods or higher rent for equivalent housing than are charged in the white areas of the city. Do you know that a can of beans almost always costs a few cents more in grocery chain stores located in the Negro ghetto than in a store of that same chain located in the upper-middle-class suburbs, where the median income is five times as high? The Negro knows it, because he works in the white man's house as a cook or a gardener. And what do you think this knowledge does to his soul? How do you think it affects his view of the society he lives in? How can you expect anything but disillusionment and bitterness? The question that now faces us is whether we can turn the Negro's disillusionment and bitterness into hope and faith in the essential goodness of the American system. If we don't, our society will crumble.

It is a paradox that those Negroes who have given up on America are doing more to improve it than are its professional patriots. They are stirring the mass of smug, somnolent citizens, who are neither evil nor good, to an awareness of crisis. The confrontation involves not only their morality but their self-interest, and that combination promises to evoke positive action. This is not a nation of venal people. It is a land of individuals who, in the majority, have not cared, who have been heartless about their black neighbors because their ears are blocked and their eyes blinded by the tragic myth that Negroes endure abuse without pain or complaint. Even when protest flared and denied the myth, they were fed new doctrines of inhumanity that argued that Negroes were arrogant, lawless and ungrateful. Habitual white discrimination was transformed into white backlash. But for some, the lies had lost their grip and an internal disquiet grew. Poverty and discrimination were undeniably real; they scarred the nation; they dirtied our honor and diminished our pride. An insistent question defied evasion: Was security for some being purchased at the price of degradation for others? Everything in our traditions said this kind of injustice was the system of the past or of other nations. And yet there it was, abroad in our own land.

Thus was born—particularly in the young generation—a spirit of dissent that ranged from superficial disavowal of the old values to total commitment to wholesale, drastic and immediate social reform. Yet all of it was dissent. Their voice is still a minority; but united with millions of black protesting voices, it has become a sound of distant thunder increasing in volume with the gathering of storm clouds. This dissent is America's hope. It shines in the long tradition of American ideals that began with courageous minutemen in New England, that continued in the Abolitionist movement, that re-emerged in the Populist revolt and, decades later, that burst forth to elect Franklin Roosevelt and John F. Kennedy. Today's dissenters tell the complacent majority that the time has come when further evasion of social responsibility in a turbulent world will court disaster and death. America has not yet changed because so many think it need not change, but this is the illusion of the damned. America must change because 23,000,000 black citizens will no longer live supinely in a wretched past. They have left the valley of despair; they have found strength in struggle; and whether they live or die, they shall never crawl nor retreat again. Joined by white allies, they will shake the prison walls until they fall. America must change.

A voice out of Bethlehem 2000 years ago said that all men are equal. It said right would triumph. Jesus of Nazareth wrote no books; he owned no property to endow him with influence. He had no friends in the courts of the powerful. But he changed the course of mankind with only the poor and the despised. Naïve and unsophisticated though we may be, the poor and despised of the 20th Century will revolutionize this era. In our "arrogance, lawlessness and ingratitude," we will fight for human justice, brotherhood, secure peace and abundance for all. When we have won these—in a spirit of unshakable nonviolence—then, in luminous splendor, the Christian era will truly begin.

INDEX